T0135397

Lecture Notes in Computer Science 13051

More information about this subseries at http://www.springer.com/series/7412

Halimah Badioze Zaman · Alan F. Smeaton ·
Timothy K. Shih · Sergio Velastin ·
Tada Terutoshi · Bo Nørregaard Jørgensen ·
Hazleen Aris · Nazrita Ibrahim (Eds.)

Advances in Visual Informatics

7th International Visual Informatics Conference, IVIC 2021
Kajang, Malaysia, November 23–25, 2021
Proceedings

 Springer

Editors
Halimah Badioze Zaman
Universiti Tenaga Nasional
Selangor, Malaysia

Alan F. Smeaton
Dublin City University
Dublin, Ireland

Timothy K. Shih
National Central University
Jhongli, Taiwan

Sergio Velastin
Queen Mary University of London
London, UK

Tada Terutoshi
Toyo University
Tokyo, Japan

Bo Nørregaard Jørgensen
University of Southern Denmark
Odense, Denmark

Hazleen Aris
Universiti Tenaga Nasional
Selangor, Malaysia

Nazrita Ibrahim ⓘ
Universiti Tenaga Nasional
Selangor, Malaysia

ISSN 0302-9743   ISSN 1611-3349 (electronic)
Lecture Notes in Computer Science
ISBN 978-3-030-90234-6   ISBN 978-3-030-90235-3 (eBook)
https://doi.org/10.1007/978-3-030-90235-3

LNCS Sublibrary: SL6 – Image Processing, Computer Vision, Pattern Recognition, and Graphics

This Springer imprint is published by the registered company Springer Nature Switzerland AG
The registered company address is: Gewerbestrasse 11, 6330 Cham, Switzerland

Preface

Visual informatics – a multidisciplinary field of computer science, information technology, and engineering is dynamic and ever-enriching, in a world that is experiencing tremendous challenges such as the COVID-19 pandemic, climate change, security, unemployment, low education standards, and corruption. Despite all these challenges, the world, including the developing countries, is making brave strides towards becoming a digital economy and a digital society. The pandemic has opened the eyes of policy makers, regulators, businesses, and the population at large to the advantages of digitally enabling a wide range of economic activities that would help reinvent organizations and nations. With the fourth industrial revolution (4IR) being at the cusp and the advent of the fifth industrial revolution (5IR) already being discussed, the researchers of this multidisciplinary field were excited when it was again time to organize this conference. Emphasizing its multidisciplinary nature, this year the International Visual Informatics Conference, which has its new home at the Malaysian Information Technology Society (MITS), was hosted for the first time by the Institute of Informatics and Computing in Energy (IICE) at Universiti Tenaga Nasional or The Energy University (UNITEN), Malaysia. IICE is a center of excellence in energy informatics but has visual informatics as one of its research areas integrated into the energy domain. IICE and the other institutional partners of this conference conduct research in various specialized areas of visual informatics which are integrated into their fundamental domains. We have seen these areas of visual informatics grow since the conference first began in 2009 through 2021. We are grateful to all our partners, locally and internationally, for making the 7th International Visual Informatics Conference (IVIC 2021) possible.

IVIC 2021 was conducted at an unprecedented time (due to the COVID-19 pandemic) which did not allow participants to meet face to face. For the first time, the conference was conducted virtually on a platform which allowed members to still interact with each other but through an online forum and chats. They also met at the virtual exhibition space to look at posters as well as a special exhibition related to the theme of the conference. As usual, the main objective of the conference was to bring together experts to discuss and share new knowledge, ideas, and innovations in this research area so that more concerted efforts can be undertaken nationally and globally. Like the previous IVIC conferences, this year's conference was organized collaboratively by the visual informatics community from various public and private universities, professional institutions, and industry players from various parts of the world (their names are listed in the proceedings).

The theme of the conference, 'Digital Innovation, Transformation, and Sustainable Technology in Reinventing Nations', reflects the importance of the need for organizations and nations to transform and reinvent themselves to meet digitalization innovation needs, to ensure security, to improve governance, and to fight against corruption and global challenges such as the COVID-19 pandemic. A human-centric future society (Society 5.0) requires new, secure digital innovations driven by artificial intelligence (AI), smart technology, and big data analytics; it also requires digital transformation through strategic digital adoption and sustainable technologies for better economic growth. Thus, the theme of the conference was relevant, apt, and timely.

IVIC 2021 took place during November 23–25, 2021. The conference focused on four tracks: Visualization, Engineering, Cyber Security and Machine Learning, and Energy Informatics, and it ended with six half-day workshops that ran concurrently: Innovation in Educational Technology for Online Teaching and Learning Environment; Introduction to Multi-criteria Decision Making Models (MCDM); Holistic Energy Modeling for Building Performance Improvement; Neural Networks and Deep Learning Using Python and PyTorch; Data Visualization with Tableau; and Munch Big Data with Apache Spark and Python. There were five keynote speakers and 60 paper presentations based on topics covered by the four main tracks. The reviewing of the papers was conducted by experts who represented the Program Committee locally and internationally. Each paper was reviewed by three reviewers and the acceptance rate was 51%. The reviewing process was managed using the system EasyChair. The conference also included an exhibition entitled "Transformation through Digital Energy Comfort" shown in the form of video art, to show how scientific and technological research can have aesthetic value and impact on public awareness on the beauty of the convergence of knowledge to solve problems related to humanity.

On behalf of the organizers and Program Committee of IVIC 2021, we thank all authors for their submissions and camera-ready copies of papers, and all participants for their thought-provoking ideas and active participation in the conference. We also thank the vice-chancellor of UNITEN (the host university) and the vice-chancellors and deans of all IT faculties of the Malaysian Institutions of Higher Learning for their support in organizing this conference. We also acknowledge the sponsors, members of the organizing committees, Program Committee members, and other supporting committees and individuals who gave their continuous help and support in making the conference a success. We believe that IVIC will grow from strength to strength and will one day be hosted by not only different institutions in Malaysia but also in different countries in Asia and the rest of the world.

November 2021

Halimah Badioze Zaman
Alan F. Smeaton
Timothy K. Shih
Sergio Velastin
Tada Terutoshi
Bo Nørregaard Jørgensen
Hazleen Aris
Nazrita Ibrahim

Organization

The 7th International Visual Informatics Conference (IVIC 2021) was organized by the Malaysian Information Technology Society (MITS) and the Institute of Informatics and Computing in Energy (IICE), Universiti Tenaga Nasional (UNITEN), in collaboration with local public and private universities in Malaysia.

Local Executive Committee

General Chair

Halimah Badioze Zaman   UNITEN/MITS, Malaysia

Deputy Chairs

Hazleen Aris   UNITEN, Malaysia
Azlina Ahmad   MITS, Malaysia

Secretaries

Nazrita Ibrahim (Head)   UNITEN, Malaysia
Faridah Hani Mohamed Salleh   UNITEN, Malaysia
Ummul Hanan Mohamad   UKM/MITS, Malaysia
Nor Hidayah Bukhari   UNITEN, Malaysia

Treasurers

Naziffa Raha Md Nasir (Head)   UNITEN, Malaysia
Azimah Abdul Ghapar   UNITEN, Malaysia
Rabiah Abdul Kadir   UKM/MITS, Malaysia

Program Committee

Program Co-chairs

Halimah Badioze Zaman   UNITEN/MITS, Malaysia
Alan F. Smeaton   Dublin City University, Ireland
Bo Nørregaard Jørgensen   University of Southern Denmark, Denmark
Sergio A. Velastin   Queen Mary University of London, UK
Tada Terutoshi   Toyo University, Japan
Timothy K. Shih   National Central University, Taiwan

Technical Program Chairs

Salman Yussof (Head)	UNITEN, Malaysia
Azlina Ahmad	UKM, Malaysia
Fatimah Dato Ahmad	UPNM, Malaysia
Hazleen Aris	UNITEN, Malaysia
Moamin A. Mahmoud	UNITEN, Malaysia

Publicity Committee

Hazleen Aris (Head)	UNITEN, Malaysia
Abbas M. Al-Ghaili	UNITEN, Malaysia
Ang Mei Choo	UKM, Malaysia
Azlan Yusof	UNITEN, Malaysia
Dahlan Abdul Gani	UniKL, Malaysia
Hafizhah Suzana Hussien	UKM, Malaysia
Hawa Shamsudin	UNITEN, Malaysia
Iskandar Shah Mohd Zawawi	UiTM, Malaysia
Mohammed Najah Mahdi	UNITEN, Malaysia
Nora Annuar	UNITEN, Malaysia
Noramiza Hashim	MMU, Malaysia
Norma Hassan	UNITEN, Malaysia
Nur Azlida Ahmad	UNITEN, Malaysia
Nurshariah Wahab	UPNM, Malaysia
Sumayyah Dzulkifly	UPSI, Malaysia

Sponsorship Committee

Azlina Ahmad (Head)	UKM, Malaysia
Halimah Badioze Zaman	UNITEN/MITS, Malaysia
Noor Afiza Mat Razali	UPNM, Malaysia
Saraswathy Shamini Gunasekaran	UNITEN, Malaysia
Wan Fatimah Wan Ahmad	UTP, Malaysia

Logistic Committee

Sunarti Abdullah (Head)	UNITEN, Malaysia
Aziah Ali	MMU, Malaysia
Azreen Azman	UPM, Malaysia
Fadzlin Md Yunus	UNITEN, Malaysia
Ismail Bin Azmi	UNITEN, Malaysia
Mohamad Taha Ijab	UKM, Malaysia
Mohd Faizam Bin Hilmy	UNITEN, Malaysia
Nadri bin Ahmad	UNITEN, Malaysia
Noor Ashikin Abdullah	UNITEN, Malaysia
Siti Noor Farahzawanni Che Omar	UNITEN, Malaysia
Suhaina Bte Abd. Sukor	UNITEN, Malaysia
Syed Nasir Alsagoff bin Syed Zakaria	UPNM, Malaysia

Exhibition Committee

Ahmad Hanif Ahmad Baharin (Head)   UKM, Malaysia
Dahlan Abdul Ghani   UniKL, Malaysia
Suzaimah Ramli   UPNM, Malaysia

Workshop Committee

Juhana Salim (Head)   MITS, Malaysia
Dhanapal Durai Dominic P.   UTP, Malaysia
Esmadi Abu Abu Seman   UMS, Malaysia
Kasturi Dewi Varathan   UM, Malaysia
Nur Hanani Binti Azami   UNITEN, Malaysia
Wong Seng Yue   UM, Malaysia

Conference System Committee

Sera Syarmila Binti Sameon (Head)   UNITEN, Malaysia
Ely Salwana Mat Surin   UKM, Malaysia
Eszleen Sies   UNITEN, Malaysia
Norshita Mat Nayan   UKM, Malaysia
Nor Zaity Zakaria   UNITEN, Malaysia
Nor Zakiah Gorment   UNITEN, Malaysia
Nur Aimi Syaqilah Binti Aziz   UNITEN, Malaysia

Special Task Committee

Eddren Law Yi Feng (Head)   UNITEN, Malaysia
Bavani Ramayah   University of Nottingham, Malay
Low Loi Ming   UNITEN, Malaysia
Norshita Mat Nayan   UKM, Malaysia
Siti Norazimah Bt Ahmat   UKM, Malaysia

Tour/Virtual Visit Committee

Prasanna A./P. Ramakrishnan   UiTM, Malaysia

Virtual Platform Committee

Rajeshkumar A./L. Sugu (Head)   UNITEN, Malaysia
Ahmad Ikhsan Bin Abd. Aziz   UNITEN, Malaysia

Technical Program Committee

International

Alan Smeaton	Dublin City University, Ireland
Aisha Umair	University of Southern Denmark, Denmark
Andino Maseleno	Gadjah Mada University, Indonesia
Cho Cô Nguyệt	Hanoi University, Vietnam
Dhiraj Shrestha	Kathmandu University, Nepal
Ehab Alsammak	Directorate General of Education of Karbala, Iraq
Emanuele Trucco	University of Dundee, UK
Farrukh Zeshan	COMSATS University Islamabad, Pakistan
Huy Nguyen	Vietnam National University, Vietnam
Irum Inayat	FAST National University, Pakistan
Li Kuan-Ching	Providence University, Taiwan
Malcolm Munro	Durham University, UK
Marta Fairén	Universitat Politècnica de Catalunya, Spain
Mohammed Subhi	Al Hikma University College, Iraq
Muhyiddine Jradi	University of Southern Denmark, Denmark
Neil Gordon	University of Hull, UK
Nick Holliman	Newcastle University, UK
Qais Saif Qassim	Ibri College of Technology, Oman
Qingde Li	University of Hull, UK
Sergio Velastin	Queen Mary University of London, UK
Shree Raj Shakya	Tribhuvan University, Nepal
Theng Yin Leng	Nanyang Technological University, Singapore
Timothy K. Shih	National Central University, Taiwan
Tony Pridmore	University of Nottingham, UK
Wenyu Liu	Huazhong University of Science and Technology, China
Yunis Ali	Simad University, Somalia

Local

Afida Jemat	UNITEN, Malaysia
Ahmad Sufril Azlan Mohamed	USM, Malaysia
Amelia Ritahani Ismail	IIUM, Malaysia
Anusha A./P. Achuthan	USM, Malaysia
Bahari Belaton	USM, Malaysia
Dayang Rohaya Awang Rambli	UTP, Malaysia
Ely Salwana Mat Surin	UKM, Malaysia
Fatimah Dato Ahmad	UPNM, Malaysia
J. Joshua Thomas	KDU Penang University College, Malaysia
Kher Hui (Marina) Ng	University of Nottingham, Malaysia

Mohd Hafiz Faizal Mohamad Kamil	UniKL, Malaysia
Mohd Khairul Azmi Bin Hassan	IIUM, Malaysia
Mohd Nadhir Ab Wahab	USM, Malaysia
Mohammad Nazir Ahmad	UKM, Malaysia
Nazlena Mohamad Ali	UKM, Malaysia
Nor Hidayati Zakaria	UTM, Malaysia
Nur Intan Raihana Ruhaiyem	USM, Malaysia
Nurul Amelina Binti Nasharuddin	UPM, Malaysia
Puteri Nor Ellyza Nohuddin	UKM, Malaysia
Rosalina Abdul Salam	USIM, Malaysia
Siti Nur Hidayah Ab Malek	UNITEN, Malaysia
Suhaidi Hassan	UUM, Malaysia
Suraya Hamid	UM, Malaysia
Suraya Yaácob	UTM, Malaysia
Suziah Sulaiman	UTP, Malaysia
Wan Mohd Nazmee Wan Zainon	USM, Malaysia
Zainab Abu Bakar	MEDIU, Malaysia
Zuraini Zainol	UPNM, Malaysia

Additional Reviewers

Abdul Syafiq Abdull Sukor	USM, Malaysia
Abdul Syukor Mohamad Jaya	UTEM, Malaysia
Alfian Abdul Halin	UPM, Malaysia
Aliza Abdul Latif	UNITEN, Malaysia
Ammuthavali Ramasamy	UNITEN, Malaysia
Amr Ahmed	University of Nottingham, Malaysia
Aslina Baharum	UMS, Malaysia
Asmidar Abu Bakar	UNITEN, Malaysia
Azizah Suliman	UNITEN, Malaysia
Azrul Hazri Jantan	UPM, Malaysia
Nurfadhlina Mohd. Sharef	UPM, Malaysia
Sa'Adah Hassan	UPM, Malaysia
Aymen Dheyaa	UNITEN, Malaysia
Azir Rezha Norizan	UniKL, Malaysia
Azleena Mohd Kassim	USM, Malaysia
Azlin Sharina Abdul Latef	UMK, Malaysia
Azrina Kamaruddin	UPM, Malaysia
Chia Yi Quah	University of Nottingham, Malaysia
Fahrul Hakim Huyop	UPM, Malaysia
Fiza Abdul Rahim	UTM, Malaysia
Hairoladenan Kasim	UNITEN, Malaysia
Intan Soraya Rosdi	MMU, Malaysia
Noris Mohd Norowi	UPM, Malaysia
Shafinah Kamarudin	UPM, Malaysia
Sulfeeza Md Drus	UNITEN, Malaysia

Fairuz Abdullah	UNITEN, Malaysia
Fatihah Ramli	UNIMAS, Malaysia
Fauziah Kasmin	UTEM, Malaysia
Husna Sarirah Husin	UniKL, Malaysia
Ibrahim Ahmad	UTEM, Malaysia
Iman Liao	University of Nottingham, Malaysia
Izzatul Nabila Sarbini	UNIMAS, Malaysia
Je Sen The	USM, Malaysia
Leong Yeng Weng	UNITEN, Malaysia
Mad Helmi Ab. Majid	UPSI, Malaysia
Mohammad Aazam	University of Nottingham, Malaysia
Mohana Shanmugam	UNITEN, Malaysia
Mohd Fadhil Harfiez Abdul Muttalib	UPSI, Malaysia
Mohd Hafeez Osman	UPM, Malaysia
Mohd Sidek Fadhil Mohd Yunus	UPSI, Malaysia
Norziana Jamil	UNITEN, Malaysia
Nur Faraha Hj. Mohd. Naim	UMS, Malaysia
Nur Syahela Hussien	UniKL, Malaysia
Nurdatillah Hasim	UniKL, Malaysia
Sami Salama Hussen Hajjaj	UNITEN, Malaysia
Sharifah Mashita Syed Mohamad	USM, Malaysia
Sharul Azim Sharudin	UNITEN, Malaysia
Siti Norul Huda Sheikh Abdullah	UKM, Malaysia
Suhaila Saee	UNIMAS, Malaysia
Syahaneim Marzukhi	UPNM, Malaysia
Yeng Weng Leong	UNITEN, Malaysia
Zarina Che Embi	UNITEN, Malaysia

Collaborators and Sponsoring Institutions

Yayasan Canselor UNITEN (YCU)
Tenaga Nasional Berhad (TNB)
Malaysian Information Technology Society (MITS)
National Professors' Council (MPN)
Al-Madinah International University (MEDIU)
International Islamic University Malaysia (IIUM)
Multimedia Universiti (MMU)
Universiti Kebangsaan Malaysia (UKM)
Universiti Kuala Lumpur (UniKL)
Universiti Malaya (UM)
Universiti Malaysia Sabah (UMS)
University of Nottingham, Malaysia
Universiti Pertahanan Nasional Malaysia (UPNM)
Universiti Pendidikan Sultan Idris (UPSI)
Universiti Putra Malaysia (UPM)

Universiti Sains Islam Malaysia (USIM)
Universiti Sains Malaysia (USM)
Universiti Teknologi Malaysia (UTM)
Universiti Teknologi Petronas (UTP)
UOW Malaysia KDU Penang University College

Contents

Engineering and Digital Innovation

Cyber Security & Machine Learning and Digital Innovation

Energy Informatics and Digital Innovation

Keynote

Computer Vision for Supporting Image Search

Alan F. Smeaton$^{(\boxtimes)}$ (ORCID)

Insight Centre for Data Analytics, Dublin City University,
9, Glasnevin, Dublin, Ireland
`alan.smeaton@dcu.ie`

Abstract. Computer vision and multimedia information processing have made extreme progress within the last decade and many tasks can be done with a level of accuracy as if done by humans, or better. This is because we leverage the benefits of huge amounts of data available for training, we have enormous computer processing available and we have seen the evolution of machine learning as a suite of techniques to process data and deliver accurate vision-based systems. What kind of applications do we use this processing for? We use this in autonomous vehicle navigation or in security applications, searching CCTV for example, and in medical image analysis for healthcare diagnostics. One application which is not widespread is image or video search directly by users. In this paper we present the need for such image finding or re-finding by examining human memory and when it fails, thus motivating the need for a different approach to image search which is outlined, along with the requirements of computer vision to support it.

Keywords: Image/video search · Information retrieval · Computer vision · Human memory

1 Introduction

Digital forms of multimedia now assault our senses and is embedded into our lives for work, leisure and entertainment. Technology support for creating, capturing, compressing, storing, transmitting and rendering multimedia are now mostly solved while the technology we use for finding multimedia information, or for having it find us, has not developed as much.

We use computer vision techniques to analyse visual imagery and across a range of applications, computer vision supports those applications well. Systems for medical diagnosis based on imaging, for autonomous driving, for event detection and classification in surveillance video, for highlights detection and video summarisation in broadcast media, and now even image and video generation and style transfer all use different forms of computer vision.

In this paper we are particularly concerned with visual search, searching for images and videos, for which there are many use cases. Finding, or re-finding

H. Badioze Zaman et al. (Eds.): IVIC 2021, LNCS 13051, pp. 3–12, 2021.
https://doi.org/10.1007/978-3-030-90235-3_1

images is a niche scenario in which we want to locate or re-locate an image or video clip we think we may have seen in the past. This could be an image on a web page, or in an advertisement, or in a movie, or on social media and we may be able to recall certain aspects of it but not describe it fully. The challenges presented here are much more complex than re-finding an equivalent text document because when re-finding text we will generally recall the words or phrases used and will have enough recollection to adequately describe the document's content. When re-finding imagery we will usually have only a partial recollection of the image and thus we cannot describe it fully. Furthermore, we know that since as much as 40% of searching is re-finding information [6] then an even greater % of image search must be re-finding.

When we examine the kind of computer vision used to support visual information seeking we see a mis-match and in this paper we re-examine the relationship between searching to find or re-find visual content, and the computer vision used to support it. Since so much of our visual information seeking is re-finding, human memory is core to this so the paper will also include an overview of human memory and why we forget and thus have to re-find information. We will see how we are wrapping ourselves around the existing search technology behind computer vision and not how the technology is wrapping itself around us, to support us. This "technology first, human second" approach is bad because it makes us change or to develop technology for visual search systems in this case, that are less than they could be and instead of supporting us, we are forced to change.

In the next section of this paper we provide a recap on human memory and how it works and why it sometimes fails, followed by an overview of information seeking and how search is just one part, the final part. We then look at search systems and how they have developed and then we examine computer vision as it is used in visual information seeking. Finally in the conclusions section we argue for visual search as a conversation between searcher and repository, and what form of computer vision is needed for this.

2   Human Memory

The human brain is made of approximately 86 billion neurons, known as grey matter, connected by trillions of connections (synapses) along which electric pulses are transmitted. This architecture of a huge number of simple connected processors, is now realised as being very good for solving very complex problems, like vision, and learning. Human memory, a core component of all brain processing, is a brain-wide process and is broadly divided into 3 types:

1. Sensory or short term memory where we see, hear or feel something and which has a rapid decay unless it is refreshed;
2. Sensor memories are then passed to our short term memory but retained only if we are attentive to those senses. Usually we can only retain up to 7 items or chunks of information in our short term memory, and these are then discarded unless we consciously decide to store them in our long term memory;

3. Long term memory is a more permanent form of memory and is made of (1) declarative memory which is facts and events, like the answers to quiz questions and (2) procedural memory which is like muscle memory, playing piano or performing some work-related tasks like composing and sending an email.

There are many commonly-observed memory phenomena like false memories in autobiographical recall, Proustian moments of recall where sensing something, like the smell of garlic or hearing a certain song triggers a cascade of recollections about something else, or flashbulb memories where we have vivid recollection around significant events in our lives, like where we were and what we were doing when we heard the news about a significant world event or a personal event like the bereavement of a close friend.

Throughout our lifetime, our memory fails, naturally. Sometimes it can fail from a mild degree to a severe degree, and this is always from neurological damage. This can be immediate damage such as with a trauma, or it can be progressive such as with age. It can be caused by drugs like alcohol, by dementias like Alzheimer's, by diseases like Huntington's or Parkinson's, by OCD, schizophrenia, stroke, or Tourette's syndrome. But even without any of these factors, we just forget things anyway during our lives at work and at leisure, and in our social interactions with others. This is because not everything moves from our short term memory to our long term memory and even within our long term memory our memories will decay.

Investigations into how long we remember were first carried out by Hermann Ebbinghaus in the 1880s [3], and the results of his work still hold true, that there is an exponential loss from our long term memory unless information is reinforced [5]. That means that last-minute cramming before an examination usually won't work and it means that the best way is to learn something, forget some of it but learn it all again, forget some again but less than before, then learn it all again, etc.

How steep is this forgetting curve and how long are we likely to remember things? In the time it takes to make and drink a cup of tea we forget up to 42% of what we learned, in an 8-h work day we forget 64%, and in a week it will be 75% of what we learned and wanted to remember, that will be forgotten.

To stop memories from decaying and fading, we need to rehearse and to repeat, and to revise through spaced repetition. What is attractive about the forgetting curve is the steepness of the tail-off. The first time something new is learned it is quickly forgotten, the second time is less quickly forgotten and as you review and review, what's learned remains remembered for longer. So repetition—especially spaced repetition—helps us remember more, and for longer.

There are memory "tricks" we can do to re-enforce our memory like connecting something new we want to remember with existing information we recall, thus weaving it into things we already know. This is achieved using things like mnemonics, word association, visualisation, chunking or breaking complex information or that big picture into smaller bits. The internet and popular science is full of resources which claim to improve your memory but they are basically exploiting these two tricks . . . repetition to overcome the forgetting curve, and the weaving of new information into your existing knowledge.

We would like to believe that technology, in all its forms, is developed to help people. We have, and we use, technologies to help our sight (glasses, contact lens, smartphones which automatically caption our surroundings), our hearing (cochlear implants), and our movement (bionic prosthetics). This is quite accepted because we have used technology for some of our other basic needs like transport and communications.

Human memory already benefits from the use of supporting technology. A trivial example is phone numbers, which we now don't have to remember when we call somebody because they are replaced with aliases, the destination person's name, on our phones. We have notepads and post-its and chunking and tracking devices for our keys, calendars and diaries and more, but we have not planned a technology from scratch to help our memories, we have evolved it over time, especially in recent times and almost by stealth. Because so much of our lives are spent online and digital, we have learned that we do not have to remember things to the same degree as previously because we can always search for things from our past. This includes our emails, our documents, our browsing history, our enterprise systems and our social media feeds.

So before we take a look at how we find things among these enormous, up-to-date, always available information resources, and see how easily accessible they really are, let us take a look at information seeking more generally.

3   Searching and Information Seeking

Searching for information or finding information is known in the research world as "information retrieval" (IR) and as a scientific topic within the broad computing area it is not new. IR pre-dates web search engines and was not a research backwater but a slowly maturing discipline. It takes time for the science behind a research area like information science to develop, it cannot be pushed or forced and by the 1990s we had evolved to a model of search based on a ranked list of search outputs. This ranked list was based on the statistical distributions of words in documents and in queries. We were developing interaction models where searches were incremental, looking beyond simple search ranking. We were looking at aspects like the incremental value of additional information in a ranking and relevance feedback in mid-search so as to re-rank as yet unseen documents. Though these were computationally demanding they would support searching as an interaction, a journey between the searcher and the information repository with the final destination being a user with a satisfied information need.

Throughout the intervening years IR developed to include things like the vector space model, term weighting approaches like BM25 and then language modeling, all built around the frequency of word occurrences in text and document representation based on a bag-of-words or more correctly a list of words. More recently we have seen retrieval based on learning-to-rank approaches, leveraging logged data from previous searches and advancements in machine learning.

Figure 1 taken from [4] illustrates the relationship between tasks we are performing, for work or for leisure, how these tasks generate information needs which we verbalise as a query which is then used as input to a search engine. What should be clear is that there is a large gap between what our task wants us to do, and the words we type into a search system, a kind of semantic gap.

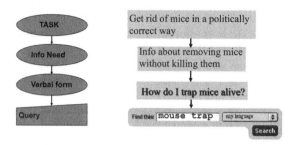

Fig. 1. How we go from information need, to search query (taken from [4]).

Then in the mid-1990s came the web, and the need or opportunity to provide search across all of the web and this was realised using a model of stateless search with no continuity or supporting the information seeking goal that enveloped each individual search. Instead the focus was on really fast response time to re-enforce the illusion that you were getting somewhere fast with your search. That was, and remains, the business model of fast response time and targeted advertising, and we accepted it because it was fast and it was free. Very quickly we grew used to this as being the way that search operated and it was superb engineering because it delivered fast response time in searching up-to-the-minute repositories of information.

In the intervening years the effort in terms of deployed web and enterprise searching has been towards crawling and indexing, and the search function has developed things like a multitude of positive and negative ranking factors for web pages and for websites and link importance and PageRank, and all of the "smarts" like Panda/Farmer and Penguin, but the search remains the same ...fast response time but stateless search. There have been some exceptions like the knowledge graph, introduced by Google in 2012, which presented facts extracted from pages instead of ranking.

As a service, search is free, even though we pay for it with our data, but as a quality service it is not very good. That is because we have grown accustomed to searching poorly because the incremental cost to us of doing another search is so little, precisely because it is so fast. Web search and enterprise search use a brute force approach and our over-arching tasks, the things we actually want to find in terms of our information seeking, information finding, information discovery, these are a mis-match to the rapid-fire, stateless searching on the web and on our enterprises. There is no support for negotiated discovery, no information exploration, no information seeking, and as users we do not miss this because we never had it.

Information retrieval is hard, and it is difficult not because of the information we search for but because of us, the people who do the searching. We are all different and our diversity is what makes humankind. That means that building a search system with a one-size-fits-all and no tailoring for the individual, is already a flawed choice.

When we want to find information, we need it in order to make decisions, and that might be tasks related to work, leisure, or social interactions during interactions with others. When we look at these information needs we discover that there are different kinds of information need. Our information needs may be verificative or explorative so for example *"who is the President of the European Commission"* vs. *"tell me about the European Commission"*. Our needs might be precise or vague such as *"Where was the movie Castaway shot?"* vs. *"tell me about the movie Castaway"*. We may be interested in topics over a long lived or a short duration and finally our needs might cost-dependent or inconsequential with respect to cost, where cost is measured as our own time.

This interpretation of information seeking is not new and information scientists have been developing theories of information seeking for decades. This is done in an attempt to understand the processes behind information seeking so we can then build tools to support different stages. Often this is done within narrowly defined tasks, like information seeking to support journalists writing articles, or in seeking information about health. Figure 2 taken from [7] shows research areas that have come and gone over the last several decades as major foci for IR research and most of these still subscribe to this single query, stateless, ranked output model of searching rather than addressing information seeking.

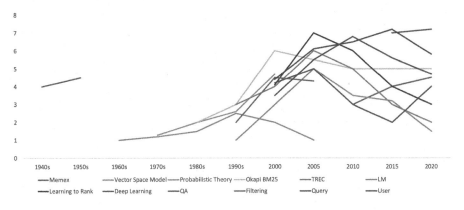

Fig. 2. History of the major research topics in information retrieval (taken from [7]).

Meanwhile the rate at which our information access is evolving is so fast that the models of information seeking cannot keep up with the technology. Think of things we use now, every day, which were not present a decade ago, or even just a couple of years ago. The Apple iPhone was introduced in 2007 and iPad in 2010, Amazon Echo was introduced in 2017, Twitter started in 2006, Snapchat in 2011 and TikTok was founded in 2016. The reason for mentioning these is to show how the information seeking landscape, the ways we can find information or it find us, the kinds of information, delivery platforms, all this changes hugely, so modelling information seeking is really difficult as a result.

As yet another further complication, nowadays we all have continuous partial attention as we work and relax. Many of us now do a kind of multi-tasking because our devices – smartphones, tablets and laptops – are multi-purpose. Sometimes this happens when we mindwander which we all do, all the time, skimming the surface of incoming information as it is presented to us, picking out relevant details and moving on to the next stream in a continuous rather than episodic fashion, casting a wide net across our tasks, but not often giving any of them our full attention.

If we accept that there is a "semantic gap" between our information seeking and the search tools that we use, what does search look like, and we answer that in the next section.

4   Search Systems

We know that search is not easy, it is indefinite, with lots of uncertainty and with complex inter-dependencies, user requirements are incomplete, sometimes contradictory and always changing as searchers' needs evolve, even in mid-search. The standard search interface and affordance allows for the very simple concepts of a search query as a set of words or query terms, a ranked list of documents as an output, a serial examination of documents in that list with the assumption that all documents in the list have at least one query term. The user is expected to browse this list until the information need is satisfied and if not, at some point the user will re-formulate and re-issue the query and repeat the process, including seeing documents already viewed in a previous search.

There is no support for a searcher's assessment of relevance, no opportunity for the searcher to indicate to the system that a document is a good, or a bad document in terms of their information need, each search operation in the sequence is independent of other searchers and thus the system is stateless with no learning, and no conversation or interaction between searcher and search system.

This model is used in web search, enterprise search, search through emails and social media and searches on our own computer filespace. The takeaway message from looking at search is that search systems do not help individuals, they tune parameters to optimise for the average person, thus diluting any personalisation or benefit to an individual person, let alone for an individual search.

An interesting use of search tools is re-finding, the phenomenon whereby a user is searching for information s/he had previously located, but cannot now find and needs to re-read or review it for the task at hand. The concept has been around for more than a decade and one of the of the earliest studies on this was [6] who found that 40% of search queries at that time, were associated with information re-finding. Recently re-finding has morphed into what is called personalised search where stateless search systems are augmented with external resources, like contextual information [8] in order to re-find information. We shall return to the importance of re-finding later.

5   Computer Vision and Image Search

Computer vision and multimedia information processing have made extreme progress within the last decade and many tasks in some domains can be performed with the same level of accuracy as if done by humans, or better. This is mostly because we leverage the benefits of having huge amounts of data available for training, we have an enormous increase in the amount of computer processing and emergence through using GPUs in parallel, and we have seen the evolution of machine learning as a suite of techniques to combine data and processing and deliver accurate vision-based systems. While issues of bias, explainability, compute cost and carbon footprint in training each remain as hurdles, there is now such momentum in the neural networks approach to visual information processing that these hurdles will be overcome in time.

Given that we can automatically process some forms of visual information better than humans what do we use this processing for? We use this in autonomous vehicle navigation though that is a narrow and niche application as are security applications when searching CCTV for a particular individual or when classifying crowds of people for shopping and footfall analysis. Computer vision is also used for medical image analysis for healthcare diagnostics, for remote monitoring of premises for outlier detection or monitoring of animals or crops in agriculture. All these applications and many more are widespread and established yet one which is not so widespread is image or video search directly by users. Most of the images and videos delivered to us as part of work or leisure or entertainment come from recommendations, or are included as part of a larger multimedia "package" like a movie, a news article, or a social media post where other aspects of that package are used to select it for delivery to us.

The types of image search which are available to us include searching for duplicates or near duplicates through reverse image search with systems like TinEye (https://tineye.com/). We also have image similarity where given an image as a search query, systems like those offered by the major web search systems, visually similar images can be found, with visual similarity based on low level features, with lots of options to filter the results. But what if we don't have a query image that we want to search against? In such cases we are faced with having to sketch a query image, which we are terrible at doing, or we have to use words to describe what we think might be in the image we are looking for. If we are searching for an image which we have already seen at some point in the past and we wish to re-find it, then likewise there is no support except to re-trace the route used to locate it first time, by following your browsing history for example to try to formulate a query using words. That is because the way we index and represent images in most systems is by low level features like colours and shapes combined with tagging them with a bag of words representation and that is done at indexing time, not at search time. This is a clear mis-match to the kind of image representation we would like to see when we try to find or re-find images. It ignores all the characteristics of human memory that lead us to need to find or to re-find the image in the first place. So no connecting an image with things we already know so it comes to mind more easily, no repeated exposure to an image so that its forgetting curve is less steep, no interaction during search or information discovery except the stateless rapid-fire query-examine-query cycle. In the final section of this paper we will look at the opportunity for a better form of image search.

6   Image Search Should Be a Conversation

Given the mis-match between on the one hand human memory and its characteristics of forgetting and our typical information seeking behaviours where we have tasks that require information in order to complete them, and on the other hand the typical feature representation of images, this is both a problem, and an opportunity for computer vision to do something differently. Each image or video clip will have a natural inherent memorability associated with it, as demonstrated in the annual MediaEval video memorability benchmark evaluation [2] and some systems based on a typical machine learning paradigm of training against manually annotated memorability scores and using an ensemble of models, show excellent performance in predicting such memorability [1]. However just because some visual imagery is more memorable does not mean we are going to actually remember it when we need to.

Human memory will fail, naturally and when it does then this will lead to the need for re-finding images, for which we currently have to use the same form of search tools as we do for all our other kinds of searching. We have grown accustomed to this because it has been the default search modality for decades. Yet re-finding of imagery is much more complicated than re-finding text documents or web pages because we have this phenomenon of continuous partial attention as we work and hence we are less likely to be able to describe or verbalise a description of it for input to a search engine. Image searching is not as widespread or as common or as much used as it should be because we are tied to the search model developed for searching through text, whose characteristics are enough to deliver something that works for text, but not for images.

If we were able to start again from scratch and build image search tools based on user needs rather than convenience to existing systems then image search would be interactive, conversational and incremental rather than a rapid-fire iterations of query re-formulations. The selection of candidate images to present to the searcher during such an interactive conversation would be based on novelty as well as similarity to any positive indications already provided by the searcher through relevance feedback. Relevance feedback would present alternative images to choose from rather than a ranked list, along the lines of "which of these two images is closer to what you are looking for" because rapid differentiation is something for which we are good at, and would re-enforce and clarify our actual information need.

In turn this would require computer vision to be incremental and run in real time, analysing and representing images and videos in some generic initial form and then, at query time, re-analysing in the context of a specific query in order to determine whether the image has or has not got the features the user is looking for. That means searching would be slower to complete because of the additional query-time computation required, but more accurate and satisfactory for the user because the user would be more engaged in the search process, and once the computation of query-specific features of an image or video was done it would be kept and re-used for subsequent querying. Building systems such as outlined here is now within our scope and would allow image search to be more integrated and useful, within our information seeking and discovery activities.

Acknowledgements. This work is part-funded by Science Foundation Ireland under Grant Number SFI/12/RC/2289_P2, co-funded by the European Regional Development Fund.

References

1. Azcona, D., Moreu, E., Hu, F., Ward, T., Smeaton, A.F.: Predicting media memorability using ensemble models. In: Proceedings of the MediaEval 2019 Workshop, 27–30 October 2019. vol. 2670. http://ceur-ws.org/Vol-2670/ (2019)
2. De Herrera, A.G.S. et al.: Overview of MediaEval 2020 predicting media memorability task: What makes a video memorable? In: MediaEval Multimedia Benchmark Workshop. http://ceur-ws.org/Vol-2882/ (2020)
3. Ebbinghaus, H.: Urmanuskript "Ueber das Gedächtniß." Passavia Universitätsverlag, Passau (1880)
4. Manning, C.D., Raghavan, P., Schütze, H.: Introduction to Information Retrieval. Cambridge University Press, Cambridge (2008)
5. Murre, J.M., Dros, J.: Replication and analysis of Ebbinghaus' forgetting curve. PloS One **10**(7), e0120644 (2015)
6. Tyler, S.K., Teevan, J.: Large scale query log analysis of re-finding. In: Proceedings of the Third ACM International Conference on Web Search and Data Mining, pp. 191–200. WSDM 2010. ACM (2010). https://doi.org/10.1145/1718487.1718512
7. Yang, G.H.: Information Retrieval Fundamentals. Slides from talk presented at AFIRM: ACM SIGIR/SIGKDD Africa Summer School on Machine Learning for Data Mining and Search, January 2019. http://sigir.org/afirm2019/. Accessed 21 Aug 2021
8. Zhou, Y., Dou, Z., Wen, J.R.: Enhancing re-finding behavior with external memories for personalized search. In: Proceedings of the 13th International Conference on Web Search and Data Mining, pp. 789–797 (2020)

Visualisation and Digital Innovation

Color Aesthetic Enhancement for Categorical Data Visualization

Wei Chuan Lim[1]([✉]), Chee Onn Wong[1], and Lai Kuan Wong[2]

[1] Faculty of Creative Multimedia, Multimedia University, Cyberjaya, Malaysia
cowong@mmu.edu.my
[2] Faculty of Computing and Informatics, Multimedia University, Cyberjaya, Malaysia
lkwong@mmu.edu.my

Abstract. Data visualizers are usually experts in statistics and the field they involved. Most of them have lack of knowledge in arts. This leads to the condition where visualization created by them most of the time are not pleasant in terms of color, or they will be limited to the palette choices provided in the platform if they want to get a better output. This reduced the potential of visualization to act as an effective medium for marketing or awareness-raising purposes. In this paper, we study on the coding of colors in the way that is closer to human perception, together with the concept of color harmonization based on existing research. By integrating them, we get a framework that can retrieve the range of colors that looks harmony based on any request color. Our aim is to enhance the aesthetics and beauty of data visualization diagram through color modification. In the process of harmonizing the colors, our approach uses a distance scaling method on the hue dimension. This approach can better preserve the intended relationship between different colors from the original visualization. In most cases, the scaling process would be scale down, decreasing the distance between colors. Therefore, we need to take additional precautions to make sure that the scaled colors can still be perceived differently. We conducted a color difference calculation on all colors with the colors that are closest to them. Through the numerical method, we can set a minimum value and computationally identify that whether does the two colors are safe enough to distinguish. The visualization can perform an entire hue shifting process by adding a constant value to the hue of all colors after being harmonized through our approach. Our proposed approach helps data visualization artist or automated program to create a more color harmonized output, as well as providing the ability to freely change its entire color theme, which is useful to match the presenting environment, without needing to consider the problem of color difference.

Keywords: Visualization · Color harmony · Human visual perception · Aesthetic

© Springer Nature Switzerland AG 2021
H. Badioze Zaman et al. (Eds.): IVIC 2021, LNCS 13051, pp. 15–26, 2021.
https://doi.org/10.1007/978-3-030-90235-3_2

1 Introduction

The technology nowadays is matured enough to generate data visualization diagrams computationally with minimal human effort, and the outcome has reached a certain level of satisfaction. Apparently, the demands of data visualization skills will go on for the following decades as data processing and analysis is continuing to emerge in many new fields. Apart from the professionals that highly depending on data visualization in their work, business companies also started to use data visualization as a persuasive method while approaching their clients. Besides that, organizations are starting to show data visualization diagram to the public to raise awareness regarding some specific topics too. Therefore, the beauty of data visualization has become more important, as it needs to ensure the visualization is effective, in such a way that it can attract the target audiences' attention and enhance their interest to read it.

One of the key factors to evaluate the aesthetic value of visualization is the color. Based on Burchett [1], colors seen together to produce a pleasing affective response are said to be in harmony. In data visualization, color is often use as a notation for data classification, or representing one or multiple dimensions of the data. Meanwhile, visualization that is constructed with harmony colors will be more appealing.

Visualization tools such as ColorBrewer and the charts function in Microsoft Excel provides several choices of preset color palettes that seems pleasant. However, choices are still limited, and fine adjustment process will be challenging when the creator is required to follow certain criteria in color for specific data category. Besides, color palettes generated through algorithmic method such as the linguistic approach [2, 3] are also lacking in harmonious value when they are viewed together.

In this paper, we are going to improve the pleasantness of categorical data visualization diagram by modifying its colors, so that it will be more attractive, and readers will feel more comfortable while looking at it, under the premise that the modified colors will not lose their original role. Our main intention of this work is to provide a significant improvement in terms of aesthetics for the continuous development of automated data visualization.

2 Background and Related Work

Our work consists of color transform based on harmonic schemes, with the integration of perceptually uniform color space.

2.1 Color Theory and Color Harmonization

Color theory is the set of guidelines on mixing various colors onto a visual presentation to imperceptibly leads the viewer to perceived the feeling based on the creator's intention.

Using the layout of color wheel, people starts to discover the relation between colors based on their position in terms of rotation angle and their effects. There are five widely accepted basic color schemes adopted in Adobe Color, which consists of analogous, monochromatic, triad, complementary, and split complementary.

Color harmony is one of the topics that always being discussed and generally adopted by designers for arts creation. Matsuda [4] proposed that a creation looks harmonious if all the colors exist in the creation follows certain patterns on a hue plane. Based on that, he developed eight harmonic patterns as shown in Fig. 1. These patterns are mostly named using the alphabets that look like their appearance (i, V, L, I, T, Y, X) on the plane, and the only exception (N) is a Neutral type that is used for the grayscale (between white and black) color sets. In Matsuda's research, the patterns can be rotated to any angle based on user preferences, and the harmonization value should be preserved. These harmonic patterns are widely used in the later research till now [5–8]. Cohen-Or [5] showed the harmonized output of photographs and posters, [6] emphasize the use of those patterns to generate color palette for fashion design, [7, 8] referred to the patterns in the creation and assessment of data or information visualization.

Carlos [6] categorized five out of the eight patterns into three basic color schemes – analogous (i, V), complementary (I, X), and triad (Y). However, we preferred to consider Type-i as monochromatic, which works better with the changes in tone (saturation and lightness) due to the potential ambiguity of minimal hue difference. Type-Y also should be better considered as split-complementary based on the shape of its pattern, and Type-X should be a combination of analogous with complementary.

In this paper, we use Matsuda's harmonization approach to enhance the aesthetic value by recoloring the existing visualization into one that adheres to the harmonization pattern.

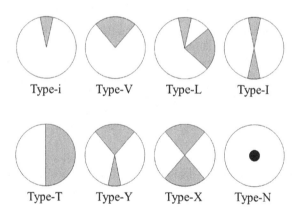

Fig. 1. Matsuda's color harmonic templates on a hue wheel.

2.2 Perceptually Uniform Color Space

During the process of choosing colors for arts creation, various kinds of color wheels will be used by different artists. As the common ones will be the RGB and RYB color wheels. The visible difference between those color wheels are the distance between hues. For example, distance between red and green in RGB is 120°, while the distance of that in RYB is 180°. Therefore, the color palette output will be different when the same color scheme is applied on these color wheels, and we need to consider the best color wheel for human perception.

In the first decade of 20th century, Albert H. Munsell introduced the Munsell color system. The Munsell system defined colors in a three-dimensional space, the hue value changes along the angle on a hue circle plane, contrast value depending on the distance from the center of circle, and lightness changes following the height of the hue circle. As compared to RGB and RYB, Munsell system divided the hue circle into five reference hues which are red, yellow, green, blue, and purple. Approximately, the angle distance between red and green is 144°. It is the first color space that take human perception into consideration [9]. Matsuda's color harmonic templates are defined based on this color system.

In this paper, we attach to the importance of user intuition on the relation between colors. The CIELAB color space defined later by International Commission of Illumination (CIE) is intended to be a perceptually uniform color space. By showing the hues on a color circle or hue plane, humans should perceive the same difference between two colors in any angle rotation when their angle distance is the same.

2.3 Visualization of Categorical Data and Continuous Data

In data visualization, the type of data determines how it should be presented. Color can be used in various ways to represent data.

For categorical data, different color will be representing different data group for readers to compare between the underlying value. The data group is distinct and there is a finite number of colors exist in the visualization (usually less than 10). For example, we use a pie chart to show the number of different fruits in a collection. Red will be suitable to represent the apple category whereas yellow will suit for banana. Based on the difference in size of the red pie and yellow pie, we can compare the percentage of both fruits in the entire collection. The choice of color for categories is important that it should highly achieves the color-concept associations [10], and research such as [2, 3] are relying on machine learning methods to assign the most suitable color to the respective terms.

The use of colors to represent continuous data usually will make use of tone (chroma and lightness) changes. Normally a high tone indicates a positive or active value of data and vice versa, and the range between the preset highest and lowest value consists of all the values available. Theoretically, the available values are potentially infinite. However, due to the limitation of colors in all kinds of displays and ease for mathematical calculation, the value will be rounded onto a specified precision. But it can still be hundreds of available colors between the highest and lowest tones. For continuous data, as in Fig. 2 [11], the actual value of each single data sometimes is not important. The purpose of this kind of diagram is more to visualize the collection as a whole to show the trend of data changes.

Our proposed approach is focusing on categorical data, where each color usually symbolizes a different class or group. In this type of data, hue variation possesses a higher importance compared to tone.

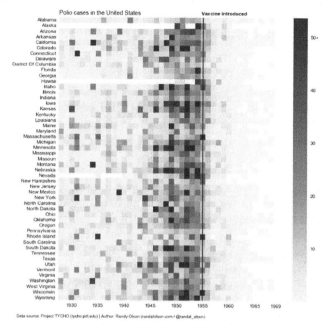

Fig. 2. Example of continuous data visualization which focus on the whole view rather than providing the ability to look for the precise value.

2.4 Color Discriminability

A main concern of constructing palette for visualization is the ability to identify different data group immediately based on the colors. Color appeared differently to human when the color angle changes [12]. A simple way of color discriminability evaluation can be done by calculation based on the Euclidean distance between two colors in a color space, known as the color difference.

Besides the standard calculation, CIE had introduced some formulas based on their CIE color spaces, more concerning on perceptual uniformity, and named their distance metric as ΔE^*. $\Delta E^* = 1$ supposed to be the Just Noticeable Differences (JND), which is the minimum difference that people able to distinguish between two different colors at 50% of all the time. [13] found out the 50% noticeable difference for colors varies under different visualization type and colored areas. This paper then has conducted tests to calculate the 50% noticeable difference for points, bars, and lines type of data visualization in different sizes.

Maji [14] proposed an Equilibrium Distribution Model (EDM) to achieve a higher color discriminability between different sections in visualization. This approach has shown a higher effectiveness on image that consists of more than 30 features to be differentiated, and is theoretically proven will be applicable on image with 100 features. However, a perceivable color difference for usual data visualization diagram need to be guaranteed when compared with any color in the whole diagram. This is because we are not just considering the discriminability between two colors when comparing side by side. We also need to make sure that the readers will not be confused when they are referring different colors from the legend.

3 Methods

Our enhancement methodology adopts the idea in [15, 16], where the harmonized palette is generated by extracting color from the original visualization and perform adjustment based on specific algorithms. This approach can be better to retain the original color characteristics.

The colors in an existing visualization image can be retrieved through k-means algorithm. This algorithm is able to look for the set of most representative colors in an image. Then, on a hue circle each color will move towards the nearest segment of the harmony pattern, decided by which segment has the least hue difference from the original color. The colors are listed in lightness, contrast, hue form according to the CIELCH (polar form of CIELAB space) measurement.

Based on the chosen color harmony pattern on a hue plane, we look for the two furthest colors that will be grouped into the same region. Then, we scale the hue distance down until the two colors reach the highest acceptable distance of that region. The scale then will be applied to all the other colors with the point next to it in anticlockwise direction. The output of this process will remain the color differences under the same scale and all colors are able to be fully covered in the harmony segments.

3.1 Hue Values Normalization

Before starting the harmonization, we need to take a preliminary step to make sure the hue is valid for calculation. For a set of colors that going to be merged into the same segment, if the 0°/360° border lies between the two furthest hue point (in terms of degree), the hue value of colors after the border will start from 0°, thus will not be continuous following the anticlockwise direction. Therefore, for each color we need to get the continuous hue values H_c based on the following condition.

$$H_c = \begin{cases} H + 360, & \text{if } H < H_0 \\ H, & \text{otherwise} \end{cases}$$

H represents the original hue and H_0 is the first hue of the set according to anticlockwise direction.

3.2 Hue Transformation

In data visualization, the similarity level between colors that representing data categories may consists of some underlying intentions. Colors that looks nearer to each other is expected to have a closer relationship. This information should not be lost after the aesthetic enhancement. For the hue transformation process, we use the distance scaling approach so that we can preserve the distance ratio between different colors.

For each segment, given a hue range limit l. We can get the hue scale s using the following equation:

$$s = \frac{l}{H_n - H_0} \tag{1}$$

where the set $H = \{H_0, H_1, H_2, \ldots, H_n\}$ is the list of hues (adopt H_c if it is different from the original hue value) of all colors to be grouped, in ascending order. H_n represents the highest hue and H_0 is the lowest hue.

The first hue H_0' will remain the same while applying scale transformation, then for all following hues, the harmonization value, H' can be calculated by.

$$H_i' = H_{i-1}' + (H_i - H_{i-1})s \tag{2}$$

After the harmonization scaling is done, we need to shift the colors to match the pattern by adding a constant value to all the hues in H'. This step can be skipped for those patterns that only have one segment (Type-i, Type-V and Type-T).

By moving along the hue plane with a constant distance from the origin, only the hue value will be changed, the chroma and lightness remain the same as the original color.

Additionally, by adding the same shift value to all the hues on the plane, we can get the same effect as rotating all colors on a hue plane, giving the effect of shifting the hue of the entire output.

3.3 Minimum Color Difference

In 2001, CIE published the CIEDE2000 formula after the CIE76 and CIE94 for distance metric calculation. CIEDE2000 is the to date formula that best resolve the perceptual uniformity issue [17, 18]. The distance matric value can be calculated with the formula.

$$\Delta E_{00}^* = \sqrt{\left(\frac{\Delta L'}{k_L S_L}\right)^2 + \left(\frac{\Delta C'}{k_C S_C}\right)^2 + \left(\frac{\Delta H'}{k_H S_H}\right)^2 + R_T \left(\frac{\Delta C'}{k_C S_C}\right)\left(\frac{\Delta H'}{k_H S_H}\right)} \tag{3}$$

$\Delta L'$, $\Delta C'$, $\Delta H'$ are the lightness, contrast and hue difference of the two colors for comparison. k_L, k_C, k_H are the correction factors of the observation environment. S_L, S_C, S_H are the compensation for visual perception. R_T is representing the hue rotation term to overcome the blue region problem.

In this research, we adopt a minimum color difference (ΔE_{min}^*) of 10 between each color to ensure that the color is obviously distinct when referring to the legend. This value is an integer round up based on the noticeable difference found out in [13] for bar charts with the visual angle of 2°. In case of low color difference detected, manual shifting process should be done by human action.

3.4 Color Theme Modification

Based on the CIEDE2000 formula, we acknowledge that in the CIE color space, the calculated color difference will always be the same when a constant value is added to (or subtracted from) either the lightness, contrast, or hue of all the colors.

In the perspective of hue, which ranged between 0° and 360°, adding or subtracting a constant value of all colors is same as the process of rotating all colors together on a color hue wheel. This rotation will change the theme and feel of the visualization, while ensuring that all colors can still be perceived differently.

4   Results

Based on the methodology, we apply our approach on a sample data visualization chart with random picked colors. All the colors are collected and ordered based on the hue value. Type-V pattern is used for this harmonization. Due to the V segment crossing the 0°/360° of hue circle, we added 360 to hue value of the colors after the 0° border to make the value continuous.

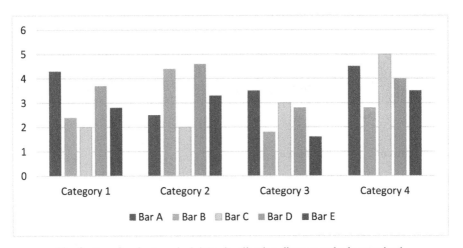

Fig. 3. Sample of categorical data visualization diagram to be harmonized.

Using Eq. (1), we set the hue range limit l to 60°, and we will get the value of s as 0.312, rounded to 3 decimal places. Based on the s value we get, we apply harmonization with Eq. (2). The harmonized hue values for each color (H') are listed in Table 2. For this example, we take an additional step by adding a constant shift of 88.548 to all hues to remain the third color (red) constant after harmonization. By referring that as the base point, all other hues will move towards it after transformation.

Based on harmonized color Table 3, we calculate the ΔE^* between each color and the color that is nearest to it in anticlockwise direction using Eq. (3). Hue value is retrieved from Table 2 while lightness and contrast is referring from Table 1 because our harmonization method did not make any modifications on the lightness and contrast value.

All color differences are higher than 10. This means that the harmonized outcome of this visualization can be perceived clearly and will not confuse the readers in terms of color discriminability.

Table 1. Lightness, contrast, hue and continuous hue values of the data representation colors in Fig. 3.

Bar	Color	Lightness	Contrast	Hue (H)	Continuous hue (H_c)
D	Light Blue	65	17.047	270.682	270.682
E	Dark Blue	35	38.283	274.999	274.999
A	Red	51	99.541	39.471	399.471
B	Orange	72	77.742	70.435	430.435
C	Yellow	95	93.574	102.709	462.709

Table 2. Original hue and transformed hue values after harmonization of the data representation colors in Fig. 3.

Bar	Original hue (H)	Harmonized hue (H')	Transformed hue after harmonization	Final color
D	270.682	270.682	359.230	Light purple
E	274.999	272.031	0.579	Dark purple
A	39.471	310.923	39.471	Red
B	70.435	320.598	49.146	Orange
C	102.709	330.682	59.230	Light orange

Table 3. Color difference of each harmonized color with the color next to it in anticlockwise direction on a hue plane.

Base Bar	Bar with color next to the base bar color in anticlockwise direction on hue plane	Color difference (ΔE^*)
D	E	31.570
E	A	29.445
A	B	20.173
B	C	17.734
C	D	38.451

Figure 4 shows the outcome after harmonization. As compared to Fig. 3 the original version, this outcome is presented with a more comfortable look and feel, and still able to perform well as a data visualization diagram, showing the classification of data clearly.

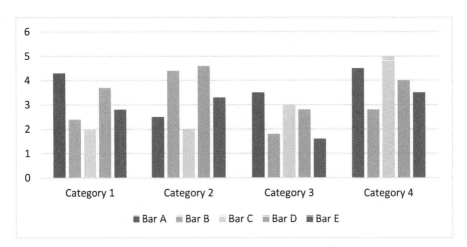

Fig. 4. Harmonized data visualization diagram of Fig. 3.

Using the harmonized visualization in Fig. 4, we can perform a color theme modification process by shifting all the hues of the colors in the entire image. Figure 5 is the outcome after applying a hues rotation of 180°. This rotation can be interpreted as an action to convert the color temperature from a warm color set (as in Fig. 4) to a cool palette.

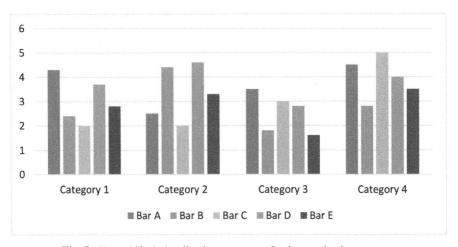

Fig. 5. Hues shifted visualization outcome after harmonization process.

5   Conclusion and Future Works

The result shows that our method can enhance the aesthetic value of categorical data visualization. By grouping the hues based on a certain pattern, we can improve the harmonization of visualization. Choosing the appropriate hue pattern also will help to indicate the relation between data categories, presenting more information to the viewer. However, this selection process still requires human action because humans can comprehend the relation of the categories better.

The proposed method does not take lightness and contrast into consideration, maintaining their original value in harmonization process. The utilization of lightness and contrast dimension has the potential to apply a monochrome scheme (Type-i) to show a different kind of data relationship. This will be helpful when showing numerical data. Moreover, by using hue and tone in the same visualization, we can increase the dimension of data representation. For example, different hue may represent different data category, while tone symbolize the numerical value. Further research can be done to identify the practicality of this concept and improve our model.

Beside the aspect of harmonization, it is also important that the readers need to be able to discriminate colors that represent different categories. Therefore, the transformation methodology needs to consider the minimum color difference.

For our future work, we plan to construct an algorithm that can be applied on the colors to computationally adjust them until all the colors adhere to the minimum perceptual difference, while preserving the aesthetic value as a whole. This will make our approach more integrated to achieve the realization of automated data visualization.

Acknowledgement. The authors would like to express appreciation for the support of the Fundamental Research Grant Scheme [FRGS/1/2019/SSI07/MMU/02/1] in providing adequate resource and guidance to complete this research.

References

1. Burchett, K.E.: Color harmony. Color. Res. Appl. **27**(1), 28–31 (2002). https://doi.org/10.1002/col.10004
2. Lin, S., Fortuna, J., Kulkarni, C., Stone, M., Heer, J.: Selecting semantically-resonant colors for data visualization. Comput. Graph. Forum **32**(3pt4), 401–410 (2013). https://doi.org/10.1111/cgf.12127
3. Setlur, V., Stone, M.C.: A linguistic approach to categorical color assignment for data visualization. IEEE Trans. Visual Comput. Graph. **22**(1), 698–707 (2015). https://doi.org/10.1109/TVCG.2015.2467471
4. Matsuda, Y.: Color design. Asakura Shoten **2**(4), 10 (2002)
5. Cohen-Or, D., Sorkine, O., Gal, R., Leyvand, T., Xu, Y.Q.: Color harmonization. In: ACM SIGGRAPH 2006 Papers, pp. 624–630 (2006). https://doi.org/10.1145/1179352.1141933
6. Lara-Alvarez, C.: Reyes, T: A geometric approach to harmonic color palette design. Color Res. Appl. **44**(1), 106–114 (2019). https://doi.org/10.1002/col.22292
7. Einakian, S., Newman, T.S.: An examination of color theories in map-based information visualization. J. Comput. Lang. **51**, 143–153 (2019). https://doi.org/10.1016/j.cola.2018.12.003

8. Zaeimi, M., Ghoddosian, A.: Color harmony algorithm: an art-inspired metaheuristic for mathematical function optimization. Soft. Comput. **24**(16), 12027–12066 (2020). https://doi.org/10.1007/s00500-019-04646-4

9. Cochrane, S.: The Munsell color system: a scientific compromise from the world of art. Stud. Hist. Philos. Sci. A **47**, 26–41 (2014). https://doi.org/10.1016/j.shpsa.2014.03.004

10. Rathore, R., Leggon, Z., Lessard, L., Schloss, K.B.: Estimating color-concept associations from image statistics. IEEE Trans. Visual Comput. Graph. **26**(1), 1226–1235 (2019). https://doi.org/10.1109/TVCG.2019.2934536

11. Olson, R.S.: Revisiting the Vaccine Visualizations. http://www.randalolson.com/2016/03/04/revisiting-the-vaccine-visualizations/ (2016)

12. Fairchild, M.D.: Color Appearance Models. 3rd ed. John Wiley & Sons (2013). https://doi.org/10.1002/9781118653128

13. Szafir, D.A.: Modeling color difference for visualization design. IEEE Trans. Visual Comput. Graph. **24**(1), 392–401 (2017). https://doi.org/10.1109/TVCG.2017.2744359

14. Maji, S., Dingliana, J.: Perceptually optimized color selection for visualization. Tetrahedron **4**(1.63299), 1–63299 (2018)

15. Zhang, Q., Xiao, C., Sun, H., Tang, F.: Palette-based image recoloring using color decomposition optimization. IEEE Trans. Image Process. **26**(4), 1952–1964 (2017). https://doi.org/10.1109/TIP.2017.2671779

16. Tan, J., Echevarria, J., Gingold, Y.: Palette-based image decomposition, harmonization, and color transfer. arXiv preprint arXiv:1804.01225 (2018)

17. Luo, M.R., Cui, G., Rigg, B.: The development of the CIE 2000 colour-difference formula: CIEDE2000. Color. Res. Appl. **26**(5), 340–350 (2001). https://doi.org/10.1002/col.1049

18. Yang, Y., Ming, J., Yu, N.: Color image quality assessment based on CIEDE2000. Adv. Multimedia (2012). https://doi.org/10.1155/2012/273723

A Preliminary Model of Learning Analytics to Explore Data Visualization on Educator's Satisfaction and Academic Performance in Higher Education

Nur Maisarah Shahril Khuzairi[✉] and Zaihisma Che Cob

Universiti Tenaga Nasional, Jalan Ikram-Uniten, 43000 Kajang, Selangor, Malaysia

Abstract. With the rapid proliferation of online learning due to the Covid-19 pandemic, learning management solutions and software has gained an extraordinary importance in tertiary education. This shift has created large amounts of data from online learning systems that need to be translated into meaningful information, hence data visualization has come into prominent focus as a solution that provides a powerful means to drive Learning Analytics to assess and support educators and students alike in decision-making and sense-making activities from the data collected. Although many research works have been published on data visualization focusing on techniques, tools and best practices, there is still a lack of research in the context of online learning to meet this urgent need of quality data visualization for successful decision-making. In this paper, we explore data visualization that is currently used in learning analytics and present an integrated preliminary model based on DeLone and McLean's IS Success model to examine the role and significance of data visualization by incorporating it as an antecedent to the Information Quality construct of the IS success model, which will support teaching and learning in an online learning environment for improved educators and student performance. This paper adds to the existing literature by incorporating data visualization to support educators decision-making and its performance impact of online learning through the consideration of the IS success model's elements. This integrated preliminary conceptual model aims to support online teaching and learning by addressing the research gap that has emerged from the expansion of learning analytics in educational technology.

Keywords: Data visualization · Learning analytics · IS success · Technology-acceptance model

1 Introduction

The world has drastically changed since the emergence of the Covid-19 pandemic. Most in-person activities have been either diminished or modified to reduce contact between persons which includes all learning activities have been moved predominantly to an online setting. This transition has caused many difficulties [1–3] in the delivery and consumption of educational content.

© Springer Nature Switzerland AG 2021
H. Badioze Zaman et al. (Eds.): IVIC 2021, LNCS 13051, pp. 27–40, 2021.
https://doi.org/10.1007/978-3-030-90235-3_3

Also new applications and tools have been adopted to facilitate online teaching and learning such as learning management systems, teleconferencing platforms and so on. This use of technologies has prompted an exponential creation of educational data which is readily available and more accessible than ever before. But there is glaring issue of how do we transform this large amounts of raw data to meaningful and actionable information which can be used by educators to improve their pedagogical approaches?

As such there is a need for learning analytics tools that have a versatile data visualization module to take advantage of complex information, by break it down to easy to understand graphical translations that convey meaningful insights to educators for enhanced decision-making.

The use of data visualization for better comprehension and decision- making is not something new. The graphical translation of raw information has its roots in early map-making and has grown into the current statistical charts, graphs, heatmaps and etc. [4]. Today, there are various definitions to data visualization such as visual representations of statistics and patterns to visual text, but the context of 'data visualization' is generally understood as graphical representations of data to facilitate understanding [5, 6] and sense-making. With the growth of technology, computers can now process large amounts of data for analysis and render vibrant and informative visualizations very quickly and efficiently for consumption by the user.

The well-known advantages to data visualization has been adopted in many domains of research such as meteorology [7], healthcare [8], and business intelligence [9], to significantly improve overall compression and decision-making.

The education domain has also embraced data visualization for decision-making. This is because the educational data generated is relatively large and complex, making it challenging to understand as it is [10]. Data visualization has the ability to expand human working memory by reducing cognitive load using visual aids, providing space efficient visualization to represent complex data, identify patterns through visually explicit representation and also making it easier to monitor larger datasets with aggregated views of it [8].

Data visualization which is used in the educational context, it is often associated with learning analytics. Learning analytics is defined as "the measurement, collection, analysis and reporting of data about learners and their contexts, for purposes of understanding and optimizing learning and the environments in which it occurs" [11]. Overall, the direction of data visualization is consistent with the growing movement of learning analytics research and practice, which is to optimize the teaching and learning process with the analysis of relevant data. Over the last decade online learning management systems have been enhanced with data visualization as part of learning analytics to track and visualize educational data to reveal actionable insights.

However, a concern within the emerging area of data visualization in learning analytics is how to determine when a visualization is communicating information successfully to its intended user and how that success can be measured [12]. The majority of research has focused on how to utilize data visualization in learning analytics and techniques to inform choices and action among stakeholders [10, 13], limited research has been conducted on data visualization's impact on learning analytics when it is in use for online learning. There are various ways to determine the successful implementation of data visualization in learning analytics depending on its goal and context. Notably when it comes to teaching and learning, the success of an online learning system is measured based on students' performance metrics and retention rate.

Research has suggested the importance of evaluating a variety of factors of an online learning system [14] in order to be effective at achieving its intended outcomes. Specifically more attention is needed with respect to the quality of information presented in the online learning system when data visualization is involved.

It is also suggested that not only the relevance and comprehensiveness of content determines the success of an online learning system but also the data visualization and its design is notably associated with successful outcomes too [15]. Although there is a need to ensure a comprehensive examination of data visualization as an element of information quality. To date there is a lack of research which systematically models and validates its actual impact in learning analytics for online learning. Therefore an investigation of data visualization as the determinant of a successful learning analytics system is vital. This study explores the impact of data visualization in learning analytics towards educators' satisfaction and students' academic performance. The Information System success model [16] and Technology Acceptance model [17] were integrated as a solution to this research problem.

2   Literature Review

Before a successful implementation of an online learning system, it is vital for us to examine theories to identify key elements and its attributes [18]. This is because the systems for learning is a complex process involving different stakeholders (i.e. students, educators, administrators), especially when more elements are introduced such as data visualization in learning analytics. Although a 'one-size-fits-all' format would be ideal but not all stakeholders are driven by the same goals and have the same interest in the same sets of data or have the same visualization [19]. For example, educators are interested with data visualization on their course materials to understand student behavior and engagement with the content, while administrators strive to utilize data visualization for retention and enrolment purposes. As such what is needed is a more comprehensive understanding of the role of data visualization in learning analytics that goes beyond merely presenting information in visual form instead it should be examined from the perspective of data visualization's impact on the overall system success.

2.1   Data Visualization in Learning Analytics

Data visualization is defined as a graphical representation of collected data to aid understanding of complex information that is sometimes difficult to be conveyed in words [20] or to identify patterns of specific situational behaviors. It can be said that data visualization is a core aspect of learning analytics work in relation to the provision of data to support the teaching and learning environment [19, 21, 22]. It is not only critical in visualizing large datasets but also creating meaningful insights for actionable decisions.

The benefits of data visualization are straightforward, as mentioned above, learning is a complex process involving different stakeholders and large amounts of collected data. Hence effective data visualizations for comprehension of collected data in learning analytics research is crucial and extremely valuable. A recent study by Paiva et al. [23] indicated that data visualizations are indeed an effective component to make information extracted from learning analytics understandable among educators. A study by Knight et al. [13] examined the web-based writing analytics tool by including data visualization in the formative feedback to students. Results showed that the visualization aspects provided additional writing support to students within and outside the classrooms. A similar result was reported in a study examining the students' outcomes and the use of e-portfolio where the inclusion of data visualization positively impacted their performance over time. The findings from Schaaf et al. [24] posited that data visualization enables students to interpret their development better with indicators for further improvement.

The varying positive value of data visualization to different stakeholders is shown when visual representations of data interact with human knowledge construction and inference-making, there is evidence for interpretative bias among different stakeholders and their visualization literacy [25]. But Yalcin et al.'s [26] comparative analysis on novice and skilled users in visual data exploration revealed that even novice users were able to gain data insights from visualization at the same level of skilled users. This two findings suggest even though there may be interpretative bias due to different levels of visualization literacy and stakeholders, there is value to be gained from visual representation of data no matter who the end user is.

A review of existing literature to date on data visualization for learning analytics in an online learning system validates data visualization as a pivotal determinant in an information system. For example, according to Roca, Chiu and Martinez [27], data visualization that is appealing and easy to understand significantly influences the system use and user satisfaction of an online learning system. This indicates that users of an online learning system require a high level of information quality where the visualized information presented will improve their productivity in performing tasks. Vazquez-Ingelmo et al. [28] observed that data visualization to be an indicator of information quality in learning analytics. This is because data visualization supports not only educators but also students in gaining insights about their teaching or learning. Another study by Park and Jo [29] indicated that although the learning analytics system used in the mentioned study did not significantly impact students' academic performance, but when students viewed the data visualization of the analytics data they had an increased understanding of their subject matter and overall satisfaction of the learning analytics system. Another example that presents the power of data visualization is the Social Networks Adapting Pedagogical Practice (SNAPP) tool which incorporates the social network analysis in learning analytics [30]. The networking visualized students' interaction in the learning management system which helped to identify patterns of their discussion activities effectively. Course Signal in Purdue University also utilized data visualization to give alarm signals that helped prevent students dropping-out and enhances their success [31]. Wise and colleagues [32] also provided a good example of how data visualization can be effectively conducted in learning analytics to promote quality of knowledge construction among students.

But there is an important gap that should be addressed, there is a need for data visualization in learning analytics to be grounded by theory rather than just being functionality and feature centric. Gasevic, Kovnovic & Joksimovic [15] mentioned previous studies rather focused on the functionality and features of data visualization in learning analytics, highlighting its potential impact on online learning and neglected to relate it to established theories in technology acceptance. Liu, Nersessian and Stasko [33] criticized that just building data visualization based on established principles is insufficient to contribute to body of research knowledge nor guide evaluation in the field of information system. Data visualization should be more than just attractive designs but instead we should incorporate theoretical considerations pertinent to the purpose a visualization aims to achieve such as support for computer aided learning [34]. In short, the crucial role of data visualization towards a successful online learning system has to be designed based on existing related theory, in order to validate its associations between the related system constructs.

It is worth noting here that many research work that focus on learning analytics are grounded by learning theories such as self-regulated learning [62], constructivism [63], collaborative learning [64] and others [65]. But only a few from the perspective of information systems [36] and with Technology Acceptance Model (TAM) [17] most frequently used [42]. However, TAM overlooks assessment of technology utilization [66]. DeLone and McLean's Information Systems (IS) Success model on the other hand assesses the technology used by looking at the impact of overall quality (information, system and service). With the implementation of online learning system, it is important to explore the overall quality of the system. Due to its simplicity and predictive accuracy in the field of technology acceptance, IS Success model and TAM have been widely used in various domains, including education technology [36–38, 42–44, 47], as such this is believe to an important addition to the research model. Hence in view of this, this research puts forth an integrated IS Success Model with perceived ease of use and usefulness from TAM to explore the relationship of data visualization and learning analytics in its impact on academic performance.

2.2 Information Systems Success Model

DeLone and McLean's, IS success model is regularly used in the field of technology to examine the factors affecting IS success and its impact. It is also consistently cited in various research works throughout the years. The original model includes six major variables that measure different aspects of IS success, which are information and system quality, and use, user satisfaction, individual impact and organizational impact [35].

Information quality and system quality was highlighted as the primary two antecedents for predicting system use and user satisfaction. This model differentiates from other models by focusing on users' beliefs and perceptions as an indicator of system use. In the IS success model, system quality refers to the features or characteristics required for a good IS system such as ease of use, flexibility, reliability and functionalities, while information quality refers to the effectiveness of how an IS system captures input and generates output such as its timeliness, accuracy, completeness and usability.

The causal relationships in the model have been used and tested in numerous studies especially in the field of online learning [36–38]. These studies are mostly aimed to investigate the success factors responsible for the implementation of an online learning system which contributes to the performance of students, and the results obtained generally found that the hypothesized relationships to be significant.

However years later, DeLone and McLean [16] made changes to their original model by adding another determinant of system use and user satisfaction into the model, which is service quality (see Fig. 1). This new determinant focuses on quality of support in terms of ease of maintenance and end-user support to the system user. Hence in total there are three major dimensions of qualities that contributes to the system use and user satisfaction, but the strength of their significance depend on the context of the studies and the type of statistical analyses applied. In general, information and system quality are advocated to measure success of information system for individual level while service quality inclines towards organizational level.

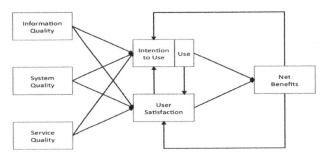

Fig. 1. The updated IS success model.

An ineffective development and implementation of IS systems that lack quality functionalities, inconsistent user interface design, and end-user support can be costly for higher education institutions as it requires a substantial amount of resources and monetary investment to remedy [40]. Thus DeLone & McLean IS success model's system quality, information quality and service quality are vital in ensuring the successful implementation of technology for its users and the organizations as a whole.

2.3 Technology-Acceptance Model

TAM another accepted and consistently cited model was conceptualized based on Fishbein and Ajzen's [41] Theory of Reasoned Action, which proposed two crucial factors for understanding behavioral intention – perceived usefulness and perceived ease of use of technology. Perceived usefulness is the degree to which an individual believes the technology will help his/her productivity, while perceived ease of use is the degree to which an individual believes that such technology can be used with minimum to little mental effort [17].

Due to its simplicity and predictive accuracy in the field of technology acceptance, TAM has been widely used in various domains, such as learning analytics [42–44], mobile learning [45], virtual laboratory [46], e-learning [47], e-procurement [48], healthcare systems [49], sustainable energy technology [50] and also ride-sharing application

[51]. Many studies in the related domains have shown that the perceived usefulness is one of the stronger drivers influencing one's behavioral intention in using the technology for practice.

In the following years, the original TAM was revised with a new proposed addition by Venkatesh and Davis [52] by including cognitive instrumental processes (output quality, result demonstrability, and job relevance), social influence elements (image, subjective norm, and voluntariness) and also experience to explain on the factor usage intention as well as perceived usefulness. With that the enhanced model is known as TAM2. Venkatesh [53] further investigated the significant role of perceived ease of use by including two classes of antecedents, which are anchors (self-efficacy, facilitating conditions, computer playfulness and anxiety) and adjustments (system-specific perceived enjoyment, system usability) (Fig. 2).

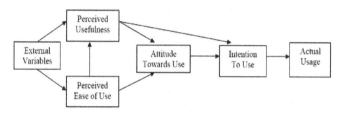

Fig. 2. Technology acceptance model (TAM) [67].

In 2008, Venkatesh and Bala proposed another extended model known as TAM3 that integrated TAM2 and the extended perceived ease of use variable by reviewing available research works in relation to determinants of perceived ease of use and usefulness. And subsequently a new comprehensive integrated model encompassing both variables antecedents were posited and empirically analyzed. The results indicated that they were generally consistent with those obtained from earlier research and most importantly, none of the determinants of perceived ease of use had significant effect on perceived usefulness and vice versa. However, perceived usefulness still emerged as the stronger predictor of behavioral usage intention [54].

3   Conceptualizing of the Integrated Learning Analytics Model

This research intends to integrate the IS success model and TAM to determine the impact of data visualization of learning analytics on educator's satisfaction and academic performance. The research model of the present study is illustrated in Fig. 3.

In this research model the following previous constructs from IS success model are renamed to create a more relevant label aligned to the present study: User Satisfaction is renamed to "Educator's Satisfaction", Intention to Use/Use to "Learning Analytics (LA) Use in System" and Net Benefits to "Academic Performance". The rest of the constructs are maintained as they are, which includes System Quality and Information Quality. The constructs integrated from TAM are Perceived Usefulness and Perceived Ease of Use. In addition, two new constructs are added as antecedent to System Quality and Information Quality, which are LA Features and Data Visualization respectively.

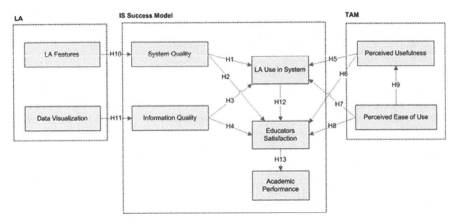

Fig. 3. Integrated learning analytics model.

These nine constructs proposed from literature review and the associated hypotheses are described below.

3.1 System Quality

This construct measures the system's features and functionalities related to the online learning system. The empirical research by Aldholay et al. [38] showed that system quality has positive effect on the use of an online learning system. The hypotheses are as follows.

H1: System Quality is positively associated with the LA Use in online learning system.

H2: System Quality is positively associated with Educator's Satisfaction on using online learning system.

3.2 Information Quality

This construct measures information generated by the online learning system specifically on students learning data. Previous studies showed that Information Quality affect both User Satisfaction and their Use of it [14, 55]. The hypotheses are as follows.

H3: Information Quality is positively associated with the LA Use in online learning system.

H4: Information Quality is positively associated with Educator's Satisfaction on using online learning system.

3.3 Perceived Usefulness

This construct measures the degree of a user's subjective belief that using the online learning system would promote and ease their task/problem within an organizational context. Theoretically, perceived usefulness affect both system use and user satisfaction of an online learning system [39]. Studies by Rienties et al. [44] and Al-Fraihat et al.

[56] showed that perceived usefulness is a pivotal factor in determining user satisfaction and their intention to use educational technologies. The hypotheses are as follows.

H5: Perceived Usefulness is positively associated with the LA Use in online learning system.

H6: Perceived Usefulness is positively associated with Educator's Satisfaction on using online learning system.

3.4 Perceived Ease of Use

This construct measures the degree of user's subjective belief that using the online learning system would be free of cognitive effort. Studies have investigated the relationship between Perceived Ease of Use and System Use and User Satisfaction on learning management system [57]. The findings confirmed that Perceived Ease of Use is a strong predictor of User Satisfaction. Thus, the hypotheses are as follows.

H7: Perceived Ease of Use is positively associated with the LA Use in online learning system.

H8: Perceived Ease of Use is positively associated with Educator's Satisfaction on using online learning system.

H9: Perceived Ease of Use is positively associated with Perceived Usefulness.

3.5 Learning Analytics Features

This construct measures the LA functionalities and features offered by the online learning system such as student content interaction analytics, quiz analytics, module analytics, single lesson analytics and social interaction analytics. Studies have shown the importance of System Quality in affecting the use of the system [14]. With the introduction of analytics into the online learning system, it will influence the system quality offered, which subsequently lead to higher user satisfaction as well as increase use of it. This leads to the following hypothesis.

H10: LA Features is positively associated with System Quality.

3.6 Data Visualization

This construct measures the desired visual content characteristics that are valued by users. As mentioned in Sect. 2.1, the type and design of data visualization provided will have an impact on the online learning system. Schaaf et al. [24] suggested that data visualization has a direct effect on the information one received. Learning analytics for online learning systems rely heavily on the information collected, hence it is believe data visualization is one of the factors which affect the information generated, having the characteristic quality of actionablity and explanability on the data presented. Thus, the hypothesis is as follows.

H11: Data Visualization is positively associated with Information Quality.

3.7 Learning Analytics Use in System

This construct measures the extent of which learning analytics is used in the online learning system such as the analytics and reporting elements are actually used/accessed. The LA Use in System is most useful in a setting where the usage of learning analytics is voluntary rather than mandatory [58]. A recent study by Koceska and Koceski [55] on factors affecting students satisfaction of online learning systems concluded that usage has a significant effect on one's satisfaction and their performance, which is also in-line with previous work done [59]. The hypothesis is as follows.

H12: LA Use in System is positively associated with Educator's Satisfaction on using online learning system.

3.8 Educator's Satisfaction

This construct measures the expectation of educators on the adopted online learning system, as compared to the available information. It is considered to be one of the most important constructs in the IS success model as it will determine the overall success of a system. Many studies have investigated the mediating effect of user satisfaction on performance impact of online learning [36, 39]. DeLone and McLean [16] also stressed that user satisfaction affect the use of a learning system. If they are satisfied with the system, their adoption of it into their activities are higher. The hypothesis is as follows.

H13: Educator's Satisfaction is positively associated with overall Academic Performance.

3.9 Academic Performance

This construct measures the net benefit or impact caused by the implementation of data visualization to the online learning system. The ultimate objective of the online learning systems use is to enhance learning pedagogy and improve academic performance. Hence student academic performance indicators (e.g. grades) is used as an assessment of individual students' to measure the impact of the change introduced. It has been a focus of many studies in this field [55, 60].

4 Discussion and Limitations

A conceptual model is a very valuable guide to real-world implications of a system [61]. This section will discuss on the implication and limitations of the integrated Learning Analytics model for an online learning system.

This paper proposes that data visualization as a construct is a significant influence in producing quality information for decision-making in the integrated model. The nature of data visualization is to present large amounts of data in visually actionable information that can ease the decision-making process as well as justifying findings. This factor must be recognized in learning analytics systems as it will influence the information quality produced, leading to effective decision-making among stakeholders such as educators in improving their teaching approaches.

This research has expanded the IS success model [16] along with TAM [17] to be put into operation for a new targeted context. A range of online learning systems have been studied in respect to its adoption as such this research provides an insight into an integrated model that takes into account the value of LA Features and Data Visualization as an antecedents to System Quality and Information Quality of IS success model, with the aim to create a more comprehensive model for use in the online learning context.

Although this research provides new insight in theory, an experimental study with the implementation of the proposed model should be conducted to further justify its relevant. The model is presented as a theoretical means of addressing the role of data visualization in learning analytics systems. It is envisioned that upon analysis and further investigation of the model, it may support the development of effective and efficient learning analytics systems so that the potential of data visualization can be fully exploited to optimize the teaching and learning environment.

5 Conclusion

With data easily captured and available via online learning systems, data visualization is a fast growing field with new research work on techniques and tools to enhance the efficiency and effectiveness of online teaching and learning. Though the benefits of data visualization is evident, it must be grounded in proper theory and it is important that we focus on its impact in an overall system for an effective uptake instead of simply implementing it as an ornamental add-on. Therefore, a preliminary model which integrates the IS success model and TAM with an extension of LA Features and Data Visualization as antecedents are presented to investigate the role of data visualization and its impact. This preliminary integrated model aims to support researchers, practitioners and software designers who aspire to implement data visualization in an online learning setting. A prototype is currently being trialed and enhanced based on the proposed model and its result will be used to further develop, refine and validate the proposed model.

Acknowledgements. We are sincerely grateful to BOLD RESEARCH GRANT 2021 (BOLD 2021-J510050002/2021054) funded by Universiti Tenaga Nasional (UNITEN), Malaysia to carry out this study.

References

1. Mailizar, M., Almanthari, A., Maulina, S., Bruce, S.: Secondary school mathematics teachers' views on E-learning implementation barriers during the COVID-19 pandemic: the case of Indonesia. Eurasia J. Math. Sci. Technol. Educ. 16(7), em186 (2020)
2. Kerres, M.: Against all odds: education in germany coping with covid-19. Postdigit. Sci. Educ. 2(3), 690–694 (2020)
3. Wang, C.J., Ng, C.Y., Brook, R.H.: Response to COVID-19 in Taiwan: big data analytics, new technology, and proactive testing. JAMA 323(14), 1341–1342 (2020)
4. Friendly, M.: A brief history of data visualization. In: Chen, C.H., Hardle, W., Unwin, A. (eds.) Handbook of Data Visualization, pp. 15–56. Springer, Berlin (2008)
5. Kirk, A.: Data Visualization: A Handbook for Data Driven Design. Sage, London (2016)

6. Kennedy, H., Engebretsen, M.: Data Visualization in Society. University Press, Amsterdam (2020)
7. Zhang, X., Yue, P., Chen, Y., Lei, H.: An efficient dynamic volume rendering for large-scale meteorological data in a virtual globe. Comput. Geosci. **126**, 1–8 (2019)
8. Khan, A., Mukhtar, H., Ahmad, H.F., Gondal, M.A., Ilyas, Q.M.: Improving usability through enhanced visualization in healthcare. In: 13th International Symposium on Autonomous Decentralized Systems, pp. 39–44. IEEE, Bangkok (2017)
9. Warestika, N.E., Sugiarto, D., Siswanto, T.: Business intelligence design for data visualization and drug stock forecasting. Intelmatics **1**(1), 9–15 (2020)
10. Vieira, C., Parsons, P., Byrd, V.: Visual learning analytics of educational data: a systematic literature review and research agenda. Comput. Educ. **122**, 119–135 (2018)
11. Siemens, G., Long, P.: Learning analytics & knowledge (LAK) call for paper. In: 1st International Conference on Learning Analytics and Knowledge. Banff (2011)
12. Hung, Y., Parsons, P.: Affective Engagement for communicative visualization: quick and easy evaluation using survey instruments. In: Visualization for Communication (VisComm) Workshop. IEEE, Berlin (2018)
13. Knight, S., et al.: AcaWriter: a learning analytics tool for formative feedback on academic writing. J. Writing Res. **12**(1), 141–186 (2020)
14. Seliana, N., Suroso, A.I., Yuliati, L.N.: Evaluation of e-learning implementation in the university using DeLone and McLean success model. J. Appl. Manage. **18**(2), 345–352 (2020)
15. Gasevic, D., Kovanovic, V., Joksimovic, S.: Piercing the learning analytics puzzle: a consolidated model of a field of research and practice. Learn. Res. Pract. **17**(1), 63–78 (2017)
16. DeLone, W.H., McLean, E.: The DeLone and McLean model of information system success: a ten-year update. J. Manage. Inf. Syst. **19**(4), 9–30 (2003)
17. Davis, F.D.: Perceived usefulness, perceived ease of use, and user acceptance of information technology. MIS Q. **13**(3), 319–340 (1989)
18. Petit dit Dariel, O., Wharrad, H., Windle, R.: Exploring the underlying factors influencing e-learning adoption in nurse education. J. Adv. Nurs. **69**(6), 1289–1300 (2013)
19. Vazquez-Ingelmo, A., Garcia-Penalvo, F.J., Theron, R.: Information dashboards and tailoring capabilities – a systematic literature review. IEEE Access **7**, 109673–109688 (2019)
20. Ward, M.O., Grinstein, G., Keim, D.: Interactive Data Visualization: Foundations, Techniques, and Applications, 2nd edn. CRC Press, Boca Raton (2015)
21. Clow, D.: An overview of learning analytics. Teach. High. Educ. **18**(6), 683–695 (2013)
22. Verbert, K., et al.: Learning dashboards: an overview and future research opportunities. Pers. Ubiquit. Comput. **18**(6), 1499–1514 (2014)
23. Paiva, R., Bittencourt, I.I., Lemos, W., Vinicius, A., Dermeval, D.: Visualizing learning analytics and educational data mining outputs. In: Penstein Rosé, C., et al. (eds.) AIED 2018. LNCS (LNAI), vol. 10948, pp. 251–256. Springer, Cham (2018). https://doi.org/10.1007/978-3-319-93846-2_46
24. Schaaf, M., et al.: Improving workplace-based assessment and feedback by an E-portoflio enhanced with learning analytics. Educ. Technol. Res. Dev. **65**, 359–380 (2017)
25. Alhadad, S.S.J., Thompson, K., Knight, S., Lewis, M., Lodge, J.M.: Analytics-enabled teaching as design: reconceptualisation and call for research. In: 8th International Conference on Learning Analytics and Knowledge, pp. 427–435. ACM, New York (2018)
26. Yalcin, M.A., Elmqvist, N., Bederson, B.B.: Keshif: Rapid and expressive tabular data exploration for novices. IEEE Trans. Visual Comput. Graph. **24**(8), 2339–2352 (2018)
27. Roca, J.C., Chiu, C., Martinez, F.J.: Understanding e-learning continuance intention: an extension of the technology acceptance model. Int. J. Hum. Comput. Stud. **64**(8), 683–696 (2006)

28. Vazquez-Ingelmo, A., Garcia-Penalvo, F.J., Theron, R.: Capturing high-level requirements of information dashboards' components through meta-modeling. In: Conde-Gonzalez, M.A., Rodriguez-Sedano, F.J., Fernandez-Llamas, C., Garcia-Penalvo, F.J. (eds.) TEEM 2019 Proceedings of the Seventh International Conference on Technological Ecossytems for Enhancing Multiculturality, pp. 815–821. ACM, New York (2019)
29. Park, Y., Jo, I.: Development of the learning analytics dashboard to support students' learning performance. J. Univ. Comput. Sci. **21**(1), 110–133 (2015)
30. Bakharia, A., Dawson, S.: SNAPP: a bird's-eye view of temporal participant interaction. In: 1st International Conference on Learning Analytics and Knowledge, pp. 168–173. ACM, Banff (2011)
31. Arnold, K.E., Pistilli, M.D.: Course signals at purdue: using Learning Analytics to increase student success. In: 2nd International Conference on Learning Analytics and Knowledge, pp. 267–270. ACM, Vancouver (2012)
32. Wise, A., Zhao, Y., Hausknecht, S.: Learning analytics for online discussions: embedded and extracted approaches. J. Learn. Anal. **1**(2), 48–71 (2014)
33. Liu, Z., Nersessian, N.J., Stasko, J.T.: Distributed cognition as a theoretical framework for information visualization. IEEE Trans. Visual Comput. Graph. **14**(6), 1172–1180 (2008)
34. Marbouti, F., Wise, A.F.: Starburst: a new graphical interface to support purposeful attention to others' posts in online discussions. Educ. Technol. Res. Dev. **64**(1), 87–113 (2016)
35. DeLone, W.H., McLean, E.R.: Information system success: the quest for the dependent variable. Inf. Syst. Res. **3**(1), 60–90 (1992)
36. Uddin, M.D.M., Isaac, O., Alrajawy, I., Maram, M.A.: Do user satisfaction and actual usage of online learning impact students performance? Int. J. Manage. Hum. Sci. **3**(2), 60–67 (2019)
37. Yakubu, M.N., Dasuki, S.: Assessing eLearning system success in Nigeria: an application of the DeLone and McLean information system success model. J. Inf. Technol. Educ. Res. **17**, 183–203 (2018)
38. Aldholay, A., Abdullah, Z., Isaac, O., Mutahar, A.M.: Perspective of Yemeni students n use of online learning: extending the information systems success model with transformational leadership and compatibility. Inf. Technol. People **33**(1), 106–128 (2019)
39. Balaban, I., Stancin, K., Sobodic, A.: Analysis of correlations between indicators influencing successful deployment of ePortfolios. In: 41st International Convention on Information and Communication Technology, Electronics and Microelectronics (MIPRO), pp. 788–793. IEEE, Opatijia (2018)
40. Toquero, C.M.: Challenges and opportunities for higher education amid the COVID-19 pandemic: the philippine context. Pedagogical Res. **5**(4), em0063 (2020)
41. Fishbein, M., Ajzen, I.: Belief, Attitude, Intention, and Behavior: An Introduction to Theory and Research. Addison-Wesley, Reading, USA (1975)
42. Alharbi, H., Sandhu, K.: Digital learning analytics recommender system for universities. In: Sandhu, K. (ed.) Digital Innovations for Customer Engagement, Management, and Organizational Improvement, pp. 184–199. IGI Global, Australia (2020)
43. Herodotou, C., Rienties, B., Boroowa, A., Zdrahal, Z., Hlosta, M.: A large-scale implementation of predictive learning analytics in higher education: the teachers role and perspective. Educ. Technol. Res. Dev. **67**, 1273–1306 (2019)
44. Rienties, B., Herodotou, C., Olney, T., Schencks, M., Boroowa, A.: Making sense of learning analytics dashboards: a technology acceptance perspective of 95 teachers. Int. Rev. Res. Open Distrib. Learn. **19**(5), 187–202 (2018)
45. Al-Emran, M., Mezhuyev, V., Kamaludin, A.: Technology acceptance model in m-learning context: a systematic review. Comput. Educ. **125**, 389–412 (2018)
46. Estriegana, E., Medina-Merodio, J., Barchino, R.: Student acceptance of virtual laboratory and practical work: an extension of technology acceptance model. Comput. Educ. **135**, 1–14 (2019)

47. Salloum, S.A., Alhamad, A.Q.M., Al-Emran, M., Monen, A.A., Shaalan, K.: Exploring students' acceptance of e-learning through the development of a comprehensive technology acceptance model. IEEE Access **7**, 128445–128462 (2019)
48. Brandon-Jones, A., Kauppi, K.: Examining the antecedents of the technology acceptance model within e-procurement. Int. J. Oper. Prod. Manag. **38**(1), 22–42 (2018)
49. Rahimi, B., Nadri, H., Afshar, H.L., Timpka, T.: A systematic review of the technology acceptance model in health informatics. Appl. Clin. Inform. **9**(3), 604–634 (2018)
50. Chen, C., Xu, X., Arpan, L.: Between the technology acceptance model and sustainable energy technology acceptance model: investigating smart meter acceptance in the United States. Energy Res. Soc. Sci. **25**, 93–104 (2017)
51. Wang, Y., Wang, S., Wang, J., Wei, J., Wang, C.: An empirical study of consumers' intention to use ride-sharing services: using an extended technology acceptance model. Transportation **47**(1), 397–415 (2018)
52. Venkatesh, V., Davis, F.D.: A theoretical extension of the technology acceptance model: four longitudinal field studies. Manage. Sci. **46**(2), 186–204 (2000)
53. Venkatesh, V.: Determinants of perceived ease of use: integrating control, intrinsic motivation and emotion into the technology acceptance model. Inf. Syst. Res. **11**(4), 342–365 (2000)
54. Venkatesh, V., Bala, H.: Technology acceptance model 3 and a research agenda on interventions. Decis. Sci. **39**(2), 273–315 (2008)
55. Koceska, N., Koceski, S.: Measuring the impact of online learning on students' satisfaction and student outcomes using integrated model. In: International Conference on Information Technology and Development of Education, pp. 96–101. ITRO, Serbia (2020)
56. Al-Fraihat, D., Joy, M., Masa'deh, R., Sinclair, J.: Evaluating e-learning systems success: an empirical study. Comput. Hum. Behav. **102**, 67–86 (2020)
57. Ohliati, J., Abbas, B.S.: Measuring students satisfaction in using learning management system. Int. J. Emerg. Technol. Learn. **14**(4), 180–189 (2019)
58. Al-Sabawy, A.: Measuring E-Learning Systems Success (PhD dissertation). University of Southern Queensland (2013)
59. Balaban, I., Mu, E., Divjak, B.: Development of an electronic portfolio system success model: an information system approach. Comput. Educ. **60**(1), 396–411 (2013)
60. Zogheib, B., Daniela, L.: Students' perception of cell phones effect on their academic performance: a latvian and a middle eastern university cases. Technol. Knowl. Learn. (2021)
61. Barbour, C., Schuessler, J.B.: A preliminary framework to guide implementation of the flipped classroom method in nursing education. Nurse Educ. Pract. **34**, 36–42 (2019)
62. Roger, T., Dawson, S., Gasevic, D.: learning analytics and the imperative for theory-driven research. In: Haythornthwaite, C., Andrews, R., Fransman, J., Meyers, E.M. (eds.) The SAGE Handbook of E-learning Research, 2nd edn, pp. 232–250. SAGE (2016)
63. Tan, J P.L., Yang, S., Koh, E., Jonathan, C.: Fostering 21st century literacies through a collaborative critical reading and learning analytics environment: user-perceived benefits and problematics. In: Proceedings of the Sixth International Conference on Learning Analytics & Knowledge, pp. 430–434. ACM, Edinburgh (2016)
64. Hatala, M., Beheshitha, S.S., Gasevic, D.: Associations between students' approaches to learning and learning analytics visualizations. In: Proceedings of the Sixth International Conference on Learning Analytics & Knowledge, pp. 3–10. ACM, Edinburgh (2016)
65. Beheshita, S.S., Hatala, M., Gasevic, D., Joksimovic, S.: The role of achievement goal orientations when studying effect of learning analytics visualizations. In: Proceedings of the Sixth International Conference on Learning Analytics & Knowledge, pp. 54–63. ACM, Edinburgh (2016)
66. Islam, N.A.K.M.: Investigating e-learning system usage outcomes in the university context. Comput. Educ. **69**, 387–399 (2013)
67. Davis, F.D., Bagozzi, R.P., Warshaw, P.R.: User acceptance of computer technology: a comparison of two theoretical models. Manag. Sci. **35**, 983–1003 (1989)

An Analytical Reasoning Framework for Visual Analytics Representation

Suraya Ya'acob[1], Sharida Mohd Yusof[2(✉)], Doris Wong Hooi Ten[1], and Norziha Megat Zainuddin[1]

[1] Faculty Technology and Informatics Razak, Universiti Teknologi Malaysia, Kuala Lumpur, Malaysia
{suraya.yaacob,doris.wong,norziha.kl}@utm.my
[2] Ministry of Communication and Multimedia Malaysia, Putrajaya, Malaysia

Abstract. Analytical Reasoning is the foundation of visual analytics, assisted via interactive and dynamic visualization representation. The main concern of visual analytics is the analytics process itself, it is important to facilitate the human mental space during the analysis process by embedding the analytical reasoning in the visual analytics representation. This paper aims to introduce and describe the essential analytical reasoning features within visual analytics representation. The framework describes analytical reasoning features from three parts of visual analytics representation which are higher-level structure, interconnection and lower-level structure. For higher-level structure, we proposed the features of big picture, analytics goal and insights through storytelling to ensure the analytics output becomes knowledge and applicable to facilitate the business decision. For interconnection, the features of trend, pattern and relevancy induce a relationship between higher and lower-level structures. Finally, analytical reasoning features for lower-level structure are quite straightforward which are benchmarking, ranking, decluttering, clueing and filtering. It is hoped that this framework could help to shed some light in terms of understanding analytical reasoning features that can facilitate the business decision.

Keywords: Analytical reasoning · Visual analytics · Visualization · Representation

1 Introduction

Visual analytics is an outgrowth of the fields of information visualization and data visualization that focuses on analytical reasoning facilitated by interactive visual representation. [1] Describe visual analytics as a discovery technology that incorporates automated analysis with interactive visualization representation. Hence, [2] highlighted the importance of visual analytics to enhance the effective and competent decision making. It consists of the combination of visualization techniques, statistical methods and the analytics process to extract usable data from a larger set of raw data to become meaningful and able to facilitate business decisions. Furthermore, visual analytics also can

© Springer Nature Switzerland AG 2021
H. Badioze Zaman et al. (Eds.): IVIC 2021, LNCS 13051, pp. 41–52, 2021.
https://doi.org/10.1007/978-3-030-90235-3_4

be described as an interactive knowledge discovery system which purpose is to guide the user for critical insights via data exploration and understanding [3]. Visual analytics is to make the tools visually enabled, coupling visualization-analytical reasoning and interaction with human understanding and judgement.

The seminal visual analytics researches are describing analytical reasoning at a high level and yet lack detailed discussion on it. As such, [4] has identified five spaces within visual analytics structure which namely as information, computer, representation, interaction and mental spaces. This categorization is at a high level and numerous sub-spaces are yet to be identified at different levels of granularity. As representation is one of the essential spaces in visual analytics, it influences how users perceive the information and analytics output. This is because representation space will facilitate cognitive activities and the partnership is formed between internal mental processes and external representation which provides a number of benefits to perform analytical activities. In consequence to the visual analytics building model from [1, 5] also describes the visual analytics building model by explaining the reality, computer and human parts. It highlighted the importance of visualization to represent data and how it can improve the knowledge and model schemata of users. Furthermore, the model argues that the main goal of doing visual analytics is to build a mental and/or formal model of a certain piece of reality reflected in the data. As to complement the visual analytics building model [5] and visual analytics space, we found the essential of analytical reasoning for visualization representation to be put inside the visual analytics framework as a whole. Therefore, this research will enrich analytical reasoning within the visualization representation space as shown in the visual structure in Fig. 1.

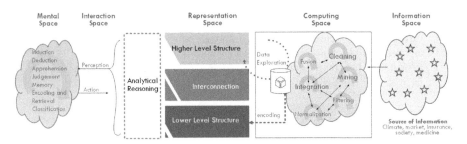

Fig. 1. Five spaces of visual analytics.

2   Working Background

Visualization has been recognized to facilitate the information overload in the Information Communication and Technology (ICT) world. Since the 1980's, the field of data visualization has been evolving dramatically from information graphics to Information Visualization, Knowledge Visualization and Visual Analytics. In the big data era, data visualization has become more significant in representing the 5Vs of data which are identified by volume, velocity, variety, veracity and value. This concurs with knowledge transformation and technology growth that has accelerated the evolution of data arena

[6]. There are a large number of complex, noisy and heterogeneous mass data sets in the big data. Therefore, data visualization is now an important research task for numerous areas that includes various questions relating to data storage, query and indexing [7]. Data visualization is the collection of techniques for easy comprehension and visual impact that transform information from its numerical to graphical presentations. The analytics demand for data visualization is increasing due to the awareness of its benefit to the business, organization and community. One of the current demands is to visualize the analytics results effectively to the end users. In precedent time, most of the analytics are used for scientific data and have been presented for expert users. Today, data analytics has been demanded by business and in needs for organizational data. Therefore, the way to develop the visualization for data analytics and to be easily understood by the end users need to be revised extensively. Hence, the field of visual analytics has emerged within the data visualization.

When using visual analytics, facilitating the reasoning is critical during data and information analyzing stage. Usually, visual analytics are used for complex cognitive activities such as decision making, problem solving and sensemaking which are higher-level thinking and require the facilitation of reasoning (why knowledge). Thus, guiding and supporting the reasoning will improve the capabilities of users when using visual analytics. Analytical reasoning is about the ability to analyze the situation, explore in a step-by-step approach to reason all the alternatives and find the best logical conclusions or solutions for the problem in hand. The process of analytical reasoning is important to be inferred because it facilitates the users to look and identify the problem within the situation. Usually, analytical reasoning will break the situation into smaller problems and reasons it out in a multi-dimensional way. Within each of the smaller problems, analytical reasoning will break down information and find a discern pattern or trends from the information. Analytical reasoning can be viewed as a process to understand, perceive and reason in regards to the dynamic and complicated data as to gather evidence for judgement in the decision making.

Sensemaking as one of the complex cognitive activities happened when using visual analytics. Through interacting with the visualization within visual analytics, the users are able to explore possible connections, gain insight and match the goal. It composes from the divergence and convergence part. sensemaking composes from divergence to convergence which are mentioned as foraging and synthesis. Foraging refers to the stages of the process to collect and filter the relevant and interesting information. While synthesis describes stages of the process where users create and test hypotheses about how foraged information may relate. In general, foraging lends itself to more computational support, while synthesis leverages human intuition for establishing relationships between information. Thus, the goal of visual analytics is to develop visualizations that are tightly coupled with mathematical models to provide computational support for the user – integrating foraging and synthesis. In this kind of process, the coupling between the system and human cognitive is important for sensemaking. The analytical reasoning is being produced during this dynamic coupling process. Throughout the tightly coupling cognition [8] engages in a process known as analytical discourse, where several, iterative dialogues with information available are conducted [1]. Sets of information are sought and processed, preferably from various sources, assert and test key assumptions.

Knowledge structures are then constructed using a series of reasoning to integrate new information into existing knowledge in possession.

Analytical reasoning is rarely a straightforward process to be handled in direct ways. Mainly because it is often intensified by time pressure, high uncertainty, high stakes and multiple tasks to be done and various information to be connected at the same time. Oftentimes, users work with information that is incomplete, dynamic, evolving and often deceptive. Hence, any attempt to find insights using this information involves dissecting the data into components, analyzing the patterns to expose evidence, gathering and connecting evidence, and compiling and synchronizing multiple varieties of insights from separate observations. Visual analytics representation (after this, the paper will use the term visualization) will be able to facilitate analytical reasoning of human cognition. Visualization in which as a tool will not only be linked together to the human cognition but also dependent upon each other. The visualization within visual analytics can be designed through the production of reasoning framework which is known as the science of analytical reasoning, as mentioned by [9]. This paradigm emphasizes the significance of visualization to facilitate human analytical reasoning in the process of integrating data to facilitate decision making and judgment.

3   An Analytical Reasoning Framework

The research extends an analytical reasoning framework based on the systemic visual structure developed by [23]. The visual structure used systemic approach as a basis for the visualization framework to synthesize the analytics outcomes. The framework only focuses on representation space because it is the most explicit and quite straightforward to be embedded with the analytical features. The concept of systemic is closely related to understanding interconnection and providing the big picture in the sense of holism. For this reason, the framework theorizes the use of synthesis visual structure by extending the overview concept towards the systemic view. Then using General System Theory, the research proposed the systemic view by embedding the underlying structure to underpin the concept of the synthesis visual structure. Moreover, the cycle of formation will help to strengthen the needs for higher-level and lower-level of multiple view visual structure as to support synthesis as higher-level thinking as shown in Fig. 2. There are three levels of the representation framework, each will be explained in the following paragraph.

3.1   Higher-Level Structure

The higher-level structure should be able to provide an overview of the visual analytics representation. For this reason, the analytical reasoning for higher-level structure should be able to synthesize the big picture, main goal and insights within the data analytics context of use. Among the benefits of applying higher-level visualization is to support logical formats and structures for users' mental model, disclosure of the existence of all information and the relationship between the key points as a whole and finally to encourage exploration of the information. Above all, the higher-level structure will govern the whole output of visual analytics. There are metaphoric phrases for higher-level structure such as "broad overview", "bird's eye view", "global overview" and "big picture". To ease the understanding, the researchers use the big picture term. This in turn describes the mental model and cognitive processes presented in Bloom's Taxonomy [11]. By gaining the big picture, the users should be able to clarify the analytics goal as the main driver while exploring visual analytics. Then, they should be able to see and draw the key points between various perspectives. The big picture also takes the lower-level structure into consideration. Based on the relationship of the data, the users should be able to find an adequate level of details or abstraction, be aware of discussing irrelevant issues and able to relate how a specific key point related to the more specific or general topic of the discussion.

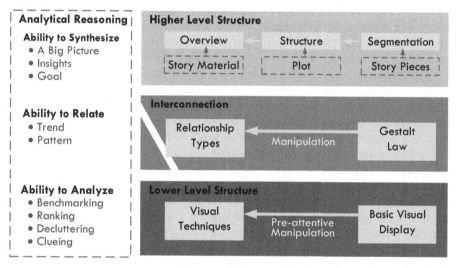

Fig. 2. Analytical reasoning framework for visual analytics representation

The framework proposed to embed visual-related analogy (e.g. similes, metaphor) as to convey meaning in addition to the straightforward reality of data. Metaphor has the capacity to link new concept and ideation with something that they are familiar with. As such, it can make sense to connect between details of analysis and application in the reality world. It also can convey an idea and emotion using literal statement which will encourage insight for non-straightforward statistics. It can be done by implying comparison that brings together two entities such as treemaps to portray containment. Finding the relevant visual-related analogy from identified storytelling can help users to refer and relate in order to emphasize on certain data. As an example, the usage of metaphor such as shrinking boats is used to indicate economic recession. While analogy such as the economy is like a coiled spring or a much straightforward related pictures of money or calculators could be used to indicate financial analysis. It is imperative for users to be able to comprehend a visualization and how its analytics will drive towards the main goal. It should be accurate and comprehensible to users in order to reduce confusion and misinterpretation [12]. Fulfilling the main goal is critical to ensure the analytics outcomes are valuable and can be used to facilitate the business decision. The visual analytics outcomes will be considered successful when the users are able to fulfill their analytics goal and become valuable to the business decision. Furthermore, business goals should be chunked into related use cases and insights. Then the visual techniques at the lower-level will be developed based on these insights. In terms of identifying the business goal, we suggest that more comprehensive elicitation of business requirement processes need to be done at the information space to ensure the business goal has been well taken care of.

The storytelling is the main feature to govern the visual analytics representation. The storytelling aims to create stories to tell data narrative, supply context and provide how the business decision can be facilitated using the outcomes from visual analytics. In representing visualization, storytelling may include text and images but essentially must be based on data. According to [13], in visual analytics, storytelling is a sort of controlled presentation of information that must relate to human emotion and analytics. It can be with or without a predefined temporal or narrative structure. It is always made up of components that form the story (structures, elements and concepts) and the telling part of storytelling (people, tools and channels). We proposed the development of storytelling concepts based on the structure and elements of analytics data that need to be presented to the users. The theme of story material will be proposed based on the overall business requirements, goals and its context of use. Then the overview concept will be segmentized into a few story pieces. Bear in mind, the structure of storytelling is the key elements to give flow to the story based on the overall concept. It can be done by following the concept of typical storytelling narration such as conflict-resolution and adding the element of surprise, emotions and punchline. The framework suggests at least each of the story pieces must contain at least a story point so it is easier for lower-level structure to provide detail explanation, justification and depth on it. It will become meaningful based on the story point for each of them. Each of the story pieces will be further developed using visualization techniques at the lower-level structure. Finally, all of the story pieces will be plotted and arranged according to the structure identified in the story material.

3.2 Interconnection

Interconnection is a relationship between two or more things within the representation data. In terms of analytical reasoning, this level should be able to relate data by identifying trend, pattern and relevancy. Contextual representation must at least show the interconnection between higher-levels of the information space (abstraction, key points, and perspectives) and lower-levels (concrete details). It is important to handle the analytical and synthetical process and furthermore the divergence to the convergence phase. This is because the users develop abstractions of the higher-levels by accessing and manipulating the lower-level details. Therefore, the relationship between these lower and higher-level elements is important to facilitate the reasoning process. To support the process, the cycle of formation can strengthen the main relationship between the higher and lower-level of visual structures.

We propose the interconnection as an organization of representation structure from an assumption of going from divergence to convergence – from lower-level details to the higher-level structure. The lower part is to encourage discussion of lower details, and is meant to help the understanding of the 'state of the art' of each of the elements, perspectives or departments. The upper level has been placed to guide the analysis process towards the synthesis of the cognitive process so that convergence of ideas can take place over time. As a whole, the users are able to view the higher and lower-level at the same time. They can view, relate and refer to the details during the reasoning for higher-level abstraction. Moreover, through the organization of representation, our emphasis is on guiding the users to discuss details according to any of their particular needs. The whole representation structure will act as explicit guidelines to be shared across several mental models so that there would be shared understanding among the users. By knowing what to do through the representation structure, it makes the process more focused on relevant elements. Nevertheless, since the research is about the complex domain, the interconnection between elements is not limited between the higher and lower-level visual structures. For this reason, the relationship can also be formed either between the elements in the same key component, between different key components or lower-level details.

Previous research from [14] has further identified and classified visualization techniques based on the six types of relationship which are correlation, comparison, distribution, differences and relationship outliers. From these six relationships of visualization, it is applied to fit into all dataset in the organizations to be used in visualizing their data for further decision making. Nowadays, due to varieties of visualization tools, methods and requirements, multiple observations and parameters of the data have to be combined in a single image in order to identify a meaningful relationship within the representation. Meaningful relationship means the users are able to identify the pattern, trend and relevancy of the data. This identification is the most important part of analytical reasoning within the interconnection of the representation level.

Trend is a general direction of elements over a period of time. It is a specific type of pattern distinguished by continuous gradational transition from one data point to another which is usually influenced by a driver parameter, such as time, process stage, etc. [15]. Generally, there are three basic concepts of trend. The first being uptrend that shows the overall elements direction in ascending manner. Then, there is the downtrend which displays the overall of elements direction in the form of descending. Lastly, is the sideway that demonstrate stagnant or nonmoving direction of the overall element. Pattern is a repeated form by a series of data in a recognizable way. Our brains are built to see structure and patterns in order for us to better understand the environment that we are living in. We visually and psychologically attempt to make order out of chaos, to create harmony or structure from seemingly disconnected bits of information [16]. Analytical reasoning is the ability to recognize and determine the meaning of patterns in a variety of information. As mentioned before, it refers to the ability to look at information, be it qualitative or quantitative in nature, and discern patterns within the information. At the same time, getting historical data is of importance in order to demonstrate patterns of classification, clustering, regression and outlier analysis. Classification is a form of supervised learning by relating the data with class labels. Meanwhile, clustering is a type of unsupervised learning by a group data without pre-labeled classes. In addition to that, regression is categorized under supervised learning for continuous data type. Lastly, outlier analysis is use to identify and reveal anomaly from the data. Relevancy is the quality and condition of the relationship between data. It can become a strong supportive evidence for visual analytics by showing the level of relevancy, consistency, clarity and similarity depending on the scenario in use. One dimensional view from a single source should be avoided while data source accuracy and dynamism of varying data perspective is highly essential.

We suggest that developers utilize and manipulate all the visualization techniques that are currently available. However, to induce analytical reasoning of pattern, trend and relevancy, the visual analytics developers must understand the manipulation of Gestalt Law. By understanding it, the developer will know why and how to show and emphasize pattern, trend or relevancy within the relationship types. Gestalt means pattern and it offers nine principles of grouping to facilitate visual perception based on the capacity of human brain to see structure, logic, and patterns. It is a natural human ability that helps make sense of the world. According to [16], Gestalt Law is about the theory around how people perceive the world around them and focused on how people interpret the world. It offers a principle of grouping to facilitate visual perception. This is because human visual working memory has limited storage, by using Gestalt, the human brain can reduce the amounts of items that need to be stored. There are six individual principles commonly associated with Gestalt theory: similarity, continuation, closure, proximity, continuity, connectedness, figure/ground, pragnanz and symmetry & order. There are also some additional, newer principles sometimes associated with Gestalt, such as common fate. In the simplest terms, Gestalt theory is based on the idea that the human brain will attempt to simplify and organize complex images or designs that consist of many elements, by subconsciously arranging the parts into an organized system that creates a whole, rather than just a series of disparate elements [17]. This approach facilitates the maintenance and retrieval of information in the visual working memory.

3.3 Lower-Level Structure

Lower-level structure is the details of analytics information within the visual analytics representation. It provides in depth analytics for each aspect of the data. As a result, users would be able to view complex information in smaller segments. Each of these segments will be understood in detail, in order find evidence and reason to support the business decision. It is quite straightforward and much of the visualization research is focused on developing this component. We suggest that developers utilize and manipulate all the visualization techniques that are currently available. However, to facilitate analytical reasoning that is able to justify decision making in a more convincing and less cluttering manner, developers must first master the visual concept mapping. By understanding it, the developer will know why and how to provide analytical reasoning in the representation. The framework proposed that lower-level structure should be able to facilitate analytical reasoning via benchmarking, ranking, decluttering, clueing and filtering.

The concept of visual mapping (encoding) is the most important part in lower-level structure. There are three important parts in visual concept mapping which are basic visual display, pre-attentive manipulation and the visual techniques. Basic visual display is the basic element in the visualization field. Using multiple terms such as graphical display, visual glyph/form and visual representation [18], basic visual display is a simple elementary thing that is visible in the visual analytics representation. There are four types of basic visual display which are point, line, spatial position and colors with comprised of attributes such as position, length, color, orientation and shape can be manipulated to amplify cognition using pre-attentive elements. Simple visual attributes can be processed extremely fast in parallel and high volume by using pre-attentive elements without any conscious effort by the iconic memory. The visual analytics representation should be made to prioritize on important data to be manipulated by the pre-attentive element that could catch the users' attention. Based on data selected from computer space, the lower-level structure will encode the information (from data/attributes) to be presented as basic visual display (e.g., form, line, picture etc.). Hence, the visual technique can be developed by composing a few elements of basic visual display and manipulating some of pre-attentive elements.

The framework suggests that lower-level details to be based on the insights identified to fulfill the business goals. The selection of the key components and the development of visual techniques will then rely on the priority business requirements and analytics goal – either depending on its function, tasks or knowledge in the context of use. Indirectly, this condition will complement the overall theme of visual analytics context of use. The categorization of lower-level structure will be governed by the overall story material and segmentation that has been identified from the higher-level structure. The lower-level structure can develop multiple visualization techniques for each story piece based on severity and depth of its analytics. Usually, for important and critical story points – multiple and in-depth visualization techniques need to be developed to provide rich insights and more potential exploration for that particular story point and how it implicates others.

The research has identified five features that can be used to support analytical reasoning at the lower-level structure. These features are quite straightforward and yet significant to reduce the cognitive load during the analysis process. The first one is benchmarking. In general, it is a mechanism of progressive activity to attain improved results and performance as well as a basic analysis feature to clarify comparisons. It could also be used as a tool to reveal how to achieve significant performance height rather than just a way to evaluate performance measure. Benchmarking helps users to identify current performance by comparing the subject of interest and recognize the gap to fill-in. It can compare the performance, process and strategy that involves internal, competitive, functional or any generic quantitative comparison such as target, maximum, median or minimum.

The second feature is ranking. It is about giving the positions by grading the items in order to have a sense of hierarchical importance. Ranking helps to prioritize the most significant/insignificant items in the dataset, which in turn, will give a more effective view of the analysis data. Ranking is defined as one of the simplest methods in performing evaluation. It is a relationship between a set of items such that, for any two items, the first is either 'ranked higher than', 'ranked lower than' or 'ranked equal to' the second". Rankings are among universal and popular method in organizing or arranging a chaotic assortment of objects through calculating a rank for all elements according to the value of one or more of its components. This permits the prioritization of assignments or in evaluating the performance of items comparative to each other. The interpretation of ranking's visualization is not as straightforward as its visual representation. This is due to the fact that ranking only signifies the summary of a possibly more complex association among its elements and the rest of the attributes [19]. Nevertheless, ranking can also lead on the overall assessment or achievement especially in the scoreboard cases.

The third feature is decluttering. It aims to reduce messy and cluttered visualization that could improve and assist targeted audience to get at the data by significantly making the data stands out more. Evidential studies have proved the advantages of decluttering, which can be done by removing unnecessary items and properly structuring the information elements [20]. Visual clutter builds up unnecessary burden to the cognitive load which could interfere with the message communicated. By understanding the cognitive load theory and manipulating the pre-attentive elements, users will be able to boost their focus and understanding on the demanded visualization [21]. The fourth feature is clueing and it is about giving hints or cue to guide its audience to somewhere meaningful during the analysis process. There a few ways to give clue in the lower-level structure by leveraging on the effectiveness of pre-attentive attributes [21]. This is done by including annotation, providing tips and summary, adding contrast color tone to distinguish and highlight important consent, put in border to differentiate or separate certain visualization points and using color highlights to amplify and attract users to voluntarily pay more attention to what is important. Studies have shown that visual cues or clueing could act as anchors to enhance accuracy and produce positive impact (Redmond, 2019).

Finally, the fifth feature is filtering. It is the process to focus on a smaller dataset in order to have better sense of direction on attributes of interest and conceal unwanted or insignificant ones. This can be done by removing unwanted data or choosing a specific part of the dataset and using subsets for analysis. It provides flexible and adjustable environment for users over their data view. As a result, it offers additional benefits by simplifying patterns, reducing visual clutter, complexity and data congestion, which allow for a more visible correlation between data [22]. Filtering is a temporary process. It allows data to be dissected through different viewpoint or drill down to a deeper level which make for an excellent method to allow user-driven, extensive data exploration and analysis. All this, while the complete data set is kept but only part of it is utilized for analysis in current demand.

4 Conclusion

Throughout this study, a substantial review and discussion regarding analytical reasoning features was conveyed. A discernment of business and technical issues related to visual analytics were explained and a significant value of analytical reasoning was unveiled to improve the representation, interaction and communication of visualization. It is relevant due to the current demand of end-users and decision makers, in assisting them to understand the analytics outcomes. Henceforth, an analytical reasoning will be able to facilitate the business decision and stimulate the analytics outcomes to evolve into knowledge in their context of use. However, analytical reasoning in visual analytics is not easy to define, due to its implicit mental space thinking process and the usual usage within complex cognitive activities in nature. Furthermore, analytical reasoning specifically the ones in relation to visual analytics are quite new, with limited publications, most of which dating from year 2000 onwards. However, reasoning and analytical reasoning by themselves are mature subjects which came from a diverse, multi-disciplinary nature with a wide variety of application areas, such as science, philosophy, cognitive, psychology, mathematics and so forth. Hence it is challenging to find quality publications that best fit the real research intent and interest without peering into or rather adopting relevant ideas from these frontiers. In short, the visual analytics developer gave positive feedback and was able to improve the analytics output when embedding these features inside the visualization. On the other hand, through respondents' feedback, there are various improvements that could be performed in order to improve the meaning, and reasoning facilitation. Hence, we hope to expand, demonstrate and clarify these features in a more holistic detail in the future.

Acknowledgement. This work was supported by the Research University Grant from Universiti Teknologi Malaysia (UTM RUG: Q.K130000.2656.17J23).

References

1. Thomas, J.J., Cook, K.A.: Illuminating the Path – The R&D Agenda for Visual Analytics.pdf. National Visualization and Analytics Center (2005)
2. Keim, D., Andrienko, G., Fekete, J.-D., Görg, C., Kohlhammer, J., Melançon, G.: Visual analytics: definition, process, and challenges. In: Kerren, A., Stasko, J.T., Fekete, J.-D., North, C. (eds.) Information Visualization. LNCS, vol. 4950, pp. 154–175. Springer, Heidelberg (2008). https://doi.org/10.1007/978-3-540-70956-5_7
3. Sips, M., Köthur, P., Unger, A., Hege, H.C., Dransch, D.: A visual analytics approach to multiscale exploration of environmental time series. IEEE Trans. Visual Comput. Graph. **18**(12), 2899–2907 (2012)
4. Sedig, K., Parsons, P., Babanski, A.: Towards a characterization of interactivity in visual analytics. **3**(1) 17 (2012)
5. Chen, S., et al.: Supporting story synthesis: bridging the gap between visual analytics and storytelling. IEEE Trans. Visual Comput. Graph. **26**(7), 2499–2516 (2018)
6. Yang, C., Huang, Q., Li, Z., Liu, K., Hu, F.: Big data and cloud computing: innovation opportunities and challenges. Int. J. Digit. Earth **10**(1), 13–53 (2017). https://doi.org/10.1080/17538947.2016.1239771
7. Bikakis N.: Big data visualization tools. arXiv preprint arXiv:1801.08336 (2018)
8. Bradel, L., et al.: How analysts cognitively "connect the dots". In: 2013 IEEE International Conference on Intelligence and Security Informatics, pp. 24–26. IEEE, Seattle, WA, USA (2013)
9. Cai, G., Graham, J.: Semantic data fusion through visually-enabled analytical reasoning. In: IEEE Conferences (17th International Conference on Information Fusion (FUSION)), pp. 1–7 (2014)
10. Brophy, J.: Connecting with the big picture. Educ. Psychol. **44**(2), 147–157 (2009)
11. Yaacob, S., Liang, H.N., Mohamad, A.N., Maarop, N., Haini, S.I.: Business Intelligence Design: Consideration of Convergence Challenges
12. Lavalle, A., Mate, A., Trujillo, J., Rizzi, S.: Visualization requirements for business intelligence analytics: a goal-based, iterative framework. In: 2019 IEEE 27th International Requirements Engineering Conference (RE), pp. 109–119. IEEE, Jeju Island, Korea (South), September 2019
13. Erete, S., Ryou, E., Smith, G., Fassett, K.M., Duda, S.: Storytelling with data: examining the use of data by non-profit organizations. In: Proceedings of the 19th ACM Conference on Computer-Supported Cooperative Work & Social Computing, pp. 1273–1283, 27 February 2016

14. Shabdin, N.I., Ya'acob, S., Sjarif, N.N.A.: Relationship types in visual analytics. In: Proceedings of the 2020 6th International Conference on Computer and Technology Applications, pp. 1–6. ACM, Antalya Turkey, 14 April 2020

15. Xu, Y., Qiu, P., Roysam, B.: Unsupervised discovery of subspace trends. IEEE Trans. Pattern Anal. Mach. Intell. **37**(10), 2131–2145 (2015)

16. Wagemans, J.: Historical and Conceptual Background: Gestalt Theory. Oxford University Press (2014)

17. Palmer, S., Rock, I.: Rethinking perceptual organization: the role of uniform connectedness. Psychon. Bull. Rev. **1**(1), 29–55 (1994)

18. Card, S.K., Mackinlay, J.D., Shneiderman, B.: Readings in Information Visualization: Using Vision to Think, Interactive Technologies. Elsevier Science (1999)

19. Gratzl, S., et al.: LineUp: visual analysis of multi-attribute rankings. IEEE Trans. Visual Comput. Graph. **19**(12), 2277–2286 (2013)

20. Deacon, J., et al.: 2020. Introduction to data visualization. In: Casualty Actuarial Society E-Forum, p. 217 (Summer 2020)

21. Knaflic, C.N.: Storytelling with Data. John Wiley & Sons Inc. (2015)

22. Idrus, Z., Zainuddin, H., Ja'afar, A.D.M.: Visual analytics: designing flexible filtering in parallel coordinate graph. J. Fundam. Appl. Sci. **9**(5S), 23 (2018)

23. Ya'acob, S., Ali, N.M., Nayan, N.M.: Systemic visual structures: design solution for complexities of big data interfaces. In: International Visual Informatics Conference, pp. 25–37. Springer, Cham, 17 November 2015

Literature Survey on Aircraft Maintenance Issues with Human Errors and Skill Set Mismatch Using Document Mining Technique

T. Nanthakumaran Thulasy[1]([envelope]) [iD], Puteri N. E. Nohuddin[2] [iD],
Norlizawati Abd Rahim[3] [iD], and Astuty Amrin[4] [iD]

[1] Razak Faculty of Technology and Informatics, Universiti Teknologi Malaysia,
54100 Kuala Lumpur, Malaysia
tnanthakumaran@graduate.utm.my
[2] Institute of IR4.0, Universiti Kebangsaan Malaysia, 43600 Bangi, Malaysia
[3] Department of Science, Management & Design, Razak Faculty of Technology and
Informatics, Universiti Teknologi Malaysia, 54100 Kuala Lumpur, Malaysia
[4] Department of Engineering, Razak Faculty of Technology and Informatics,
Universiti Teknologi Malaysia, 54100 Kuala Lumpur, Malaysia

Abstract. Aviation encompasses a wide range of mechanical flights as well as the aircraft business. The industry is quickly expanding as travelers choose to travel by air due to the concept of a world without borders, lower rates, and global business activities. Thus, aircraft maintenance and repair are critical jobs in the aviation sector for improved aircraft service and safety. Despite this, numerous aviation disasters occur due to a variety of factors such as malfunctioning equipment, hazardous weather conditions such as turbulence, and human error. In this research, we used text mining to explore a set of internet articles and reports about aviation occurrences and difficulties. The method retrieves frequent and significant terms from the document set. The experiment is divided into four (4) modules: (i) collecting of web articles and reports, (ii) document preprocessing, (iii) text analytics, and (iv) visualization. The experiment's results show that the bulk of records describe aircraft maintenance, skill mismatch, and training shortages.

Keywords: Aviation · Industry revolution 4.0 · Aircraft maintenance issues · Skill mismatch · Document mining

1 Introduction

The combination of Artificial Intelligence and engineering automation is driving the growth of Industry Revolution 4.0. (IR4.0). As a result, it sort of creates surplus and shortage in specific groups of employees and specialists especially in which the workforce requires the replacement of appropriately skilled personnel. Some work tasks can be replaced by machines to reduce production costs. In general, many work skills are acquired through formal schooling (TVET, colleges, and universities), but they can also be acquired through alternative means [1]. The changes in the IR4.0 workforce setting

© Springer Nature Switzerland AG 2021
H. Badioze Zaman et al. (Eds.): IVIC 2021, LNCS 13051, pp. 53–64, 2021.
https://doi.org/10.1007/978-3-030-90235-3_5

have necessitated the acquisition of new skills and competences in order to keep up with the advancement of current innovations [2]. The recent situation revealed that many job domains have become extremely demanding, and as a result, current employees' skill sets are insufficient to sustain a significant transformation in the entire area of work. As a result, additional efforts should be made to implant critical job skills in recent graduates and even present employees, so that they are in sync with the current needs of the organization.

Graduates should be exposed to appropriate skill sets in order to guarantee their work and remain employed in a constantly changing industry and innovation climate. As such, the purpose of this article is to support claims that one of the aircraft maintenance skill sets is challenging. The aviation sector is being shaped by IR4.0 to adopt current technologies in its aircrafts and human resources [3]. In the production of aircrafts and related equipment, the aviation sector is moving forward with the use of technology such as artificial intelligence, machine learning, automation, sensors, and remote monitoring. Therefore, maintaining modern aircrafts has become a difficult undertaking and it is critical to guarantee that engineers and technicians have a broad skill set and the best competences. According to the Malaysian Aerospace Industry Blueprint 2030 [4], some education and training programs are not being developed sufficiently, and there is a skills mismatch between academics and industry. Graduates from academies do not meet workforce requirements for the proper talent. Recently, skill mismatch among aircraft maintenance professionals has emerged as a widespread personnel management issue in the aviation industry [5].

The aim of this paper is to outline a document mining experiment conducted on a set of documents pertaining to human factors, issues and aircraft maintenance using a text mining algorithm. The following is how the paper is structured: Sect. 2 goes over the backdrop and associated work on the influence of IR4.0 on aircraft maintenance, skill sets issues and incidents, and document mining or document analytics procedures. Sections 3 and 4 elaborate on document mining framework and the results of document analytics utilizing the proposed methodology. Finally, Sect. 5 concludes with a summary and recommendations for further research.

2   Literature Review

This section covers a variety of topics relating to IR4.0, such as aircraft maintenance and skill set concerns and mishaps, as well as document mining.

2.1   The Effects of IR4.0 on Aviation

IR4.0 ushers in Industry 4.0 by transforming the manufacturing sector to embrace digital transformation through the incorporation of sensing devices in virtually all manufacturing parts, products, and equipment. The implementation of a ubiquitous system enhances the ability to examine digital data and physical equipment, allowing every worldwide industrial sector to progress much more quickly [6]. [7] defines Artificial Intelligence (AI), Big Data, the Internet of things (IoT), the Internet of services (IoS), cyber-physical systems (CPS), and smart production are all listed as essential components of IR4.0.

As a result, this gyration is the culmination of all preceding revolutions' inventions. According to the literature, this revolution will convert and have an irreversible impact on the built environment business as profoundly and irreversibly as each of its three predecessors, and faster.

In the aviation industry, one example of IR4.0 adaptation is the development of predictive maintenance systems, which include the function of sensors and IoT in maintaining and monitoring aircraft components to be replaced before obvious flaws arise. This approach teaches a valuable lesson in how regular aircraft maintenance processes can be translated by the smart factory [8]. Similarly, in the manufacturing industry, components of smart factories are introduced as part of engineering science integrations. The distributed manufacturing branches or alliances are linked by leveraging technological improvements such as big data analytics and remote monitoring to assist factories in increasing productivity, creating a safe environment, and maintaining safe operations [8].

2.2 Aircraft Maintenance and Skill Sets Issues and Incidents

Aircraft maintenance refers to the repair and servicing actions conducted to maintain the aircraft operational and reliable. Aircraft maintenance is a critical responsibility for ensuring flight safety throughout the aircraft's life cycle [9]. Despite the fact that aircraft maintenance is considered a high-risk job assignment in aviation due to its critical impact on aviation safety, it nevertheless plays a substantial role in aircraft accidents and incidents [10].

Saleh et al. [11] did a study to explore maintenance safety issues. Human factors analysis in both studies reveals that the majority of the factors impacting the maintenance event are related to incorrect component inspection and installation methods, as well as transitory factors that come from the organizational and management levels.

According to Khan et al. [12] based on International Civil Aviation Organization (ICAO) official statistics, around 0.9 percent of aircraft incidents involved maintenance. It also said that maintenance accidents were 20% more likely to result in one or more deaths than all official ICAO mishaps (14.7%). Nonetheless, it was discovered that the number of accidents caused by maintenance errors each year dropped over the study period, and the statistic rate decreased from 5% per year to 2% per year. The findings revealed that aircraft with maintenance contributions were typically between the ages of 10 and 20 years, with aircraft over 18 years old being more likely to result in fleet loss and aircraft over 34 years old being more likely to result in death. [13] discovered that the primary causes of technical failures were inadequate repair processes, irresponsibility, and erroneous installations, which might be caused by worker skill sets.

Many of the previous publications explored key concerns concerning human factor errors in aircraft maintenance. This paper offers a study on document analytics on additional published publications about these topics. As a result, it is projected that this analysis will reveal human factors mistake, particularly skill mismatch among aircraft maintenance personnel, as a common talent management issue in the aviation business.

2.3 Document Mining

Document mining is one of the Data Mining (DM) approaches [14]. It seeks knowledge in a stack of documents that may contain comparable conversations and arguments by determining phrase frequencies and word connections in the texts. DM is well-known as a method of obtaining nontrivial, valuable, and meaningful insights from databases, also known as Knowledge Discovery in Databases (KDD) [15]. The KDD stages are as follows:

(i)   Selection – For the mining process, data set is carefully selected.
(ii)   Preprocessing – The selected data is preprocessed into an acceptable data format and data type.
(iii)   Transformation – The cleaned data is turned into appropriate data ranges and aggregations.
(iv)   Data Mining – The primary process of discovering knowledge in terms of patterns and rules.
(v)   Interpretation – Patterns and rules are translated into knowledge and information for users, stakeholders, and decision makers.

A document is commonly regarded as a single piece of information, and a collection of them is referred to as a document dataset. A proper document collection is essential for both formal and informal readers to access material as part of knowledge and information sharing [16]. Many documents, such as articles, contracts, reports, and news, can be collected as data files produced or converted into digital papers thanks to ICT. Thus, document mining can be used to process digital documents for speedier information transmission. Document mining is mostly used to directly find term relationship and similarity in a document dataset [17].

In this study, document mining utilizes Text Mining (TM) which is one of the data mining approaches used to derive insights from text data. TM is a text analytics methodology that uses NLP and DM to convert free (unstructured) text in documents and databases into standardized and structured data patterns. During the preprocessing stage, NLP is used to clean, convert, and standardize text data (text terms) formatting.

In TM, cleaned terms are ranked using Term Frequency-Inverse Document Frequency (TF-IDF) to apply term count and weighting to each term that appears in a set of documents or corpus. As a result, it generates a list of keywords ranked by TF-IDF. Then, in a corpus, a Term Document Matrix (TDM) is built, which is a two–dimensional matrix or table with rows representing words and columns containing document ids. The goal of TDM generation is to record calculated word frequency counts across documents in a corpus [18].

TF-IDF is a popular method for computing word frequency counts and weights across documents in a corpus, and it is widely used in information retrieval and TM. It is intended to assess how important a term is to a document in a corpus. As a result, TF is the term frequency for terms that appear in a document, whereas IDF is used to determine how relevant a term is for a collection of documents or corpus [19]. Each term has its own TF and IDF score, as well as its own TF*IDF weight, as indicated in Eq. 1:

$$w_{i,j} = tf_{i,j} \times \log\left(\frac{N}{df_i}\right) \tag{1}$$

- $tf_{i,j}$ is total of frequencies of i in j.
- df_i is the number of documents have i.
- N is total number of documents in a corpus.

The $w_{i,j}$ value of a term grows in proportion to the number of terms that appear in the documents. It is used to determine the significance of a phrase across all papers in a corpus. Non-data science experts may find document mining to be technical, yet there are several useful text or document analytics products on the market, such as SAS, WordStat, Voyant Tools, RapidMiner, and many more. Some of these are beautifully designed, powerful, and ready to be used by non-technical users in constructing their own text or document analytics tasks. In this work, we employ a document analytics technique to evaluate a collection of internet articles about aircraft incidents, maintenance personnel issues and skill mismatch difficulties. As an absolute combination method, we combine NLP and TF-IDF.

3 Document Analytics on Aircraft Maintenance Issues

3.1 Document Mining Framework

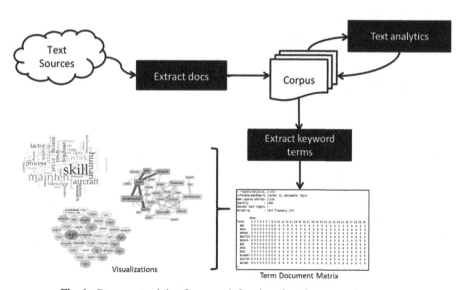

Fig. 1. Document mining framework for aircraft maintenance documents.

This proposed document analytics process includes multiple integrated procedures in this study. Figure 1 depicts the framework, Document Mining Framework (DMF), which consists of four (4) stages: (i) online articles and report collections on aircraft maintenance and incidents, and. (ii) preprocessing of document data (iii) text analytics (iv) visualizations. The goal of this experiment is to identify the key keywords that appear in the document set, also known as the corpus.

Initially, DMF gathers online papers that particularly explain and discuss aircraft maintenance faults and incidents, engineers' and technicians' competence and competency, and aircraft maintenance personnel training. These web articles and reports are gathered at random, but the extent of document content descriptions is carefully chosen. The documents are in text (.txt) file format. The files are then subjected to a document preprocessing mechanism. The R programming language was used to create the module. The module is built on the (NLP) principle, with two (2) key processes: (i) removing stop words and (ii) stemming terms to become root words. Document preprocessing is an important step in document analytics since it is a standard approach used to clean original documents to reduce noise, unstructured data, and inconsistent data.

The following module extracts relevant terms for use in creating the TDM. The ranking and extraction of these keywords is based on the TF-IDF methodology. Text analysis is carried out in accordance with their important values and word occurrences. The framework uses the TF-IDF algorithm to rank and count keywords at this level. A TDM is created throughout the mining process. The TDM is then used as the data input for term pattern visualization using the Voyant application [20], which is an open-source web-based program that reads and analyses texts in a variety of formats. It facilitates scholarly text analytics of texts or corpora, primarily by analysts, students, and the general public. Finally, the identified term patterns are represented in three (3) forms of visualization graphics, such as word clouds, term links and term berry. From here, we can identify the gist of document contents amongst various studies undertaken under the areas of aircraft maintenance and repair, technician skills, human errors, and aviation mishaps.

4   Results and Discussion

The experiment's results are reported and discussed in this subsection. The document analytics data are displayed in a variety of visualizations, including a word cloud, term links and termberry. Each visualization shows the key phrases that describe the gist of the document's contents.

The corpus includes 43 documents, including (i) 20 Web of Science indexed journals, (ii) 3 Scopus indexed journals, and (iii) 20 technical reports and white papers. Maintenance and Reliability (Web of Science), Human Factors: The Journal of the Human Factors and Ergonomics Society (Sage Journals), International Journal of Industrial Ergonomics (Scopus), Aerospace, and other indexed journals are among those chosen. These articles discussed and reviewed aircraft maintenance, repair, and overhaul, technician skills, human errors, and aviation incidents. This document dataset was published between 2010 and 2020.

All 43 documents were subjected to the document preprocessing module in the second stage of DMF to remove stop words and stemming. All papers are integrated as a corpus during document preprocessing. The text in the papers is then transformed to lowercase, and all symbols and numerals are eliminated. The next step is to remove all numbers, symbols, stop words such as 'a', 'an', 'the', and white space from the corpus. The goal of this method is to improve the quality of the corpus by removing nonsensical phrases. Finally, stemming is a critical procedure. Stemming is a process in which terms are trimmed down to their underlying term. For example, the terms 'running' and 'runner' are trimmed down to their base word 'run'. The stemming procedure is essential to ensure that terms with the same root words are referred to as the same separate term.

Table 1. Part of the term document matrix.

	file1	file2	file3	file4	file5	file6
Accept	3	4	4	5	3	4
Access	9	1	25	1	23	0
Accord	1	34	8	1	2	13
Activ	1	6	10	4	6	12

The third stage of DAF then employs the TF-IDF equation on the cleaned corpus to generate TDM. Table 1 depicts a portion of TDM's rows and columns used to store documents and phrase frequencies. These frequency counts are used to determine the links between terms and documents.

The summary sheet, as shown in Fig. 2, contains information corpus and term details such as document length, vocabulary density, average words, most frequent words, and distinctive words. This corpus contains 43 documents with a total of 278,807 words and 13,045 unique terms. The longest and shortest documents in the corpus are described by document length. The top five longest documents are file7 (32757 terms), file27 (30792 words), file29 (21910 words), file14 (21425 terms), and file3 (12706 terms). The shortest documents, on the other side, are file24 with 353 terms, followed by file26 with 581 terms, file21 with 589 phrases, file16 with 658 terms, and file20 with 794 terms.

It also reveals that the most often occurring terms in the corpus are 'skill', 'mainten', 'aircraft', 'error', and 'human'. Other visualization statistics use these keywords to demonstrate word relevance and relationship in the document contents.

Figure 3 depicts a word cloud, which is a graphical representation of the frequency of words in the corpus. The larger the words appear in the word cloud, the more frequently the terms are used. The word cloud indicates larger words for 'skill' (4350 frequencies), which indicates it appears 4350 times in relation to the 43 long datasets, followed by 'mainten' (2719 frequencies), 'aircraft' (1968 frequencies), 'error' (1772 frequencies), and 'human' (1772 frequencies) (1673 frequencies). The terms in the word cloud have a high phrase count among the 13,045 unique terms. Terms such as 'employ' (1191 frequencies), 'technolog' (939 frequencies),'mismatch' (756 frequencies), 'industry' (1494 frequencies), 'educ' (942 frequencies),'safeti' (1167 frequencies), 'aviat' (1436 frequencies), 'factor' (1359), 'train' (1058 frequencies), and 'accid' (1046 frequencies). We may determine from the word cloud visual that the corpus contains many document

This corpus has 43 documents with 278,807 total words and 13,045 unique word forms. Created 2 seconds ago.

Document Length:
- Longest: file7 (32757); file27 (30792); file29 (21910); file14 (21425); file3 (12706)
- Shortest: file24 (353); file26 (581); file21 (589); file16 (658); file20 (794)

Vocabulary Density:
- Highest: file24 (0.688); file25 (0.529); file20 (0.526); file26 (0.504); file21 (0.499)
- Lowest: file27 (0.073); file29 (0.093); file14 (0.104); file7 (0.113); file3 (0.151)

Average Words Per Sentence:
- Highest: file7 (32757.0); file27 (30792.0); file29 (21910.0); file14 (21425.0); file3 (12706.0)
- Lowest: file24 (353.0); file26 (581.0); file21 (589.0); file16 (658.0); file20 (794.0)

Most **frequent words** in the corpus: skill (4350); mainten (2719); aircraft (1988); error (1772); human (1673)

Fig. 2. Summary of information corpus and term.

contents about aircraft maintenance, human factors, accidents and errors, skill mismatch, the aviation industry, and education and training.

Fig. 3. A word cloud.

Figure 4 depicts the link analysis of the frequent phrases found in the 43 documents in this text analytics. Term links associate terms with how they are written or described in texts. As a result, the created term linkages provide support for details pertaining to term representation in a word cloud. The term links display the descriptive terms associated with the primary keywords. For example, the term 'skill' associated to 'mismatch', 'technician', and 'requir' described that many of the documents described the technician having mismatch skills required for their aircraft maintenance job responsibilities. The thicker the ties between two (2) keywords, the greater their association.

Fig. 4. Term links.

We may use the term link to zoom in and see what other terms are related to the core keywords. Figure 5 depicts the sub term connection, which reveals a connection analysis of more related keywords associated with the 43 documents' common keywords. In this graphic, we will get a larger picture of how the issues in these publications are comparable. Many publications addressed skill mismatch and inadequacy, as well as aircraft maintenance. The words 'technician' are synonymous with 'learn', 'program', and 'aircraft'. The connections between 'human', 'error', 'mainten' and 'accid' emphasize one of the critical challenges that require more attention from the allied parties. Overall, the link analysis correlates the primary keywords and terms such as 'skill', 'aircraft', 'technician', 'error', 'human', 'mismatch', 'measur' and 'train'.

A TermsBerry representation is depicted in Fig. 6. The TermsBerry aims to integrate high frequency terms with co-occurring phrases. In this way, it is an extension of displaying how close the terms appear to one another. It is also used in the same way as word cloud visualization, but it is more effective because it includes term statistics and corpus coverage information. In this figure, we highlight the term 'mismatch' which has 756 frequencies and appears in 20 publications and is strongly connected to keywords such as 'skill', 'educ', 'employ', 'use' and 'studi' (high statistics).

Overall, we can deduce from the visualizations that the document dataset focuses and discusses on aircraft maintenance incidents and skill set issues. Because aircraft maintenance is seen as a complicated problem to solve [21], it is critical to address issues of talent inadequacy and mismatch among aircraft maintenance specialists.

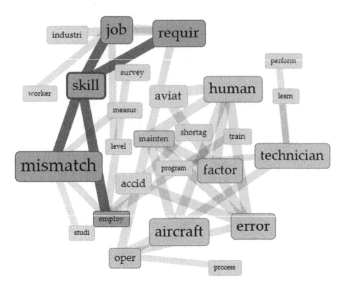

Fig. 5. Sub-term links.

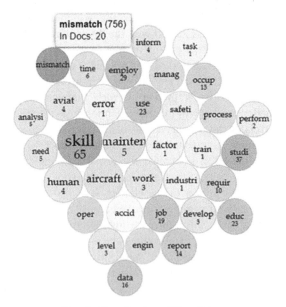

Fig. 6. Visualization of TermBerry

5 Conclusion

We use a document mining technique to analyze a collection of web articles and reports on aircraft incidents and aviation competence problems in this study. The impact of IR4.0 on aviation, aircraft maintenance and competence challenges and incidents, document mining, TDM, and the TF-IDF technique are also discussed in this paper. It introduces the DMF and shows the results of document analytics performed with the framework in question. We can deduce that the document collection under consideration focuses mostly on aircraft maintenance and skill set problems. According to the publications reviewed, aircraft maintenance is considered a challenging topic to solve, and it is critical to address skill gaps and mismatch among aircraft maintenance professionals. The importance of aircraft maintenance, repair, and safety were emphasized in these contents. According to reports and news, many aviation disasters occur due to a variety of factors, including malfunctioning equipment, hazardous weather conditions, such as turbulence, human mistake, and worker technical skill. To address IR 4.0 and skill mismatch concerns in aircraft maintenance, the research will be developed in the future to address the need for a competency-based skill evaluation and training mapping model for Royal Malaysian Air Force technicians.

References

1. Verhaest, D., Omey, E.: The relationship between formal education and skill acquisition in young workers' first jobs. Manch. Sch. **81**, 638–659 (2014). https://doi.org/10.1111/j.1467-9957.2012.02305.x
2. Mohd Kamaruzaman, F., Hamid, R., Mutalib, A.A., Rasul, M.: Comparison of engineering skills with IR 4.0 skills. Int. J. Online Biomed. Eng. (iJOE). **15,** 15 (2019). https://doi.org/10.3991/ijoe.v15i10.10879
3. Xu, M., David, J., Kim, S.: The fourth industrial revolution: opportunities and challenges. Int. J. Finan. Res. **9**, 90 (2018). https://doi.org/10.5430/ijfr.v9n2p90
4. Samah, S.K.: Advancing Malaysian Aerospace Industry Through Research. Malaysian Industry-Government, Kuala Lumpur (2015)
5. Kumar, P., Kamalakannan, P.: Skill gap analysis and training needs in Indian aerospace industry. J. Airl. Airpor. Manag. **6**, 115–132 (2016). https://doi.org/10.3926/jairm.56
6. Mrugalska, B., Wyrwicka, M.: Towards lean production in industry 4.0. Procedia Eng. **182**, 466–473 (2017) https://doi.org/10.1016/j.proeng.2017.03.135
7. Maskuriy, R., Selamat, A., Maresova, P., Krejcar, O., David, O.: Industry 4.0 for the construction industry: review of management perspective. Economies **7**, 14 (2019) https://doi.org/10.3390/economies7030068
8. Tat, M., Kushan, M.: Impact of Industry 4.0 to aircraft maintenance, repair and overhaul. In: Conference: VII International Symposium Engineering Management and Competitiveness 2017 (2017)
9. PCAA: Approved Maintenance Organisations-Air Navigation Order, 3rd ed Pakistan Civil Aviation Authority, Karachi, Pakistan (2019)
10. Rajee, O.D., Miller, M., Mrusek, B.M.: Managing safety risks in airline maintenance outsourcing. Int. J. Aviat. Aeronaut. Aerosp. **7**, 7 (2020)
11. Saleh, J.H., Tikayat, R.A., Zhang, K.S., Churchwell, J.S.: Maintenance and inspection as risk factors in helicopter accidents: Analysis and recommendations. PLoS ONE **14**, e0211424 (2019)
12. Khan, F.N., et al.: A preliminary investigation of maintenance contributions to commercial air transport accidents. Aerospace **7**(9), 129 (2020). https://doi.org/10.3390/aerospace7090129
13. Habib, K., Turkoglu, C.: Analysis of aircraft maintenance related accidents and serious incidents in Nigeria. Aerospace **7**(12), 178 (2020). https://doi.org/10.3390/aerospace7120178

14. ECM Connection: Data mining and document mining. https://www.ecmconnection.com/doc/data-mining-and-document-mining-0001. Access Online on 21 Jan 2021

15. Fayyad, P., Shapiro, S.: From data mining to knowledge discovery: an overview. In: Fayyad, P.-S., Smyth, U. (eds.) Advances in Knowledge Discovery and Data Mining, pp. 1–34. AAAI Press/The MIT Press, Menlo Park, CA (1996)

16. O'Neil, B.: Framework for managing knowledge, content and documents. https://tdan.com/framework-for-managing-knowledge-content-and-documents/21065 (2017). Last Accessed 21 Jan 2021

17. Nohuddin, P.N.E., Noormanshah, W.M.U., Zainol, Z.: Content analytics based on random forest classification technique: an empirical evaluation using online news dataset. Int. J. Adv. Appl. Sci. **8**(2), 77–84 (2021). https://doi.org/10.21833/ijaas.2021.02.011

18. Robertson, S.: Understanding inverse document frequency: on theoretical arguments for IDF. J. Doc. **60**, 503–520 (2004). https://doi.org/10.1108/00220410410560582

19. Qaiser, S., Ali, R.: Text mining: use of TF-IDF to examine the relevance of words to documents. Int. J. Comput. App. **181**(1), 25–29 (2018). https://doi.org/10.5120/ijca2018917395

20. https://voyant-tools.org/ (2018)

21. Ward, M., McDonald, N., Morrison, R., Gaynor, D., Nugent, T.: A performance improvement case study in aircraft maintenance and its implications for hazard identification. Ergonomics **53**(2), 247–267 (2010). https://doi.org/10.1080/00140130903194138

Interactive Tangible Game for Collaborative Play Between Children with Cerebral Palsy

Chloe Hue Tung San and Kher Hui Ng[(✉)] [iD]

School of Computer Science, University of Nottingham Malaysia, Jalan Broga,
43500 Semenyih, Selangor, Malaysia
{hcycs1,marina.ng}@nottingham.edu.my

Abstract. Cerebral refers to the brain, specifically the outer layer while palsy refers to the loss or impairment of motor function. Interactive tangible systems have been widely designed with aims of rehabilitation for users with cerebral palsy. However, there is still a lack of tangible systems that can support collaborative play between children with cerebral palsy. This paper describes the process of research, design, and development as well as evaluation of an interactive tangible game system with the purpose of supporting collaborative play as well as rehabilitation. Based on results of a pilot study, a new prototype iteration of tangible system incorporates multiplayer games with an accessible tangible interface. Two user experiments were conducted virtually with 8 participants from the Spastic Children's Association of Selangor and Federal Territory (SCAS&FT) who provided positive feedback and to gain a general population's point of view on system's usability, with results of 75 on the System Usability Score (SUS) showing that the system's functionalities were deemed effective and easy to use. Main findings of this paper are that children with cerebral palsy prefer playing with friends rather than alone and the system provides motivation for rehabilitation as well as social collaboration during use due to its multiplayer function. We further discuss future work that can improve the development of interactive tangible game for collaborative play between children with cerebral palsy.

Keywords: Interactive tangible system · Collaborative play · Game · Rehabilitation · Cerebral palsy

1 Introduction

Cerebral palsy (CP) is the most common motor disability in childhood and affects approximately 17 million people worldwide. In every 2000 babies born, 1–2 of them are diagnosed with cerebral palsy. Caused by damage to or abnormalities inside the developing brain during pregnancy of birth or within the first 2 to 3 years of a child's life, this permanently affects a person's ability to move and maintain balance [1]. There are three types of CP namely spastic CP (stiff muscles), dyskinetic CP (uncontrollable movements) and ataxic CP (poor balance and coordination) [2]. The severity of these disabilities' ranges from mild to severe in correlation with the degree of injury to the brain. Some children are diagnosed with a level of intellectual disability and impaired sensations as well as

© Springer Nature Switzerland AG 2021
H. Badioze Zaman et al. (Eds.): IVIC 2021, LNCS 13051, pp. 65–76, 2021.
https://doi.org/10.1007/978-3-030-90235-3_6

other medical disorders. This impairs the quality of life, independence, and all aspects of health ranging from physical to emotional.

Children with cerebral palsy may experience mobility limitations due to problems in fine motor control, strength, and range of motion [3]. This reduces their ability to participate in community and leisure activities such as sports and games which leads to disassociation from the community and the feeling of exclusion. Differences in their functional abilities can be seen in their daily activities such as sitting, walking and mobility. Children with cerebral palsy may also have impacted speech especially if the muscles of the tongue, mouth and throat are affected. This makes it difficult for a child to verbally express themselves with confidence. Hence, they are unable to make friends easily in comparison to healthy peers and this affects their ability to develop a concept of self and find meaning in life [4], causing them to develop a shy and reserved personality due to lack of social interaction.

Besides, collaboration is an important aspect in a child's growth and is a skill they must hone. The ability for a child to collaborate when they grow up is increasingly important in an era where work is done in teams of people rather than in isolation. Collaboration can be in the form of social interaction, engagement, and cooperative activities. Developing collaboration as a skill allows children to engage with each other It enables them to discover each other's strengths, weaknesses, interests, and capabilities [5]. In this environment of positivity, self-confidence and self-esteem may be boosted, allowing them to communicate comfortably. Clear and effective communication is a vital skill to have to convey ideas and messages [6]. There have been attempts to develop tangible interfaces for children with CP, however they do not place an emphasis on collaborative play, rather on single player games. There is research ongoing for designing tangible interfaces for collaborative play, however they have less focus on children with limited physical movement [7].

Therefore, this project aims to design an interactive tangible game system that allows collaborative play for children with CP between the ages of 12 to 17. The project incorporated games and an accessible interface inclusive to wheelchair bounded users. The system consists of multiplayer games to encourage socialization and collaboration when children play together. Having multiple games to choose from that are both fun and engaging increases the replay value of the system. The games included different level of difficulties to cater for children with varying severities. The project investigated ways that an interactive tangible game system could support both physical rehabilitation as well as social interaction between children with CP.

This paper begins with reviewing related work to give an overview of necessary background and describe the methods used for design to include initial ethnography and pilot study and user evaluation. Next, design guidelines and implications are discussed before final discussions and conclusions are made.

2   Related Work

Tangible interactive systems are perceptible by touch and require significant amounts of interaction between users and the system. It can provide feedback in the form of visual or auditory in response to an interaction with the user. Through extensive research, we have come across several tangible interactive systems designed for cerebral palsy users.

2.1   Interactive Rehabilitative Game Systems for Children with Cerebral Palsy

Previous work on interactive rehabilitative systems shows positive effects in training the upper limbs of children with CP. They include hand therapy exercises that include wrist and thumb extension and flexion, wrist stretch, wrist side movement, finger curl, finger flexion and extension as well as finger spread [8]. There is evidence that passive stretching increases the overall agility of children [9]. For example, Kinect2Scratch is a motion game that focuses on improving the upper extremities of children with CP with training on shoulder holding, hand-eye coordination and reaction time [10]. Results of the study show that although the system allows them to enjoy training, it was highlighted in the paper that a lack of multiplayer game mode eventually cause the children to lose interest gradually. Another similar project uses a multi-touch Microsoft Surface display combined with tangible inputs – wands with custom grips, foam balls and wearable kinematic sensor for monitoring [11]. It focuses on improving the fine motor skills of the upper limbs in children with CP by combining an immersive play environment and rehabilitative exercises.

Other studies further explored the use of tangible user interface with gamification in the rehabilitation of children with CP. For example, ShaRki is a tangible system that incorporates gamification to encourage enhanced hand movement for children with unilateral cerebral palsy [12]. Users will have to grasp a cylindrical tangible controller, equipped with sensors to measure arm movements, to play a game of feeding the crocodile. Grasping and releasing the tangible closes and opens the crocodile's mouth and rotating the wrists turns the crocodile's head. There are different levels and game modes designed for each motoric level. The system shows some success in using a tangible user interface to meet the therapeutic needs of targeted users. However, it does not support multiplayer and social engagement. There still exists a gap in understanding how to design tangible systems that can provide sustained interest and motivation in children's physical rehabilitative exercises.

2.2   Interactive Tangible Game System for Collaborative Play

There are several projects that aim to support collaborative play among children with special needs. However, current research on the development of collaborative technology for children with cerebral palsy is still lacking as most have focused on designing for children with Autism Spectrum Disorder (ASD) [7]. For example, Mazi is a tangible user interface which encourages play between 6 and 9-year-olds diagnosed with ASD [13]. However, this system is not suitable for children with a more severe case of cerebral palsy since it requires full body movement to fully engage with the system. In another example, POMA uses pretend play toys equipped with conductive foam to create unique touch-point patterns to use with an iPad in a gameplay [14]. However, collaborative gameplay only begins at level 6 which most children are unable to reach due to an eventual lack of interest to its repetitiveness.

There are only a few interactive tangible game systems that have been designed for children with CP to support collaborative play. For example, in PhysiTable, a programmable board game uses an accelerometer to detect the smoothness of the hand movement of children with CP [15]. It is a multiplayer game, where two children compete to see who can move the object to the destination first. However, the result of the study shows that children with severe CP tend to dislike the game as it is difficult for them to maintain smooth movements. The game mainly functions as an assessment tool hence there is little replay value as the game could easily become repetitive. Another study explores the use of interactive toy modules with sensors, light, and audio feedback, which can be combined with basic blocks from LEGO for specific hand and arm functional exercises [16]. It proposes collecting user performance data and tracking the systems' long-term effect in rehabilitation training and more tangible systems to support competitive and cooperative gameplay for both physical exercises and social development to help children with CP communicate with peers properly.

3   Context and Design Requirements

This project is carried out as part of research collaboration with Spastic Children's Association of Selangor & Federal territory (SCAS&FT). The SCAS&FT runs a spastic children's centre that provides services, facilities and activities that are used to care and treat these special children. Initial ethnographic study and interview sessions were conducted at the centre involving teachers and parents over a 2-month period which results showed that encouraging actions that rely on hands and/or fingers and stretching are extremely important to increase their motor movements and intellectual development by giving meaning to their movement. Furthermore, any features of the systems developed should aim to build confidence, be enjoyable as this will lead to prolonged attention and concentration spans and promote creative expression. We further identified the following 4 rehabilitation requirements that an interactive tangible system for children with CP should support: 1) Movement of the shoulder, 2) Pronation or flexion of the wrist, 3) Extension of the fingers, and 4) Smiling or laughing while interacting. A pilot study was carried out at the centre showcasing our early idea of a tangible musical soundscape developed using a Bare Conductive Touch Board. The system was designed to support physical rehabilitation and recreation for children with CP in the form of music playing and making. Suggestions from the study given by the teacher and parents was to introduce game elements to motivate users to interact with the system. Participants also expressed wishes to play together.

4   System Iteration

4.1 System Design

Based on results of the pilot study, our new prototype iteration became focused on supporting collaborative play as well as rehabilitation. Figure 1 shows the system architecture of the improved interactive tangible game system consisting of two sets of tangible input controllers to support collaborative play involving two players. To set up the system, users will have to plug in the Arduino USB cable into their computers to power up the controller. The controller consists of an Arduino and touch sensors. The touch sensors used to design the controllers are Trill Sensors in the shape of a Bar, Square,

Ring, and TTP223 Capacitive Touch Sensor Modules. Users can then play and control the games using the touch sensor equipped controller. The sensors can read the touch inputs, made by children with CP when they extend their fingers to tap on the sensors and translating them to in-game actions.

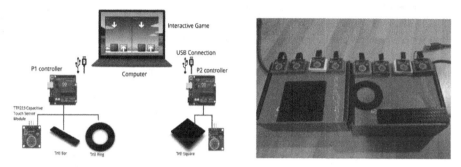

Fig. 1. General layout of the interactive tangible system (left), P2 and P1 controller (right)

4.2 Hardware

Arduino and Unity. The games can be played by two players, thus requiring the use of two Arduino controllers. Player 1's Arduino Uno controller has the Trill Bar, Trill Ring, and 4 capacitive touch sensors attached. Player 2 has the Trill Square and 4 capacitive touch sensors attached. The Arduino controllers were programmed to read the values from sensors continuously. It will then send the data information through the COM3 port, signaling that the third capacitive touch sensor has been pressed. Port COM4 was used for player 2. In Unity, a library called Ardity was used to receive data from the serial ports. Ardity allows Unity to read and process serial data. The data is stored in a queue and can be processed by a message listener. The message listener oversees the interpreting of data, translating them into in-game actions.

Tangible Input Controller. A cardboard box was used to develop the tangible input controller (Fig. 1). The 4 capacitive sensors were placed on top of a foam sheet to absorb pressure since users will have to press on them and the pins on this sensor are at the bottom. The foam was then covered with color paper to improve the aesthetics and allowed easy understanding of the Rhythm game.

4.3 Game Design

The games in the system were designed based on guidelines for making video games accessible to users with CP [17]. Motivation both in the form of extrinsic (external incentive) and intrinsic (personal satisfaction) are key to designing a fun game. Besides, progressiveness also allows users to enter a state of flow when playing the game. To establish a flow, there is a structure of levels so that users will feel accomplished when they overcome a level. The following game features were integrated into the system:

- Dual player gameplay in either cooperative or competitive mode.
- Various game difficulty to cater for children with different abilities.
- High score system which logs user's performance and can record any improvements throughout usage. This also acts as a motivational factor.
- Children can play freely with minimal supervision.
- Incremental difficulty to enhance motivation.
- Trial and error where mistakes should be forgiving so users can learn from errors.
- Immediate feedback allowing cause-effect learning when immediate feedback is given upon every action.
- Social component to encourage collaboration and social interaction between players.

4.4 Software Development

The programming platform used in developing the interactive game system is Unity which uses C# for game creation. The sensors were set up correctly on the Arduino controllers before connecting to Unity. This is essential to allow the sensors to sense touch input and send the data to Unity for in-game actions. Two new games were developed to support collaborative as well as competitive play modes respectively:

Asteroids. The Asteroids game detects touch input from Trill Bar sensor for Player One and Trill Square sensor for Player Two. The sensor input will be translated to position a player's spaceship. The Trill Ring sensor input is used to adjust the volume. The game interface consists of the Main Menu, Difficulty setting and Game Play. The game play is cooperative where both players share 5 lives and work together to increase player scores by destroying asteroids and aliens. There are two spaceships and each player control their respective sprites by dragging along the sensors. The spaceships automatically shoot bullets, so no additional controls are required (see Fig. 2).

The difficulty of the game gradually increases as the number of asteroids increases with each level progression. An alien will spawn targets and attack a player. So, players will have to work together to destroy it. Each level ends when the alien and asteroids are cleared. Lastly, there is a scoreboard which acts as a motivational factor for players to improve and beat their previous best score.

Rhythm. The Rhythm game processes touch input from a total of 8 capacitive touch sensors, each player uses 4 capacitive touch sensors respectively. The Trill Ring sensor is used to adjust the volume. The sensor input will be translated into a note hit if players tap on the sensor when a falling arrow enters a colored tile. The game interface consists of the Main Menu, Difficulty setting, Song Selection and Game Play. There are three song choices that may be selected by players, each ranging between 30 to 45 seconds, in a length not to be too tiresome for users. The Game Play corresponds to a chosen difficulty. There are a few differences between each level besides the speed of arrows falling down. In the easy and medium modes, two fingers are required to tap on the sensors whereas in hard mode four fingers are required illustratied in Fig. 2. Users can use either their dominant or non-dominant arm. The speed increases with difficulty but it is set at a managable speed for CP users. The square tiles decrease in size for harder difficulties.

During game play, player scores and visual feedbacks will be displayed depending on how precise the players tap on the sensor once an arrow enters a tile. Higher scores will be awarded if the accuracy in players' response improve. A scoreboard will be shown at the end of game play.

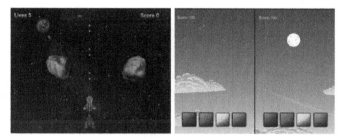

Fig. 2. Game play of asteroids (left) and rhythm (right)

5 Results

5.1 Results of Remote Usability Evaluation

An initial user evaluation was conducted to involve a general population sample. Due to the pandemic and Movement Control Order (MCO) imposed in Malaysia, the user evaluation was carried out remotely and limited to virtual demonstrations in order for participants to have an in-depth understanding of the system and also learn how users can interact with the system using the tangible input controller. The evaluation involved 52 participants in total. 28 of the participants were male, while 24 were female. 90.4% of the participants were in the age range of 18–25 years old, while others in the age range of 26 and above. The standard System Usability Scale (SUS) was used to investigate the usability of the interactive tangible game system. The SUS consists of ten questions, implemented on a 5-point Likert scale which 1 represented 'Strongly Disagree' and 5 represented 'Strongly Agree'. Additional closed and open-ended questions were included in the questionnaire to gain feedback on the perceived ease of use and effectiveness of the system to support collaborative play, in addition to recommendations on possible ways to improve the system. Table 1 shows the results of the SUS test. Overall, the SUS score is 75 which lies on the 3rd quartile, within the rating of 'Good'. Results indicated the system's functionalities were perceived as usable and acceptable, and participants were clear with the objective of the app. This would allow the system to be tested and used by children with CP in future.

In response to the questions to gain feedback on the effectiveness of collaborative play: a) to motivate users to use the system more often, and b) to increase social interaction during use, results showed that most participants agreed, where the average score to both questions was 4 (Agree) (see Fig. 3). Hence, most participants believed that using the interactive tangible game system in multiplayer mode may encourage users to use the system as they get to play along with a peer and engage in social interactions. Results also suggest that majority of participants consider the controller as straightforward and easy to use with an average score of 2.

Table 1. Results of system usability scale test

No	System usability scale questions	Average score
1	I think that I would like to use this system frequently	3
2	I found the system unnecessarily complex	2
3	I thought the system was easy to use	4
4	I think that I would need the support of a technical person to be able to use this system	2
5	I found the various functions in this system were well integrated	4
6	I thought there was too much inconsistency in this system	2
7	I would imagine that most people would learn to use this system very quickly	4
8	I found the system very cumbersome to use	2
9	I feel very confident using the system	4
10	I needed to learn a lot of things before I could get going with this system	2

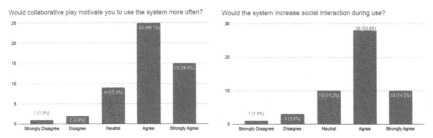

Fig. 3. Users' feedback on effect of collaborative play – (a) motivation (left) and (b) social interaction (right)

The questionnaire also included 2 open-ended questions where participants were asked to suggest genres of games that they would like to see added into the tangible interactive game system. 20% of participants suggested including retro or classic games such as Tetris. 18% of participants proposed including adventure games with an interactive story, while 16% of participants suggested fighting or first-person shooting games. Another 16% of participants suggested educational games such as puzzles. 11% of participants suggested racing games. 4% of participants suggested games of other genres such as horror. Virtual instruments and more music-based games were suggested by 7% of participants. Lastly, 4% of participants hoped to see sports related games.

Finally, participants were asked to suggest improvements to be made to the system. A total of 23% of participants commented on the design of the controller with suggestions to make it more compact, aesthetic, with a robust casing. 17% of the participants gave some suggestions to improve the games. For instance, rewards or powerups in the game to encourage players. Furthermore, 6% of participants suggested improvements to the portability of the system by using wireless controller and providing compatibility of the game with mobile phones. 8% of participants suggested improvements to the game user interface. For instance, they suggested to place instructions at the start of the game rather than using a separate instruction button and to combine all games into a single application. The rest of the participants commented that the system was great and hoped to see more games on the system.

5.2   Results of User Evaluation Involving Participants from SCAS&FT

Due to the pandemic, we were unable to conduct a physical user evaluation with targeted users involving children with CP at SCAS&FT. A virtual evaluation was conducted via Zoom to involve a live demonstration of the developed prototype system, followed by an interview session. The evaluation objectives were to evaluate the usability and effectiveness of the interactive tangible game system in motivating children to carry out physical rehabilitative exercises and encouraging social interaction through collaborative play. The participants involved were eight in total to include 3 children with CP, 1 female (F1) aged 14 years old, and 2 males (M1 and M2) aged 15 and 13 years old respectively. The three children have only mild CP with high functioning mobility and can move their fingers well. Other participants included 3 teachers and 2 parents. The interview questions aimed to gain feedback on various evaluation aspects such as usability, feasibility, ease of adaptation and accessibility.

Results of the interview showed that the system would be easy to use by all 3 children (F1, M1 and M2) where the children feedback that they would be able to play the games themselves without any assistance. One of the teachers affirmed this by saying, "It is easy for M3 to play as he can move his fingers very well. M2 also enjoys playing video games. He can type on his iPad, but it takes some time." The children confirmed that they would be able to reach out to touch the sensors easily and the arrangement of the sensors were comfortable. When participants were asked if they agree that the system would increase social interaction among children with CP, all of them agreed. Additional feedback revealed that the user interaction with the system was similar to physical occupational therapy that the children carry out in the center. As highlighted by a teacher, the system supports "typing" movements with fingers that the children carry out. She further suggested that extending the system to support the stretching of the shoulders and arms would increase the rehabilitative benefits to children with CP. All participants agreed that the incorporation of games would increase children's motivation to carry out physical therapy. The children were particularly interested in the multiplayer feature of the system.

Lastly, a suggestion was made by one of the teachers to allow the Rhythm game to be played with only one hand in the medium mode as it would be hard for children with CP to interact with 3 sensors. So, changes were made to the arrangement of sensors to allow the board to be placed horizontally such that upper arm movement is encouraged.

6 Discussion

Play is vital for a child's development in areas ranging from motor, cognitive, emotional, and social. Most participants believed that collaborative play is a preferred game mode for children, and has the potential of enhancing their social skills. This result built on existing evidence that children with cerebral palsy prefer multiplayer conditions [18]. Positive effects that collaborative play bring included motivation for rehabilitation as well as social collaboration. However, this requires more concrete confirmation and to study the systems' long-term effect on rehabilitation training and social collaboration. Despite the benefits that collaborative play brings, it should also be used with caution as users may be too involved in gaming, resulting in them using their dominant arm more instead of the affected arm that requires rehabilitation [18].

Results of our evaluation suggested good perceived ease of use and effectiveness of the system to support collaborative play. Future work would involve adding a game tutorial at the start of the game to demonstrate use of the sensors. Additionally, the system could be improved to allow users to fully use the system without the need of a mouse and keyboard interaction. Currently, typing players' names in the scoreboard and pausing the game required keyboard pressing. Hence interface improvements could be made to include additional touch sensors for pausing the game and a virtual keyboard for in-game input. Some participants also suggested that more arcade style games could be included in the interactive tangible game system to give players more choices to play with to prevent children with CP from getting bored with the system easily.

Based on participant feedback, further improvements could be made to the tangible input controller to improve its physical design to become more ergonomic and to achieve rehabilitation goals such as stretch outing or lifting arms to interact with the system. We propose using projection mapping, a technique to turn a wall or board into a display surface for digital projection. These digital projections of visual game interface onto a display surface embedded with touch sensors will allow for direct manipulation and seamless interaction with the interactive board or wall. Creating a sensor-based tangible board or wall with projection mapping that is physically larger in size would mean that bigger movements will be required to interact with the system and may be suitable to support multi-player group experience to facilitate healthy emotional development. To improve the accessibility of a tangible system, it could be designed in a modular way allowing it to be adjusted according to each child's height or reach.

From this research, the use of touch interfaces appeared to fit the needs of children with CP [19]. The touch sensors used in the system were sensitive and easily accessible. The Trill sensors can sense multiple touch points so children with CP can carry out tapping motions instead of dragging their fingers along. More research will be needed to explore the design and use of touch interfaces to encourage various motor movements to achieve higher rehabilitation goals such as movement of the shoulder and pronation or flexion of the wrist. For example, there are many user modes and readings that may be taken from Trill sensors such as pressure of finger. It is also possible to tune the sensitivity of the touch sensors to adjust the difficulty of the games.

All in all, the proposed touch based tangible system showed potential as an easy-to-use controller for children with CP. Our future work will focus on understanding how to design better tangible input controller to achieve higher physical rehabilitation goals with inclusion of suitable multiplayer games.

7 Conclusion

In conclusion, this paper presents a new tangible interactive game system that can support collaborative play between children with cerebral palsy. Previous studies involving design of tangible systems for collaborative play have less focus on children with limited mobility, while tangible systems for children with CP tend to cater for single users. Results from usability testing suggested that the developed system achieved good perceived ease of use and effectiveness to engage players in collaborative play. Future game design iteration should allow players to select their game difficulty level to include assigning placement of touch sensors based on physical rehabilitation goals and their music of choice to be played. The potential benefit of the interactive tangible game system is two-fold – to motivate children with CP to engage in their physical therapy exercises while encouraging social interactions and communication. Future work will involve studying the system on-site with actual children with CP in SCAS&FT and studying the effect of collaborative play in comparison to single user play.

Acknowledgements. We would like to thank the teachers, parents, and children at SCAS&FT for participating in this project.

References

1. Cerebral Palsy: Hope through research. https://www.ninds.nih.gov/Disorders/Patient-Car egiver-Education/Hope-Through-Research/Cerebral-Palsy-Hope-Through-Research/. Last Accessed 24 June 2021
2. Cerebral Palsy. https://www.cerebralpalsyguidance.com/cerebral-palsy/. Last Accessed 24 June 2021
3. Lin, C., Chen, W., Lin, C.: The effects of interactive music and bubble feedback using Arduino on enhancing physical activities for children with cerebral palsy. In: Proceedings of the 2017 International Conference on Education and Multimedia Technology, pp. 1–7. ACM New York, USA (2017)
4. Kang, L., Palisano, R., Orlin, M., Chiarello, L., King, G., Polansky, M.: Determinants of social participation—with friends and others who are not family members—for youths with cerebral palsy. Phys. Therapy **90**(12), 1743–1757 (2010)
5. Why Kids Should Develop Collaboration as A Life Skill. https://funacademy.fi/collaboration-as-a-life-skill/#:~:text=Collaboration%20helps%20children%20to%20discover,a%20fun%20and%20efficient%20wa. Last Accessed 24 June 2021
6. Ananiadou, K., Claro, A.: 21st Century Skills and Competences for New Millennium Learners in OECD Countries. OECD Education Working Papers (41), pp. 6–34 (2009)
7. Baykal, G., Van Mechelen, M., Eriksson, E.: Collaborative technologies for children with special needs. In: Proceedings of the 2020 CHI Conference on Human Factors in Computing Systems, pp. 1–13. ACM, New York, USA (2020)
8. Hand Therapy Exercises: 39 Ways to Restore Mobility. https://www.flintrehab.com/hand-the rapy-exercises/#stretching. Last Accessed 24 June 2021

9. Stretching as an intervention for Cerebral Palsy. https://www.physio-pedia.com/index.php?title=Stretching_as_an_intervention_for_Cerebral_Palsy&oldid=204753. Last Accessed 24 June 2021

10. Hung, J.-W., Chang, Y.-J., Chou, C.-X., Wen-Chi, W., Howell, S., Wei-Peng, L.: Developing a suite of motion-controlled games for upper extremity training in children with cerebral palsy: a Proof-of-Concept Study. Games Health J. **7**(5), 327–334 (2018). https://doi.org/10.1089/g4h.2017.0141

11. Dunne, A., Do-Lenh, S., Laighin, G., Shen, C., Bonato, P.: Upper extremity rehabilitation of children with cerebral palsy using accelerometer feedback on a multitouch display. In: Proceedings of the Annual International Conference of the IEEE Engineering in Medicine and Biology, pp. 1741–1754. IEEE, Buenos Aires, Argentina (2010)

12. Mittag, C., Leiss, R., Lorenz, K., Siebold, D.: Designing a tangible solution to encourage playful hand usage for children with cerebral palsy. Curr. Dir. Biomed. Eng. **6**(2), 20202008 (2020). https://doi.org/10.1515/cdbme-2020-2008

13. Nonnis, A., Bryan-Kinns, N.: Mazi: tangible technologies as a channel for collaborative play. In: Proceedings of the 2019 CHI Conference on Human Factors in Computing Systems, pp. 1–13. ACM, New York, USA (2019)

14. Mahmud, A., Soysa, A.I.: POMA: a tangible user interface to improve social and cognitive skills of Sri Lankan children with ASD. Int. J. Hum. Comput. Stud. **144**, 102486 (2020). https://doi.org/10.1016/j.ijhcs.2020.102486

15. Mandil, M., Jamil, N., Gupta, S., Ahirrao, S., Sorathia, K.: PhysiTable: tangible interactive system for physical rehabilitation of children with cerebral palsy. In: Proceedings of the 7th International Conference on HCI, pp. 149–153. ACM, New York, USA (2015)

16. Bian, Y., Wang, X., Han, D., Sun, J.: Designed interactive toys for children with cerebral palsy. In: Proceedings of the Fourteenth International Conference on Tangible, Embedded, and Embodied Interaction, pp. 473–478. ACM, New York, USA (2020)

17. Compañ-Rosique, P., Molina-Carmona, R., Gallego-Durán, F., Satorre-Cuerda, R., Villagrá-Arnedo, C., Llorens-Largo, F.: A guide for making video games accessible to users with cerebral palsy. Univ. Access Inf. Soc. **18**(3), 565–581 (2019). https://doi.org/10.1007/s10209-019-00679-6

18. Lopes, S., et al.: Games used with serious purposes: a systematic review of interventions in patients with cerebral palsy. Front. Psychol. **9**, 1712 (2018). https://doi.org/10.3389/fpsyg.2018.01712

19. Spiller, M.G., Audi, M., Braccialli, L.M.P.: Motor performance of children and adolescents with cerebral palsy during the execution of computer tasks with different peripherals. Rev. CEFAC **21**, 4 (2019). https://doi.org/10.1590/1982-0216/20192140319

Establishing Field of Study: Towards Development of a Multilingual Model for Auto-detection of Cyberbullying Using Fuzzy-Crisp Rules and Internet Crowd Data

Marina Md Din[1]([✉]) [iD], Fiza Abdul Rahim[1,2] [iD], Rina Md. Anwar[1] [iD],
Asmidar Abu Bakar[1] [iD], and Aliza Abdul Latif[1] [iD]

[1] Institute of Informatics and Computing in Energy (IICE), Universiti Tenaga Nasional,
Putrajaya Campus, Jalan Ikram-Uniten, 43000 Kajang, Selangor, Malaysia
{marina,mrina,asmidar,aliza}@uniten.edu.my
[2] Universiti Teknologi Malaysia, Jalan Sultan Yahya Petra, 54100 Kuala Lumpur, Malaysia
fiza.abdulrahim@utm.my

Abstract. This paper is about establishing field of study on the proposed development of a multilingual model for auto-detection of cyberbullying using fuzzy-crisp rules and Internet crowd data among Malaysian. From the time of preliminary study conducted, there was no cyberbully detection tool reported in Malaysia. This study intends to formulate an improved algorithm using fuzzy and crisp rules that is able to detect cyberbullying incidents in Malaysia society based on English and Malay languages. Some literature reviews and preliminary findings are attached and discussed to give more view about the research. This paper also encompasses on the methodology and activities to be carried out in achieving the objectives, along with the research expectations.

Keywords: Cyberbullying detection · Cyberbullying · Content extraction · Fuzzy logic · Crisp rule

1 Introduction

The explosive growth of internet and growing popularity of social media platform, allow everyone to connect with each other all over the world and express their opinions and interests openly. However, this does not come without side effects, which among others, is the increase in cyberbullying. Cyberbullying is the online repeated misbehavior carried out by typically a teenager by means of posting rumors, threats, sexual remarks and victims' personal information with an intent to harm.

Cyberbullying is the bullying or harassing others on the internet or digital spaces, particularly on social media sites. Popular current methods in dealing with cyberbully is to create awareness of it in events and activities. Diana Chai [1] reported the nationwide campaign by UNICEF and the Malaysian government to ensure every child has the opportunity to grow healthy and happy, live safely, and achieve their full potential.

© Springer Nature Switzerland AG 2021
H. Badioze Zaman et al. (Eds.): IVIC 2021, LNCS 13051, pp. 77–89, 2021.
https://doi.org/10.1007/978-3-030-90235-3_7

Other campaigns like Anti-Bullying Campaign [2], #DareToShout [3] and Nickelodeon's Together for Good anti-bullying campaign [4] were targeted at school and college students. They aimed to educate children and students about bullying and proposed methods to stop it, such as by contacting Malaysia's Talian Kasih (care hotline) [5].

Social media users can lodge bullying instances reports via many channels; for example, in Facebook, via Facebook Bullying Prevention Hub [6]. There are useful guides on how to report and block postings on Facebook. There are resources provided for teens, parents and educators seeking support and help on issues related to bullying. These resources are provided by Non-Governmental Organizations (NGOs), government agencies or personal blogs that explain a great deal about cyberbullying and how to prevent it.

In the social media site Instagram, offensive or inappropriate behavior can result in the user being blocked [7] and the Instagram help center explains how to report these problems. The site recently introduced shadow banning (restricting posting or commenting on a post) as a mechanism to combat cyberbullying [8]. For Twitter [9], it provides step-by-step guides to reporting abusive or threatening behavior. Multiple Tweets can be packaged within the same report.

Locally in Malaysia, CyberSecurity Malaysia (CSM) has launched the CyberSAFE program to educate Malaysian public on cyber safety and the threats they may face online. CyberSAFE is a platform where online users who face cyber threats can lodge complaint to Cyber999 Help Centre via email by sending email to cyber999@cybersecurity.my or mycert@mycert.org.my. The public can also call the hotline number 019-2665850 or use the Cyber999 mobile application on their mobile phones [10].

All of the above initiatives are necessary and should be continued in curbing or at least reducing future cases of cyberbullying. Detecting cyberbullying early is found to be effective to prevent it further. Various methods and techniques have been used to overcome cyberbullying problem by automatically detecting them. To determine whether any postings can be considered cyberbullying (or not), there are lists of terms or words considered inappropriate, as part of the vocabulary in cyberbullying.

In Malaysia, as many internet users post comments in social media in both English and Malay, this research attempts to develop an automatic multilingual system for detection of cyberbully for both English and Malay languages. The main function is to detect and filter potential cyberbullying communications and at the same time it may potentially help the authorities to take actions before any real cyberbullying occur. This effort will rely on utilizing the Internet itself to crowd source the required data and then using machine learning for building the detection model. It is also envisaged that fuzzy-crisp rules method will be specifically used. Eventually, the proposed tool with fuzzy capabilities will be able to detect words used to intimidate cyber-victims. It can be used to detect potential cyberbully postings in a variety of social media sites. It may also find acceptable usage in a wide range of other platforms where massive textual communication takes place which has postings that are abusive and offensive in nature.

2   Literature Review

Bullying is defined as an act to hurt, intimidate or threaten a weaker person and it can took many forms including cyberbullying. To some cases, physical violence can leed to severe injuries and even death.

In 2017, Malaysians were shocked by a series of physical bullying incidences that ended in the death of T Nhaveen and a military college student Zulfarhan Osman at the hands of their peers. The late T Nhaveen was beaten with helmets, suffered burns on his back and sodomised by an object by five youths aged between 16 and 18 [11]. Zulfarhan, in another case, was believed to have been abused after being accused of stealing his friend's laptop. He suffered from burns on the chest, arms and legs believed to have been caused by a steam iron [12].

In the era of digital world, there has been many cyberbullying cases and with the continuous and heavy worldwide usage of social media, those numbers seem unlikely to drop. In addition, with the Covid-19 pandemic, people tend to spend more time on social media which may increase the chances of them becoming cyberbullies or the victim.

In 2019 The United Nations Children's Fund (UNICEF) reported that three out of ten young Malaysians have been a victim of cyberbullies in the country [13]. There was a survey conducted on cyberbullying by IPSOS [14] in 2018 which involved 20,793 respondents worldwide. The survey revealed that Malaysia was ranked sixth among twenty-eight countries in the number of parents who have reported that their children are experiencing cyberbullies. When compared to only among Asian countries, Malaysia was ranked second after India. The survey also reported the platforms used for cyberbullying and the types of cyberbullies. The statistics indicated that Malaysia was among the top countries having cyberbullying problem as illustrated in Fig. 1 and Table 1.

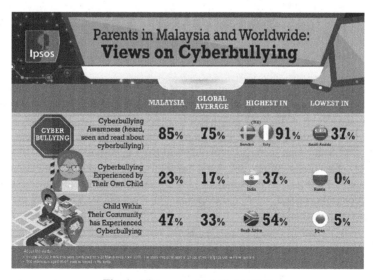

Fig. 1. Views on cyberbullying [14]

Table 1. Platform used for cyberbullying [14]

Platforms used for cyberbullying	Malaysia (%)	Global average (%)
Social media	71	65
Mobile	57	45
Online messaging	33	38
Online chatroom	31	34

Cyberbully victims of abusive online behavior are subjected to anything from threats, humiliation (this includes body shaming), impersonation, hate speech, stalking, sexual harassment, and discrimination based on religion, race, or sexual identity. Kids and adults can say hateful vicious things, and they can keep it up relentlessly. They say harsh words such as, *"you are fat"*, *"bimbo"*, *"stupid"*, *"weirdo"*, *"I can see you but you can't see me,"* *"no one likes you,"* *"I wish you were dead"*, *"I hate you"*, *"prepare to die"*, *"you should kill yourself"* and much worse they send a red splatter image as a symbol of blood. Some of these are as illustrated in Fig. 2 and Fig. 3 when it is a group of people that they know do this, it can be traumatizing.

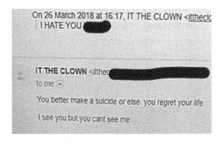

Fig. 2. Hateful words said to a person   **Fig. 3.** Sample of e-mail

People say much more hateful and vulgar things online than they would say in person. It causes significant emotional, psychological, and physical distress. They might experience anxiety, fear, depression, low self-esteem, mental health issues, and some have even been driven to suicide. From a victim's perspective, a study reported that around 25% of Malaysian teenagers encountered from cyberbullying from moderate to severe levels. This also resulted in cyber-related anxiety, depression, and stress among more than 44% of Malaysian teenagers [15]. In addition to feeling distressed, they also may feel embarrassed, hurt, and even fear for their safety. They may even blame themselves for the cyberbullying.

Cyberbully is real in today's society. There are many instances of cyber-bullying involving Malaysians. In one case, a man had his and his wife's personal details posted online after they were involved in a traffic accident [16]. In 2019, a 16-year-old girl in Sarawak jumped to her death from the third floor of a building in Kuching after her Instagram poll she posted the day before. She had posted a poll to her followers to help her decide whether or not she should continue living, or kill herself. From the poll, 69%

of her followers voted for her to commit suicide [17]. It's impossible to know how the girl felt after reading all replies but all we know is that she took her own life the very next day. In 2020, a young lady aged 20 from Bukit Mertajam, who was a victim to cyberbullying took her own life after a Tik-Tok video of her and a Nepali colleague drew criticism on Facebook and went viral [18].

Cyberbullying is a critical issue that needs specific legislation. Those who have fallen victims to cyberbullies not only affecting these individuals themselves but also their family members. Existing laws such as the Computer Crime Act 1997, Communications and Multimedia Act 1998 and Children's Act 2001 may be adequate to deal with cyberbullying but a more specific law is needed to penalize bullies as well as to protect online users.

3 Cyberbullying Detection

A measure in combating and reducing cyberbullying perpetration is needed whenever the bullies are trying to carry out a cyberbully attack. Many studies have been conducted in detecting cyberbullying. Salawu et al. [19] outline that there are four features used in cyberbullying detection:

i.   Content-based features.
ii. Sentiment-based features.
iii. User-based features.
iv. Network-based features.

In content-based, cyberbullying classification is done by investigating the comments (the textual content of postings, emails, blog or any sort of text-based platform), image content or contextual features as conducted by [20–24]. Sentiment-based is done by detecting and categorizing sentiments expressed or emotion in a piece of text or in a whole content, especially in order to decide whether the writer's attitude towards a particular topic is positive, negative, or neutral. In this process, a sentence is considered positive if it has a positive keyword and is considered negative if it has a negative keyword. To extract emotion or sentiment in detecting cyberbullying, [25, 26] investigated the content of the posts which contain the emoticons that show the sentiment.

However, there is also a situation involve '*backhanded compliment*' where the statement is using positive words but somehow it shows negativity to intimidate the victim. Statement like "*you are gorgeous if you are slim*" or "*you are beautiful if you are fairer and no pimple scars like a moon on your face*". If this is the case, some artificial intelligent algorithm is needed to capture this based on the structural of the statement.

Alongside content-based and emotion-based features, researchers have explored incorporating user-related features into cyberbullying detection systems. These include features like age, gender, and race as done by [19, 26]. Most studies were conducted to characterize the public either cyberbully or non-cyberbully [22, 27, 28]. With the advancements used in social media, network data such as number of followers, friends, likes of every postings, number of uploads and etc., are being used as features in detecting cyberbullying as conducted by [28, 29]. Table 2 represents a summary of related studies on cyberbullying detection which include the technique used and some of it revealed the accuracy level of their technique. It is observed that Support Vector Machine (SVM), Naïve Bayes (NB) and Random Forest (RF) are among classification techniques used in comparative study to test the accuracy level as conducted by [23, 25–28]. Recent studies have used Natural Language Processing (NLP) techniques to detect and prevent cyberbullying [20, 29] because of its capabilities of extracting emotions related texts and doing sentiment analysis. Another approach made by [21, 22] implementing convolutional neural network (CNN) algorithm (deep learning) for classification with word embedding (GloVe) in their models/experiments. CNN showed great results when used with different text mining tasks. The study presented in [23] compares the Fuzzy Fingerprint (FFP) with Logistic Regression (LR), NB and SVM, and proved that FFP is better compared to the other three.

4   Proposed Methodology

This research will be carried out based on the following proposed framework (see Fig. 4) for detecting cyberbully activities. For the initial stage, platforms to be used in collecting data related to cyberbullying incidents will be identified. Next step is to collect the dataset (input) from the identified text based digital platforms. This study will use content-based data collected from the identified platforms. In this phase, the main task involves activities with regards to filtering and excluding all data noise such as extra characters, whitespace, special characters like hash (#), dash (−), exclamation mark (!), question mark (?), hyperlink as well as stop words like "a", "as", "have", "is", "the", "or", etc.

Preprocessed and filtered will be prepared for characterizing process. This is to identify noun, adjective, pronoun, usage of capital letters, spelling checking (purposely miss-spell the word such as *shaddap, biatch, dafuq, r-tard, k33l*) and internet slang (*stfu, wth, wtf, fub, fugly, idttu*). The statistics on occurrence of word in the text are also extracted. A complete glossary for cyberbullying incidents is expected to be produced as the first deliverable.

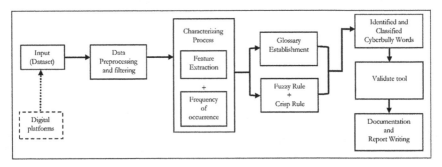

Fig. 4. Proposed framework

The next phase in this study will be proceed with the development of the detection tool. The development is using Fuzzy-Crisp rules to train all words and value of every

Table 2. Summary of related studies on cyberbullying detection

Ref	Data source			Detection technique	
	Country and language	Selection of training dataset and duration (year/no. of posts)	Related feature(s)	Classification technique(s)	Evaluation parameter(s) and results
[20]	India, English	14200 tweets	Textual	Reinforcement Learning along with NLP techniques	F1 score Proposed Q-bully Algo utilizing Reinforcement Learning gives consistent accuracy avg. of 88% on randomly sampled datasets
[21]	India, English	69874 tweets	Text-based	Deep learning - CNN Implemented in Python and TensorFlow Utilizing word embedding GloVe	Accuracy, 93.97%
[22]	Arab Saudi, English	20,000 random tweets	Textual-based	CrowdFlower to do labeling (bullying vs non-bullying) Deep learning CNN, use word embedding GloVe (Global Vector) to capture semantic and similarities between words	Accuracy, precision and recall 81.60% of accuracy

(*continued*)

Table 2. (*continued*)

Ref	Data source			Detection technique	
	Country and language	Selection of training dataset and duration (year/no. of posts)	Related feature(s)	Classification technique(s)	Evaluation parameter(s) and results
[23]	Portugal, English	formsrping.me dataset comprises of 17846 text and emoticons (13160 labeled text)	Textual	Amazon's Mechanical Turk and 3 workers to label the text FFP copared with LR, NB and SVM	Precision (prec), recall (rec), F1-score (F1) FFP is better compared to the other three
[24]	Malaysia, English	5453 tweets	User features such as personalities, sentiment and emotion	NB, RF and J48 User persoalities were determined using Big Five and Dark Triad models	Cyberbullying detection improved using J48 when user personalities and sentiments were used Accuracy of 91.88% and AUC of 0.97
[26]	Turkey, Turkish text	900 messages in Turkish collected manually from Instagram and Twitter	Textual and emoticons (content)	SVM, decision tree (C4.5)-J48, NB and kNN Using WEKA data mining tool	Information gain and chi^2 feature selection methods on F-measure only NB improved up to 84% for the dataset used based on accuracy and running time

(*continued*)

Table 2. (*continued*)

Ref	Data source			Detection technique	
	Country and language	Selection of training dataset and duration (year/no. of posts)	Related feature(s)	Classification technique(s)	Evaluation parameter(s) and results
[27]	Malaysia, English	10,007 geo tagged tweets between January 2015 and February 2015	Features based: Network features, activities features, user features include (personality, gender, age), content features (Vulgarities feature, Specific social network cyberbullying features, First and second person)	Compare among NB, SVM, RF, KNN	Precision (prec), recall (rec), F1-score (F1), and weighted area under the ROC curve (AUC) chi^2 test, information gain, and Pearson correlation run on SMOTE and Cost Sensitive RF using SMOTE showed the best AUC (0.943) and f-measure (0.936
[28]	Greece, English	9484 tweets over a period of 3 months	User, Textual (content), Network Frequency, type of topics discussed	Crowdsourcing worker (834) to do labeling process – aggressor, bully, spammer, normal Machine Learning classifiers used are NB, RF, Ensemble, Neural Network (NN) Utilizing WEKA data mining toolkit and NN setup use Keras with Theano	Precision (prec), recall (rec), F1-score (F1), and weighted area under the ROC curve (AUC) Run on Twitter from Nov 2016 – Sept 2018. Twitter suspended the majority of them (only ~5% of the bully users are still active)

(*continued*)

Table 2. (*continued*)

Ref	Data source			Detection technique	
	Country and language	Selection of training dataset and duration (year/no. of posts)	Related feature(s)	Classification technique(s)	Evaluation parameter(s) and results
[29]	Global, English	2235 tweet dataset	Analyze texts and predicting abusive behavior	Comparative study that utilizing NLP and Machine Learning classifiers such as LR, RF, SVM and Gradient Boosting Machine	model accuracy score, test accuracy score, cross validation score and AUC score LR and RF classifier trained on the feature stack performed better than SVM and Gradient Boosting Machine
[30]	Malaysia, English	Twitter	User based feature (to extract name, gender, age)	Combine NB and RF	Integration of cyberbully detection and rumor detection in a single application makes the detection easier
[31]	Malaysia, Malay	427,108 Tweets from between 18–25 April 2018 A Questionnaire were distributed to 125 undergraduate students on March 21, 2019	Linguistic features for Intelligence-Related Insults Questionnaire Text and image on Twitter	Manually distinguished, coded and categorized	No experiment conducted

individual cyberbully terms will be calculated. Figure 5 shows the Fuzzy-Crisp algorithm in obtaining the desired output. It is anticipated to give an improved result by incorporating both Fuzzy-Crisp rules in the experiment. This algorithm will be implemented on the established cyberbully glossary that to be trained. The cyberbully glossary will be the crisp input to the model and fuzzification with the suitable rules will be used to train the data. The process iteratively takes place for a few times until the crisp output is obtained and classified as cyberbully word.

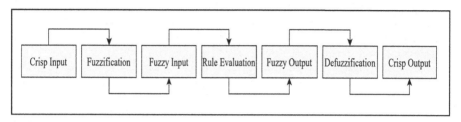

Fig. 5. Fuzzy-crisp algorithm

At the final stage of this study, we will simulate and validate the accuracy of developed model through several samples and test vectors, the validation will be based on its performance in detecting the cyberbullying using real data from the selected digital media.

5 Conclusion

Day by day we can see the rapid growth of the internet and technology which to some extent, people might misuse it. In the case of cyberbullying, some countries are already done their study on what can be done in order to curb it. These previously carried out studies implied that cyberbullying can be detected by various machine learning methods. Different methods yield different results, depending on the algorithm and techniques used in the method. However, there was no specific tool developed to generate automatic multilingual detection for both English and Malay language. Our study intends to formulate an improved algorithm using Fuzzy-Crisp rules that is able to detect cyberbullying incidents on different digital platforms such as social media, email and chatting applications.

References

1. Chai, D.: Standing together to curb bullying I UNICEF Malaysia. https://www.unicef.org/mal aysia/stories/standing-together-curb-bullying. Last Accessed June 2021
2. R.E.A.L Education Group: Anti-bullying campaign. https://real.edu.my/anti-bullying-cam paign/. Last Accessed 30 June 2021
3. Quah, E.: Beauty queen takes on cyberbullying I The Star. https://www.thestar.com.my/metro/ metro-news/2018/10/15/beauty-queen-takes-on-cyberbullying. Last Accessed 30 June 2021

4. theSundaily: Nickelodeon announces its anti-bullying campaign in Malaysia. https://www.thesundaily.my/archive/nickelodeon-announces-its-anti-bullying-campaign-malaysia-XTARCH468385. Last Accessed 30 June 2021

5. R.AGE team: Support – #StandTogether: ending school bullying through kindness. https://standtogether.my/support/. Last Accessed 30 June 2021

6. Facebook: Bullying prevention hub. https://web.facebook.com/safety/bullying. Last Accessed 30 June 2021

7. Instagram: Instagram help Centre. https://help.instagram.com/. Last Accessed 30 June 2021

8. mint: Instagram is taking cyberbullying seriously, introduces "shadow ban". https://www.livemint.com/technology/tech-news/instagram-is-taking-cyberbullying-seriously-introduces-shadow-ban-1562648818682.html. Last Accessed 30 June 2021

9. Twitter: How to report abusive behavior on Twitter | Twitter Help. https://help.twitter.com/en/safety-and-security/report-abusive-behavior. Last Accessed 30 June 2021

10. CyberSecurity Malaysia: CyberSAFE. https://www.cybersafe.my/en/. Last Accessed 30 June 2021

11. The Straits Times: Malaysia teen Nhaveen dies after brutal assault by bullies, SE Asia news & top stories – the straits times. https://www.straitstimes.com/asia/se-asia/malaysia-teen-nhaveen-dies-after-brutal-assault-by-bullies. Last Accessed 30 June 2021

12. Gunaratnam, S.: Bullied, murdered UPNM naval cadet: five students charged with murder. https://www.nst.com.my/news/crime-courts/2017/06/248852/bullied-murdered-upnm-naval-cadet-five-students-charged-murder. Last Accessed 30 June 2021

13. Nortajuddin, A.: Does Malaysia have a cyberbullying problem? The ASEAN Post. https://theaseanpost.com/article/does-malaysia-have-cyberbullying-problem. Last Accessed 30 June 2021

14. IPSOS: Malaysian and Global Views on Cyberbullying

15. Meikeng, Y., Lee, L.M., Clarissa, S.: Our teens are bullies. https://www.thestar.com.my/news/nation/2018/03/18/behaving-badly-in-cyberspace-malaysian-teens-more-likely-to-be-cyberbullies-than-victims-says-study. Last Accessed 22 Aug 2021

16. Nur, A.: Malaysia surpasses 26 countries to become 2nd in Asia for … cyber-bullying. https://www.thesundaily.my/local/malaysia-surpasses-26-countries-to-become-2nd-in-asia-for-cyber-bullying-DD2948511. Last Accessed 30 June 2021

17. Adams, D.: Teen commits suicide after Instagram poll, Digit. https://digit.fyi/teen-commits-suicide-after-instagram-poll/. Last Accessed 30 June 2021

18. Chern, L.T.: Cyberbullying victim leaves suicide note. https://www.thestar.com.my/news/nation/2020/05/22/cyberbullying-victim-leaves-suicide-note. Last Accessed 24 Sep 2020

19. Salawu, S., He, Y., Lumsden, J.: Approaches to automated detection of cyberbullying: a survey. IEEE Trans. Affect. Comput. **11**, 3–24 (2020). https://doi.org/10.1109/TAFFC.2017.2761757

20. Aind, A.T., Ramnaney, A., Sethia, D.: Q-Bully: a reinforcement learning based cyberbullying detection framework. In: 2020 International Conference for Emerging Technology (INCET), pp. 1–6 (2020). https://doi.org/10.1109/INCET49848.2020.9154092

21. Banerjee, V., Telavane, J., Gaikwad, P., Vartak, P.: Detection of cyberbullying using deep neural network. In: 2019 5th International Conference on Advanced Computing & Communication Systems (ICACCS), pp. 604–607 (2019). https://doi.org/10.1109/ICACCS.2019.8728378

22. Al-Ajlan, M.A., Ykhlef, M.: Optimized twitter cyberbullying detection based on deep learning. In: 2018 21st Saudi Computer Society National Computer Conference (NCC), pp. 1–5 (2018). https://doi.org/10.1109/NCG.2018.8593146

23. Rosa, H., Carvalho, J.P., Calado, P., Martins, B., Ribeiro, R., Coheur, L.: Using fuzzy finger-prints for cyberbullying detection in social networks. In: 2018 IEEE International Conference on Fuzzy Systems (FUZZ-IEEE), pp. 1–7 (2018). https://doi.org/10.1109/FUZZ-IEEE.2018.8491557

24. Van Hee, C., et al.: Automatic detection of cyberbullying in social media text. PLoS One **13**, (2018). https://doi.org/10.1371/journal.pone.0203794

25. Balakrishnan, V., Khan, S., Arabnia, H.R.: Improving cyberbullying detection using Twit-ter users' psychological features and machine learning. Comput. Secur. **90**, 101710 (2020). https://doi.org/10.1016/j.cose.2019.101710

26. Özel, S.A., Saraç, E., Akdemir, S., Aksu, H.: Detection of cyberbullying on social media messages in Turkish. In: 2017 International Conference on Computer Science and Engineering (UBMK), pp. 366–370 (2017). https://doi.org/10.1109/UBMK.2017.8093411

27. Al-Garadi, M.A., Varathan, K.D., Ravana, S.D.: Cybercrime detection in online communi-cations: The experimental case of cyberbullying detection in the Twitter network. Comput. Human Behav. **63**, 433–443 (2016). https://doi.org/10.1016/j.chb.2016.05.051

28. Chatzakou, D., et al.: Detecting cyberbullying and cyberaggression in social media. ACM Trans. Web. **13**, (2019). https://doi.org/10.1145/3343484

29. Nandhini, B.S., Sheeba, J.I.: Online social network bullying detection using intelligence techniques. Procedia Comput. Sci. **45**, 485–492 (2015). https://doi.org/10.1016/j.procs.2015.03.085.

30. Saravanaraj, A., Sheeba, J.I., Devaneyan, S.P.: Automatic detection of cyberbullying from Twitter. Int. J. Comput. Sci. Inf. Technol. Secur. **6**, 2249–9555 (2019)

31. Sood, S.M.M., Hua, T.K., Hamid, B.A.: Cyberbullying through intellect-related insults. Malaysian J. Commun. **36**, 278–297 (2020)

Identifying the Presence of Cyberbullying in Tamil-English Phonetic Words Using Browser Plugin

Rina Md. Anwar[1]([✉]) [iD], Puven Alvin Victor[1], Fiza Abdul Rahim[1,2] [iD],
Marina Md Din[1] [iD], Asmidar Abu Bakar[1] [iD], and Aliza Abdul Latif[1] [iD]

[1] Institute of Informatics and Computing in Energy (IICE), Universiti Tenaga Nasional, 43000 Putrajaya Campus, Jalan Ikram-Uniten, 43000 Kajang, Selangor, Malaysia
{mrina,marina,asmidar,aliza}@uniten.edu.my,
fiza.abdulrahim@utm.my
[2] Universiti Teknologi Malaysia, Jalan Sultan Yahya Petra, 54100 Kuala Lumpur, Malaysia

Abstract. While social media provides excellent communication opportunities, it also exposes people to potentially threatening situations online. The rising popularity of various social media platforms has enabled people worldwide to freely exchange views, ideas, and interests. But that does not come without consequences, including an increase in cyberbullying. Early identification of cyberbullying has been proven to be beneficial in preventing it from spreading. We have tested a web browser plugin over few social media platforms to identify offensive comments or posts. Furthermore, research on cyberbullying identification has been done in many languages, but none has been done on Tamil and English phonetic words until the time of conducting this study. Therefore, this study attempts to elicit keywords or phrases relating to cyberbullying incidents in both Tamil and English phonetic words. The study results might be helpful to the research community to create further tools and prepare a training dataset for cyberbullying identification.

Keywords: Social networking · Cyberbullying · Detection · Language

1 Introduction

The rise of the Internet has sparked a debate over the influence of social interactions in cyberspace. When you have a platform in which its community can communicate smoothly using social media, there are numerous classes of netizens who, by means of different forms of behaviours, can or may not contribute to a healthy atmosphere. One such dark side of human behaviour is cyberbullying perpetration.

Cyberbullying is a phrase often used amongst netizens, but only a few fully comprehend its true meaning and its detrimental impacts on any victim, regardless of age or background. Cyberbullying occurs when a person or group utilizes the Internet or technologies with the intent to harass, intimidate, disgrace, or abuse someone else [1]. Because humiliation of the victim can "go viral" and become public in a short time, cyberbullying may do more damages than traditional bullying [2].

© Springer Nature Switzerland AG 2021
H. Badioze Zaman et al. (Eds.): IVIC 2021, LNCS 13051, pp. 90–97, 2021.
https://doi.org/10.1007/978-3-030-90235-3_8

Worldwide statistics reveal that cyberbullying incidents have increased gradually between 2011 to 2018, as reported in [3]. This raised a lot of concern for the public as social media gets toxic every day. Cyberbullying has brought a swirl of adverse effects from suicide to increased and persistent mental health issues such as social anxiety disorder and depression worldwide.

As cyberbullying occurs around the globe, it immediately diversifies regarding its inflected language depending on the nation it "visits". Cyberbullying can take place in different languages, depending on one's language proficiency. It can also be presented in a mixture of languages, especially in a multiracial country such as Malaysia. A mixture of languages is utilized for hurting or reaching a wider "audience" with various language proficiency.

Indeed, Malaysian cyberbullies tend to communicate and, in some instances, employ all their harmful words in a range of languages. However, there is limited research in cyberbullying that uses different types of languages or a mixture of multiple languages. The likelihood of the cyberbullying victim feeling the same or perhaps worse effects using a mix of language that may convey more hurtful meanings. Hence, there is a serious need to investigate methods for identifying potentially offensive mixed languages on social media platforms.

2   Background

There have been numerous instances of cyberbullying in the digital world, and the constant and intensive use of social media worldwide makes it unlikely that these figures will fall. In addition, people have more time spent on social media through the Covid-19 pandemic, raising their chances of becoming cyberbullies or victims.

A 2018 poll was carried out with 20,793 people worldwide on cyberbullying by IPSOS [3]. The results showed that 3 out of 10 young Malaysians had been victims of cyberbullies in the country. Malaysia ranks second in Asia, where parents have reported their children experiencing cyberbullies.

Most research in cyberbullying identification was based on either a filters program or machine learning approaches [4–7]. As multiple uncertainties are inherent in one language, several identification cyberbullying techniques for different contexts have been investigated by scholars. For example, Saravanaraj et al. (2016) suggested a cyberbullying identification model using Naïve Bayes, where the presence of an abusive word indicates cyberbullying, and the absence indicates otherwise [7].

In addition to content, researchers have examined user-related factors in cyberbullying identification systems. This includes age, gender, sexual orientation, and race, as discovered by [8, 9]. Many studies also were conducted to classify between cyberbully or non-cyberbully [10–12].

It is believed that the integration of user knowledge, features, and post-harassing behaviour, for example, by readdressing their harassment experiences by placing a new status on another social network, will increase the cyberbullying identification's accuracy [13]. These strategies have over the years been repeated and enhanced to better match modern language nuances and the expansion of social media features.

In this study, we focused on the identification of the most commonly used Tamil-English phonetic offensive words. A wide search of existing journals and publications was conducted, and no previous work was found on the identification of cyber-bullying in used Tamil-English phonetic words. Since Tamil is also a language that transcends the multiracial people of Malaysia, it may also be utilized as a medium for harm and distress online.

3   Browser Plugin Testing

The browser plugin used in this study was adapted from two other Google Chrome Browser Plugins or Extensions, "NO SPOILERS" [14] and "CODAR" [15]. "NO SPOIL-ERS!" was created by a Malaysian named Ng Khai Yong, which will automatically blur out any posts talking about Avengers: Endgame movie. The other plugin is called "CO-DAR" or "Cyber Offense Detecting and Reporting Framework" which performs Text Toxicity Prediction on public Facebook posts or comments using BeautifulSoup and Facebook API. Both plugins are integrated to test the sample dataset in this study.

Figure 1 illustrates the workflow of the testing activities, from preparing the dataset preparation to configuring the manifest file, modifying the sample dataset and finally testing the adapted plugin.

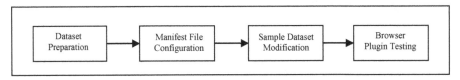

Fig. 1. Browser plugin testing workflow

Dataset Preparation. The key challenge in this study is the availability of a suitable dataset, which is necessary to identify the presence of cyberbullying. In this study, we have developed a Tamil-English phonetic words dataset obtained from the comment sections of public posts of some popular Facebook pages and Twitter accounts. We select a sample of 45 offensive Tamil-English phonetic words from the dataset for testing purposes.

Configuration, Modification and Testing. The manifest file was coded and tested, similar to all Google Chrome Browser plugins. The manifest is the Google Chrome Browser plugin' backbone or the central nervous system. If the manifest file is success-fully coded and loaded into the Google Chrome web browser, this is visible in the plugins menu at chrome://extensions on the same browser, as shown in Fig. 2. When the plugin is selected, it is displayed the entire name, version number, description, and unique ID number. Each plugin is allocated an ID number since each plugin has its own unique ID.

The next step was to align manifest.json script with a jquery-3.6.0.min.js script. The jquery-3.6.0.min.js script is available to download on the jquery website. After downloading it, it is saved to the same directory as the manifest.json script, as shown in Fig. 3.

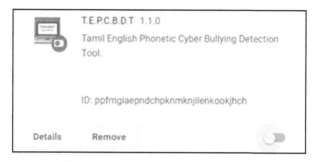

Fig. 2. The activation menu of the plugin

Fig. 3. The manifest.json and jquery-3.6.0.min.js scripts working under the same directory

After the manifest file is configured, the block.js file, adapted from the NO SPOIL-ERS! and CODAR extensions, is equipped with a new dataset that consists of 45 offensive Tamil-English phonetic words. However, certain concerns with the security policies on Facebook, Twitter, Instagram, and Youtube have prevented the detection procedure from operating on these websites. Despite that, the Google Chrome search bar detects and blocks photos from the same search. After several adjustments have been made, the adapted plugin still could not bypass Facebook, Twitter, Instagram, and Youtube's security policies.

If the offensive words are found, a message will appear in red font colour showing "[Text Blocked: Offensive content warning.]", indicating a clear warning that the word or phrase being searched contains an offensive word. As shown in Fig. 4 and Fig. 5, the plugin can identify and block out the offensive phrases in the Chrome and standard Incognito web browsers.

Fig. 4. Search result using standard Chrome tab

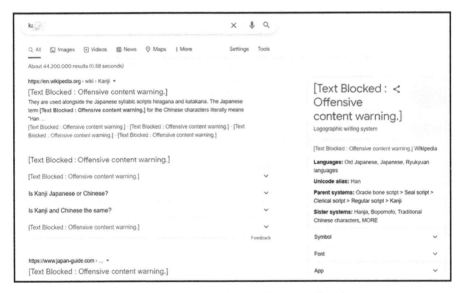

Fig. 5. Search result using standard Incognito tab

Figure 6, Fig. 7 and Fig. 8 show the adapted plugin running on Facebook, Twitter, and YouTube. The adapted plugin works to identify harmful phrases on Facebook, but it does not work on Twitter and YouTube, which is due to the security policies established by these social networking sites to ensure that no foreign application or plugins can

Fig. 6. The adapted plugin running on Facebook

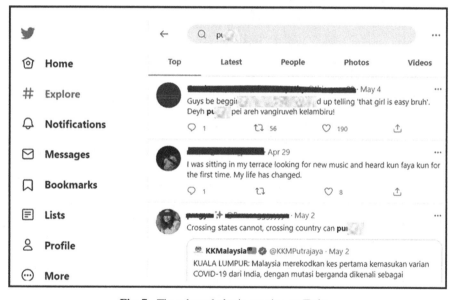

Fig. 7. The adapted plugin running on Twitter

comb through any information, even in the background on their websites. The constant changes in their privacy policies can also be attributable to this.

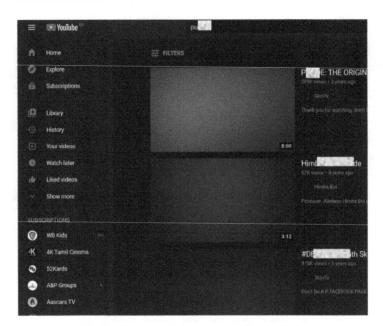

Fig. 8. The adapted plugin running on YouTube

4 Conclusion

The adapted browser plugin focused on identifying inappropriate words and phrases in a mixture of Tamil and English phonetic words. However, much future work is needed to improve the usability and performance of the plugin or develop sophisticated tools that can automatically identify offensive words. Developing a complete dataset is also essential in multiple languages for conducting tests and development to identify cyberbullying.

Hence, this study will be extended to apply different machine learning models for identification purposes. Secondly, we intend to complete the dataset development of the words and phrases in a mixture of Tamil and English phonetic words. Finally, we plan to validate our approach and generalize the results using different datasets from social media sites.

Acknowledgment. This study was funded by BOLD Research Grant 2021 Universiti Tenaga Nasional (J510050002/2021046). We would like to thank UNITEN Innovation & Research Management Centre (iRMC) for fund management.

References

1. Park, M.S., Golden, K.J., Vizcaino-vickers, S., Jidong, D., Raj, S.: Sociocultural values, attitudes and risk factors associated with adolescent cyberbullying in east Asia : a systematic review. Cyberpsychol. J. Psychosoc. Res. Cybersp. **15** (2021)

2. Sood, S.M.M., Hua, T.K., Hamid, B.A.: Cyberbullying through intellect-related insults. Malaysian J. Commun. **36**, 278–297 (2020)
3. IPSOS: Malaysian and Global Views on Cyberbullying
4. Ghosh, R., Nowal, S.: Social media cyberbullying detection using machine learning in Bengali language. Int. J. Eng. Res. Technol. **10**, 190–193 (2021)
5. Van Hee, C., et al.: Automatic detection of cyberbullying in social media text. PLoS ONE **13**, 1–22 (2018). https://doi.org/10.1371/journal.pone.0203794
6. Saravanaraj, A., Sheeba, J.I., Devaneyan, S.P.: Automatic detection of cyberbullying from twitter. Int. J. Comput. Sci. Inf. Technol. Secur. **6**, 2249–9555 (2019)
7. Balakrishnan, V., Khan, S., Arabnia, H.R.: Improving cyberbullying detection using twitter users' psychological features and machine learning. Comput. Secur. **90**, 101710 (2020). https://doi.org/10.1016/j.cose.2019.101710
8. Salawu, S., He, Y., Lumsden, J.: Approaches to automated detection of cyberbullying: a survey. IEEE Trans. Affect. Comput. **11**, 3–24 (2020). https://doi.org/10.1109/TAFFC.2017.2761757
9. Özel, S.A., Saraç, E., Akdemir, S., Aksu, H.: Detection of cyberbullying on social media messages in Turkish. In: 2017 International Conference on Computer Science and Engineering (UBMK), pp. 366–370 (2017). https://doi.org/10.1109/UBMK.2017.8093411
10. Al-Garadi, M.A., Varathan, K.D., Ravana, S.D.: Cybercrime detection in online communications: the experimental case of cyberbullying detection in the Twitter network. Comput. Human Behav. **63**, 433–443 (2016). https://doi.org/10.1016/j.chb.2016.05.051
11. Al-Ajlan, M.A., Ykhlef, M.: Optimized twitter cyberbullying detection based on deep learning. In: 2018 21st Saudi Computer Society National Computer Conference (NCC), pp. 1–5 (2018). https://doi.org/10.1109/NCG.2018.8593146
12. Chatzakou, D., et al.: Detecting cyberbullying and cyberaggression in social media. ACM Trans. Web. **13** (2019). https://doi.org/10.1145/3343484
13. Dadvar, M., de Jong, F.: Cyberbullying detection: a step toward a safer internet yard. In: Proceedings of the 21st International Conference on World Wide Web. pp. 121–126. Association for Computing Machinery, New York, NY, USA (2012). https://doi.org/10.1145/2187980.2187995
14. Ng, K.: NO SPOILERS!. https://chrome.google.com/webstore/detail/no-spoilers/anbpdfddbjchiihmibgakojddmhbfmeb?hl=en
15. Krishnakanth, A., Mahalakshumi, V., Vignesh, S., Nivetha, M.: CODAR – Cyber Offense Detecting and Reporting Framework. https://github.com/axenhammer/CODAR. Last Accessed 30 June 2021

Visual Learning Application in Mathematics Using Holographic Display Based on Multi-touch Technology

Khoo Shiang Tyng[1]([⊠]), Halimah Badioze Zaman[2], Ummul Hanan Mohamad[1], and Azlina Ahmad[1]

[1] Institute of IR4.0 (IIR4.0) formerly known as Institute of Visual Informatics (IVI), Universiti Kebangsaan Malaysia, 43600 Bangi, Selangor, Malaysia
ummulhanan@ukm.edu.my
[2] Institute of Informatics and Computing in Energy, Universiti Tenaga Nasional, Jalan Ikram Uniten, 43000 Kajang, Selangor, Malaysia

Abstract. The Malaysian Education System have recently implemented the home-based teaching and learning or *Pengajaran dan Pembelajaran di Rumah* (PdPR) classes due to the outbreak of the pandemic COVID19. Since students were not able to go to schools during the lockdown period, teachers and parents have resorted to creating various methods to engage students in their learning process. Multi-touch technology on tablet appears as a promising tool in visual learning especially during this pandemic out-break. This paper presents a preliminary study conducted on a research project in developing a Visual Learning Application for Mathematics using Holographic Display for the topic on *Shape and Space* based on Multi-Touch Technology called MEL-VIS. A preliminary study was conducted on fifteen (15) primary school teachers. The results of the preliminary study showed that the topic on Shape and Space is a topic that most students had major problems when learning Mathematics at three (3) primary schools. Students were found to have difficulty in understanding the concepts being taught due to factors such as: abstractive phenomena and concepts; as well as possessing low imagination.

Keywords: Tablet technology · Multi-touch technology · Hologram · Visual learning · Visual informatics

1 Introduction

The topic on *Shape and Space* in Mathematics is widely used in the fields of engineering, architecture, science, and technology. The most notable shape and space applications are used in architectural design and architectural layout. Due to this clear demand, the education system in Malaysia adopts the themes related to shape and space in all the national syllabi from pre-kindergarten to higher education, especially in the fields of design and architecture. Space and shape learning not only learns the meaning or hypothesis of geometric concepts, but also learns the ability to analyse the features

H. Badioze Zaman et al. (Eds.): IVIC 2021, LNCS 13051, pp. 98–110, 2021.
https://doi.org/10.1007/978-3-030-90235-3_9

of two-dimensional (2D) and three-dimensional (3D) shapes in geometric shapes. In addition, students are also expected to be able to discuss geometric relationships to identify position and space in geometric relationships, then modify and use symmetry, visualisation, spatial thinking and geometric models to solve open problems.

Technologies related to holography and holograms with multi-touch tablets have a significant impact on the teaching and learning process of STEM subjects, especially for students in primary schools. This is because multi-touch tablets can enhance and enhance teachers' perception and understanding of STEM education [1, 2]. For students learning mathematics, using multi-touch tablets, can make them to be more active and also encourage them to develop their mathematics skills in an enjoyable and interesting way [3]. The use of holographic pyramid floating image technology has many advantages in students learning mathematics, and its use is in 360-degree view that can be viewed in many different angles [4]. Multi-touch technology on tablets allow users to interact with the system through multi-finger use, and students will be able to see what they are doing on the same device they are operating. Due to easy access and accessibility, the multi-touch and hologram display can easily improve the learning ability level of primary school students. Figure 1 shows a primary school student using multi-touch tablet with hologram display to solve Mathematics problem.

Fig. 1. Student solving mathematics problem on a multi-touch tablet with hologram display

2 Multi-Touch Technology in Learning Mathematics

Multi-touch technology is used in a variety of industries, but more so in the education industry. This technology, for some time now, has been used as a teaching aid in schools to help students learn more successfully. Many instructional possibilities exist in a mobile learning environment with multi-touch technologies that are difficult to be realised in conventional learning settings [5, 6]. Many research have shown that multi-touch tablet approaches can help students learn and teachers teach more effectively [7]. Some of them believe that multi-touch tablet can help students learn at a higher level of personality, enhance student freedom, and boost collaborative chances in learning [7, 8]. There have also been numerous researches on multi-touch technology-based mathematics learning exercises. By using multi-touch technologies in mathematics learning can help students to improve their arithmetic abilities [9]. They will be more willing to experiment with new ideas and more interested in learning Mathematics [10, 11].

A holographic pyramid is a floating image technology that is reflected on the pyramid's surface from a digital picture display [12]. The holographic pyramid setting method is very simple and is most commonly used in holographic presentations. This technique requires a four-sided glass or acrylic pyramid, as well as an LCD screen, tablet, or mobile phone screen. Images reflected on the screen appear to float in the air inside the pyramid, separated from the physical display screen. Through this holographic pyramid, students can get a true visual view of the object from various locations [13]. Students will be able to understand more complicated 3D structures and phenomena as a result of this [14].

3 Multi-Touch Tablets in Learning Mathematics

Studies show that the usage of multi-touch tablets may attract primary school students in learning mathematics [2]. Generally, primary school students are visual learners, which means they retain knowledge better when it is provided concretely, in the form of 2D and 3D visual images rather than voice and text. To develop a playful learning environment, it is important to combine visuals, music, animation, and video in a digital environment. This technology might create a game-based learning environment in primary schools. Moreover, the use of multi-touch tablets may motivate primary school students to learn mathematics more effectively. Besides, utilising a holographic display on a multi-touch tablet can increase primary school students' learnability, since interaction and 3D visualisation make them more engaged in their learning process. The students can observe any angle of 3D shapes which float on the multi-touch tablet screen. With all of the multi-touch and holographic display's potential uses in education, the goal of this study is to create and build a visual learning application for elementary or primary school students learn mathematics using a holographic display based on a multi-touch tablet (MEL-VIS).

A preliminary research was conducted on fifteen (15) primary school teachers/instructors and 40 primary school children in order to have a better understanding of the problems experienced by primary school students in the teaching and learning of Mathematics. The preliminary study's objectives, procedures, and findings will be described in the parts that follow.

4 Objectives of Preliminary Study

Preliminary analysis, design, development, and evaluation are the three primary steps of MEL-VIS design and development. This paper highlights the preliminary study conducted as part of the MEL-VIS development process. Thus, the objectives of the preliminary study were as follows:

i. To investigate on the types of teaching aids that was in current use by the Mathematics teachers, as well as the issues they confronted.

ii. To identify topics in primary Mathematics syllabus which the primary school students found difficult to comprehend.

iii. To identify which topic in the Mathematics syllabus is most challenging for the primary school students.

5 Design of Preliminary Study

In order to fulfil the main objectives of the preliminary study, the process involved was designed to obtain the necessary data required in order to understand the problems faced by the teachers and students in the teaching and learning of mathematics in the primary schools. It was concluded that an interview and survey methods were the best approach to conduct this preliminary study to obtain the necessary data. Thus, the interview schedule/tool and the questionnaire were designed to be administered to the samples/respondents (teachers and primary school students, respectively) of the preliminary study.

The sampling of the study was based on three (3) primary schools in the Klang Valley which were approved by the schools. The respondents comprised of fifteen (15) primary school mathematics teachers with a combined mathematics teaching experience of 10 to 20 years from the three (3) schools; and 40 primary school students participated in the preliminary study. Thus, this study was implemented using two instruments: Teacher's Interview Schedule (TIS) or tool; and a questionnaire to be administered to teachers and primary school students on the challenging topics on Mathematics (QCT). The procedures that were followed in the preliminary study were as follows:

- Step 1: Conduct Interview session with teachers based on the instrument: TIS.
- Step 2: Administer Questionnaire on Techers and primary school Students based on the instrument: QCT.
- Step 3: Quiz conducted on primary school students on topic Shapes and Space.
- Step 4: Collect and analyse data based on the interview and questionnaire administered.

6 Findings of Preliminary Study

This section highlights preliminary study findings from the interview session and questionnaire survey.

The findings of the first preliminary analysis study conducted can be seen based on Table 1. The table shows the results of statistical analysis for the questionnaire instrument administered to teachers. The results revealed that the topic on Shape and Space is the most challenging topic for students in year four (4), with a Mean of 4.73 and an SP of 0.46, followed by the topic on Division with the Highest Dividend of 10 000, with a Mean of 4.27 and an SP of 0.46. While the topics on Combined Operations, Decimals, and Percentages had achieved Mean = 4.07 and SP = 0.59, respectively. The next topic was Fractions (Mean = 3.93, SP = 0.59). For the topic of Time, Coordinates, and Ratios and Proportions, respectively, are Min = 3.67, SP = 0.49. The next topics were Data Handling (Mean = 3.6, SP = 0.51), Volume of Liquid (Mean = 3.4, SP = 0.51), Length (Mean = 3.33, SP = 0.49), Money Up to RM100 000 (Mean = 2.73, SP = 0.46), Multiplication with the Highest Product of 10 000 (Mean = 2.53, SP = 0.74), Mass (Mean = 2.4, SP = 0.51) Subtraction within the Range of 10 000 (Mean = 2.07, SP = 0.59), Addition with the Highest Total of 10 000 (Mean = 1.13, SP = 0.35), and the easiest topic was Whole Numbers Up to 100 000 (Mean = 1.07, SP = 0.26).

Table 1. Questionnaire for teachers: most difficult mathematics topic for students

Topic	N	Mean	Standard deviation
Whole numbers Up to 100 000	15	1.07	0.26
Addition with the highest total of 10 000	15	1.13	0.35
Subtraction within the range of 10 000	15	2.07	0.59
Multiplication with the highest product of 10 000	15	2.53	0.74
Division with the highest dividend of 10 000	15	4.27	0.46
Combined operations	15	4.07	0.59
Fraction	15	3.93	0.59
Decimals	15	4.07	0.59
Percentage	15	4.07	0.59
Money to RM100 000	15	2.73	0.46
Time	15	3.67	0.49
Lengths	15	3.33	0.49
Mass	15	2.40	0.51
Volume of liquid	15	3.40	0.51
Shape and Space	**15**	**4.73**	**0.46**
Coordinate	15	3.67	0.49
Ratios and proportions	15	3.67	0.49
Data handling	15	3.60	0.51

According to Table 2, a total of eight (8) teachers, 53.33% believed that the students who were having difficulties were not getting a clear understanding of the topic due to their inability to imagine the right image. Whilst eleven (11), 73.33% of the teachers believed that the students did not comprehend the context of the Mathematics concept taught. Thus, findings of this preliminary study also showed that primary school students, generally have difficulty understanding the solution process and explanation of the idea of Space and Shape, when it is presented in the form of abstract and difficult-to-understand when presented in text, in a form of writing. When the concept of Space and Shape is provided in the form of visual learning via graphics, animation, or three-dimensional (3D) objects, the students were more ready and were more engaged in the learning process. Table 2 reveals that there is also a scarcity of teaching aids in schools. There were more than 25 students in the class, and the teacher only had one set of shape blocks to show everyone in the class. This limited the effectiveness of the teaching and learning process conducted in the class between the teacher and students.

Table 2. Teachers' interview schedule/tool to ascertain problems

Problems faced	Percentage(frequency) %
Students did not get clear picture on what they study	53.33 (8)
Students found it difficult to remember mathematical formulas	46.66 (7)
Students did not understand the context of the mathematics presented	73.33 (11)
Students lack interest or were not motivated in learning mathematics	26.67 (4)
There are not enough teaching aids	60.00 (9)

In addition to questionnaires and interview session conducted amongst the experienced teachers, a third preliminary analysis process took place. A quiz was implemented amongst the primary school students, to ensure that the problem of the topic on Shapes and Space did really exist amongst primary school students. Data were obtained based a Mathematics quiz administered to the students, that covered topics related to Space and Shape for primary school students. The Mathematics Quiz was tested on 40 students at the primary school level.

Results of the Mathematics quiz tested amongst the students at the primary school level can be observed in Table 3. Based on the table, it was found that there were real problems faced by the primary school students in understanding the concept of Space and Shape. A total of 40.0% of the students that took part in the study failed (scored between 0%–39%) the test, which comprised of a total of 16 students out of the total number of students involved in the study.

Table 3. Mathematics quiz test results of primary school students

Score	Grade	Status	Percentage (%)	Frequency
80–100	A	Passed	10.0	4
60–79	B	Passed	17.5	7
40–59	C	Passed	32.5	13
20–39	**D**	**Fail**	**27.5**	**11**
1–19	**E**	**Fail**	**12.5**	**5**
0	Absent	Fail	0.0	0

Therefore, summary of the Preliminary Study's findings are as follows:

i.   The mathematics topic on Shape and Space is a major problem in the learning of Mathematics at the primary school level.
ii. The abstract concept of Space and Shape is difficult for primary school students to understand.
iii. Primary school students find it difficult to understand the concept of Shape and Space due to the lack of teaching tools and reference resources on the topic available in the classrooms in schools.

7   Conceptual Framework of MEL-VIS

The conceptual framework was created based on the preliminary study, as presented in Fig. 2. The MEL-VIS conceptual framework is divided into two aspects:

i.   Prototype Development of MEL-VIS
ii. Usability Evaluation of MEL-VIS Prototype

The preliminary Studies were conducted at the first stage to identify problems as well as system requirements specifications or System Requirements Specification (SRS) of the system. The Preliminary studies involved data collection through questionnaires administered with teachers and surveys through questionnaires and interview schedule/tool administered to teachers and primary school students.

The second stage is the design and development stage. This stage involved the analysis of the System or System Design Specification (SDS). This specification can help in designing and developing the ID model (Instructional Design Model) and scaffolding models as well as the storyboards. The ID model was built on sound learning and cognitive theories.

The fourth stage is the implementation stage. At this stage all integration processes were implemented. All media developed were integrated in the relevant modules. Similarly, each module that has been built was integrated into one meaningful application based on the themes and concepts built.

The last stage was the evaluation stage. At this stage, a usability testing of the Visual Learning Application Prototype (MEL-VIS) was conducted. The constructs developed to measure the attributes of the prototype were as follows:

- Effectiveness
- Ease of learning
- Ease of Use

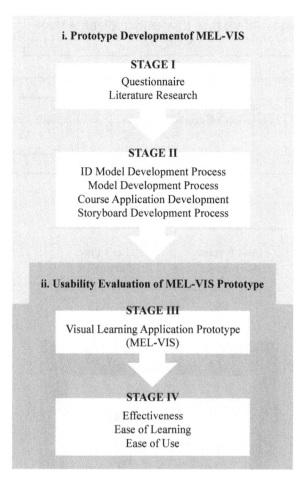

Fig. 2. Conceptual framework of MEL-VIS

8   Modules of MEL-VIS

The MEL-VIS Visual Learning Application consists of three (3) main modules: *Let's Read Module, Let's Recognize Shapes Module, and Let's Learn Shapes Module* as can be seen in Fig. 3. For each module mentioned, there are two (2) important parts that need to be completed by students, namely: *Let's Practice Submodule* and *Let's Play Submodule*. Overall, the learning process in the MEL-VIS modules are based on the *5E Approach, Learning While Playing*, and *Serious Game-based digital Exploration*.

Let's Read Module. The reading module introduces 3D shapes with a poem. Learning shapes and colours allow primary school students to group or classify items. These poem with narration and animation assists students in learning the names of 3D shapes. Primary school students learn to establish logical connections, which is essential for learning mathematic and language. Figure 4 shows an example of *Let's Read Module.*

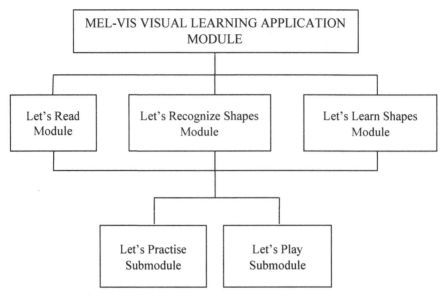

Fig. 3. Modules of MEL-VIS

Fig. 4. Let's read module of MEL-VIS

Let's Recognize Shapes Module. The 3D Shapes Recognition Module introduces 3D shapes such as cylinder, cone, cuboid, cube, and pyramid. In this module, primary school students will recognise by touching the 3D shapes button on the screen. There will be animation and narration explaining the 3D shapes. Figure 5 shows the *Let's Recognize Shapes Module.*

Let's Learn Shapes Module. Figure 6 shows the *Let's Learn Shapes Module* introduces faces, Edges, and corners of a 3D Shape. Primary school students can also watch hologram display of the 3D shape for understand more on the topic as shown in Fig. 7.

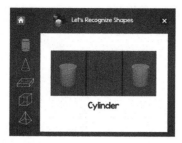

Fig. 5. Let's recognize shapes module of MEL-VIS

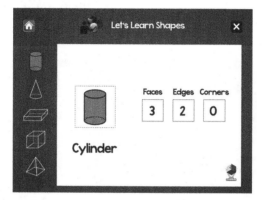

Fig. 6. Let's learn shapes module of MEL-VIS

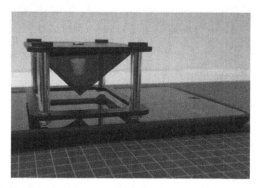

Fig. 7. Let's learn shapes module of MEL-VIS (hologram display)

Let's Practice Submodule. The *Let's Practice Submodule* has 12 questions. The primary school student must log in by entering their username and password. All tasks performed by the student will be saved in their own profile. Teachers may keep track of the date, total score, average score, and activities completed by the students. Figure 8 shows the *Let's Practice Submodule*.

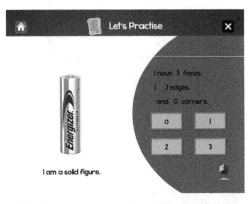

Fig. 8. Let's practice submodule of MEL-VIS

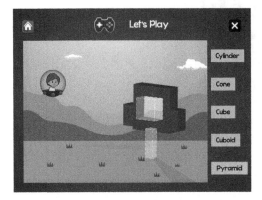

Fig. 9. Let's play submodule of MEL-VIS

Let's Play Submodule. In this module, the primary school students must locate the shapes that correspond to the question and solve the question in order to go to the next stage. Figure 9 shows the *Let's Play Submodule.*

9 Conclusion

Based on the study conducted, it was found that primary school students having problem on learning Mathematic especially the topic *Shape and Space*. Multi-touch tablets when integrated with the right content and technology, can help primary school students develop three (3) main domains of learning, namely the cognitive domain, affective domain, and psychomotor domain, by stimulating their various senses. Moreover, the studies [15–19] showed that when integrated well, the technologies can help learners be engaged in their learning and can help them in understanding mathematics concepts more effectively. In the specific case of this study, the development of the visual learning application prototype, designed and developed to teach the topic *Shape and Space* using a holographic display and multi-touch tablet technologies (MEL-VIS), gave positive expectations that can help motivate primary school students' interest in learning mathematics, specifically on the topic of shape and space. Further studies to be conducted will see whether *'learning through play'* via a new technology and media such as Mel-VIS amongst the primary school students would provide a better understanding on mathematics concepts and thus would make it possible for them to solve arithmetic problems more effectively. The complete findings of this study later would be useful not just for teachers and curriculum developers on mathematics, but also critical for policymakers to ensure that Malaysian education system do not fall behind other countries in terms of the use of modern educational technology to enhance students' learning on Mathematics. Primary school students who represent the new digital Z generation and the use of modern educational technologies are without doubt, important elements in the process of reinventing nations.

References

1. Pitiporntapin, S., Chantara, P., Srikoom, W., Nuangchalerm, P., Hines, L.M.: Enhancing Thai in-service teachers' perceptions of STEM education with tablet-based professional development. Asian Soc. Sci. **14**, 13–20 (2018)
2. Nedungadi, P., Raman, R., McGregor, M.: Enhanced STEM learning with online labs: empirical study comparing physical labs, tablets and desktops. In: 2013 IEEE Frontiers in Education Conference (FIE), pp. 1585–1590. IEEE (2013)
3. Nang, H., Harfield, A.: A framework for evaluating tablet-based educational applications for primary school levels in Thailand. Int. J. Interact. Mob. Technol. **12** (2018)
4. Luo, X., Lawrence, J., Seitz, S.M.: Pepper's cone: an inexpensive do-it-yourself 3D display. In: Proceedings of the 30th Annual ACM Symposium on User Interface Software and Technology, pp. 623–633 (2017)
5. Lin, M.-H., Chen, H.: A study of the effects of digital learning on learning motivation and learning outcome. Eurasia J. Math. Sci. Technol. Educ. **13**, 3553–3564 (2017)
6. Seibert, J., Heuser, K., Lang, V., Perels, F., Huwer, J., Kay, C.W.M.: Multitouch experiment instructions to promote self-regulation in inquiry-based learning in school laboratories. J. Chem. Educ. (2021)
7. Pegrum, M., Howitt, C., Striepe, M.: Learning to take the tablet: how pre-service teachers use iPads to facilitate their learning. Australas. J. Educ. Technol. **29** (2013)
8. Burden, K.J., Kearney, M.: Investigating and critiquing teacher educators' mobile learning practices. Interact. Technol. Smart Educ. (2017)
9. Trongtortam, S., Sophatsathit, P., Chandrachai, A.: An interactive multi-touch teaching innovation for preschool mathematical skills. Appl. Sci. Eng. Prog. **5**, 19–25 (2012)
10. Tzeng, H.C.: Learning math with tablet devices: An exploratory study examining time spent on the app in academic performance. In: EdMedia+ innovate learning, pp. 982–987. Association for the Advancement of Computing in Education (AACE) (2017)
11. Zhang, M., Trussell, R.P., Gallegos, B., Asam, R.R.: Using math apps for improving student learning: an exploratory study in an inclusive fourth grade classroom. TechTrends **59**, 32–39 (2015)
12. Chehlarova, T., Chehlarova, K.: Managing pepper's ghost illusion using intelligent methods. In: 2020 IEEE 10th International Conference on Intelligent Systems (IS), pp. 415–420. IEEE (2020)

13. Zhou, H.: The development, special traits and potential of holographic display technology (2015)
14. Xu, S., Wu, B., Ge, D., Chen, L., Yang, H.: Building an inverted pyramid display for group learning. In: Xiao, T., Zhang, L., Fei, M. (eds.) AsiaSim 2012. CCIS, pp. 394–405. Springer, Heidelberg (2012). https://doi.org/10.1007/978-3-642-34387-2_45
15. Abrahamson, D.: Mathematics Education in the Digital Era
16. Matzavela, V., Alepis, E.: M-learning in the COVID-19 era: physical vs digital class. Educ. Inf. Technol. 1–21 (2021)
17. Leung, A., Baccaglini-Frank, A. (eds.): Digital Technologies in Designing Mathematics Education Tasks: Potential and Pitfalls. Springer International Publishing, Cham (2017)
18. Turnbull, D., Chugh, R., Luck, J.: Encyclopedia of education and information technologies. Encycl. Educ. Inf. Technol. 0–7 (2020)
19. Orcos, L., Jordán, C., Magreñán, A.: 3D visualization through the hologram for the learning of area and volume concepts. Mathematics **7**, 247 (2019)

Systematic Review of Common Factors Used to Measure Individuals' Career Choice

Feninferina Azman[1]($\boxtimes$) ⓘ, Azimah Abdul Ghapar[1] ⓘ, Masyura Ahmad Faudzi[1] ⓘ,
Hasventhran Baskaran[1] ⓘ, and Fiza Abdul Rahim[1,2] ⓘ

[1] Institute of Informatics and Computing in Energy (IICE), Universiti Tenaga Nasional, 43000
Putrajaya Campus, Jalan Ikram-Uniten, 43000 Kajang, Selangor, Malaysia
{ferina,azimah,masyura}@uniten.edu.my, fiza.abdulrahim@utm.my
[2] Razak Faculty of Technology and Informatics, Universiti Teknologi Malaysia, Jalan Sultan
Yahya Petra, 54100 Kuala Lumpur, Malaysia

Abstract. Many individuals are faced with the challenge of a career choice that
is appropriate for them. This is due to the fact that decisions are made up of
a variety of subjective judgments. As a result, selecting a career path without
first assessing an individual's suitability as a foundational step can result in an
unfavorable outcome. This paper aims to investigate and summarize the evidence
of common factors used in the domain of career guidance. This study adapts
Systematic Literature Review (SLR) techniques by utilizing research questions
and Boolean search strings to identify prospective studies from three established
databases that are related to the research area. In this study, 28 articles, consisting
of 17 journals and 11 conference proceedings, were selected through a systematic
process. All articles underwent a rigorous selection protocol to ensure content
quality according to formulated research questions. We categorize and document
the common factors in career selection which can benefit in the development of a
career decision-making system that helps individuals visualize their future career
path.

Keywords: Employment · Career selection · Decision support

1 Introduction

Decision-making is an essential process in each individual, and one of it is in deciding
career of choice. Deciding what career they will pursue could be challenging as career
decision-making involves complex processes [1]. One must understand how to determine
what they want to do and explore various career options with the help of guidance and
planning. In choosing the right career path, one needs to determine what he or she wants
to do in the future and then explore the career options [2].

One of the methods that can assist the students in increasing their knowledge of
potential careers is by implementing career counseling interventions or programs [3].
Such interventions aim to enable them to make informed decisions whenever choices
have to be made and understand the reality of work to know what skills they need to

© Springer Nature Switzerland AG 2021
H. Badioze Zaman et al. (Eds.): IVIC 2021, LNCS 13051, pp. 111–126, 2021.
https://doi.org/10.1007/978-3-030-90235-3_10

succeed [4]. These efforts may increase the readiness of young people for their transition to their post-school lives and empower them to plan for their future.

In most practices, counselor teachers stationed in schools are the main reference point for seeking career guidance advice. Meanwhile, at the tertiary level, the psychology officer will often act as a career counselor who will usually conduct a psychological test to determine the student's inclination towards a certain career.

There have been several published works on predicting a student's career path. Since counselors have considered the best area of specialization that suits a student, a decision support system (DSS) is developed to assist in determining the right career for students [5]. In another study, a DSS employs a rule-driven approach that assists students in selecting the best faculty for them based on their skills [6]. Kinanee in [7] proposed a DSS for academic orientation that used a collaborative filtering technique that provides advice to counselors in order to help them make better choices while assisting students in selecting the right career path in their academic area.

In line with the development of fuzzy technology, a fuzzy logic-driven career recommendation system is developed by receiving career recommendations based on a career test [8]. Another application involves an AI-based fuzzy expert system that was developed to assist students in giving a basic idea or insight of possible career opportunities depending on the student's grade, IQ, hobbies, interests, and other prominent specifications entered by the student [9]. The most recent study on career guidance by [10] proposed two hybridized distance measures using Hausdorff, Hamming, and Euclidian distances under a picture fuzzy environment where the evaluating information about students, subjects, and student's features is provided in picture fuzzy numbers.

Given the increasing numbers of career guidance applications, it is important to examine the scope and range of research activities available in the area of career decision-making, particularly in relation to influencing factors to measure individuals for suggesting their career path. A study conducted by [1] on one campus of the largest university in South Africa discovered that interpersonal, intrapersonal, and career outcomes expectancy influenced the decision to pursue a career in science, technology, engineering, and mathematics (STEM).

Meanwhile, a significant relationship is revealed between internal influence and career decision-making among nurses [7], which means people-oriented values significantly influence individuals aspiring to go in for the nursing profession. Yuan and Li [11] examined the influences of childhood experiences on early career choice and discovered that male youths are generally more sensitive to childhood experiences than female ones. Another study within the congenital heart disease (CHD) community suggests integrating educational and career counseling within patient education curricula to ensure positive impacts on the lifestyle and livelihood of adults with CHD [12].

To the best of our knowledge, less research has been dedicated to reviewing existing literature available in career decision-making. Therefore, this systematic review aims to examine the measurement factors used in career guidance-related studies. With better insight into various perspectives on career decision-making, proper recommendations can be developed for comprehensive career guidance reference.

2 Review Method

The objective of this SLR is to investigate and summarize the evidence of current approaches used in the domain of career guidance decision-making. In our study, career guidance refers to the entire process, from the educational level of choosing a major to profession choice and preferences, through career decisions and career adaptability. In order to achieve this objective, this study formulated two research questions (RQ) relating to the aim of this study:

RQ1: What are the common approaches, research types, and contributions for career guidance decision-making studies?

RQ2: What are the common factors used to measure individuals for suggesting their career path?

The scope of this review identifies the common approaches and criteria that help in predicting and suggesting career paths or professions for students. The review process consists of five stages, as described in the next subsections. Figure 1 summarizes the stages involved.

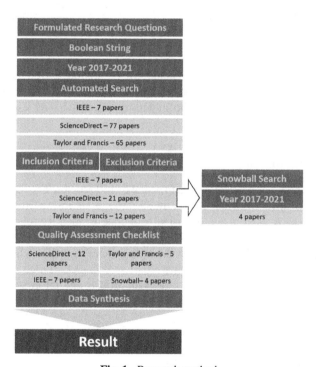

Fig. 1. Research method

2.1 Selection of Databases

We use three databases in this study, namely Institute of Electrical and Electronics Engineers (IEEE) Xplore, Taylor and Francis, and Science Direct to get a full coverage of relevant articles elicitations. The work we compile is a set of 149 articles ranging from the year 2017 to 2021 post of duplication deletion based on search term that is already set.

2.2 Keyword Search

To locate articles related to career guidance, we used keywords and combine with their synonyms. Keywords used are "job" and "career" as well as their synonyms such as "occupation" "personnel". "employment", "work", "profession selection", "decision", "decision-making", "decision support", "decision support system", "prediction", "classification approach", "method", "technique", and "scheme" is also used in this study.

To get wider results, wildcard is also used in our searching technique. In wildcard technique, special characters are used to represent a letter or letters in words when database searching is happening. This allows for the variations of the usage of a particular word to be elicited without having to focus on the grammar and the formatting used in the articles searched. In example, "*career*" could elicit career or careers, career-, as well as –career, and perhaps many more.

Besides keywords and wildcard, we include string searching as well which is ("career guidance" OR "career decision" OR "career selection" OR prediction") AND ("decision-making" OR "decision support") to help in getting career not only wider, but almost precise results.

2.3 Articles Filtering: Inclusion, Exclusion and Snowball

Execution of the previous search resulted in a total of 149 articles. The result was further refined via the inclusion and exclusion criteria through an abstract reading. A set of predefined features is used in the inclusion technique to identify relevant articles to be included in this particular study. This is the same for exclusion criteria, we use the predefined features to guide us to select the right article, as well as eliminating those that are irrelevant for this study.

The inclusion criteria are set to elicit relevant articles and information needed for this review. Articles searched are included if the criteria below are met:

1. Articles published in English language;
2. Articles with decision-making/support methods/approaches, techniques and evaluation/measurement/metrics implemented;
3. Articles involving decision-making or decision support system.

The exclusion criteria on the other hand, is also firmly set to remove irrelevant articles and information. This is crucial to ensure that the articles chosen helps in optimizing the validity of this study. Articles searched are excluded if the criteria below is found:

1. Articles published in languages other than English;
2. Articles that discuss only about application development and does not implement any evaluation/testing/analysis;
3. Articles that present study other than decision-making or decision support system.

After execution of the inclusion and exclusion criteria, 40 articles are screened, and 24 articles are finally taken into account for manual searching using snowball or citation tracking technique. In this study, we refer to the term "snowballing" as a practice of identifying other articles using a paper's reference list. We "start set" with a small number of articles that are currently available, and snowball from there. There are four additional articles included to the total above for the next process.

2.4 Quality Assessment

Articles from the filtering process using inclusion criteria, exclusion criteria and manual searching are then further analysed using quality assessment checklists. The content of the article is read carefully and a point will be given based on the quality assessment below:

Table 1. Quality assessment questions

Number	Quality assessment questions
QA1	Does the paper clearly describe the method/methods of career guidance decision-making used? "Yes" = 1, "Partly" = 0.5, or "No" = 0
QA2	Does the paper highlight the career guidance criteria clearly? "Yes" = 1, "Partly" = 0.5, or "No" = 0
QA3	Does the paper clearly present the contribution of study? "Yes" = 1, "Partly" = 0.5, or "No" = 0

The quality markers for each quality assessment question defined are "Yes" that carries 1 mark, "Partly" that carries 0.5 mark, and "No" that carries zero value. The total points is the summation of the quality marker as shown in Table 1. Articles with score 1.5 points and above is taken into consideration for this study, however those lower are disregarded. A total of 28 articles are successfully elicited by our team after the completion of quality assessment.

2.5 Data Synthesis

The main purpose of this phase is to present and demonstrate data from 28 selected studies that could help in addressing the research questions. This procedure involves identifying, synchronizing, and analyzing data. The process will then provide information that can answer the research questions. Data collected for RQ1 and RQ2 are articulated to show findings through visualization instruments such as structured tables and charts. Findings from the research questions also presented the respective classification of studies, presented contributions, methodologies, contributions and measurement factors.

3   Results of the Systematic Review

This section is specifically composed for this study to answer the first research question RQ1 as stated above in Sect. 2. Summarization of the systematic review is broken into four parts, and are elaborated clearly in Sect. 3.1 to 3.2 respectively. Types of studies is explained in Sect. 3.1, number of research publications in the given years is tabled in detail in Sect. 3.2, domains are listed in Sect. 3.3, and thorough explanation on methods and contributions is in Sect. 3.4.

3.1   Types of Studies

Four types of studies have been identified in this review; survey, experiment, survey and experiment and review, as shown in Table 2. A majority of 17 studies carried out surveys, followed by five experimental studies, three studies conducted both experiment and survey and another three studies performed review.

Table 2. Types of studies for career guidance

Types of studies	Statistics of usage	Cited literatures
Survey	17	[11, 13–28]
Experiment	5	[29–33]
Experiment and survey	3	[34–36]
Review	3	[37–39]

3.2   Number of Research Publications in the Given Years

This study selected a total of 28 papers from three major databases and categorized them into two different clusters; 17 papers (60.7%) are from journal publications and 11 (39.3%) from conference proceedings. The majority of papers are extracted from 2018 (eight papers), followed by 2020 (seven papers), 2021 (six papers), 2017 (four papers), and 2019 (three papers), as shown in Fig. 2. As the paper selection process is carried out in the middle of 2021, the paper search deadline was decided in June 2021 to allow other SLR processes could be carried out as planned. Table 3 provides information about each paper based on publication type, publication name, year, and reference.

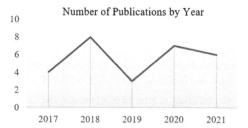

Fig. 2. Publication years (duration)

Table 3. List of publications

Pub. type	Year	Publication name	Refs.
Journal	2017	Journal of work and organizational psychology	[20]
Journal	2017	Health psychology and behavioral medicine	[16]
Journal	2017	Labour economics	[22]
Proceeding	2017	IOP conference series	[31]
Journal	2018	Personality and individual differences	[18]
Journal	2018	Journal of career assessment	[23]
Journal	2018	Social science research	[25]
Journal	2018	Kasetsart journal of social sciences	[28]
Proceeding	2018	4th International conference on education and technology (ICET)	[30]
Proceeding	2018	4th International conference on computing communication control and automation (ICCUBEA)	[32]
Proceeding	2018	17th International conference on computer and information science (ICIS)	[33]
Proceeding	2018	2nd International conference on electrical engineering and informatics (ICon EEI)	[29]
Journal	2019	Saudi pharmaceutical journal	[24]
Proceeding	2019	International conference on electrical, computer and communication engineering (ECCE)	[37]
Proceeding	2019	International conference on virtual reality and visualization (ICVRV)	[36]
Journal	2020	International journal of adolescence and youth	[11]
Journal	2020	Heliyon	[17]
Journal	2020	Higher education pedagogies	[15]
Proceeding	2020	Procedia computer science	[21]
Proceeding	2020	International conference on power electronics & IoT applications in renewable energy and its control (PARC)	[13]

(continued)

Table 3. (*continued*)

Pub. type	Year	Publication name	Refs.
Proceeding	2020	3rd International conference on mechanical, electronics, computer, and industrial technology (MECnIT)	[34]
Proceeding	2020	2nd International conference on computer and information sciences (ICCIS)	[35]
Journal	2021	British journal of guidance & counselling	[14, 38]
Journal	2021	Journal of vocational behavior	[39]
Journal	2021	International journal of hospitality management	[19]
Journal	2021	Heliyon	[26]
Journal	2021	Nurse education today	[27]

3.3 Domain

Nine categories of research domain are identified during the data synthesis process, which are education, family/gender, medical/healthcare, social network, working adult, service provider, sports, unemployed, and general field, as shown in Table 4. Among the 13 publications in the education domain, six publications are referring to high school students, four on college students, two on general education and one is on recent graduates. In the family/gender domain, family income and childhood experience is the focus area. Pharmacy and nursing, each contributed one publication for the medical/healthcare domain. For working adult domains, two contradictory areas are being explored which are working professionals and workers without formal qualification.

Table 4. Career guidance domain

Domain	Statistics of usage	Cited literatures
Education	13	[13, 15, 17, 18, 22, 25, 28–32, 34, 35]
General field	4	[23, 26, 33, 39]
Family/gender	2	[11, 37]
Medical/healthcare	2	[24, 27]
Social network	2	[21, 36]
Working adults	2	[20, 38]
Service provider	1	[19]
Sports	1	[16]
Unemployed	1	[14]

3.4 Methods and Contributions

All the 28 articles that is reviewed contribute to career guidance study in terms of their main contributions to career guidance and the methods that is used in their study.

There are 20 articles that study career guidance through a survey. The survey study is on the factors contributing to career guidance including in selecting the right majoring, choosing the preferences career, deciding career and on career adaptability. In analysing their survey, the authors use methods and theory to come out with their findings. One of the methods being used by three authors is Career Adapt-Ability Scale (CAAS) [16, 18, 38]. A study by [38] used the CAAS to study the connection between work experience with career adaptability and decent work, while [16] used CAAS to study the impact of dual career for an athlete. CAAS with Career Decision-making Difficulties Questionnaire (CDDQ) and Self-Perceived Employability Scale (SPES) used by [18] in studying the relationship between trait emotional intelligence, career indecision, and self-perceived employability in career adaptability.

Social Cognitive Career Theory is used by [15] to study the needs for employability development for STEM students. Investigation of the impact of childhood experiences to early career choice by [11] also used Social Cognitive Career Theory. [37] has done a survey on several regression algorithms to be used in their study and they used Linear Model (glm) and Linear Regression (lm) to their dataset in finding the most affected class of adolescents having difficulties making a proper career decision based on family incomes. [23] is implementing the Career Decision-making Profile (CDMP) methods to German community in validating the German career decision-making profile. A person's readiness in career decision-making is done by Sampson & Toh [14] using Career State Inventory method before the person starts a job.

Meroni & Vera-Toscano [22] study about overeducated jobs that has an impact on the mismatched career of graduates. The author used sensitivity analysis onto their data. [26] study on how parenting styles, thinking styles, and gender affect career decisions using Career Decision Self-Efficacy (CDSE) as their method. Jamal et al. [33] has done a study on factors that contribute to a career of choice. The author uses Fuzzy and the Technique for Order Preference by Similarity to Ideal Solution (TOPSIS) in identifying key factors for career of choice. Apart from the method mentioned above, social media data can be used for career guidance [21]. These data need to be further analysed using a machine learning technique to come out with career guidance decisions. Marcia's Interview Protocol is used by [17] to identify career identity formation and this protocol completely supported the findings.

The remaining eight articles is identified to have methods that can be used in developing the career guidance systems in processing the input and analysing the information given by the user. The career guidance system is developed to help in determining the majoring, career selection, career decision, and intuitive career system. The methods that are being highlighted are Certainty Factors, Decision Tree, Data Mining, Naïve Bayes, Neuro Fuzzy System, K-Nearest Neighbour and Linear Classification [13, 30–32, 34, 35]. All the highlighted methods are machine learning methods used for processing and analysing data. Cruz, Orozco & Gonzales [36] has done a study on the current guidance system thatis developed focusing on usability study. The five usability factors are learnability, efficiency, memorability, reliability in use and acceptability or satisfaction of use.

4 Discussion

In answering RQ2, it can be seen in Table 5 that the majority of studies are mainly focused on factors related to family (nine), followed by academics (eight), gender (seven), interest (seven), profession (seven), skills (six), and, personality (six). Other common factors such as age, economic status, friends, study duration, religion, community, and experience appear in two different studies. Each of the remaining factors such as psychology, location, confidence, politics, culture, media, and commitment are found in a separate study.

Table 5. Factors studied by selected studies

Factor	Fr.	Refs.
Family	9	[11, 17, 24–28, 33, 37]
Academics	8	[11, 13, 15, 22, 30, 32, 34, 35]
Gender	7	[11, 13, 18, 25, 32, 33, 37]
Interest	7	[13, 16, 17, 24, 28, 30, 34]
Profession	7	[14, 20, 33, 35, 37–39]
Skills	6	[21, 26, 31, 32, 34, 35]
Personality	6	[13, 18–20, 31, 32]
Health	3	[14, 21, 39]
Age	2	[32, 37]
Economic status	2	[11, 17]
Friends	2	[17, 24]
Study duration	2	[35, 37]
Religion	2	[11, 17]
Community	2	[11, 17]
Experience	2	[24, 33]
Others	4	[11, 17, 30, 37]

4.1 Family

Family is the closest person to an individual. Based on the findings, family influences become the most factor included in the studies. Family factors include experience, level of education, and support of the family member. A study by Chen, Peng & Yu [33] integrates the typical and atypical factors to build a comprehensive factor model for career planning. Among the key factors suggested in their study are parental education and family background. Meanwhile, Halim et al. [28] examined the opportunities provided by parents to their children intending to facilitate science learning and promote science-related careers. They found that parental support and parental academic expectations play an important role in cultivating the interest of their children in science and science-related careers.

From another point of view, Satu et al. [37] explores the most affected class of adolescents about career decision difficulties considering family income ranges in Bangladesh. They observed that middle-level family income ranges of adolescents had more difficulties choosing proper careers than others.

Alhomoud et al. [24] conducted a cross-sectional survey of undergraduates from several pharmacy colleges in Saudi Arabia to identify pharmacy students' career choices and examine the factors that influence their choices. Surprisingly, the influence of family was the least important factor that influences students' career choices. The results of Batool & Ghayas [17], on the other hand, indicate that adolescents were being influenced by their parent's choices and dreams for their children's careers.

Individual choices, including career choices, can be imposed by early childhood experiences. According to Yuan and Li [11], a stratified random sampling survey of life history in China reveals that lower quality childhood experiences are likely to increase young people's chances of working in the government sector after adulthood. A study by Shahbazian [25] revealed that there is an association between siblings and the likelihood of choosing a STEM educational field. If this probability is high, siblings may choose a career in the same field.

4.2 Academics

An individual's career choice can be identified as early as selecting the appropriate major when entering high school. Damayanti et al. [30] used an adaptive neuro-fuzzy inference system (ANFIS) to determine students' suitable high school major as the first step in career selection. A dataset of students' academic records, interests, and psychology test results is used to input the system. Rangnekar et al. [32] used their proposed "Intuitive Career System," which consists of a series of aptitude questions, to help students find a career that matches their aptitude and personality. They emphasize the importance to include interest assessment test in career prediction because aptitude test would only helps ascertain the field in which the student is academically sound.

Shankhdhar et al. [13] proposed using academic grades to determine students' ability to pursue a particular predicted career. In addition to academic grades, the proposed career system takes into account students' interests, personality traits, and skills. Another study conducted by Tulus & Situmorang [34] used students' grades, interests, and skills obtained from questionnaires to determine student careers using K-Nearest Neighbor algorithm. In another study, Jamal et al. [35] discovered that academic achievement through Cumulative Grade Point Average (CGPA) is one factor that determines the suitability of alumni careers with their fields.

A study carried out by Bennett et al. [15] explored how STEM students' perception of their future careers and employability compared to non-STEM fields. The study concluded that employability and career guidance development should be aligned with disciplinary knowledge, skills, and practices within the core curriculum.

In observing the effect of accepting an overeducated job, Meroni & Vera-Toscano [22] suggested that graduates must wait for the right job offer rather than choosing a position that is overeducated at the beginning of their career. In the same study, they discovered that an overeducated job not only results in the same employment probability as waiting longer for unemployment, but it also increases the chances of landing an unsuitable job.

4.3 Gender

Gender is one of the measuring element for the majority of survey studies. For example, Chen, Peng & Yu [33] include gender as one of the atypical factors in their study by examining the interaction between typical, atypical factors and occupational elements. Similar to studies in [13, 25, 37].

A study conducted by Yuan and Li [11] examining the influences of early professional experience showed that male youngsters are more sensitive than females to children in general. In a study conducted by Shahbazian [25], the choice of the STEM field between younger siblings is obvious where girls are likely to select a STEM field if they have an old sister who participated in STEM rather than an older brother in a comparable program.

4.4 Interest

In recent years, many new career opportunities have sprung up and provided more options to those who are new to the field of employment. Knowing a person's interests can be one of the indicators to be matched with a suitable job [13]. This is also aligned with Alhomoud et al. [24], which revealed that personal interest influenced the students' career choices.

An exploratory study on the roles played by the parents in cultivating interest toward science subjects and careers by Halim et al. [28] revealed the encouragement from parents toward science subjects might cultivate their children's interest in science and science-related careers. The encouragement from parents such as sending their children to extra classes, providing financial support for science activities, and encouraging a science culture at home.

Ryba et al. [16] also include "interest" as a measurement factor to understand the specific competencies of young athletes to succeed in combining sport and training in a dual career path. The measurement of "interest" is included in a Dual Career Form of the Career Adapt-Abilities Scale (CAAS-DC) for young student-athletes.

4.5 Profession

The career choices among young professionals could also be influenced by the market value given to each profession. In a study conducted by Bargsted [20], the professions with high market value involve Engineering, Economics, Construction, and Medicine. The medium level includes Law, Nursing, Chemistry, Education, Architecture, Psychology, Nutrition, Kinesiology, and Aquaculture. The low level was Science, Biology, and Journalism.

An individual's abilities may also influence the choice of career in that profession. Chen, Peng and Yu [33] include professional ability as one of the atypical factors in their study, which can help to understand an individual's capability. A survey conducted by Jamal et al. [35] revealed that alumni of tafseer and hadith who have excelled in their academics would have a profession consistent with their field.

A study by Vilhjálmsdóttir [38] found that young workers without formal qualifications wish to work in professional or technical jobs. With high expectations of future career aspirations, young low-qualified people should focus on improving their ability to adapt to careers different from their current profession.

4.6 Skills

Individual skills in a certain domain are also one of the measuring factors in career choice. For example, a specialization program on interactive multimedia taken by students may enhance their skills in that area and influence their career decisions [31]. Students may also experience difficulties in their careers if the required skills in the field in which they work are still weak [34].

In predicting career decisions among Tafseer and hadith graduates, Jamal et al. [35] emphasized the importance of students being equipped with additional skills such as proficiency in foreign languages and IT. These additional skills can be acquired not only from formal education but can also be acquired with students' initiative to learn on their own to ensure their competitiveness in the job market.

4.7 Personality

Many existing career decision-making systems employ personality tests to suggest suitable jobs. A study carried out by Rangnekar et al. [32] indicated that personality factors are related to student's career choices. Individual personalities may also be derived based on their interest in the career field.

A proposed counseling application developed by Irwan et al. [31] also includes personality factors in facilitating students' future career choices. The proposed application is expected to assist students in making career choices that suit their personalities and other relevant factors.

5 Conclusion

This paper has successfully reviewed and identified related factors that influence individuals in choosing their career path. The SLR technique had assisted in narrowing down the relevant works of literature in the career guidance domain. A total of 28 primary studies are used in the review process, 16 factors influencing career choice are established, and seven common factors are identified. Family and academics are the most common factors attributed to career decision-making. This study also exhibits other factors; skills, gender, interest, profession, and personality.

The findings from this review may benefit the design, development, and implementation of an operational career decision-making system. The system should be able to produce a visualization of suitable careers by using the factors highlighted in this study as its input. Future research on the application of functional systems will also provide insights into the implications for certain target groups, such as young adults who have doubts about choosing a suitable career.

Acknowledgment. This study was funded by BOLD Research Grant 2021 Universiti Tenaga Nasional (J510050002/2021042). We would like to thank UNITEN Innovation & Research Management Centre (iRMC) for fund management.

References

1. Abe, E.N., Chikoko, V.: Exploring the factors that influence the career decision of STEM students at a university in South Africa. Int. J.STEM Educ. **7**(1), 1–14 (2020). https://doi.org/10.1186/s40594-020-00256-x
2. Akosah-Twumasi, P., Emeto, T.I., Lindsay, D., Tsey, K., Malau-Aduli, B.S.: A systematic review of factors that influence youths career choices—the role of culture. Front. Educ. (2018). https://doi.org/10.3389/feduc.2018.00058
3. Poh Li, L., Aqeel, K., Abdullah, H.S., Fong Peng, C.: The effectiveness of career exploration program for high school students. Int. Conf. Humanit. Soc. Cult. IPEDR **20**, 226–230 (2011)
4. Dodd, V., Hanson, J., Hooley, T.: Increasing students' career readiness through career guidance: measuring the impact with a validated measure. Br. J. Guid. Couns. (2021). https://doi.org/10.1080/03069885.2021.1937515
5. Balogun, V.F., Thompson, A.F., State, O.: Career master : a decision support system (DSS) for guidance and counseling in Pacific. J. Sci. Technol. **10**, 337–354 (2009)
6. Castellano, E.J., Martínez, L.: A web-decision support system based on collaborative filtering for academic orientation. Case study of the spanish secondary school. J. Univers. Comput. Sci. **15**, 2786–2807 (2009)
7. Kinanee, J.B.: Factors in the career decision-making of nurses in rivers state of Nigeria : implications for counselling. J. Psychol. Couns. **1**, 134–138 (2009)
8. Razak, T.R., Hashim, M.A., Noor, N.M., Halim, I.H.A., Shamsul, N.F.F.: Career path recommendation system for UiTM perlis students using fuzzy logic. In: ICIAS2014: 2014 5th International Conference on Intelligent and Advanced Systems (ICIAS) (2014)
9. Gupta, M.V., Patil, P., Deshpande, S., Arisetty, S., Asthana, S.: FESCCO: Fuzzy expert system for career counselling. Int. J. Recent Innov. Trends Comput. Commun. **5**, 239–243 (2017)
10. Sahu, R., Dash, S.R., Das, S.: Career selection of students using hybridized distance measure based on picture fuzzy set and rough set theory. Dec. Mak. Appl. Manag. Eng. **4**(1), 104–126 (2021). https://doi.org/10.31181/dmame2104104s
11. Yuan, B., Li, J.: Social-economics, community, campus and family: a nationwide empirical investigation on the association between adverse childhood experiences and early career choice of youths and adolescents. Int. J. Adolesc. Youth **25**, 221–239 (2020). https://doi.org/10.1080/02673843.2019.1608274
12. Girouard, H.S., Kovacs, A.H.: Congenital heart disease: education and employment considerations and outcomes. Int. J. Cardiol. Congenit. Hear. Dis. **1**, 100005 (2020). https://doi.org/10.1016/j.ijcchd.2020.100005
13. Shankhdhar, A., Agrawal, A., Sharma, D., Chaturvedi, S., Pushkarna, M.: Intelligent decision support system using decision tree method for student career. In: 2020 International Conference on Power Electronics and IoT Applications in Renewable Energy and its Control, PARC 2020, pp. 140–142 (2020). https://doi.org/10.1109/PARC49193.2020.246974
14. Sampson, J.P., Toh, R.: Improving career decision-making of highly skilled workers: designing interventions for the unemployed and discouraged. Br. J. Guid. Couns. **49**, 228–241 (2021). https://doi.org/10.1080/03069885.2021.1892589

15. Bennett, D., Knight, E., Dockery, A.M., Bawa, S.: Pedagogies for employability: understanding the needs of STEM students through a new approach to employability development. High. Educ. Pedagog. **5**, 340–359 (2020). https://doi.org/10.1080/23752696.2020.1847162

16. Ryba, T.V., Zhang, C.-Q., Huang, Z., Aunola, K.: Career adapt-abilities scale – dual career form (CAAS-DC): psychometric properties and initial validation in high-school student-athletes. Heal. Psychol. Behav. Med. **5**, 85–100 (2017). https://doi.org/10.1080/21642850.2016.1273113

17. Batool, S.S., Ghayas, S.: Process of career identity formation among adolescents: components and factors. Heliyon **6**, e04905 (2020). https://doi.org/10.1016/j.heliyon.2020.e04905

18. Udayar, S., Fiori, M., Thalmayer, A.G., Rossier, J.: Investigating the link between trait emotional intelligence, career indecision, and self-perceived employability: the role of career adaptability. Pers. Individ. Dif. **135**, 7–12 (2018). https://doi.org/10.1016/j.paid.2018.06.046

19. Lee, P.C., Xu, S., Yang, W.: Is career adaptability a double-edged sword? The impact of work social support and career adaptability on turnover intentions during the COVID-19 pandemic. Int. J. Hosp. Manag. **94**, 102875 (2021). https://doi.org/10.1016/j.ijhm.2021.102875

20. Bargsted, M.: Impact of personal competencies and market value of type of occupation over objective employability and perceived career opportunities of young professionals. J. Work Organ. Psychol. **33**, 115–123 (2017). https://doi.org/10.1016/j.rpto.2017.02.003

21. Kiselev, P., Kiselev, B., Matsuta, V., Feshchenko, A., Bogdanovskaya, I., Kosheleva, A.: Career guidance based on machine learning: social networks in professional identity construction. Procedia Comput. Sci. **169**, 158–163 (2020). https://doi.org/10.1016/j.procs.2020.02.128

22. Meroni, E.C., Vera-Toscano, E.: The persistence of overeducation among recent graduates. Labour Econ. **48**, 120–143 (2017). https://doi.org/10.1016/j.labeco.2017.07.002

23. Ebner, K., Thiele, L., Spurk, D., Kauffeld, S.: Validation of the German career decision-making profile—an updated 12-factor version. J. Career Assess. **26**, 111–136 (2018). https://doi.org/10.1177/1069072716679996

24. Alhomoud, F.K., AlGhalawin, L., AlGofari, G., AlDjani, W., Ameer, A., Alhomoud, F.: Career choices and preferences of Saudi pharmacy undergraduates: a cross sectional study. Saudi Pharm. J. **27**, 467–474 (2019). https://doi.org/10.1016/j.jsps.2019.01.009

25. Shahbazian, R.: Under the influence of our older brother and sister: the association between sibling gender configuration and STEM degrees. Soc. Sci. Res. **97**, 102558 (2021). https://doi.org/10.1016/j.ssresearch.2021.102558

26. Situmorang, D.D.B., Salim, R.M.A.: Perceived parenting styles, thinking styles, and gender on the career decision self-efficacy of adolescents: how & why? Heliyon **7**, e06430 (2021). https://doi.org/10.1016/j.heliyon.2021.e06430

27. Wei, L., Zhou, S., Hu, S., Zhou, Z., Chen, J.: Influences of nursing students' career planning, internship experience, and other factors on professional identity. Nurse Educ. Today **99** (2021)

28. Halim, L., Abd Rahman, N., Zamri, R., Mohtar, L.: The roles of parents in cultivating children's interest towards science learning and careers. Kasetsart J. Soc. Sci. **39**, 190–196 (2018). https://doi.org/10.1016/j.kjss.2017.05.001

29. Desnelita, Y., Rukun, K., Syahril, S., Nasien, D., Gustientiedina, G., Vitriani, V.: Intelligent decision support system using certainty factor method for selection student career. In: Proceedings – 2018 2nd International Conference on Electrical Engineering and Informatics: Toward the Most Efficient Way of Making and Dealing with Future Electrical Power System and Big Data Analysis, ICon EEI 2018, pp. 18–23 (2018). https://doi.org/10.1109/ICon-EEI.2018.8784143

30. Damayanti, A.S., Wibawa, A.P., Pujianto, U., Nafalski, A.: The use of adaptive neuro fuzzy inference system in determining students' suitable high school major. In: 2018 4th Int. Conf. Educ. Technol, ICET 2018, pp. 1–4 (2018). https://doi.org/10.1109/ICEAT.2018.8693933

31. Irwan, G., Sunarti, Y.D.: Counseling model application: a student career development guidance for decision maker and consultation. IOP Conf. Ser. Earth Environ. Sci. **97**, 012045 (2017). https://doi.org/10.1088/1755-1315/97/1/012045

32. Rangnekar, R.H., Suratwala, K.P., Krishna, S., Dhage, S.: Career Prediction model using data mining and linear classification. In: Proceedings – 2018 4th International Conference on Computing, Communication Control and Automation, ICCUBEA 2018, pp. 1–6. IEEE (2018). https://doi.org/10.1109/ICCUBEA.2018.8697689

33. Chen, Y.T., Peng, W.C., Yu, H.Y.: Identify key factors for career choice by using TOPSIS and fuzzy cognitive map. In: Proceedings – 17th IEEE/ACIS International Conference on Computer and Information Science, ICIS 2018, pp. 104–109. IEEE (2018). https://doi.org/10.1109/ICIS.2018.8466384

34. Tulus, N., Situmorang, Z.: Analysis optimization k-nearest neighbor algorithm with certainty factor in determining student career. In: MECnIT 2020 – International Conference on Mechanical, Electronics, Computer, and Industrial Technology, pp. 306–310 (2020). https://doi.org/10.1109/MECnIT48290.2020.9166669

35. Jamal, K., Kurniawan, R., Husti, I., Zailani, Nazri, M.Z.A., Arifin, J.: Predicting career decisions among graduates of tafseer and hadith. In: 2020 2nd International Conference on Computer and Information Sciences, ICCIS 2020 (2020). https://doi.org/10.1109/ICCIS49240.2020.9257663

36. Cruz, A.F., Orozco, L., Gonzales, C.: Intelligent web platform for vocational guidance. In: Proceedings – 2019 Int. Conf. Virtual Real. Vis. ICVRV 2019. 205–207 (2019). https://doi.org/10.1109/ICVRV47840.2019.00049

37. Satu, MS, Ahamed, S., Chowdhury, A., Whaiduzzaman, M.: Exploring significant family income ranges of career decision difficulties of adolescents in Bangladesh applying regression techniques. In: 2nd International Conference on Electrical, Computer and Communication Engineering, ECCE 2019, pp. 1–6. IEEE (2019). https://doi.org/10.1109/ECACE.2019.8679415

38. Vilhjálmsdóttir, G.: Young workers without formal qualifications: experience of work and connections to career adaptability and decent work. Br. J. Guid. Couns. **49**, 242–254 (2021). https://doi.org/10.1080/03069885.2021.1885011

39. Spurk, D.: Vocational behavior research: Past topics and future trends and challenges. J. Vocat. Behav. **126**, 103559 (2021). https://doi.org/10.1016/j.jvb.2021.103559

Interaction Design for Digital Saron Musical Instruments Using Call and Response System and Rhythmic Emphasis Weighting Methods

Salsabila Putri Jatiningtyas[✉] [iD], Danang Junaedi[✉], and Veronikha Effendy[✉]

Telkom University, Bandung, Indonesia
salsabilaputri@student.telkomuniversity.ac.id, {danangjunaedi,
veffendy}@telkomuniversity.ac.id

Abstract. Gamelan digitization is one of the efforts to introduce and preserve traditional Indonesian musical instruments not to become extinct. The focus of digitization in research is only on one type of saron musical instrument because the saron instrument is the main melody in a gamelan instrument that can be played individually and is more harmonious when played in collaboration. The most important thing in playing gamelan instruments is playing several types of musical instruments at the same time, especially the saron instrument. In using the saron instrument itself must be played collaboratively according to the tempo. For this reason, to make the interaction design model, the Call and Response System method is used, which has a "your turn" indicator and the Rhythmic Emphasis Weighting method connected to the "Techno Rhythm Monitor". The application of the two methods above, the interaction design modeling design uses the Design Thinking method. The research testing using the System Usability Scale (SUS) because the results have a high level of validity for a study. The test results from research using the Call and Response System and Rhythmic Emphasis Weighting methods resulted in an interaction design model playing the saron musical instrument that can collaborate according to the tempo. For the test results using SUS, which obtained a final result of 85%, it is at level B and means that the interaction design model that has been designed is acceptable because it has met the user's goals (proper).

Keywords: Call and response system · Design thinking · Interaction design · Rhythmic emphasis weighting · Saron · System usability scale

1 Introduction

[1]With the development of the era in the current generation of globalization, there are many significant changes, including human evolution towards the modern era [1]. One of the impacts of the current era of globalization is a decrease in public interest and understanding of the preservation of Indonesian traditional culture and arts [2]. Based

---

[1] *Supported by Telkom University.

© Springer Nature Switzerland AG 2021
H. Badioze Zaman et al. (Eds.): IVIC 2021, LNCS 13051, pp. 127–138, 2021.
https://doi.org/10.1007/978-3-030-90235-3_11

on these conditions, there was a desire to seek efforts. In modern times like today, Indonesian traditional culture and arts can still be preserved and introduced to the broader community. One of the efforts made to protect and introduce Indonesian traditional culture and skills to the younger generation or the wider community is by utilizing the current era of technological development [3]. Traditional Indonesian arts that need to be preserved include traditional musical instruments, one of which is gamelan [4].

Gamelan is a traditional Indonesian musical instrument that needs to be preserved so as not to become extinct. One of the efforts in protecting the gamelan, among others, is to continue to introduce it and invite the public to understand how to play it. In playing gamelan, each player must be able to collaborate [5]. With the introduction of traditional gamelan musical instruments, a solution was made by utilizing digitalization technology. This study only focused on one type of musical instrument among other types of musical instruments found in the gamelan, namely the saron musical instrument only. The reason is that saron is the main melody in gamelan, and saron also has a unique way of playing it, which can be played individually or in collaboration [6].

In this study, the Call and Response System method is used, which has a "your turn" indicator to respond to the interaction of the players in collaborating to play music. This is done by making the interactive instrument beat the original saron musical instrument by making it into digital form, namely by entering the original saron audio into the interaction design model. While the method used to visualize the suitability of the tempo of the saron musical instrument, the Rhythmic Emphasis Weighting method is used, which is connected to the "Techno Rhythm Monitor" [7]. The way of testing is by trying various levels of tempo to adjust the emphasis of the rhythm. This method selected is because of the players who cannot participate in the game collaboratively according to the tempo. To facilitate applying the two methods above, the Interaction Design Modeling was designed using the Design Thinking method. Furthermore, the product usability level was tested using the System Usability Scale (SUS) method [8, 9].

2 Related Work

2.1 Call and Response System

The call and Response System serves to regulate the pattern of music playing. The call pattern functions as the initial player, followed by the second player by copying the way from the initial player, which becomes a cue to play music (respond). Each other can react in the interaction of the players when collaborating on music. The "your turn" indicator is used in the Call and Response System method. If the players already understand the game's rules, then the opportunity to improvise can be done by playing music. There are several essential elements in the Call and Response System, including:

1. Background, which is a visual picture as a whole to show the music part.
2. Caller, which is giving an initial sample of music to be played by the players.
3. Response Cues, namely the rhythm played by the players.
4. The "your turn" indicator, which is a hint to give a signal to the player when to start playing music.

This Call and Response System method succeeded in uniting the players to collaborate in playing music because apart from being able to respond to each other, imitate each other's rhythm patterns, they could also improvise [7].

2.2 Rhythmic Emphasis Weighting

Rhythmic Emphasis Weighting there are several opinions, among others, expressed by Jae Hun Roh and Lynn Wilcox in a paper entitled Exploring Tabla Drumming Using Rhythmic Input, that Rhythmic Emphasis Weighting is a method for suppressing rhythm or volumes that serves to assist players in playing music according to the tempo [10]. Meanwhile, the opinion expressed by Tina Blaine and Tim Perkins, that to provide a visualization of the appropriateness of the tempo in playing a musical instrument, is marked by Rhythmic Emphasis Weighting which is connected to the "Techno Rhythm Monitor" [7].

2.3 Interaction Design

Design Thinking is a comprehensive thinking process that focuses on creating solutions and innovations as needed. The stages carried out in the Design Thinking method are shown in Fig. 1 below [11].

Fig. 1. Phase of design thinking method

2.4 System Usability Scale (SUS)

System Usability Scale (SUS) is a survey used to assess the functionality of a product. The SUS Characteristics consists of ten questions, each of which has a five-point scale, ranging from a score of Strongly Disagree to Agree Strongly. In the SUS, there are five positive statements and five negative statements, making it easier for the scoring system to be completed quickly. This SUS result is a single score with a rating scale ranging from 0 to 100, which is relatively easy to understand. SUS is a technology that a group of practitioners can use to evaluate all types of interaction designs, for example, in interactive voice response applications and systems. Formula of SUS method have values of '5' and '−1' for calculating the SUS value in data processing, and the steps are as follows [8]:

– SUS calculation:

a. Odd Numbe: (Value Obtained) − 1

b. Even Numbe: 5 − (Value Obtained)

− Calculation of the average:

$$SUS\ Score = \frac{(Value\ obtained\ per\ respondent \times 2.5)}{respondent} \tag{1}$$

An explanation of the variables used in the formula are:

1. Value obtained per respondent: adding up the scores of each respondent starting from question number 1 until number 10.
2. Respondent: number of people who are doing the test.

3 Modeling

The flow of interaction design modeling in this study uses the Design Thinking method. Figure 2 described the modeling flow carried out in carrying out the final project research.

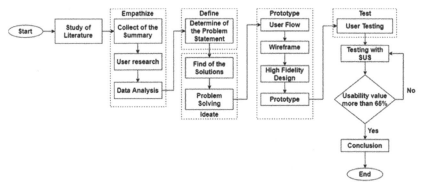

Fig. 2. The flow of the process using design thinking method

3.1 Empathize

At this empathize stage, user research is carried out to users to understand what users' needs are. User research is carried out using a survey method in the form of a questionnaire because it can reach many people quickly for data collection in the form of quantitative data [12]. The survey was conducted on 15–20 April 2021 to the traditional music community in Bandung, namely Gentra Wirahma Putra. The contents of the survey questions are about the user's identity, the user's busyness, the difficulties and problems faced by the user in recognizing and playing the saron musical instrument, and the expectations desired by the user in playing the saron musical instrument. After conducting the survey, the results were obtained in user identity data, user habits, existing problems, goals, and motivation. The output obtained at this empathize stage include:

User Persona. User persona with two different fictitious characteristics, namely beginner persona and expert persona.

Empathy. Map Empathy map is a visualization to deepen understanding of user needs. Generated one empathy map for each user persona.

Journey Mapping. Journey mapping is a visualization of the steps taken by users to reach a goal. The contents of the journey mapping consist of 2 parts, namely zone A and zone B. Where Zone A contains user personas, scenarios, and goals. At the same time, zone B or, in other words, the vertical axis includes touchpoints and strategic actions, including actions, questions, happy moments, pain points, and opportunities.

3.2 Define

After doing the empathize stage, the next stage is the define stage to determine the problem statement obtained from the results of survey data analysis. The aim is to focus on the existing problems, and a solution will be produced later [13]. The first thing to do before determining the problem statement is to determine the question "How Might We" whose function is to provide a short question. How Might We be a collection of questions converted into a problem statement generated at the introduction stage [14, 15].

3.3 Ideate

The purpose of ideate is to create a prototype design that will be used at a later stage [13]. The collection of solution ideas at this ideate stage serves to be implemented in the interaction design model. The following is the implementation resulting from the ideate stage:

First Implementation. Digitizing the saron musical instrument by applying the Call and Response System method has a test method by making an interactive instrument beat the original saron musical instrument by making it into digital form. Then, editing and custom shaping each stroke with several tone samples to play repeatedly. In more detail, the steps are, the first thing to do is look for pictures of the saron musical instrument and its Panakol, after which the Daminatilada notes are given in the form of numbers and letters on the saron. So that saron can be played by making sounds, first, a search for the notes contained in the saron is carried out, then an audio drum search is also carried out as a caller element as a sign of the initial music (intro) to start playing saron. Then, according to the tone in the saron, the existing tones are combined and put into a prototype form. Then proceed with applying the "your turn" indicator in the collaborative game section. This indicator works by giving cues in the form of instructions to the player when playing music. This method also applies a reinforcing background element in the visual representation to distinguish saron 1 and saron 2 when playing. The location of the visual presentation is in a position in the middle of the screen. The way is by putting different marks on the song notation. The distinguishing mark is a blue circle for Saron 1 and a red triangle for Saron 2.

Second Implementation. The digitization of the saron instrument also applies the Rhythmic Emphasis Weighting method in connection with the "Techno Rhythm Monitor" which provides a visualization of the tempo. The test is by trying various beat levels starting from 8 taps to 64 taps to adjust the rhythm or tempo emphasis. Its application provides a tempo visualization on the song notation to give instructions played according to the tempo. If the play is not according to the tempo, then there is an information display in the form of a pop-up "Tempo is not appropriate. Please continue playing." However, if the game matches the tempo, the information is not displayed because the method tries to regulate the rhythmic emphasis on playing musical instruments.

3.4   Prototype

The prototype in the modeling flow is the stage of making the initial design of the interaction design model for the saron musical instrument learning application that is by the user's goals [13]. Several steps were taken at this prototype stage are creating a user flow, low fidelity wireframe, and high fidelity prototype. The following is an explanation of the prototype stages:

User Flow. User flow is the output generated from the application design stage that requires steps to work on the task for users in carrying out learning activities for the saron musical instrument. The outcome of this stage is illustrating by the activity diagram in Fig. 3 below.

Wireframe Wireframe. Low Fidelity is a design framework that displays the structure and layout of the playing saron in collaboration according to the tempo.

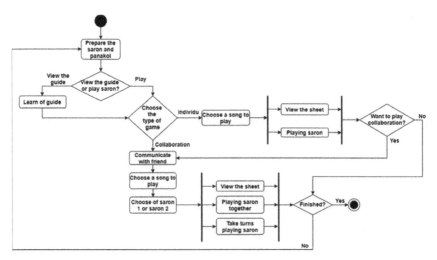

Fig. 3. User flow

Prototype High Fidelity. The High Fidelity prototype is the final product in the design to create an application. The implementation of the Call and Response System method is in the "your turn" indicator as a hint to give a signal to players when to start playing saron, and a visual representation to distinguish the roles of Saron 1 and Saron 2 when playing with a blue circle and a red triangle. The implementation of the Rhythmic Emphasis Weighting method is in the visualization of the song notation started from 8 taps to 64 taps to set the rhythm emphasis. Before that, a design guideline was made which contained a guide regarding the design requirements of an application such as layout, color, icons, and typography [16]. Figure 4 described a high fidelity prototype in playing saron in collaboration according to the tempo.

3.5   Test

The last stage in the modeling flow is testing. In this case, testing is carried out on users to validate whether the solutions made are appropriate and solve user problems. Testing in this final project was carried out on 7 respondents consisting of 4 beginner respondents and 3 expert respondents because the results were valid enough to conclude the product that had been designed [17]. This test takes place online by including a prototype link and a google form link to fill out a questionnaire on the application design that has been tested. The stages carried out in this test are testing purpose, test preparation scenarios, test scenarios, test results, and analysis of test results.

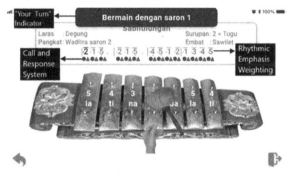

Fig. 4. Prototype of 'playing saron in collaboration according to the tempo' page (color figure online)

Testing Purpose. The purpose of this study is to ensure that applying the Call and Response System and Rhythmic Emphasis Weighting methods can function to playing saron in collaboration according to the tempo, and analyze that the usability results that have been designed can be accepted and used by users.

Test Preparation Scenario. The test preparation scenario is making of the steps before do testing to respondents.

Test Scenario. Test scenarios are the steps used to assist respondents in completing their tasks when using the prototype.

Test Result. The final test in this study was conducted on 7 respondents consisting of 4 beginner respondents and 3 expert respondents. The test is on July 14, 2021, online using the prototype link and google form link. Based on the results of using the prototype with Maze, 85.7% or 6 out of 7 respondents were able to complete the task with the specified path, 11.1% misclicked, and it took 22.1 s to complete the task. After analyzing the questionnaire conducted by 7 respondents consisting of 4 beginner respondents and 3 expert respondents, an average value is 85% for the interaction design for digital saron musical instruments.

Analysis of Test. Results the analysis of test results using Maze is, judging from running task of playing Saron in collaboration according to the tempo, for 3 out of 4 respondents the beginner persona was successful in carrying out their task, but there was one respondent who did not understand the task and resulted in the wrong button choosing to start the collaborative. Some respondents experience click errors because they do not match the predetermined path. While 3 respondents the expert persona succeeded in carrying out this task. Based on the analysis, 85.7% or 6 of 7 respondents completed the task with the specified path, but there was an 11.1% misclick which had 15 click errors on this task. That is because some respondents clicked wrongly when the game start count pop-up appeared. This causes the execution time when running this task is 22.1 s. It means that takes a long time to complete the task because respondents try to click to complete the task of playing saron collaboration according to the tempo.

Figure 5 and Fig. 6 describe bar graphs of beginner persona and expert persona for showing the percentage results of each question of the SUS method. The analysis of test results from the calculation of SUS are:

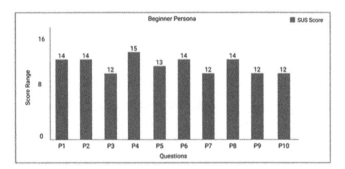

Fig. 5. The result of SUS score from beginner persona

1. Judging from the results of answer number 1, where the question is more directed to how often you want to use this application, a score of 14 points isobtained from 4 beginner respondents and 12 points from 3 expert respondents. The respondents

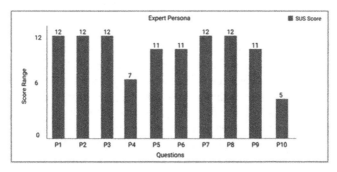

Fig. 6. The result of SUS score from expert persona

feel they want to use this application. After all, it is unique, interesting, innovative, has never been found before, and is a traditional saron musical instrument game application that can be done collaboratively.

2. Judging from the results of answer number 2, where the question is more directed to the perceived complexity when using the application, a score of 14 points is obtained from 4 beginner respondents and 12 points from 3 expert respondents. The respondents do not feel this application is complicated to use because in the high fidelity prototype that has been designed, there is clear and easy-to-understand information.

3. Judging from the results of answer number 3, where the question is more directed to the ease of application to use, a score of 12 points is obtained from 4 beginner respondents and 12 points from 3 expert respondents. The respondents are easy to use the high fidelity prototype that has been designed. After all, respondents are 85,7% successful in carrying out tasks, but some respondents do not understand when running each lesson, so there are several mistakes in clicking on the existing scheme.

4. Judging from the results of answer number 4, where the question is more directed to the need for assistance when using the application, a score of 15 points is obtained from 4 beginner respondents and 7 points from 3 expert respondents. The respondents need help when using the high-fidelity prototype that has been designed. After all, respondents are still not used to using the application.

5. Judging from the results of answer number 5, where the question is more directed to features that are well integrated into this application, a score of 13 points is obtained from 4 beginner respondents and 11 points from 3 expert respondents. The existing features are well integrated because the display and the information are obvious, but not all the devices used by the respondents are well supported.

6. Judging from the results of answer number 6, where the question is more directed to consistency in the application, a score of 14 points is obtained from 4 beginner respondents and 11 from 3 expert respondents. The respondents agree that there is no inconsistency in this high-fidelity prototype. After all, the existing features and menus are following the screen they should be, but several things need to be improved, namely when respondents play saron, the sound produced is slow to hear.

This is because the tools used to make this high-fidelity prototype lack support in terms of audio.

7. Judging from the results of answer number 7, where the question is more directed to the understanding of others when using the application quickly, a score of 12 points is obtained from 4 beginner respondents and 12 points from 3 expert respondents. The respondents agree that other people will understand how to use this application quickly. After all, the average duration of respondents running the task is less than 10 s. But some respondents experience errors in clicking on the existing task.

8. Judging from the results of answer number 8, where the question leads to confusion when using the application, a score of 14 points is obtained from 4 beginner respondents and 12 points from 3 expert respondents. The respondents disagree that this high-fidelity prototype is confusing to use. After all, the existing features can already operate properly, and when one button is pressed, it will display the screen correctly.

9. Judging from the results of answer number 9, where the question is more directed to discovering obstacles in using the application, a score of 12 points is obtained from 4 beginner respondents and 11 points from 3 expert respondents. The majority of respondents do not experience obstacles when using the high fidelity prototype that has been designed. However, some respondents still encounter obstacles

10. Judging from the results of answer number 10, where the question is more directed to studying first before using the application, a score of 12 points is obtained from 4 beginner respondents and 5 points from 3 expert respondents. Some respondents still need to get used to using this application because there are still many who ask what needs to be done when running the tasks in this high fidelity prototype.

Based on the analysis of testing using the Maze and SUS methods, it was found that users can play the saron musical instrument collaboratively according to the tempo. Based on the category of acceptability range, the results obtained can be accepted in class B very well, with an average rating of 85%. This application is well received because it has fulfilled the user's goal of collaborating with the saron musical instrument according to the tempo.

4   Conclusion

From the results of this study, it can be concluded that including the original saron tone sample with technology found the most effective form of interaction in playing the saron musical instrument in collaboration, namely by physical responses between players that produce rhythmic patterns and rhythmic improvisations spontaneously. Meanwhile, the use of the "your turn" indicator is applied by giving different signs in Saron 1 and Saron 2 with a blue circle and a red triangle. A balance of playing music was also found to give each other creativity in the game by the direction of tempo visualization. According to the tempo, where play collaborative music is visualized using the "Techno Rhythm Monitor" on the song notation contained in the application. Based on the analysis of testing the implementation of Call and Response System and Rhythmic Emphasis Weighting methods on the interaction design model using Maze and SUS methods, it was found that users can play the saron musical instrument collaboratively according to the tempo. The test result using Maze obtained an average 85.7% completed the task with the specified path and using the SUS method obtained an average value of 85%, which is at level B, which is excellent, with a category including acceptable. Based on the final results of these tests, the interaction design modeling for the collaborative learning application of the saron musical instrument by the tempo can be accepted because it has met the user's goals (proper). The results of Interaction Design for Digital Saron Musical Instruments that collaborate according to the tempo can be used by users, both beginners, and experts, as well as artists and the general public. From the research experience, suggestions for the future are that this research can be further expanded and developed to conduct collaborative learning of other types of traditional musical instruments, both similar musical instruments and with different types of musical instruments.

References

1. Osterhammel, J., Petersson, N.P.: Globalization: A Short History. Princeton University Press (2021)
2. Walton, S.P.: Aesthetic and spiritual correlations in Javanese gamelan music. J. Aesthet. Art Criticism **65**(1), 31–41 (2017)
3. Born, G., Devine, K.: Music technology, gender, and class: digitization, educational and social change in Britain. Twentieth-Century Music **12**(2), 135–172 (2015)
4. Purwadi: Seni karawitan Jawa: ungkapan keindahan dalam musik gamelan. Hanan Pustaka, Yogjakarta (2006)
5. Walton, S.P.: Collaboration, feeling and the partnership of the spiritual and musical in Javanese Gamelan music. J. Asian Music Res. Inst. **23** (2001)
6. Becker, J.: Traditional Music in Modern Java: Gamelan in a Changing Society. University of Hawaii Press (2019)
7. Blaine, T., Perkis, T.: The Jam-O-Drum interactive music system: a study in interaction design. In: Proceedings of the 3rd Conference on Designing Interactive Systems: Processes, Practices, Methods, and Techniques, pp. 165–173 (2000)
8. Kaya, A., Ozturk, R., Gumussoy, C.A.: Usability measurement of mobile applications with system usability scale (SUS). In: Calisir, F., Cevikcan, E., Akdag, H.C. (eds.) Industrial Engineering in the Big Data Era: Selected Papers from the Global Joint Conference on Industrial Engineering and Its Application Areas, GJCIE 2018, June 21–22, 2018, Nevsehir, Turkey, pp. 389–400. Springer International Publishing, Cham (2019). https://doi.org/10.1007/978-3-030-03317-0_32
9. Sharfina, Z., Santoso, H.B.: An Indonesian adaptation of the system usability scale (SUS). In: 2016 International Conference on Advanced Computer Science and Information Systems (ICACSIS), pp. 145–148. IEEE (2016)
10. Roh, J.H., Wilcox, L.: Exploring tabla drumming using rhythmic input. In: Conference Companion on Human Factors in Computing Systems, pp. 310–311 (1995)
11. Plattner, H., Meinel, C., Weinberg, U.: Design-Thinking. Mi-Fachverlag, Landsberg am Lech (2019)
12. Sauro, J., Lewis, J.R.: Quantifying user research. In: Quantifying the User Experience, pp. 9–18. Elsevier (2016). https://doi.org/10.1016/B978-0-12-802308-2.00002-3
13. Wolniak, R.: The design thinking method and its stages. Systemy Wspomagania w Inz'ynierii Produkcji. **6**(6), 247–255 (2017)
14. Carlgren, L., Rauth, I., Elmquist, M.: Framing design thinking: the concept in idea and enactment. Creat. Innov. Manage. **25**(1), 38–57 (2016)

15. Diderich, C.: Design Thinking for Strategy. MP, Springer, Cham (2020). https://doi.org/10. 1007/978-3-030-25875-7
16. Schlatter, T., Levinson, D.: Visual usability: principles and practices for designing digital applications. Newnes (2013)
17. Woolrych, A., Cockton, G.: Why and when five test users aren't enough. In: Proceedings of IHM-HCI 2001 Conference, vol. 2, pp. 105–108. C´epadu´es Editions, Toulouse, France (2001)

A User Experience Model for Designing Educational Mobile Application

Kiranjeet Kaur, Khairul Shafee Kalid$^{(\boxtimes)}$ ⓘ, and Savita K. Sugathan

Department of Computer Information Sciences, Universiti Teknologi PETRONAS, Seri Iskandar, Malaysia
{khairulshafee_kalid,savitasugathan}@utp.edu.my

Abstract. The use of mobile application facilitates an interactive and innovative learning experience for students. While there are many studies emphasizing on the use of mobile application but less focuses on the student's experience in using those applications. Mobile application designers tend focus on user interfaces but neglects user experience (UX) as their approach in designing educational application for children. Thus, this paper aims to present a model called EduMobile UX model, a user experience model that designers can adopt when designing educational applications for children. To develop the model, an extensive literature was performed to determine the dimensions for the model. The elements for each dimension of the model were identified through semi-structured interviews and observation respondents from two public school in Tronoh, Perak. This study contributes to the development of a UX model that designers can use to develop education mobile applications based on UX principles.

Keywords: User experience · Children educational application · Cognitive skills

1 Introduction

According to the Ministry of Education of Malaysia, the Science, Technology, Engineering and Mathematics (STEM) in Malaysia aims to develop students with necessary skills which could face the challenges of science and technology [1]. Thus, it is important for Malaysia to focus on producing enough qualified graduates in STEM [2, 3] though the student's interest in STEM is gradually declining [4]. The Minister of Science, Technology and Innovation Ministry stated further that low number of STEM student is worrying [5]. There are many studies that have been conducted to investigate the factors that lead to declining number of student's enrolment on STEM education. One of the factors that contributed to these concerns with student's learning experience. Reference [6] conducted a study on the factors affecting effective instructional practices in teaching mathematics stated that classroom culture is the most important factor in teaching mathematics in STEM education. Thus, it is important for teachers to understand the elements that makes teaching of STEM more interesting to the students so that teachers can facilitate the student's learning. To enhance student's learning experience on STEM, the use of technologies such as mobile application, virtual reality, augmented reality, and

© Springer Nature Switzerland AG 2021
H. Badioze Zaman et al. (Eds.): IVIC 2021, LNCS 13051, pp. 139–150, 2021.
https://doi.org/10.1007/978-3-030-90235-3_12

others to support teaching and learning seem to be an opportunity. In addition, with the COVID-19 outbreak, the use of these technologies has becoming more prevalent than before. Mobile devices and applications enhance student's engagement by transforming the way educational content is being delivered. There are many studies that demonstrate the effectiveness of mobile devices in teaching and learning on student's performance [7] but there seems to be limited number of studies on children's user experience in using mobile devices and applications for learning. It is argued that existing mobile applications were designed based on a one-size-fits-all user interface design and not based on user experience (UX) principles. Children that use these applications that are design based on user interface design principles are accustomed to the behavior of the application because they are familiar with the placements of the icons and activities that the applications provide [8]. This could be attributed to the tendency of mobile application designers in using a 'one-size-fits-all' approach in which the same interface design principles are used for both children and adult users. It is argued in this paper that existing educational mobile application are designed without taking into consideration the user's experience.

Thus, this study explores the concept of UX in designing educational mobile application. The objective of this paper is to present a UX model called the EduMobile UX model that guides mobile application designers to design educational mobile application based on user experience principles.

2   Literature Review

2.1 Overview of User Experience

User Experience (UX) is a well-defined consequence of presentation, functionality, system performance, interactive behaviour, and assistive capabilities of an interactive system for hardware as well as software [9]. UX has evolved into one of the core concepts of human computer interaction (HCI) where wide range of disciplines' researchers and practitioners daily work on these concepts. Despite several attempts of understanding, defining and scoping UX, no secured consensus has been reached on this concept [10]. Donald Norman coined the term "User Experience" to describe all the person's experience aspects with a system he believed "usability" to be narrowed deeply for representing a holistic vision of HCI [10]. According to Jacob Nielsen and Don Norman, UX encompasses "all aspects of the end-user's interaction with company, its services and its products" [11] yet not all associated with UX have agreed on this definition [12]. Generally, developers who are interested in UX design, not only focuses on what the product does but on how the users tend to interact with it. Thus, a positive experience requires substantial benefits to users and a negative experience entails frustration and failure [13]. The UX approach in mobile application development in Malaysia is still limited. Mobile application development companies often focus on product-oriented metrics [14]. For example, pre-defined product goals are referred on creating operational goals and functional achievement.

2.2   The Role of UX

The role of UX in user interface design is of paramount importance. The interaction between a user and the application leads to a unique experience in different context of use [15] which includes users perceptual and emotional aspects [9]. It also portrays a paradigmatic shift of how a user anticipates about the interface [12] and the results will then represent usability of a system, product, or service [16]. Furthermore, user interface design is the key factor to produce the best interaction of beauty [14] for users to accept the application because their dislikes could lead to anxiety or discomfort [17]. The function of the application is important for anticipating the usage of the application through a user's perception and responses [16] for maintaining an experience full of engagement and fun [18]. Reference [19] conducted a review on UX design principles in education contexts. The authors stated that the purpose of UX implementation in STEM education is to design educational experiences such as redesigning curriculum and pedagogy and the design of educational tools such as online repository, productivity tools, interfaces, and others. Most of the studies on UX implementation in STEM settings is on designing educational experiences but lack on designing educational tools. Therefore, the adoption of UX to improve innovation has the unique contribution to STEM education researchers.

2.3   UX Dimensions

There are existing UX models such as [20], UI/UX model [21] and Experience-Centered Web Design Model [22]. Each model composed of its own dimension. From all three models, the Experience-Centered Web Design model's dimensions are clearly understood and suitable with the educational context of this study. Furthermore, user experience concerns with the feelings of the users in using the mobile application that is triggered by the properties of the app and the context of use as cited in [23]. The Experience-Centered Web Design model includes all the necessary dimensions for user experience. Table 1 shows the description of each of the dimension of the Experience-Centered Web Design model.

Table 1. Dimensions in the Experience-Centered Web Design Model [20]

Dimensions	Description
Emotional	The emotional dimension relates to a person's feeling, response, and sentiment on the application
Functional	The functional dimension refers to the functionality and usability of the application's
Aesthetic	Aesthetic dimension contributes all visual attributes of the interface such as colours, texture, images, and graphic composition

2.4   The Cognitive Dimension

The existing UX model focuses on experience. Children's user experience in using mobile application is crucial but the learning aspect must not be neglected thus, for an educational mobile application, the learning aspect needs to be part of the design of the application. The cognitive dimension is based on Piaget's theory of cognitive development. Piaget's theory focuses on the children's progress by referring to the development stages qualitatively [24] namely sensorimotor stage (birth–2 years), preoperational stage (2–7 years), concrete operational stage (7–11 years) and formal operational stage (12 years–adult). The scope of study is for primary school children aged 10–12, therefore this study focuses on the concrete operational stage of Piaget's theory. Children at this stage tends to be very concrete, they grow to be more logical and sophisticated in their thinking in this stage. This stage includes genuine exercise of logic, resolving difficulties, reasoning, problems and undergo hindrances in a logical way. Children in the concrete operational stage practice solving logical problems in their mind.

3 Methodology

This study is an extension of a study by [25]. The previous study focuses on a school in which the analysis of the data is a within case analysis. This study extends that by conducting another case study and compare that with the previous case study in which the analysis of the data is cross-case.

The methodology of this study consists of two main parts. The first activity is the development of the proposed EduMobile UX model. The main dimensions of the proposed model were based on the Experience-Centered Web Design Model [22] and Piaget's theory of cognitive development [24]. The dimensions are emotional, functional, aesthetic, and cognitive. The elements for each of the dimensions were identified through a systematic literature review in educational mobile application. The second part is the identification of the elements for each of the dimension in the EduMobile UX model through two case studies. Two schools in Tronoh, Perak were selected as for this case study which is named as Case Study 1 and Case Study 2 respectively. For Case Study 1, five students participated in the study and six students participated in Case Study 2. The data collection stage was conducted in 2019 before the pandemic and the movement control order was implemented. Thus, the approval to conduct interview and observation sessions in the schools was obtained from education department and a letter of consent was prepared for the parents to grant their permission to invite their children as participants. An educational mobile application was chosen for this study. The application was used by the participants to see their reaction in terms of user experience. The application, "Environment Current Affairs 2018" is an Android-based educational mobile application that contains materials and assessments on topics related to the environment. The focus is not on the content of the application but on the user's experience of the school children in using the application. The device used was a smartphone.

The interview questions were developed based on the four dimensions of the EduMobile UX model and reviewed by an experienced qualitative researcher to ensure that the questions are reliable and easily understood. The data from the interview sessions were transcribed and analyzed based on qualitative data analysis principles using Atlas.ti, a qualitative data analysis software. The data analysis process follows the steps outlined by [26]. Using these steps, the data is codified and categorized according to the four dimensions. The transcripts and observation notes were prepared after each completed data collection session. From these transcripts and notes, the coding process commenced. The coding process are based on the steps outlined by [27]. The coding process consists of two cycles. In the first cycle coding process, the student's emotion, feelings, and perception were observed. The output of the first cycle coding is the regarded as open codes. These open codes are then synthesized in which that the occurrence and meaning of the codes were observed. Based on this synthesis, the codes were put through the second cycle of coding. In this cycle, patterns and core categories were observed and identified. The analysis is done for within case and cross case analysis. For cross-case, the similarities, and differences between the two cases are observed. The outcome of the second cycle coding is the categories which are the grouped into the dimensions of the UX model. From the analysis, the elements for each of the dimensions in the EduMobile UX model were identified.

3.1 Case Study 1

The first case study involves a school in Tronoh that consist of 237 students and 20 teachers. There are also Orang Asli and Indian students registered in the school, but majority consists of Malay students. Due to the student's examination was around the corner the researcher was only allowed to conduct the data collection for 1.5 h with each participant. Furthermore, the data collection could only be conducted in the morning on Tuesday(s) and Thursday(s). Thus, looking into the school's conditions the researcher decided to limit the observation period to 5 min and the rest of the time was utilized for interview session. The researcher would reach at the venue 10 min earlier for setting up the data collection tools to avoid wasting the allocated time. The observation session was video recorded, and interview was voice recorded for analyzing purpose. The data collection was completed once the researcher could find the saturation of data from the participants answers and through the observation pattern. Hence, the data collection was conducted with 5 participants where 3 of them were standard 5 students and 2 of them were standard 4 students. 4 of them were female and only one participant was male.

3.2 Case Study 2

The second case study involves a vernacular school in Tronoh. This school consist of 53 students and 11 teachers. All the students were only Hindu. The research data collection was not allowed to be held during school hours thus, it was conducted during extra-curricular hours on Wednesday(s) from 1.30 pm to 3.00 pm. Firstly, the observation session was held for 5 min, and video recorded for analyzing. Later, semi-structured interview session was conducted with the participants upon their experience with the mobile application. Since, the participants native language was Tamil thus, the researcher was appointed a translator to communicate with the participants during the interview session. The translator later would also transcribe the voice recording into script document for researcher to analyze. The researcher found the data saturated after collecting data from total of 6 participants. 3 of them were standard 4 and the others were from standard 5. There were 3 female and 3 male participants.

4   EduMobile UX Model

Figure 1 shows the proposed EduMobile UX Model. This model is based on the Experience-Centered Web Design model with an additional dimension named Cognitive. The Cognitive dimension signifies the learning aspects of the model. The cognitive dimension refers to the children's thinking skills while using the mobile application.

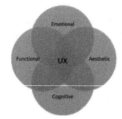

Fig. 1. EduMobile UX model

Interview sessions and observations were conducted in both Case Study 1 and Case Study 2 based on the dimensions of the EduMobile UX model. The outcome of the two case studies has revealed the elements for each of the dimension. Table 2 shows the elements for each of the dimension.

Table 2. EduMobile UX model dimensions and elements

Dimension	Elements
Emotional	Attractiveness, pleasure, satisfaction, enjoyment, motivation
Functional	Technology fit, effective, efficient, convenience, gesture interaction
Aesthetic	Text, audio, animation, colour, layout, video
Cognitive	Learnability, memorability, complexity, discoverability

5   Results and Discussion

The findings identified the important elements for each of the four dimensions of the EduMobile UX model. The emotional dimension claims to be the first dimension to be designed because the user experience will be conceived here [20]. The most individual and often idiosyncratic of human phenomena are probably emotions [21]. Overall interaction with mobile application is the focus of the study and the experience should be re-created, modified and amplified in real world. This dimension focuses on the user interactivity which enhances users' motivation through better participatory activity. Children's helping behaviour emerges early in concrete operational stage, suggesting that pro sociality is rooted deeply in human nature [25].

5.1 Emotional

For the emotional dimension, the data collection activities demonstrate the participant's emotion towards using the educational mobile application. The application "Environment Current Affairs 2018" does not give the participants the utmost user experience. Participants believed that the user interface was not attractive due to the style of the content being presented to them. Participants did not feel the enjoyment from using the application because they feel that the content is dull with lack of interaction with the user. This affects the motivation of the user to continuously use the application for learning as participant 3 from Case Study 2 stated.

> *"The colours are also very like not so attractive or like dull cause it uses only one colour and too small words makes me hard to read so I don't get motivated to read more" [19:45 CASE_2 INTERVIEW 3].*

The emotional aspects seem to be related with other dimensions. For example, aesthetic dimension elements such as content layout, use of colours, animation and others could impact the emotions of the user. The two case studies indicate the use of colours affect the participant's emotion. Colours have been seen as a source of attraction for the students to use the application in both case studies. The use of colours in the application impacts the participants somehow. For example, participants of Case Study 1 felt that colorful design delivers enjoyable experience to them whereas participant in Case Study 2 commented that colours motivates them in using the application. Both case studies show similar findings on the impact of colours and content design towards user experience. The findings from the Case Study 1 and Case Study 2 indicated that interesting and multiple content style with colorful design provide pleasure in using the educational mobile application.

The findings from the two case studies also indicates the elements of interactivity and engaging experience in delivering meaningful knowledge brings satisfaction the participants. This can be seen from the two case studies in which the participants felt that interactive feedbacks and design would satisfy them as it enhances their learning abilities. Interactive activities in the application provides enjoyment feeling to the children. The study by [28] corroborate this finding. The study, despite not using in any specific mobile application, indicates that the experience of using educational mobile application should be fun and motivating. This could be achieved through activities with good usability factors.

5.2 Functional

The functional dimension concerns with the features and functionality of the application and the usage of the application itself by the user. Mobile application needs to operate fast, provide reliable content, contain all workable user interface elements, enables the user to personalize learning, provide both open and secured access, able to adjust the content according to the new settings and perform all relevant task or functions without any manner of interference. As one participant stated,

"Here there is only one icon back button so, it is nice and clear. The size is also just nice for the button not so big and not so small so with this size is just nice to see it clearly" [18:1 CASE_2 INTERVIEW 2].

Moreover, educational mobile application should be delivering high quality standards to keep pace with the growing mobile technology. The navigation of the application needs to be economical and convenient. The findings indicated that children find touch/gesture interaction of the mobile application to be easily detected and performed softly. This is due to children prefer performing gesture using their own method rather than following instructions [29], which delivers accurate single/multitouch gestures since, they are regularly using smart gadgets at home.

The findings of the two cases have shown that the school children prefer mobile application that is laden with the latest features which would help them in completing a task easily and faster. The participants of this study are regarded as Gen Z which has been exposed to mobile devices and applications. Thus, designers should be aware of all the technological features which are necessary to be included in designing the application for children. Nonetheless, the mobile application design for school children cannot to be too complicated. A less complicated design makes the application more effective. Participants in Case Study 1 and Case Study have different views regarding the effectiveness of the "Environmental Current Affairs" mobile application. Participants in Case Study 1 defines effectiveness as when all the interface elements are easily visible. Participants in Case Study 2 views speed, responsiveness and non-interfered task as the elements that makes an application to be effective. The efficiency of the mobile application, however, relates to how convenient the user performs a task in the mobile application. Participants for Case Study 1 focus on gesture interaction on how easy for them to navigate the application. Thus, the mobile application should consist of all the latest gesture interaction as children are aware of all the available gestures and can perform without any assistance. Participants for Case Study 2 commented further that the efficiency of an application is depending on how organized the layout of the application is. An application with an organized layout design would ease the children in navigating the application and perform any tasks within the application faster. Overall, children mobile application designers should take into consideration the layout design of the application to enhance the children's experience in using the application. The designers should ensure the mobile application is designed to produce responsive, errorless, and fast tasks but with simple as well as highly noticeable presentation. The challenge in developing mobile application for learning is on how to balance between information and the display size, navigation, and storage [30].

5.3 Aesthetic

Aesthetic dimension contributes all visual attributes of the interface such as colours, texture, images, and graphic composition. This aesthetic dimension represents the other two dimensions of UX. Picturing the concept and functionality may interest the user for experiencing the design [22]. In this paper, it is important that visibility, text, colour, images, audio and animation can contribute a big portion to interactivity since, human respond better to visual arrangements. Research has confirmed that images prove to interest, create emotion, and stimulate curiosity. Text needs to integrate with images since text create the meaning of the image. The use of colors and audio not only enhance the mobile application aesthetically but also improves student's overall satisfaction in using the application [31]. The use of appropriate font size and colours is crucial for delivering clear readability. Thus, the two case studies have uncovered that font which are big and clear would be easy to read and understand the content. The animation is useful believed to catch the users' attention. The use of animation could eliminate boredom when using the application but in Case Study 2, the participants claimed that too many and animation in reading content would distract children. However, in Case Study 1 animation are appreciated as it contributes to the content awareness more seriously. Moreover, participants in Case Study 2 find animation which are used for guidance interest them in using the application more. Participant from Case Stud 1 stated,

They should present (the information) the animation in way where the water is like clean and beautiful but suddenly changes to dirty and polluted. (The use of) animation will make us realize that the nature is getting polluted. [2:9 | 2 CASE_1 INTERVIEW 2]

Therefore, inclusion of animation should be done carefully as its misplacement and amount could disrupt children's loyalty towards the application. Nonetheless, it can be agreed that animation plays an important role in sustaining their fun while maintaining their seriousness in understanding the content.

The use of sound helps in setting the mood of the user however, it should appropriate and not overused as it could affect the users focus on learning. The use of colors affects the student's interest in using the application. Colours play an important role in content visibility as found from Case Study 2. On the other hand, children in Case Study 1 believed that colours play a role of excitement which intrudes them in choosing bright colours. As the following participants commented,

That loud music will make me irritated, and I will get distracted" [1:26 CASE_1 INTERVIEW 1].

Sound is a tool that will keep us alert. Like example when we are pressing something like button, with the help of sound we will be aware of what we are pressing" [17:33 CASE_2 INTERVIEW 1].

It can also be seen that the participants are prefer objects such as icons, pictures, and others to be well-organized. A well-organized layout allows user to find information more easily. From Case Study 1, the participants prefer layout arrangement that focus on the visibility of the interface elements. Participants from Case Study 2 mentioned about a well-organized layout that contributes to effectiveness of the application. Therefore, mobile application designers should ensure the layout are best to fit with mobile application screen that ensures clear visibility, help in doing task correctly and could provide comfortable environment. Pictures should be included in the application to contribute in relevant visual information. The pictures and text should be presented clearly as these contributes to learning and avoiding misinterpretation of information.

5.4 Cognitive

The cognitive dimension is the learning dimension of the model. The findings from Case Study 1 and Case Study 2 indicate that school children could use mobile application for learning if the content is aligned to the student's level of understanding and comprehension. Children could learn better if the derived knowledge is easily understandable. The participants feel that the content of the application is too complex for them. Thus, it is important for an educational mobile application to have content that suited the user's level of capabilities. Content complexity affects the student's learnability. One participant stated,

> *This information is not for my age kids can understand and work. So, better like in our textbooks they show and then which I can do like in book I got read that there must be 3 bins to throw rubbish so this I can do at home also" [18:50 CASE_2 INTERVIEW 2].*

One of the approaches to make the content less complex is to make it bite-sized which means avoiding long sentences or presenting the content using mind maps. The aesthetic dimension affects the cognitive dimension. The use of animation, videos and sounds in education mobile application impact student's learning. According to [28], the excitement created through animation, virtual objects, sound, and video could improves children memory. The use of technologies such as 3D animation, multimedia are able to enhance student's understanding on science subjects [32]. Reference [31] studied the use of mobile application with augmented reality capabilities in learning of the topic Solar System called AR-SiS. Their findings show that students perceived could improve their understand and knowledge on the solar system using augmented reality mobile application. Interactive activities promote memorability in children as discovered from Case Study 1 and Case Study 2. Additionally, these two case studies have also uncovered that child tend to remember content better when it is highlighted using colours and unique fonts.

6 Conclusion

This study proposed a UX model called the EduMobile UX for education mobile application for school children. The dimensions of the model were proposed based on the Experienced-Centered Web Design model and Piaget's Theory of Cognitive Development. The model consists of four dimensions namely emotional, functional, aesthetic, and cognitive. The elements for each of the model were identified through a single case study. This study presents this model as the first step towards developing a UX guideline for education mobile application. Overall, this study contributes to the mobile application industry, children, and the education system. From a practical standpoint, the EduMobile UX model can be adopted by mobile application designers to design education mobile application for school children using UX principles.

References

1. Recsam, S.: Curriculum reform: the Malaysian experience. https://home.kku.ac.th/crme/Fil epaper/apec2016/MALAYSIANEDUCATIONSYSTEM.pdf (2016). Accessed 06 Sept 2021
2. Ramli, N.F., Talib, O., et al.: Can education institution implement STEM? From Malaysian teachers' view. Int. J. Acad. Res. Bus. Soc. Sci. **7**(3), 721–732 (2017)
3. Shahali, E.H.M., Halim, L., Rasul, M.S., Osman, K., Zulkifeli, M.A.: STEM learning through engineering design: impact on middle secondary students' interest towards STEM. EURASIA J. Math. Sci. Technol. Educ. **13**(5), 1189–1211 (2016)
4. Krajcik, J., Delen, I.: How to support learners in developing usable and lasting knowledge of STEM. Int. J. Educ. Math. Sci. Technol. **5**(1), 21–28 (2017)
5. Bernama: Low number of STEM students worrying - Khairy. https://www.bernama.com/en/general/news.php?id=1899173 (2020, November 09). Accessed 14 Nov 2020
6. Rasid, N.S.M., Nasir, N.A.M., Singh, P., Han, C.T.: STEM integration: factors affecting effective instructional practices in teaching mathematics. Asian J. Univ. Educ. **16**(1), 56–69 (2020)
7. Sung, Y.-T., Chang, K.-E., Liu, T.-C.: The effects of integrating mobile devices with teaching and learning on students' learning performance: a meta-analysis and research synthesis. Comput. Educ. **94**, 252–275 (2016)
8. Ruiz-Iniesta, A., Melgar, L., Baldominos, A., Quintana, D.: Improving children's experience on a mobile EdTech platform through a recommender system. Mob. Inf. Syst. **2018**, 1374017 (2018)
9. Pucillo, F., Cascini, G.: A framework for user experience, needs and affordances. Des. Stud. **35**(2), 160–179 (2014)
10. Lallemand, C., Gronier, G., Koenig, V.: User experience: a concept without consensus? Exploring practitioners' perspectives through an international survey. Comput. Human Behav. **43**, 35–48 (2015)
11. Normman, D., Nielsen, J.: The definition of user experience (UX). https://www.nngroup.com/articles/definition-user-experience/. Accessed 06 Sept 2021
12. Mullins, C.: Responsive, mobile app, mobile first: untangling the UX design web in practical experience. In: Proceedings of the 33rd Annual International Conference on the Design of Communication, pp. 1–6 (2015)
13. Park, S., Oh, D.-S.: An exploratory study on the content design of mobile edutainment for preschool children. Int. J. Softw. Eng. Appl. **8**(11), 55–66 (2014)
14. Wong, C.Y., Chu, K., Pauzi, M.A.M.: Advocating UX practice in industry: lessons learnt from UX innovate bootcamp. In: 2016 4th International Conference on User Science and Engineering (i-USEr), pp. 204–209 (2016)
15. Nagalingam, V., Ibrahim, R.: Finding the right elements: user experience elements for educational games. In: Proceedings of the 2017 International Conference on E-commerce, E-Business and E-Government, pp. 90–93 (2017)
16. Nagalingam, V., Ibrahim, R.: A review of user experience (UX) frameworks for educational games, June, pp. 134–143 (2015)
17. Al-Khalifa, H.S., Garcia, R.A.: Website design based on cultures: an investigation of saudis, filipinos, and indians government websites' attributes. In: International Conference of Design, User Experience, and Usability, pp. 15–27 (2014)
18. Ariffin, S.A.: Needs and potentials for studying local malaysian culture through mobile learning. In: Proceedings of the 3rd International Conference on Human-Computer Interaction and User Experience in Indonesia, pp. 60–66 (2017)
19. Minichiello, A., Hood, J.R., Harkness, D.S.: Bringing user experience design to bear on STEM education: a narrative literature review. J. STEM Educ. Res. **1**(1), 7–33 (2018)

20. Stern, C.: CUBI: a user experience model for project success | UX Magazine. https://uxmag.com/articles/cubi-a-user-experience-model-for-project-success (2014, September 25). Accessed 06 Sept 2021

21. Herasymenko, A.: UX design for beginners: what is UI/UX Design? | by Andrey Herasymenko | UX Collective. https://uxdesign.cc/ux-design-for-beginners-what-is-ui-ux-design-89bc4da54cbf (2019, January 15). Accessed 06 Sept 2021

22. Fadel, L.M.: Experience-centered web design model. In: International Conference of Design, User Experience, and Usability, pp. 92–103 (2014)

23. Yang, B., Liu, Y., Liang, Y., Tang, M.: Exploiting user experience from online customer reviews for product design. Int. J. Inf. Manage. **46**, 173–186 (2019). https://doi.org/10.1016/J.IJINFOMGT.2018.12.006

24. Feldman, D.H.: Cognitive development in childhood: a contemporary perspective. In: Handbook of Psychology, vol. 6, Second edn. DEF publishers, Champaign, IL (2012)

25. Kaur, K., Kalid, K.S., Sugathan, S.: Exploring children user experience in designing educational mobile application. In: 2021 International Conference on Computer Information Sciences (ICCOINS), pp. 163–168 (2021). https://doi.org/10.1109/ICCOINS49721.2021.9497234

26. Erlingsson, C., Brysiewicz, P.: A hands-on guide to doing content analysis. Afr. J. Emerg. Med. **7**(3), 93–99 (2017)

27. Saldaña, J.: The Coding Manual for Qualitative Researchers. Sage, Thousand Oaks, CA (2021)

28. Ariffin, S.A., Yatim, M.H.M., Daud, F.: Identification of usability impact of mobile learning STEM in a local university context. In: Proceedings of the 5th International ACM In-Cooperation HCI and UX Conference, pp. 106–115 (2019)

29. Hussain, N.H., Wook, T.S.M.T., Noor, S.F.M., Mohamed, H.: Multi-touch gestures in multimodal systems interaction among preschool children. In: 2017 6th International Conference on Electrical Engineering and Informatics (ICEEI), pp. 1–6 (2017)

30. Abd Samad, M.R., Ihsan, Z.H., Khalid, F.: The use of mobile learning in teaching and learning session during the covid-19 pandemic in Malaysia. J. Contemp. Soc. Sci. Educ. Stud. (JOCSSES)(E-ISSN 2785-8774)**1**(2), 46–65 (2021)

31. Zaki, N.A.A., Zain, N.Z.M., Zanilabdin, A.: AR-SIS: augmented reality application to encourage STEM teaching and learning. Int. J. Multimedia Appl. **10**(6), 1–13 (2019)

32. Lok, W.F., Hamzah, M.: Student experience of using mobile devices for learning chemistry. Int. J. Eval. Res. Educ. **10**(3), 893–900 (2021)

Evidence-Based of Interactive Multimedia-Based Nutrition Education Package Efficacy on Obesity Outcomes Through Game and Video Intervention

Hafzan Yusoff[1]([⊠]) [iD], Wan Putri Elena Wan Dali[1] [iD],
and Nur Intan Raihana Ruhaiyem[2] [iD]

[1] School of Health Sciences, Universiti Sains Malaysia, Health Campus,
16150 Kota Bharu, Kelantan, Malaysia
hafzany@usm.my
[2] School of Computer Science, Universiti Sains Malaysia, Main Campus,
11800 Gelugor, Penang, Malaysia
intanraihana@usm.my

Abstract. This paper presents the effectiveness evaluation of interactive multimedia-based nutrition education package (IMNEP), a game and video-based intervention tool targeting in improving obesity outcomes among obese children. The IMNEP stands for Interactive Multimedia-based Nutrition Education Package which comprise of a digital game namely *MakanSihatSaya* and 6 animated explainer videos, supported with physical activity component using Xbox 360 exergame. The intervention aims at providing the children and parents or caretaker with precise dietary guideline related to childhood obesity and encourage them to practice healthy eating and be active physically. The package was developed based on literature and pilot study, followed by evaluation through a 6-month randomized-controlled trial among obese primary school children in Kota Bharu, Malaysia. Significant improvement in obesity outcomes were evidenced among the children at the end of the trial. In summary, video and game are highly effective modes of intervention, particularly in the prevention and management of obesity problems among children due to their attention-grabbing and engaging features.

Keywords: Obesity · Interactive multimedia · Children · Video-based

1 Introduction

1.1 Background of Research Project

According to the recent National Health and Morbidity Survey, 29.8% of the Malaysian children aged between 5 to 17 years were overweight (15%) and obese (14.8%) [1]. The rate is growing, thus calls for appropriate interventions to improve the healthy eating practice and physical activity status among children. A handful of related studies were carried out to identify the best approaches that deem effective in addressing obesity

H. Badioze Zaman et al. (Eds.): IVIC 2021, LNCS 13051, pp. 151–162, 2021.
https://doi.org/10.1007/978-3-030-90235-3_13

among children, ranging from using board game [2], to comic book storytelling [3–5], and even web-based interactive comic [6]. All these studies reported positive impact of intervention on the children's knowledge, attitude, and healthy eating outcomes. However, the new generation which are born as digital natives need intervention that suits their interest the most. We evidenced the popularity of video and game streaming by the younger generation on social media platforms such as YouTube [7], thus the same modes of communication can become an enabler in delivering health-promoting messages to these target population. Previous studies had also demonstrated that computer-assisted instruction or education could improve the nutrition knowledge and results in behavior change among children [8, 9]. Implementation and evaluation of such intervention are still limited in this country, thus, we developed IMNEP, a multimedia nutrition education package which integrates explainer video and education game as possible solution to the obesity problem among school age children in Malaysia. The package development and week 1 evaluation both have been previously published elsewhere [10–12]. This paper will report on the findings of the randomized controlled trial examining the effectiveness of IMNEP on obesity outcomes.

2   Methodology

2.1   Implementation and Evaluation of the Intervention

A 4-arm randomized controlled trial has been conducted involving 139 obese school children from Kota Bharu, Kelantan. The participants were assigned into three intervention groups (**CPI**: Children + Parents Intervention, **COI**: Children only Intervention, **POI**: Parents only Intervention), and one control group (**COC**: Children only Control). They underwent three waves of obesity outcomes measurement at baseline (week 1), post-intervention (week 12) and followed up after withdrawal period (week 24). Only intervention groups received the IMNEP package. The intervention was started soon after the baseline measurements taken. During the intervention period, the CPI group were subjected to watch the explainer videos, play the *MakanSihatSaya* game, and play exergame at school. The parents in POI group are subjected to watch the videos only, and their children will be given access to the tools after the intervention study ends. The children in COI will receive both tools during school session only. The parents of CPI and POI were also contacted either face to face at school or via phone call to identify any problems regarding their child's food habits. A CD-ROM comprised of all the intervention videos and games was then provided to parents in CPI and POI groups for their reference which allowed repeated use of videos and game during their convenient time. This effort further ensures the objectives of this study can be achieved. The children in all intervention groups were also subjected to play exergame at school during physical activity (PA) class. Meanwhile, those in the control group (COC) continued with their normal school activity without any information provided about physical activity, healthy eating, or weight loss throughout the intervention period. However, upon completion of the study period, participants in the COC group were provided with a one-hour video viewing session on healthy eating topics. The flow and retention of the study participants were shown in Fig. 1. Data entry and statistical analyses were performed using IBM Statistical Package for the Social Sciences version 22.0 (SPSS 22.0). Normal distribution of data was evaluated based on histogram pattern and Kolmogorov-Smirnov test value. A repeated measure ($2 \times 2 \times 2$) analysis of variance (RMANOVA) was used to analyze the effect of the intervention within each group based on time. $P < 0.05$ indicates statistical significance.

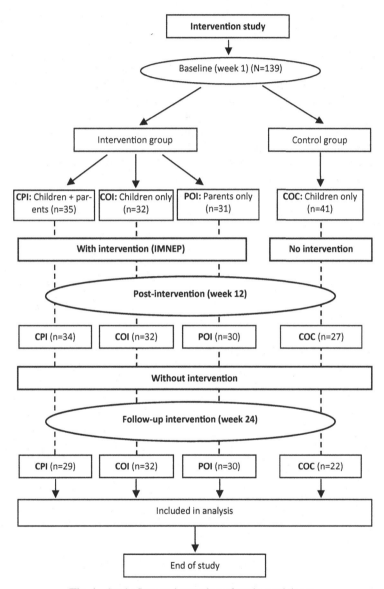

Fig. 1. Study flow and retention of study participant.

3 Findings

3.1 General Characteristics

A total of 2986 Year 5 primary students were screened for obesity status. One hundred and thirty-nine students were finally recruited for the randomized controlled trial. 16.5% and 83.5% of them was in overweight and obese categories based on the BMI z-scores. Most of the children came from families with low household income category [13]. Majority of the parents work either in private or government sectors in Kota Bharu with 48.9% of their children having regular breakfast every day (n = 68). The detailed description on the week 1 characteristics of the participants have been published elsewhere [10]. Out of 139 respondents enrolled at the baseline (week 1), 121 (87.1%) finished the 12-week IMNEP program and 113 (79.1%) completed the whole 24-week intervention trial, with a 20.9% dropout rate - Fig. 1. The remaining 27 students (20.9%) did not submit complete end-line data due to being moved to other schools, being away from school throughout the intervention period and follow-up (2 times consecutively) or refusing to participate due to a busy school schedule.

Table 1. Comparison of obesity outcomes within each group based on time (n = 113).

Measure	Week	CPI (n = 29)	COI (n = 32)	POI (n = 30)	COC (n = 22)
		MD (95% CI) p value	MD (95% CI) p value	MD (95% CI) p value	MD (95% CI) p value
BW (kg)	1–12	0.36 (−0.04, 0.76) 0.094	−0.30 (−0.81, 0.21) 0.439	−0.89 (−1.58, −0.21) 0.007	−0.18 (−0.49, 0.12) 0.411
	12–24	−2.23 (−3.67, −0.79) 0.001	−3.28 (−4.31, −2.24) <0.001	−2.12 (−2.79, −1.45) <0.001	−0.53 (−0.86, −0.20) 0.001
	1–24	−1.87 (−3.38, −0.36) 0.012	−3.58 (−4.73, −2.43) <0.001	−3.01 (−4.13, −1.89) <0.001	−0.71 (−1.13, −0.29) 0.001
BMI	1–12	0.71 (0.37, 1.05) <0.001	0.10 (−0.31, 0.52) >0.950	0.54 (0.13, 0.95) 0.007	−0.05 (−0.25, 0.16) >0.950
	12–24	−0.14 (−0.66, 0.38) >0.950	−0.17 (−0.70, 0.36) >0.950	+0.30 (−0.69, 0.09) 0.187	0.17 (−0.08, 0.42) 0.170

(continued)

Table 1. (*continued*)

Measure	Week	CPI (n = 29)	COI (n = 32)	POI (n = 30)	COC (n = 22)
		MD (95% CI) p value	MD (95% CI) p value	MD (95% CI) p value	MD (95% CI) p value
	1–24	0.57 (−0.15, 1.30) 0.162	−0.07 (−0.65, 0.51) >0.950	0.24 (−0.41, 0.89) >0.950	0.12 (−0.02, 0.27) 0.123
FM (kg)	1–12	0.58 (−0.58, 1.75) 0.636	0.57 (−0.59, 1.73) 0.674	0.85 (0.04, 1.65) 0.037	−0.09 (−0.24, 0.06) 0.369
	12–24	−1.22 (−2.89, 0.44) 0.214	−0.69 (−2.01, 0.62) 0.572	−0.67 (−2.00, 0.67) 0.646	−0.31 (−0.44, −0.17) <0.001
	1–24	−0.64 (−2.52, 1.24) >0.950	−0.13 (−1.72, 1.47) >0.950	0.18 (−1.45, 1.81) >0.950	−0.40 (−0.64, −0.16) 0.001
Waist (cm)	1–12	0.64 (−0.66, 1.94) 0.666	0.26 (−1.63, 2.15) >0.950	1.69 (0.32, 3.05) 0.012	−0.24 (−0.59, 0.12) 0.288
	12–24	−4.12 (−5.72, −2.52) <0.001	−0.98 (−2.84, 0.87) 0.563	−2.24 (−3.62, −0.87) 0.001	−0.68 (−0.85, −0.50) <0.001
	1–24	−3.48 (−5.65, −1.32) 0.001	−0.72 (−2.53, 1.08) 0.949	−0.56 (−2.36, 1.25) >0.950	−0.91 (−1.31, −0.52) <0.001
Hip (cm)	1–12	−0.26 (−1.53, 1.02) >0.950	1.40 (−0.16, 2.95) 0.090	2.16 (1.25, 3.08) <0.001	−0.29 (−0.61, 0.03) 0.090
	12–24	−1.10 (−2.85, 0.64) 0.354	−0.97 (−2.49, 0.56) 0.354	−2.79 (−3.98, −1.61) <0.001	−1.25 (−1.61, −0.90) <0.001
	1–24	−1.36 (−3.01, 0.29) 0.134	0.43 (−1.18, 2.04) >0.950	−0.63 (−1.92, 0.65) 0.665	−1.54 (−1.98, −1.10) <0.001

3.2 Effect of IMNEP on Obesity Outcomes

Body Weight (BW). The body weight of the group CPI declined from week 1 to week 12 (MD = 0.36, 95% CI: −0.04, 0.76) before increasing significantly following the intervention (week 12–24) (MD = −2.23, 95% CI: −3.67, −0.79). The other groups steadily gained weight throughout trial (MD = −1.87, 95% CI: −3.38, −0.36). The estimated marginal means plot of body weight throughout trial is shown in Fig. 2(a).

BMI. Based on time, there was a significant difference in mean BMI within each group (F = 11.37, p 0.001). Table 1 shows that only during the intervention period (week 1–12) did respondents in groups CPI (MD = 0.71, 95% CI = 0.37, 1.05) and POI (MD = 0.54, 95% CI = 0.13, 0.95) experience a decrease in BMI (p 0.05). Figure 2(b) shows it clearly in a profile plot.

Fat Mass (FM). Based on time, there was a significant difference in mean fat mass within each group (F = 6.88, p = 0.002). Only during baseline and week 12 (MD = 0.85, 95% CI = 0.04, 1.65; p = 0.037) did POI participants recorded fat mass reductions. Respondents in the COC control group (MD = −0.40, 95% CI = −0.64, −0.16; p = 0.001), on the other hand, experienced fat mass increases from baseline to the end of the study – Table 1 and Fig. 2(c).

Waist and Hip Circumference. There were significant variations in the mean waist (F = 21.49, p < 0.001) and hip (F = 15.48, p < 0.001) circumferences within each group based on time, according to the multivariate test results. Result shows that throughout the intervention period, the waist circumference of the intervention group reduced insignificantly in POI and COI, but significant reduction was observed in CPI (MD = 3.48, 95% CI = −5.65, −1.32) as compared to the control group. In regard to the hip circumference, POI shown a dramatic reduction throughout the intervention (week 1–12) but increased significantly following the intervention period until the completion of the trial (week 12–24), as shown in Table 1, Fig. 2(d) and (e).

4 Discussion

4.1 Impact of IMNEP on Obesity Outcomes

The RMANOVA findings indicated that the IMNEP resulted in significant improvement of BMI among participants in CPI (0.71 kg/m^2 week1–week 12) and POI (0.54 kg/m^2 week 1–week 12) groups; body fat among participants in POI (0.85 kg week 1–week 12) group; and hip circumference among participants in POI (2.16 cm week 1–week 12) group in comparison to the children in COI and COC (without intervention) groups. Active participation from both children and parents could be the reason for the improvement in anthropometric parameters for all groups except COI and COC.

Additionally, waist circumference, which is a highly predictive cardiovascular risk factor [14] reduced significantly (1.69 cm) among participants in POI group during the intervention period (week 1 to week 12). The effect of IMNEP intervention on BMI was rather smaller for COI group than the CPI group, showing the parents' participation was

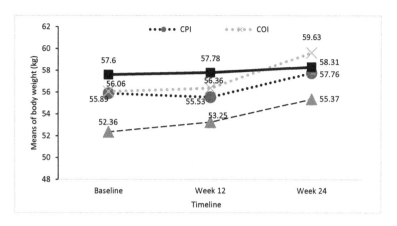

(a) Changes in body weight (kg)

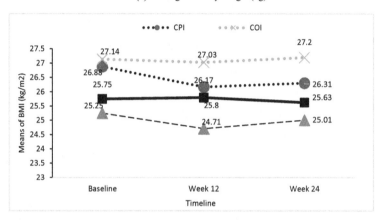

(b) Changes in BMI (kg/m²)

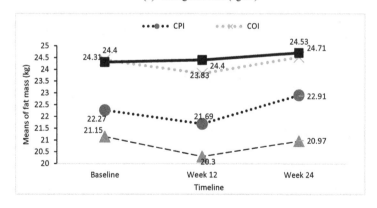

(c) Changes in fat mass (g)

Fig. 2. Estimated marginal means plot

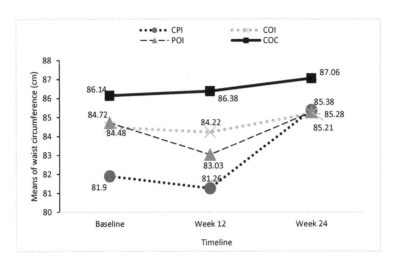

(d) Changes in Waist Circumference (cm)

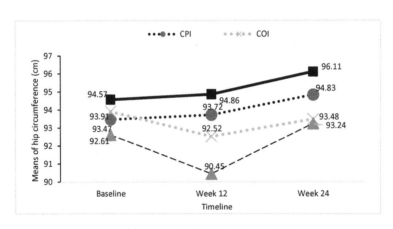

(e) Changes in Hip Circumference (cm)

Fig. 2. continued

notably effective in slowing the rate of undesirable weight gain to promote the growth of healthy children [15]. As regards to the time-interaction effect, the profile plot showed that participants in the CPI group experienced a significant decrement of body weight, BMI, fat mass and waist circumference within 12 weeks of the intervention period. Participants in the COI and POI groups portrayed similar reduction pattern except for body weight outcome. A previous study also showed that intervention targeting both parents and children as represented by the CPI group in this study is more effective than intervention focusing only children or without target specified in the treatment of intervention program [16].

Other than that, establishing a well-designed nutrition education program with consistent positive effects on anthropometric measurements is of great public health importance [17]. A multicomponent intervention study which involved modification in dietary intake, increase in physical activity, classroom curriculum focused on healthy eating and lifestyle and family-involvement program was carried out among American Indian school children over three consecutive years [18]. However, this study found no significant reduction in BMI and body fat of the children. This was due to no target was specified for excess body weight participants and the study included all the children at the school. Thus, it is evident that setting up a target population is crucial for significant study outcomes besides designing a well-planned intervention.

In contrast, the body weight increased significantly among participants in the POI within-group analysis from week 1 to week 12 and continuous increment of body weight was observed for all groups including control group from week 12 to week 24. However, participants in the CPI group showed an insignificant decrement in body weight during the intervention period (week 1 to week 12). Another study stated that children grow according to the third percentile with an average height of 5.1–6 cm per year and body weight of 2.5 kg per year until the onset of puberty [19]. Other possible reason could be the limited time available for the intervention (12 weeks). Thus, it was difficult to observe the changes as a reasonable timeline for 5% to 10% weight loss of overweight individuals is between three to six months, with a safe weight loss of 0.5 to 1 kg per week [20].

The findings from this study suggest that parents are highly concern about their children's health. Many previous studies reported a significant reduction in body weight among obese children as affected by healthy eating behavior, increased physical activity, and improved parent-youth relationship [21–24]. Parents play a vital role in nourishing their children with healthy and good quality foods [25]. Parents who are concerned about their children's weight and the associated negative health consequences due to overweight should adopt child-feeding practices [26]. A high BMI during childhood has been associated with coronary heart disease in adulthood [27]. Therefore, parent participation in any interventions could pose positive effects on both parents and their children and results from intervention studies should be considered by relevant authorities for larger-scale nutrition-related educational program implementation for a specific community.

Other positive change noted include the decrease in the number of obese children towards the end of this study. The number of obese children in POI group reduced from 26 to 20 at week 12, whereas the number of overweight children reduced from 10 to

7 at week 24 for intervention groups as compared to control group. The reduction in the number of obese and overweight children was consistent with the reduction in fat mass (total mean change $= 0.79$ kg) after 12 weeks of intervention which was coherent with findings by Gortmaker et al. [28]. The intervention by the authors over two school years focused on decreasing television viewing time, decreasing consumption of high-fat foods, increasing fruits and vegetables intake, and increasing moderate and vigorous physical activity. Previous research also showed an insignificant reduction in the number of overweight and obese participants below the 1-year duration of the intervention [29, 30]. It is difficult to expect a behavioral change in a short time and in an environment which promotes a sedentary lifestyle [31].

5   Conclusion

The findings from the present intervention study propose the use of Interactive Multimedia Nutrition Education package which include explainer video and game-based strategy to improve the anthropometric status, nutrition knowledge, and enhance children's physical activity. Implementation of such intervention that targets both children and their parents should be encouraged to reduce the alarming rate of obesity cases among children.

Acknowledgement. The authors wish to thank Universiti Sains Malaysia for the support it has extended in the completion of the present research through University Short Term Grant No.: 304/PKOMP/6315321.

References

1. Institute for Public Health: National Health and Morbidity Survey 2019. Non-communicable diseases, healthcare demand, and health literacy: key findings (2020)
2. Roszanadia, R., Norazmir, M.N.: Knowledge, attitude and practice on healthy eating among special needs boarding school students. Int. J. Dairy Sci. **6**, 1–9 (2011)
3. Branscum, P., Sharma, M., Wang, L.L., Wilson, B.R., Rojas-Guyler, L.: A true challenge for any superhero: an evaluation of a comic book obesity prevention program. Fam. Community Health **36**(1), 63–76 (2013)
4. Amresh, A., Sinha, M., Birr, R., Salla, R.: Interactive cause and effect comic-book storytelling for improving nutrition outcomes in children. In: Proceedings of the 5th International Conference on Digital Health 2015, pp. 9–14 (2015, May)
5. Tarver, T., Woodson, D., Fechter, N., Vanchiere, J., Olmstadt, W., Tudor, C.: A novel tool for health literacy: using comic books to combat childhood obesity. J. Hosp. Librariansh. **16**(2), 152–159 (2016)
6. Leung, M.M., Mateo, K.F., Verdaguer, S., Wyka, K.: Testing a web-based interactive comic tool to decrease obesity risk among minority preadolescents: protocol for a pilot randomized control trial. JMIR Res. Protoc. **7**(11), e10682 (2018)
7. Thompson, D.: Designing serious video games for health behavior change: current status and future directions. J. Diabetes Sci. Technol. **6**(4), 807–811 (2012)
8. Kim, S.H., Hyun, T.S.: Evaluation of a nutrition education website for children. Korean J. Community Nutr. **11**, 218–228 (2006)

9. Matheson, D., Achterberg, C.: Ecologic study of children's use of a computer nutrition education program. J. Nutr. Educ. **33**, 2–9 (2001)
10. Dali, E.W., Putri, W., Mohamed, H.J.J., Yusoff, H.: Development and evaluation of interactive multimedia-based nutrition education package (IMNEP) to promote healthy diet for overweight and obese children. Health **8**, 124–148 (2017)
11. Dali, E.W., Putri, W., Mohamed, H.J.J., Yusoff, H.: Nutrition knowledge, attitude and practices (NKAP) and health-related quality of life (HRQOL) status among overweight and obese children: an analysis of baseline data from the Interactive Multimedia-based Nutrition Education Package (IMNEP) Study. Malays. J. Nutr. **23**(1), 17–29 (2017)
12. Dali, E.W., Putri, W., Mohamed, H.J.J., Yusoff, H.: Nutrient intakes status and physical inactivity among overweight and obese school children in Kota Bharu, Kelantan Malaysia. Iran. J. Public Health **47**(8), 1098–1107 (2018)
13. Department of Statistics Malaysia: Household income & basic amenities survey report 2019, Kuala Lumpur (2019). https://www.dosm.gov.my/v1/index.php?r=column/ctheme ByCat&cat=120&bul_id=TU00TmRhQ1N5TUxHVWN0T2VjbXJYZz09&menu_id=amV oWU54UTl0a21NWmdhMjFMMWcyZz09
14. Reinehr, T., Wunsch, R.: Relationships between cardiovascular risk profile, ultrasonographic measurement of intra-abdominal adipose tissue, and waist circumference in obese children. Clin. Nutr. **29**, 24–30 (2010)
15. Maddison, R., Foley, L., Mhurchu, C.N., Jiang, Y., Jull, A., Prapavessis, H., et al.: Effects of active video games on body composition: a randomized controlled trial. Am. J. Clin. Nutr. **94**, 1–8 (2011)
16. Epstein, L.H., Gordy, C.C., Raynor, H.A., Beddome, M., Kilanowski, C.K., Paluch, R.: Increasing fruit and vegetable intake and decreasing fat and sugar intake in families at risk for childhood obesity. Obes. Res. **9**(3), 171–178 (2001)
17. Kriemler, S., et al.: Effect of school based physical activity programme (KISS) on fitness and adiposity in primary schoolchildren: cluster randomised controlled trial. BMJ **340**, c785 (2010)
18. Caballero, B., Clay, T., Davis, S.M., Ethelbah, B., Rock, B.H., Lohman, T., et al.: Pathways: a school-based, randomized controlled trial for the prevention of obesity in American Indian schoolchildren. Am. J. Clin. Nutr. **78**, 1030–1038 (2003)
19. Rogol, A.D., Clark, P.A., Roemmmich, J.N.: Growth and pubertal development in children and adolescents: effects of diet and physical activity. Am. J. Clin. Nutr. **72**, 521–528 (2000)
20. National Coordinating Committee on Food and Nutrition (NCCFN): Recommended Nutrient intakes for Malaysia. A report of the technical working group on National Coordinating Committee on Food and Nutrition, Ministry of Health Malaysia, Putrajaya (2005)
21. Golan, M., Kaufman, V., Shahar, D.R.: Childhood obesity treatment: targeting parents exclusively v. parents and children. Br. J. Nutr. **95**(5), 1008–1015 (2006)
22. West, F., Sanders, M., Cleghorn, G.J., Davies, P.S.: Randomized clinical trial of a family-based lifestyle intervention for childhood obesity involving parents as the exclusive agents of change. Behav. Res. Ther. **48**(12), 1170e9 (2010)
23. Van Ryzin, M.J., Nowicka, P.: Direct and indirect effects of a family-based intervention in early adolescence on parent-youth relationship quality, late adolescent health and early adult obesity. J. Fam. Psychol. **27**(1), 106–116 (2013)
24. Kim, H.S., Park, J., Park, K.Y., Lee, M.N., Ham, O.K.: Parent involvement intervention in developing weight management skills for both parents and overweight/obese children. Asian Nurs. Res. **10**, 11–17 (2016)
25. Stang, J., Loth, K.A.: Parenting style and child feeding practices: potential mitigating factors in the etiology of childhood obesity. J. Am. Diet. Assoc. **111**(9), 1301–1305 (2011)

26. Birch, L.L., Davidson, K.K.: Family environmental factors influencing the developing behavioral controls of food intake and childhood overweight. Pediatr. Clin. North Am. **48**, 893–907 (2001)
27. Baker, J.L., Olse, L.W., Soensen, T.I.: Childhood body mass index and the risk of coronary heart disease in adulthood. N. Engl. J. Med. **357**, 2329–2337 (2007)
28. Gortmaker, S.L., Peterson, K., Wiecha, J., Sobol, A.M., Dixit, S., Fox, M.K., et al.: Reducing obesity via a school-based interdisciplinary intervention among youth. Arch. Pediatr. Adolesc. Med. **153**, 409–418 (2009)
29. Warren, J.M., Henry, C.J.K., Lighttowler, H.J., Bradshaw, S.M., Perwaiz, S.: Evaluation of a pilot school programme aimed at the prevention of obesity in children. Health Promot. Int. **18**(4), 287–296 (2003)
30. Sichieri, R., Trotte, A.P., de Souza, R.A., Veiga, G.V.: School randomized trial on prevention of excessive weight gain by discouraging students from drinking sodas. Public Health Nutr. **12**(2), 197–202 (2008)
31. Swinburn, B., Egger, G.: Preventive strategies against weight gain and obesity. Obes. Rev. **3**(4), 289–301 (2002)

Evidence-Based of Improved Electron Tomogram Segmentation and Visualization Through High-Pass Domain Kernel in Bilateral Filter

Nur Intan Raihana Ruhaiyem$^{(\boxtimes)}$ (iD) and Noor Shariah Ismail

School of Computer Sciences, Universiti Sains Malaysia, Main Campus, Penang 11800 Gelugor, Malaysia
intanraihana@usm.my

Abstract. Segmentation is the most challenging task in image processing. To date, there is still no superior method can segment all types of images either in 2D or 3D. A popular technique: bilateral filter, a non-linear method used to efficiently eliminate noise while preserving object's edges, has two parameters: domain and range kernel, and widely used for medical image segmentation. Unlike medical images, noise on electron tomogram, are diverse in terms of its density and intensity. Therefore, this research proposed a modification on the two kernels: the existing Gaussian domain kernel replaced by Sobel and Canny edge detector to improve the edge detector element and the existing Gaussian range kernel replaced by an inverted Gaussian kernel serves to highlight different regions. The results of bilateral filter using Canny as the high-pass domain kernel show efficient detection accordingly as the pixel intensity changes, in comparison to the results of Sobel as domain kernel, and to the techniques engaging filter along: Sobel and Canny edge detectors.

Keywords: Bilateral filter · Electron tomogram segmentation · Gaussian filter · High-pass domain kernel · Sobel edge detector · Canny edge detector

1 Introduction

Segmentation is one of the most used processes in image processing, particularly in the medical world. The goal of segmentation is to simplify or change the representation of an image into something that is more meaningful and easier to analyze. If the edges of images are identified correctly, the overall objects can be placed proficiently, and performance can be calculated smoothly. In the medical world, edge detection is a significant task for object gratitude of the human organ, and it is a vital to have pre-processing stage in medical image segmentation and 3D reconstruction [1]. Intensities level are change along the edges. Detection of image edges plays an important role in medical image processing, segmentation, and computer vision application. Finding the boundaries of objects within images is known as edge detection. It is also used to detect

© Springer Nature Switzerland AG 2021
H. Badioze Zaman et al. (Eds.): IVIC 2021, LNCS 13051, pp. 163–170, 2021.
https://doi.org/10.1007/978-3-030-90235-3_14

discontinuities of image brightness. Common edge detection algorithms include Sobel, Canny, Prewitt, Roberts, and fuzzy logic methods.

For many years, full attention is given to develop robust edge detection algorithms. Derivatives technique is the popular approach for edge detection. Gradient-based methods and Laplacian-based methods are two alternatives of derivative-based methods. It is important to note that detection solely specifies that an edge is present near a pixel in an image but does not essentially deliver a precise estimation of the edge location or orientation. The errors in edge detection are usually caused by misclassification: false edges and missing edges. The errors in edge estimation are modelled by probability distributions for the location and orientation estimates. A bilateral filter is a non-linear, edge preserving and noise-reduction smoothing filter for images. This filter is one of the best edge detectors that is widely used for tracing medical images. The intensity value at each pixel in an image is replaced by a weighted average of intensity values from nearby pixels. The weights depend on the spatial distance and the strength of the pixels. It depends only on two parameters to specify the size and differentiate the features to preserve. This weight is based on a Gaussian distribution, preserves edges while eliminates noise.

2 Background and Related Work

Edge provides a very important role in many image processing applications. Detected edges technique in the image are expected to symbolize object boundaries and applied to recognize these items [2]. Edges generally correspond to points in the image where the grey value moves expressively from one pixel to the next. Thus, in extracting the useful knowledge characteristics of the image where there are abrupt changes is supported by detecting edges. The edge detection technique is one of the structural methods of the image segmentation [3]. The edge detection treats the confinement of imperative varieties of a grey level image and the detection of the physical and geometrical properties of objects of the scene in image processing. It is an essential procedure detects and outlines of an object and boundaries among objects and the background in the image. Detecting significant discontinuities in intensity values is the most familiar approach for edge detection [4].

2.1 Sobel Operator Algorithm

Sobel is one of the well-known edge detectors, which it creates an image emphasizing edges. In theory at least, the operator consists of a pair of 3×3 convolution kernels as shown in Fig. 1. One kernel is simply the other rotated by $90°$.

One kernel for each of the two perpendicular orientations, these kernels are intended to react maximally to edges running vertically and horizontally with respect to the pixel grid. The kernels can be applied independently to the input image to deliver separate measurements of the gradient component in each orientation (call these Gx and Gy). These procedures can then be combined to look for the absolute gradient magnitude at each point and the gradient orientation. The gradient magnitude is given by:

$$|G| = \sqrt{Gx^2 + Gy^2} \tag{1}$$

-1	0	1
-2	0	2
-1	0	1

1	2	1
0	0	0
-1	-2	-1

Fig. 1. Sobel convolution kernels 3×3 dimensions [5]

where Gx is Gradient x and Gy is Gradient y.

Ordinarily, an approximate magnitude is figured using: $|G| = |Gx| + Gy|$ which is much faster to compute. Where Gx is Gradient x and Gy is Gradient y.

Pseudocode for Sobel Edge Detection [5]:

```
Input: A sample image.
Output: Detected edges.
Step 1:  Accept the input image.
Step 2:  Mask Gx, Gy is applied to the input image.
Step 3:  Algorithm of Sobel edge detection is applied and
the gradient.
Step 4:  Masks manipulation of Gx, Gy separately on the
input image.
Step 5:  Results combined to find the absolute magnitude
of the gradient.
Step 6:  The absolute magnitude is the output edges.
```

2.2 Canny Operator Algorithm

Canny edge detection is the valuable structural information extraction from dissimilar vision objects and intensely decreases the amount of data to be processed. It has been broadly used in numerous computer vision systems. Canny has found that the necessities for the application of edge detection on various vision systems are comparatively similar. Therefore, the solution of edge detection to handle these requirements might be applied in a wide range of situations. The edge detection general criteria consist of; (a) the detection must precisely catch as many edges shown in the image as possible which equivalent to edge detection with low error rate, (b) the operator detects the edge point, so it should precisely localize on the edge entre, and (c) image noise should not generate false edges; the image edge should only be marked once. The optimal function in Canny detector can be approached by the first derivative of a Gaussian by defining the total of four exponential terms. It became one of the most popular algorithms for edge detection due to optimality to meet with the over three criteria for edge detection and the straightforwardness of process for execution. The process of Canny edge detection algorithm consists of five steps [6]:

```
Step 1: A Gaussian filter is used to smooth the image to
remove noise in an image
Step 2: Compute the intensity gradients of the image
Step 3: Get free of false edge detection by applying non-
maximum suppression
Step 4: Determine potential edges by applying double
threshold
Step 5: Track edge by hysteresis: Suppressing all the
other edges that are weak and not connected to strong
edges to finalize all the edge detection.
```

2.3   The Bilateral Filter Segmentation for Cellular Tomography Approaches

Allner et al. developed a novel generalized 3D bilateral filter, where the reduction and phase images created with filtered back-projection renovation from grating based phase-contrast tomography. This image-based denoising algorithm feats additional information and noise statistics from multi-modal images [7]. This filter has successfully enhanced noise reduction and improved the preservation of edges in the images compared to established bilateral filters [7]. More sophisticated segmentation method such as by integrating the edge information with noise decrease reconstruction images. Quantitative evaluations of noise reduction and segmentation performance are conducted using simulated and real electron tomography datasets [8].

3   Methodology

3.1   Bilateral Edge Detection Filter

In bilateral filter edge detection, there are two important parameters; (1) domain kernel standard deviation (σd) smooths the large features and blurs the detailed textures upon increasing, (2) range kernel standard deviation (σr) along with the weight (W). As the range component increases, it smoothens and widens, resulting in an increase in dynamic range of the image intensity, so it is very likely to fine the identification of intensity gradient present at the edges [9]. The response of the bilateral filter is the multiplication of its constituent domain and range kernel respectively. For a large spatial Gaussian multiplied with narrow range Gaussian achieves limited smoothing despite the large spatial extent. The range weight enforces a strict preservation of the gradient contours [9]. The evaluation has been made by comparison between the proposed method; the bilateral edge detection using Canny domain kernel and existing method; bilateral edge detection using Sobel domain kernel [10]. The next comparison is between the proposed method and Canny edge detector. Parameters for evaluation used in this research work are Mean Square Error (MSE) and Peak Signal to-Noise-Ratio (PSNR). The outcome then will be match with the existing edge detector.

3.2 Modified Domain Kernel

The process of smoothing an image while preserving the edges is called a non-linear method in bilateral filtering, contradict to bilateral edge detector. The bilateral filter of Gaussian domain kernel is converted to an edge detection filter, and Gaussian range kernel is converted to an inverted Gaussian kernel. The altered range kernel helps to highlight different regions. The resultant technique efficiently adjusts the detection filter accordingly as the pixel intensity changes. The idea of the proposed methodology by [10] is to highlight edges in images so that can select the domain and range kernels correctly. For achieving this objective, engaging functions of Gaussian as domain and range kernels is needed. Notice that the bilateral edge detector can be understood by appropriately choosing the range kernel as per the application of the domain kernel filtering. High frequency content in an image is suitable for edge that requires a domain kernel that performs derivative operation. In that case the existing edge detection technique, the range kernel that highlights different regions should be assigns weights changing directly as the pixel intensity difference.

A couple of domain and range kernel that contribute to sustain the above two conditions are the one engaging a high-pass domain kernel and an inverted Gaussian range kernel. The current bilateral filter algorithm from [11] needs some modification to make the bilateral edge detector work very well. Modification is needed for domain kernel and range kernel. A domain kernel needs changes because it performs the derivative operation that is required a high frequency content in an image to get the better impact of bilateral edge detector. Therefore, instead of employing Gaussian smoother as a low-pass domain kernel, they employed high-pass domain kernel, i.e., Sobel edge detection in their experiment together with inverted range kernel [10]. This inverted range kernel produced optimal outputs because it emphasizes different regions. In this work, electron tomograms were used, and thus, deploying high-pass domain kernel (i.e., Sobel and Canny to see the results) and inverted range kernel are most helpful in designing a bilateral edge detector for electron tomogram (Fig. 2).

4 Experimental Results

Based on the process flow of bilateral edge detector in Fig. 3, the comparison is done on the performance of the bilateral edge detection technique between Sobel as domain kernel, Canny as domain kernel, and between the original Sobel and Canny edge detector. In each case, the comparative analysis is made on two quantitative measurements, i.e., PSNR and MSE, based on the root MSE of the reconstructed image. All experiment was tested on *.jpeg* and *.bmp* image types. To test, the images of insulin granules from electron tomography dataset were used. Figure 4 shows the sample of experiment with the optimized parameters after tweaking, $\sigma d = 5$ and $\sigma r = 0.4$. Here, test also done on standard image and magnetic resonance imaging (MRI) besides electron tomography image data. Obviously, the values of PSNR and MSE are substantial from the Canny as domain kernel in bilateral filter for all three types of images. With a slightly different with Sobel as domain kernel, this proves that Canny has improved the results of segmentation and visualization of electron tomography particularly.

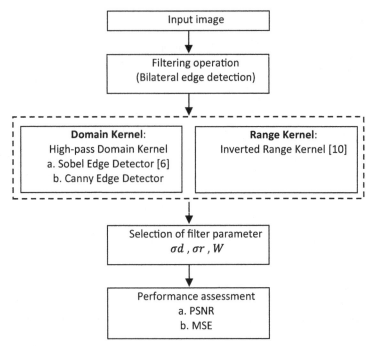

Fig. 2. The proposed process of segmentation using bilateral edge detection (the modified parameter highlighted in a dashed box)

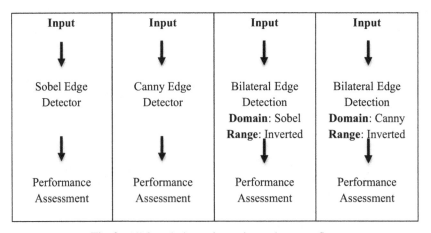

Fig. 3. All four designs of experimental process flow

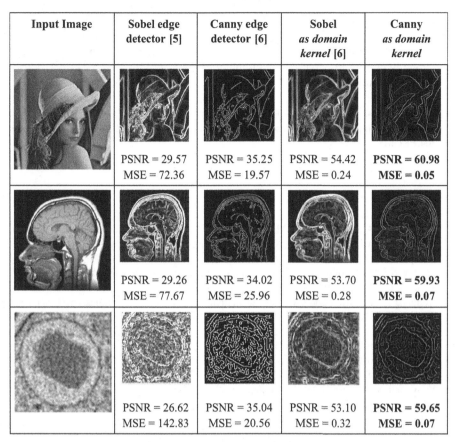

Input Image	Sobel edge detector [5]	Canny edge detector [6]	Sobel *as domain kernel* [6]	Canny *as domain kernel*
	PSNR = 29.57 MSE = 72.36	PSNR = 35.25 MSE = 19.57	PSNR = 54.42 MSE = 0.24	**PSNR = 60.98** **MSE = 0.05**
	PSNR = 29.26 MSE = 77.67	PSNR = 34.02 MSE = 25.96	PSNR = 53.70 MSE = 0.28	**PSNR = 59.93** **MSE = 0.07**
	PSNR = 26.62 MSE = 142.83	PSNR = 35.04 MSE = 20.56	PSNR = 53.10 MSE = 0.32	**PSNR = 59.65** **MSE = 0.07**

Fig. 4. Experiment results with $\sigma d = 5$, $\sigma r = 0.4$, and $W = 1$ for (top) standard image, (middle) magnetic resonance imaging (MRI) and (bottom) electron tomography of insulin granule

5 Conclusion and Future Work

In this research, the bilateral edge detector filter is presented with Sobel and Canny filter for noise removal. This bilateral edge detector is created with the combination of inverted gaussian range kernel and high-pass mask domain kernel and to help in smoothen and reduce noise in the image while enhancing edges and textures in the images. This research focuses on modifying the existing bilateral filtering parameter, domain kernel and range kernel to get better in preserving and highlighting edges and produced an improved segmentation results particularly for electron tomogram data. A proven robust bilateral edge detector can be intended by choosing a domain kernel that does a derivative operation, and a range kernel that adaptively emphasizes its high-pass impact at edges. The calculated PSNR and MSE values are promising in showing clear results for both segmentation and 2D visualization. For future enhancement, a test to evaluate 3D images of electron tomography data can be carried out, with the assistance of organelles morphologies identified in previous research [12]. It is believed that with this combination would provide prominent outcomes as the organelles' shapes are varies across its maturity levels [12]. Semi-automated process is still a popular option in image denoising particularly for electron microscopy data [13]. Significant diversion has also been done in current research on small-angle tomography [14] which can be another possibility for future work.

Acknowledgments. The authors wish to thank Universiti Sains Malaysia for the support it has extended in the completion of the present research through Short Term Grant University Grant No: 304/PKOMP/6315321.

References

1. Elaraby, A.E.A., El-Owny, H.B.M.A., Heshmat, M., Abdel Rady, A.S.: New algorithm for edge detection in medical images based on minimum cross entropy thresholding. Int. J. Comput. Sci. Issues **11**(2), 196–200 (2014)
2. Pandey, N.: Review of literature of image processing filters and fundamental steps. Int. J. Inf. Technol. Comput. Sci. Perspect. **4**(3), 1581–1591 (2014)
3. Kumar, J., Kumar, R., Reddy, V.: Review on image segmentation techniques. Int. J. Sci. Res. Eng. Technol. **26**(9), 1277–1294 (1993)
4. Muthukrishnan, R., Radha, M.: Edge detection techniques for image segmentation. Int. J. Comput. Sci. Inf. Technol. **3**(6), 259–267 (2011)
5. Gupta, S., Mazumdar, S.G.: Sobel edge detection algorithm. Int. J. Comput. Sci. Manage. Res. **2**(2), 1578–1583 (2013)
6. Vijayarani, S., Vinupriya, M.: Performance analysis of canny and sobel edge detection algorithms in image mining. Int. J. Innovative Res. Comput. Commun. Eng. **1**(8), 1760–1767 (2013)
7. Allner, S., et al.: Bilateral filtering using the full noise covariance matrix applied to x-ray phase-contrast computed tomography. Phys. Med. Biol. **61**(10), 3867–3856 (2016)
8. Yang, Q., Maier, A., Maass, N., Hornegger, J.: Edge-preserving bilateral filtering for images containing dense objects in CT. In: IEEE Nuclear Science Symposium Conference Record, pp. 0–4 (2013)
9. Pal, C., Chakrabarti, A., Ghosh, R.: A brief survey of recent edge-preserving smoothing algorithms on digital images. In: Science Direct Procedia Computer Science, pp. 1–40 (2015)
10. Jose, A., Chandra, S.S.: Bilateral edge detectors. In: Proceedings of the IEEE International Conference on Acoustics, Speech and Signal Processing, pp. 1449–1453. Vancouver, Canada (2013).
11. Kaur, H., Gupta, N.: Evaluating the efficiency of bilateral filter. Int. J. Eng. Res. Gen. Sci. **2**(5), 276–280 (2014)
12. Ruhaiyem, N.I.R., Mohamed, A.S.A., Belaton, B.: Optimized segmentation of cellular tomography through organelles' morphology and image features. J. Telecommun. Electron. Comput. Eng. **8**(3), 79–83 (2016)
13. Roels, J., et al.: An interactive ImageJ plugin for semi-automated image denoising in electron microscopy. Nat. Commun. **11**, 771 (2020)
14. Chang, J., Li, L., Abuellail, A., Soldatov, A., Soldatov, A., Kostina, M.: Bilateral filter for small-angle ultrasonic tomography using linear arrays. In: IEEE 22nd International Conference of Young Professionals in Electron Devices and Materials (EDM), pp. 247–250 (2021)

VR-Based Relaxation Therapy for Customer Service Staff: A Pilot Study

Nazrita Ibrahim[1,2]([✉]) [iD], Eze Manzura Mohd Mahidin[2], Azmi Mohd Yusof[2],
Mohd Ezanee Rusli[2], Nur Suria Iskandar[3], Farhah Amaliya Zaharuddin[3],
and Imran Mahalil[3]

[1] Institute of Informatics and Computing in Energy, Universiti Tenaga Nasional,
Kajang, Malaysia
nazrita@uniten.edu.my
[2] College of Computing and Informatics, Universiti Tenaga Nasional, Kajang, Malaysia
[3] UNITEN R&D Sdn Bhd, Kajang, Malaysia

Abstract. Customer service staff are the frontliners of any organisation. They act as the first stop centre for customer or client to report complaints or feedback. However, this job also comes with a stressful working condition. For this reason, XperionVR™, a Virtual Reality-based relaxation therapy system was developed with the intention of providing easy access for employees to manage their stress by practising relaxation techniques. This paper describes the evaluation of XperionVR™ conducted among the staff of a customer service unit of a large utility company. This pilot study aims to gather participants' perception of the effectiveness of each element in the therapy component of the VR-based relaxation therapy system in helping them to relax or reduce their stress level. The procedure involves participants going through the therapy session, and feedback on the experience was gathered using questionnaire, direct observation, and interview. Forty participants had voluntarily participated in the pilot study. Based on the result of the analysis, it could be observed that most participants felt that the system managed to make them feel more relaxed and reduce their stress level. However, two challenges observed were i) due to the nature of customer service staff who only have short break time, it is important for any VR-based relaxation therapy system to be designed with the ability to provide optimal therapy outcome within a short period of time and ii) the system should consist of a feature that can provide a quick demonstration for users with no experience of using a virtual reality system on how to navigate the system. Without the demonstration, users will have difficulty using the system, which in turn, will cause adverse effect to the overall therapy experience.

Keywords: VR-based relaxation therapy · VR-based therapy · VR-based stress therapy · Stress and workplace · Organisation wellbeing

1 Introduction

The stress level of individuals working in an organisation has become an important issue in organisational wellbeing. Many studies reported that excessive work stress causes

H. Badioze Zaman et al. (Eds.): IVIC 2021, LNCS 13051, pp. 171–183, 2021.
https://doi.org/10.1007/978-3-030-90235-3_15

negative impacts on individuals' mental and physical health as well as their wellbeing. A report released in 2019 by AIA Vitality as result of a survey conducted to understand how the workplace can affect employees' health, which relates the health of employees to their performance and engagement at work shows that Malaysian employees, consisting of mainly the working adults are overworked, stressed, and led unhealthy lifestyles [1]. This unbalanced work-life routine has basically contributed to the increment of mental health problems. Based on the survey, it is reported that among the main cause of mental health issues suffered by Malaysian workforce is overwork stress. Additionally, it is also reported that 51% of the employees suffer from at least one dimension of work-related stress mainly due to personal financial problem, long working hours and workplace bullying.

Another survey published by Statista Research Department in June 2019 also reported that the percentage of respondents experiencing mental health issues in Malaysia within the age range of 18 to 24 is much higher than those who are 55 years old and above [2]. This result shows that young adults are likely to struggle and adapt themselves to Malaysia's demanding working culture. Most of Malaysian employee starts to enter the workforce at the age of 18 to 24 years old, depending on their education level. A high number of young adults experiencing mental health problems indicate an early sign of our unhealthy working culture or the decline in our current generation's ability to deal with issues at workplace. This survey also reported that respondents with earnings of at least seven thousand Ringgit Malaysia (RM7000) per month are more likely to experience mental health issues. It is assumed that people with higher salaries are more likely to deal with complicated issues, which requires urgent and accurate decision-making processes. The quick and precise decision required put more pressure on these individuals.

The above statistics show an alarming sign for our society to be more aware and concerned about mental health-related issues. Therefore, it is imperative to address these issues among the Malaysian population in general and specifically among the Malaysian workforce before it is too late. Many studies reported that excessive work stress causes negative impact on individuals' mental and physical health [3]. Consequently, work stress is observed to cause health problems like cardiovascular diseases [4], musculoskeletal pain [5], depression [6] and cancer [7]. It has also been identified that work stress among workers have negative implication on their work performance, including high rate of absenteeism [8], inefficient work performance, and decreased work performance and motivation [9].

A new method for relaxation therapy that leverages the strength of Virtual Reality (VR) in reducing stress levels is being proposed. The fully immersive technology-based VR devices enable users to feel the virtual environment realistically. The usage of the Head-Mounted Displays (HMD) offers a fully immersive virtual reality experience. In VR technology, the virtual environment responds to the user's actions. Once equipped with HMD, a user is virtually isolated from the real-world surroundings; which hence, will help users to stay focused on the therapy and yield a better therapy outcome. At the minimum, the solution is to help those experiencing mild to moderate levels of mental health-related issues. The solution is not to replace mental health experts or mental healthcare support systems but to complement these existing services. Many studies on virtual reality technology in the field of psychology have yielded promising results, where its benefits outweigh its disadvantages [10, 11] There is a growing research supporting the efficacy of Virtual Reality based treatment for stress and anxiety [12, 13], including the use of VR based relaxation therapy in workplace [14–16]. However, studies to evaluate VR based relaxation therapy with participants coming from customer service unit in an organisation (other than the healthcare field) is quite limited.

Therefore, this paper presents a pilot study conducted on real users who work in a busy customer service unit of a large utility company. The objective of the study is to gather the participants' perceptions of the effectiveness of each element in the therapy component of the VR-based therapy system in helping them relax or reduce their stress level. Apart from the effectiveness of therapy outcome, the pilot study also aims to observe the proposed system setup in real working environment and the real user approach to the solution.

2 XperionVR™

Along with the idea of providing easy access for workers to manage their stress by practising relaxation techniques, the project team has developed a VR-based relaxation therapy system named XperionVR™. The development of the VR-based relaxation therapy system has started since 2018. Each of the components of the VR-based relaxation therapy system and the elements associated with the components were carefully designed based on literature and few iterations of prototype development-evaluation-refinement cycles. In each cycle, the prototype was evaluated by a group of users and further refinements were made in the next iteration cycle, either incorporating new elements or refining existing elements to address issues and shortcoming observed during the user evaluation stage. Our past works can be found from the following publications [17–21].

XperionVR™ was designed to provide mental and emotional relaxation therapy for users while also helping them to regulate positive emotions within a minimal duration. Using stand-alone virtual reality head-mounted display (HMD), the application can be used by users anytime and anywhere. XperionVR™ provides two types of therapy scene option: 3D virtual environment and high quality 360° video. Each type of therapy scene option includes four types of audio: enchanting background music, soothing sound of nature, zikr and meditational recitative. The zikr provided were from a well-known Malaysian local artist, Hafiz Hamidun, while the writing of the meditational recitatives was supervised by a clinical psychologist. XperionVR™ also provide users with two language options: English and Bahasa Melayu. The 3D virtual environment scene option also includes relaxing games. The objective of the games is to distract the users from thinking about their problem for a while. However, the games are made optional since not all users would like to play games while going through the relaxation therapy. The duration of the therapy session for 3D environment scene and 360° video scene are 10 min and 5 min respectively. XperionVR™ also provides a before and after mind-framing session to the users. This mind-framing session is important as it prepares the mind of the users for the transitional stage, from the real world to the virtual world (mind-framing before the therapy session) and from the virtual world back to the real world (mind-framing at the end of the therapy session). During a therapy session, relevant data were captured and submitted to the XperionVR™ database for analytics purposes. Figure 1 shows the snapshot of some of the 3D environments available in XperionVR™.

Fig. 1. Snapshots of 3D environments in XperionVR™

3   Procedure

The project team has conducted a pilot study to evaluate the effectiveness of XperionVR's system among the staff members of a customer service unit of a utility company. Since the utility company is a big corporation, the customer service unit is constantly busy with customer calls, putting the employees under constant pressure and stress. The customer service unit employees are usually given two 15 min break and a one-hour break during their work shift. The pilot study was carried out from 14th April until 5th May 2021. The original plan was to carry out the pilot study for three months. However, due to the rising cases of Covid-19, the unforeseen event of movement control order and further lockdown issued by the Government of Malaysia has halted the evaluation study.

This pilot study aimed to promote awareness of XperionVR™ system and gather feedback on the effectiveness of the system through surveys. More than forty (40) participants tried the system. However, only 40 participants answered the provided survey since not all users have the luxury of time to answer the survey due to insufficient break time and workload.

The system was placed in a small room dedicated to function as a 'therapy room' to avoid unnecessary interruptions (shown in Fig. 2). A 360° rotatable chair with wheel was provided to allow the participants to enjoy the 360° viewing experience while sitting on the chair. Participants were encouraged to sit during the therapy session to maximise the therapy outcome. However, the participants were also free to go through the therapy session while standing.

Participation in the survey were on voluntary basis. The participants were welcome to come to the therapy room at any time of the day. However, most of the participants visited the therapy room during their break time. Although instructions on how to use the system were provided in the therapy room, almost all participants did not read through the instruction. Instead, they preferred a quick demonstration to be given to them. To accommodate to this, our team member would provide a quick demonstration on how to use the VR controller and a brief explanation on how to navigate the system. The participants were then left to enjoy the therapy session by themselves. The session for

3D virtual environment option lasted for 10 min, while the 360° video option, lasted for 5 min. All participants completed the full session, i.e., none of them stop in the middle of viewing the session. Upon the completion of the therapy session, the participants were asked to fill in a set of questionnaires.

Fig. 2. Room setting for XperionVR™ pilot study

The questionnaire aimed to gather data on the usability and effectiveness of XperionVR™ as a relaxation tool. There were 15 questions included which consists of a combination of closed-ended and open-ended questions. However, there were also six questions on the selection preferences of participants on the system options, such as language preference, type of virtual environment, audio preference and type of games played, which will not be discussed in this paper. The rest of the questions aimed to gather participants' perception of the effectiveness of each element in the therapy component and the overall effectiveness of the solution in helping them to relax or reduce their stress level. Table 1 shows the questions included in the questionnaire pertaining the demographics and system effectiveness as well as its objectives.

Two methods used in analysing the gathered data were descriptive analysis and qualitative analysis. Descriptive analysis was used to analyse the collected data from the closed-ended questions, while the qualitative analysis method was utilised to interpret collected data from the open-ended question.

4   Results and Discussion

4.1   Demographics Information and Frequency of Use

This section describes demographics data and captures the frequency of use among the participants. Based on the analysis, 26 male (65%) and 14 female (35%) participated in this evaluation. Twenty-eight (28) participants (75.7%) were in the age range between 18 to 30 years old. Seven (7) participants (18.9%) were between the age range of 31 to 40 years old, and another 2 participants (5.4%) were between 41 to 50 years old. A question on the system usage frequency was also included in the questionnaire. Since the participants were free to use the system voluntarily, some participants used the system repeatedly during the three weeks of the evaluation period. Based on the analysis, 34 participants (85%) tried the system only once, while 6 participants (15%) tried the system more than once.

Table 1. Provided questions and objective of the questions

No	Question	Objective
1	Gender	To identify the participant's gender
2	Age range	To identify the participant's age group
3	Frequency of using XperionVR™	To identify the participant's XperionVR™ usage frequency
4	The system is easy to use	To identify the usability of the system
5	The therapy session helps me to feel relaxed	To identify the effectiveness of the system as a relaxation tool
6	The audio helps me to feel relaxed	To identify the effectiveness of the audio provided as a mean to induce relaxation
7	The 3D environment/360° video helps me to feel relaxed	To identify the effectiveness of the environment provided as a mean to induce relaxation
8	The provided games help me to feel relaxed	To identify the effectiveness of the games provided as a mean to induce relaxation
9	Overall, I am satisfied with the whole experience provided by XperionVR™	To identify the user satisfaction level with the therapy session provided through XperionVR™
10	On a scale of 1–10, how would you rate your overall experience with XperionVR™	To identify the overall experience provided by XperionVR™

4.2   Results on System Effectiveness

This section provides an overview and summary of the analysis for the system effectiveness questions. For each question, participants were asked to rate the answers using a 10-point Likert scale; 1 (Strongly disagree) to 10 (Strongly agree).

Perceived Usability of the System. It was required for participants to rate the system's usability based on how easy it is to operate the system. Based on the analysis done, 34 (85%) of the participants has agreed that it is easy to use the system (with the usability rating between 8 to 10). The result indicates that the system is easy to be used as a relaxation tool. Figure 3 shows the rating on the perceived usability of the system.

Perceived Effectiveness of the System as a Relaxation Alternative. The effectiveness of the system was rated based on how effective the system has assisted the participants in achieving their tranquil state. The analysis shows that most of the participants (33 or 82.5%) agreed that the system is effective in assisting them in the relaxation process (with an effectiveness rating of 8 to 10). The result indicates that the system is effective as a relaxation alternative. Figure 4 illustrated the perceived effectiveness level of the system.

Perceived Effectiveness of the Audio Selections Provided in Inducing Relaxation.
The system is equipped with four types of audios which are nature, zikr, meditation and

Fig. 3. Rating on the perceived usability of XperionVR™ for relaxation purposes

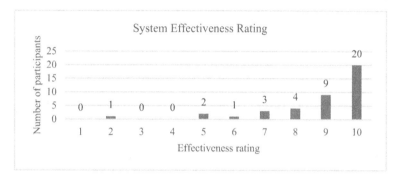

Fig. 4. Rating on the perceived effectiveness of XperionVR™ as a relaxation alternative

instrumental. The participants were free to choose their preferred audio for the therapy session. Therefore, to identify the effectiveness of the audio provided, the participants were required to rate on how helpful the audio in assisting them to relax. The result of the analysis shows that the audios included in the system are effective in inducing relaxation (30 participants or 75% with an effectiveness rating between 8 to 10). However, since many of the participants only used the system once, they might have accidently chosen unsuitable audio for their therapy session, which lead to some of them feeling that the audio was not as helpful in assisting them to relax. Figure 5 shows the rating on the perceived effectiveness of the audio.

Perceived Effectiveness on Environment Selections Provided in Inducing Relaxation. The system is equipped with two types of environments; 3D environment and 360° video. Each type has seven and six options, respectively. The participants were asked to rate the effectiveness of the environment in inducing relaxation. The analysis shows that the environment selections included in the system are effective in aiding the relaxation process (33 participants or 82.5% with an effectiveness rating between 8 to 10). However, there were one participant who rated 1 (strongly disagree) and 4 (somewhat disagree). The reasons given during the interview was that the person who rated 1 mentioned that he did not like the 3D cartoony look of the environment and prefer 360° video instead. Another person who rated 4 indicated that she felt a bit dizzy since it was

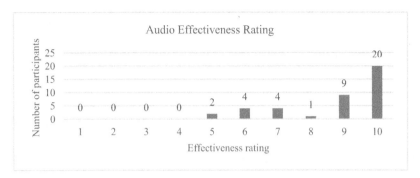

Fig. 5. Rating on the perceived effectiveness of audio selections in inducing relaxation

her first experience trying virtual reality application. Figure 6 illustrates the perceived effectiveness level of the system.

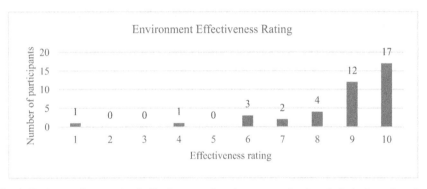

Fig. 6. Rating on the perceived effectiveness of environment selections in inducing relaxation.

Perceived Effectiveness of the Game Selections Provided in Inducing Relaxation. XperionVR™ offers several games to the users as an alternative interaction in the relaxation process. The participants were required to rate how useful the games were in assisting them to feel relax. The rating was used to identify the effectiveness of the games in aiding the relaxation process. However, there were three participants who did not give any rating to the question which may be due to the reason that they did not play any of the games. Despite that, the analysis shows that the game selections included in the system are effective in assisting the relaxation process with 29 of them give a high rate (with an effectiveness rating of 8 to 10). Figure 7 shows the rating on the perceived effectiveness of the game's selections.

User Satisfaction. The user satisfaction on the system is rated based on a 10-points Likert scale; 1 (Strongly disagree) to 10 (Strongly agree). The participants were required to rate the system based on how satisfied they feel with the system performance in assisting them to relax. Based on the analysis, the result shows that 34 (85%) participants

Fig. 7. Rating on the perceived effectiveness of games selections in inducing relaxation

were delighted with the performance of the system (with a satisfaction rating of 8 to 10). Figure 8 illustrates the perceived users' satisfaction level of the system.

Fig. 8. Rating on users' satisfaction towards XperionVR

User Overall Experience. The participants were requested to rate their overall experience with XperionVR™. The rating is based on a 10-points Likert scale; 1 (Worst) to 10 (Best). The analysis result shows that most of the participants (34 or 85%) had a good experience using the system (with an overall experience rating of 8 to 10). Figure 9 shows the rating for the overall users' experience with XperionVR™.

Based on the results, it can be concluded that the therapy experience provided by XperionVR™ is capable of assisting its users in achieving a relaxation state or reducing the stress level the users experienced before they undergo the therapy session. From 40 participants who had participated in this study, six participants (15%) have repeated the therapy session, indicating that the system is somehow useful to them, especially in assisting them to feel relaxed.

4.3   Participants' Feedbacks on the XperionVR System

The participants may provide any feedback, suggestions, and comments on their experience with XperionVR on the last question in the survey. The responses have been

Fig. 9. Rating for the overall users' experience with XperionVR

categorised into two; positive feedback and feedback for improvements. Eighteen (18) participants provided positive feedback, which directly shows that the system has successfully assisted them in the stress reduction and relaxation process. Among the feedbacks received that shows the good impact of the system on the participants were: *"it's a good trail for stress relieve"*, *"interesting and exciting"*, *"good idea"*, *"good. I like it. It may change mood for a while. Definitely helping"*, *"it was really relaxing and kinda (kind of) nice. Appreciating this effort and I'm doing this for my second time"*, *"good experience"*, *"helping a lot"*, and *"I'm trying this for my 3rd time and it's nice for relaxation. This time I've tried to select new 360 mode. The 360 mode is realistic"*.

Six participants provided suggestions for future improvement. Among the suggestions received were: *"can be improved – use video instead of animation"*, *"feel dizzy since this is my first time using the system. Guide not clear. Can be improved"*, *"improve the visual to be more real next time"*, and *"the 360 mode is realistic and would suggest if there is some movement can be done means would be better"*.

4.4 Observation Notes

Based on the observations made during the pilot test, several feedbacks on the system were received either through observing participants' actions or by interview. Generally, the spontaneous actions and comments received during or after the therapy session show that the participants were generally satisfied and happy with the system that acts as a relaxation alternative. Among the good feedback received were:

a. VR-based relaxation therapy is a good initiative since before this, the users need to go to other places like the nearby park to relax their minds.
b. The meditation audio is effective partly due to the voice of the actor used in the system, which most participants find as 'lovely'.
c. The immersive environments make the users feel that they are physically in it.
d. The games make users feeling excited.

Despite that, there were also a few negative aspects in terms of a technical and controlled environment that needed to be improved and should be considered for future enhancement. Among the observed comments were:

a. A chair without a headrest made the participants feel uncomfortable since they are not sitting in a comfortable position due to being unable to rest their heads while experiencing the therapy.
b. The HMD model used feels quite heavy when users wear it, especially when they tilt their heads.
c. Several first-time users are clueless on how to press enter, scroll and drag using the controller since they are new to VR technology, requiring some demonstration to be done before they use the system.

Another observation found is that for staff working in a customer service unit, their break time is limited and hence, they need to be able to utilise their break time effectively. For this reason, in order to make any VR-based relaxation therapy useful to the staff of any customer service unit, it is important to develop a system capable of delivering therapy outcomes within a short time. It was also observed that the first timers did not really know what to expect with VR. Some of them just sat still and looked straight ahead. Our team will observe the participants's behaviour, and in the case where participants behaved as such, the team members will gently inform them that they can turn their head, look around and even rotate the chair to enjoy the 360° viewing experience. Once they realised the effect of 360 viewing experience, most of the participants will start turning their head to look around, rotating the chair (because they are sitting so that rotating the chair will have the same effect as if they turn around full body) and even standing up to play the game. Some of the first-time users and those who were not familiar with virtual reality applications also tend to spend a considerable amount of time getting themselves familiar with how to use the VR controllers instead of enjoying the therapy session. However, once they got a grasp on how to use the controllers, they enjoyed the therapy experience. This scenario is something that every VR designer need to think about when designing VR application. A feature to offer a short training session on how to navigate or experience the virtual environment might be helpful. However, this feature must be made optional since users who are already familiar with VR would want to skip going through the training session.

The decision to place the therapy system in a dedicated therapy room seems to be a correct decision. The participants can truly enjoy the session without being interrupted. With the therapy room being located outside of their workspace area, the participants had the chance to take a break from the place which had caused them to be in a stressful state. By being away from their workspace area, their break time are not interrupted by friends or immediate manager, but instead, they get to enjoy an exclusive 'me time' by themselves. A few of the participants also asked for the door of the therapy room to be closed for privacy. This observation is important to suggest how the system should be set up in the real working environment.

5 Conclusion

Overall, this pilot study has successfully fulfilled the objective of getting feedback on the effectiveness of the solution as an alternative relaxation tool from the participants. Forty (40) participants have participated in the survey. Based on the results, most of the participants gave a high value rating on the usability and effectiveness of the system, user satisfaction level and user overall experience, indicating that the participants felt that the VR-based relaxation therapy has helped them to relax to a certain extent. The results suggested that VR-based relaxation therapy has the potential to be used as an alternative tool for stress management and relaxation for employee working under stressful condition, such as customer service unit.

However, the study had some limitation. Due to the limited time available for the participants, the survey can only be conducted very briefly to give the users more time to experience the therapy session. Hence, the questions that we asked only revolved around the usability and the effectiveness of the system in terms of helping the users to relax. It would be more helpful if questions on their stress level before and after using the system are also administered. For future evaluation, these items will be included in the evaluation procedure. Future plans include having the evaluation of VR-based therapy system effectiveness with different type of frontliners, such as those serving the customer directly (face-to-face encounter), general office worker, and different target group like the resident of senior home care. Additionally, the plan would also include conducting an evaluation on users who would be using the application repeatedly on a regular basis, in order to study the long-term effect of VR-based relaxation therapy to users.

Acknowledgement. The work reported in this article is funded by TNB Innovation and Commercialisation Fund (U-TE-PC-19-03). Special thanks to Tenaga Nasional Berhad for the funding opportunity and UNITEN R&D Sdn Bhd for assistance in fund management.

References

1. AIA Vitality: Media Release, Malaysian Workforce: Sleepless and Overworked ? Kuala Lumpur. https://healthiestworkplace.aia.com/www/assets/malaysia/eng/press-release-2019.pdf (2019, November). Accessed July 2021
2. Prevalence of mental health issues in Malaysia as of 26th June 2019, by demography, Statista Research Department. https://www.statista.com/statistics/1019587/malaysia-prevalence-of-mental-health-issues-by-demography/ (2019, June). Accessed July 2021
3. Seňová, A., Antošová, M.: Work stress as a worldwide problem in present time. Procedia Soc. Behav. Sci. **109**(2014), 312–316 (2014)
4. Chandola, T., Brunner, E., Marmot, M.: Chronic stress at work and the metabolic syndrome: prospective study. BMJ **332**, 521 (2006)
5. Marcatto, F., et al.: Work-related stress risk factors and health outcomes in public sector employees. Saf. Sci. **89**, 274–278 (2016)
6. Wang, J.: Work stress as a risk factor for major depressive episode (s). Psychol. Med. **35**(06), 865–871 (2005)
7. Blanc-Lapierre, A., Rousseau, M.-C., Weiss, D., El-Zein, M., Siemiatycki, J., Parent, M.-É.: Lifetime report of perceived stress at work and cancer among men: a case-control study in Montreal, Canada. Prev. Med. **96**(2017), 28–35 (2017)
8. Park, J.: Work Stress and Job Performance, Perspectives on Labour and Income. Statistic Canada, Ottawa (2007)

9. Siu, O.L.: Job stress and job performance among employees in Hong Kong: the role of Chinese work values and organisational commitment. Int. J. Psychol. **38**(6), 337–347 (2003). https://doi.org/10.1080/00207590344000024

10. Jerdan, S.W., Grindle, M., Van Woerden, H.C., Kamel Boulos, M.N.: Head-mounted virtual reality and mental health: critical review of current research. J. Med. Internet Res. **20**(7), 1–12 (2018). https://doi.org/10.2196/games.9226

11. Taneja, A., Vishal, S.B., Mahesh, V., Geethanjali, B.: Virtual reality based neuro-rehabilitation for mental stress reduction. In: 2017 Fourth International Conference on Signal Processing, Communication and Networking (ICSCN), pp. 1–5, IEEE (2017) https://doi.org/10.1109/ICSCN.2017.8085665

12. Anderson, P.L., Molloy, A.: Maximizing the impact of virtual reality exposure therapy for anxiety disorders. Curr. Opin. Psychol. **36** (2020). https://doi.org/10.1016/j.copsyc.2020.10.001

13. Cieślik, B., Mazurek, J., Rutkowski, S., Kiper, P., Turolla, A., Szczepańska-Gieracha, J.: Virtual reality in psychiatric disorders: a systematic review of reviews. Complement. Ther. Med. **52** (2020). https://doi.org/10.1016/j.ctim.2020.102480

14. Thoondee, K.D., Oikonomou, A.: Using virtual reality to reduce stress at work. In: Proceedings of Computing Conference 2017, Institute of Electrical and Electronics Engineers Inc., vol. 2018-January, pp. 492–499 (2018). https://doi.org/10.1109/SAI.2017.8252142

15. Pretsch, J., Pretsch, E., Saretzki, J., Kraus, H., Grossmann, G.: Improving employee well-being by means of virtual reality – REALEX: an empirical case study. Eur. J. Econ. Bus. Stud. **6**(1) (2020). https://doi.org/10.26417/ejes.v6i1.p95-105

16. Straßmann, C., et al.: Relax yourself - using virtual reality to enhance employees' mental health and work performance. In: Extended Abstracts of the 2019 CHI Conference on Human Factors in Computing Systems (CHI EA '19). Association for Computing Machinery, New York, NY, USA, Paper LBW0286, pp. 1–6 (2019). https://doi.org/10.1145/3290607.3312946

17. Zaharuddin, F.A., Ibrahim, N., Yusof, A.M., Mohd Mahidin, E.M., Rusli, M.E.: Active interaction design for stress therapy virtual environment. In: 8th International Conference on Information Technology and Multimedia (ICIMU2020), pp. 292–296 (2020). https://doi.org/10.1109/ICIMU49871.2020.9243456

18. Mahalil, I., Yusof, A.M., Ibrahim, N., Mahidin, E.M.M., Rusli, M.E.: Virtual reality mini map presentation techniques: lessons and experience learned. In: IEEE Conference on Graphics and Media (GAME), pp. 26–31 (2019). https://doi.org/10.1109/GAME47560.2019.8980759

19. Mahalil, I., Yusof, A.M., Ibrahim, N., Mahidin, E.M.M., Rusli, M.E.: Implementation of an effective locomotion technique in virtual reality stress therapy. In: IEEE Conference on Graphics and Media (GAME), pp. 1–6 (2019). https://doi.org/10.1109/GAME47560.2019.8980987

20. Zaharuddin, F.A., Ibrahim, N., Mohd Mahidin, E.M., Yusof, A.M., Rusli, M.E.: Virtual reality application for stress therapy: issues and challenges. Int. J. Eng. Adv. Technol. **9**(1), 2325–2329 (2019)

21. Zaharuddin, F.A., Ibrahim, N., Yusof, A.M., Rusli, M.E., Mohd Mahidin, E.M.: Virtual environment for VR-based stress therapy system design element: user perspective. In: Badioze Zaman, H., Smeaton, A.F., Shih, T.K., Velastin, S., Terutoshi, T., Mohamad Ali, N., Ahmad, M.N. (eds.) IVIC 2019. LNCS, vol. 11870, pp. 25–35. Springer, Cham (2019). https://doi.org/10.1007/978-3-030-34032-2_3

Fusion Technology and Visualisation to Share STEM Data Using PETS Robots (i-COMEL) for Open Data Readiness Amongst Primary School Children

Halimah Badioze Zaman[1]($\boxtimes$), Hanif Baharin[2], and Azlina Ahmad[3]

[1] Institute of Informatics and Computing in Energy (IICE), Universiti Tenaga Nasional (UNITEN), Jalan IKRAM-UNITEN, 43000 Kajang, Selangor, Malaysia
[2] Institute IR4.0, Universiti Kebangsaan Malaysia, 43600 Bangi, Selangor, Malaysia
[3] Malaysian Information Technology Society (MITS), Bandar Baru Bangi, Malaysia

Abstract. The world is seeing rapid and dynamic technological innovations in the form of applications, tools, systems, or software that can help a nation's population, organisations and Government, make their administration and management more effective and efficient and most importantly at a more affordable price. Fusion technology, a hybrid concept practiced in Japan, Germany, which involves the integration of two or more technologies to develop products that can revolutionise the market. Thus, this paper highlights a fusion technology innovation (integration of vision and motion as well as analytical technologies) in the form of Box Robot application or PETS Robots that are programmable, called i-COMEL, to share STEM data in a class activity on a lesson related to Solar Systems. This activity was conducted to help primary school students enhance critical and scientific thinking through the use of Computational Thinking (CT) across STEM. In this activity students share data with other groups of students to prepare them for open data readiness. This was done through the use of PETS Robots that would use both vision and motion technologies to collect data based on the questions set, and these data were uploaded to the ThinkSpeak server on the Internet to visualise the data and displayed for all students to share during the presentation in the classroom. Learning to share data amongst the very young generation of the population, is important as Malaysia reinvents itself and moves towards a smart and digital data driven society, Malaysia 5.0. Findings of the proof of concept (POC) conducted on i-COMEL, showed that fusion technology used in the form PETS Robots and integrated with Computational Thinking (CT) across STEM for primary school students not only was a fun method of learning STEM subjects and acquiring critical and scientific skills but also an effective approach to open data readiness practice amongst primary school students.

Keywords: Malaysia 5.0 · Fusion technology strategy · Fusion technology innovation · Visualisation · Open data readiness · STEM data

© Springer Nature Switzerland AG 2021
H. Badioze Zaman et al. (Eds.): IVIC 2021, LNCS 13051, pp. 184–194, 2021.
https://doi.org/10.1007/978-3-030-90235-3_16

1 Introduction

As is happening globally, the 21st century, especially post-COVID19 pandemic, sees the world accepting the economy of digital innovation as something that needs to continue to happen more rapidly. Malaysia responded to the launching of the Digital Economy Blueprint (MyDIGITAL) [1] initiative. This policy outlines the importance of all sectors and groups of the population to see digitalisation and digital adoption as critical and needs to be improved at all levels: government, businesses and society. This also means that knowledge, data and technology will play a key role in ensuring that all parties: government, business and the general public can obtain, share and use data to improve the country's digital economy for the well-being of the society. To ensure that the government, businesses and the general public are data driven entities, each entity needs to be prepared to share data and use data as efficiently as possible. Therefore, the concept of open data needs to be understood by all levels of the Malaysian society as it moves towards Malaysia 5.0.

In a society such as Malaysia 5.0 [2], fusion technologies that use more than one type of technology can solve problems either in providing specific functions, control systems that can analyse situations, and make data -based decisions are inevitable. Typically, fusion technology involves the transformation of core technologies into hybrid technologies, i.e. combining knowledge from different technologies, different fields, different companies, different industries and different geographies. Research related to fusion technology can be distinguished from technology research that only focuses on one technology or one basic area commonly known as break-through approach, which is a long and horizontal technology development (linear technological development). The fusion technology approach takes over old generation technology methods while focusing on incorporating the technologies needed to build hybrid products that can revolutionise the market in this digital innovation economic era.

2 Fusion Technology and Visualisation in Digital Innovation Economy

In this digital innovation economy era, fusion technology and visualisation has become inevitable. Organisations can invest in research (R&D) based on a 'breakthrough' approach or focus on the existing fusion technology with visualisation approach. The first approach uses a sequential approach (linear), a step-by-step strategy, while the second approach is non-sequential (nonlinear), complementary and collaborative. It mixes additional technical improvements from a variety of different technology fields to create products that can revolutionise the market. For example, combining optics with electronics to create optoelectronics, which has successfully produced optic-fiber communication systems with visualisation; fusing mechanical and electronic technologies to give birth to the mechatronic revolution and visualisation, which has transformed the machine-tool industry in Japan [3, 4]. Similarly, a smart factory in Germany (which has a branch in Kulim Hitech Park, Kedah, Malaysia) produces integrated microwave chips. The process involved in producing microwave chips is extremely complicated and time consuming. The steps involved are also too many. Thus, the plant has used fusion technology and visualisation [5–7]: augmented reality technology, virtual reality and robotic technology as well as data analytics technology that is able to visualise and determine the microwave chips in the oven are ready to be produced and packaged for marketing.

In this era of digital innovation economy too, the old adage "one technology-one industry" is no longer appropriate because breakthrough strategies are not comprehensive; companies need to combine both approaches i.e. breakthrough approach and fusion approach in the technology strategy adopted. Relying only on breakthrough approaches fails because the focus on R&D efforts is too narrow (for example, within one specialised field of electronics), ignoring the possibility of combining technologies to produce innovations in more than two areas of technology. In this paper, the emphasis is on the fusion of motion and vision-based technologies and analytical technology using PETS Robots called i-COMEL through the process of collecting, visualising and sharing STEM learning data in primary schools in Malaysia. Technology fusion application built and described in this paper, is an application that combines technology fusion in helping primary school students collect, visualise and share data based on the concept of Computational Thinking (CT) and open data for learning purposes.

The justification for the fusion of motion and vision as well as analytical technologies used in this study is to ensure that the programmable PETS Robot (i-COMEL) can see its surroundings and move as programmed and collect data as it moves and visualise it through a visualisation server to be shared by the groups in the classroom for discussion.

3   Open Data and STEM in the Digital Innovation Economy

Primary school students who are the future generation of a smart society (Malaysia 5.0) need to be a generation that is not only savvy (has digital skills), but also has knowledge of STEM in addition to the arts, and has the skills to think logically, critically, creatively and scientifically. To solve problems effectively, they need to be trained with the skills of computational thinking (CT) across STEM [8–10]. To ensure that results of problem solving are effective, primary school students also had to share as much information and data with other students. This means, open data practices should be practiced amongst students and it must begin in primary schools.

Open data (OD) in this era of digital innovation economy, includes three (3) important elements, namely: use (use), share (share) and reuse (reuse) [11, 12]. Use involves the user obtaining information or data from an authentic source and using it for a specific purpose. Sharing involves users sharing information or/and authentic data obtained with other users to solve complex or complex problems. Reuse, on the other hand, involves users using information or/and authentic data obtained to produce a new digital innovation.

STEM data was shared amongst primary school students through an activity conducted based on Computational thinking (CT). CT is a concept that was initially created to help students who are studying computer science to be able to think logically, scientifically, critically and creatively before implementing programming and coding that showed more effective results [13, 14]. However, various studies have shown that students can benefit from CT in any subject in addition to computer science subjects such as STEM subjects or literature such as Language, Geography and History. Computational

Thinking (CT), is a concept that includes elements such as logic, algorithms, composed, abstraction, plotting, visualization, evaluating and presenting [15].

4   PETS Robot Application (i-COMEL) for Open Data Readiness

As mentioned earlier, the i-COMEL application-based fusion technology strategy is a Box Robot application called PETS Robot, which was designed and built to help primary school students code and program to solve problems, whilst preparing them to practice open data readiness. This is important to prepare young students to be aware that problem solving in the present and the future is data-driven. The availability of open data for future generations is the only way that will be accepted as an authentic method and will be believed as truth [16, 17]. Thus, a validation based on a proof of concept study (POC) on the use of i-COMEL robot was implemented to ensure that primary school students can solve problems based on fusion technology strategies using COMEL teaching and learning modules to train them coding and programming using i-COMEL and at the same time encouraging them to share data.

4.1   Reengineering Design of PETS Robots: i-COMEL

PETS Robot is a Robot Box used by many overseas schools such as Taiwan, USA and Japan to teach primary school students to learn to code and program through a fun gaming approach [18, 19]; with some integrating AI technology in solving complex problems [20]. For the purpose of this study, the design of i-COMEL was reengineered to meet the objectives of the study. Figure 1 shows the re-engineered exterior design of the i-COMEL from the top view. Figure 2, on the other hand, shows the redesigned i-COMEL from the bottom view. The visible wheels allow i-COMEL to move and be controlled based on the programming done by the primary school students.

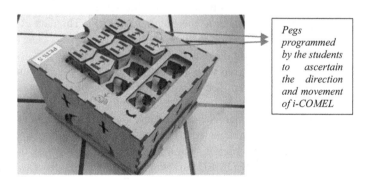

Pegs programmed by the students to ascertain the direction and movement of i-COMEL

Fig. 1. Top view of the reengineered i-COMEL

To ensure that i-COMEL can move smoothly, stably, be able to collect data, able to be linked to databases in the internet, and to ensure that the data can then be visualised using online visualisation tools, it was necessary to re-engineer i-COMEL, in order to implement specific functions. For that purpose, some hardware were loaded on the Robot as follows:

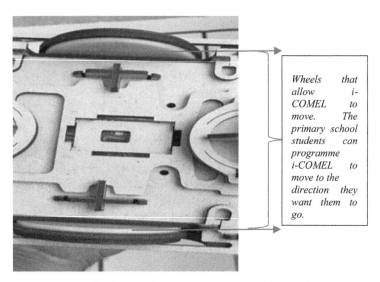

Wheels that allow i-COMEL to move. The primary school students can programme i-COMEL to move to the direction they want them to go.

Fig. 2. Bottom view of the reengineered i-COMEL

a. Near Field Communication (NFC) card reader
b. Board ES8266
c. Rechargeable battery

The reader board on the original Robot was augmented with a Near Field Communication (NFC) card reader, plus an ES8266 board and a rechargeable battery. This allowed i-COMEL to function more efficiently and effectively. The program in the main board that existed, was modified to allow i-COMEL to detect and collect data from NFC cards using an NFC card reader. The main board on the Robot was added with an ES8266 board to enable i-COMEL to connect to the Internet via WiFi. The data collected by i-COMEL was sent to an IoT server on the internet called ThinkSpeak. The server is a visualisation tool that can visualise the data collected by i-COMEL.

The original battery was replaced with a rechargeable battery because the replaced battery had more electrical power. The combination of technology to ensure that i-COMEL can implement the fusion technology strategy on i-COMEL is very important. This is because it enabled the primary school students to perform coding and programming activities, while solving problems based on cross - STEM teaching and learning modules for open data readiness. Figure 3 shows a simple sketch showing the changes that have been implemented to i-COMEL through the reengineering process.

4.2   Design Reengineering Sketch from Internal Perspective of i-COMEL

To understand the reengineering that has been implemented on PETS Robot, i-COMEL to achieve the objectives of the study, a sketch of the design engineering from an internal perspective as shown in Fig. 4, 5, 6 and 7.

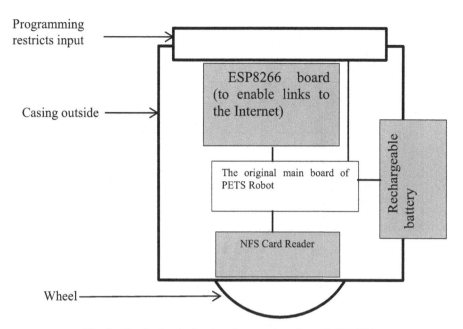

Programming restricts input

Casing outside

Wheel

Fig. 3. Simple sketch showing the reengineering of i-COMEL.

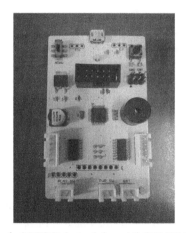

Fig. 4. PETS Robot sub-board (i-COMEL) before being reengineered

Fig. 5. NFC reader card connected to PETS Robot sub-board (i-COMEL)

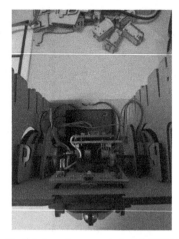

Fig. 6. ESP8266 board added to PETS Robot sub-board (i-COMEL)

Fig. 7. Sub-board augmented with ESP8266 and NFC card reader mounted on PETS Robot casing (i-COMEL)

5 POC of PETS Robot Application (i-COMEL) for Open Data Readiness

Proof of the concept (POC) of PETS Robot application, i-COMEL for open data readiness is implemented to enable students to make simple coding and programming to move the robot in order to solve a problem and achieve a specific goal. In addition, data is collected and visualised and then shared with other students for open data readiness. Fusion technology strategies combined with analytical technology, visualization and movement technology are being extensively studied, suitable for 21st century teaching and learning use. PETS Robot also known as robot box is widely studied for primary school teaching and learning use. However, its use in the teaching and learning of coding and programming, especially in the context of CT across STEM has never been implemented both nationally or globally.

This study observed how i-COMEL was integrated with fusion technology strategy, moved, collected, visualised and shared STEM data with other students using an online visualisation server. Through i-COMEL Robot, STEM-themed data and information were shared by primary school students who contributed to the practice of open data readiness. This is a very important effort in the digital innovation economy era towards the formation of a technological smart society (Malaysia 5.0).

5.1 POC: Programming Activities Based on CT Across STEM Using i-COMEL

Teaching and learning activities using i-COMEL were implemented based on the teaching of English (Unit 9: Solar System) at a primary or elementary school called *Sekolah Kebangsaan Sri Jelok, Kajang, Selangor, Malaysia.* Five (5) PETS Robots, i-COMEL, were used in the activity implemented in a classroom at the selected school. The students were divided into five (5) groups (five (5) persons in each group). Due to the fact that the POC needed to be implemented in detail, the detailed observational study was implemented based on only one group from Grade 4. These students were categorised as students with high academic achievement.

The students were given two sets of problems to solve using i-COMEL. Both of these problems required them to create a programming program. For both tasks, they needed to discuss in groups (using CT and TRIZ skills) and plan before programming the robot together.

The decision made must be the group decision. The first task (T1) required them to solve a given problem using linear programming and the second task (T2) required them to solve a given problem using a loop programming function. In both tasks, students had to move the i-COMEL robot on a display (board) specially designed for the movement of the robot. The display should be smooth, but can be detected by the app to stop at a specific pit stop, where students were instructed to collect as much data (points) as possible on the display. Then the students had to direct i-COMEL to move to a pit stop to upload the obtained data to the ThinkSpeak server in the internet, to visualise the data. Figures 8, 9 and 10 show a CT-based across STEM teaching and learning process session, based on fusion technology strategy and visualisation using i-COMEL.

5.2 POC: Results of Task Based Activities Using i-COMEL

Observational Results of the POC conducted on primary school students in a selected school, based on task - based activities using i-COMEL were as follows:

i. All the students (100%) acquired coding and programming skills quickly. It is assumed that they have implemented the activity based on an interesting theme and students found the theme undertaken as relevant to their lives.

ii. All the students (100%) were active and they seemed to have fun working and playing with the PETS Robot, i-COMEL. This is important because the COMEL teaching and learning model created (model has already been published earlier) based on Computational Thinking (CT) across STEM was intended to make the learning process active and fun.

iii. Majority of the students in the group (80%) learned that in the process of programming, they needed to plan the programming in advance. This involved a process of thinking as well as a process of systematic, logical and scientific discussion with peers in the group.

iv. All students in the group (100%) learned to work as a team through the division of tasks (planning, programming, re-analysing data calculations) made with those downloaded by i-COMEL online. This is a skill that is to be taught to students through the COMEL model based CT across-STEM.

v. All students (100%) successfully completed both assigned tasks in one (1) hour. This had met the expectations of the researchers. Thus, indicated that the fusion technology strategy and visualisation, through the use of i-COMEL successfully helped primary school students performed the tasks given based on the CT across STEM COMEL model.

vi. All the students (100%) appreciated how data could be shared from one device to the Internet and that the data collected can then be visualised using the online server,

ThingSpeak. This simple fusion technology strategy and visualisation, demonstrated that fusion technology and visualisation, can be applied in; a more sophisticated and complex contexts at the industry level. This had helped young students to practice open data readiness and data sharing.

5.3 POC: Improvements of Future i-COMEL

The use of fusion technology strategy through the use of PETS Robot called i-COMEL which has been validated through a Proof of Concept, found that the strategy successfully helped primary school students to learn English based on a computational thinking (CT) across STEM model. However, based on the findings, future i-COMEL can be further improved as follows:

i.   The speed performance of the future i-COMEL robot needs to be improved. Four (4) out of the five (5) students (80%) in the group, indicated they felt it was a bit long waiting for the first move to be made by i-COMEL when the programmed distance was quite far.

ii. All the students, five (5) out of five (5) students (100%) in the group had agreed that the battery power used in i-COMEL should be increased so that there is no need to frequently charge the battery while performing the tasks.

ii. All the students, five (5) out of five (5) students (100%) in the group agreed that the display that can be recognised by the robot needs to be enlarged so that the robot route is more interesting and it is easier to plan the i-COMEL route in order solve the problem.

vi. The researchers realised that the databases and visualization tools need to be created on a regular basis and placed in a cloud server for use so that data can be collected and reused for other students not just from day to day, but from year to year for many years to come.

v.   The researchers also realised that adding AI to the PETS Robots would make the problem solving approach more exciting and effective. Thus, future i-COMEL could be improved with the integration of AI technology (Fig. 11).

Fig. 8. Primary school students conducting T1 using i-COMEL Robots

Fig. 9. Primary school students conducting T1 using i-COMEL Robots

Fig. 10. Primary school students conducting T2 using i-COMEL Robots

Fig. 11. Primary school students conducting T2 using i-COMEL Robots

6 Conclusion

The Proof of Concept (POC) conducted on the application called i-COMEL based on fusion technology and visualisation for STEM data sharing to facilitate practice on open data readiness, was implemented amongst primary school students in a school in Malaysia. Findings of the POC showed that the strategy used was positive and the students had successfully performed the tasks assigned to them. The i-COMEL Robots successfully helped primary school students to code and do programming effectively. At the same time, these young students also acquired computational thinking (CT) across STEM skills. The fusion technology and visualisation strategy through i-COMEL Robots also made it easier for the students to share STEM data for learning purposes an exciting and innovative way. This strategy not only strengthen their STEM knowledge, but also prepares the young students to deal with data, for the future modern and smart society (Malaysia 5.0) which will be a data driven society. Therefore, the observational POC based on the task-based activities using PETS Robot, i-COMEL, implemented on year 4 primary school students, had successfully proven that the strategy used can prepare students for open data readiness. The problem solving functionalities of i-COMEL can be further improved in the future by integrating fusion technology with AI technology.

References

1. Economic Planning Unit (EPU): Malaysia Digital Economy (MyDIGITAL). Economic Planning Unit (EPU), Putrajaya (2021)
2. Zaman, H.B., Ahmad, A.: Teknologi Fusion dan Pemikiran Komputational bagi Kesediaan Data Terbuka. Universiti Kebangsaan Malaysia, Bangi (2020)
3. Kadoma, F.: Fusion technology and new R&D. Harv. Bus. Rev. **70**, 1–15 (2020)
4. Chandler, D.: Validating the physics behind the new MIT designed fusion experiment. MIT News (2020)
5. Healy, K.: Data Visualisation: A Practical Introduction. Princeton University, Princeton (2019)
6. Tufte, E.: The Visual Display of Quantitative Information, 2nd edn. Graphic Press, New York (2021)
7. Naflic, C.: Storytelling with Data: A Data Visualisation Guide for Business Professionals. Wiley, New York (2021)
8. Mailund, T.: Introduction to Computional Thinking: Problem Solving, Algorithms, Data Structures, and More. Apress, New York (2021)
9. Zingaro, D.: Algorithmic Thinking: A Problem-Based Thinking. No Strach Press, New York (2020)
10. Denning, P., Tedre, M.: Computational Thinking. MIT Press, Cambridge (2020)
11. Kayla, M.: Productivity Bytes. KNIME Platform 4.4. (2021)
12. Wheelan, C.: Naked Statistics. W.W. Norton & Co., New York (2020)
13. Roehrig, G., Dare, E., Ring-Whalen, E., Weiselmann, J.: Understanding coherence and integration in integrated STEM curriculum. Int. J. STEM Educ. **8**(2), 1–25 (2021)
14. Seage, S., Turegun, M.: The effects of blended learning on STEM achievement of elementary school students. Int. J. Res. Educ. Sci. **6**(1), 133 (2019). https://doi.org/10.46328/ijres.v6i1.728
15. Zaman, H.B., et al.: Integrating Computational Thinking (CT) with English across STEM: Proposal. Universiti Kebangsaan Malaysia, Bangi (2016)
16. Spradlin, D.: Are you solving the right problem? Harv. Bus. Rev. **90**(9) (2019)
17. Eilerts, K., Filler, A., Pinkwart, N., Rosken-Winter, B., Tiemann, R., Zu Belzen, A.U.: A framework to foster problem solving in STEM and computing education (2019). https://doi.org/10.1080/02635143.2019.1600490
18. Ihamaki, P., Heljakka, K.: Social and emotional learning with a robot dog: technology, empathy and playful learning in kindergarten. In: 9th Annual Arts, Humanities, Social Sciences and Education Conference, Honolulu, Hawaii, USA, 6–8 January, 2020 (2020)
19. Hao, K.: This robot taught itself to walk entirely on its own: AI powered robots that navigate without human intervention. MIT Techno. Rev. (2020)
20. Timms, M.J.: Letting artificial intelligence in education out of the box: educational cobots and smart classrooms. Int. J. Artif. Intell. Educ. **26**(2), 701–712 (2016). https://doi.org/10.1007/s40593-016-0095-y

Interactive Multimedia Kolb Experiential Learning Model Using Logistic Regression Algorithm to Improve Student Cognitive

Azizah Nurul Khoirunnisa[1]([✉]), Munir[1], Rasim[2], Eka Fitrajaya Rahman[2], and Laksmi Dewi[1]

[1] Curriculum Development Study Program, School of Postgraduate Studies, Indonesia University of Education, Bandung, Indonesia
`azizahnurulk@student.upi.edu`, {`munir,laksmi`}`@upi.edu`
[2] Computer Science Education Study Program, Department of Computer Science Education, Indonesia University of Education, Bandung, Indonesia
{`rasim,ekafitrajaya`}`@upi.edu`

Abstract. The differences of each student become a challenge for educators in delivering learning materials. More often than not, students often find it difficult to process study materials. Conventional study-based learning may not always have a profound impact on students. Consideration of interactive multimedia as a tool for student-centered learning has not been widely discussed in scientific research. In this paper, the authors investigate interactive multimedia using Kolb's experiential learning model in improving students' cognitive abilities. This study uses a pre-experimental method and one-group pre-and post-test design type with the research population in class XI RPL and a sample of SMK students in Bandung. The results show that the application of interactive multimedia using Kolb's experiential learning model is effective in improving students' cognitive abilities. On the other hand, it is found that combining abstract learning materials with interactive visuals and activities that involve students' participation could create exceptionally positive feedback from students.

Keywords: Interactive multimedia · Experiential learning · Logistic regression algorithm · Student cognitive

1 Introduction

The 4th Industrial Revolution has proven that the digital era has advanced significantly. This advancement shows by the digitalization and computerization in the education sector. In this age of digital education, it is imperative to encourage educators to consider integrating technology with teaching methodology and base the said integration on students' preferences [1]. This means that the difference among the individual students and teaching methods to be the most important variables in education [2]. Through student-centered learning, educational institutions will improve the quality of their student's

© Springer Nature Switzerland AG 2021
H. Badioze Zaman et al. (Eds.): IVIC 2021, LNCS 13051, pp. 195–204, 2021.
https://doi.org/10.1007/978-3-030-90235-3_17

education. This will help them develop critical thinking and communication skills, as well as independence and responsibility [3].

More often than not, students often find it difficult to process study materials. This difficulty then affects the outcome of their study, be it cognitively, psychometrically, and aphetically [4]. Among the three, the cognitive or knowledge aspect gets the spotlight since it is considered as the most related to students' performance and ability in terms of understanding school materials [5].

The database design material emphasizes the analysis of factual, conceptual, and procedural knowledge based on curiosity, and the SQL material emphasizes management, reasoning, and presentation in the concrete and abstract realms [6]. In line with research conducted by Fathansyah [7], a database material is considered as one of the abstract materials which causes it to require a medium to create a proper data model. As a result, students who are struggling in a database learning often find difficulties in material concept achievements, both collaboration and interaction, as well as problem-solving [8]. Therefore, database subjects require the students to have a good understanding in order to solve problems in accordance with the concept of the database itself.

Traditional classroom-based learning may not always make a lasting impression on students due to its standard nature. Hence, by engaging in real-life activities, students can easily transfer their knowledge into an understanding of certain subjects or topics [9]. *Experiential learning*, or also known as learning through real-life activities, emphasizes the need for students' involvement in all educational activities and discusses the concept of making meaningful learning through experience. In other words, this type of learning considers experience as the foundation of learning [10]. With the advancement of technology, learning from real-life activities can be organized regardless of time and learning the environment by using interactive media.

Multimedia is the combination of text and images. Texts may refer to a series of words and letters displayed on a computer screen or in the form of recorded spoken text that is played on a loudspeaker. Meanwhile, images may come in the form of photos, illustrations, figures, tables, videos, or animations [11]. Both of these items help students to better understand information or knowledge conveyed by educators through its use of a combination of various media [12]. Interactive media may also help educators to increase the overall quality and efficacy of their teaching as well as emphasizes a student-centered learning approach [13].

Interactive multimedia also has several benefits that could support a better learning experience, including multisensory activities, students' participation, individual learning, and simulation [14]. It also provides students with feedback for instance of various arguments and explanations assist students in improving their conceptual understanding, and application of learned concepts, data analysis, as well as provide an overview of concrete and specific problems; in addition, interactive media may also develop their problem-solving intuition [15, 16]. Furthermore, research suggests interactive multimedia are a suitable learning medium for practical materials and a wider range of groups of classes [17, 18].

In order to determine learning styles in multimedia, Logistic Regression (LR) may be used to analyze and determine students' learning styles. This is because LR is a general method of data mining and machine learning as well as a type of regression that relates one or more dependent variables to independent variables in the form of categories; these categories usually come in forms of 0 and 1 or Boolean. This then corresponds to the type of KLSI question, which is a two-choices question, appropriate or not appropriate [19].

The development of learning media has been massively carried out, with the help of the logistic regression algorithm, we designed interactive multimedia system that increases students' cognitive abilities in database subjects as well as investigates students learning styles. The main purpose of interactive multimedia is to present material with the Kolb learning cycle and several tests that will determine the level of understudies' cognitive comprehension of the material provided.

2 Methodology

2.1 Research Design

This research used a pre-experimental one-group pre-and post-test design that involves one group being given pretest (O) and given treatment (X), and the final result can be seen in the posttest. The design was taken based on research objective to examine the effects of the media and the application of the learning styles toward students' cognitive understanding. The design pattern of the pre-experimental one-group pre- and post-test can be seen in Table 1.

Table 1. The design pattern of the pre-experimental one group pre-and post-test

Pretest	Treatment	Posttest
O_1	X	O_2

The Explanation:

O1: Pretest
O2: Posttest
X: Treatment, an application of Interactive Multimedia

Site and Participant. The research was conducted at a vocational high school (SMK) in Bandung. The selection was based on the comparable quality of the three schools and taking into account accessibility and other considerations.

Therefore, the participants of this study are SMK students. Subjects were selected based on the non-probability sampling technique of purposive sampling. The selection of samples with certain considerations that the selected sample was in accordance with the criteria and problems raised by the researcher.

Development of Research Instrument. Interviews were carried out with teachers and questionnaires were shared among students to investigate what is needed which was eventually used as general analysis in the development of interactive multimedia.

The media expert an assessment instrument used a questionnaire from the *Judge's Rubric* to assess the feasibility of interactive learning multimedia developed by researchers in terms of graphics, language, and presentation of material.

Meanwhile, the instrument in determining student learning styles uses a questionnaire from the Kolb Learning Style Inventory (LSI) developed by David Kolb, which contains 80 questions and provides spending on four learning style groupings, namely Assimilator, Converger, Accommodator, and Diverger.

Data Analysis. The collected data in this research are then processed and analyzed. As mentioned earlier, this research used a qualitative design, and the qualitative analysis by observing non-participants. Then, the results of the observations could be directly explained.

In the interactive multimedia evaluation data analysis, the data were obtained from the *Student Checklist*. Meanwhile, the questionnaire was processed using quantitative descriptive statistical techniques with the following formula:

$$P = \frac{data\ collection\ score}{Number\ of\ criteria\ score} \times 100\% \tag{1}$$

The Explanation:

P: Percentage eligibility of the media
Criteria Score: The Highest score × number of respondents × number of items

Student Learning Results Analysis. In this study, the Normalize-Gain value was calculated to determine the increase in student understanding and the effectiveness of interactive multimedia with the following formula:

$$g = \frac{T_2 - T_1}{T_3 - T_1} \tag{2}$$

The Explanation:

g: The average gain of normalization
T_1: Pretest
T_2: Posttest
T_3: Maximum Score

2.2 Multimedia Development

The interactive multimedia' development using the Kolb learning cycle, where the learning flow starts from doing/having activities that can be used as experiences (Concrete Experience/CE), reviewing the experience gained (Reflective Observation/RO), then concluding from the experience gained (Abstract Conceptualization/AC), and practice/application of the experience (Active Experimental/AE).

Fig. 1. Concrete experience stage

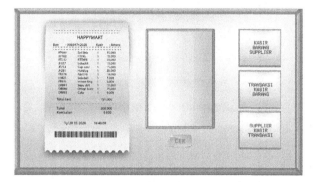

Fig. 2. Reflective observation stage

In the Concrete Experience stage, students are given orders to shop according to the instructions, this stage is shown in Fig. 1.

In the Reflective Observation stage, students are given commands in the form of drag and drop to analyze what they previously did and expressed opinions regarding what they have done, this stage is shown in Fig. 2.

Meanwhile, Abstract Conceptualization Stage provides confirmation in the form of video presentations to help students conceptualize a theory from the experience gained, this stage is shown in Fig. 3.

Lastly, in the Active Experimental stage, students are given exercises with varied types of questions, including drag and drop, multiple choices, and input value, this stage is shown in Fig. 4.

Logistic Regression (LR) is used in determining learning styles. LR works by counting the number of 'yes' answers then divided by the number of times students have tried to complete the questionnaire. It is then stored to examine the results of learning styles which can be seen in Fig. 5.

Fig. 3. Abstract conceptualization stage

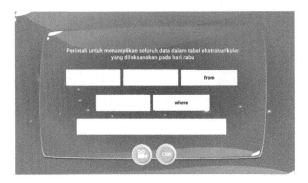

Fig. 4. Active experimental stage

Fig. 5. Kolb learning style questionnaire

3 Results

3.1 Students Cognitive Improvement

The results of the average pre-and post-test shown in Fig. 6., As seen in the table, The students' post-test scores have a significant increase compared to their pre-test scores before using Kolb's Experiential Learning Model's interactive multimedia. From the results of the average pre- and post-test scores, there is a difference of 33.08 meaning that there is an increase between two scores.

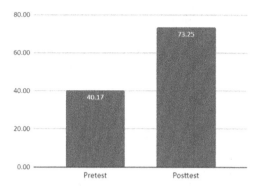

Fig. 6. Pretest and posttest average scores

The increase of students' pre-and post-test scores after using the interactive multimedia can be seen from the analysis of the Normalize-gain results in Table 2. Between two scores, it can be seen that there is an overall gain of 0.57 for the group with high scores. Meanwhile, the middle group students had an average gain of 0.56. Lastly, the overall gain for the lower scoring group indicates a gain of 0.55. According to this gain test in three different groups of scores, three gain values are categorized as a *medium* since the overall gain of the three is 0.56 and the said score is considered as a medium in terms of learning effectiveness criteria.

Table 2. Normalize-gain value of pre-and post-test

Group	Information	Pretest	Posttest	Gain
High	Maximum value	60	90	0.57
	Minimum value	55	70	
	Average	57.27	81.82	
Middle	Maximum value	60	90	0.56
	Minimum value	35	60	
	Average	45.57	75.91	
Low	Maximum value	30	70	0.55
	Minimum value	15	60	
	Average	23.21	65.36	

3.2 Determining Learning Style by Using Logistic Regression

The use of LR in interactive multimedia can be seen in Fig. 7. The accuracy of using the LR algorithm in determining learning styles is 81.3%. From this percentage, it can be interpreted that LR in determining learning styles is quite accurate. This finding can be improved by checking the student learning styles over time so that the machine can be more familiar with patterns based on the items that determine the learning style.

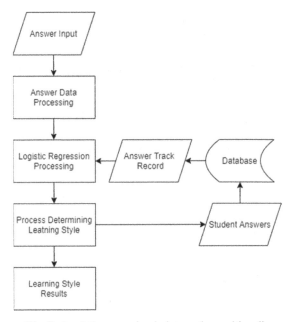

Fig. 7. Logistic regression in interactive multimedia

4 Discussion

Findings indicate that using interactive multimedia is effective in improving students' cognitive ability. This relevant study supports the effectiveness of the learning model. Mutmainah, Rukayah, and Indriayu [20] found that the student group that was given experiential learning model learning materials achieved higher scores compared to the one that was not. Sediyani and Budisantoso [21] also found that the experiential learning model imprinted a higher impression among students compared to problem-based learning with the difference lies in the average score; the experiential learning model scored 76.19 while problem-based learning only scored 72.137. On the other hand, experiential learning could also help develop a higher level of understanding and problem-solving skills for students. It can also motivate them to solve problems and develop effective solutions based on experience [22–24].

The participants were asked about their experiences, particularly in their satisfaction with the use of interactive multimedia. This was done in order to create an adjustment for future research. The test was conducted on 60 students using the Multimedia Mania 2004 – Student Checklist questionnaire. As seen in the responses of the questionnaire, interactive multimedia is considered very interesting and is able to support the students since it uses various types of visuals/images. In addition, most of the students also think that, interactive multimedia is easy to use thanks to its user-friendly interface that annihilates any obstacles from using the said multimedia.

5 Conclusion

As previously mentioned, the application of interactive multimedia by using Kolb's Experiential Learning model is able to increase the students' cognitive ability. This finding is based on the N-gain scale. It is found that combining abstract learning materials with interactive visuals and activities that involve the students' participation could create exceptionally positive feedback from students.

The findings of this study have valuable applications for teachers and students. It can be used to improve the teaching techniques of teachers or can be used to innovate learning activities.

Acknowledgment. We would like to appreciate and thank PMDSU Scholarship under Direktorat Jenderal Pendidikan Tinggi, Kementerian Pendidikan dan Kebudayaan Republik Indonesia for support throughout this research, and vocational high school students for lending their precious time aiding in the success of research.

References

1. Hussin, A.A.: Education 4.0 made simple: ideas for teaching. Int. J. Educ. Lit. Stud. (2018). https://doi.org/10.7575/aiac.ijels.v.6n.3p.92
2. Tuncer, M., Dikmen, M., Akmençe, A.E.: Investigation of higher education students' learning styles and attitudes towards mobile learning according to various variables. Int. J. Soc. Sci. Educ. Res. 4(3) (2018). https://doi.org/10.24289/ijsser.412095
3. Saputro, S.D.: The application of student centered learning through lesson study on quality and learning results. J. Intensive Stud. Lang. Lit. Art Cult. 84–91 (2018).https://doi.org/10.17977/um006v2i22018p084
4. Biabani, M., Izadpanah, S.: The study of relationship between Kolb's learning styles, gender and learning American slang by Iranian EFL students. Int. J. Instr. 517–538 (2019). https://doi.org/10.29333/iji.2019.12233a
5. Sudjana, N.: Penilaian Hasil dan Proses Belajar Mengajar. Rosda Karya, Bandung (2011)
6. Munif, A.: Basis Data Semester 1, Jakarta: Direktorat Jenderal Peningkatan Mutu Pendidik & Tenaga Kependidikan (2013)
7. Fathansyah, Basis Data, Bandung: Informatika Bandung (2012)
8. Dahri, N.: Learning development of database systems to overcome learning difficulty. UNES J. Educ. Sci., 107–117 (2018). https://doi.org/10.30998/jidr.v1i1.237
9. Chan, C.K.Y.: Exploring an experiential learning project through Kolb's learning theory using a qualitative research method. Eur. J. Eng. Educ., 405–415 (2015). https://doi.org/10.1080/03043797.2012.706596

10. Kolb, A.Y., Kolb, D.A.: The Kolb learning style inventory- version 4.0: a comprehensive guide to the theory. Psychom. Res. Valid. Educ. Appl. (2013)
11. Mayer, R.E.: Multimedia learning. Psychol. Learn. Motiv. **41** (2002)
12. Topano, A., Asiyah, Basinun, Walid, A., Alimi, Febrini, D.: Improving student cognitive learning outcomes through the development of interactive multimedia-based biology learning at Muhammadiyah University, Bengkulu, Young Scholar Symposium on Science Education and Environment (YSSSEE) (2020). https://doi.org/10.1088/1742-6596/1796/1/012042
13. Bujeng, B., Kamis, A., Hussain, M.A M., Rahim, M.B., Soenarto, S.: Validity and reliability of multimedia interactive making clothes (MIMP) module for home science subjects. Int. J. Innov. Technol. Explor. Eng. (IJITEE), 2278–3075 (2019)
14. Pujiriyanto: Teknologi untuk Pengembangan Media dan Pembelajaran. UNY Press, Yogyakarta (2012)
15. Syawaludin, A., Gunarhadi, Rintayati, P.: Development of augmented reality-based interactive multimedia to improve critical thinking skills in science learning. Int. J. Instr., 331–344 (2019). https://doi.org/10.29333/iji.2019.12421a
16. Cardenas, L., Izquierdo, J.L., Cardenas, E.: Interactive multimedia application for teaching and learning in analytical geometry. IEEE Lat. Am. Trans., 3461–3466 (2016). https://doi.org/10.1109/TLA.2016.7587655
17. Pardjono, P., Syauqi, K., Prasetya, W.A., Baihaqi, S.: Multimedia interactive learning of pictorial projection mechanical engineering skills in vocational high schools. In: International Conference on Vocational Education of Mechanical and Automotive Technology (ICoVEMAT) (2020). https://doi.org/10.1088/1742-6596/1700/1/012009
18. Untari, R.S., Kamdi, W., Dardiri, A., Hadi, S., Nurhadi, D.: The development and application of interactive multimedia in project-based learning to enhance students' achievement for 2D animation making. Int. J. Emerg. Technol. Learn. (iJET), 17–30 (2020). https://doi.org/10.3991/ijet.v15i16.16521
19. Ran, J., Zhang, G., Tong Zheng, W.W.: Logistic regression analysis on learning behavior and learning effect based on SPOC data. In: The 13th International Conference on Computer Science & Education (2018). https://doi.org/10.1109/ICCSE.2018.8468834
20. Mutmainah, R., Indriayu, M.: Effectiveness of experiential learning-based teaching material in mathematics. Int. J. Eval. Res. Educ. (IJERE), 57–63 (2019). https://doi.org/10.11591/ijere.v8i1.15903
21. Sediyani, L., Budisantoso, H.T.: Comparing problem-based learning and experiential learning on civil servant training program. Indones. J. Curric. Educ. Technol. Stud. 104–108 (2019). https://doi.org/10.15294/ijcets.v7i2.24045
22. Hill, B.: Research into experiential learning in nurse education. Br. J. Nurs. (2017). https://doi.org/10.12968/bjon.2017.26.16.932
23. Pherson-Geyser, G.M., Villiers, R.d., Kavai, P.: The use of experiential learning as a teaching strategy in life sciences. Int. J. Instr., 877–894 (2020). https://doi.org/10.29333/iji.2020.13358a
24. Giac, C.C., Gai, T.T., Hoi, P.T.T.: Organizing the experiential learning activities in teaching science for general education in Vietnam. World J. Chem. Educ., 180–184 (2017). https://doi.org/10.13189/ujer.2019.070129
25. Sumarmi, S., Bachri, S., Irawan, L.Y., Putra, D.B.P., Risnani, Aliman, M.: The effect of experiential learning models on high school students learning scores and disaster countermeasures education abilities. J. Educ. Gifted Young, 61–85 (2020). https://doi.org/10.17478/jegys.635632

Performance Analysis of Machine Learning Techniques for Sentiment Analysis

Muhamad Hariz Izzat Ahmad Hapez, Noor Latiffah Adam$^{(\boxtimes)}$, and Zaidah Ibrahim

Faculty of Computer and Mathematical Sciences, Universiti Teknologi MARA,
40450 Shah Alam, Malaysia
{latiffah508,zaidah782}@uitm.edu.my

Abstract. Sentiment analysis determines the sentiment or opinion of a given text. A sentiment analysis model can classify whether a given text data is positive or negative by extracting meaning from the natural language. The growth of social media such as Twitter, forum discussions and reviews, contributed to the huge data repository in digital form. Analyzing these huge data manually is very time consuming and challenging. Thus, applying machine learning techniques can automatically classify the sentiment effectively. This research compares the performance of five popular machine learning techniques for sentiment analysis namely, Support Vector Machine (SVM), Logistic Regression, Naïve Bayes, Random Forest and K-Nearest Neighbor using a publicly available dataset from kaggle.com. Their classification performances are compared based on accuracy and training time where fine tuning of some of the hyperparameters are per-formed to improve the accuracy. Experimental analysis indicates that SVM with linear kernel function produces the highest accuracy but a slower training time. On the other hand, Naïve Bayes requires the shortest training time but with a slightly lower accuracy compared to SVM.

Keywords: Sentiment analysis · Support vector machine · Logistic regression · Naïves Bayes · Random Forest · K-nearest neighbor

1 Introduction

Sentiment analysis or also known as opinion mining is a natural language processing technique used to determine whether the data is positive, negative or neutral. People are eager to share their comments and reviews on social media. This kind of short review could highlight their preference on certain topic [1–3]. Sentiment analysis is often performed on textual data which may use slang phrases, misspellings, short forms, recurring characters, the use of dialects and modern emoticons [4, 5]. The same words and phrases can be used in a different context, thus making it difficult to be determined. Such analysis, for example, may help businesses on monitoring the brand and product sentiment in the customer feedback and understanding the customers' needs [6, 7]. It is extremely crucial because it helps businesses to quickly understand the overall opinions of their customers. By automatically sorting the sentiments behind those reviews, social media conversations, and more, you can make faster and more accurate decisions.

© Springer Nature Switzerland AG 2021
H. Badioze Zaman et al. (Eds.): IVIC 2021, LNCS 13051, pp. 205–213, 2021.
https://doi.org/10.1007/978-3-030-90235-3_18

An example of this application in the real world, is when we want to study the people's opinion on the Covid-19 [8, 9] vaccine. One way to do that is by doing a survey, interview, questionnaire, etc. However, these methods take an enormous amount of time and cost. Therefore, instead of doing these traditional methods, we can scrap people's opinions from the social media, and then running a sentiment analysis towards the scrapped text [10]. Not only that it will save time and any unnecessary costs, but we can also get up to millions of samples from all over the world. However, the accuracy of this prediction is also dependent on the models that were being applied. Some of the machine learning approaches that help classify the sentiments are Logistic Regression [11], Support Vector Machine [12], Random Forest [11], K-Nearest Neighbors [11] and Naïve Bayes [7, 13]. Thus, the goal of this study is to find the best machine learning algorithms out of these five models. We will be tuning the hyper-parameters of each model so that we can find an optimal combination of hyperparameters that minimizes a predefined loss function to give better results.

2 Literature Review

One good reason why opinion mining worth to be explored is that, we have massive data recorded in digital form which have potential to be examined [4, 11, 14–16]. The growth of social media such as Twitter, forum discussions and reviews, contributed to the huge data repository. To handle such big data, require intelligent approach such as machine learning. This section will elaborate on the machine learning approaches used to classify the sentiments.

Support Vector Machine (SVM) is a powerful machine learning model algorithm which is used for both classification and regression. But generally, it is used in the classification problem. The strength of an SVM rooted from its ability to learn the data classification patterns with balanced accuracy and reproducibility [17].

Logistic Regression is a regression model that utilizes binary on the targeted variables. In other words, the dependent variable is binary in nature having data coded as either 1 (stands for success/yes) or 0 (stands for failure/no). Study in [18], reported that, the classifier has confidence when predicting the positive sentiments but biased when predicting negative reviews.

The Naïve Bayes classifier assumed that the presence of a particular feature in a class is unrelated to the presence of any other features of Naïve Bayes. It is widely used for text classification and spam detection. Despite the simplicity of this model, it works surprisingly well for document classification [19]. Naïve Bayes on text classification require a small data set for training [2]. Conditional probability can be used to classify words into their respective categories.

Random forest was introduced by Breiman [20]. It is a tree-based technique that uses a large number of decision trees built out of randomly selected sets of features. Contrary to the simple decision tree, it is highly uninterpretable, but it is generally produced good performance makes it a popular algorithm.

The K-Nearest Neighbor algorithm, commonly known as k-NN, is a nonparametric approach where the response of a data point is determined by the nature of its K-Nearest Neighbors from the training set. It is suitable to be used in both classification and regression settings [21]. The higher the parameter k, the higher the bias, and the lower the parameter k, the higher the variance.

3 Methodology

3.1 Data Description

The data that we obtained is from Kaggle. It contains 1,600,000 number of rows and extracted using the twitter API. There are a total of 800,000 rows for Positive Sentiment and another 800,000 for Negative Sentiment which is perfectly balanced. However due to time complexity, we decided to take a sample of 40,000 number of samples with a balanced Positive and Negative ratio. The data contains 6 number of columns, and the description of the data is on Fig. 1.

```
1. target: the polarity of the tweet (0 = negative, 2 = neutral, 4 = positive)
2. ids: The id of the tweet ( 2087)
3. date: the date of the tweet (Sat May 16 23:58:44 UTC 2009)
4. flag: The query (lyx). If there is no query, then this value is NO_QUERY.
5. user: the user that tweeted (robotickilldozr)
6. text: the text of the tweet (Lyx is cool)
```

Fig. 1. Data description

Figure 2 shows the snippet of the data that we obtained from Kaggle. As you can see, there are a total of six columns, namely Target, Ids, Date, Flag, User, and Text. However, we will only be using the Target and Text columns. As you can see from Fig. 3, there are a total 40,000 rows of data that we have selected with a balance between the positive and negative sentiment.

	Target	Ids	Date	Flag	User	Text
0	0	2323066693	Wed Jun 24 23:50:25 PDT 2009	NO_QUERY	iKarimah	talking to... no one
1	0	2323067072	Wed Jun 24 23:50:28 PDT 2009	NO_QUERY	PsychobillyCass	wanna listen to "my girl" but can't ...
2	0	2323067309	Wed Jun 24 23:50:30 PDT 2009	NO_QUERY	originald	OK, finally threw everything out. Trying some...
3	0	2323067331	Wed Jun 24 23:50:30 PDT 2009	NO_QUERY	pariahriot	My dumbass wiped the micro sd card I had in my...
4	0	2323067540	Wed Jun 24 23:50:31 PDT 2009	NO_QUERY	Rubyam	@HorseCrazyBoy1 oh apologies dear friend - i w...

Fig. 2. Data snippet

3.2 Data Pre-processing

One of the common steps that we did when we do data pre-processing is to remove null values if there is any. Null values can cause misleading results. Besides that, we also remove any duplicate values of the 'text' column. Duplicate values will only put unnecessary weight to a certain parameter in the model that might cause the model to be biased or overfit.

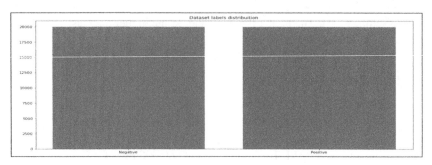

Fig. 3. Bar plot of the sentiment data

Then for the text analysis, the data cleaning step applied is very important for the data to be reliable. There are a lot of possible data noise for the text, such as the inconsistency use of the upper and lower cases, unexpected words such as symbols or emojis, also some useless words like nouns and others. This is expected since the text is one of the most unstructured data forms [22].

In this study, we will be using the stopwords list from the NLTK library to remove any unnecessary words in the text such as 'a', 'and', 'how' and others. Next, we also normalise the text data by using the snowball stemmer from NLTK to convert the words into its root form. For example, from 'stemmed' into 'stem', from 'kicks, kicked, kicking' into 'kick', etc.

3.3 Machine Learning

We have tested five different types of machine learning algorithms to find the best model to classify the sentiments of a Twitter text, namely, SVM, Logistic Regression, Naïve Bayes, Random Forest and K-Nearest Neighbors. We have tuned the hyper-parameters in each model to find out the best model in this study. We compared the speed of the training time and the accuracy of each model. The following subsection will describe the parameters of each algorithm that will be tested.

SVM. The goal of support vector machines is to find the line that maximizes the minimum distance to the line. The parameters that will be tested will be as follows:

- Kernel Specifies the kernel type to be used in the algorithm. [linear, poly, rbf]
- Gamma Kernel coefficient. [scale, auto] 5
- Decision function shape: Whether to return a one-vs-rest ('ovr') decision function of shape (n_samples, n_classes) as all other classifiers, or the original one-vs-one ('ovo') decision function of libsvm which has shape (n_samples, n_classes * (n_classes - 1)/2). [ovo, ovr]

Logistic Regression. The parameters that will be tested will be as follows:

- Solver Algorithm to be used in the optimization problem. [liblinear, lbfgs, saga]
- Penalty Used to specify the norm used in the penalization. [l2, none]

- C Inverse of regularization strength; must be a positive float. [1, 4, 10]

Naïves Bayes. The parameters that will be tested will be as follows:

- Alpha Additive (Laplace/Lidstone) smoothing parameter (0 for no smoothing). [0, 1]
- Fit prior Whether to learn class prior probabilities or not. If false, a uniform prior will be used. [True, False]

Random Forest. The parameters that will be tested will be as follows:

- Criterion The function to measure the quality of a split. [gini, entropy]
- Number of estimators is the number of trees in the forest. [50, 100, 200]

K-Nearest Neighbors. The parameters that will be tested will be as follows:

- Number of neighbors Number of neighbors to use by default for kneighbors queries. [5, 15, 40]
- Weights Weight function used in prediction. [uniform, distance]
- Power parameter (p) for the Minkowski metric. When p = 1, this is equivalent to using manhattan_distance (l1), and Euclidean distance (l2) for p = 2. [1, 2]

4   Finding and Results

Table 1 shows the summary of the overall results by comparing the accuracy and training time. The first row of SVM described the comparison by using different Kernel parameters. Based on the results, we can say that the 'linear' kernel has a higher accuracy compared to 'rbf' and 'poly'. However, the 'rbf' kernel takes less time to train. The second row of SVM shows the results by using different Gamma parameters. The results illustrate that the 'scale' kernel coefficient has the higher accuracy compared to the 'auto' kernel coefficient. But the 'auto' kernel coefficient takes shorter time to train. The last row of SVM shows the results by using different parameters of the Decision Function Shape. The results show no significant difference on the accuracy and the time training of the model.

In this study, we have tested three parameters of Logistic Regression. The first one is the Solver parameters. It did not cause any significant different on the accuracy and the time training of the model. It takes only a few seconds of difference between these solver types. As for the different Penalty parameters, by using the 'l2' penalization, it has a higher accuracy compared to the 'none' penalization. Besides, the 'none' penalization also takes a bit longer to train the model. The C parameters exhibited that using the 'l0' regularization strength has a greater accuracy compared to '1' and '4' regularization strength. However, we also noticed that the greater the regularization strength is, the longer it takes for the model to be trained. We tested two parameters for the Naïve Bayes. The Alpha parameters, when using the additive smoothing one (1) has a greater accuracy compared to the no smoothing zero (0), while for the training time, they are only a few milliseconds apart. When using Fit Prior parameters, if we set the fit prior to True or False, it would not cause any significant differences on the accuracy and the training time of the model. It only takes a few milliseconds in difference between these solver types.

Table 1. Summary of results.

Machine Learning Model	Parameter Tested				
	Kernel		linear	poly	rbf
		Accuracy	0.76125	0.719625	0.756375
		Training time	12min 33s	11min 3s	7min 3s
SVM	Gamma		scale	auto	
		Accuracy	0.756375	0.49825	
		Training time	8min 23s	2min 57s	
	Decision function shape		One versus one (ovo)	One versus rest (ovr)	
		Accuracy	0.756375	0.756375	
		Training time	6min 13s	6min 2s	
	Solver		liblinear	lbfgs	Saga
		Accuracy	0.752875	0.752625	0.752875
		Training time	487 ms	3.64 s	641 ms
Logistic Regression	Penalty		12	none	
		Accuracy	0.752625	0.735000	
		Training time	1.18s	3.85s	
	Maximum iteration	C	1	4	10
		Accuracy	0.752625	0.75975	0.761000
		Training time	1.34s	5.27s	7.45s
	Alpha Additive		0	1	
		Accuracy	0.710500	0.755875	
Naïve Bayes		Training time	57 ms	29 ms	
	Fit prior		True	False	
		Accuracy	0.755875	0.756125	
		Training time	29 ms	27 ms	
	Criterion		gini	entropy	
		Accuracy	0.739250	0.739500	
Random Forest		Training time	6min 11s	5min 49s	
	Number of estimators		50	100	200
		Accuracy	0.73575	0.736625	0.7425
		Training time	2min 49s	6min 19s	11min 53s
	Number of neighbors		5	15	40
		Accuracy	0.546625	0.525375	0.519000
		Training time	5.25 ms	11.4 ms	8.84 ms
K-Nearest Neighbors	Weights		uniform	distance	
		Accuracy	0.546625	0.5495	
		Training time	8.12 ms	8.69 ms	
	p		1	2	
		Accuracy	0.542875	0.546625	
		Training time	8.01 ms	8.63 ms	

Using Random Forest, we tested two parameters. The criterion parameters also show that, there is no significant difference in accuracy by setting the criterion to either 'gini' or 'entropy'. The 'gini' criterion takes a slightly longer time to train the model compared to the 'entropy' criterion. The Different Number of Estimators parameters also presented no significant difference in accuracy by setting the criterion to either '50, '100' or '200'. However, there is a significant difference for the time taken to train the model, that is the greater the number of estimators, the longer it takes to train the model.

We tested three parameters of K-Nearest Neighbour. We have set a different number of the Neighbors parameters and it shows that, the '5' neighbors have a higher accuracy compared to '15' and '40' neighbors. However, there is no actual pattern in the time taken to train the model, since the result is inconsistent when the number of neighbors increased. Weights parameters shows that when setting the weights to 'uniform' or 'distance', does not cause any significant difference on the accuracy and the training time of the model.

It takes only a few milliseconds of difference between these weight types. The P parameters shows that by setting P to '1 or '2, they do not cause any significant difference on the accuracy and the training time of the model. It only takes a few milliseconds of difference between these power parameter types.

5   Conclusion and Recommendation

The main purpose of this study is to find the best hyper parameters setup that can be used for the sentiment analysis for each model. By using SVM, we noticed that it has the highest accuracy compared to other models, however it also takes longer time to train. For the 'kernel' parameter, by setting it to linear, it has the highest accuracy compared to other kernel type. But it also causes the model to train longer. Next, for the 'gamma' parameter, by setting it to scale, it has a much higher accuracy when compared to the auto scale. However, it made the model to train longer. Furthermore, for the 'decision function shape', we do not notice any difference between the various decision function shapes. The difference between the time taken to train the model is also unnoticeable.

Besides, for the Logistic Regression model, we observed that it has one of the highest accuracies compared to other models and takes shorter time to train the model. For the 'Solver' parameter, there is no significant difference on the accuracy and the training time of the model. 'lbfgs' have a slightly longer time to train the model but in mere seconds. For the 'penalty' parameter, we can say that the 'l2' penalization has a greater accuracy compared to the 'none' penalization. It also causes the model to have a slightly less time to train the model. On top of that, for the regularization strength of the 'C' parameters, there is no significant difference on the accuracy performance between the value of the regularization strength. However, we noticed that the higher the regularization strength, the time it takes to train the model will also increase.

Furthermore, for the Naïve Bayes model, overall, we can say that it has a decent performance on the accuracy and the time taken to train the model. For the 'alpha' parameters, by setting it to 1 (additive smoothing), causes the model to be extra magnificent compared with no smoothing, 0. Not only that it causes the model to have better accuracy, but also a slight less time to train the model. Next, for the 'fit prior' parameters, there is no significant difference on the accuracy and time taken to train the model when setting it up to True or False.

Next, for the model Random Forest, it also has a decent performance on the accuracy, however it is quite the opposite for the time taken to train the model. For the 'criterion' parameters in the Random Forest model, even though there is a slight difference on the time taken to train the model, but there is no significant difference on the accuracy either when setting it up to gini or entropy. For the 'number of estimators' parameters, there is also no significant difference in accuracy when setting the criterion to either '50, '100' or '200'. However, there is a significant difference for the time taken to train the model, that is; the higher the number of estimators, the longer it takes to train the model.

Finally, for the model K-Nearest Neighbors, we can say that the accuracy performance of the model is quite terrible compared to other models even though it causes only a few milliseconds to train. For the 'number of neighbors' parameters, we noticed that by setting the number lower, it will cause the model to have a slightly better accuracy on the prediction. However, there is no real pattern on the time taken to train the model. Next for 'weights' parameters, by setting it up to either uniform or distance, there is still no significant difference on the performance of the model. Besides that, by setting the power parameter (P) to '1 or '2, it does not cause any significant differences on the accuracy and the time training of the model. It only takes a few milliseconds in difference between these power parameter types. Therefore, out of all 5 models, we can say that the Naïve Bayes and the Logistic Regression performed extremely well compared to other models. Not only the fact that they have good accuracy, the time they took to train the model are also nominal. However, if the time taken to train the model is not the main concern, the Support Vector Machine would be the best model due to its sharp accuracy. Additionally, we would also say that the K-Nearest Neighbors is not suitable for sentiment analysis due to its below-average accuracy despite having less training time.

However, the result of this study focuses only on one single text processing and vectorizing technique. Therefore, it is recommended for future researchers to try different vectorizing techniques of the text, such as different n-grams of the vector, etc. According to Subarno et.al. (2018), LSTM RNNs are more effective than Deep Neural Networks and conventional RNNs for sentiment analysis. Hence, we would also recommend future researchers to try LSTM RNNs and compare it with different models so that various results could be attained.

References

1. Naresh, A., Venkata Krishna, P.: An efficient approach for sentiment analysis using machine learning algorithm. Evol. Intell. **14**(2), 725–731 (2020). https://doi.org/10.1007/s12065-020-00429-1
2. Singh, J., Singh, G., Singh, R.: Optimization of sentiment analysis using machine learning classifiers. HCIS **7**(1), 1–12 (2017). https://doi.org/10.1186/s13673-017-0116-3
3. Maskat, R., Faizzuddin Zainal, M., Ismail, N., et al.: Automatic labelling of malay cyber-bullying twitter corpus using combinations of sentiment, emotion and toxicity polarities. In: ACM International Conference Proceedings Series (2020). https://doi.org/10.1145/3446132.3446412
4. Liu, B.: Sentiment Analysis and Opinion Mining: A Survey. Morgan & Claypool
5. Adam, N.L., Rosli, N.H., Cik Soh, S.: Sentiment analysis on movie review using Naïve Bayes. In: 2nd International Conference on Artificial Intelligence and Data Sciences (AiDAS2021), pp 1–6 (2021)

6. Wah, Y.B., Abdullah, N., Abdul-Rahman, S., Peng Tan, M.L.: Text mining and sentiment analysis on reviews of proton cars in Malaysia. Malaysian J. Sci. **37**, 137–153 (2018). https://doi.org/10.22452/mjs.vol37no2.5

7. Mohamed Shuhidan, S., Hamidi, S.R., Kazemian, S., et al.: Sentiment analysis for financial news headlines using machine learning algorithm. Adv. Intell. Syst. Comput. **739**, 64–72 (2018). https://doi.org/10.1007/978-981-10-8612-0_8

8. Das, S., Kolya, A.K.: Predicting the pandemic: sentiment evaluation and predictive analysis from large-scale tweets on Covid-19 by deep convolutional neural network. Evol Intell. (2021). https://doi.org/10.1007/s12065-021-00598-7

9. Ramya, B.N., Shetty, S.M., Amaresh, A.M., Rakshitha, R.: Smart simon bot with public sentiment analysis for novel Covid-19 tweets stratification. SN Comput. Sci. **2**(3), 1–11 (2021). https://doi.org/10.1007/s42979-021-00625-5

10. Du, J., Xu, J., Song, H., et al.: Optimization on machine learning based approaches for sentiment analysis on HPV vaccines related tweets. J Biomed. Semant. **8**, 1–7 (2017). https://doi.org/10.1186/s13326-017-0120-6

11. Shah, K., Patel, H., Sanghvi, D., Shah, M.: A comparative analysis of logistic regression, random forest and KNN models for the text classification. Augment. Hum. Res. **5**(1), 1–16 (2020). https://doi.org/10.1007/s41133-020-00032-0

12. Kharde, V.A., Sonawane, S.S.: Sentiment analysis of twitter data: a survey of techniques. Int. J. Comput. Appl. **139**, 5–15. (2016). https://doi.org/10.5120/ijca2016908625

13. Yuri, M.N., Mohd Rosli, M.: TelcoSentiment: sentiment analysis on mobile telecommunication services using Naive Bayes technique. In: 2nd International Conference on Information Security and Computer Technology (ICISCT2021), pp 1–8 (2021)

14. Yue, L., Chen, W., Zuo, W., Yin, M.: A survey of sentiment analysis on social media. Knowl. Inf. Syst. **60**, 617–663 (2019). https://doi-org.ezaccess.library.uitm.edu.my/10.1007/s10115-018-1236-4

15. Singh, J., Singh, G., Singh, R.: A review of sentiment analysis techniques for opinionated web text. CSI Trans. ICT **4**(2–4), 241–247 (2016). https://doi.org/10.1007/s40012-016-0107-y

16. Hemmatian, F., Sohrabi, M.K.: A survey on classification techniques for opinion mining and sentiment analysis. Artif. Intell. Rev. **52**(3), 1495–1545 (2017). https://doi.org/10.1007/s10462-017-9599-6

17. Pisner, D.A., Schnyer, D.M.: Support vector machine. Mach. Learn., 101–121 (2020)

18. Al Omari, M., Al Hajj, M., Hammami, N., Sabra, A.: Sentiment classifier: logistic regression for arabic services' reviews in Lebanon. In: 2019 International Conference on Computer and Information Sciences (ICCIS), pp 1–5. IEEE , (2019)

19. Murphy, K.P.: Naive Bayes classifiers, pp. 1–8 (2006)

20. Breiman, L.: Random Forests. Mach. Learn. **45**, 5–32 (2001)

21. Dey, L., Chakraborty, S., Biswas, A., et al.: Sentiment analysis of review datasets using Naïve Bayes' and K-NN classifier. Int. J. Inf. Eng. Electron Bus. **8**, 54–62 (2016). https://doi.org/10.5815/ijieeb.2016.04.07

22. Jones, A.B.: Sentiment analysis of reviews: Text Pre-processing (2018). https://medium.com/@annabiancajones/sentiment-analysis-of-reviews-text-pre-processing-6359343784fb

National Sport Institute Case: Automated Data Migration Using Talend Open Studio with 'Trickle Approach'

Suzaimah Ramli[1]([⊠]), Izzuddin Redzuan[1,2], Iqbal Hakim Mamood[2], Norulzahrah Mohd Zainudin[1], Nor Asiakin Hasbullah[1], and Muslihah Wook[1]

[1] National Defence University of Malaysia, Kuala Lumpur, Malaysia
suzaimah@upnm.edu.my
[2] National Sport Institute, Kuala Lumpur, Malaysia
iqbal@isn.gov.my

Abstract. In the current era of globalization, old systems are replaced or improved daily. Before the transition happens, IT experts need to carefully plan the best course of action to move the massive amount of data from old to new systems. If there are flaws unnoticed, the data may be lost during the migration process where it will feed unreliable data to the end-users. Recently, National Sports Institute had launched a new system the National Coaching Academy System where it was outsourced and developed by a vendor. Unfortunately, the system cannot be used immediately because there are no data from the old system in its database. This kind of problem occurs when data migration is not considered during the development phase of a new system. Because of this, the staff need to manually navigate between the two old and new systems to obtain accurate data of their coaches. Thus, in this paper, we will discuss the process that needs to be analyzed and what are the best strategies to solve the problem. The result should be able to increase the efficiency and make it easier for the staff when working with the coach's data.

Keywords: Automation · Data migration · ETL process · Talend open studio

1 Introduction

Data migration is the process of transferring data between storage systems, data formats, or computer systems. Data migration projects are undertaken for a number of reasons, including changing or upgrading servers or storage devices, transferring data to third-party cloud providers, merging websites, maintaining infrastructure, migrating applications or databases, updating software, corporate mergers, or relocating data centers [1]. A project that involves data migration has been quiet challenging to most IT experts where they must time the project so there is minimal impact to an organization. Depends on the budget, not only they have to keep an eye on the cost but also the time taken for the project to finish. IT experts need to allocate most of their time to maintain

H. Badioze Zaman et al. (Eds.): IVIC 2021, LNCS 13051, pp. 214–223, 2021.
https://doi.org/10.1007/978-3-030-90235-3_19

data integrity to avoid problem occurs during the migration where it will risk of a prolong disruption and downtime to an active organization.

As part of the extract/transform/load (ETL) process, each data migration includes at least the transformation and loading steps. This means that the extracted data must go through a number of preparatory functions before it can be loaded into the target locale. Companies migrate data for several reasons. You may need to upgrade the entire system, upgrade the database, build a new data warehouse, or combine new data from acquisitions or other sources. Data migration is also important when implementing other systems in addition to existing applications [2]. The data must be relevant for the purpose of the new system. This often requires data validation, correcting database problems, changing data formats, or combining values.

Talend Open Studio is an open architecture for data integration, data profiling, big data, cloud integration and data migration. It is a GUI environment that offers more than 1000 ready-made connectors. This makes it easy to perform operations such as changing files, loading data, moving files, and renaming files. This allows each component to define complex processes. Integration tasks are created by configured Talend components, not coded. In addition, tasks from the development environment or as stand-alone scripts can be executed [2]. Talend offers components that include database administration, auditing, and monitoring. This component helps with the administration of user accounts, permissions, and project permissions. The audit database helps evaluate various aspects of the workplace to develop the ideal process-oriented decision support system.

2 Literature Review

2.1 Type of Data Migration

There are a few types of migration that can be done depends on the organization needs such as the storage migration moves data off existing arrays into more modern ones that enable other systems to access it. It offers significantly faster performance and more cost-effective scaling while enabling expected data management features such as cloning, snapshots, and backup and disaster recovery. Next is cloud migration where it moves data, application, or other business elements from either an on-premises data center to a cloud or from one cloud to another. In many cases, it also entails a storage migration. Application migration moves an application program from one environment to another. It may include moving the entire application from an on-premises IT center to a cloud, moving between clouds, or simply moving the application's underlying data to a new form of the application hosted by a software provider [3]. The importance of choosing the correct strategy is crucial in a data migration project due to the compatibility of the system especially when the system uses a different architecture and formats.

2.2 Data Migration Strategies

Organizations need to consider which data migration strategy will best suit their needs. Depending on the project requirements and the available editing windows, you can choose from several strategies. There are two main types of migration: "Big Bang" and "trickle". When migrating Big Bang data, all data is migrated in one operation. While this may take some time, there will come a time when users will no longer be able to use the old data and the new system will take effect. The change was made in the event "Big Bang". The Big Bang migrations typically have significant setup times and short downtime for which systems are not available [4]. The ideal Big Bang migration has no downtime, but this is not the case for every project.

Trickle Migration takes a step-by-step approach to data migration. Instead of completing the entire event in a short amount of time, Trickle migration operates the old and new systems in parallel, and data is migrated step by step. This method essentially provides zero downtime that critical 24/7 applications need [8]. Migration can be implemented with a real-time process to move data, and this process can also be used to maintain data and bypass future changes in the target system. Adopting the Jet approach adds complexity to the design as it should be possible to track what data has been migrated. In the context of system migration, this can also mean that the source and target systems run in parallel and users have to switch between the two, depending on where they need the information they need. Alternatively, the old system may continue to function until all migrations are complete before the user switches to the new system. In this case, changes to the data in the source system should cause the associated data records to be migrated again so that the target is updated correctly [5].

3 Methodology

The methodology used is the commonly known waterfall model (Fig. 1) where it is broken down into 5 phases. Not only the model is easy to understand but it also provides a better way to present a documentation of a project development. For a data migration project, this is the best model to reflect the details and explanation of each process that have been taken throughout the project.

3.1 Planning

In the first phase, we must define what is possible in theory and reasonable approach to solve the problem. From the organization perspective they cannot afford to spend high budget on data because it is not their core business. Therefore, we turn into open-source software to help with the data migration. Not only it will speed up the process, but also help us to monitor the database. But it is not only the case, open-source software usually has locked content for free users where the tools provided is limited, thus we must come up with other way to fill in the weaknesses. Data migration projects needs to be executed carefully by prioritizing the required data to run the system effectively. Considering the best software to use is also one of the factors for a successful data migration.

3.2 Analysis

The purpose of the analysis phase of a data migration project is to identify the source data to be extracted from the source system and then modify it so that the subject or data type fits the new system and is loaded into the new system. In a data migration project, analysts

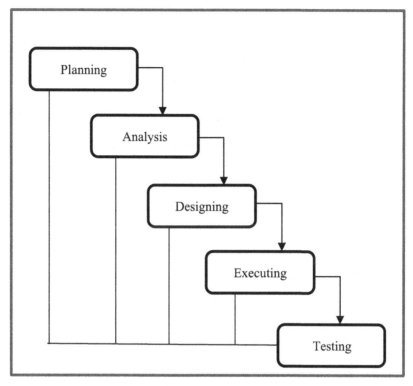

Fig. 1. Waterfall model

identify the mappings between source and target data models at a conceptual level using informal textual descriptions for the ETL process where it must be correctly stated on which data that needs to undergo the process [9]. At this stage we need to consider whether the data quality is good or not. The most common solution is to migrate the source data to a new platform whose data structure is identical to that of the source system. This allowed us to shut down old systems and issue new ones with confidence and without losing historical data [6]. Moreover, it provides clear visibility and access to all data issues with the ability to investigate anomalies at any required depth. In addition, inconsistencies regarding the scope of the data to be migrated are eliminated and their impact on the overall migration project assessed. Therefore, the best strategies to use is the trickle migration where it meets all the criteria for the project.

3.3 Designing

The flow process is shown in Fig. 2. The process starts with extracting data from old AKK System's Database and map the schema with the new database schema before executing the data migration. Unsuccessful migrations can lead to inaccurate data containing redundancy and unknowns. This can happen even if the output is fully usable and adequate. In addition, any existing problems in the data source can be amplified

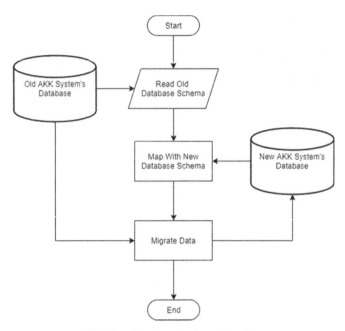

Fig. 2. Flowchart for data migration

when incorporated into new and more complex systems. Common data migration strategies prevent low-level experiences that end up creating more problems than they solve. Incomplete design can lead to a complete failure of the migration project (Fig. 3).

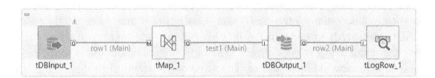

Fig. 3. Talend open studio models for failure

In the next step, is to create models using Talend Open studio (TOS) workspace. Chosen components will determine how the product looks after running the job. 'tDBInput_1' reads the database and retrieves fields based on the query [7]. It executes queries against the database in a strictly defined order which must correspond to the schema definition. The "row1(Main)" link then takes you to the list of fields for the next component. Next, 'tMap_1' is an advanced component that is integrated in addition to the TOS. It converts and routes data from one or more sources to one or more destinations where in this case it is linked via 'test1(Main)'. 'tDBOutput_1' writes, updates, makes changes or suppress database entries. It takes the specified action for the data in the table, based on the flow incoming from the preceding component in the Job where it linked via 'row2(Main)'. Finally, 'tLogRow_1' Displays data or results in the run console and is used to monitor data processed.

3.4 Executing

Once the model has been created, data is extracted from the source system, modified, prepared, and loaded to the target system according to the migration rules. At basic run tab, there is a route run button and clicking it will execute the job according to prior setting. the console show progress in implementation. The log contains each error message as well as the start and end messages. It also shows the output for the operation if the tLogRow component is used in the job design. Talend Open Studio offers a variety of information functions that are displayed while running the framework, such as statistics and tracks, which make monitoring and debugging easier (Fig. 4).

Fig. 4. Job execution

3.5 Testing

Finally, the testing phase requires the model to be tested to see the quality and integrity of the migrated data. The test will be performed on a platform that has similar setting to the actual system's database to increase the rate of success, especially when implement it on a live system (Fig. 5).

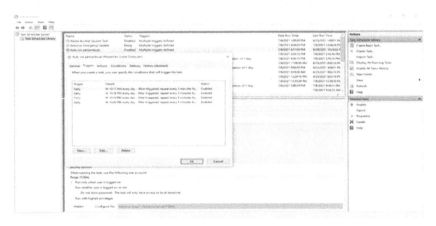

Fig. 5. Windows task scheduler

If the test is successful with no errors or anomalies, the next step is to create a standalone job where it can automate and execute the job on a schedule. This can be done with the help of Windows Task Scheduler. The actual system needs to be updated every 1 min but the task scheduler can only run the job at every 5-min time intervals. This can be solved by navigating to triggers tab and create 4 triggers where each one of it is set 1 min late than their predecessor. After 1 min the first trigger ran the job, the second trigger will run the job again and the cycle continues where it will loop back at the first trigger after 5 min. Therefore, the scheduler can by past the 5-min minimum limit.

4   Result and Discussion

According to the phases stated in the methodology section, every finding is recorded and explained in this section.

4.1 Effectiveness of Using Trickle Migration

Throughout the experiment it is not as smooth as expected. Even if the theories behind the strategies match the main problem, there are other factors that also contribute to the success of the data migration. In this case, the data from the older system during their service is not well managed by the organization because of there are no employee who hold the position to overlook the qualities of the data gathered. Thus, creating more complication for the project. Therefore, we had to separate the usable data to avoid 'blanks and redundancies before executing the data migration. At the end, we had to do data preparation and validation first where the data is transmitted by batch to a newly database before it could be extracted into the new system to eliminate the uncertainty. From the experiment, we have observed the effectiveness of the Trickle Migration. It is as follows:

1. Zero downtime required.
2. Start old and new systems in parallel and transfer data in small steps.
3. If the single-phase phase fails, only this failed phase needs to be rolled back and repeated the process again.

4.2   Talend Open Studio and Automation Performance

After finishing the testing phase, we find that TOS software is capable to solve most of the problem besides capable to adept with any data migration strategies. It offers not only tools such as cloud, big data, enterprise application integration, data quality, and master data management, but also a unified repository for storing and reusing Metadata. In addition, the Talend ETL tool improves the design efficiency of data migration jobs by setting and configuring them in a graphical interface where we can simply drag and drop the necessary component.

Fig. 6. Talend open studio output

Figure 6 is the output when the job is executed for the first time on a similarly structured of the new system database. This is considered a success when it can extract data from other database then transform the data to match the destination database and lastly load it to the destination database. When new data are inserted or updated, the destination database also updates at the same time. Next, there are no noticeable anomalies, blank space, or redundancy after the job is complete.

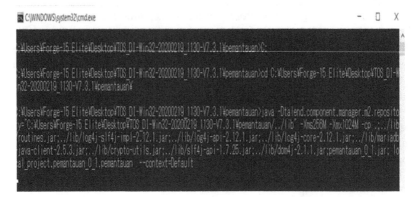

Fig. 7. Window command prompt automatically execute data migration

Figure 7 is the windows command that pop up every 1 min after the job is executed. The finished design in TOS is converted into.bash file format where it can be executed like a normal application. To automate the execution of the file, window task schedular was used and the result is similar to our main objective.

5   Conclusion

In conclusion, data migration can improve an organization performance and deliver advantages in their industry. In terms of efficiency, it is far better than transferring the data manually when technology can do the labor of data migration automatically. Generally, to move all the foundation data structures in the source system to the new system is time consuming where the plan needs to be laid out carefully to get the best result. At some point in the future, there is a high chance for organizations that use IT system will need to transfer a huge set of data from one platform to another. Therefore, it is a mistake if data migration simply considered as part of a larger project. Some organization might be convinced to handle it by themselves, but this can lead to decreased efficiency and increased costs down the road. If an organization is planning to migrate large sets of data, it's essential to do research on the best practices for a successful data migration.

Even with the right data migration tools, the migration process can be long and arduous. By educating oneself on the why and how of the process, it will help deciding what type of data migration the organization needs to undergo. Having a reliable team of experienced employees and consultants can help an organization ensure this process goes smoothly.

References

1. Lelii, S., Hefner, K.: What is data migration? - definition from whatis.com. SearchStorage 28 April 2017. https://searchstorage.techtarget.com/definition/data-migration
2. Data migration: Strategy and best practices - talend. Talend Real-Time Open-Source Data Integration Software, 2 October 2020. https://www.talend.com/resources/understanding-data-migration-strategies-best-practices/

3. NetApp. What is data migration? – how to plan a data migration. NetApp, 1 January 1 1970. https://www.netapp.com/knowledge-center/what-is-data-migration/
4. CloverDX. (n.d.). Data migration. CloverDX. https://www.cloverdx.com/explore/data-migrat ion#:~:text=A%20'big%20bang'%20data%20migration,single%20'big%20bang'%20event.
5. Oracle Successful Data Migration, October 2011. https://www.oracle.com/technetwork/mid dleware/oedq/successful-data-migration-wp-1555708.pdf
6. Joseph, R.H.: An Overview of Data Migration Methodology. An overview of data migration methodology, April 1998. https://dulcian.com/articles/overview_data_migration_method ology.htm
7. Talend Open Studio Components Reference Guide. Welcome to Talend help center. (n.d.). https://help.talend.com/reader/hCrOzogIwKfuR3mPf~LydA/_KmjKFtYUBb9Wd_P~whPcg
8. Nyeint, K.A., Soe, K.M.: Database migration based on trickle migrations approach. Natl J. Parallel Soft Comput. 81–86, (2019)
9. Yeddula, R.R., Das, P., Reddy, S.: A model-driven approach to enterprise data migration. In: Zdravkovic, J., Kirikova, M., Johannesson, P. (eds.) CAiSE 2015. LNCS, vol. 9097, pp. 230–243. Springer, Cham (2015). https://doi.org/10.1007/978-3-319-19069-3_15

Engineering and Digital Innovation

Mudahnya BM: A Context-Aware Mobile Cloud Learning Application Using Semantic-Based Approach

Sufri Muhammad(✉) 📵, Novia Admodisastro📵, Hafeez Osman📵,
and Norhayati Mohd Ali📵

Faculty of Computer Science and Information Technology, Department of Software Engineering
and Information System, Universiti Putra Malaysia, 43400 Seri Kembangan, Selangor, Malaysia
sufry@upm.edu.my

Abstract. A great potential of various learning environment in mobile learning application can clearly be seen in current pandemic situation. The accessibility of the learning resources needs to be available from anywhere anytime despite having strong or poor internet connection. It has motivated researchers to imply context-aware capability in improving the accessibility of the learning resources. This paper presents a development process of *Mudahnya BM* mobile application that follows a fundamental concept of Mobile Cloud Learning (MCL). *Mudahnya BM* is an application to learn basic Malay language for learner 7–12 years old. The injection of extrinsic and intrinsic context-aware help the application to improve the reasoning process for finding available learning resources from service providers. Semantic-based approach is applied in the reasoning process. This study involved the end users for evaluation purposes. 33 randomized scenarios have been tested using One-Sample Wilcoxon Signed Rank test. The result shows a positive impact to the population.

Keywords: Context-aware · Mobile cloud learning · Semantic-based approach

1 Introduction

The evolution of education paradigm is based on the evolution of technology. Numbers of mobile applications are developed in accordance with the needs of users. Mobile application needs to serve their content to users by integrating with service providers. This integration helps in diversification of mobile application which will be beneficial to many users through academic, health, work, or online learning activities.

MCL is one of the examples of Service-Based Application (SBA) that has a composition of services in a single application [1]. MCL application is substantial in providing a suitable learning contents where the system itself can track the learner's performance real-time based on the status of learner activities. To ensure that each user receive a correct learning resources, this is where context awareness is considered.

The usage of context aware in MCL has enable the application to aware with the changes of the contextual information such as internet connectivity, device configuration

© Springer Nature Switzerland AG 2021
H. Badioze Zaman et al. (Eds.): IVIC 2021, LNCS 13051, pp. 227–238, 2021.
https://doi.org/10.1007/978-3-030-90235-3_20

status, learner's input, and activities as well as the Quality of Services (QoS). This contextual information needs semantic representation to facilitate in reasoning process [2]. Semantic-based approach has been used in various domain as it has the great potential and ability to provide a meaningful and formal representation of the context as well as the services.

Thus, this resulted in our motivation to devise a context-aware mobile cloud learning application using semantic-based approach. Section 2 presents the background study. Followed by Sect. 3 which discussed the related works. Section 4 shows the design and development processes of *Mudahnya BM*. Section 5 presents the evaluation. While Sect. 6 will conclude the study.

2 Background Study

In general, this section explained on Mobile Cloud Learning (MCL), Context-Aware and Semantic-Based Approach.

2.1 Mobile Cloud Learning (MCL)

Mobile cloud learning term is used when two platforms which are mobile application and cloud computing integrate with each other in education environment [3, 4]. This integration is achieved through network connection. Mobile application will requestion the educational resources from service provider via middleware. In this case, service provider is located in the cloud computing and middleware will be the network bridge between frond-end and back-end.

MCL consists of four main recursive components. Learning, Assessment, Analysis and Feedback are basics components that need to be included in MCL application [3, 5]. The first component in MCL recursive model is the Learning. Learners may access learning resources using their mobile devices which connected to cloud computing. Since learners could be different in their learning preferences from one another, learning resources are delivered to the learners' mobile application based on their current contextual information. Learning component helps learners to prepare themselves by studying the learning materials to make them feel confident during the assessment process.

The second component is the Assessment. Assessment is one of the most important components in MCL. Learners' performance will be analyzed based on the result of the assessment. Learners may self-assess their knowledge level by answering online multiple-choice questions (MCQs) or online quizzes in the subject matter.

Analysis is the third component of MCL model. It comprises statistical analysis of learners learning outcome which is helpful in tracking their learning process. Learners may view their performance based on their assessments result. Their score and their feedbacks are used to develop learning strategy. This strategy is helpful to identify learners' path and their learning contents.

The fourth component is the Feedback. Learners may provide their opinions or recommendations on each of the assessment items or complexity of the learning materials. These feedbacks will be useful for critical analysis on learners' performance which will then be rectified and identified to promote better services in the future. Thus, good quality learning resources will beneficial a larger number of MCL users.

2.2 Context-Aware System

Context can be defined as "… any information that can be used to characterize the current situation on an entity. Entity can be in the form of object, person or place that associate between the system or application" [6]. Contextual information can be further classified into two types which are extrinsic and intrinsic.

External contextual information or extrinsic is normally be acquired using sensor such as sound, light, location, touch, temperature, and others. While intrinsic is the internal contextual information that acquired within the learner prospect such as learner goal, their knowledge background, emotional state, input and interaction, their activities, and others relevant contexts [7].

These two types of contexts can either be static or dynamic. Contextual information can be classified into static of the value of the context does not change over time such as central processing unit (CPU) specification and other. Whereas dynamic context is the context can be changed over time such as status of battery level, network connection strength, date, and time and other.

Thus, the application of contextual information in MCL helps to provide a personalized learning resources to the learners. By leveraging context-aware, it helps MCL become more flexible and allows for adjustments depending on the learners' needs.

2.3 Semantic-Based Approach

There are many approaches offered by current technology to represent contextual information and services (learning resources). One of the promising approaches that broadly used is semantic-based approach. It is implicit approach that semantically provided a comprehensive representation and description of the service and context to support reasoning process during runtime.

Semantic-based approach comprises of six different techniques: Model Driven, Code-Level, Message Interception, Middleware, Rule-Based and Ontology-Based Solution [8, 9]. Based on the hierarchical concept in Fig. 1, ontology-based solution is used to shows the association between the learner and respective contextual information that involved this British Education Ontology [10]. The context as in the figure is categorized into learner and mobile context. Mobile context represents the learning environment and device configuration status, while learning context represents the objective of the learning.

The combination of these techniques can provide better formal representation and expressiveness of the service and contextual information to support reasoning process. Thus, next section will discuss on several research in context aware of MCL that combined these different techniques.

3 Related Works

Some works have introduced extrinsic and intrinsic contextual information in performing adaptation process such as user's location, user's profile, preferred language, device configuration, user's goals, interaction, or time. It is important to mention that most of

Fig. 1. MCL ontology

these works are followed a fundamental concept of dynamic service adaptation process and MCL recursive model. Ten research in the dynamic service adaptation in context-aware systems using semantic-based approaches were reviewed. The studies are Units of Learning mobile Player (UoLmP) [11], Mobile Semantic Web Assessment Personalization (MobiSWAP) [12], Ubiquitous Learning Framework (ULF) [13], Mobile Response System (MRS) [14], and Web-Based Learning Platform (WLP) [15], Dynamic Adaptation in Context-Aware Mobile Cloud Learning (DACAMoL) [16], Hybrid Recommender System (HRS) [17], Interactive Video-Based M-Learning System (IVB-MLS) [18], Dynamic Mobile Adaptive Learning Content and Format (D-MALCOF) [19] and Context-Aware Mobile Learning System (CAMLS) [20]. The following paragraphs describes all the related works in detail.

UoLmP [11] system is semi-auto adaptation that facilitates students to find available facilitators according to the facilitators' expertise and availability based on input inserted by the students. Adaptability and personalization in mobile learning are referred to the process of fitting the system's functionalities and behavior correspond to the educational goals, location, and movement of the users and well as their learning style [21]. Model-driven approach is used for context modeling that consists of five dimensions which are information, place, artefact, time, and physical condition [22]. Adaptation rules (if/then/else) are considered according to the learner's mobile context dimensions. Apart from that, adaptation algorithms are derived and used such as similarity algorithm, heuristic algorithm, and decision-based algorithm which are processes according to the learner's context dimensions.

MobiSWAP [12] is a mobile application that used semantic-based approach to perform the adaptation process. Contextual information is varied depending on the learner's need in mobile assessment situation. Different learners have their own abilities, profiles, and needs. The framework is divided into three layers which are mobile assessment context layer, semantic layer, and assessment resources layer. The contextual information is acquired from the front layer which is mobile context assessment context layer. The dynamic service adaptation takes places within the middleware layer which is semantic layer. The discovery, ranking, and selection of the services are explicitly stated.

Whereas assessment resources layer is responsible for managing the ontologies, rules, and services.

ULF [13] is developed using selected pedagogical strategies for designing personalized learning path. The framework consists of Adaptation Layer, Adaptation layer, and Personal Data Locker (PDL). Presentation layer is responsible to support the understanding the content of PDL reasoning process. Adaptation Layer comprises of rules for selecting both concept and content for learning path. Learning goals integrated with domain ontology are for sharing knowledge purposes.

MRS [14] facilitates in-class interactive problem solving using mobile devices. MRS is designed as a three-tier architecture. MRS client would gather as much contextual information from the user side as possible such as device's battery level and internet connection. Whereas cloud IaaS (Infrastructure as a Service) is used as a middleware to facilitate dynamic service adaptation that act as a broker between the clients and the server. IaaS is used to minimize the instructor's workload. Thus, it helps students to have transparent access and enables the system to be extensible to any disciplines. This system automatically prompts the students' devices to do exercises that synchronize with lecturers' materials. Hence, students will actively interact by providing feedback, question, or vote to existing pool to lecturer since MRS supports anonymous communication and MRS also provides analysis on students' performance.

WLP [15] adapts learning contents according to the learner's contexts. WLP acquire their contextual information from web-based application and mobile-based application. The dynamic service adaptation is operated within the web server. Rule-based approach for content adaptation is performed based on two parameters which are (i) context awareness such as user maturity, device configuration, and cognitive load of the learner, and (ii) content adaptation such as network, device, and resource adaptation.

DACAMoL [16] is a framework developed for MCL environment that provides personalized learning resources to the learner's according to device context and learner context such as network status, device battery level, learner's input, and learner's profile. These contexts help in reasoning process to provide correct and effective services to the learner. Ontology-based and rule-based approaches are used in the framework via Semantic Web Ontology Language (OWLS) technology.

HRS [17] adapts it learning contents according to learner's contextual information such as learning goals, knowledge level and sequential access patterns. Hybrid approach using sequential pattern mining (SPM) and CF algorithm help to improve the reasoning process. Contextual information and services are represented using model driven approach as well as ontology-based solution. HRS provides self-adaptation process help to improve the QoS and accuracy of the service substitution.

IVB-MLS [18] implies a self-adaptive smart learning environment that provides streaming video as well as prerecorded lecture session to the students. The video is served to the students according to mobile device contexts as well as students' contexts such as network transmission, mobile device type, learners' profile as well as learners' activity. The framework used the combination of approaches which are code level, message interception and model driven. Real-Time Transport Protocol (RTP) technology is used in the system.

D-MALCOF [19] is a mobile learning system that facilitates students to improve their learning skills. This framework can detect knowledge level of the learner, learner's profile, and their learning style through different sensors. Hence, the system will provide a suitable learning style to respective students according to their contextual information. Model driven approach, middleware and rule-based solution has been used for the reasoning process via Simple Object Access Protocol (SOAP) technology.

CAMLS [20] is a mobile learning system provide a comprehensive system to the students and lecturers to keep updating about current state of the system that they used. Thus, they will be aware about what is happening during the interactions. Users can have full control over the system which helps to motivate users in teaching and learning aspect. Contextual information such as learner profile, their activity and disabilities are acquired to provide real time services via augmented reality environment.

Based on these findings, to develop context aware MCL application, self-automation is substantial as it will remove the interruption while learner uses the application. It also enables the application to continuously monitor the context changes during run-time and provide correct learning resources to the learner. Whereas the semantic-based approach should be combined within the technique for better service and context representation.

4   Design and Development

Developing a mobile application must follows fundamental knowledge of the chosen domain. MCL recursive model is the main guideline for developing *Mudahnya BM* mobile application. Figure 2 shows the low-level UML component diagram of the application. Three main components involved are the device or mobile application itself, web server and service provider.

Users interact with the application via the device component. Six different component that integrate with the users are Learning, Assessment, Feedback, Performance, QoS and DeviceStatus. Each of these components required the input from the sensor or user and provide their output to the web server as a reasoning mechanism.

This is where extrinsic and intrinsic contexts are acquired such as (Extrinsic: network status, device battery status) and (Intrinsic: learner profile, learner input, QoS). Since *Mudahnya BM* is a real-time application, the contextual information will change over time.

The contextual information is then passed to the web server component in the web server via Hypertext Transfer Protocol (HTTP) request using Representational State Transfer (RESTful) web service. DACAMoL web service will become as a controller that transform the context using ontology semantically. Rule-based techniques is also used to discover the available learning resources from service provider.

DACAMoL web service will discover the available services from service provider. Service provider will bind their service when the request meet the equivalence service that they have. There are three main services stored in service provider which are: (1: Service with image, 2: Service with grey out image, 3: Service without image).

These three services will be served according to the contextual information. Based on the list of rules in Table 1, the three main rules are; Rule 1 (i.e. service discovery rule), Rule 2 (i.e. service ranking rule), Rule 3 (i.e. service binding rule).

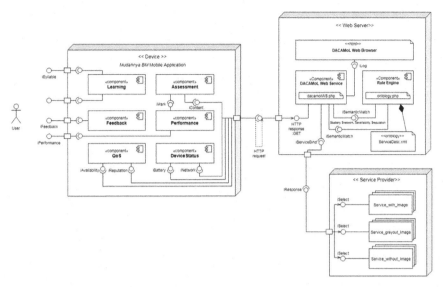

Fig. 2. Low-level component diagram of *Mudahnya BM*

As stated in Rule 1.3 and Rule 1.4b from Table 1, network status is categorized into two different scales which are poor and strong. Network is considered as poor if it is 66 kilobits per second (Kbps) and below. Higher than this value is considered as strong network. Whereas battery level is considered as low if the value is 49% and below [23].

As for selecting the services, availability is the higher priority ranking where the services should be in available state that score 98% or higher. Reputation on the other hand is defined as a rating of the service from user in a specific period which is an important factor for users to select the best service among many services. Scores of 1, 2 and 3 is considered low while 4 and 5 is considered as high score.

The screenshot of the application is shown in Fig. 3. The screenshot is captured from assessment module where it comprises of three different level. Figure 3 shows the lowest level which is level 1.

Learner needs to answer what would be the small letter for the question. For example, learner needs to find what will be the small letter for capital B. There user interface will be based on the context changes. If the network connection is strong, device battery level is optimum, QoS is high, thus learner will receive color image. If some of the contexts are not in the optimum value, grey out image will be provided. If each context is in its lowest value, only textual information will be displayed.

5 The Evaluation

The objective of this evaluation is to measure the correctness of the chosen learning resources based on the context changes and QoS. The correct application is correct if it exhibits the correct services for all correct scenarios. Thus, the correctness of *Mudahnya BM* is based on the number of correct scenarios which must correct more than 32 scenarios out of 33 scenarios. This is because 32 is represent 95% of the population.

Table. 1. List of rules

Rule	Description
Rule 1: Service Discovery	Rule 1 uses to discover available services based on context changes from learner or device such as learner's age, mark, network status, or battery level.
Rule 1.1	Age = 7, 8, 9,10, 11, 12 If Age = 7 | 8 | 9 | 10 | 11 | 12 Then Service = [Learning_Resources]
Rule 1.2	Mark = 0 to 100 If $0 \leq$ Mark ≤ 100 Then Service = [Assessment Level 1] else if $80 \leq$ Mark Level 1≤ 100 Then Service = [Assessment Level 1, Level 2] else if $80 \leq$ Mark Level 2≤ 100 Then Service = [Assessment Level 1, Level 2, Level 3]
Rule 1.3	Network = strong connection or poor connection If Network_strong ≥ 67 Kbps Then Service = [Assessment Level 1, Level 2, Level 3 with color image] else If Network_poor ≤ 66 Kbps Then Service = [Assessment Level 1, Level 2, Level 3 greyed out image/ textual]
Rule 1.4	Rule related to battery level of the device
Rule 1.4a	int contextValue = getContext (LowContext) if X == contextValue(true) { HighContext = convertContext} Return HighContext
Rule 1.4b	If HighContext $\geq 50\%$ Then Service = [Assessment Level 1, Level 2, Level 3 with color image] else Then Service = [Assessment Level 1, Level 2, Level 3 greyed out image/ textual]
Rule 2: Service Rank	Rule 2 uses to rank the service from service candidate according to QoS values

Rule 2.1	If (QoSValue_Availability $\geq 98\%$) && ($4 \leq$ QoSValue_Reputation ≤ 5)
	Then Service = [Assessment Level 1, Level 2, Level 3 with color image]
	else
	Then Service = [Assessment Level 1, Level 2, Level 3 greyed out image/ textual]

Rule 3: Service Binding	Rule 3 uses to enact the adaptation
Rule 3.1	If Rule2.1 success Then Service = [Assessment Level 1, Level 2, Level 3]

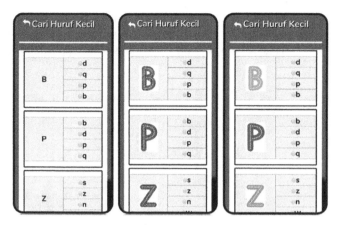

Fig. 3. Screenshot of *Mudahnya BM*

The 33 scenarios are separated into six subcategories. These subcategories have been clearly justified which are based on the probability that might arise during runtime such as the combination between high battery level ($\geq$50%), high internet network ($\geq$67 Kbps), high QoS in availability ($\geq$98%), high QoS in service reputation ($\geq$4). These data can be varied among participant in term of their context changes. Sometimes the battery level can be low, but the internet connection is high, and they might be charging their phone or unplugged the charger. We have simulated these scenarios to cover each 33 scenarios during runtime since it is impossible to control the battery level and the internet network connection.

After the pilot study was approved by the expert reviewers, the experiment with real participants was conducted. This evaluation is a Quasi-experiment where we prior selected 30 Software Engineering third years' students from Universiti Putra Malaysia. They should be skilled in SOA, service adaptation and able to understand Malay language since *Mudahnya* BM mobile application is in Malay language. They must own an Android-based mobile device, or they will be provided with a device if they do not own any device for the purpose of this evaluation. Next, they must install *Mudahnya* BM mobile application in their mobile devices. The participants need to run the application and monitor from time to time and answer the checklist according to the stated scenarios.

Based on the result from 30 participants (N = 30), they managed to score 30 and above. 80% of participant manage to get all correct scenarios which are 24 participants. While five participants only received 32 correct scenarios which is 17%. At least only one participant received 31 correct scenarios which is 3%.

Two hypotheses are deduced prior the evaluation which are: -

1: *Null Hypothesis (H_0): m $\leq$ 32*
2: *Alternative Hypothesis (H_1): m > 32*
    m = median

Since the median of this evaluation is 33, the null hypothesis can be rejected Since Shapiro-Wilk normality test is less than 0.05, a further statistical test which is Wilcoxon Signed Rank test is conducted to verify the correctness of the application.

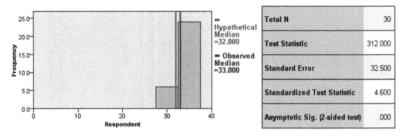

Fig. 4. Wilcoxon signed rank test result

Based on the result from Fig. 4, 4.600 Standardized Test Statistic resulting 0.00 for the p-value of Asymptotic Sig (2-sided test). The bar graph illustrates the observed median which is 33 is higher than the hypothetical median; 32 value that priorly been set up. Null hypothesis can be rejected since m $\leq$ 32. The objective of the study achieved.

6 Conclusion

This paper has presented a study on context-aware mobile cloud learning using semantic based approach. A mobile application called Mudahnya BM is developed based on the background study of related works and follows fundamental concept of MCL. The correctness of the adapted learning resources is verified based on the evaluation within the end user. To conclude, a specific contextual information might affect the correctness of the application which will promote better learning experience to the users. As for the future work, different contextual information might be considered as well as different approach such as machine learning might me combined with the current method which is semantic-based approach.

Acknowledgement. Thank you to Faculty of Computer Science and Information Technology, Universiti Putra Malaysia (UPM) for the financial support.

References

1. Muhammad, S., Admodisastro, N., Osman, H., Ali, N.M.: The dynamic web services adaptation framework in context-aware mobile cloud learning using semantic-based method. Int. J. Eng. Adv. Technol. **9**(1), 2353–2357 (2019). https://doi.org/10.35940/ijeat.A2652.109119
2. Papazoglou, M., Parkin, M., Pohl, K., Metzger, A.: Service Research Challenges and Solutions for the Future Internet (2010)

3. Gurung, R.K., Alsadoon, A., Prasad, P.W.C., Elchouemi, A.: Impacts of mobile cloud learning (MCL) on blended flexible learning (BFL). In: IDT 2016 - Proceedings of the International Conference on Information and Digital Technologies 2016, pp. 108–114 (2016). https://doi.org/10.1109/DT.2016.7557158

4. Wang, M., Chen, Y., Jahanzaib Khan, M.: Mobile cloud learning for higher education: a case study of moodle in the cloud. J. Educ. Pract. **7**, 6 (2016)

5. Muhammad, S., et al.: The correctness of service in runtime adaptation for context-aware mobile cloud learning. Turkish J. Comput. Math. Educ. **12**(3), 2236–2241 (2021). https://doi.org/10.17762/turcomat.v12i3.1173

6. Abowd, G.D., Dey, A.K., Brown, P.J., Davies, N., Smith, M., Steggles, P.: Towards a better understanding of context and context-awareness. In: Gellersen, H.-W. (ed.) HUC 1999. LNCS, vol. 1707, pp. 304–307. Springer, Heidelberg (1999). https://doi.org/10.1007/3-540-48157-5_29

7. Mizouni, R., Matar, M.A., Al Mahmoud, Z., Alzahmi, S., Salah, A.: A framework for context-aware self-adaptive mobile applications SPL. Expert Syst. Appl. **41**(16), 7549–7564 (2014). https://doi.org/10.1016/j.eswa.2014.05.049

8. Guermah, H., Fissaa, T., Hafiddi, H., Nassar, M., Kriouile, A.: A semantic approach for service adaptation in context-aware environment. Procedia Comput. Sci. **34**, 587–592 (2014). https://doi.org/10.1016/j.procs.2014.07.077

9. Peinado, S., Ortiz, G., Dodero, J.M.: A metamodel and taxonomy to facilitate context-aware service adaptation. Comput. Electr. Eng. **44**, 262–279 (2015). https://doi.org/10.1016/j.compeleceng.2015.02.004

10. Casals, A., Paulo, S., Alves Franco Brandão, A.: Modeling a mobile learning context data ontology. IEEE World Engineering Education Conference (EDUNINE) (2017)

11. Gomez, S., Zervas, P., Sampson, D.G., Fabregat, R.: Context-aware adaptive and personalized mobile learning delivery supported by UoLmP. J. King Saud Univ. Comput. Inf. Sci. **26**(1), 47–61 (2014). https://doi.org/10.1016/j.jksuci.2013.10.008

12. Harchay, A., Cheniti-Belcadhi, L., Braham, R.: A context-aware approach for personalized mobile self-assessment. J. Univers. Comput. Sci. **21**(8), 1061–1085 (2015)

13. Karoudis, K., Magoulas, G.: Ubiquitous learning architecture to enable learning path design across the cumulative learning continuum. Informatics **3**(4), 19 (2016). https://doi.org/10.3390/informatics3040019

14. Fuad, M.M., Deb, D.: Cloud-enabled hybrid architecture for in-class interactive learning using mobile device. In: 5th IEEE International Conference on Mobile Cloud Computing, Services, and Engineering (MobileCloud), pp. 0–3 (2017). https://doi.org/10.1109/MobileCloud.2017.15.

15. Curum, B., Chellapermal, N., Kumar, K.: A context-aware mobile learning system using dynamic content adaptation for personalized learning. Emerg. Trends Electr. Electron. Commun. Eng. **416**(1), 379–384 (2017). https://doi.org/10.1007/978-3-319-52171-8.

16. Muhammad, S., Admodisastro, N., Osman, H., Ali, N.M.: Dynamic service adaptation framework for context aware mobile cloud learning using semantic-based approach. Int. J. Eng. Technol. **7**(4.31), 182–190 (2018)

17. Tarus, J.K., Niu, Z., Kalui, D.: A hybrid recommender system for e-learning based on context awareness and sequential pattern mining. Soft. Comput. **22**(8), 2449–2461 (2017). https://doi.org/10.1007/s00500-017-2720-6

18. Pal, S., Pramanik, P.K.D., Choudhury, P.: A step towards smart learning: designing an interactive video-based m-learning system for educational institutes. Int. J. Web Based Learn. Teach. Technol. **14**(4), 26–48 (2019). https://doi.org/10.4018/IJWLTT.2019100102

19. Ennouamani, S., Mahani, Z., Akharraz, L.: A context-aware mobile learning system for adapting learning content and format of presentation: design, validation and evaluation. Educ. Inf. Technol. **25**(5), 3919–3955 (2020). https://doi.org/10.1007/s10639-020-10149-9

20. Pensabe-Rodriguez, A., Lopez-Dominguez, E., Hernandez-Velazquez, Y., Dominguez-Isidro, S., De-la-Calleja, J.: Context-aware mobile learning system: usability assessment based on a field study Telemat. Inform. **48,** 101346 (2020). https://doi.org/10.1016/j.tele.2020.101346

21. Wu, G., Li, J., Feng, L., Wang, K.: Identifying potentially important concepts and relations in an ontology. In: Sheth, A. et al. (eds.) ISWC 2008. LNCS, vol. 5318, pp. 33–49. Springer, Heidelberg (2008). https://doi.org/10.1007/978-3-540-88564-1_3

22. Mohamed, R., Perumah, T., Sulaiman, M.N., Mustapha, N.: Multi-resident activity recognition using label combination approach in smart home environment. In: IEEE International Symposium on Consumer Electronics (ISCE), pp. 69–71 (2017)

23. Benlamri, R., Zhang, X.: Context-aware recommender for mobile learners. HCIS **4**(1), 1–34 (2014). https://doi.org/10.1186/s13673-014-0012-z

Software Redocumentation Using Distributed Data Processing Technique to Support Program Understanding for Legacy System: A Proposed Approach

Sugumaran Nallusamy[1](✉) , Hoo Meei Hao[1](✉) ,
and Farizuwana Akma Zulkifle[2](✉)

[1] Universiti Tunku Abdul Rahman, Sungai Long Campus, Jalan Sungai Long,
Bandar Sungai Long, 43000 Kajang, Selangor, Malaysia
{sugumaran,hoomh}@utar.edu.my
[2] Universiti Teknologi MARA, Kuala Pilah Campus, 72000 Shah Alam,
Negeri Sembilan, Malaysia
farizuwana@uitm.edu.my

Abstract. Source code is the most updated source among all the available software artifacts. The majority of existing software redocumentation approaches relied on source code to extract the necessary information for program comprehension in order to support software maintenance tasks. However, performing Extract, Transform and Load (ETL) using a parser from the source code becoming a challenging task. The traditional approach is no longer able to handle the ETL efficiently due to the effect of the analysis efficiency, especially for large source code. This paper proposed to use distributed data processing technique to extract legacy source code components to generate detailed designed or technical software documentation at source code level to support program understanding. The objective of this paper is to apply the distributed data processing technique to the parser by using Hadoop Distributed File System and Apache Spark. Legacy java source code used as a case study to apply our proposed approach to extract the source code components and generate the technical software documentation.

Keywords: Software redocumentation · HDFS · Spark · Legacy system · Program understanding · Software maintenance

1 Introduction

Industry practitioners perceived legacy systems as business critical and reliable system operated for more than ten to twenty years, but inflexible to adapt to new changes [1]. In respect of legacy system modernization, lacking of knowledge [2] and high maintenance cost [3] are the main drivers [1]. Similarly, it is a challenge for software developers to maintain and support the legacy systems due to lacking the latest documentation and increasing complexity of source codes as times are passing. Thus, software redocumentation is essential to rebuild the documentation of existing resources in order to

© Springer Nature Switzerland AG 2021
H. Badioze Zaman et al. (Eds.): IVIC 2021, LNCS 13051, pp. 239–252, 2021.
https://doi.org/10.1007/978-3-030-90235-3_21

give a better understanding of the system for the purpose to generate documentation for the modified programs, update the system changes, and creating alternative views. The redocumentation process can be carried out at several stages of the software design process, such as source code, design, or requirement. However, according to a survey conducted by Souza et al. [4], source code level documentation is more relevant documentation or technical that may be classified as technical documentation or functional documentation to aid in program comprehension and maintenance tasks. As specified by Geet et al. [5], the technical document contains features such as a summary of the source code, source code metrics, forms, and method dependencies that are derived from current redocumentation tools [6].

The redocumentation process is comprised of five major components: source code, parser, system knowledge base, view composer, and software documentation [7]. We concentrated on the parser in this study because it is critical for extracting the necessary information to build the documentation. The present limitation of the existing parser is its inability to extract the pieces required for technical documentation from huge amounts of old source code. Existing parsers are embedded into software tools that place a premium on traditional extraction methods, which reduces the effectiveness of extracting pertinent information due to the enormous source code size. Additionally, retrieval should be performed in a timely manner in order to comprehend the program and assist with software maintenance tasks. The limitations of the parser in the redocumentation tool in terms of handling huge source code, the explosion of big data, and the evolution of data processing technologies all encourage the investigation of the proposed approach in the process of software redocumentation.

Analysing software systems and extracting source code components requires processing of source code and rebuild the structure of information. There are many existing studies related to different techniques used in extracting the data [8, 9]. Nevertheless, those approaches used Extract, Transform, Load (ETL) based on relational query approach unable to handle streaming or near real-time data and stimulating environment which demands high availability, low latency and scalability features [10]. Although the traditional ETL may prove to be effective in managing structured, batch-oriented data which, up to date and within scope for corporate insights and decision making [10, 11], it is not suitable for source code that consists of semi structured or unstructured data [12].

Thus, we proposed an approach to use Hadoop Distributed File System (HDFS) and Spark which provide a cluster computing model for distributed computing platforms intended to run the process of redocumentation. The proposed approach would assist software developers maintain the source code efficiently and effectively solving the problems of processing, analyzing and redocument the massive source codes.

This paper is organized as follows: The first section is a background of software redocumentation and related works that gives an overview of some studies and research carried out involved big data processing. In the methodology section, we describe the proposed approach of distributed data processing in software redocumentation. The Case Study section presents the initial work following the proposed approach. We end with a conclusion and give some future works to complete the process of redocumentation.

2 Background and Related Work

As defined in the IEEE Standard for Software Maintenance (IEEE 14764-2006-ISO/IEC), after development and delivery, software maintenance undergoes a similar process as in software development to modify the software product to correct faults, improve performance, or to adapt the product to the modified environment. Software maintenance aims to preserve the software product over time. Christa et al. [13] indicated that the legacy system is a contributor to maintenance cost, effort, and productivity. A significant challenge for software developers is taking over development work if the source code is the only source of understanding the written codes and system documentation is out-of-date, lacking, or incomplete. The software developer spent more time with existing code than creating new software. These are emphasized by [13].

Nallusamy et al. [7, 14] mentioned that software redocumentation is a software documentation update created within the same abstraction and in line with the latest developments of the code. Additionally, it includes analyzing a static representation of a software system to give a different perspective. Earlier studies examined software redocumentation to support software evolution and software maintenance. Essentially, re-documentation is intended to help developers comprehend programs [15, 16]. The results of a four-year long case study [17] demonstrate a significant decrease in maintenance costs and effort due to redocumentation effort. Methods and approaches to solve program understanding have attracted the software engineering community. Such development in this area can be seen from the studies on the category of redocumentation approaches comprise of XML based approach, incremental redocumentation, model-oriented redocumentation, island grammar, doclike modularized graph, ontology-based approach [7], and reverse engineering to transform the source code to UML diagrams such as [18–20].

Most evaluation studies of format, granularity, and efficiency showed that all approaches were of low quality when it came to granularity and efficiency [14]. Comparison of two approaches of incremental and model-oriented had shown different usage and purposes [21]. This approach works if outdated or missing documentation is an issue. Rebuild the documentation incrementally, while using a model-oriented approach will produce models from existing systems and generate documentation based on the models. As a result, model-oriented approach is best for redocumenting a legacy system from source code. In other words, effective and efficient software maintenance is necessary. Moreover, code analysis keeps evolving in terms of technique and application development.

As software becomes more complex over time, the number of lines of source code increases, particularly for huge legacy systems. The team has spent several years writing and maintaining these program codes. When new programmer takes over the maintenance job including change request, new programmer required an efficient tool to extract the software components from the source code which handle by the parser in the software redocumentation process. Current parsers in re-documentation tools may be incapable of handling this massive volume of data, as they were not designed for high-volume data processing [22].

As a result, the endeavor to leverage contemporary technology in the management of big legacy systems continues to evolve, as indicated by Wolfart et al. [23]. On the other hand, the work of Ruchir Puri et al. [24] emphasized the necessity of artificial intelligence in acquiring information from huge amounts of source code in order to assist software maintainers in performing maintenance activities. Verena Geist et al. [22] used machine learning to analyze source code comments. These studies focus the strategies used to circumvent the current difficulties connected with digesting large volumes of source code in order to comprehend and conduct software maintenance activities on time. Additionally, several of these investigations used cutting-edge data processing methods to redocument the source code. As a result of these investigations, we have begun to investigate data processing using distributed computing frameworks based on commodity cluster designs, such as Hadoop and Apache Spark. This approach is widely utilized in a variety of fields for the processing of large amounts of data and is constantly evolving [25]. Recent examples include processing and analyzing YouTube big data to determine the success of films and items in comparison to competitors [26] and analyzing airline delays using Spark [27].

Apache Spark is distributed computing system designed to run in a cluster, it is also fast and general purpose. Spark extends the MapReduce model of Hadoop to efficiently support more types of computations, including interactive queries and stream processing [28]. One of the main features Spark offers for speed is the ability to run computations in memory, but the system is also more efficient than MapReduce for complex applications running on disk. The core data units in Spark are called Resilient Distributed Datasets (RDDs). They are only read only collections which partitioned to multiple machines and can be rebuilt if the partitions are lost. RDDs are collections of elements that are distributed, immutable, and fault-tolerant. They can be produced by performing a series of actions on either stable storage data or other RDDs. RDDs can be stored in memory, on disk, or in a combination of the two storage media types. Furthermore, RDD is adopting the Lazy Evaluation approach in order to complete the action task. This is done in order to ensure that compute and memory are used as less as possible. As RDDs are not cached in RAM by default, a persist method is required when data is reused to avoid re-computation [27]. One of the advantages of the Spark environment is provide Application Programming Interface in Scala, Phyton and Java. Furthermore, Spark provides Spark Context as a master node and distributed to worker node through cluster manager. Spark allows to configure properties such as the number of executors, the number of cores per executor, and the amount of memory per executor for each application [29].

Hadoop Distributed File System (HDFS) a reliable and has scalable storage and processing system for a large volume of distributed unstructured data. On the other hand, Apache spark used to speed the processing power which is 100 times faster in memory and 10 times faster by running on disk. Thus, HDFS is an ideal technique to develop a highly scalable application that able to process massive data as compared to a traditional method such as database management systems [25]. As far as our knowledge goes until this paper is written, none of the study that using distributed data processing techniques in the field of software maintenance. This paper shows the approach of using HDFS and Spark environment to generate documentation to assist in software maintenance.

3 Proposed Approach

Our main contribution to the suggested solution is the development of a parser that is utilized to extract the source code component using HDFS and Apache Spark via a distributed data processing technique. As a result, the parser processes raw source code using a distribution strategy to accelerate the process of extracting source code components within the constraints of limited run times.

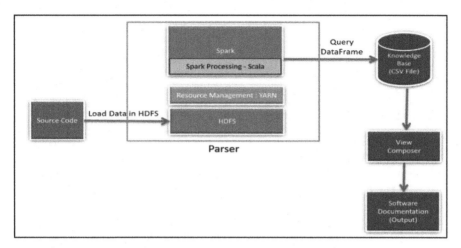

Fig. 1. Software redocumentation using distribution data technique

Figure 1 illustrates the system architecture for locating and generating source code components via the HDFS and Spark environments. Each component is thoroughly explained as follows:

3.1 Legacy Source Code (LSC)

A software work product or artefact consists of source code, configuration files, built scripts, and auxiliary artifacts [7, 30]. However, this study looked at only LSC during the redocumentation process [4]. SWPs were excluded for two main reasons. First, the most up-to-date or reliable source is the source code. SWPs contain greater precision when compared to other data sets. Second, SWPs are poorly maintained when compared to the source code [31]. Legacy systems undergo numerous changes. Additionally, these changes include numerous software maintainers, who must spend almost half of their time understanding the program's functionality versus their total time spent on maintenance. This problem affects the software maintenance efficiency.

3.2 Parser

The parser is used to extract necessary information from the SWP and store it in the repository. The proposed approach utilized HDFS for storing, processing, and analyzing the LSC across multiple nodes of commodity hardware. There will be a master node (Name Node) and a slave node (Data Node) [27]. A Name node distributes the works to data node at load time and blocks from the same file are all on different machines. When a data node is failed, it is replicated across multiple data nodes. Yarn acts as a distributed container for the master node's resources. Figure 2 shows how the source code is distributed across the network through the data nodes. Distributed computing has multiple advantages. It's scalable and makes it easier to share resources. It also speeds up computation tasks.

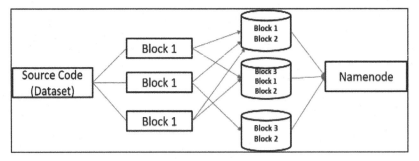

Fig. 2. Block replication of the source code dataset in Hadoop cluster

In our proposed context, Spark plays an important role as a parser [29], performing ETL from source code and providing source code components. Yarn is a distributed container manager, like Mesos for example, whereas Spark is a data processing tool. Spark can run on Yarn. We used Scala as the programming language and the Databricks Community Cloud (DCC) platform [32] to execute the Scala code, which includes a notebook (workspace) and a spark session. Figure 3 illustrates the Spark data processing flow in DCC:

Fig. 3. Spark data processing flow

3.3 Knowledge Based

A repository component is used in the software redocumentation knowledge based on the data process and produce documentation as defined by Nallusamy et al. [7]. It provides appropriate semi-structured data on source code for building documentation content as well as allowing browsing and searching for relevant content in the documentation [33]. In the redocumentation, some current repositories used conventional models like flat archives, databases, or knowledge bases [34]. These repositories must be used to locate and create different views or documents that software maintainers have requested. These capabilities save software maintainers time and effort in learning about the application domain. As a result, in our proposal, we used a Command Separated Values (CSV) file to store the flat file in the repository and convert it to a data frame during document generation. Data frames enable the query for specific data to be used in the documentation.

3.4   View Composer

View Composer is a user interface that is used to interact with a knowledge-based system in order to retrieve specific components [7]. In addition to a list of modules, the interface needed to be able to see the dependencies between them. Understanding the dependencies between the components is a crucial problem during software maintenance tasks. Software maintainers must be aware of the change impact of making improvements to a specific piece of source code. Therefore, it's critical to use the search and browsing functions to locate the relevant item.

3.5   Technical Documentation

According to a survey conducted by Souza et al. [4], the most important documents for software maintenance are the source code and comments. However, the problem with outdated comments in the source code can lead to the wrong interpretation of the meanings of the code. Moreover, experts are not available and new software maintainers may find it difficult to understand the current system for carrying out the maintenance tasks. In this perspective, Van Geet et al. [5] emphasized a redocumentation technique to generate a detailed design document. This document is related to the technical documents containing the structure with all the functions, database tables, screens, batch jobs, dependencies among the components and the slices of the program [35].

Table 1. Software technical documentation schema

Technical documentation section	Components
Source code metrics	• Finding out the number of method in a class • Total lines of code • Total number of imported libraries • Total number of class in a class • Total word counts • Total number of public function • Total number of the private method • Total number of a protected method
Object and descriptions	• Find out what are the available packages in the application • List the classes, interfaces, abstract classes in the packages • List the functions that are in the classes

(continued)

Table 1. (*continued*)

Technical documentation section	Components
Dependency diagram	• Dependency analysis – Package level analysis – Class level analysis – Function level analysis

In the proposed approach, as shown in Table 1, the documentation generated is the technical document that consists of certain elements, such as the source code summary, source code metrics, classes, packages and functional dependencies. The functionalities and elements in this technical documentation are defined to retrieve only relevant parts of the source code using the HTML based documentation, as suggested by Van Geet et al. [5].

4   Case Study

The implementation of this approach is still in the initial stage. In this stage, we have created a simple prototype and have implemented each process specified in Fig. 1. The detailed process of implementation is described in the following sections.

4.1   Legacy Source Code

We used Restaurant Management System legacy source code for this proposed model. This software, which was built ten years ago in Java, provides restaurant management for customers. This end-to-end restaurant management system manages orders, inventory, and employee management. All orders and employee data will be stored in a database. The application has 14905 lines of code. These java files include the backend database code until the front-end GUI interfaces.

4.2   Parser

Once the LSC identified, the first step is to load LSC into HDFS environment. As specified earlier, we used Scala as a programming language and DCC as a cloud platform. We have created the cluster and notebook space to execute the Scala commands. During data preparation, we have identified and grouped java files on Restaurant Management system as specified in the previous section loaded in the data directory of the cloud platform. Next step, we load the source code into RDD which is the fundamental storage unit of Spark in order to extract some information from the source code to do analysis. Spark automatically and transparently divides the data in RDDs into partitions which are distributed across worker nodes in the cluster and parallelize the data performed on these partitions as specified in Fig. 2. Figure 4 shows the command to load the source code into RDD for each 14 java file. After loading all the files into their respective RDD,

```
1    val file1 = sc.textFile("/FileStore/tables/src/Controller.java")
2    val file2 = sc.textFile("/FileStore/tables/src/Controller_GUI.java")
3    val file3 = sc.textFile("/FileStore/tables/src/Database.java")
4    val file4 = sc.textFile("/FileStore/tables/src/DatabaseException.java")
5    val file5 = sc.textFile("/FileStore/tables/src/Employee.java")
6    val file6 = sc.textFile("/FileStore/tables/src/Manager.java")
7    val file7 = sc.textFile("/FileStore/tables/src/MenuItem.java")
8    val file8 = sc.textFile("/FileStore/tables/src/Order.java")
9    val file9 = sc.textFile("/FileStore/tables/src/OrderDetail.java")
10   val file10 = sc.textFile("/FileStore/tables/src/RMS.java")
11   val file11 = sc.textFile("/FileStore/tables/src/RMS_GUI.java")
12   val file12 = sc.textFile("/FileStore/tables/src/Staff.java")
13   val file13 = sc.textFile("/FileStore/tables/src/UserInterface.java")
14   val file14 = sc.textFile("/FileStore/tables/src/UserInterface_GUI.java")
```

Fig. 4. Load source code into RDD

we created a list to store all the RDD so that created RDD it is easy to use later by using loop structure instead of typing a command that works for each RDD repeatedly.

In data transformation, the process of classification done through the process of filtration in the data loaded in RDD using Action and Transformation operation. The main classification that needs to be done in this source code is based on the documentation section specified in Table 1. RDD transformation commands such as filter, map, flatMap used in our proposed approach to filter the source code by extracting java packages, classes, interfaces and abstract class in java packages. On the other hand, RDD

```
1    //read class files
2    val readClassFile = sc.textFile("/FileStore/tables/src/Classes/*")
3
4    //get all libraries name used in class
5    val findLibrariesInClasses = readClassFile.filter(lines => lines.contains("import") && lines != "").map(x =>
     x.replace(";","")).map(x => x.replace("import", "")).map(x => x.trim).distinct
6    //transform into dataframe
7    import spark.implicits._
8    // for implicit conversions from Spark RDD to Dataframe
9    val librariesInClassDf = findLibrariesInClasses.toDF("Libraries")
10
11   librariesInClassDf.show
12   //save the dataframe into csv
13   // librariesInClassDf.repartition(1).write.format("com.databricks.spark.csv").option("header",
     "true").save("dbfs:/FileStore/tables/librariesInClass.csv")
```

Fig. 5. Partial Scala code to extract component

Actions such as count and aggregate used to perform aggregation functions to provide the source code metrics such as finding the total line of codes, imported libraries, classes, packages and other relevant components. Figure 5 shows the partial Scala command use RDD Transformation and Action used to extract source code components in Spark environment.

On the other hand, one more important component that needs to be extracted is the dependency which in our implementation emphasize Package, class and function dependency analysis. Figure 6 shows partial Scala code to extract the functional dependency.

```
1   //Using Databricks Community Edition
2
3   //remove file if exist
4   dbutils.fs.rm("/FileStore/tables/ClassDependency",true)
5
6   //remove ; and comments
7   def trimming(item:String) :(String) = {
8     val pos = item.indexOf(";")
9     item.substring(0,pos)
10  }
11
12  //find all class name to act as filepath later
13  val allClass = sc.textFile("/FileStore/tables/Classes/*")
14  val findClass = allClass.filter(x => (x.contains("public class") || x.contains("public enum"))).map(line => line.split(" "))
15  val extractClass = findClass.map(x => x(2))
16
```

Fig. 6. Extract the dependency code

The next process is to load dataset to dataframe. Source code components are extracted and dependencies loaded into a DataFrame. We performed column transformation, and query the DataFrame to get useful information such as code metrics, source code component list and component dependencies to save into CSV file.

4.3 Knowledge Based

The extracted source code components stored in few CSV files based on documentation elements namely source code metrics, and list the components and dependencies among the components.

4.4 View Composer

View Composer or in our context called web-based user interface provides related function to extract the components and present them as HTML documentation. The user interface will use the data from CSV and loaded it into dataframe.

4.5 Technical Documentation

As specified in Sect. 4.2, once data loaded into dataframe, SPARK SQL used to query and retrieve relevant source code components and classified according to documentation

Class	Total number of methods	lines of code	number of	number of	number of class	Total of words counts	Total Number of public method	Total Number of private method
Controller.java	35	1887	318	3	1	35004	4	31
Controller_GUI.java	37	633	104	2	1	13025	36	1
Database.java	42	835	148	4	3	17565	38	4
DatabaseException.java	2	10	0	0	1	154	2	0
Employee.java	4	26	0	0	1	465	4	0
Manager.java	4	29	0	0	1	488	4	0
MenuItem.java	12	85	0	0	1	1209	12	0
Order.java	12	112	8	1	1	1664	12	0
OrderDetail.java	7	47	3	0	1	841	7	0
RMS.java	1	11	1	0	1	161	1	0
RMS_GUI.java	1	11	0	0	1	175	1	0
Staff.java	21	176	4	2	1	3588	16	0
UserInterface.java	33	500	42	2	1	12773	30	3
UserInterface_GUI.java	84	2219	518	8	13	50921	50	34
Total	295	6581	1146	22	28	138033	217	73

dependency	function name	dependent function	class
Iterator<OrderDetail> it = orderDetailList.iterator();	addItem	iterator	Order
while(it.hasNext() && !found)	addItem	hasNext	Order
re = it.next();	addItem	next	Order
if(rNewMenuItem.getID() == re.getItemID())	addItem	getID	Order
re.addQuantity(quantity);	addItem	addQuantity	Order
orderDetailList.add(detail);	addItem	add	Order
orderDetailList.remove(index);	deleteItem	remove	Order
//System.out.println(e.toString() + ":" + e.getMessage());	deleteItem	println	Order
Iterator<OrderDetail> it = orderDetailList.iterator();	calculateTotal	iterator	Order
while (it.hasNext()) {	calculateTotal	hasNext	Order
re = it.next();	calculateTotal	next	Order
total += re.getTotalPrice();	calculateTotal	getTotalPrice	Order

Fig. 7. Generate software technical documentation

section as shown in Table 1. The sample technical documentation generated can be referred to Fig. 7.

On other hand, the functional dependencies also shown in Fig. 8 below generated from the Scala code in Fig. 6.

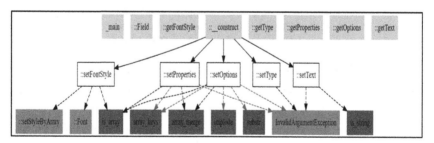

Fig. 8. A function call graph

5   Conclusions and Future Work

In this paper, we have presented our proposed approach for software redocumentation that employs the distribution data technique. As an initial effort, we present the system architecture for locating and generating the source code component through HDFS and Spark environments. Our experiments focus on the parser used to extract the source code components from the SWP and store it in the repository. As a result, Sparks plays an important role as a parser to perform ETL on legacy java source code. The significance of the experiment shows the process of a raw source code by using a distribution technique. This technique helps to speed up the extraction process of the source code component within limited run times. For future work, we plan to use the same approach in different languages and other large legacy systems with precise evaluation to improve the efficiency of our proposed approach.

References

1. Khadka, R., Batlajery, B.V., Saeidi, A.M., Jansen, S., Hage, J.: How do professionals perceive legacy systems and software modernization? In: Proc. Int. Conf. Softw. Eng., pp. 36–47 (2014). https://doi.org/10.1145/2568225.2568318
2. Matthiesen, S., Bjørn, P.: Why replacing legacy systems is so hard in global software development: an information infrastructure perspective. In: Proceedings of the 18th ACM Conference on Computer Supported Cooperative Work & Social Computing, pp. 876–890 (2015)
3. Crotty, J., Horrocks, I.: Managing legacy system costs: a case study of a meta-assessment model to identify solutions in a large financial services company. Appl. Comput. Inform. **13**, 175–183 (2017)
4. de Souza, S.C.B., Anquetil, N., de Oliveira, K.M.: Which documentation for software maintenance? J. Braz. Comput. Soc. **12**(3), 31–44 (2007). https://doi.org/10.1007/BF0319 4494
5. Van Geet, J., Ebraert, P., Demeyer, S.: Redocumentation of a legacy banking system: an experience report. In: Proceedings of the Joint ERCIM Workshop on Software Evolution (EVOL) and International Workshop on Principles of Software Evolution (IWPSE), pp. 33–41 (2010)
6. Tadonki, C.: Universal Report: a generic reverse engineering tool. In: 12th IEEE International Workshop on Program Comprehension (IWPC 2004), pp. 266–267 (2004)
7. Nallusamy, S., Ibrahim, S., Mahrin, M.N.: A software redocumentation process using ontology based approach in software maintenance. Int. J. Inf. Electron. Eng. **1**, 133 (2011)
8. Dorninger, B., Moser, M., Pichler, J.: Multi-language re-documentation to support a COBOL to Java migration project. In: SANER 2017 – 24th IEEE Int. Conf. Softw. Anal. Evol. Reengineering, pp. 536–540 (2017). https://doi.org/10.1109/SANER.2017.7884669
9. Kienle, H.M., Müller, H.A.: Rigi – an environment for software reverse engineering, exploration, visualization, and redocumentation. Sci. Comput. Program. **75**, 247–263 (2010). https://doi.org/10.1016/j.scico.2009.10.007
10. Sabtu, A., et al.: The challenges of Extract, Transform and Loading (ETL) system implementation for near real-time environment. In: Int. Conf. Res. Innov. Inf. Syst. ICRIIS, pp. 3–7 (2017). https://doi.org/10.1109/ICRIIS.2017.8002467
11. García, S., Ramírez-Gallego, S., Luengo, J., Benítez, J.M., Herrera, F.: Big data preprocessing: methods and prospects. Big Data Anal. **1**, 1–23 (2016). https://doi.org/10.1186/s41044-016-0014-0
12. Ragab, M., Tommasini, R., Awaysheh, F.M., Ramos, J.C.: An In-depth Investigation of Large-Scale RDF Relational Schema Optimizations Using Spark-SQL (2021)
13. Christa, S., Madhusudhan, V., Suma, V., Rao, J.J.: Software maintenance: from the perspective of effort and cost requirement. In: Proceedings of the International Conference on Data Engineering and Communication Technology, pp. 759–768. Springer (2017)

14. Sugumaran, N., Ibrahim, S.: An evaluation on software redocumentation approaches and tools in software maintenance. In: Commun. IBIMA, pp. 1–10 (2011). https://doi.org/10.5171/2011.875759

15. Kaur, U., Singh, G.: A review on software maintenance issues and how to reduce maintenance efforts. Int. J. Comput. Appl. **118**, 6–11 (2015). https://doi.org/10.5120/20707-3021

16. Kaur, P.: The study of software re-engineering. WWJMRD **4**, 381–383 (2018)

17. Rostkowycz, A.J., Rajlich, V., Marcus, A.: A case study on the long-term effects of software redocumentation. In: IEEE Int. Conf. Softw. Maintenance, ICSM, pp. 92–101 (2004). https://doi.org/10.1109/ICSM.2004.1357794

18. Nanthaamornphong, A., Leatongkam, A.: Extended ForUML for automatic generation of UML sequence diagrams from object-oriented Fortran. Sci. Program. (2019). https://doi.org/10.1155/2019/2542686

19. Singh, K.: Transformation of source code into UML diagrams through visualization tool. Int. J. Adv. Sci. Technol. **29**(8), 4861–1114 (2020)

20. Sheer, A., Tahrawi, A., Jeesh, J., Al Ibrahim, Y.: A Framework for software re-documentation by using reverse engineering approach. Int. J. Comput. Appl. **118**, 1–21 (2016)

21. Pathania, Y., Bathla, G.: A review on re-documentation approaches and their comparative study. Int. J. Comput. Sci. Trends Technol. **2**, 48–51 (2014)

22. Geist, V., Moser, M., Pichler, J., Beyer, S., Pinzger, M.: Leveraging machine learning for software redocumentation. In: SANER 2020 – Proc. 2020 IEEE 27th Int. Conf. Softw. Anal. Evol. Reengineering, pp. 622–626 (2020). https://doi.org/10.1109/SANER48275.2020.9054838

23. Wolfart, D., et al.: Modernizing legacy systems with microservices: a roadmap. In: Evaluation and Assessment in Software Engineering, pp. 149–159. Association for Computing Machinery (2021)

24. Puri, R., et al.: Project CodeNet: A Large-Scale AI for Code Dataset for Learning a Diversity of Coding Tasks. https://arxiv.org/abs/2105.12655 (2021)

25. Casado, R., Younas, M.: Emerging trends and technologies in big data processing. Concurr. Comput. **27**, 2078–2091 (2015). https://doi.org/10.1002/cpe.3398

26. Shaikh, F., Pawaskar, D., Siddiqui, A., Khan, U.: YouTube data analysis using MapReduce on Hadoop. In: 2018 3rd IEEE International Conference on Recent Trends in Electronics, Information and Communication Technology, RTEICT 2018 – Proceedings, pp. 2037–2041 (2018). https://doi.org/10.1109/RTEICT42901.2018.9012635

27. Nibareke, T., Laassiri, J.: Using Big Data-machine learning models for diabetes prediction and flight delays analytics. J. Big Data **7**(1), 1–18 (2020). https://doi.org/10.1186/s40537-020-00355-0

28. Jonnalagadda, V.S., Srikanth, P., Thumati, K., Nallamala, S.H., Dist, K.: A review study of apache spark in big data processing. Int. J. Comput. Sci. Trends Technol. **4**, 93–98 (2016)

29. Han, Z., Zhang, Y.: Spark: a big data processing platform based on memory computing. In: Proc. – Int. Symp. Parallel Archit. Algorithms Program, PAAP, pp. 172–176 (2016). https://doi.org/10.1109/PAAP.2015.41

30. Chikofsky, E.J., Cross, J.H.: Reverse engineering and design recovery: a taxonomy. IEEE Softw. **7**, 13–17 (1990)

31. Müller, H.A., Kienle, H.M.: A Small Primer on Software Reverse Engineering (2009)

32. Databricks Community Edition. https://community.cloud.databricks.com. Accessed 10 November 2020

33. Van Deursen, A., Moonen, L.: Documenting software systems using types. Sci. Comput. Program. **60**, 205–220 (2006)
34. Canfora, G., Di Penta, M., Cerulo, L.: Achievements and challenges in software reverse engineering. Commun. ACM **54**, 142–151 (2011)
35. Freeman, R.M., Munro, M.: Redocumentation for the Maintenance of Software. In: Proceedings of the 30th Annual Southeast Regional Conference, pp. 413–416 (1992)

System Design and Usability Evaluation of Ghana Music Documentation System Using the System Usability Scale

Alimatu-Saadia Yussiff[1] (✉) ⓘ, Florian Carl[2] ⓘ, Wan Fatimah Wan Ahmad[3] ⓘ,
Simon Mariwah[4] ⓘ, Otchere Eric Debrah[2] ⓘ, and Abdul-Lateef Yussiff[1] ⓘ

[1] Department of Computer Science and IT, University of Cape Coast, Cape Coast, Ghana
{asyussiff,ayussif}@ucc.edu.gh
[2] Department of Music and Dance, University of Cape Coast, Cape Coast, Ghana
{florian.carl,eric.otchere}@ucc.edu.gh
[3] Department of Computer and Information Sciences, Universiti Teknologi PETRONAS,
Seri Iskandar, Malaysia
fatimhd@utp.edu.my
[4] Department of Geography and Regional Planning,
University of Cape Coast, Cape Coast, Ghana
smariwah@ucc.edu.gh

Abstract. Ghana lacks proper establishment of primary sources of information on Ghanaian music, musicians, artists, and performance group. In addition, there is lack of a channel for acquiring such data. In an attempt to solve these problems, an online system entitled, Ghana Music Documentation System (GMDS) was developed and evaluated. The research aim at developing and evaluating a sustainable, usable and interactive online database of institutions, musical practices, musicians, artists, cultural entrepreneurs, performance groups, producers, as well as other stakeholders in the fields of music performance, education, production, promotion, and dissemination. In addition, the GMDS will allow users to browse, search for musical information and mapped Ghanaian music information for further analysis and visualization. In order to achieve these objectives, the development we followed five development approach: background study, identification of need and establishing requirements, designs, building an interactive system, and evaluation. We employed the System Usability Scale (SUS) instrument to evaluate the usability of GMDS and the result shows that the GMDS has an average SUS score of 81.6. This demonstrated that the GMDS system is acceptable, has a grade scale of B and the rating adjective is excellent. Based on the evaluation result, we concluded that the system proposes an innovative mapping technique, and will serve as a powerful primary repository for mapping Ghanaian music thereby becoming a reliable, effective and efficient research tool for all.

Keywords: System Usability Scale · Ghana Music Documentation · System design · Ghana music database · Usability evaluation · SUS

© Springer Nature Switzerland AG 2021
H. Badioze Zaman et al. (Eds.): IVIC 2021, LNCS 13051, pp. 253–264, 2021.
https://doi.org/10.1007/978-3-030-90235-3_22

1   Introduction

Cultural globalization and the growing importance of digital technology are realities that artists, cultural entrepreneurs, as well as researchers and policy makers today must face. Scholars of cultural globalization have identified two opposing trends: One points towards an increased cultural homogenization, mainly associated with Western culture, but also taking place at the inter-regional level, where larger cultural markets often dominate smaller ones. The opposite trend, described as cultural heterogenisation, fostered by the diffusion of images, sounds, ideas, and cultural products through mass media as well as through increased inter-cultural exchange and transnational mobility [1–6]. Policy makers, practitioners and other stakeholders are therefore confronted with the question of how to respond to these contradictory global forces [7, 8].

At the national level, a response to the challenges of cultural globalization was Ghana's Cultural Policy, which came into effect in 2004" [9]. The Cultural Policy set out to define Ghana's cultural heritage and identify measures for its sustainable development, with the ultimate goal to promote "unity in diversity". In 2016, Ghana also ratified the UNESCO Convention on the Protection and Promotion of the Diversity of Cultural Expressions, which was the most explicit response to the threat of cultural homogenization at the international level.

Nevertheless, Ghanaian music culture from the past has been lacking behind as compared to other countries and continents in the globe. A major concern is that the interested persons find it difficult to find and locate Ghanaian musician across the world, especially when it comes to the native or cultural music which most of the traditional people and tourists are so much desperate. Currently, Ghana lacks proper establishment of primary sources of information on Ghanaian music, musicians, artists, and performance group. In addition, there is lack of a channel for acquiring such data. These has been a major problem for some time and the GMDS implementation has made it a concern to provide an appropriate solution by developing and evaluating an all-inclusive database of Ghanaian music culture.

In this regard, the goal of the research is to develop and evaluate a sustainable and interactive online database of institutions, musical practices, musicians, artists, cultural entrepreneurs, performance groups, producers, as well as other stakeholders in the fields of music performance, education, production, promotion, and dissemination. This will represent Ghanaian music culture on the globe for easy reach to all interested persons. It will also go a long way to benefit stakeholders, tourist and the public at large in promoting Ghanaian music culture.

The fundamental questions the research addressed are; what is the state of cultural and musical diversity in Ghana? Can we use GMDS to document and map a musical diversity in Ghana? Also, to build interactive digital online database as a tool to help achieve musical sustainability? How usable and satisfactory is the GMDS for the users?

The benefit of the system include the development of a sustainable tool for the betterment of all stakeholders. Secondly, the system would provide a database environment that would help in organizing, storing and retrieving information on Ghanaian music culture. This will be convenient and efficient to use by stakeholders, artistes, tourists, and policy makers in different ways that best serve their respective interests. In addition, the System also addresses five out of the six-implementation areas stated in Ghana Cultural Policy document. These are; "preservation and conservation of culture," "development and promotion of culture," "presentation of culture," "establishment of appropriate administrative structures," and finally "establishment of linkages with various sectors of national development" [10].

Thus, the paper presents first the introduction to the research. Followed by review of related work then the methodology employed in the study. In addition, we present the main interfaces and evaluation results. Finally, we present conclusions and future works.

2 Related Work

This section presents literature review on Ghana music culture, usability evaluation, System Usability Scale (SUS) and related work on the topic.

2.1 Ghana Music and Culture

Music has always been an integral part of the Ghanaian community even prior to the contact with European colonialists. Music is use to mark the cycles of life, animate religions, during rituals, and to communicate the social values of the various ethnolinguistic groups that inhabited the Ghana-Togoland sub regions.

Music performs a great function in ceremonies, religion, funerals, festivities and many social gatherings of the Ghanaian communities, coupled with the art of dancing and drumming.

According to Collins [11], the Ghanaian trans-cultural popular music can be divided into three broad epochs or eras with its roots far from the early 1880s. Colonialism then influenced the way of traditional music-culture and introduced some foreign elements, which continued up to the Second World War and erected several forms of music and musical groups; popular among them was the Ghanaian Highlife, which started from the Fante-lands and Adaha and Konkoma music groups. By the 1940's the term highlife became the generic term for all the new forms of Ghanaian music.

Innovations in current times has metamorphosed traditional music culture all over the world especially with the introduction of media, internet and other forms of coordinating musical components and composing music. This means that modern technology, innovation and globalization trends has accounted for the current state of the Ghanaian music culture. According to [12], technology is currently the means for the transformation and advancement of culture. Considering day-to-day practices, it was realize that music documentation was not taken seriously and there was very little research in this domain. Although there is an emerging and growing literature on the subject of preservation of digital documents since the beginning of this century, to the best of our knowledge the subject of documenting the Ghanaian music culture and mapping of the information have not yet been addressed [13].

2.2 Usability Evaluation

ISO (9241-11) defines usability as "...the extent to which a product can be used by specified users to achieve specified goals with effectiveness, efficiency and satisfaction in a specified context of use" [14]. Usability is an important attribute for ensuring the quality of products or systems in order to meet user's satisfaction [15]. Usability engineering was characterized into five; Learnability, Memorability, User's Satisfaction, Efficiency, and Few errors [16]. Usability in this regard is mainly about users understanding and effective use of system or product to satisfy their needs or wants.

Usability evaluation is a systematic assessment of the degree to which a given product, software, or service has met the usability needs of its intended user. It focuses on easy to learn, easy to use, and users' satisfaction [17].

2.3 System Usability Scale

John Brook developed the System Usability Scale (SUS) in 1986 for measuring the usability of systems and software products. Since then, researchers have been using the instrument to measure the usability of numerous products including hardware, software, mobile devices, websites and applications. More importantly, the SUS can be used as a "post-test questionnaire for the assessment of perceived usability" [18]. The SUS consists of ten-item Likert scale questionnaire with five responses for each question namely "strongly agree", "agree" "neutral", "disagree", and "strongly disagree" [19, 20]. Thus, the SUS as a measure of usability "provides a global measure of system satisfaction and as sub-scales of usability and learnability"[21]. While items 4 and 10 can calculate the measure of learnability, the remaining 8 items measure the system usability as shown in Fig. 1. It is therefore, a good tool for collecting quantitative data about users' opinions.

The main goal of SUS is to help measure "people's subjective perceptions"[22] quickly and easily [18]. It has become an industry standard for evaluating a given system or product and as a measure of users satisfaction. The SUS is reliable, free, easy to set up and administer to participants online or in print [22], and "scores can be compared regardless of the technology" [23]. In addition, SUS provides a clearer understanding about users perceived usability and attitudes towards a system or products being tested

	The System Usability Scale Standard Version	Strongly Disagree				Strongly Agree
		1	2	3	4	5
1	I think that I would like to use this system frequently.	o	o	o	o	o
2	I found the system unnecessarily complex.	o	o	o	o	o
3	I thought the system was easy to use.	o	o	o	o	o
4	I think that I would need the support of a technical person to be able to use this system.	o	o	o	o	o
5	I found the various functions in this system were well integrated.	o	o	o	o	o
6	I thought there was too much inconsistency in this system.	o	o	o	o	o
7	I would imagine that most people would learn to use this system very quickly.	o	o	o	o	o
8	I found the system very awkward to use.	o	o	o	o	o
9	I felt very confident using the system.	o	o	o	o	o
10	I needed to learn a lot of things before I could get going with this system.	o	o	o	o	o

Fig. 1. Standard usability scale

[19, 21]. Not all, [24] summarizes the characteristics of SUS to be valid, reliable, not diagnostics, scores are not percentages, measures of learnability & usability, and SUS scores have a modest correlation with task performance.

2.4 Music Documentation and Information Systems

The Ewha Music Database (EMDB) system [25] was developed to store and share music information of East Asia. The goal of the system was to deliver a meaningful database system for East Asian music through technical solutions as well as experience in collecting and analyzing music materials. The implemented system accumulates educational music data from East Asia by creating a database that allows users to share the collected music database. The system also allow user to register and search for East Asia music information on the go. Other research using the EMDB system is entitled, "Enhancement of Understanding East Asian Music through Technical Innovation of the EMDB (Ewha Music Database)" [26]. This paper seeks to find out how useful two innovative search methods are for finding specific data in large volumes of data. Even though the EMDB provided the above-mentioned capabilities, the limitation is that it generated un-mapped.

Also, [27] developed a data and meta-data model for use in a music digital library system to support search and navigation of music content in multiple formats. This development was entitled, the Variations2 digital music library project at Indiana University. The goal of the project was to overcome the limitations identified in a traditional library databases and to accommodate the special needs of the music domain in several. First, it identifies, separates, and relates the logical and physical layers of musical works and their physical manifestations into four entities: work, instantiation, container and media object. In our view, the goals for developing Variations2 are very different from that of GMDS as stated above.

In addition, the Tuscan Music Documentation Centre (CeDoMus) is a service promoted by the Tuscan Regional Administration and Music School of Fiesole. The Center created an online database of musical collections to offer support to the music collections owned by Tuscan libraries, archives, and cultural institutions. The database offers information about provenance, nature, and extent of each collection, its history and place, relevant bibliographic information, links to catalogues, and other documentary resources available on the Web. The search schedule permits queries by name of the collection, name of the previous and actual owner, type, age and genre of the musical documents, and geographical coordinates. The website provide a global visualization of the dissemination of musical collections and their owners in the region through mapping [28]. Considering the kind of data stored in CeDoMus, it is different to that stored in [28] the GMDS database. However, we generated the idea of mapping data from this paper.

Not all, [29] developed a 3D technologies to document and disseminate information about ancient Maya musical instruments. The main purpose of the documentation is to address the inaccessibility of instruments housed in archaeological labs and museums across Mesoamerica. "In order to facilitate the study of ancient Maya music, it is necessary to create a database of numerous instruments from the Maya area that transcends geographical and temporal boundaries" [29]. Having a 3D printed replica of physical musical object and the ability to interact with them by students and researchers allowed them to learn about the archaeological sites and excavated instruments. They were also able to visit the virtual sites and finally, learned how to play the instruments. Thus, the original object is preserved and protected while its duplicates continue to produce music. We therefore concluded from the Maya Musical database study that it deals with the development of 3D musical instruments for storage and use by both students and researchers. This is however different from the kind of data being considered under GMDS.

Overall, the idea of creating a database of musical objects and the ability of users to interact with an intuitive interface is an added advantage for our proposed GMDP system derived from the review of the above existing system. However, we derive the idea of mapping the data from both CeDoMus and the Ewha Music Database system.

3   Methodology

Based on the proposed topic, the system design and evaluation of the GMDS followed five stages as shown in Fig. 2.

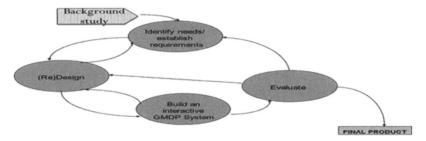

Fig. 2. Research methodology

The first phase, background studies, involved literature reviews of existing musical systems to identify concepts, gaps, issues, and measurable objectives. Needs identification and establishment of requirements in the second phase immediately followed this. In order to capture the right requirements for the system there was the need to identify the key stakeholders, those that the GMDS will affect either positively or negatively. This include representatives of the GMDS team from University of Cape Coast, developers, representatives from the Centre for National Culture, representative from Music Association of Ghana (MUSIGA) Cape Coast branch. We conducted Focus group discussions with stakeholders on three different occasions to elicit and establish requirements. In addition, we identified the functional requirements, usability requirements, performance requirements and non-functional requirements.

At the third phase, we designed the architecture, interaction model, object model and user interfaces. The fourth phase witnessed the development of an interactive GMDS using web technologies and multimedia elements. Some of the technologies employed include programming languages such as HTML, JavaScript, CSS, Bootstrap, PHP and SQL to build an impressive user interface for simple and clear user interactivity; Google map for database mapping to show the exact locations of the various music groups and more description to the kind of music they perform and other information. Users will be able to browse, search and locate various music groups and organizations. Finally, the evaluation of the GMDS was done using SUS instruments and by following the systematic steps below.

3.1 Evaluation

The evaluation of the GMDS was done using SUS instruments and by following the systematic steps below. Criteria

3.1.1 Instrumentation, Participants Selection and Procedure

The evaluation process used a convenience sample from participants. Overall, 60 participants volunteered to take part in the study. The study adapted standardized SUS items (see Fig. 1) by replacing the word "system" in the original item with "GMDS", i.e. the product that is being evaluated.

This approach is supported by the work of [21]. We then designed Google Form using the SUS questionnaire with a link to the GMDS website. We also gave the participants the instructions i.e. list of tasks to perform on GMDS. Participants were introduce to GMDS, the expected tasks and the main purpose of evaluation. Immediately after completing the tasks listed in Table 1, participants filled the SUS survey online.

Table 1. List of tasks performed on GMDS

Number	Task
1.	Type the provided URL into a browser: https://gmdp.ucc.edu.gh
2.	Explore the interfaces by navigating through the pages
3.	Register a musician/artist/musical band, etc.
4.	Search the GMDS database by region/by name of artist/musician/musical band, etc.
5.	Fill out the SUS questionnaire based on your exploration of the GMDS

3.1.2 System Usability Scale Data Analysis

At this stage, we downloaded data from Google form in excel format and analyzed it using SUS standardized calculation format proposed by [19, 20]. First, we assigned a value for the SUS score calculation with 1 being Strongly Disagree; 2 being Disagree; 3 being Neutral; 4 being Agree and 5 being Strongly Agree. After that for all even numbered Likert scale numbered response items (i.e. 2, 4, 6, 8, and 10); we subtracted the participants' response score from 5. In addition, for all odd numbered Likert scale numbered response items (i.e. 1, 3, 5, 7, and 9); we subtracted 1 from the participants' response score. At the end of this stage, all users' response values were scaled from 0 to 4 with 4 being the most positive response. Finally, we calculated the overall value of SUS by summing up all individual scores and multiplied it by 2.5. This convert the range of possible values from 0 to 100. This format of calculation is supported by [18–20]. We then interpreted the results of the analysis using Fig. 3. It illustrates how the percentile ranks are associated with SUS scores and the letter grades.

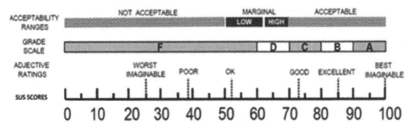

Fig. 3. SUS scores interpretations guide

4   Results and Discussion

This section presents and discusses the results of the study. First, it presents the GMDS interfaces and related functionalities. Then we present the SUS evaluation results.

4.1   The Ghana Music Documentation System

The GMDS is a web application with intuitive and usable interfaces that promote effective and efficient usage. Figure 4 illustrate the GMDS homepage and can be located at https://gmdp.ucc.edu.gh/en/. The homepage illustrates seven main menu (about, team, join, database, search, find out more, and homepage) for easy interactivity.

The system has three groups of users: the general users, the surfer and administrator. A surfer is a person who came to the site to explore and search for information. A general user is either an artist, music producers, performing group, etc. who is interested in joining the GMDS database. The main activity of the general user is registering the information about its organization by inputting data through the form into the GMDS

Fig. 4. GMDS homepage

database system. A general user can also search the GMDS database just as a surfer does and perform all the activities of a surfer. The final group of user for the GMDS is the administrator and his roles in addition to that of the surfers and general users include managing user accounts, publishing and mapping users' information, backup the database, and performing system configuration.

4.2 SUS Evaluation Results and Interpretation

Figure 5 presents the GMDS SUS scores, percentile ranks and letter-grades (from A to D) for users (N = 60). Considering the results of the SUS analyses performed within the data obtained, the usability of the developed GMDS proved to be at a higher rate with the overall average SUS score of 81.6 (i.e. sum of individual SUS score/number of participants = 4897.5/60). It also shows a high mean SUS score across all participants.

Table 2: Ghana Music Documentation Project SUS Scores

Respondents	Odd Items	Even Items	SUS Score (/100)	Grades
1.	14	19	82.5	B
2.	17	12	72.5	C
3.	15	13	70	C
4.	14	14	70	C
5.	13	15	70	C
6.	17	14	77.5	C
7.	16	14	75	C
8.	20	15	87.5	B
9.	14	15	72.5	C
10	12	12	60	D
11	15	12	67.5	D
12	18	13	77.5	C
13	19	12	77.5	C
14	20	17	92.5	A
15	20	17	92.5	A
16	15	18	82.5	B
17	20	17	92.5	A
18	20	17	92.5	A
19	19	14	82.5	B
20	16	15	77.5	C
21	16	15	77.5	C
22	16	15	77.5	C
23	20	17	92.5	A
24	20	17	92.5	A
25	16	15	77.5	C
26	20	15	87.5	B
27	20	17	92.5	A
28	20	15	87.5	B
29	20	15	87.5	B
30	20	15	87.5	B

Respondents	Odd Items	Even Items	SUS Score (/100)	Grades
31	20	17	92.5	A
32	20	15	87.5	B
33	20	15	87.5	B
34	20	17	92.5	A
35	20	14	85	B
36	20	17	92.5	A
37	20	15	87.5	B
38	20	14	85	B
39	16	13	72.5	C
40	12	12	60	D
41	13	13	65	D
42	15	13	70	C
43	16	15	77.5	C
44	20	15	87.5	B
45	15	13	70	C
46	20	12	80	B
47	20	15	87.5	B
48	20	17	92.5	A
49	20	15	87.5	B
50	15	13	70	C
51	15	13	70	C
52	20	15	87.5	B
53	16	15	77.5	C
54	15	15	75	C
55	20	15	87.5	B
56	12	20	80	B
57	19	15	85	B
58	20	17	92.5	A
59	20	15	87.5	B
60	20	17	92.5	A
		Average score	81.625	

Fig. 5. GMDS SUS scores

4.2.1 Acceptability, Grade Scale, Adjective Rating of GMDS Result

To determine the acceptability, grade scale, and adjective rating of the GMDS, we compared GMDS SUS evaluation result in Fig. 5 with the SUS Scores Interpretations Guide in Fig. 3. In addition, there are six SUS grade scale, ranging from A, B, C, D, E and F where:

- Grade A: with a score greater than or equal to 80.3
- Grade B: with the same greater score with 74 and smaller 80.3
- Grade C: with a score greater than 68 and smaller 74.
- Grade D: with the same greater score with 51 and smaller 68.
- Grade F: with a score less than 51.

In conclusion, comparing our overall SUS score of 81.6 in Fig. 5 with interpretation scale (A - F) and Fig. 3 demonstrated that the GMDS has the following levels of acceptability, grade scale, and adjective rating:

- Level of user acceptance falls into the acceptable category,
- The grade scale is included in category B, and
- The rating adjective of GMDS is excellent category.

Thus, the GMDS is usable, has good utilities and efficient to support the goal of its development, which means the end user can find it easy to learn, easy to use, and satisfactory.

4.3 User Suggestions for Future Improvement of GMDS

When we asked participants under item 11 of the questionnaire to provide us with any suggestion for upgrading the GMDS system. Many agreed that the GMDS is good, has nice interface with good application, has nice layout and easy to locate artists/groups and that the system will help promote Ghanaian culture to the world. Alternatively, some suggested we should add necessary items to the GMDS, help its usage with every other Operating system. Some also suggested that the satellite view of the map should focus more on Ghana and finally to educate people on GMDS.

5 Conclusion

This study developed and evaluated GMDS featuring an interactive on-line database of institutions, musical practices, musicians, artists, cultural entrepreneurs, performance groups, producers, as well as other stakeholders in the fields of music performance, music education, and music production, promotion, and dissemination.

The system provide users the opportunity to add their information into the database for further query, mapping and use by stakeholders. The system provided users the answers to the fundamental questions on how to access or locate a particular musician or music-group via near-by facilities, finding route, and contacting them. This is possible through searching GMDS user-friendly interface and the resulting mapped output. This helps the users to find the most relevant information or locate various institution with ease. The results of the evaluation conducted on GMDS with 60 participants resulted in the mean score of 81.6, has a grade scale of "A" and the rating adjective is excellent. Overall, the GMDS offer powerful, clear and user-friendly access to Ghanaian music data with great benefits to users. In future, we hope to add more features to the system by introducing music groups and artists' performance photographs and the satellite view of the mapped data to focus more on Ghana.

References

1. Appadurai, A.: Modernity at Large: Cultural Dimensions of Globalization, vol. 1. University of Minnesota Press (1996)
2. White, A.: Manuel Castells's Trilogy the Information Age: Economy, Society, and Culture. Taylor & Francis (2016)
3. Friedman, J.: Cultural Identity and Global Process, vol. 31. Sage (1994)
4. Hannerz, U.: Cultural complexity: Studies in the social organization of meaning. Columbia University Press (1992)
5. Hannerz, U., Ulf Hannerz, H.: Transnational Connections: Culture, People, Places. Taylor & Francis, USA (1996)
6. Meyer, B.E., Geschiere, P.E.: Globalization and Identity: Dialectics of Flow and Closure. Blackwell Publishing (1999)
7. De Beukelaer, C., Pyykkönen, M., Singh, J.P.: Globalization, Culture and Development (2015)
8. Kagan, S., Kirchberg, V.: Music and sustainability: organizational cultures towards creative resilience – a review. J. Clean. Prod. **135**, 1487–1502 (2016)
9. N. National Commission on Culture: The Cultural Policy of Ghana, Ghana, (2004)
10. GMDP: Ghana Music Documentation System. https://gmdp.ucc.edu.gh (2020)
11. Collins, J.: A social history of Ghanaian popular entertainment since independence. In: Transactions of the Historical Society of Ghana, pp. 17–40 (2005)
12. Collins, J.: Popular performance and culture in Ghana. Ghana Stud. **10**, 9–64 (2007)
13. Lemouton, S., Bonardi, A., Pottier, L., Warnier, J.: On the documentation of electronic music. Comput. Music. J. **42**, 41–58 (2019)
14. Bevan, N., Carter, J., Earthy, J., Geis, T., Harker, S.: New ISO standards for usability, usability reports and usability measures. In: International Conference on Human–Computer Interaction, pp. 268–278 (2016)
15. Roy, S., Pattnaik, P.K.: Some popular usability evaluation techniques for websites. In: Proceedings of the International Conference on Frontiers of Intelligent Computing: Theory and Applications (FICTA) 2013, pp. 535–543 (2014)
16. Nielsen, J.: The usability engineering life cycle. Computer **25**, 12–22 (1992)
17. Sharfina, Z., Santoso, H.B.: An Indonesian adaptation of the system usability scale (SUS). In: 2016 International Conference on Advanced Computer Science and Information Systems (ICACSIS), pp. 145–148 (2016)
18. Lewis, J.R., Sauro, J.: Item benchmarks for the system usability scale. J. Usability Stud. **13** (2018)
19. Klug, B.: An overview of the System Usability Scale in library website and system usability testing. Weave J. Libr. User Experience **1** (2017)
20. Webster, R., Dues, J.F.: System usability scale (SUS): Oculus Rift® DK2 and Samsung Gear VR®. In: 2017 ASEE Annual Conference and Exposition (2017)
21. Lewis, J.R., Sauro, J.: The factor structure of the system usability scale. In: International Conference on Human Centered Design, pp. 94–103 (2009)
22. Brooke, J.: SUS: a retrospective. J. Usability Stud. **8**, 29–40 (2013)
23. Sauro, J.: SUPR-Q: a comprehensive measure of the quality of the website user experience. J. Usability Stud. **10** (2015)
24. Sauro, J.: A Practical Guide to the System Usability Scale: Background, Benchmarks & Best Practices (2011)
25. Chae, H.K., Kim, E.-H., Lee, M.-S., Myagmar, O.: Challenges to music documentation: design and implementation of a web-based content management system for East Asian Music education documents. Fontes Artis Musicae, pp. 249–259 (2014)

26. Chae Hyun-Kyung, L.G.-J.: Enhancement of understanding East Asian music through technical innovation of the EMDB (Ewha Music Database). Ewha Music Collection **19**, 137–150 (2015)
27. Minibayeva, N., Dunn, J.W.: A digital library data model for music. In: Proceedings of the 2nd ACM/IEEE-CS Joint Conference on Digital Libraries, pp. 154–155 (2002)
28. Grigat, F., Bonn, B.-H.: The Tuscan music documentation center (CeDoMus—Centro di documentazione. Fontes Artis Musicae J. Int. Assoc. Music Libr. Arch. Document. Centres **63**, 145–146 (2016)
29. Katz, J.: Digitized Maya music: the creation of a 3D database of Maya musical artifacts. Digit. Appl. Archaeol. Cult. Herit. **6**, 29–37 (2017)

Static Indoor Pathfinding with Explicit Group Two-Parameter Over Relaxation Iterative Technique

A'qilah Ahmad Dahalan[1]([✉]) [iD] and Azali Saudi[2] [iD]

[1] Centre for Defence Foundation Studies, National Defence University of Malaysia,
Kuala Lumpur, Malaysia
a.qilah@upnm.edu.my

[2] Faculty of Computing and Informatics, Universiti Malaysia Sabah, Kota Kinabalu, Malaysia
azali@ums.edu.my

Abstract. A solution to Laplace's equation referred to as harmonic potential fields is commonly employed in robot pathfinding as an indication for robot navigation in an identifiable environment. The simulations computation of these harmonic functions frequently requires a high-performance computer. In the quest to address the pathfinding problem, the article presents a technique called Block Two-Parameter Over-Relaxation, otherwise known as Explicit Group Two-Parameter Over-Relaxation (EGTOR). The simulations of robot pathfinding were executed in a static known enclosed environment to validate the competency of EGTOR. Multiple tests are provided to assess the effectiveness of the suggested technique. Different departure and goal positions, in particular, are used to assess the paths generated by the simulations. The outcomes demonstrate the advantages of the proposed technique. In the context of iteration number, EGTOR improves by around 4.4% when compared to EGAOR and 17.1% in comparison with EGSOR. While as to computational timing, EGTOR outperforms EGAOR and EGSOR by 6.3% and 14.5%, respectively. The study concludes that the suggested method in computing harmonic functions is appealing and attainable for solving path planning problems.

Keywords: Self-directed · Harmonic potential · Collision free · Optimal path

1 Introduction

Developing intelligent autonomous motion planning is among of the most complex tasks in robotics practices. Presently, intelligent self-directed robots are in high demand in a variety of areas including space [1], industrial [2], manufacturing [3], transportation [4], military and security [5]. A successful autonomous mobile robot should be efficient and dependable in designing a path from any launch point to a finish point without colliding with obstructions. Path-planning with artificial potential fields [6] proposes an excellent approach for a navigational path selection through the formation of an artificial potential function which "draws" the robot towards the destination and "repulse" the robot from

© Springer Nature Switzerland AG 2021
H. Badioze Zaman et al. (Eds.): IVIC 2021, LNCS 13051, pp. 265–275, 2021.
https://doi.org/10.1007/978-3-030-90235-3_23

the obstacles. However, as discussed in [7], a potential field without residual local minima is extremely difficult to establish, which might mistakenly lead the robot passing over the field's negative gradient, eventually become stranded in the inaccurate position. Koren [8] has addressed additional well-known challenges, such as oscillations over the obstacle borders, escaping the entrance of extremely small tunnels, and oscillations while moving across tapering channels.

The notion of analytically addressing the Laplace equation for path planning purposes was led by Connolly [9]. He illustrated how numerical solutions may be used to search pathways in two and three-dimensional configuration spaces for certain simple and motionless environments. His approach has been executed utilizing the technology available at the time, which resulted in unacceptable time frames nowadays, with the computation of simple environments taking within 23 to 188 s. He projected that with adequately powerful computers, path formation consuming this technique would be an attainable choice.

Later, Sasaki [10] proposed by exploiting the elliptic PDE to tackle heat conduction issues in order to generate a potential field with no local minima. He successfully designed a potential field which ensures a route from start to the goal (assuming it exists) that free of local minima by viewing the start as a hot point, the goal as a cold, and the obstacles as an unknown adiabatic object. Sasaki's approach is, however, solely appropriate for motionless and thoroughly recognized environments. The starting point was given a high temperature and was designated as a local maximum. Since the study was completed in 1998, computer restrictions/limitations at the time prevent or at least discourage its usage for higher-dimensional problems or in difficult environments.

This article introduces the problem of mobile robot pathfinding expressed as a heat transfer analogy. The heat transmission is illustrated by Laplace's equation. One of the most essential features of heat transfer is its ability to exceed the difficulty of local minima, which makes it particularly promising for robot navigation control. The solutions to Laplace's equation a.k.a harmonic function, symbolize the temperature values in the environment of the path formation model. Several methods were applied for the achievement of harmonic functions, but the most general approach is through numerical techniques owing to the obtainability of rapid processing machines and their elegance and competence in addressing the problem [11–13]. Three experiments i.e. Explicit Group Successive Over-Relaxation (EGSOR), Explicit Group Accelerated Over-Relaxation (EGAOR), and Explicit Group Two-Parameter Over-Relaxation (EGTOR), were executed in this article to assess the proficiency of the accelerated iterative approach employed in constructing routes of a portable robot for various size of environments. This article is divided into four different sections. The next section mainly will address the materials and techniques that will be used in this study, including the formulation and algorithms that describe the entire pathfinding process. Whereas Sect. 3 describes the results and discussion, along with some figures and tables reflecting the study's outcome. Finally, in Sect. 4, the conclusion will be explained.

2   Materials and Methods

Rather than employing a genuine robot mobile, we recreate the idea of an autonomous mobile robot depicted by a roaming nodal point in a known motionless confined environment. The predicament of identifying the robot's course is classified as a problem of steady-state heat transfer. The goal should be regarded, in the resemblance of heat transmission, as a sink drawing heat in. The environment's obstacles/barriers and boundary walls are referred to as heat sources, and they are preserved at consistent temperatures. The temperature dispersion expands along the heat diffusion course, and the contour of heat flux spreading toward the sink that floods in the environment. Such condition may be considered as a means of communication among the goal, barriers, and the points functioning as robots. The temperature distribution inside the environment is then utilized as a controller to lead the robot to travel from the departure location to the target spot by directing the heat flow beginning at the highest to the lowest temperature point in the given environment. The temperature distribution in the environment is calculated by practicing the harmonic function to describe the setup space.

The domain Ω (denoted by $\partial\Omega$) in subject to generate the path planning consists of several components such as the walls, borders, obstacles/hindrances/barriers, multiple start locations, and goal point. A harmonic function in a domain $\Omega \subset R^n$ is a function that satisfies Laplace's equation, as follow

$$\nabla^2 U = \sum_{i=1}^{n} \frac{\partial^2 U}{\partial x_i^2} = 0 \tag{1}$$

with x_i indicates the i-th coordinates of Cartesian and the dimension be represented as n. Owing to the benefits of harmonic functions that satisfy the minimum-maximum condition, the formation of local minima in the domain can be prevented. As a result, harmonic functions are highly useful in robot pathfinding because they give exact path algorithms that allow smooth and efficient autonomous robot navigation [14]. It is widely known in the literature that Laplace's equation can be efficiently solved numerically through conventional techniques [15] for instance Jacobi, Gauss-Seidel (GS), and Successive Over-Relaxation (SOR). In pursuit to speed up the computation, this article aims to define Eq. (1) using an accelerated iterative approach called EGTOR.

In the pathfinding problem, the potential field is computed globally. Solving the Laplace expression, as indicated in Eq. (1), yielded the harmonic function. It is used to determine a route that progressively advances the point robot upon the starting location to the destination position while never colliding with any obstacles. The hindrances are always quantified as new sources, while the target is defined as the sink with the lowermost potential value. This all adds up to the application of Dirichlet boundary conditions, $U|\partial\Omega = c, \ c = $ constant. Later, by executing a Gradient Descent Search-Distance Transform (GDS-DT) on the potential field, a sequence of potential points with lower values will lead to the lowermost value, which is the goal point, to be discovered.

This study applied the above-mentioned framework for the path planning problem to aid in expressing the results of Laplace expression Eq. (1). The objective is to use the notion of how temperature and heat stream function in generating potential value and path lines for robot navigation. The experiment is carried out in a 2D domain with several types of obstacles. The proposed iterative scheme, EGTOR is employed to compute Laplace's equation as well as to obtain the values of temperature at each node. Comparisons with the EGSOR and EGAOR iterative techniques were used to evaluate its performance.

As mentioned before, a nodal point in the grid-form structure (see Fig. 1) portrayed the robot in this simulation. Meanwhile, Fig. 2 illustrates a part of a computational molecule for a five-point approximation from the configuration space, at which h indicates the length among nodal points at each direction. The numerical approach then calculates the function values for every node iteratively so as to meet Eq. (1). The departure location is assigned with the uppermost temperature, while the target spot is appointed as the lowest, and varying departure temperature values are allocated to the boundaries wall and barriers/obstacles. After obtaining the potential values in the configuration area, a smooth trajectory can be established by tracing the temperature dissemination through the steepest descent approach, in which the algorithm tracks the negative gradient at the lowermost temperature goal point from the start to lower temperature consecutive points.

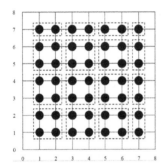

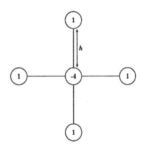

Fig. 1. Grid-form structure of nodes.   **Fig. 2.** Five-point approximation computational molecule.

2.1 Explicit Group Two-Parameter Over-Relaxation Iterative Technique

The conventional GS [9] and SOR [16] from robotics writings were employed as remedies for the problem (1). In this investigation, the solution to Laplace's equation is found by employing a quicker numerical approach, the Explicit Group Two-parameter Over-Relaxation (EGTOR) iterative technique. In reality, the TOR method is an extension of the AOR method (which has two parameters, r and ω). The AOR method, on the other hand, is an extension of the SOR method (that has one parameter, ω). SOR, AOR and TOR techniques are all within over-relaxation family scheme. Former work on block iterative techniques [17–20] uses various points of Explicit Group (EG) techniques to demonstrate that block iterative approaches outperform the conventional point techniques.

Let the two-dimensional Laplace's equation given in (1), be viewed as

$$\nabla^2 U = \frac{\partial^2 U}{\partial x^2} + \frac{\partial^2 U}{\partial y^2} = 0. \tag{2}$$

Equation (2) approximation, as frequently represented in the following equation, allows to reduced using 5-point second-order finite difference formula,

$$u_{i-1,j} + u_{i+1,j} + u_{i,j-1} + u_{i,j+1} - 4u_{i,j} = 0. \tag{3}$$

The TOR method comprising three distinct optimal relaxation parameters denoted by r, r', and ω. From Eq. (3), the iterative scheme for conventional TOR iterative method is given as

$$\begin{aligned}
U_{i,j}^{(k+1)} &= \tfrac{r}{4} U_{i,j-1}^{(k+1)} + \tfrac{r'}{4} U_{i-1,j}^{(k+1)} + \tfrac{\omega}{4} \left(U_{i,j+1}^{(k)} + U_{i+1,j}^{(k)} \right) \\
&+ \left(\tfrac{\omega-r}{4} \right) U_{i,j-1}^{(k)} + \left(\tfrac{\omega-r'}{4} \right) U_{i-1,j}^{(k)} + (1-\omega) U_{i,j}^{(k)}
\end{aligned} \tag{4}$$

By considering the approximation in Eqs. (3) and (4), the general iterative scheme for EGTOR may be expressed as

$$\begin{bmatrix} U_{i,j} \\ U_{i+1,j} \\ U_{i,j+1} \\ U_{i+1,j+1} \end{bmatrix}^{(k+1)} = \frac{1}{24} \begin{bmatrix} 6S_1 + S_a \\ 6S_2 + S_b \\ 6S_3 + S_b \\ 6S_4 + S_a \end{bmatrix} + (1-\omega) \begin{bmatrix} U_{i,j} \\ U_{i+1,j} \\ U_{i,j+1} \\ U_{i+1,j+1} \end{bmatrix}^{(k)} \tag{5}$$

where

$$\begin{aligned}
S_1 &= r\left(U_{i-1,j}^{(k+1)} - U_{i-1,j}^{(k)} \right) + r'\left(U_{i,j-1}^{(k+1)} - U_{i,j-1}^{(k)} \right) + \omega\left(U_{i-1,j}^{(k)} + U_{i,j-1}^{(k)} \right), \\
S_2 &= r'\left(U_{i+1,j-1}^{(k+1)} - U_{i+1,j-1}^{(k)} \right) + \omega\left(U_{i+1,j-1}^{(k)} + U_{i+2,j}^{(k)} \right), \\
S_3 &= r\left(U_{i-1,j+1}^{(k+1)} - U_{i-1,j+1}^{(k)} \right) + \omega\left(U_{i-1,j+1}^{(k)} + U_{i,j+2}^{(k)} \right), \\
S_4 &= \omega\left(U_{i+2,j+1}^{(k)} + U_{i+1,j+2}^{(k)} \right), \\
S_a &= 2(S_2 + S_3) + S_1 + S_4, \\
S_b &= 2(S_1 + S_4) + S_2 + S_3.
\end{aligned}$$

The ambiguous optimal values of all parameters imposed no constraints on obtaining the smallest iterations number. According to Hadjidimos [21], the amounts of r and r' are generally chosen to lie as close as the value of related SOR ω, with $\omega = [1, 2)$. As a result, sensitivity analysis was performed in this study to determine the best values of optimal relaxation parameters using $\omega = [1, 2)$ as a benchmark and following Hadjidimos's [21] motion. The implementation of EGTOR to solve problem (2) is described in Algorithm 1.

Algorithm 1: EGTOR technique	
i	Setup the configuration space with specified start and goal position
ii	Initializing starting point U, $\varepsilon \leftarrow 10^{-15}$, $iteration \leftarrow 0$
iii	Set the variables $$S_1 \leftarrow r\left(U_{i-1,j}^{(k+1)} - U_{i-1,j}^{(k)}\right) + r'\left(U_{i,j-1}^{(k+1)} - U_{i,j-1}^{(k)}\right) + \omega\left(U_{i-1,j}^{(k)} + U_{i,j-1}^{(k)}\right),$$ $$S_2 \leftarrow r'\left(U_{i+1,j-1}^{(k+1)} - U_{i+1,j-1}^{(k)}\right) + \omega\left(U_{i+1,j-1}^{(k)} + U_{i+2,j}^{(k)}\right),$$ $$S_3 \leftarrow r\left(U_{i-1,j+1}^{(k+1)} - U_{i-1,j+1}^{(k)}\right) + \omega\left(U_{i-1,j+1}^{(k)} + U_{i,j+2}^{(k)}\right),$$ $$S_4 \leftarrow \omega\left(U_{i+2,j+1}^{(k)} + U_{i+1,j+2}^{(k)}\right).$$ $$S_a \leftarrow 2(S_2 + S_3) + S_1 + S_4$$ $$S_b \leftarrow 2(S_1 + S_4) + S_2 + S_3$$
iv	For all non-occupied node points of type $\bullet$ using Eq. (5), calculate $$U_{i,j}^{(k+1)} \leftarrow \tfrac{1}{24}[6S_1 + S_a] + (1 - \omega)U_{i,j}^{(k)},$$ $$U_{i+1,j}^{(k+1)} \leftarrow \tfrac{1}{24}[6S_2 + S_b] + (1 - \omega)U_{i+1,j}^{(k)},$$ $$U_{i,j+1}^{(k+1)} \leftarrow \tfrac{1}{24}[6S_3 + S_b] + (1 - \omega)U_{i,j+1}^{(k)},$$ $$U_{i+1,j+1}^{(k+1)} \leftarrow \tfrac{1}{24}[6S_4 + S_a] + (1 - \omega)U_{i+1,j+1}^{(k)}.$$
v	Compute the remaining group of points (with one or two points) near to the boundary via direct method by using equation $$U_{i,j}^{(k+1)} \leftarrow \tfrac{1}{4}\left[U_{i-1,j}^{(k+1)} + U_{i+1,j}^{(k)} + U_{i,j-1}^{(k+1)} + U_{i,j+1}^{(k)}\right]$$
vi	Check the convergence test for $\varepsilon \leftarrow 10^{-15}$. If yes, proceed to step (vii). Else, back to step (iii)
vii	Execute GDS-DT to create path from departure to target location

3   Results and Discussion

The simulation environments employed were 300×300, 600×600, 900×900, 1200×1200, 1500×1500, and 1800×1800. In the configuration space, various numbers of hindrances of various forms have been established. All the obstacles and the walls were initially set to high temperatures. Meanwhile, the target point has been set to a very low temperature, but the departure point has no initial value. All other points were set to a zero temperature. The experiments were done out on a personal computer executing at 2.50 GHz speed with 8GB of RAM using Robot 2D Simulator [22]. The looping progression proceeded to calculate the temperature values at each point while waiting for the stopping criterion to be fulfilled. Specifically, when there has no change in the temperature value from one iteration process to the next or when it has converged at a predetermined value 1.0^{-10}. Such a configuration is required to avoid flat areas, which result in failure to generate a path to the goal location. Tables 1 and 2 respectively showed the iteration counts and time taken (in seconds) needed by each iterative algorithm based on these simulations. These result tables are separated into three different methods executed in four different environments, namely Event 1 to Event 4. In terms of iteration count, it is shown that the EGTOR produced the best results compared to the EGAOR (approximately by 4.4%) and EGSOR (approximately by 17.1%). Whereas in terms of CPU time, the EGTOR reduces roughly 6.3% over EGAOR and 14.5% over EGSOR.

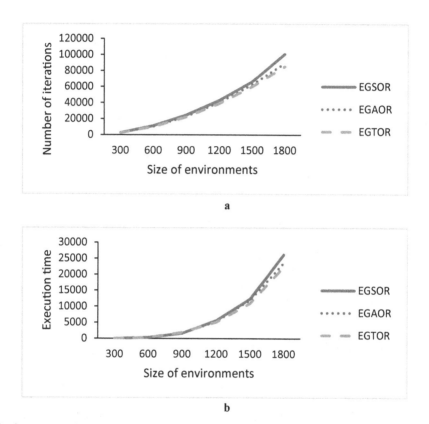

Fig. 3. (a) Overall performances concerning the iteration counts. (b) Overall performances concerning the time taken

The performance graph of the suggested methods relating to iteration counts (see Fig. 3a) and time taken (see Fig. 3b) are also illustrated. In reference to Fig. 3, EGTOR exhibited the least computing time with the fewest number of iterations needed in comparison with other existing methods. Clearly, it proved to be the fastest of all. This is because three distinct optimal parameters for this approach have been added. The EGAOR and EGSOR, on the other hand, required two and one parameters, respectively. These optimal parameters have a positive effect on the acceleration of computation.

Table 1. The implementation of the projected methods based on iteration counts.

| | Methods | N | | | | | |
		300	600	900	1200	1500	1800
Event 1	EGSOR	1258	5899	12844	22227	34055	48446
	EGAOR	1042	4994	10928	19107	29306	41775
	EGTOR	997	4812	10581	18549	28445	40524
Event 2	EGSOR	1729	6782	14874	26007	39968	56858
	EGAOR	1610	6368	13953	24429	32926	46923
	EGTOR	1489	5957	13062	22905	31552	45197
Event 3	EGSOR	2666	11076	24519	42897	65977	100842
	EGAOR	2480	10389	22995	40322	62423	89182
	EGTOR	2371	9977	22111	38917	59912	85272
Event 4	EGSOR	1629	6487	14194	24913	38195	54508
	EGAOR	1392	5648	12367	21724	33518	48120
	EGTOR	1328	5428	11907	20963	34842	49772

Table 2. The implementation of the projected methods based on time taken (in seconds).

| | Methods | N | | | | | |
		300	600	900	1200	1500	1800
Event 1	EGSOR	6.88	163.72	871.66	2694.80	6286.69	12675.73
	EGAOR	6.05	137.87	751.78	2442.66	5551.02	10459.68
	EGTOR	5.05	133.00	720.29	2394.62	5404.33	10316.42
Event 2	EGSOR	7.67	199.59	1009.48	2827.46	6925.80	14336.95
	EGAOR	8.25	185.36	926.49	3003.98	5909.85	12802.89
	EGTOR	7.64	169.39	867.20	2787.69	5700.19	12312.08
Event 3	EGSOR	13.24	315.87	1602.81	5591.93	12331.17	26171.60
	EGAOR	13.83	301.27	1633.35	5261.60	11975.63	23616.21
	EGTOR	11.66	296.46	1883.36	5094.93	10921.11	22338.11
Event 4	EGSOR	7.80	187.33	990.20	2979.14	6919.25	13843.15
	EGAOR	7.56	167.65	891.51	2609.11	6139.29	12833.82
	EGTOR	7.10	163.21	850.26	2573.12	6494.66	13381.51

When the configuration space potential values are obtained, the trail is generated by employing the steepest descent search from any departure location to the given target spot. The algorithm monitors the negative gradient and repeatedly selects the lowest temperature around the neighborhood points up until the constructed path reaches its goal point. Figure 4 illustrates the successful development of a path from numerical computation in a known stationary environment. All of the starting points (green/square) manage to end at the specific target point (red/circle) while escaping multiple obstacles in the given environment.

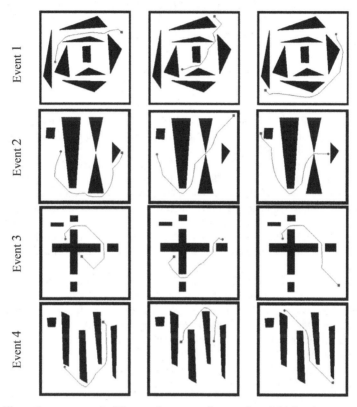

Fig. 4. The pathways created of four environments from various initial and target positions.

4   Conclusion

To summarize, the investigations in this article highlights that harmonic functions give a promising and feasible way of generating routes in a point robot environment due to advanced finding numerical techniques, together with the new sophisticated computing technologies. The simulation results confirmed that the EGTOR iterative scheme is faster than the conventional method (families of SOR and AOR). While the number of obstacles has risen, the effectiveness of the suggested technique is not affected. In reality, the computation becomes quicker as the obstacle zones are omitted along the calculation process. It is worth emphasizing once more that EGTOR results surpass the EGAOR (by approximately 4.4%) and EGSOR (by approximately 17.1%) as to iteration count. While in terms of computational time, the EGTOR saves around 6.3% over EGAOR and 14.5% over EGSOR. Furthermore, the originality/novelty of this study is the use of the TOR scheme families in robot pathfinding and on Algorithm 1.

Acknowledgement. This research was supported by **Ministry of Education (MOE) through Fundamental Research Grant Scheme (FRGS/1/2018/ICT02/UPNM/03/1).** We also want to thank National Defence University of Malaysia for the funding of this article. The researchers declare that there is no conflict of interest regarding the publication of this study.

References

1. Shyam, R.B.A., Zhou, H., Umberto, M., Shilip, D., Arunkumar, R., Yang, G., Gerhard, N., Saber, F.: Autonomous robots for space: trajectory learning and adaptation using imitation. Front. Robot. AI **8**, 638849 (2021)
2. Bahrin, M.A.K., Othman, M.F., Azli, N.H.N., Talib, M.F.: Industry 4.0: a review on industrial automation and robotic. J. Teknol. **78**(6–13), 137–143 (2016)
3. Miguel, A.M., Diego, C, Paulo, D.: Autonomous robots and CoBots: applications in manufacturing. In: Enabling Technologies for the Successful Deployment of Industry 4.0, Chapter 3 (2020)
4. Giles, B., Simon, H., Beate, K., Sophie, P.: The role of robotics and artificial intelligence in public transportation and urban mobility for cities. Whitepaper in TravelSpirit Open Mobility Evidence Base (2017)
5. Stephanie, M.P., Jose A.C.: The future of wars: artificial intelligence (AI) and lethal autonomous weapon systems (LAWS). Int. J. Secur. Stud. **2**(1), Article 2 (2020)
6. Andrews, J.R., Hogan, N.: Impedance Control as a Framework for Implementing Obstacle Avoidance in a Manipulator, M.S. Thesis. MIT Cambridge, USA (1993)
7. Rimon, E., Koditschek, D.E.: Exact robot navigation using artificial potential functions. IEEE Trans. Robot. Autom. **8**(5), 501–581 (1992)
8. Koren, Y., Borenstein, J.: Potential field methods and their inherent limitations for mobile robot navigation. In: Proceedings of the IEEE International Conference on Robotics and Automation, pp. 1398–1404 (1991)
9. Connolly, C.I., Burns, J.B., Weiss, R.: Path planning using Laplace's equation. In: Proceedings of the IEEE International Conference on Robotics and Automation, pp. 2102–2106. Cincinnati, OH, USA (1990)
10. Sasaki, S.: A practical computational technique for mobile robot navigation. In: Proceedings of the IEEE International Conference on Control Applications, pp. 1323–1327 (1998)
11. Chou, H., Kuo, P., Liu, J.: Numerical streamline path planning based on log-space harmonic potential function: a simulation study. In: 2017 IEEE International Conference on Real-time Computing and Robotics (RCAR), pp. 535–542 (2017)
12. An, Y., Wang, S., Xu, C., Xie, L.: 3D path planning of quadrotor aerial robots using numerical optimization. In: Proceedings of the 32nd Chinese Control Conference, pp. 2305–2310 (2013)
13. Silva, M.O., Silva, W.C., Romero, R.A.F.: Performance analysis of path planning techniques based on potential fields. In: 2010 Latin American Robotics Symposium and Intelligent Robotics Meeting, pp. 115–119 (2010)
14. Connolly, C.I., Gruppen, R.: On the applications of harmonic functions to robotics. J. Robot. Syst. **10**(7), 931–946 (1993)

15. Ibrahim, A.: The Study of the Iterative Solution of Boundary Value Problem by the Finite Difference Method, PhD Thesis. Universiti Kebangsaan Malaysia, Malaysia (1993)
16. Saudi, A., Sulaiman, J., Hijazi, M.H.A.: Fast robot path planning with laplacian behaviour-based control via four-point explicit decoupled group SOR. Res. J. Appl. Sci. **9**(6), 354–360 (2014)
17. Dahalan, A.A., Saudi, A., Sulaiman, J., Din, W.R.W.: Numerical evaluation of mobile robot navigation in static indoor environment via EGAOR iteration. J. Phys. Conf. Ser. **890**, 012064 (2017)
18. Chew, J.V.L., Sulaiman, J.: Application of four-point Newton-EGSOR iteration for the numerical solution of 2D porous medium equations. J. Phys. Conf. Ser. **890**, 012075 (2017)
19. Lee, M.K., Ali, N.M.: New explicit group iterative methods in the solution of three dimensional hyperbolic telegraph equations. J. Comput. Phys. **294**, 382–404 (2015)
20. Saudi, A., Sulaiman, J.: Robot path planning using four point-explicit group via nine-point Laplacian (4EG9L) iterative method. Procedia Eng. **41**, 182–188 (2012)
21. Hadjidimos, A.: Accelerated overrelaxation method. Math. Comput. **32**(141), 149–157 (1978)
22. Saudi, A.: Robot Path Planning using Family of SOR Iterative Methods with Laplacian Behavior-Based Control, PhD Thesis. Universiti Malaysia Sabah, Sabah Malaysia (2015)

Use of Faceted Search: The Effect on Researchers

Mohammed Najah Mahdi[1]([⊠]), Abdul Rahim Ahmad[2], Qais Saif Qassim[3], and Mohammed Ahmed Subhi[4]

[1] Informatics and Computing in Energy, Universiti Tenaga Nasional, Kajang, Selangor, Malaysia
`Najah.Mahdi@uniten.edu.my`
[2] Systems and Network Department, College of Computing and Informatics (CCI), Universiti Tenaga Nasional, Kajang, Selangor, Malaysia
[3] Ibri College of Technology, Ibri, Sultanate of Oman
[4] Al Hikma University College Department of Computer Engineering, Baghdad, Iraq

Abstract. The extensive amount of results obtained from any Web search operation and loads of related and/or irrelevant hits presented on the user's screen are still poses challenges in the information retrieval field of study; especially if the user is an academic researcher and is looking for reliable and focused results. Therefore, improving the performance of Web search engines continues to be an active research topic. One of the biggest challenges to search engine optimization is when a user submits incomplete query statements or fragmented keywords. Using broken or fragmented keywords the semantic correlation will fail to result in inconsistent and outsized search results. This oversized (or overloaded) problem can be mitigated by utilizing the Exploratory Search technique with a faceted search refining mechanism. This study's main goal is to present a short review of the existing Exploratory Search techniques and faceted search implementations and shed light on the main limitations and shortcomings.

Keywords: Exploratory search · Faceted search · Faceted energy · Information overload · Search engine

1 Introduction

Today we live in an information and data environment. Practically everybody on the planet owns a cell phone which provides unhindered connection to virtually all human information. This paradigm shift to a more connected world has radically altered what is meant by knowledge and information as related to how it is accessed and maintain in an accurate and timely manner. A search engine is a method for obtaining a huge volume of data. It is also a type of information Retrieval system that identifies and prioritizes the importance of the searched query, and returns the correct and most relevant results to the user for timely use.

In IR, academicians and researchers are more concerned with the search precision; for instance, they want fewer results, which suit the queried information closely. However,

© Springer Nature Switzerland AG 2021
H. Badioze Zaman et al. (Eds.): IVIC 2021, LNCS 13051, pp. 276–286, 2021.
https://doi.org/10.1007/978-3-030-90235-3_24

most returned results have little to do with the queried information, and are found in irrelevant documents on the web [1, 2]. The method employed to query for a particular information depends on a question [3–5], typically conducted in unstructured records, an example include a sample of text from a wide range, closely related to the standard materials in computers.

This essay reviews the difficulties of "easy access to information" endured by researchers. This requires retrievals, consolidation, and presentation of information using specialized tools such as SE from large database databases. As most of them do not return important information on a regular basis, searchers must enter precise queries to get accurate information. This is challenging and often leads to information overload as the SE usually returns droves of relevant and irrelevant information.

The rest of this article is structured as follows. The second section contains a review of the previous works on faceted search. While in Sect. 3, we present issues in traditional search engines and information retrieval. Also reviews some exploratory comparisons with existing faceted search systems. And it also focuses on unresolved questions and difficulties faced in this area of research, and presents some possible future research directions of faceted search in Sect. 4. Finally, conclusions of the research.

2   Related Work

Exploring the Internet is not simply about browsing the results to particular keywords. Exploratory search (ES) helps a searcher expand his/her knowledge on a specific area and learn new subjects. However, the features and models for ES are much less mature than those of traditional search. The primary focus of this paper is to study and review the state-of-the-art features and paradigms of ES; to develop standards, and techniques for evaluating the search results returned by ES engines and to prevent information overload. The amount of information returned to users is a crucial problem of SE that has been investigated in several papers. Table 1 contains the literature reviewed in this study and are further discussed as follows:

The authors in Mahdi, et al. [6] comprehensively reviewed several academic papers that primarily deals with (1) faceted search; (2) availability of excessive information and (3) data filtering. Which classified into four categories, (a) review and survey (b) developing theoretical frameworks, (c) Software framework or model for big data filtering, (d) investigate data filtering methods. This work provides additional level of knowledge to the field of information overload and proposes relevant and important directions for researchers to explore. And further reinforces the efficiency of using dynamic faceted filters in reducing information overload.

Marie and Gandon [7] examined the accomplishments and mechanisms in the rapidly developing area of ES to guide future research in this area. Also, she proposed a review of such models from the elementary semantic navigator to the latest one and significant ones. Their work primarily aimed to establish a relation between the task characteristics and system features of ES. From these features, they discovered the desired effects of ES models and combined them with their widely implemented characteristics. The survey presented based on (1) the browsers linked data, (2) the recommenders based linked-data; (3) the linked data-based ES models. The wide usage of ES-based linked data functionalities and models can greatly facilitate future web search experiments and improve the quality of their results.

Table 1. Summary of previous surveys on features of ES

Authors and reference	Survey features	Year
Mahdi, et al. [6]	Presented reduction of information overload using dynamic faceted filers	2020
Marie and Gandon [7]	The ES function between relation common systems features and characteristics	2014
Zheng, et al. [8]	Refine search results by a faceted taxonomy	2013
Palagi, et al. [9]	Characteristics of ES	2017
Hoeber [10]	Information visualization and visual search interfaces	2018
Jiang [11]	Presenting the classified search results based on faceted classification, dynamic clustering, social classification, and visualization support	2014
Zheng and Vaishnavi [12]	Visual exploration systems	2009
Tvarožek [13]	Focus on faceted browsing approaches and visualization approaches	2011
Tzitzikas and Analyti [14]	Faceted taxonomy-based information sources	2007
Seifert, et al. [15]	Visualization for navigation and refinement of search results	2014
Athukorala, et al. [16]	Review the characteristics of ES behavior	2016

The authors in Zheng, et al. [8] examined typical faceted search concepts, the construction of hierarchy, investigated relevant architectures and frameworks, and researched how to derive, and rank effective compound facet terms. Furthermore, they emphasised the key characteristics of the common FS solution and investigate metrics used to test their performance. Some recommendations for future research were also presented. Zheng et al. also provided a comparative study on FS with form-based, directory, and keyword search in terms of these search mechanisms' main characteristics. They have also investigated the efficiency of many advanced FS systems, conducted a comprehensive survey of 20 FS models, compared them in terms of their data source, extraction of facet terms, a ranking of facets, and hierarchy construction.

Palagi, et al. [9] discussed the complexities and obstacles in ES as can be seen in the lack of strategies for evaluating ES models. To enhance these models, they developed several evaluation models that adopt a user-centered ES method. They also identified the features of ES and used them to build an evaluation grid for assessing various information search methods. They tested this grid by using the information search models of Ellis and Marchionini. They found that Marchonini's model did not match Palagi evaluation models' demands and that Ellis's model can be used for ES. They aimed to develop a significant ES evaluation model that can apply a user-centered ES method.

Jiang [11] comprehensively reviewed the concept of ES and its basic theoretical grounds and explained such a complex concept by demonstrating the context of its problem and its search procedure. Based on ES models' current review, Jiang classified the ES results via faceted classification, hierarchical content classification, dynamic clustering, and social classification. The ingrained features, functions, and applications of ES models were also comprehensively reviewed and a visualization technique that provides classified search results was investigated.

Zheng and Vaishnavi [12] tested and developed a multifaceted visual examination-based model to create a precise and intelligent decision-making option for managing project portfolios. The authors also discussed problems in the design of research science, which includes how to understand, infer, recommend, and assess the evolution of the problem. These prototypes were designed, developed and tested using computer programs and surveys from users. The result of the testing showcases the convenience of adopting the proposed solution.

Tvarožek [13] explored the current (semantic) web exploration options, mostly limited to query builders and table-based metadata browsers. He also examined the design issues in ES improvements and summarised adaptive social semantic web grade contributions to end-user exploration. He also identified several extensions of this approach, outlined these extensions with a focus on legacy and semantics, took advantage of the aforementioned web initiatives, combined these methods into a highly interdisciplinary solution, and presented an in-depth survey of the existing exploration techniques from which we draw inspiration for developing semantic web exploration approaches. He partly addressed scalability by offloading server-side personalized computations onto a client-side browser that tracks and evaluates user behavior and forwards the necessary data to the backend of the server to reduce the load and to enhance end-user privacy.

Tzitzikas and Analyti [14] reviewed the various directions of controlling faceted taxonomy-based information sources. Notably, they (1) described the compound term composition algebra of semantic faceted taxonomy-based information sources, (2) designed an expression of the compound term composition algebra and reviewed the evolution of faceted taxonomies, (3) constructed navigational trees of the dynamic generation and (4) conducted personalization integration and identified the taxonomy-based sources of personalization.

Seifert, et al. [15] presented an overview of the search results refinement, which allows the user to visually construct compound Binary search terms to minimize complexity of the results returned. They relied on query previews and user interactions to give the user an effective solution to the job at hand. This survey showed the participants used the unfamiliar model and domain as efficiently and effectively as the familiar tree-like display.

Athukorala, et al.[16] provided a description of the actions of ES and examined six tasks related to how it acquires knowledge, i.e. planning, comparison, finding, navigating and answering questions. The following describes the behavior of an ES; the query length, the maximum scroll depth, and how long it takes to complete the task. The second task was borderline and exhibited mixed characteristics. These comparisons helped the compatibility of this reporting and finding on various sorting experiments.

3   Issues in Traditional Search Engines

The massive data volume on the Internet is not the only obstacle that the new SE website faces. In theory, knowledge exploration is not the primary nature of a search. Quest methods are only a way to achieve the desired goal. Therefore, SE managers need to perform exploratory discussions with customers to serve their large customer base better and know exactly why they need them. A typical example is a user heading towards a closed train station while using a navigation aid. The only thing that helps in this situation is to find the information. Searching is usually difficult because of query problems and an abundance of information as mentioned below.

3.1   Query Problems

A user normally only wants three terms or less for communicating his/her knowledge on the site. This creates a knowledge gap that prevents the searcher from producing the correct question. Many SE has thus allowed the user to define his/her realm of interests or, in order to help the search process, to best explain their interest in a profile [17]. Such methods impose some limits in the area of interest. This is not an agreed universal method that cannot be supplied by every user [18]. Occasionally users often look at some uncertainty that cannot correctly direct the SE. Besides, the researcher discontinues the initial query. It is easy to expand the search engine's scope and related documents for a question while sensibly approaching this task. At least one of these documents is thus likely to meet the user's utter needs for information.

In comparison, although it is widely recognized the utility of the present SE generation, they only show optimal performance for simple questions such as webpage searches and popular/known subjects. If we have a well-defined need for details and a good knowledge about the website(s), we will generate an appropriate question to direct the SE to return the answers. A response should be sufficient under these conditions with several keywords. Unfortunately, if the user does not have a target website or a clear understanding of the subject being sought, as is often the case with the ES and the hunt for information [19, 20], such short questions will prove unsuccessful. The technical reason for an unsuccessful response is due to several reasons [21, 22]. The following are three plausible reasons:

Ambiguity: if a question is a vague word with only one meaning, SE can always provide the best results by manipulating the senses or combining multiple senses. For instance, for the vague question 'jaguar', the first Google Results page contains at least three meanings of this term: a sports team, an animal, and a vehicle. Although the question is simplified as the 'Jaguar Team', the recipient may still have unclear responses such as a wrestling team, a Jaguar Car Team, the softball team of Jaguar Southwestern University, and the football team of Jacksonville Jaguar.

Vocabulary Mismatch: in the case of an adventurer seeking very accurate information in an area unfamiliar to him, a person might not know the correct terms for marking the details he/she wants. As a consequence, keywords may not match the terminology used in the relevant documents in the application. This might trigger a language malfunctioning problem. For instance, if an individual researcher needs to get information regarding the retrieval functions used by SE, but does not know about the correct IR terms for the search, the searcher will not use queries like "SE formula", "methods used for SE query execution" and "methods used to score SE". "Functions Recovery of SE" should be a simpler and straightforward response.

3.2 Information Overload

If something is not on the site, definitely it will not be found. To provide better user experience, the information available on the website must have high accuracy in comparison to other sources. However, detailed operating knowledge lies within the backend repositories. The desired result in an ordinary search lies in the first ten results ranking according to algorithms. Besides, this distinction is based on the presence of keywords on the webpage or more complex relation identification hypotheses, as with Google. This is also the case. Nevertheless, the utility of the first ten search results can only be calculated by the individual, given the accuracy of the first couple of results is not satisfactory [23].

Searching is fast, but finding is harder. This is a vital point given modern SE are especially tailored to search for information, and timely results are returned based on the search query. Easy search answers can be easily found, though, based on the suitability of the application or user experience. The successful quest takes time to achieve better results.

The World Wide Web (or Web, for short) is entrusted with a large quantity of fragmented, repetitive, and imprecise information that makes it difficult to use anything produced. The word "info overload" is used. Nevertheless, advanced information processing technology has overcome this problem, allowing the network SE to find resources and making things simpler. Nonetheless, these methods are inadequate as they simply ignore the actual importance of the information collected, which would make the interpretation and filtering of data more complex.

3.3 Exploratory Comparison with Existing FS Systems

To produce an efficient faceted navigation system, careful consideration of the following is needed: (1) content-based faceted taxonomy, (2) association of documents based on specified rules, and (3) a dynamic strategy to optimize the facet path in runtime. Ben-Yitzhak, et al. [24] used an open-source tool—Lucene—to the describe the fundamental design and the internal runtime of a typical FS engine. Solutions such as mSpace [27], Flamenco [25], Carsabi [28] and Parallax [26] are examples of interesting research and industrial products in FS domain. The incremental developmental progress in FS research has led to the production of Visual aided approaches (Relation Browser).

4 Possible Future Research Directions of ES Research

In this section, a future direction that we envisaged for this research field is described. The ES process is a better information search mechanism since because it finds information in a free, continuous and diverse system. Albeit, ES has been under intensive study, there are still several problems to be solved. Based on our survey, we outline some possible future research directions of ES research. The contributions of these studies and approaches are presented in Fig. 1.

The potential future research directions of ES are based on (1) improving the search operation results and (2) enhancing the interface of the system user. The ES-based engines have two distinct categories: search results and user interface depending on the behavior of the searcher. The former's main operation is to select results that tend to be more visualizing, discovering, and browsing, but in the latter, the objective is to choose a suitable user interface for the individual query (see Fig. 1).

The latest trend in the application of the Search Results is focused on the refinement of the search results, which is one of the possible paths for optimizing the results received. This approach has been used in some related works, as illustrated in Table 2.

Observations from the literature suggests that the best ways to get a better refined searched result is to use complex queries or intelligent FS. The two methods are capable of improving the search results by utilizing faceted features with constructing complex queries and increasing the refining technology to get more accurate results.

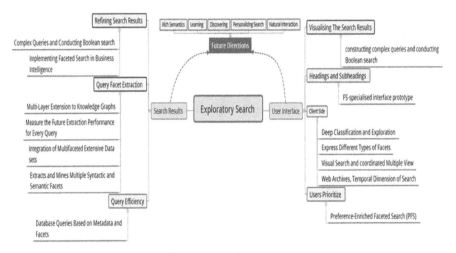

Fig. 1. Future research directions of ES

The other research direction is focusing on query facet extractions. This approach uses the knowledge graphs structuring visualizations to enhance the performance of the search results. Another scheme was to integrate extensive, multifaceted datasets to improve the search results and generate only interesting facets. An alternative approach is to extrat multiple syntactic and semantic facets from potential candidates. This depends on the characteristics of the location process, that often facilitates multifaceted, and dynamic application discovery.

Improving query efficiency is another research direction, this involves refining the returned results to present the user with more relevant results. In semantics, understanding, and experimentation, the validity of the information and human experience, apart from improving the search results, enhanced user interface has been an active area of research focused on partnership ES outperforms conventional keyword-based search techniques.

Table 2. Critical reviews of techniques in faceted search application

Name	Year	Data source	Facet term extraction	Hierarchy construction	Facet ranking	another search
Schmidt, et al. [29]	2017	Text-mining	Automatically selecting based on information extraction results	Using nodes to automatically generated queries to the users	Relevance to a Search query	Searched by keywords
Charleer, et al. [30]	2016	Websites	Auto-selection	Dependent on the user's lowest cost	Navigation price based	Keyword search
Siddiqui, et al. [31]	2016	Textual-analysis	Auto-selection	Depends on what the user selects	None	Searched by keywords
Kharlamov, et al. [32]	2017	Textual-analysis	Auto-selection	Depends on what the user selects	Dependent on the navigation charges	Keyword search
Mauro, et al. [33]	2019	System on two public datasets	Multi-facetedTrust ModelDataset	Yelp, Booking, Expedia, and LibraryThing based provided by social networks	None	Multifaceted trust framework to incorporate local trust systems, characterise by social connections,
Chantamunee, et al. [34]	2019	FS system for Thai research article	Two-level FS knowledge extraction from facets	Knowledge discovery tool	Real-time meta-data	Application of knowledge acquisition tool with respect to FS
de Campos, et al. [35]	2019	Records collected of Parliamentary Proceedings	Document filtering and Profile-based expert recommendation	Representing profiles based on different information sources expert finding	Recommendation	Based on text clustering to easily generate compound profiles for expert
Bogaard, et al. [36]	2019	Metadata-based clustering	Modelling user interests to identify the user interests and investigate the relation between them	Search behavior is related to specific parts with in the collection	Re-ranking of the results by the time	Improved system support or refined recommendations in Interactive IR
Le, et al. [37]	2019	Multimedia databases from the LSC dataset	FS lifelog system to a VR-platform	Image extracting based visual features	Ranked list of images	Provided a Life Seeker interactive lifelog SE

One of the processes described below can be used to improve the presentation of queried results:

Visualizing the search queries. One direction or approach is to improve the user interface. This approach has been used in several related works, as illustrated in Table 2. An example is to construct complicate queries with several level to create better user experience and efficiency.

The second research path relies on the method of headings and subheadings; this trend is used to identify possible responses to searches, and to make use of valuable metadata. This method can be realized by applying more sophisticated techniques. The third approach is to use visual search based on different views to enhance the client-side; this will provide deeper exploration and better classification to users. The final approach prioritizes the preference of the users qualitatively, allowing for better expressions that cannot be achieved using questionnaires. Personalizing searches to improve the user experience, the ES can incorporate users' interests into the retrieval techniques to produce user specific search results.

5 Conclusions

This paper focuses on contemporary explorative search techniques. The study of IR, the new SE grouping, SE forms with an emphasis on new search techniques. A variety of strategies for the successful enhancement of the user's SE are also discussed in this report. In essence, all strategies' main focus is to improve the value rate that consumers use in a particular operation and make relevant files available by the SE. By reviewing the detailed FS literature conducted over the last ten years, we objectively analyze these studies' SE exploratory portrayal for a search engine classification. This article compares different types of SE techniques, and these methodologies test the findings. Such approaches have shown that the IR reporting process is successfully enhanced. And techniques for ES and FS were discussed in this work. The key emphasis of these methods is to optimize the degree of satisfaction the customer gains and amplify the exposure of the related documents available to the SE. By performing comprehensive review of ten years' worth of literature on FS, we systematically analyse search engine classification with regards to how exploratory SE are represented in the reviewed literature. This paper further compares different SE techniques and discusses those methods for evaluating the quality of the results. These approaches have been shown to enhance document IR process significantly.

Acknowledgments. This research was sponsored and supported under the Universiti Tenaga Nasional (UNITEN) internal grant no J510050783 (2018). Many thanks to the Innovation and Research Management Center (iRMC), UNITEN who provided their assistance and expertise during the research.

References

1. Backhausen, D.-I.D.: Adaptive User Support in Interactive Information Retrieval Processes (2017)
2. Mahdi, M.N., Ahmad, A.R., Ismail, R., Subhi, M.: Review of techniques in faceted search applications. In: 2020 International Symposium on Networks, Computers and Communications (ISNCC), pp. 1–5 (2020)
3. Xu, J., Croft, W.B.: Quary expansion using local and global document analysis. SIGIR Forum **51**, 168–175 (2017)

4. Langville, A.N., Meyer, C.D.: Google's PageRank and beyond: The Science of Search enGine Rankings. Princeton University Press (2011)
5. Mahdi, M.N., Ahmad, A.R., Ismail, R., Subhi, M.A., Abdulrazzaq, M.M., Qassim, Q.S.: Information overload: the effects of large amounts of information. In: 2020 1st. Information Technology To Enhance E-learning and Other Application (IT-ELA), pp. 154–159 (2020)
6. Mahdi, M.N., Ahmad, A.R., Ismail, R., Natiq, H., Mohammed, M.A.: Solution for information overload using faceted search – a review. IEEE Access **8**, 119554–119585 (2020)
7. Marie, N., Gandon, F.: Survey of linked data based exploration systems. In: IESD 2014-Intelligent Exploitation of Semantic Data (2014)
8. Zheng, B., Zhang, W., Feng, X.F.B.: A survey of faceted search. J. Web Eng. **12**, 041–064 (2013)
9. Palagi, E., Gandon, F., Giboin, A., Troncy, R.: A survey of definitions and models of exploratory search. In: Proceedings of the 2017 ACM Workshop on Exploratory Search and Interactive Data Analytics, pp. 3–8 (2017)
10. Hoeber, O.: Information Visualization for interactive information retrieval. In: Proceedings of the 2018 Conference on Human Information Interaction & Retrieval, pp. 371–374 (2018)
11. Jiang, T.: Exploratory search: a critical analysis of the theoretical foundations, system features, and research trends. In: Chen, C., Larsen, R. (eds.) Library and Information Sciences, pp. 79–103. Springer, Heidelberg (2014). https://doi.org/10.1007/978-3-642-54812-3_7
12. Zheng, G., Vaishnavi, V.: A multidimensional and visual exploration approach to project prioritization and selection. In: AMCIS 2009 Proceedings, p. 129 (2009)
13. Tvarožek, M.: Exploratory search in the adaptive social semantic web. Inf. Sci. Technol. Bull. ACM Slovakia **3**, 42–51 (2011)
14. Tzitzikas, Y., Analyti, A.: Faceted taxonomy-based information management. In: 18th International Workshop on Database and Expert Systems Applications, 2007, DEXA 2007, pp. 207–211 (2007)
15. Seifert, C., Jurgovsky, J., Granitzer, M.: FacetScape: a visualization for exploring the search space. In: 18th International Conference on Information Visualisation (IV), 2014, pp. 94–101 (2014)
16. Athukorala, K., Głowacka, D., Jacucci, G., Oulasvirta, A., Vreeken, J.: Is exploratory search different? A comparison of information search behavior for exploratory and lookup tasks. J. Am. Soc. Inf. Sci. **67**, 2635–2651 (2016)
17. Kelly, R., Payne, S.J.: Collaborative web search in context: a study of tool use in everyday tasks. In: Proceedings of the 17th ACM Conference on Computer Supported Cooperative Work & Social Computing, pp. 807–819 (2014)
18. Wachsmuth, H., et al.: Building an argument search engine for the web. In: Proceedings of the 4th Workshop on Argument Mining, pp. 49–59 (2017)
19. Marchionini, G.: Exploratory search: from finding to understanding. Commun. ACM **49**, 41–46 (2006)
20. Chen, G., Lu, Z., Zhang, Z., Sun, Z.: Research on hybrid modified cuckoo search algorithm for optimal reactive power dispatch problem. IAENG Int. J. Comput. Sci. **45**, 328–339 (2018)
21. Savoy, J.: Why do successful search systems fail for some topics. In: Proceedings of the 2007 ACM Symposium on Applied Computing, pp. 872–877 (2007)
22. Leung, N.K., Lau, S.K.: No more keyword search or FAQ: innovative ontology and agent based dynamic user interface. IAENG Int. J. Comput. Sci. **33** (2007)
23. Azimi, J., Alam, A., Zhang, R.: Ads keyword rewriting using search engine results. In: Proceedings of the 24th International Conference on World Wide Web, pp. 3–4 (2015)
24. Ben-Yitzhak, O., et al.: Beyond basic faceted search. In: Proceedings of the 2008 International Conference on Web Search and Data Mining, pp. 33–44 (2008)
25. Hearst, M.: Design recommendations for hierarchical faceted search interfaces. In: ACM SIGIR Workshop on Faceted Search, pp. 1–5 (2006)

26. Huynh, D.F., Karger, D.: Parallax and companion: set-based browsing for the data web. In: WWW Conference ACM, p. 6 (2009)
27. Wilson, M., Russell, A., Smith, D.A.: mSpace: improving information access to multimedia domains with multimodal exploratory search. Commun. ACM **49**, 47–49 (2006)
28. Berner, C.: http://carsabi.com (2012)
29. Schmidt, D., Budde, K., Sonntag, D., Profitlich, H.-J., Ihle, M., Staeck, O.: A novel tool for the identification of correlations in medical data by faceted search. Comput. Biol. Med. **85**, 98–105 (2017)
30. Charleer, S., Klerkx, J., Duval, E., De Laet, T., Verbert, K.: Faceted search on coordinated tablets and tabletop: a comparison. In: Proceedings of the 8th ACM SIGCHI Symposium on Engineering Interactive Computing Systems, pp. 165–170 (2016)
31. Siddiqui, T., Ren, X., Parameswaran, A., Han, J.: FacetGist: collective extraction of document facets in large technical corpora. In: Proceedings of the 25th ACM International on Conference on Information and Knowledge Management, pp. 871–880 (2016)
32. Kharlamov, E., Giacomelli, L., Sherkhonov, E., Cuenca Grau, B., Kostylev, E.V., Horrocks, I.: SemFacet: making hard faceted search easier (2017)
33. Mauro, N., Ardissono, L., Hu, Z.F.: Multi-faceted trust-based collaborative filtering. In: Proceedings of the 27th ACM Conference on User Modeling, Adaptation and Personalization, pp. 216–224 (2019)
34. Chantamunee, S., Fung, C.C., Wong, K.W., Dumkeaw, C.: Knowledge discovery from thai research articles by solr-based faceted search. In: Unger, H., Sodsee, S., Meesad, P. (eds.) IC2IT 2018. AISC, vol. 769, pp. 337–346. Springer, Cham (2019). https://doi.org/10.1007/978-3-319-93692-5_33
35. de Campos, L.M., Fernández-Luna, J.M., Huete, J.F., Redondo-Expósito, L.: Automatic construction of multi-faceted user profiles using text clustering and its application to expert recommendation and filtering problems. Knowledge-Based Syst. **190**, 105337 (2020)
36. Bogaard, T., Hollink, L., Wielemaker, J., Hardman, L., Van Ossenbruggen, J.: Searching for old news: user interests and behavior within a national collection. In: Proceedings of the 2019 Conference on Human Information Interaction and Retrieval, pp. 113–121 (2019)
37. Le, T.-K., et al.: LifeSeeker: interactive lifelog search engine at LSC 2019: In: Proceedings of the ACM Workshop on Lifelog Search Challenge, pp. 37–40 (2019)

Sustainable Product Innovation Using Patent Mining and TRIZ

Chun Kit Chan[1], Kok Weng Ng[1], Mei Choo Ang[2(✉)], Chin Yuen Ng[3],
and Ah-Lian Kor[4]

[1] Department of Mechanical, Materials and Manufacturing Engineering, University of
Nottingham Malaysia, Semenyih, Malaysia
[2] Institute of IR 4.0, Universiti Kebangsaan Malaysia, Bangi, Malaysia
amc@ukm.edu.my
[3] Department of Electrical and Electronic Engineering, University of Nottingham Malaysia,
Semenyih, Malaysia
[4] School of Built Environment, Engineering, and Computing,
Leeds Beckett University, Leeds, UK

Abstract. Sustainable issues have become more serious due to the rapid development of the global economy. Sustainable design is an approach for designing or creating sustainable products/solutions based on sustainable development principles. Patent documents contain a lot of useful inventive information which will be useful for sustainable product design. However, they are dense and lengthy due to excessive overladen technical terminology. Automatic text mining tool in patent analysis is therefore, in great demand to assist innovators or patent engineers in their patent search. The main focus of this work is to develop a patent mining prototype to extract sustainable design information from the patent database and recommend potential solutions to the user by using Patent Mining and TRIZ. The TRIZ problem solving process and details of patent mining will be described in this paper. Patent mining techniques include tokenization, stop words filtering, stemming, lemmatization and classification. The patent mining techniques were implemented together with relevant sustainable design indicators to identify patent documents that contained the most relevant sustainable design solution or suggestions. A sustainable design problem is illustrated in this paper to demonstrate how a TRIZ user can utilize the implemented patent mining techniques and sustainable design indicators to obtain a sustainable solution for a design problem.

Keywords: Sustainable · Product innovation · Patent mining · TRIZ

1 Introduction

With rapid development of the global economy, issues such as resource shortages, air pollution, etc., have become more prevalent [1, 2] and are major causes for sustainability-related problems. It has been suggested that AI be employed for sustainability and innovation [3] to support UN 2030 sustainable development goals [4]. Sustainable product innovation (to support sustainable development) is necessary to effectively address such

© Springer Nature Switzerland AG 2021
H. Badioze Zaman et al. (Eds.): IVIC 2021, LNCS 13051, pp. 287–298, 2021.
https://doi.org/10.1007/978-3-030-90235-3_25

sustainability problem. Sustainable development includes ecological design, green or environmental design, and sustainable design [5]. Sustainable design is the higher level of green and environmentally friendly design evolution with an end goal developing a sustainable product or solution [2, 6, 7]. The entire process encompasses a systematic adaptation or embedment of sustainable development principles [8]. However, challenges faced by designers stem from the lack of suitable design tools during conceptual design phase [2, 9].

Theory of Inventive Problem Solving (TRIZ) is an innovative problem-solving tool that fosters a systematic study of patterns of invention in the global patent literature [10]. It eliminates the need for compromise and trade-off caused by conflicts as well as contradictions amongst different performance measures. Genrich Altshuller developed TRIZ in Russia [11] by analyzing huge amounts of patent documents because he recognized the fact that ideas of invention and new concepts were in published inventions. Product innovation connotes a solved problem that we are trying to solve.

Patent analysis [12–16] in high-tech management has become more prominent as the innovation process and innovation cycle becomes more complex and shorter, and therefore, resulting in an unpredictable and unstable market demand. Patents contain a lot of technical information which is a source for technological-scientific innovations. However, they are dense and lengthy due to verbose technical terminology and details. Such documents require extensive as well as intensive manual analysis. The method of reading or scanning the indexed patent documents to extract information from a long list of unprocessed results is a very time-consuming and is not a trivial process that involves careful manual selection. Data mining can be used to address this problem. Data mining is a system that automatically extract useful information from massive databases. Text mining of patent information or patent mining is similar to data mining, but for the full-text patent analysis, it specifically extracts useful knowledge from patent documents which typically comprises poorly structured texts [17]. Automatic text mining tool in patent analysis is therefore, in great demand to assist innovators or patent engineers.

A patent mining prototype is developed in this work to extract sustainability design information from a patent database and recommends Patent Mining and TRIZ solutions to potential users. The focus would be primarily on the methodology of extracting textual information from patent documents using Python. In this paper, the TRIZ problem solving process, and patent mining which mainly focus on text mining process will be introduced in Sect. 1 and Sect. 2. The details of the implemented patent mining process such as tokenization, filtering, stemming and lemmatization and classification will be elaborated in Sect. 3. A consumer product case study will also be described in this section In Sect. 4, sample results of the sustainable design recommendations will be displayed and discussed. Finally, this paper is concluded with some future work in Sect. 5.

2 TRIZ Problem Solving Process

The general process of solving an engineering problem is shown in Fig. 1. Engineers utilize all their knowledge and expertise to translate an engineering problem (specific problem) to a specific solution. In applying TRIZ problem solving, the TRIZ engineering contradiction is applied by defining an engineering problem in the form of contradicting features (general problem) which will then propose a list of possible general solutions in the form of inventive principles which are derived from learning repeating patterns of problems and solutions from patent information. From the suggested inventive principles which are actually general solution, the engineer will have to translate these inventive principles into specific solutions for the engineering problem as shown in Fig. 2. However, it is a not an easy task to define the contradiction features i.e. map a specific problem to 39 improving and worsening features [9]. In other words, it remains a very challenging task for an engineer to translate the inventive principles (general solutions) to specific solutions. However, with some general ideas from the inventive principles, the task of finding a specific solution based on the inventive principles is relatively easier compared to the problem solving process without TRIZ. However, this approach might not work in cases when there are contradictions or conflicts that are difficult to be resolved before the generation of good solutions [18].

Fig. 1. The general process of problem solving without TRIZ.

For the TRIZ problem solving approach shown in Fig. 2, engineers need to analyze a specific problem encountered. Subsequently, they map the problem into a general problem in TRIZ. The general problem will have some general TRIZ solutions generated through the application of TRIZ tools including contradiction matrix, substance-field modelling, and even ARIZ (a Russian acronym for the TRIZ tool, "Algorithm for Inventive Problem Solving").

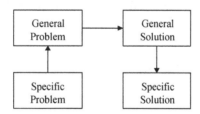

Fig. 2. The general process of problem solving with TRIZ.

However, it is common for engineers to struggle to translate general TRIZ solutions to specific solutions as the general TRIZ solutions are in the form of inventive principles which are very abstract and require in-depth domain knowledge and expertise. Based on this identified gap, in this research, a patent mining system has been developed to assist engineers in the translation of general TRIZ solutions. Patents related to the inventive principles will be identified and further manually examined to provide more specific ideas to engineers.

Thus, with the help of patent mining as illustrated in Fig. 3, engineers can speed up the process of devising specific solutions by reviewing relevant patent documents in a shorter time span before deciding on which patent they should further examine in detail. By incorporating patent mining in the TRIZ engineering contradiction framework, it will facilitate an engineer's task of designing a specific solution for an engineering problem. Undeniably, the work entailed will be much easier compared to manual individual patent search or standalone TRIZ engineering contradiction tools. Although TRIZ tools are not specifically created for sustainable design, these tools can be applied to sustainable design if engineers applied the inventive principles grounded on sustainability. Thus, with the incorporation of patent mining, our proposed patent mining system can assist engineers consider sustainability in their specific solutions based on the recommended inventive principles. This is because patent mining is a computational approach that can facilitate a faster and more focused search of large patent databases. Large amount of relevant and specific information (e.g., information related to sustainability or specific solutions) could be retrieved easily and quickly to support engineers in their sustainable solution designs.

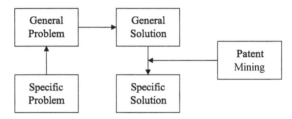

Fig. 3. TRIZ problem solving process with the help of patent mining.

3   Patent Mining and a Sustainable Consumer Product Case Study

Patent documents are divided into two categories namely structured and unstructured data [14]. Structured data refers to information that are well organized such as patent number, assignees or filing date [13]. For unstructured data, they are not well organized and normally, they are full texts of various lengths and contains, such as Title, Abstract, Claims and Descriptions [13]. Abstract, Claims and Descriptions contain useful information such as the technical features of an invention.

There are 3 main stages of Patent Mining for this research work (see Fig. 4). The first stage is patent information extraction, which includes downloading related patent documents from USPTO and extract unstructured data from all the documents. After extracting all useful unstructured data from the patent document, information that are related to sustainability will be further extracted. Relevant sustainability information will be fed into the design conceptualization process. The detail patent mining process expanded from these main stages is shown in Fig. 5.

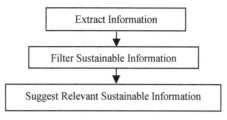

Fig. 4. Patent mining framework.

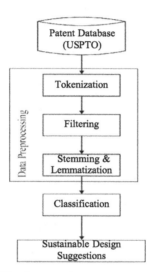

Fig. 5. Patent mining workflow.

3.1 Extraction of Patent Information

The data source is patent information which is a key element of patent data analysis. Care must be taken to ensure a sizeable dataset viewing the fact that large amount of data could be messy. Therefore, it is necessary to provide scope and boundaries of the research, only relevant design criteria and context of interest are considered. Next, patent documents are retrieved from suitable open online patent databases such as USPTO, Google Patent, SIPO, EPO, etc.

In this work, patent information that are related to sustainability and design is mainly obtained from USPTO. This is facilitated by developing an automated search program for USPTO advanced search facility. The information that is retrieved from USPTO is in a HTML format, where only title, abstract, claims and description are extracted and stored in a CSV format. Subsequently, the patent document is imported into a Python workspace and store in a dictionary format with data for the patent number, title, and abstract. A total of 22281 patent documents related to sustainability have been extracted in this research work. These patent documents are stored as csv files for further search based on sustainable design indicators. Processes encompass tokenization, stopwords filtering, and stemming as well as lemmatization.

3.2   Data Pre-processing

Extracted information from the unstructured data from all relevant patent documents are lengthy. Therefore, data pre-processing is required to reduce the size of the dataset to transform them to structured data for easy analysis. In this research work, there are 3 main processes in the data pre-processing, namely Tokenization, Filtering and Stemming as well as Lemmatization. Natural Language Toolkit (NLTK) is a Python library that work with human language data for the application in statistical Natural Language Processing (NLP) [19]. It contains text processing libraries for parsing, tokenization, stemming, semantic reasoning, classification and tagging. Therefore, the imported patent information which is stored in the Python dictionary will undergo pre-processing before classification. This is to remove unrelated information from the corpus and improve the search results through the extraction of more relevant design suggestions.

A. Text Segmentation (Tokenization). Tokenization is one of the text mining techniques that is used to split text into smaller units which is known as tokens. The non-text characters in the patent information such as tabs, punctuation, etc. are removed in this process. Tokens can be individual word, phrases or even a whole sentence. The unstructured data are segmented into smaller units for summarization [13]. Additionally, the tokens can be further processed by filtering process. NLTK provides a tokenization module which can be used to divide a text into tokens. In this work, sent_tokenize() has been used to split the patent information.

B. Stopwords Filtering. Filtering is a process to remove words from a document. Term Frequency – Inverse Document Frequency (TF-IDF) is a numerical statistic that indicates the importance of a word which relate to a text document or corpus and is widely used in text filtering process. Words with low TF and IDF are removed in indexing of a collection. However, using TF-IDF alone does not prevent undesirable words such as function words from being calculated. Therefore, stop words filtering is added into the process. Stopwords are words that do not contain any significant meaning to search queries and stopwords are commonly used in English, such as "as, the, be, are" etc. Stopwords are normally filtered out before the processing of natural language data in operation because they appear too frequently in the patent text and lose their purpose as search terms.

C. Stemming and Lemmatization. In a full text of extracted information, there are words, which has similar meaning but in different form, which need to be reduced to its base (root) form. For example, the word "play" is the root form of "plays", "playing" and "played". This could be problematic for text data analysis, and it can be solved by applying stemming and lemmatization. Stemming is a process of removing affixes from the word and transforming the word into its root form. Sometimes the root is not an actual word but might be part of the word. Lemmatization is a process of reducing the inflected words to its actual base form of word which is known as the Lemma.

3.3   Classification

Study on sustainable design indicators is very important because it can render design suggestions more related to the sustainability problem. Sustainable design indicators have been classified into three groups which are environmental, economic, and social. Sustainable design indicators are used in the extraction process to extract the most similar sentence and classified into these 3 groups.

A. Sustainable Design Indicators. In order to obtain suggestions that are related to sustainable design, relevant design indicators have been extracted from literature. Sustainable design indicators selected for this research work is shown in Table 1 [5].

Table 1. Sustainable design indicators [5].

Environmental	Economic	Social
High material utilization	Low production Costs	Practicability
Energy and resource conservation	Low transportation costs	High degree of intelligence
Biodegradable material	Low recovery costs	Security
Material easy recovery	Low maintenance costs	High reliability
Identifiable material	Low using costs	Ease of use
Material of low pollution	High economic benefits	High capacity utilization

B. Gensim. Gensim (Generate Similarity) is a topic detection modelling which is a technique that is very apt for this work. It determines the similarity between a pair of documents or at least two sets documents. Cosine Similarity and Vector Space modelling are used in Gensim. Vector Space modelling is a model for representing text document as vectors [20]. Bag-of-Words is a document representation which is used to convert document to vectors as depicted in Fig. 6.

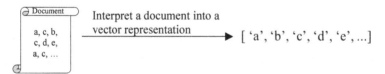

Fig. 6. Bag-of-Words.

After pre-processing, the documents will retain the meaningful words with the corpus converted to vectors for future use. All the words in the Bag-of-Words are allocated a specific integer ID as illustrated in Fig. 7. Python function "doc2bow()" was used to convert the tokenized documents to vectors. This function calculates the number of occurrences of every word before transforming a word into its integer word id and a sparse vector.

The sparse vector is used as a representation of a document and it assumes the form ("word id", "Occurrences"). Therefore, it is read as the word "a" (id 0) and word "b" (id 1) appearing once.

Assign unique ID

['a', 'b', 'c', 'd', 'e', ...] ⟶ ['a': 0, 'b': 1, 'c': 2, 'd': 3, 'e': 4, ...]

Fig. 7. Unique ID assigned to all words in Bag-of-Words.

Cosine similarity is used to measure and make comparisons of documents similarity or ascribe a rank to the documents with respect to a given vector of query words [21]. The Cosine similarity approach involves the computation of the cosine of the angle between vectors x and y. The similarity between two term-frequency vectors can be calculated using the Eq. (1) below.

$$sim(x, y) = \frac{x.y}{|x||y|} \tag{1}$$

where $|x|$ = The Euclidean distance of vector x; $|y|$ = The Euclidean distance of vector y. In Cosine similarity, when both the vectors are orthogonal (i.e., at 90° to each other) then the cosine value is zero, which implies they are not a match. If the angle is very small, the cosine value will be very close to 1, which means the vectors have greater match [19]. To prepare for similarity queries, all collected data documents are imported into Python workspace to compare against subsequent queries. A user types in the query and uses it to search for a related sentence by comparing it against a pool of collated data documents. To reiterate, an initial search based on the word 'sustainability' yields a search result of 22281 patent documents. Next, sustainable design indicators are used as query inputs for further search on this pool of retrieved documents. The final search results are grouped under the sustainable design indicators as shown in Fig. 8.

A case study has been conducted to derive a sustainable solution for home liquid detergents (with containers of diverse sizes and made of different materials) which are widely sold in the market. After use, most of these containers are not recycled nor reused and thus, causes environmental issues in the long run due to its non-biodegradable materials (i.e. polymers). Hence, the essential requirement for the design of a liquid detergent container is to facilitate recycle or reuse (duration of action of stationary object feature) to conserve resources. However, the container will not be able to accommodate different detergent volume (adaptability or versatility feature). The inventive principles can be identified using a TRIZ contradiction matrix table and the recommended inventive principle is 'Taking Out' which easily implicates the replacement of the existing container of various sizes and material to a re-usable or recyclable type. However, this leads to the pertinent question on how to design a re-usable and sustainable container that could accommodate different volumes of liquid detergent.

With this inventive principle as a guide, engineers can start looking for specific solution ideas through the patent documents recommended by a patent mining system based on sustainable design indicators shown in Table 1. Engineers can explore the search results of patent mining to elicit design suggestions which are related to the recommended inventive principle. For example, in the results of "Bio-degradable material", the design suggestion with patent number 8567660 is a patent that describes a "multi-layer packaging design that can be used to contain liquid" which can be adapted and applied to replace the existing container that concurs with the inventive principle #2 (Taking Out) which is shown in Fig. 9.

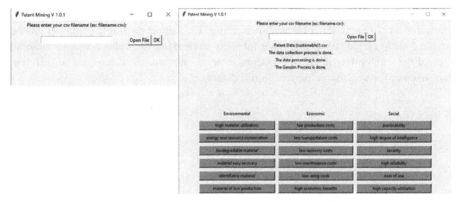

Fig. 8. The user interface for sustainable patent mining before search (left) and after search (right). The application of sustainable product innovation using patent mining and TRIZ.

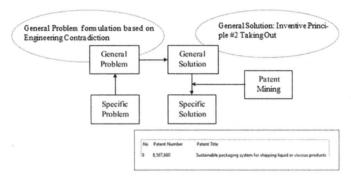

Fig. 9. Suggestion which relates to Inventive Principle 2 (Taking Out) assisted with a result from patent mining system.

Therefore, the designer can study the details of the patent which will assist engineers derive a specific solution to solve the liquid detergent container problem. This demonstrates how patent mining and TRIZ can be combined to help engineers to find solutions to the problem.

4 Results and Discussions

Figure 10 shows the results of the potential suggestions for sustainable design with the 20 top similarity results of patent documents to the sustainable design indicator "Biodegradable material", patent number, and patent title. The listing of these top similarity results of patent documents are based on their score in similarity calculated by Cosine measure (-1 to 1) where the similarity result of 1.0 is highest in regard to the sentences in the patent titles and abstracts. The search results only show the top 20 results sorted in descending order to reduce computational time. Engineers can also explore other sustainable design indicators to explore the details of potential solutions for finding specific

solutions to replace the liquid detergent container. To reiterate, with the ideas from specific solution of patent 8567660 as shown in Fig. 11, a novel re-usable container can be
designed with a rigid recyclable material such as kenaf as the outer container with an
internal detachable bag made of biodegradable plastics that is waterproof of different
sizes to cater for varying volume of liquid detergent.

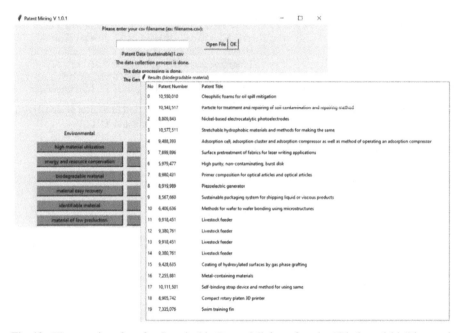

Fig. 10. The user interface for Sustainable Patent Mining after the "Biodegradable" button is
clicked.

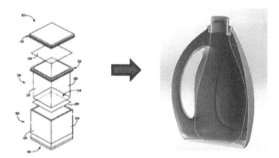

Fig. 11. Results of specific solution from USPTO Patent No. 8567660 (left) that inspire the
sustainable design (right).

5   Conclusions and Future Work

In this paper, a methodology of patent mining that used to analyze patent documents for TRIZ users is presented. Firstly, the patent document is retrieved from USPTO with HTML format and imported into Python workspace. Next the database is pre-processed to segment the lengthy database into tokens and the stopwords are filtered out. Subsequently, every individual word is normalized into its base form so that the size of the dataset can be reduced. The patent mining results are discussed and shown with an example of how patent mining result can be linked with the inventive principle of TRIZ.

For future work, the current algorithms could be further improved for enhancing the performance of document classification algorithms. Claims or descriptions can be used as the corpus because the abstracts contain less technical detail information.

Acknowledgements. The authors would like to thank the Universiti Kebangsaan Malaysia and the Ministry of Higher Education, Malaysia, for supporting the work through research grants: GUP-2018-124 and FRGS/1/2018/TK03/UKM/02/6.

References

1. Sherwin, C.: Design and sustainability: a discussion paper based on personal experience and observations. J. Sustainable Prod. Des. **4** (2004)
2. Zainali, N., Ang, M., Ng, K., Ijab, M.: A framework for sustainable eco-friendly product development based on TRIZ. In: Badioze Zaman, H., et al. (eds.) IVIC 2019. LNCS, vol. 11870, pp. 704–712. Springer, Cham (2019). https://doi.org/10.1007/978-3-030-34032-2_63
3. Kor, A.L., Rondeau, E., Andersson, K.: AI for sustainability and innovation [Special Issue]. Appl. Sci. **11** (2021)
4. UN: The 17 Goals. Department of Economic and Social Affairs (2021)
5. Cao, G., Luo, P., Wang, L., Yang, X.: Key technologies for sustainable design based on patent knowledge mining. Procedia CIRP **39**, 97–102 (2016)
6. Ahmad, S.A., Ang, M.C., Ng, K.W., Wahab, A.N.A.: Reducing home energy usage based on triz concept. Adv. Environ. Biol. **9**, 6–11 (2015)
7. Ang, M.C., Ng, K.W., Ahmad, S.A., Wahab, A.N.A., Jenal, R.: Sustainable smart autonomous visual design system in product development in 4IR for societal well-being. In: Zaman, H.B., Ahmad, A. (eds.) Sustainable Smart Technologies in Visual Informatics in the Fourth Industrial Revolution for Societal Well Being, pp. 208–233. UKM Press, Bangi (2019)
8. Waas, T., Hugé, J., Verbruggen, A., Wright, T.: Sustainable development: a bird's eye view. Sustainability **3**, 1637–1661 (2011)
9. Ang, M., Ng, K., Ahmad, S., Wahab, A.: An engineering design support tool based on TRIZ. In: Zaman, H.B., Robinson, P., Olivier, P., Shih, T.K., Velastin, S. (eds.) IVIC 2013. LNCS, vol. 8237, pp. 115–127. Springer, Cham (2013). https://doi.org/10.1007/978-3-319-02958-0_11
10. Hua, Z., Yang, J., Coulibaly, S., Zhang, B.: Integration TRIZ with problem-solving tools: a literature review from 1995 to 2006. Int. J. Bus. Innov. Res. **1** (2006)
11. Li, M., Ming, X., Zheng, M., He, L., Xu, Z.: An integrated TRIZ approach for technological process and product innovation. Proc. Inst. Mech. Eng. B: J. Eng. Manuf. **231**, 1062–1077 (2015)

12. Fischer, G., Lalyre, N.: Analysis and visualisation with host-based software – the features of STN®AnaVist^{TM}. World Patent Inf. **28**, 312–318 (2006)
13. Soo, V.-W., Lin, S.-Y., Yang, S.-Y., Lin, S.-N., Cheng, S.-L.: A cooperative multi-agent platform for invention based on patent document analysis and ontology. Expert Syst. Appl. **31**, 766–775 (2006)
14. Tseng, Y.-H., Lin, C.-J., Lin, Y.-I.: Text mining techniques for patent analysis. Inf. Process. Manage. **43**, 1216–1247 (2007)
15. Yoon, B., Park, Y.: A text-mining-based patent network: analytical tool for high-technology trend. J. High Technol. Manage. Res. **15**, 37–50 (2004)
16. Ghane, M., Ang, M.C., Kadir, R.A., Ng, K.W.: Technology forecasting model based on trends of engineering system evolution (TESE) and big data for 4IR. In: 2020 IEEE Student Conference on Research and Development (SCOReD), pp. 237–242 (2020)
17. Liang, Y., Tan, R.: A text-mining-based patent analysis in product innovative process. In: León-Rovira, N. (ed.) CAI 2007. ITIFIP, vol. 250, pp. 89–96. Springer, Boston, MA (2007). https://doi.org/10.1007/978-0-387-75456-7_9
18. Yusof, S.M., Awad, A.A.: A brief review of theory of inventive problem solving (TRIZ) methodology. Jurnal Teknik Industri – Universitas Bung Hatta **2**, 119–131 (2014)
19. Bird, S.: NLTK: The Natural Language Toolkit (2006)
20. Ballard, N., Joshi, D.: Similarity matching in news articles. J. Comput. Sci. Coll. **35**, 46–51 (2019)
21. Han, J., Kamber, M., Pei, J.: Data Mining: Concepts and Techniques. Morgan Kaufmann, Boston (2012)

Personalised Smart Mobility Model for Smart Movement During Pandemic Covid-19

Noor Afiza Mat Razali[1]([✉]), Nur Atiqah Malizan[1], Nuraini Shamsaimon[1],
Khairani Abd Majid[1]([✉]), Muhammad Narzwan Mohd Puad[1], Khairul Khalil Ishak[2],
and Muhammad Hafiz Abdul Rahim[3]

[1] National Defence University of Malaysia, Kuala Lumpur, Malaysia
{noorafiza,khairani}@upnm.edu.my
[2] Management and Science University, Shah Alam, Malaysia
[3] National Security Council, Putrajaya, Malaysia

Abstract. When a disaster such as pandemic Covid-19, flood and landslide struct, essential services and aid must reach the disaster area promptly. A mechanism that enables smooth coordination for people and vehicles especially for movement during a disaster is vital. This paper aims to present the conceptual model for personalised smart mobility for smart movement during a disaster such as Covid-19 that includes smart vehicle mobility profile and smart people mobility profile. The model was formulated by applying the smart city concept in urban Malaysia and focusing on smartphones and various IoT sensors as the enabler technologies and foundation of data gathering to be utilized for decision making in multiple circumstances. In the process, we reviewed recent advances based on Smart City and disaster management policy for Malaysia and outline relevant directions for future research of smart movement control and decision-making during a disaster including pandemic outbreaks such as Covid-19 for the Malaysia case. The focus is on a fundamental topic in the application of telematics to assist the authority and community for citizens and vehicles mobility when disaster strike.

Keywords: Smart city · Disaster management · Covid-19 · Telematics · Personalised smart mobility

1 Introduction

Natural disasters such as pandemic outbreaks, floods, earthquakes, landslides and many more can strike in so many ways at any time. Meanwhile, a human-made disaster occurs due to development, human activities that include acts of terrorism such as bombing and actions to sabotage and contribute to the malfunction of critical national infrastructures such as electricity, gas and water facilities. United Nations Sustainable Development Goals outlined the most critical items during a disaster are water, food, fuel, emergency kits, first aid, and medical supplies [1]. Thus, the availability and access to the essential items to all areas especially those affected by disaster must be highly prioritised. Disaster can result in disruption of transportation and communication that lead to confusion on the standard operating procedure during the disaster event. The natural disaster

© Springer Nature Switzerland AG 2021
H. Badioze Zaman et al. (Eds.): IVIC 2021, LNCS 13051, pp. 299–309, 2021.
https://doi.org/10.1007/978-3-030-90235-3_26

that affecting the world is the Pandemic Covid-19 outbreak that caused severe illness, including death around the globe and creating a new phenomenon such as lockdown and restriction in terms of people mobility due to the disaster. The global outbreak of Covid-19, a cluster of acute respiratory illnesses with unknown causes, which started in Wuhan, Hubei Province, China, in December 2019, had made us experience the true nature of the seriousness of disaster caused by virus pandemic. Besides providing treatments and developing vaccines, tremendous efforts are put in place to detect and break the virus's chain, including introducing movement restriction orders around the world. To control the further spread of the Covid-19 pandemic, the Malaysian government has implemented various types of Movement Control Order (MCO). However, various levels of understanding by the authority members and people who received the instruction that keeps changing due to the various level of seriousness of the event caused a different compliance level within the community and varying levels of enforcement by the authorities. This gap can be solved by the utilization of technologies to assist the coordination of disaster management and release effort when the disaster structs. Development of mechanisms that apply smart city-related technology, telematics and big data analytics can be utilised in executing the strategy for disaster management and prevention.

This study proposes the conceptual model of personalised smart mobility by integrating the smart city concept for smart movement during a disaster that is crucially needed for efficient coordination and disaster relief effort. The model considers related policies as the foundation and components of relevant factors in the decision-making process in any possible event for the mobility of vehicle and people in essential sectors when disaster strike and the people movement is limited or restricted. This paper is organised as follows: first, we briefly discuss the background and general overview of existing approaches in handling disaster management focusing on Malaysia's disaster management strategy that includes natural disasters such as pandemics, floods and landslides. This is followed by a discussion of the technologies that can be applied to manage disasters better. Then, we discuss the utilisation of data, information, and communication technologies (ICT) that can help to manage the pandemic in organised and coordinated ways. Finally, we propose a Personalised Smart Mobility Model for Smart Movement during a disaster by considering the smart city concept for urban Malaysia to ensure that people are informed with the updated situation, standard operating procedure (SOP) in real-time and advising citizens to comply with the authority instruction efficiently.

2   Background

The Malaysian government had coordinated all relevant government authorities and agencies, including public healthcare, police, defence, fire departments, welfare departments and so on, in handling the disaster including the Covid-19 pandemic disaster. Systematic and secured data sharing among all relevant government authorities and agencies is essential to enable efficient data analysis to support various decision-making, action planning, and implementation to preserve the nation's stability and security during a disaster. The knowledge domain that could be utilised in disaster management and coordination is the smart city, telematics and big data analytics using various sensors including smartphones. A disaster management strategy was also included as a pillar in the implementation strategy so that it could be applied efficiently with the assistance of technology.

2.1 Disaster Management Strategy

When disaster strike, to be able to respond to varying situations regardless of the scale of effects, decision support for disaster management requires flexibility and efficiency [3]. Involvement of expertise from different fields is essential as response involves multiple agencies and coordinating disaster management. According to the locality of the area, the precise management support system will also play a vital part when the disaster occurred [4]. In Malaysia, the National Disaster Management Agency (NADMA) handled disaster management and response under Directive 20 of the National Security Council. NADMA acts as the focal point in managing disaster with three (3) levels of disaster management that included district level, state level and national level. Each group has specific agencies that will be deployed for the relief operation during the disaster. Any disaster involving local incidents that can potentially spread will be managed by the District Disaster Management and Relief Committee (DMRC). If the disaster level escalated and the next level of support is required, the State Disaster Management and Relief Committee (SDMR) will manage the disaster. On the highest level, the Central Disaster Management and Relief Committee (CDMRC) will be in charge and responsible for forming a central, state and district level of operation team [5].

In flood and landslide scenarios, people mobility is also very significant to be handled carefully to ensure smooth evacuation of people from affected areas. It can be done by dynamically monitoring the disaster affected areas through cameras, smartphones and other IoT technologies to avoid road congestion, blockages and chaos [6, 7]. The study by [8] proposed a novel emergency response framework that facilitates the stakeholders of the urban transport systems in the decision-making during emergencies by emphasising on personalised mobility profile for evacuation during a disaster. Meanwhile, during the pandemic Covid-19, Malaysia National Security Council (NSC) commanded and decided on mobilising the pandemic response at the national level, with technical guidance from the Ministry of Health (MOH). Covid-19 was deemed a national security threat, the National Security Council (NSC) was activated via the National Security Council Act 2016 (Act 776) to command and mobilise all government and non-governmental machinery to control the pandemic on a national scale. Legislation and policy documents that applied during the pandemic disaster are the Prevention and Control of Infectious Diseases Act (Act 342), International Health Regulations 2005, the MOH Disaster Management Plan, and the Malaysia Strategy for Emerging Diseases and Public Health Emergencies (MySED) II Workplan (2017–2021) [9].

Also, the government made a recommendation to society to adhere to the SOP developed by the Ministry of Health, the National Security Council and the Prime Minister's Department. Preventive efforts to oversee individual and neighbourhood wellbeing was emphasized. Government officials are being advised to prevent Malaysia's population from misinterpreting signals or directives issued by the authorities. Municipal authorities' collaboration with the local government was established to manage Covid-19 in the community. Community councils also giving the best effort in keeping the community secure by collaborating with age-specific organisations to reach out to people in need [10].

However, for this scale of the disaster, the management of the disaster is overwhelming the responding agencies. In all aspects of disaster management, technologies that supported by various type of data and tools have great potential to expedite the coordination, decision making, save lives, limit damage and reduce the costs.

2.2 Smart City

The proliferation of the Internet of Things (IoT) devices, notably in the advancement of sensors technology, leads to the development of a Smart City worldwide. One example of such Smart City planning and development in Malaysia is the City Brain project in Kuala Lumpur [11, 12]. Smart City elements are comprised of citizens (people), transportation, healthcare, technology, governance, infrastructure, building, energy and education. Leading technologies in Smart City are sensors, cameras, mobile phones, high-speed wireless Internet and emerging new technologies that are part of the IoT. These devices generate big data for various utilisation purposes in Smart City. Big data refers to high volume, variety, velocity, and veracity [13].

2.3 Telematics for Vehicle and Citizen

Telematics refers to the transmission of information provided by sensors from various areas of the smart city using telecommunications services. Meanwhile, applications and services in the smart city can be divided into sensors, local processing, visualisation and background processing and analytics [14]. The implementations will include computational infrastructure, network facilities and data centres. The increase in worldwide smartphone penetration has gained new ways to collect data. This phenomenon resulted in benefitting people, vehicle owners, industry, government and society. A combination of sensors and smartphone usage is determined to be the best for data collection and communication sharing. A variety of connected devices and smartphones enable report writing and status update to be done in real-time. Also, based on data analysis, commands will be sent to the specific group resulted in an appropriate action that could be done [15, 16]. The mobility of smartphones triggers various research in smartphone-based vehicle telematics because it enables services based on the monitoring of devices and their surroundings. Among the research areas that need to be addressed are efficient methods for real-time decision-making. Also, smartphone usage gives the advantage in terms of application development that are optimising the user experience, human factors and improving the total cost of utilisation. A personalised mobility route planning model for campus evacuation was proposed in [17, 18]. The model includes registration functions and collecting the students' information, providing the distributed location information for general emergency evacuation in the university campus, and smart personalised students' route planning in an emergency evacuation.

3 Personalised Smart Mobility for Vehicles and People During Disaster

Based on the background studies in the previous chapter, we propose personalising citizens and vehicles for smart mobility using a unique profiling mechanism. The unique profile is created for a particular user based on their assigned role.

3.1 Supporting Technologies

The IoT devices that are embedded in the connected vehicle and installed throughout the roads and public transportation facilities for Smart City, can be exploited as telematics solutions to personalise the smart mobility profile. In a way, it provides accurate real-time smart mobility information of the vehicle, such as location, identification, capacity available and situation of the traffic. The current smartphone application that uses Global Positioning System (GPS) is handy for normal daily lives, such as knowing the route and traffic condition when travelling using cars. But in a disaster situation, GPS alone will not provide the true nature of the traffic situation. Additional IoT devices in Smart City such as Laser Detection and Ranging (LiDAR) [19], cameras and information from social media must be pooled as the input information to make a prediction of the routes. Through the information generated, authorities will have the predictive information on the fastest, safest and most efficient route [2, 20] to deliver the critical items supply to the eagerly waiting disaster victims. Using the Smart City concept, big real-time data of people and traffic mobility, for example, real-time GPS, traffic and road conditions data that are generated from the connected vehicles, various sensors and devices can be obtained and utilised in the process of labelling area according to the level of severity of the disaster. The collected data can be analysed using identified components, variables and parameters for telematics solutions to manage traffic flow and help with navigation strategies to provide emergency services. It could also be used for smooth evacuation from the affected areas, avoid congestion, minimise risk to public security and safety and minimise economic losses.

3.2 Model Conceptualisation

In this paper, we present the personalised smart mobility in the smart city for smart movement during a disaster by extending the Malaysia Smart City Framework. Our proposed model consists of 3 modules which are 1) Data obtainment module 2) Decision-making for vehicle and people mobility using big data analytics techniques module 3) Role-based profiling module as described in Fig. 1.

Based on our conceptual studies, we determine the components and variables for the proposed model based on Malaysia Smart City elements focusing on monitoring and decision making for enforcement control, coordination and assistance arrangement during a disaster. We suggested the personalised profile be allocated to people (citizens) and vehicles (people who drive the designated vehicles) using the role-based profiling concept to enable optimum movement and mobility during the disaster. Meanwhile, the data gathered using telematics and smartphones will be used for decision-making

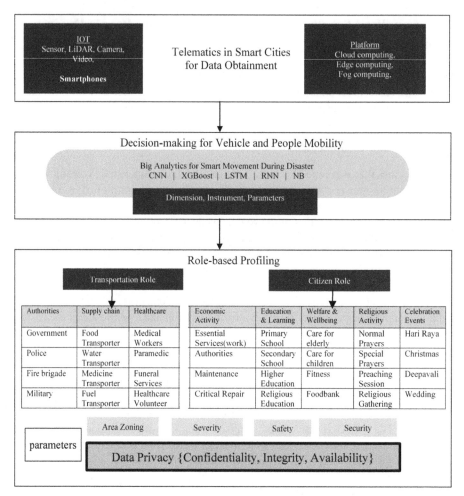

Fig. 1. Personalised smart mobility model for smart movement during disaster: Malaysia case

to monitor traffic, vehicles and people's movement in real-time. This would help the authorities in implementing assistance arrangements and mobility controls during a disaster through personalised smart mobility tailored by each user's profile.

This model also takes into consideration parameters such as area zoning according to severity, safety and security definition that must be parallel with the government policy for disaster management tailored specifically for particular events. As for the collected data, this proposed model also comprised of the data privacy perimeters to protect the Confidentiality, Integrity and Availability (CIA) of the data. We discuss the module in the sub-section as follows:

3.2.1   Module 1: Telematics in Smart City for Dataset Obtainment

In this module, the data obtainment mechanism using telematics devices in and near the smart vehicles is designed to obtain data from vehicles to accelerate data processing and data feed structured with pre-defined variables. The vehicle telematics concept is utilised to organise systematic vehicles mobility using vehicles movements data across a specific area in a smart city. Then, real-time data analysis will be executed and the finest mobility movement according to each user movement objective, will be communicated using smartphones directly to each user.

The process used for data obtainment plays an essential role in mobility controls and assistance arrangement management. The method of generating model diagrams for the data obtainment for the analysis purposes be addressed by considering the stakeholders(actor) stance because the current understanding of the detail's activities, sequence, and decisions is still not precisely defined. Data from sensors, including connected cars, LiDAR, camera and video for the smart city mapping and traffic control, will be gathered in cloud computing, edge computing and fog computing based on the processing requirement. Then, the big data generated from the sensors and devices will be analysed according to the role of the data. Users such as citizens and vehicles, especially for those with crucial functions such as ambulances, need to have their personalised profile created and be integrated into the system.

3.2.2   Module 2: Decision-Making for Vehicle and People Mobility Using Big Data Analytics Techniques

Module 2 discuss the decision-making mechanism for vehicles and people mobility using data analytic. The decision-making variables will include vehicles and people specific profiles for precise data input. Based on the input data, the decision-making mechanism for particular circumstances by utilising the data analytics technique is proposed. We are proposing traditional data analytic techniques including Naïve Bayes, Recurrent Neural Network and Long Short-Term Memory to be utilised. The data that will be used are gathered in module 1 which include data from user's smartphones, road data, event data, traffic sensors data and weather data. Under each component, variables are proposed as shown in Table 1. The decision-making is based on Malaysia's MCO scenarios when vehicles and citizens with essential roles determined by the government, need to access information about the best and safe routes to deliver food supply, clean water and healthcare supply in all areas. Meanwhile, in the case when citizens are having a symptom of the pandemic, this module will be able to guide them on the best routes to reach the medical team without risking other people's health by having unnecessary contact. This module also takes into consideration, the heavy traffic problem that occurred during the MCO due to excessive and unnecessary movement. It also will reduce the citizens' non-compliance behaviour by having passive monitoring of people movement behaviour based on the collected data and will be sending the warning when citizens breach the SOP attached to their role. We also include the attributes such as the road network context-awareness data as a component for decision-making. We set the context as events, weather and structure affection. The features also include modelling pedestrian profiles, visual clustering of users' mobility behaviour and route planning. Route planning consists of the evacuation and collaborative rescue procedure. This model also works in the evacuation during the disaster such as flood, landside, fire, terrorism and any situation deemed as a disaster by the authority.

Table 1. Decision-making element for vehicles and people mobility

Components	Variables
Data from user smartphones	Coordinate, Movement, Mode of Transportation, Timestamps
Road data	Congestion, Delay, Smooth
Event data	Disaster {Flood, Landslides}, Accident, Authority Roadblock, Mass Gathering
Traffic sensors	Conjunction {Coordinate, Timestamps}
Weather data	Storm, Heavy Rain

3.2.3 Module 3: Role-Based Profiling

When a disaster such as a flood and a landslide occurred, the movement of vehicles that carries basic essential items to the various areas during a disaster must be prioritized. The availability and access for people and vehicles carrying essential needs to the designated location must be guaranteed. On top of that, for a pandemic disaster such as Covid-19 that require movement control to be implemented, the mechanism for people and vehicle mobility need to be systematically developed.

Role-based profiling modules are suggested in our model to assign a role to citizens (including authority personnel) and vehicles. This module will enable vehicles assigned with a particular role such as ambulance, police, army, transporting critical items etc. to have a safe and smooth route during the disaster using their personalised smart mobility profile. The authorities will be able to guide them to the best possible routes for delivering the much-needed critical items to the respected facilities or victims. As an application during MCO, low-risk citizens in a designated place that is considered as a low-risk area based on the profiling will be able to perform activities categorized as allowed activities based on the SOP by employing our proposed model. The components and variables that we proposed for this module are shown in Table 2. Under each element, variables are proposed. For example, for component authorities, the variables include police, fire brigade, military and so on as per definition by the government.

Table 2. Components and variables: role-based profiling for transportation

Components	Variables
Authorities	Police, Fire Brigade, Military etc
Supply chain	Water, Food, Fuel, Emergency Goods, First Aid Kit and Medical Supplies
Healthcare provider	Hospitals, Clinic

Meanwhile, to increase the decision-making precision by utilizing data that was gathered by module 1, components to make profiling for a particular user based on their activities in the society must be defined when assigning the role. Base on the components, the specific variables that address user-specific roles for this module are shown in Table 3. Under each component, variables are proposed. The components and variables can be in concurrence with the present interpretation of the policy and situation.

Table 3. Components and Variables: Role-based profiling for People (Citizen)

Components	Variables
Economic Activity	Work, Authorities, Critical Roles
Education & Learning	School, Higher Institution
Welfare	Care for the elderly
Wellbeing	Fitness
Religious-Activity	Prayers Funeral
Celebration Events	Wedding, Gathering for Celebration

In a conclusion, in our proposed model, people personalised mobility information will be determined based on the elements, components and variables that set up for disaster management. To allow efficient role assignment for each citizen's and vehicle's personalise profile, they will be able to request their roles to the authorities and the approval will be given according to the recent SOP and policies set up by the government. Then, based on assigned role, the citizens and vehicles movement either public transport, personal transport or commercial transport during a disaster will be systematically managed. In a disaster, the dimensions, instruments, and parameters will be changing. Thus, for efficient and fast decision making, data analytics is utilised to analyse the data and provide instruction in accordance with the policies set by the government.

All 3 modules proposed for this model is designed to manage citizens and vehicles mobility according to their roles to give more flexibility and also authorization. The conceptual model is based on the disaster management strategy, literature review and case study during the events of disaster in Malaysia. As a result, this model will be contributing to systematic management and coordination during a disaster in real-time.

4 Conclusion

This research's main contribution is the elaborated concept and modelling of smart profiles for vehicles based on data gathering using telematics. The telematics ecosystem will contribute to big data generation. Thus, decision-making during a disaster that requires analysis can be done using big data analytics techniques to handle a large volume of data by taking into account all required parameters, components and variables. The application of telematics solutions for personalised smart mobility models using IoT and big data analytics in disaster management is an emerging and interdisciplinary research area that calls for collaborations between researchers with various backgrounds, government agencies and industries.

This article presented a Personalised Smart Mobility Model for Smart Movement during Disaster by applying the smart city concept in urban Malaysia. With this proposed personalised mobility profile, smart mobility can be implemented during the disaster and pandemic such as Covid-19. Even if a measure to counter the disaster such as MCO is executed, this proposed concept will help to categorise people with risk levels according to contagious patterns and map the highly affected area. The vaccination factor also must be added to the personalised profile to measure the risk of the citizen spreading the pandemic or being infected by the disease. As a result, only people with the risk of being infected will need to be quarantined until they are free from the disease. Also, geographically, only partial areas must be labelled as high risk and that area must be managed under the quarantined and restriction order precisely. Other than that, economic activity, education and learning, welfare and wellbeing, religious activity and celebration should be allowed to work as usual. This model will minimise risks and consequences related to disaster and should be included in the Malaysia disaster preparedness items [21]. As future work, an empirical analysis will be carried out by prototyping and establishing the simulation of the proposed model in the testing environment.

Acknownledgements. This work was supported under the National Defence University of Malaysia Short Grants UPNM/2020/GPJP/ICT/3.

References

1. Birrell, R.: 13-Emergency Preparedness for Natural Disasters. in Family Capital and the SDGs, pp. 203–210 (2016)
2. World Health Organization (WHO): World Health Organization Laboratory testing for 2019 novel coronavirus (2019-nCoV) in suspected human cases (2020)
3. Graves, R.J.: Key technologies for emergency response. In: Proceedings of ISCRAM 2004 - 1st International Workshop on Information Systems for Crisis Response and Management, pp. 133–138 (2004)
4. Afiza, N., et al.: Volunteer management system for disaster management. Int. J. Recent Technol. Eng. (IJRTE) **7**(5), 569–576 (2019)
5. Che Hamid, H.E., et al.: Disaster management support model for Malaysia. In: Badioze Zaman, H., et al. (eds.) IVIC 2019. LNCS, vol. 11870, pp. 570–581. Springer, Cham (2019). https://doi.org/10.1007/978-3-030-34032-2_50
6. Miah, M., Omar, A.: Technology advancement in developing countries during digital age. Int. J. Sci. Appl. Inf. Technol. **1**(1), 30–38 (2012)
7. Gawade, P., Meeankshi, A.: IOT based smart public transport system. Int. J. Sci. Technol. Res. **06**(07), 396–402 (2017)
8. Zamichos, A., Theodorou, T.I., Drosou, A., Tzovaras, D.: An evacuation management framework based on urban data and personalized mobility information. In: Proceedings - IEEE 4th International Conference on Big Data Computing Service and Applications, BigDataService 2018, pp. 121–128 (2018). https://doi.org/10.1109/BigDataService.2018.00026
9. Rahim, I.A., Nordin, A.A., Hong, T.E., Shauki, N.I.A.: Universal health coverage and COVID-19 preparedness & response, vol. 20, no. August, p. 8 (2020). https://www.who.int/malaysia/news/detail/04-09-2020-universal-health-coverage-and-covid-19-preparedness-response-in-malaysia

10. Aziz, N.A., Othman, J., Lugova, H., Suleiman, A.: Malaysia's approach in handling COVID-19 onslaught: Report on the Movement Control Order (MCO) and targeted screening to reduce community infection rate and impact on public health and economy. J. Infect. Public Health **13**(12), 1823–1829 (2020). https://doi.org/10.1016/j.jiph.2020.08.007

11. El Mendili, N., El Idrissi, S., Hmina, Y.E.B.: Big data processing platform on intelligent transportation systems. In: International Symposium on Advanced Electrical and Communication Technologies (ISAECT), vol. 8, no. 4, pp. 208–213 (2019). https://doi.org/10.30534/ijatcse/2019/4181.32019

12. Siegel, J.E., Erb, D.C., Sarma, S.E.: A survey of the connected vehicle Landscape - architectures, enabling technologies, applications, and development areas. IEEE Trans. Intell. Transp. Syst. **19**(8), 2391–2406 (2018). https://doi.org/10.1109/TITS.2017.2749459

13. Ekler, P., Balogh, T., Ujj, T., Charaf, H., Lengyel, L.: Social driving in connected car environment, In: Proceedings of European Wireless 2015; 21th European Wireless Conference, pp. 1–6 (2015)

14. Handel, P., et al.: Insurance telematics: Opportunities and challenges with the smartphone solution. IEEE Intell. Transp. Syst. Mag. **6**(4), 57–70 (2014)

15. Wahlström, J., Skog, I., Händel, P.: Smartphone-based vehicle telematics: a ten-year anniversary. IEEE Trans. Intell. Transp. Syst. **18**(10), 2802–2825 (2017)

16. Duan, P., Zhang, H., Xiong, S., Zhou, S., Chen, Z., Yang, P.: "Personalized Route Planning System Based on Wardrop Equilibrium Model for Campus Evacuation", Proceedings - 2015 2nd International Symposium on Dependable Computing and Internet of Things. DCIT **2015**, 101–105 (2016). https://doi.org/10.1109/DCIT.2015.16

17. Tsai, C.-W., Lai, C.-F., Chao, H.-C., Vasilakos, A.V.: Big data analytics: a survey. J. Big Data **2**(1), 1–32 (2015). https://doi.org/10.1186/s40537-015-0030-3

18. Najafabadi, M.M., Villanustre, F., Khoshgoftaar, T.M., Seliya, N., Wald, R., Muharemagic, E.: Deep learning applications and challenges in big data analytics. J. Big Data **2**(1), 1–21 (2015). https://doi.org/10.1186/s40537-014-0007-7

19. Sumalee, A., Ho, H.W.: Smarter and more connected: future intelligent transportation system. IATSS Res. **42**(2), 67–71 (2018). https://doi.org/10.1016/j.iatssr.2018.05.005

20. El Mendili, N., El Idrissi, S., Hmina, Y.E.B.: Big data processing platform on intelligent transportation systems. In: 2018 International Symposium on Advanced Electrical and Communication Technologies (ISAECT), vol. 8, no. 4, pp. 208–213 (2019). https://doi.org/10.30534/ijatcse/2019/4181.32019

21. Šendelj, R., Ognjanović, I.: Cyber security education in montenegro: current trends, challenges and open perspectives (2015)

Intelligent Multi-cellular Network Connectivity for Internet of Things Applications

Kisheen Rao Gsangaya[1]👤, Sami Salama Hussen Hajjaj[2(✉)]👤,
Wahidah Hashim[3]👤, and Rina Azlin Razali[3]👤

[1] Centre for Advanced Mechatronics and Robotics (CaMaRo),
Universiti Tenaga Nasional, 43000 Kajang, Selangor, Malaysia
[2] Institute of Informatics and Computing in Energy (IICE),
Universiti Tenaga Nasional, 43000 Kajang, Selangor, Malaysia
ssalama@uniten.edu.my
[3] College of Computing and Informatics (CCI),
Universiti Tenaga Nasional, 43000 Kajang, Selangor, Malaysia

Abstract. The Internet of Things (IoT) is the interconnection of computing devices embedded in everyday objects, enabling them to send and receive data via the Internet. Unfortunately, single cellular networks cannot provide the best connectivity for IoT applications due to limited coverage, network congestion, and poor data rate. A multi-cellular network modem was developed in this research work to establish reliable and cost-effective network connectivity for information broadcast in outdoor IoT applications. The prototype modem continuously monitors network parameters, including download rate, upload rate, and latency, and switches to the best available network using a selection algorithm to ensure optimum quality of service. Based on the assessment of the prototype modem, the network selection algorithm was able to continuously switch to the best available network based on the download rate with a 100% success rate at all five urban test locations. The modem also provided a significant improvement of up to 10% in terms of packet transfer speed compared to a single network system. Additionally, when connected to an IoT device, the modem achieved an impressive 100% data broadcast success rate, compared to 96% and 89% when using a single network setup.

Keywords: Internet of Things · IoT Applications · Network selection algorithms · Cellular networks · IoT Networking

1 Introduction

The Internet of Things (IoT) refers to the billions of physical devices around the world that are connected to the Internet, collecting and sharing data [1]. In addition, these devices capture and broadcast data to cloud servers for storage and processing [2]. The communication protocols they utilize for data transfer largely depend on the IoT applications and their specific needs.

© Springer Nature Switzerland AG 2021
H. Badioze Zaman et al. (Eds.): IVIC 2021, LNCS 13051, pp. 310–321, 2021.
https://doi.org/10.1007/978-3-030-90235-3_27

For example, *Smart Utility Meters* might involve networking set-up in remote and rural locations with unreliable coverages [3]. On the other hand, IoT agriculture monitoring systems are plagued by connectivity and coverage issues due to the vastness of agriculture fields [4]. As for the transportation sector, moving vehicles could experience intermittent network connectivity as they travel along their journeys [5]. As such, IoT applications require reliable and cost-effective connectivity, with good bandwidth, high data rates and low latency to support large data volumes [6]. Short-range wireless communication protocols (Bluetooth, ZigBee) are not suitable due to their limited ranges [7], medium-range protocols (Wi-Fi) are prohibitively expensive due to the use of multiple access points (APs) [8]. In contrast, long-range protocols (LoRaWAN) suffer from low bandwidths and data rates [11]. As such, cellular networks are increasingly being utilized to overcome these drawbacks while being cost-effective. Unfortunately, cellular network coverage in Malaysia varies by location and provider. Figure 1 shows the coverage by cellular network operators (CNOs) in Pergau, in Northern Peninsular Malaysia.

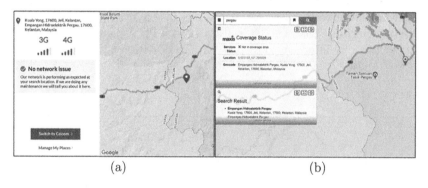

(a)   (b)

Fig. 1. a) Celcom coverage at Pergau; b) Maxis coverage at Pergau. Images developed using Celcom & Maxis Network Tracker Services [9, 10]

In fact, in the rural regions in Malaysia, cellular network coverage is limited to highways and major cities. Still, that coverage is not continuous, with only blobs of 3G and 4G services available [12]. Furthermore, users in dense urban areas such as Klang Valley could connect to 4G networks 83.7% of the time, but only 44% in the rural areas [13]. Network quality in Malaysia also depends on the time of the day wherein the 4G broadband throughput can drop to as low as 9 Mbps during peak hours [14]. In light of the cellular network issues in Malaysia, we recommend the use of multiple cellular networks (multiple CNOs), coupled with an intelligent selection mechanism. This work presents our developed system, the Multi-Cellular Network Selection (MCNS) modem, which achieves reliable connectivity by selecting and connecting to the best available CNO near the modem. The MCNS modem can be retrofitted to any IoT system for a high-quality and stable connectivity.

2 The MCNS Modem

Figure 2 shows the Multi-Cellular Network Selection (MCNS) modem developed for this work. As discussed above, the MCNS modem scans for available connections, selects the most reliable option available, and connects to it.

The main components of the MCNS modem are discussed here:

– **Network-ready Micro-controller:** For this work, the Raspberry Pi 3 Model B+ single-board computer was selected to read network information, compare parameters, switch to the best option, and upload network data to the dedicated IoT client for later analysis.
– **External SIM card Peripherals:** For the micro-controller to capture cellular networks data and perform the needed selection algorithm, we include the Huawei E8372-155 SIM card readers, which functions as a wireless router that connects to a cellular network, and the J5Create JUH340 USB 3.0 hub, which acts as an adaptor.
– **GPS Module:** The VK-172 GPS module was selected to capture location data for remote monitoring. The module consists of a built-in low-power UBlox satellite receiver core for highly accurate positioning information.
– **Display Screen:** Lastly, a 3.5-inch Raspberry Pi touch-screen was added as part of the user interface to display vital information such as device status, network data, etc.

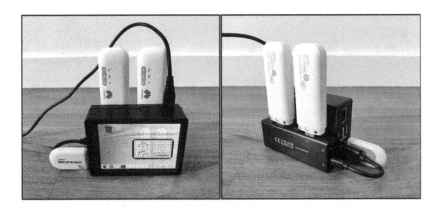

Fig. 2. Setup of the multi-cellular network modem prototype

All of these components were housed in a custom-designed 3D printed casing for protection and safekeeping. This is especially important for mobile IoT applications where the devices are expected to be installed on moving vehicles.

2.1   Elements of the MCNS Modem

The Network Selection Algorithm. For this work, the network selection algorithm was developed using two cellular networks, converted to Wi-Fi networks by the SIM card adapters, to establish a stable, reliable, and high-quality network connectivity. Unfortunately, the Raspberry Pi board cannot read data from SIM cards directly, so we added external SIM card adapters. As shown in Fig. 3, the custom network selection algorithm starts by connecting to the first network. The Python script is detailed in Fig. 4.

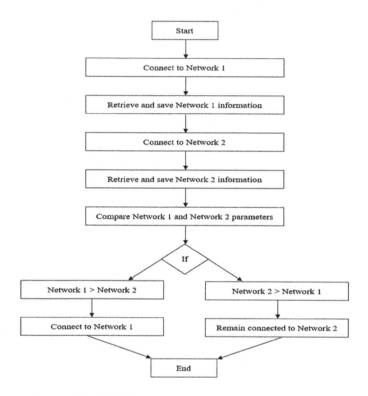

Fig. 3. The MCNS modem: Network Selection Algorithm

The next part of the script scans and lists all available Wi-Fi networks. If the targeted Wi-Fi network is in the list of available networks, the programme connects to this network. It should be noted that the Network Manager service is required to connect to Wi-Fi networks via a Python script. This concludes the first part of the network selection algorithm, wherein the programme automatically connects to Network 1. Next, Speedtest-cli, a command-line interface for testing Internet bandwidth using the popular Speedtest.net service, was utilised to retrieve network information, including download rate, upload rate,

```
class Finder:
    def __init__(self, *args, **kwargs):
        self.server_name = kwargs['server_name']
        self.password = kwargs['password']
        self.interface_name = kwargs['interface']
        self.main_dict = {}

    def run(self):
        command = """sudo iwlist wlan0 scan | grep -ioE 'ssid:"(.*|).*)'"""
        result = os.popen(command.format(self.server_name))
        result = list(result)

if __name__ == "__main__":
    server_name = "Network1"
    password = "mcnsmnetwork1"
    interface_name = "wlan0"
    F = Finder(server_name=server_name,
               password=password,
               interface=interface_name)
    F.run()
```

Fig. 4. The MCNS modem: Python script for network connection

and latency. This process typically takes around 30 s to display results. The network information retrieved by the Speedtest client is saved as variables within the Python script. Finally, this information is displayed via terminal along with a timestamp of the readings as reference. This marks the end of the second part of the network selection algorithm wherein the network information of Network 1 is retrieved and saved.

The received signal strength solely portrays the connection strength, which tells us the distance of a device to a network base station compared to network speed and latency, which characterizes the actual network condition and quality of service. As for the network plans, both maxis and Celcom do not have a data speed cap for the specific selected plans in this research. Next, the system automatically disconnects from Network 1 and connects to Network 2 instead. Similarly, the system then retrieves and saves the network parameters of Network 2 as variables. Next, the script converts the string values saved previously from the Speedtest client to float values to enable accurate comparison between the saved parameters of both networks. For this research work, the network selection algorithm compares the download rates among the networks. However, this comparison can be amended to compare the upload rates, latency, or a combination of these parameters based on user preference.

At this stage, the programme is still connected to Network 2. From the comparison, if the algorithm determines that the download rate of Network 1 is greater than Network 2, the programme disconnects from Network 2 and reconnects to Network 1. Otherwise, the programme remains connected to Network 2 instead. Finally, the programme displays a message via a terminal to indicate the currently connected network. The network selection algorithm was set to loop every 30 min, so the network selection algorithm continuously monitors and selects the best network at all times throughout the day based on the set interval. It should also be noted that while the current network selection algorithm was developed with only two networks as a proof of concept, more networks can be added to the Python script for comparison and selection in the future due to the flexible nature of the algorithm.

The Location Monitoring Algorithm. GPS technology uses signals sent by the satellites in space to ground stations on Earth, in this case, the GPS module, to determine its position accurately. The signals received from the satellites by the module contain timestamps of when the signals were transmitted. Using the information from three or more satellites, the exact position of the GPS module can be triangulated. The VK-172 GPS module connects to the Raspberry Pi board via a USB port and communicates via a simple serial connection. The GPS module transmits raw National Marine Electronics Association (NMEA) messages to the micro-controller. NMEA is a standard data format supported by GPS manufacturers.

Based on Fig. 5, a variable named data containing the NMEA strings published by the GPS module was first defined in the custom location monitoring algorithm. Then, the readline function from the serial library reads the NMEA strings from the specific serial port. The next Python script parses the data available in the $GPGGA string to create individual GPS parameters such as latitude, longitude, altitude, and others. Once the $GPGGA string parses, the latitude and longitude values are contained in variables msg.lat and msg.lon, respectively. However, the values are still in the decimal minutes format. Therefore, inputting latitude and longitude values in this format to a GPS mapping application programming interface (API) would result in a map location error. The built-in dm_to_sd function from the pynmea2 library was utilised to convert these values to the standard degree format.

```
while True:
    try:
        data = serial.Serial(port = "/dev/ttyACM0").readline()
    except:
        print("loading")

    if data[0:6] == '$GPGGA':
        msg = pynmea2.parse(data)
        print data

        latitude = (pynmea2.dm_to_sd(msg.lat))
        print 'Latitude:', latitude

        longitude = (pynmea2.dm_to_sd(msg.lon))
        print 'Longitude:', longitude
```

Fig. 5. The MCNS modem: Python script to retrieve location data

The IoT Client. The final requirement is to display the network information of both cellular networks and the modem location for user reference. To display the network and location information via the IoT client, the dweepy module was first imported. Dweet.io is a simple publishing and subscription service for machines, sensors, robots, and devices, collectively known as things. By using the Dweet.io module, messages are published as dweets, synonymous with tweets on Twitter. Each thing is assigned a unique *thing* name, and a thing may be subscribed to, which is analogous to following someone on Twitter. Dweet.io enables the machine and sensor data to become easily accessible through the Internet, allowing for simple data sharing.

To display the required data via the IoT client, the network information and location coordinates were packaged into an array, namely iot_data, to be published to the cloud server. In this case, the custom thing name, iot_mcnsm, allows the IoT client to accurately determine and retrieve the specific information from the prototype modem once it is published on the cloud server. As illustrated in Fig. 6, the IoT client utilised for this application was Freeboard.io. Both networks' download and upload readings were displayed as gauge widgets on the Freeboard.io dashboard page, while the latency information was displayed as text widgets. The currently selected network on the modem was also displayed for quick reference. Furthermore, a graph widget was added to compare historical readings for the download rate between both networks for trend analysis. Lastly, the modem location was displayed using a Google Maps widget which utilises the latitude and longitude values to pin the exact device location on the map.

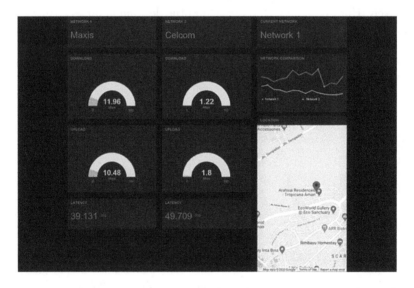

Fig. 6. Our Developed Freeboard.io dashboard with our MCNS information (can be accessed here [15])

3   Results and Discussion

3.1   Network Selection

The network switching assessment was carried out in five different locations around the Klang Valley for three days for a total assessment period of 15 d. The two CNOs selected for this research were Maxis and Celcom, as these are the two most popular options for consumers and possess comprehensive network coverage across Malaysia. Information for both networks was recorded in a data logger based on the values from the IoT dashboard and cross-referenced to the network selected by the modem as displayed via the terminal. The network information was recorded once every two hours for 12 entries over one full day and a total of 36 entries at each test location.

From Table 1, at the first location, Bandar Tropicana Aman, Kota Kemuning, it was noted that the network selection algorithm had a 100% success rate in selecting the best network in terms of download rate. However, the Maxis network performed significantly better than the Celcom network. Thus, this proves that the coverage and quality of service of Maxis are much better compared to Celcom at the first test location. Furthermore, the modem was recorded to have switched only four times to the alternate network at the first location. At the second test location, Bandar Puteri, Puchong, both networks' average download speeds were excellent. Here, the network switching mechanism was utilised extensively, with the modem switching to the alternate network 12 times in total. Finally, at the third test location, Universiti Tenaga Nasional campus, Putrajaya, the network switching mechanism has been utilised a total of seven times throughout the assessment period with a 100% success rate.

Table 1. Results of the network switching assessment (Partial data set)

No	Kota Kemuning			Puchong			Putrajaya			Petaling Jaya			Sungai Buloh		
	DR (Mbps)		SN	DR (Mbps)		SN	DR (Mbps)		SN	DR (Mbps)		SN	DR (Mbps)		SN
	N1	N2		N1	N2		N1	N2		N1	N2		N1	N2	
1	3.42	0.93	N1	16.87	18.32	N2	18.76	11.19	N1	2.84	7.37	N2	7.47	19.73	N2
2	4.67	1.17	N1	19.54	17.27	N1	16.18	14.07	N1	3.73	8.24	N2	5.38	16.48	N2
3	3.98	1.63	N1	15.23	18.34	N2	20.61	16.38	N1	3.26	6.65	N2	5.94	17.34	N2
4	7.61	1.42	N1	20.17	14.25	N1	15.47	13.2	N1	4.78	4.34	N1	6.37	20.48	N2
5	10.83	2.08	N1	22.36	11.59	N1	12.62	14.87	N2	3.37	5.86	N2	8.16	18.37	N2
6	9.54	2.64	N1	20.43	9.45	N1	16.27	15.31	N1	5.17	4.24	N1	6.49	14.86	N2
7	11.56	2.31	N1	18.87	14.18	N1	13.04	7.18	N1	4.38	6.83	N2	7.78	15.05	N2
8	8.83	3.02	N1	13.25	12.27	N1	8.28	6.52	N1	3.91	7.89	N2	10.23	10.01	N1
9	16.12	1.94	N1	12.43	21.84	N2	9.93	5.26	N1	3.79	5.7	N2	8.7	11.36	N2
10	14.75	2.57	N1	13.68	14.9	N2	15.5	11.43	N1	3.45	4.24	N2	6.18	9.23	N2

Abbreviations
DR: Download Rate SN: Selected Network N1: Network 1 N2: Network 2

Next, contrary to previous test results, the Celcom network outperformed the Maxis network at the fourth test location, Seksyen 14, Petaling Jaya. While the average download speed of the Celcom network was good, the average download speed of the Maxis network was relatively poor, with all readings below 5 Mbps. For the fourth round of testing, the modem was recorded to have switched a total of seven times to the alternate network during the test period with a success rate of 100%. The last test location for the network switching assessment was the industrial area of Sungai Buloh. Here, the modem was recorded to have switched to the alternate network four times throughout the test period

In summary, the network switching mechanism in the MCNS modem can be said to have performed as intended with an excellent 100% success rate. As for the usefulness of the network switching mechanism, it was observed that while the mechanism was used extensively in specific locations to ensure optimum network quality, it was less vital and not utilised as often in other locations where one network outperforms its counterpart. However, this assessment was conducted in predominantly developed city areas, where the network coverage and quality of service are primarily decent. Consequently, the network selection mechanism is predicted to be more useful in rural areas where cellular network coverage is intermittent and unreliable. The network switching mechanism could be critical for information transfer at locations where cellular network outages are common such as in less developed areas of the country.

3.2   Packet Transfer Speed

Based on the network switching assessment, the average download rate for the Maxis and Celcom networks were calculated based on the respective test locations as shown in Table 2. In addition, the average download rate of the prototype modem was also calculated based on the number of times the network selection algorithm was utilised to switch to the alternate network with a greater download speed. Based on these values, the percentage of improvement when utilising the prototype modem compared to a single network system can be determined. For example, in Kota Kemuning, the average download rate of the best single network, in this case, Maxis, was 7.82 Mbps, while the prototype modem was 7.97 Mbps, leading to a slight improvement of 2%. Meanwhile, in Puchong, the percentage improvement was much more pronounced at 10.1%, where the prototype modem had an average download rate of 18.58 Mbps compared to the best single network, Maxis, with 16.87 Mbps.

Table 2. Packet transfer speed comparison.

Location	Average download rate (Mbps)		Percentage improvement
	Single network system	Prototype modem	
	Network 1	Network 2		
1	7.82	2.20	7.97	2.0%
2	**16.87**	**14.53**	**18.58**	**10.1%**
3	15.68	11.70	16.21	3.4%
4	3.98	6.87	6.98	1.6%
5	6.98	14.92	15.02	0.7%

Next, in Putrajaya, the best single network, Maxis, recorded an average download rate of 15.68 Mbps, compared to 16.21 Mbps for the prototype modem, leading to an improvement of 3.4%. At areas where Celcom was the better single network, such as Petaling Jaya and Sungai Buloh, the performance improvement provided by the modem was less noticeable at 1.6% and 0.7%, respectively. In Petaling Jaya, the average download rate of the Celcom network was 6.87 Mbps, while the average download rate of the prototype modem was 6.98 Mbps. Meanwhile, in Sungai Buloh, the average download rate of the Celcom network was 14.92 Mbps, while the average download rate of the prototype modem was 15.02 Mbps. While not quite able to provide up to a 40% data rate increase as reported by similar studies performed using a multiple network setup [16], it was proven that the prototype modem can still provide a significant packet transfer speed improvement of up to 10% in a city area when compared to a single network system. This proves to be essential in applications where a high-quality communication network is required. The performance improvement achieved by the prototype modem is predicted to rise to up to 20% to 30% in a rural location setting with limited and unreliable coverage, where obtaining a decent communication network is vital for uninterrupted information transfers.

3.3   Data Broadcast Success Rate

Data broadcast success rate for the modem when connected to an IoT device–in this case, an agriculture data acquisition unit that monitors environmental parameters such as ambient temperature, ambient humidity, light intensity level, and soil moisture content in a farm, and uploads the information to a ThingSpeak IoT client dashboard–was evaluated. The IoT data broadcast success rate was assessed by monitoring the data published to the ThingSpeak dashboard over 15 days.

The data broadcast success rate was first tested with Maxis and Celcom single networks to establish a benchmark result. Then, the assessment was repeated with the prototype modem to determine if a considerable performance increase in data broadcast success rate was achieved by utilising multiple cellular networks as suggested in this research work. The IoT client was assessed at 10.00 am, 4.00 pm, and 10.00 pm daily to monitor if the agriculture data acquisition unit was functioning as expected to capture and upload environmental information to the cloud server. If the IoT client was not displaying the required readings, the data acquisition unit was not functional due to data broadcast failure. From Table 3, with the data acquisition unit connected solely to the Maxis network, data broadcast failure was detected twice over the assessment period, resulting in a data broadcast success rate of 96%. On the other hand, the Celcom network performed even poorer than its counterpart, with a total of five data broadcast failures and a data broadcast success rate of only 89%. As such, utilising a single cellular network for data broadcast in IoT devices is unsuitable due to poor reliability and a high risk of transmission failure, especially for vital information transfer.

Next, the IoT data broadcast success rate was tested with a multiple network setup provided by the prototype modem. Based on the results in Table 3, the agriculture data acquisition unit was observed to be functional throughout the assessment period with no data broadcast failures detected. Furthermore, the data acquisition unit was recorded to continuously update the information displayed on the IoT client as expected throughout the assessment period. As such, the IoT data broadcast success rate was an impressive 100%. Thus, this assessment has proven that the use of multiple cellular network connectivity can improve the data broadcast success rate, resulting in a more stable and reliable IoT functionality.

Table 3. IoT data broadcast success rate.

Day	Time	Maxis	Celcom	Prototype Modem	Day	Time	Maxis	Celcom	Prototype Modem
1	10.00 am	Success	Success	Success	6	10.00 am	Success	Success	Success
	4.00 pm	Success	Success	Success		4.00 pm	Fail	Success	Success
	10.00 pm	Success	Success	Success		10.00 pm	Success	Success	Success
2	10.00 am	Success	Success	Success	7	10.00 am	Success	Fail	Success
	4.00 pm	Success	Success	Success		4.00 pm	Success	Fail	Success
	10.00 pm	Success	Success	Success		10.00 pm	Success	Success	Success
3	10.00 am	Success	Success	Success	8	10.00 am	Success	Success	Success
	4.00 pm	Success	Success	Success		4.00 pm	Success	Success	Success
	10.00 pm	Success	Fail	Success		10.00 pm	Success	Success	Success
4	10.00 am	Success	Success	Success	9	10.00 am	Success	Success	Success
	4.00 pm	Success	Success	Success		4.00 pm	Success	Success	Success
	10.00 pm	Success	Success	Success		10.00 pm	Success	Success	Success
5	10.00 am	Success	Success	Success	10	10.00 am	Success	Fail	Success
	4.00 pm	Success	Success	Success		4.00 pm	Success	Success	Success
	10.00 pm	Success	Success	Success		10.00 pm	Fail	Success	Success

4   Conclusions

The objective of this research work was to develop a multi-cellular network modem for IoT applications to acquire reliable and cost-effective network connectivity for the broadcast of information captured by outdoor IoT devices to the cloud server. The prototype modem continuously monitors cellular network parameters, including download rate, upload rate, and latency, and switches to the best available network at all times to ensure optimum quality of service through the use of a selection algorithm. The modem location and network status are also displayed via an IoT client that can be accessed via a webpage for remote monitoring by the user.

Assessment of the prototype modem showed that it could perform as intended. The network selection algorithm continuously switched to the best available network based on the download rate with a 100% success rate at all five test locations comprising of urban areas.

In terms of packet transfer speed comparison against a single network system, the prototype modem provided a significant improvement of up to 10% in urban areas, which could prove essential in applications where a high-quality communication network is required. The performance improvement was much greater in rural locations. The modem achieved a 100% data broadcast success rate, compared to 96% and 89% when using a single network setup.

Acknowledgement. The authors would like to thank the Innovative & Research Management Centre, and the Institute of Informatics and Computing in Energy (IICE), UNITEN, for their support of this project.

References

1. Jeongyeup, P., Gaglione, A., Gnawali, O., Vieira M. A., Hao, S.: Advances in mobile networking for IoT leading the 4th industrial revolution. Mobile Information Systems Volume, 1–3 (2018)
2. Stoces, M., Vanek, J., Masner, J., Pavlik, J.: Internet of Things (IoT) in Agriculture - Selected Aspects 8(1), 83–88 (2016)
3. Samuel, S.: A review of connectivity challenges in IoT smart home. In: International Conference on Big Data and Smart City, pp. 1–4. Muscat, Oman (2016)
4. Elijah, O., Rahman, T.A., Orikumhi, I., Leow, C.Y., Hindia, N.: An overview of Internet of Things (IoT) and data analytics in agriculture: benefits and challenges. Internet Things J. 5(5), 1–17 (2018)
5. Inmarsat Research: Connectivity Challenges Threaten to Derail Logistics Sector IoT Ambitions. The Future of IoT in Enterprise (2017)
6. Ahmed, A.: Benefits and challenges of internet of things for telecommunication networks. In: Telecommunication Networks-Trends and Developments, pp. 105–124 (2019)
7. Nandurkar, S.R., Thool, V.R., Thool, R.C.: Design and development of precision agriculture system using wireless sensor network. In: International Conference on Automation. Control, Energy and Systems, pp. 1–6. Hooghly, India (2014)
8. Dagar, R., Som, S., Khatri, S. K.: Smart farming - IoT in agriculture. In: International Conference on Inventive Research in Computing Applications, Coimbatore, India, pp. 1052–1056 (2018)
9. Celcom Network Tracker (2021). https://www.celcom.com.my/support/network-checker. Accessed 26 Aug 2021
10. Maxis Network Map - Where We Are Today, Maxis (2021). https://www.maxis.com.my/en/about-maxis/maxis-network/network-map/. Accessed 26 Aug 2021
11. Ma, Y.: Toward intelligent agriculture service platform with LoRa-based wireless sensor network. In: International Conference on Applied System Innovation, Tokyo, Japan, pp. 204–207 (2018)
12. Faizah, N.A., Azian, N.M.: 4G coverage in Malaysia. Int. J. Sci. Res. 1(4), 1817–1823 (2015)
13. Khatri, H.: Malaysia's Disparity in Mobile Network Connectivity: An Operator Level View. OpenSignal. shorturl.at/nqJQW. Accessed 31 Oct 2020
14. Khatri, H.: Analysing Malaysia's Mobile Data Consumption, and its Effects on 4G Download Speed. OpenSignal. shorturl.at/jqK03. Accessed 31 Oct 2020
15. Hajjaj, S., Gsangaya, K.: IoT Client for Published work (Currently offline). Freeboard.io (2021). https://freeboard.io/board/RP4Cyh. Accessed 26 Aug 2021
16. Hashim, W., Ismail, A.F., Dzulkifly, S.: Cognitive selection mechanism for indoor propagation. Int. J. Comput. Commun. Eng. 2(4), 433–437 (2013)

A Performance Study on Emotion Models Detection Accuracy in a Pandemic Environment

Priyadashini Saravanan[1]([⊠]), Suvendran Ravindran[1], Leong Yeng Weng[2]([⊠]),
Khairul Salleh Bin Mohamed Sahari[3], Adzly Bin Anuar[1],
Muhammad Fairuz Bin Abdul Jalal[1], Zubaidi Faiesal Bin Mohamad Rafaai[1],
Prashalini Naidu A/P Raventhran[1], Husni Mohd Radzi[2], and Salman Yussof[2]

[1] Collage of Engineering (COE), Universiti Tenaga Nasional, Jalan IKRAM-UNITEN,
43000 Kajang, Selangor, Malaysia
{priyadashini,Suvendran,Adzly,mfairuz,Zubaidi,
Prashalini}@uniten.edu.my
[2] Institute of Informatics and Computing in Energy (IICE), Universiti Tenaga Nasional,
Jalan IKRAM-UNITEN, 43000 Kajang, Selangor, Malaysia
{ywleong,husni,Salman}@uniten.edu.my
[3] MQA, Jalan Teknkotrat 7, Cyber 5, 63000 Cyberjaya, Selangor, Malaysia
khairulsalleh@mqa.gov.my

Abstract. This paper studies emotion detection using deep learning on the prevalent usage of face masks in the Covid-19 pandemic. Internet repository data Karolinska Directed Emotional Faces (KDEF) [1] was used as a base database, in which it was segmented into different portions of the face, such as forehead patch, eye patch, and skin patch to be representing segments of the face covered or exposed by the mask were transfer learned to an Inception v3 model. Results show that the full-face model had the highest accuracy 74.68% followed by the skin patch (area occluded by the mask) 65.09%. The models trained on full-face were then used to inference the different face segments/patches that showed poor inferencing results. However, certain emotions are more distinct around the eye region. Therefore, this paper concludes that upper segmented faces result in higher accuracy for training models over full faces, yet future research needs to be done on additional occlusion near the eye section.

Keywords: Deep learning · Covid19 · Pandemic · Emotion

1 Introduction

Emotions are intuitive feelings that have great influence by the individual's circumstances (different cultural and ethnic backgrounds) [2]. The psychologist Paul Eckman has identified six discrete states of emotions in humans such as anger, sadness, disgust, happiness, fear, and surprise [3]. Individuals express these emotions via body language, verbal communication, and facial expression. Little did we know, fifty-five percent of effective communication generally constitutes face expressions [4]. Hence,

© Springer Nature Switzerland AG 2021
H. Badioze Zaman et al. (Eds.): IVIC 2021, LNCS 13051, pp. 322–331, 2021.
https://doi.org/10.1007/978-3-030-90235-3_28

facial expressions are crucial for daily social interaction as it possesses great importance in non-verbal communication. The movements of facial muscles (both upper and lower areas of the face) contribute to one's facial expression, With the specific facial expression, the emotion of the individual is being interpreted.

However, in the light of the current global pandemic Covid19, most countries advised their citizens to wear facial masks for everyone's safety and to minimize the risk of spreading the virus. Due to the mask mandate, covering the lower areas of the face below the eyes can be challenging for successful emotion recognition since only the forehead, eyebrows, and eye muscles will be the sole contributor to one's emotion recognition.

Since the coronavirus outbreak and the new norm of wearing face masks to protect ourselves, many researchers have studied the effect of the mask on facial and emotional recognition using various methods. M. Grahlow et al. conducted two different studies on the mask effect by using an adapted version of the Validated Emotion Recognition Task (VERT-K). In the first study, they digitally added surgical masks to the original facial stimuli, and they observed that emotion recognition was difficult when faces were covered with masks especially for angry, sad, and disgusted expressions. The second study was adapting VERT-K to cropped faces and photos of skin-toned bubbles obscuring the mouth and nose area. Emotions of fear and happiness were recognized more accurately when the only upper face was presented, and disgust has higher recognition rate for bubbled faces [5]. Hence, presenting the exposed face to the training model shows a better accuracy but not all emotions were recognized accurately.

Another study was conducted on train-test strategies in which the researcher found the result shows a higher accuracy when both training and testing data are occluded than using non-occluded data for the strategy. However, in this study, various occlusions were approached and not specifically to the lower face and upper face region [6].

Furthermore, several deep learning methods were also used to carry out face recognition for better performance [7]. One of the studies proposed cropping and attention-based approach for partially occluded faces for face recognition. The attention mechanism can significantly improve the recognition performance using model trained with Masked-Web Face datasets, but the performance is limited when testing is done on routine face recognition. The cropping method that uses integration of optimal cropping and Convolutional Block Attention Module (CBAM) module in ResNet50 network has better recognition on face-masked images [8]. Another face recognition studied by W. Hariri in which he discarded the masked region for training has concluded on high recognition performance on Real-World-Masked-Face-Dataset [9].

Even though many studies have been conducted on occluded faces and face recognition, the best performing method of cropping and discarding approach using deep learning on emotional recognition with face masks is still very limited. Training and testing on segmented face regions are essential as every section of our face contributes to a certain percentage of the emotions. Therefore, evaluating the performance of each face part is crucial in recognizing the emotion accurately on full faces and occluded faces.

This paper tries to fill this gap left out by previous research by involving and contributing to cropping and segmenting methods for training and testing data to evaluate the effect of masks occlusion on emotion recognition. The next section describes the methodology, on the overall environmental set-up and the details of segmenting the full faces into three different parts to obtain better accuracy on the recognition. Sect. 3 demonstrates the result and in-depth analysis. We compare the detection rate on full faces and segmented faces, thus further analyse the contribution of the face sections to the respective emotions. Finally, our findings are concluded and suggestion for future research is proposed in Sect. 4.

2   Methodology

2.1   Experimental Set-Up

Hardware. The environment used for this training model is Windows OS i7-8700 CPU with a clock speed of 3.20 Ghz, RAM of 16 GB, and NVIDIA GeForce GTX 1080ti GPU with 11 Gb RAM as a resource limitation and time required to train the classification model.

Software. In this experiment, MATLAB® was the only programming software used with pre-trained face detection MTCNN [10] for cropping the faces into three segments. As of the transfer learning, pretrained Inception-v3 convolutional neural network was used for image classification [11]. Inception-v3 is a 48 layers deep network that has an image input size of 299×299 [12]. This specific pretrained network is opted based on its speed, accuracy, and the compatibility of the available hardware. This model supported the system and was large enough to do the transfer learning.

Database. Karolinska Directed Emotional Faces (KDEF) database was used to train the training model. KDEF is a set of totally 4900 pictures of seven human facial expressions (anger, sad, surprise, fear, happy, disgust and neutral). Since this paper only focuses on the basic six emotions, neutral was excluded and only 4200 pictures were used for training and testing. To simply describe these KDEF subjects, they were not allowed to have beards, mustaches, wear earrings or eyeglasses, or visible make-up during the photo-session [1].

2.2   Method of Training

(See Fig. 1).

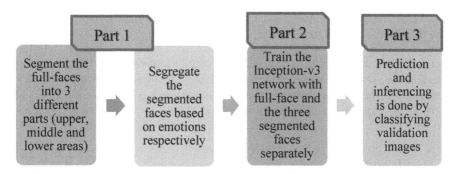

Fig. 1. The flowchart to represent the process of training the model and inferencing the validation images

Part 1. The full faces KDEF database was segmented into three different parts such as eye, forehead and skin patches using MTCNN [13]. Eye patch region is from forehead to nose which is the exposed part when face masks are being worn. Forehead region is from the top of the forehead till eyelids and the skin patch is from the nose till the lips. Figure 2 shows the examples of the KDEF full database that was cropped into three different parts. The three segmented faces are then segregated into six folders (emotions) respectively.

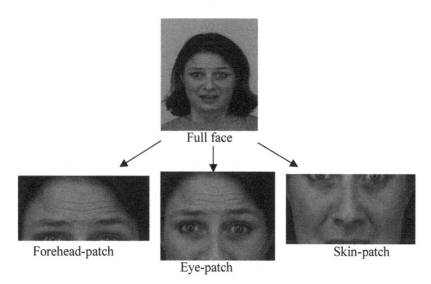

Fig. 2. Example of KDEF full-face that has been segmented into three parts

Part 2. To evaluate the full-face database on KDEF, training was done using the pre-trained Inception v3 network model (default augmentation settings) with 10 epochs, mini batch-size of 32 and the learning rate of 0.0001 using GPU for execution. The cross-validation ratio for training and testing was 70:30. The same training method was done for all three patches respectively [14].

Part 3. To calculate the prediction accuracy, confusion matrix was computed. For classification, the validating images are resized to 299 × 299 to match the input size of the Inception-v3. The comparison is then made between patch trained vs full-face trained model on the respective patch datasets and full-face datasets via the confusion matrix.

3 Result and Discussion

The transfer learning performance for each training data is shown in Table 1.

Table 1. Model transfer learning performance

KDEF model	Full face	Forehead patch	Eye patch	Skin patch
Performance (%)	74.68	44.09	51.65	65.09

Based on the above table, it can be clearly seen that the full face KDEF database has shown the highest performance over the patch model which is followed by skin patch, eye patch and the forehead patch. To further analyse its prediction on patch datasets and full-face datasets, these trained models are inferred by presenting various datasets and the true model (full face model) vs predicted model (patch model) on these datasets are populated using confusion matrix.

3.1 Discussion on Individual Patch Models vs Full-Face Model

Confusion matrix is being plotted for the full-face trained model vs the patch models on the full-face datasets and its respective datasets of KDEF (Fig. 3).

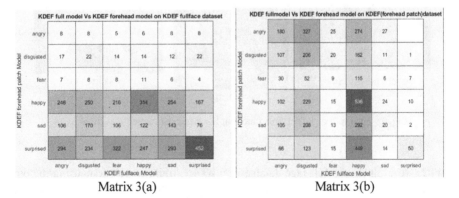

Matrix 3(a)   Matrix 3(b)

Fig. 3. Matrix 3(a) is the comparison between forehead-patch model and full model on the full-face dataset. Matrix 3(b) shows the result on validating forehead-patch datasets.

For the forehead patch model, the recognition on the forehead patch datasets is fairly better than the full-face datasets. The full-face model has least detection percentage and the forehead-patch model barely recognize angry, fear and disgust emotions when presented the full-face datasets, but has better detection rate for the sad, surprise and fear [Matrix 3a]. Meanwhile, the forehead-patch model recognizes the emotions better on forehead patch datasets, but the numbers are still not convincing since the full-face model solely recognizes more happy faces on forehead dataset [Matrix 3b] (Fig. 4).

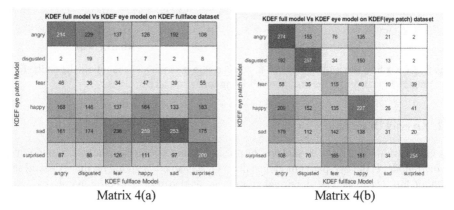

Matrix 4(a)   Matrix 4(b)

Fig. 4. Matrix 4(a) depicts the comparison between eye-patch model and full model on the full-face dataset. While Matrix 4(b) shows the result on validating eye-patch datasets.

When each emotion's prediction of the model is compared between the full-face datasets and the eye-patch datasets, the eye-patch model is able to predict five out of six emotions of the eye-patch datasets accurately whereas on the full-face datasets only four out of six are being more recognized. When we further analyze the matrix of eye-patch dataset, the full-face model was only able to detect 274/663 images (663 images are the total images identified by the full-face model) whereas the eye-patch model identified 663/700 as angry [Matrix 4b]. Further calculation using these values is done for detail analysis later.

The eye patch model hardly captures disgust and fear on full face datasets [Matrix 4a] meanwhile it only had some difficulty on determining the sad emotion when presented the eye-patch dataset [Matrix 4b]. Overall, the performance of this eye-patch model on eye-patch datasets is quite convincing for five emotions (Fig. 5).

Based on Matrix 5a, it shows the full-face model on full–face dataset has the least detection on most emotions which is lesser than five percent. While the skin patch model on the full-face datasets is the worst in detection as it all the datasets prediction is saturated in one emotion but when the model is used to predict the skin-patch datasets, it seems to have a better detection rate but still has somewhat moderate [Matrix 5b].

There is no true value for the surprise emotion in Matrix 5b, but surprise is the only emotion that was detected by the skin-patch model when full-face dataset is presented. This is because surprise facial expression is highly perceived when the eyebrows elevate [14].

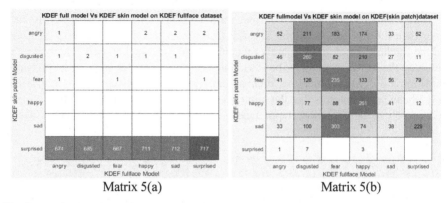

Matrix 5(a)   Matrix 5(b)

Fig. 5. Matrix 5(a) shows the comparison between skin-patch model and full model on the full-face dataset. Matrix 5(b) is the result on validating forehead-patch datasets.

3.2 Overall Discussion

By visual evaluation, it can be said among all six confusion matrices, the most convincing trained model is the eye-patch model as the model is able to capture all the six emotions without fail. Nevertheless, detail calculation is needed on each emotion categories to accept the hypothesis.

To further analyze this confusion matrix, a couple of simple calculations was made to look at the difference in the model's prediction.

True values for each emotion from the matrices were obtained to access the accuracy for the patch model vs the full-face model using Eq. 1.

$$\text{Angry eye} - \text{patch} = \frac{\text{True value of angry/}}{\text{Total images detected as angry by eyepatch model}}$$
$$= 274/663$$
$$= 0.4133 \tag{1}$$

The above equation is applied for all the true values in the confusion matrix to yield Table 2 and Table 3.

Even though the transfer learning performance of the full-face model is high, when the patch datasets have been presented to the full-face model the performance on recognition certain emotions are skewed to sad and surprise. In the previous research, M. Grahlow states on poor detection rate on anger, fear and sad when occluded faces are presented to full face models [5]. Similar result can also be seen in this experiment on Table 2 as the model has poor recognition on fear.

The full-face model's detection rate on other patch datasets is convincing since the transfer learning of full-face model is 74.68%. It can be clearly seen, the full-face model, seem to be better in detecting the sad and surprise and highly skewed to those emotions. When we further analyze the patched model on patch datasets, better accuracy is obtained for a number of emotions as derived in Table 3 based on the confusion matrix.

Table 2. Accuracy assessment for full face model to patch datasets

		Emotions accuracy (%)					
	Datasets	Angry	Disgust	Fear	Happy	Sad	Surprise
Full face model	Eye-patch	26.86	32.91	17.24	26.06	**22.96**	**70.95**
	Forehead-patch	30.51	17.99	9.28	29.32	**19.61**	**71.43**
	Skin-patch	25.74	33.29	26.37	30.53	**19.39**	0.00

Table 3. Accuracy assessment for patch models to patch and full-face datasets

		Emotions accuracy (%)					
	Datasets	Angry	Disgust	Fear	Happy	Sad	Surprise
Forehead-patch model	Forehead-patch	21.61	40.63	4.11	58.52	3.13	6.97
	Full-face	18.60	21.78	18.18	21.70	19.78	24.54
Eye-patch model	Eye-patch	**41.33**	**39.66**	**38.72**	28.73	4.98	**31.28**
	Full-face	**21.27**	**48.72**	**13.23**	17.62	20.11	**28.21**
Skin-patch model	Skin-patch	7.38	**40.88**	**35.23**	**51.38**	4.89	0.00
	Full-face	14.29	**33.33**	**33.33**	0.00	0.00	17.21

Table 4. Differences between VERT-K model and Inception v3

Emotion accuracy on eye-patch datasets	VERT-K model M. Grahlow [5]	Inception-v3
Angry (%)	56	41.33
Disgust (%)	19	39.66
Surprise (%)	(not evaluated)	31.28

From the accuracy Table 3, we can evaluate further into specific emotions for each dataset and model. As mentioned by M. Grahlow the cropping method used on full face models gives different detection rate for different emotions [5]. Based on Table 4, we can see that, the Inception-v3 eye patch models on eye patch datasets are able to recognize more emotions accurately when compared to other research. Then looking at Table 3, angry emotion has the highest recognition rate using eye-patch model on eye patch datasets. This is because eyes play crucial role in determining anger as the facial expression of anger mostly emphasizes the central and downward movement of eyebrows and glaring eyes.

Moreover, surprise and fear emotions also can be expressed by movement of eyebrows and mouth muscles. Distinct elevated eyebrows show surprise and it can be seen that eye patch model have high detection and accurate on eye-patch dataset among other patch models. As for fear, eyebrow, forehead, and more lips movements are involved.

When Table 2 is observed, the eye patch and skin patch have better accuracy for fear and skin patch gives better result in both datasets as fear involves more lips muscles [15].

On the other hand, happiness is determined by smiles and wrinkles at edge of eye. That is why the skin patch seems to be more accurate. While, disgust is perceived by nose wrinkles, eyebrows pulled down and squint eyes [15]. Due to the involvement of middle part of the face, eye patch and skin patch model have higher detection while skin patch model on skin patch dataset has higher accuracy.

From comparing Table 2 and 3, the full-face model has quite convincing detection rate on segmented faces but to gain higher accuracy retraining the model with segmented model is highly encouraged.

When comparing overall models, the accuracy table clearly shows that the patch model has higher accuracy on its own patch and the full-face datasets among the three trained models. When the accuracy values are compared between each dataset for the respective models, the eye-patch model has the greatest number of emotions recognized accurately among the three patched models. From this table, we can set the trained eye-patch model's prediction as the benchmark for this experiment. Hence, it can be evaluated that, the training the segmented regions gives better accuracy and emotion recognition for occluded datasets [6].

4 Conclusion

The current global pandemic has created a new norm of wearing facial mask in public to reduce the spread of Covid19. With this mask mandate, emotion recognition has been severely challenged as most of the face is occluded. Nevertheless, deep learning method for recognition is a big help to overcome that hurdle and different methods of training the model to maintain the high accuracy rate in emotion recognition is being deeply studied. This paper has proven that training the model with the segmented patch model is the best to recognize and predict the emotion accurately. Hence, this illustrates the significance of informing/training the learning model the presence of occlusion patterns for better recognition. Even though we ought to prove this method is resulting the best outcome, there are still several issues that need to be considered for future research on the additional occlusion of wearing sunglasses or a cap since the KDEF database is only focused on bare faces.

Acknowledgements. This research is supported by a TNB SEED grant managed by UNITEN R&D U-TD-TD-19–28.

References

1. Lundqvist, D.E., Flykt, A., Öhman, A.: The karolinska directed emotional faces - KDEF, CD ROM from Department of Clinical Neuroscience. Psychology section, Karolinska Institutet (1998). ISBN 91–630–7164–9
2. Fasel, B., Luettin, J.: Automatic facial expression analysis: a survey. PR **36**(1), 259–275 (2003). https://doi.org/10.1016/S0031-3203(02)00052-3

3. Ekman, P., Friesen, W.V.: Constants across cultures in the face and emotion. J. Pers. Soc. Psychol. **17**(2), 124 (1971)
4. Mehrabian, A.: Silent Messages - A Wealth of Information About Nonverbal Communication (Body Language). Silent Messages, Belmont (1981)
5. Grahlow, M., Rupp, C., Dernt, B.: The impact of face masks on emotion recognition performance and perception of threat (2021). https://doi.org/10.31234/osf.io/6msz8, Accessed 27 July 2021
6. Ranzato,M., Susskind, J., Mnih, V., Hinton, G.: On deep generative models with applications to recognition. In: CVPR 2011, pp. 2857–2864 (2011). https://doi.org/10.1109/CVPR.2011.5995710
7. Teoh, K.H., et al.: Face recognition and identification using deep learning approach. J. Phys. Conf. Ser. **1755**(1), 012006 (2021). https://doi.org/10.1088/1742-6596/1755/1/012006
8. Li, Y., Guo, K., Lu, Y., Liu, L.: Cropping and attention based approach for masked face recognition. Appl. Intell. **51**(5), 3012–3025 (2021). https://doi.org/10.1007/s10489-020-02100-9
9. Hariri, W.: Efficient masked face recognition method during the COVID-19 pandemic (2020). PREPRINT (Version 1) available at Research Square, https://doi.org/10.21203/rs.3.rs-39289/v1
10. Pinkney, J.: MTCNN face detection. https://github.com/matlab-deep-learning/mtcnn-face-detection/releases/tag/v1.2.4, GitHub. Accessed 26 July 2021
11. Pretrained Deep Neural Network. https://www.mathworks.com/help/deeplearning/ug/pretrained-convolutional-neural-networks.html#References, Accessed 25 July 2021
12. Inceptionv3. https://www.mathworks.com/help/deeplearning/ref/inceptionv3.html, Accessed 25 July 2021
13. Sajjanhar, A., Wu, Z., Wen, Q.: Deep learning models for facial expression recognition. In: 2018 Digital Image Computing: Techniques and Applications (DICTA), pp. 1–6 (2018). https://doi.org/10.1109/DICTA.2018.8615843
14. Salvador, R.C., Bandala, A.A., Javel, I.M., Bedruz, R.A.R., Dadios, E.P., Vicerra, R.R.P.: DeepTronic: an electronic device classification model using deep convolutional neural networks. In: 2018 IEEE 10th International Conference on Humanoid, Nanotechnology, Information Technology,Communication and Control, Environment and Management (HNICEM), pp. 1–5 (2018). https://doi.org/10.1109/HNICEM.2018.8666303
15. Zhang, L., Tjondronegoro, D.: Facial expression recognition using facial movement features. IEEE Trans. Affect. Comput. **2**(4), 219–229 (2011). https://doi.org/10.1109/T-AFFC.2011.13

IoT-Based System for Real-Time Swimming Pool Water Quality Monitoring

Afida Jemat[1]($\boxtimes$) (iD), Salman Yussof[1] (iD), Sera Syarmila Sameon[2] (iD),
and Nur Adriana Alya Rosnizam[2]

[1] Institute of Informatics and Computing in Energy, Universiti Tenaga Nasional (UNITEN),
Jalan IKRAM-UNITEN, 43000 Kajang, Selangor, Malaysia
{afida.jemat,salman}@uniten.edu.my
[2] College of Computing and Informatics, Universiti Tenaga Nasional (UNITEN),
Jalan IKRAM-UNITEN, 43000 Kajang, Selangor, Malaysia
sera@uniten.edu.my

Abstract. This paper presents an IoT based real-time water quality monitoring system for swimming pools. For most swimming pools, the maintenance work is done based on fixed schedule irrespective of the water quality condition. This may cause some issues, such as unnecessary waste of water in the case of over maintenance. In the case of under maintenance, the pool water could end up being cloudy, murky, discolored and dirty. A smart water quality monitoring system using an IoT platform is proposed to automatically monitor various water quality parameters and help to optimize maintenance work by suggesting the appropriate maintenance tasks to be performed. Technically, the proposed system consists of a controller connected to multiple sensors which read pool water parameters and transmit the data to a cloud server. The parameters read by the sensors are pH level, temperature, turbidity, chlorine residual and water flow. There is also a Web portal where users can view the collected parameters and the recommended maintenance tasks proposed by the system. In addition to making the monitoring system real time and more accessible to users, this work also aims to provide an appropriate algorithm for suggesting the maintenance task to be performed based on the water quality parameter reading.

Keywords: Water monitoring system · IoT · Sensor · Swimming pool

1 Introduction

Swimming pool is an essential amenity in modern society, where swimming for exercising or recreational purposes is considered a norm. Swimming pool is also a necessity in hotel industry to attract tourists or hotel customers. However, as more people use the pool, the water quality will degrade, and this may trigger health issues. Adequate pool maintenance to maintain good water quality is an essential requirement to ensure a swimming pool is safe for pool users. Usually, hundreds of people will use a public swimming pool every day, and this makes pool maintenance mandatory. Swimming in a dirty pool can cause infectious diseases, such as skin diseases, diarrhea, eye irritation,

© Springer Nature Switzerland AG 2021
H. Badioze Zaman et al. (Eds.): IVIC 2021, LNCS 13051, pp. 332–341, 2021.
https://doi.org/10.1007/978-3-030-90235-3_29

and respiratory tract irritation [1]. Swimming pool maintenance team would need a pool water test kit to check the pH value, temperature turbidity and chlorine contents in the pool regularly which may contribute to the maintenance cost. In addition, the maintenance of water quality in swimming pools is a challenge for homeowners with limited budgets.

The quality of pool water depends on its chemical, physical, and microbial features. Typical water quality parameters include pH, chlorine residual, dissolved oxygen, temperature, turbidity, conductivity and microbes [2]. The right amount of chemicals is needed for disinfection and ensuring the pool is safe for swimming. Mostly, the pollution in the swimming pool is from the pool users themselves. The pollutant comprises of saliva, sweat, hair, urine and sneeze. Some of the pollutants may cause the growth of microorganisms in the pool. Several diseases such as E.coli, Naegleria fowleri and Cryptosporidium parvum are linked directly to swimming pools [3]. Hence, it is necessary to disinfect the pool water in order to prevent disease outbreaks. The common and most effective disinfectant that has been used in swimming pool is calcium hypochlorite, $Ca(OCl)_2$. However, the disinfectant's effectiveness to kill microorganisms depends on pH value, temperature, and turbidity [3].

The safe pH level for swimming pool is between 7.2 and 7.8, which is categorized as a normal condition. The pH reading is a sign of the acidity level of the water and it is the most critical parameter that needs to be monitored in swimming pool water [4]. Improper maintenance of pH levels leads to bacteria breeding in the pool and this could be harmful to swimmers. According to [5], the chlorine residual of a swimming pool should be maintained between 1.5 and 2 mg/L for the pool to remain safe and healthy for users. On the other hand, according to American National Swimming Pool Foundation (NSPF), the chlorine residual should have a lower limit of 1 mg/l and an upper limit of 5 mg/l, with an ideal value between 2 and 4 mg/L [6, 7]. It is noted in [6] that the regulation for chlorine residual limit varies between regions and countries. Chlorine residual (also called chlorine level or total chlorine) is defined as the amount of free chlorine and combined chlorine in the water. However, it has been identified that to control bacterial and algae growth, chlorine residual between 0.3 and 0.6 mg/L is sufficient [8]. Free chlorine is the amount of chlorine available to sanitize contaminants in the pool. The free chlorine concentration measurement is quite challenging because it is correlated with the temperature and pH of the water sample [9]. Furthermore, the response of a pH sensor is dependent on the temperature [10]. In common practice, the standard temperature for an outdoor swimming pool is between 15 °C and 30 °C [11]. Thus, pH and temperature sensors are important and should be integrated into a monitoring system Turbidity can be explained as the degree to which the water loses its transparency due to suspended particulates. The more suspended solids in the water, the murkier the water seems and the higher the turbidity. The main reason for the required clear water for the swimming pool is to eliminate safety hazards and to ensure water cleanliness because water clarity is an indication of its cleanliness. The standard rule for safety at swimming pool is that the lifeguards and other people near or in the pool must see each other and distinguish persons that need helps. More importantly, turbid water does not look healthy and is less attractive, affecting the involved industry's reputation [12]. Moreover, the existence of turbidity caused a decrease in the effectiveness of the disinfectant.

Turbidity may affect the normal temperature of pool water because suspended particles near the surface facilitate the heat absorption from sunlight. Currently, the maximum recommended turbidity level is from 0.5 to 1.0 NTU (nephelometric turbidity units) [3, 13]. Ultrasonic sensor is used to measure the water level. It is imperative to keep water at the right level in the swimming pool for a healthy pool water filtration system. The ideal water level should be the halfway point of the skimmer's opening. The water should be at least one third up the opening of the pool skimmer [14]. If the water level is higher than that, it may slow or even stop debris from being pulled into the skimmer box through the plate or valve. However, if the water level is too low, it may cause the skimmer to suck air into the system then the pool pumps motor might be at risk of burning [15, 16].

Internet of Things (IoT) can be defined as a combination of physical things which comprise of hardware, software, and other smart technologies [17] that enable interconnecting, exchanging [18, 19] and sharing the data with a wide range of different devices and sensors via the internet. IoT is very much useful for achieving real time monitoring of sensor data. Some of the protocols and technologies used in IoT are WiFi, RFID, NFC, low-energy wireless and radio protocols, LTE-A and Bluetooth [20]. The application of IoT in the monitoring system allows the users to continuously visualize water quality analysis results in real-time. The result of data analysis can be access and display on user devices such as desktops, tablets, laptops and smartphones. A wireless sensor network (WSN) is described as a network formed by a number of sensor nodes where each node is equipped with a sensor to detect physical phenomena [21]. With the rapid technological development of sensors, WSNs become the key technology for IoT. WSN consists of multiple sensors connected through wireless channels and capable of providing digital interfaces to real-world things [22]. IoT has enabled automatic water quality monitoring systems that mitigate the challenges mentioned earlier. By using devices like sensors and probes, water parameters of a swimming pool can be measured in real-time from remote locations.

In this paper, we propose and describe the design of a system that can be applied to a swimming pool. The system enables the monitoring of a swimming pool remotely via an online platform. The contributions of the paper are as follows.

- It proposes architecture for pool water quality monitoring system that considers multiple types of sensors for measuring various water quality parameters.
- It proposes an algorithm for making pool maintenance decision based on readings from various sensors.

The remainder of the paper is organized as follows. Section 2 presents related works on water quality monitoring system. Section 3 presents the system architecture and working principle of the proposed IoT-based water quality monitoring system. This section also presents the pseudocode of the algorithm used by the system to provide maintenance recommendations based on the sensor reading. Section 4 provides some discussion on the proposed architecture and algorithm. Finally, Sect. 5 concludes the paper.

2   Related Works

Numerous studies have been carried out on water quality monitoring systems using different sensors and controllers, including Raspberry Pi [23], Raspberry Pi3B [24], ESP32 [25], Arduino Uno [23, 26], Peduino, Gaiko [27], and ATmega16 [28]. Furthermore, various wireless communication protocols to be used for water quality monitoring system including WiFi, LoRa, Bluetooth, Zig Bee and LTE have also been studied. Both the controller and the wireless technology to be used are important to ensure data from sensors can be read and transmitted to the application that will use the data. Marais et al. in [29] have developed a management system to measure water properties for swimming pools consisting of a sensor node with various sensors and actuators. This system successfully provided an accurate reading with optimum maintenance but only focused on water pH and turbidity levels. Meanwhile, Gows and Nieuwoudt [30] invented a low cost monitoring system with the purpose to save energy consumption and reduce the time the water pump is used. Initially, their system performs a test for water quality and then makes the necessary adjustments. A new smart water quality monitoring system (SWQMS) was developed by using Node MCU V3 with ESP8266 as the processing unit [31]. The systems are able to automatically update the water quality data via the IoT platform and making an instant adjustment to the pH level. The SWQMS system also proficiently provides real-time monitoring that leads to less maintenance. Nevertheless, the system only focuses on two parameters: pH and temperature. The system does not cover the other parameters like turbidity, chlorine residual and water level, which is crucial to maintain water quality, especially for an outdoor swimming pool [32]. A study in [33] on a multi-sensor network has been conducted for measuring physicochemical water parameters, enabling real-time monitoring and developing an algorithm to detect possible contaminations of drinking water. In their system, water parameters are displayed clearly on the LCD, and a warning buzzer will be activated if the parameter values are outside the normal range. However, the history of data reading is unavailable.

Duffy et al. [3] developed a water quality monitoring and control system with real-time data logging, microbiological sampling capabilities and online connectivity. They also discussed the chemicals and the control methods for each pool parameter, namely pH, temperature, chlorine residual, and turbidity. As for pH value, they suggested adding $NaHCO_3$ when the reading is above normal value and adding HCl if the value is below normal. In addition, to retain the temperature to normal condition, the cooler/heater pump must be on/off according to high or low temperature [15]. If the temperature is in a normal state, then the cooler/heater pump must be off. Furthermore, to stabilize the pool's chlorine residual, they recommended adding $Ca(ClO)_2$ in the pool water if the reading increases and diluting with raw water when the reading decreases. With respect to turbidity, they decided to take action when the value is above 1 NTU by adding $Al_2(SO_4)_3$ to maintain the normal reading. In order to maintain the water level, the inlet and drain valve plays an important role. According to [15], if the water level exceeds the normal range, the drain valve must be turned on to channel out the water until the water level is back to normal. On the other hand, the inlet valve should be opened to fill in the water to the desired level if the opposite happens.

Although several research works on pool water monitoring system have been conducted, none of them presented an algorithm on maintenance actions to be taken based on values of the water quality parameters. Such algorithm would enable the pool water quality monitoring system to either perform automated maintenance tasks, or provide recommendations to the maintenance team on the maintenance tasks to be performed.

3   System Architecture

The proposed system monitors the quality of water in real time with the help of IoT devices. Also included in the proposed system is an algorithm for recommending corrective maintenance actions that need to be done on the swimming pool to improve its condition.

The proposed system design consists of several devices like sensors, microcontroller and WiFi module. As a transducer device, the sensor provides electrical data by responding to its environment. There are five types of sensors are used in this work namely pH sensor, temperature sensor, turbidity sensor, chlorine residual sensor and water level sensor. The microcontroller acts as data processor and sends the data from sensors to the web database using WiFi. The proposed sensing system block diagram is shown in Fig. 1.

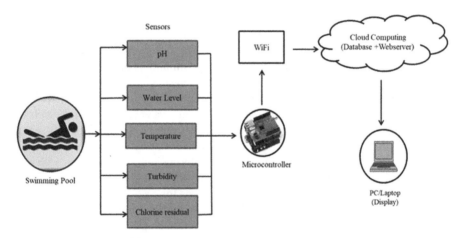

Fig. 1. System architecture for monitoring

3.1 Algorithm for Pool Maintenance

To assist the pool maintenance team, we propose an algorithm for recommending pool maintenance action based on the pool water parameters read by the sensors. The algorithm is constructed based on information from literature [3, 11, 13, 14, 16]. The corrective actions and the chemicals involved for each of the water pool parameters is summarized in Table 1 below. The flowchart of the proposed algorithm is shown in Fig. 2.

Table 1. Corrective actions for pool maintenance based on sensor values

Parameter	Readings/Corrective actions		
	Low	Normal	High
pH level	pH < 7.4 Add NaHCO$_3$	7.4 ≤ pH ≤ 7.6	pH > 7.6 Add HCl
Temperature	T < 15 °C	15 °C ≤ T ≤ 30 °C	T > 30 °C
	Turn ON heater	Turn OFF chiller and heater	Turn ON chiller
Chlorine residual	ClR < 2 mg/L	2 mg/l ≤ ClR ≤ 4 mg/L	ClR > 4 mg/L
	Add Ca(ClO)$_2$		Dilute with raw water
Turbidity level	–	TL ≤ 1 NTU	TL > 1 NTU
	–		Add Al$_2$(SO$_4$)$_3$
Water level	WL < $\frac{1}{3}$ skimmer	$\frac{1}{3}$ skimmer ≤ WL ≤ $\frac{1}{2}$ skimmer	WL > $\frac{1}{2}$ skimmer
	Open inlet valve	Close drain and inlet valve	Open drain valve

The proposed system for pool water monitoring is depicted in Fig. 3. We would like to highlight that since the scope of the work is on the monitoring system, the control system used for performing the corrective actions is not included as part of the system. As such, the proposed monitoring system remains relevant even if the maintenance work is done manually.

4   Discussion

The proposed architecture, with the use of five different sensors, is intended to be used as a guide for those who want to develop such system. Obviously, more sensors can be added if required. Similarly, the proposed algorithm was designed based on the proposed architecture. The minimum and maximum limits specified in Table 1 and subsequently Fig. 2 is based on the literature review. However, it is noted that the values may vary depending on country, region, or type of swimming pool. Therefore, for optimal results, these values may need to be adjusted accordingly to fit each implementation.

The pool monitoring system may or may not be integrated with a control system that can automate the maintenance actions. In the case where the automated control system is integrated with the monitoring system, the proposed algorithm should be implemented inside the controller, which would also control the actuators of the control system. In the absence of the control system, the proposed algorithm should be implemented in the web application so that the recommended maintenance actions can be displayed to the user. Alternatively, it is also possible to have an implementation where the control system is integrated, but the maintenance actions to be performed are manually controlled by the user. In that case, the algorithm is also implemented in the web application to display the recommended maintenance actions to the user. In addition, this implementation requires the web application to be able to send commands to the control system to perform the required maintenance actions.

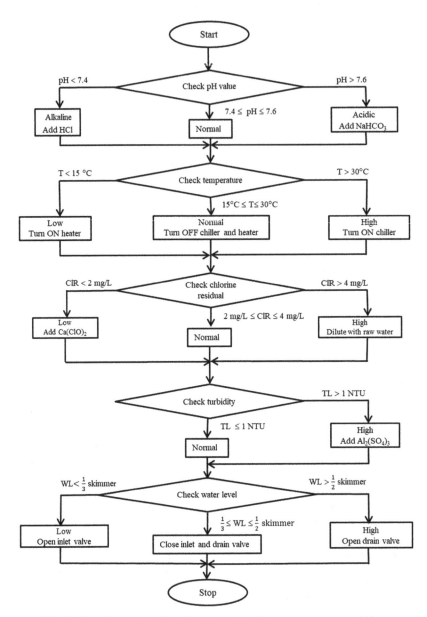

Fig. 2. Flowchart of the algorithm for pool maintenance recommendations.

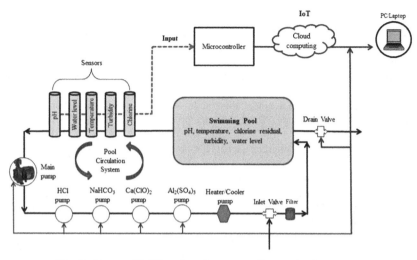

Fig. 3. Proposed IoT-based pool water quality monitoring system.

5   Conclusion

This paper proposed an IoT-based pool water quality monitoring system that can both monitor the water quality parameters and recommend appropriate maintenance tasks to be performed. The water quality parameters taken into consideration are pH level, temperature, chlorine residue, turbidity and water level. An algorithm for deciding the recommended corrective maintenance task to be performed based on the water quality parameter values is also proposed. Such system has the potential to improve water utilization and reduce pool maintenance cost. The proposed system architecture could be adapted to monitor water quality in other environments such as river, lake, reservoir, and sewage system.

Acknowledgement. The authors would like to acknowledge the Research and Innovation of Private Higher Education Network (RIPHEN) for providing research grant under the RIPHEN Digital Future Research Programme to support this research work.

References

1. Angdresey, A., Sitanayah, L., Sampul, V.J.A.: Monitoring and predicting water quality in swimming pools. EPI Int. J. Eng. **3**, 119–125 (2020)
2. Alam, A.U., Clyne, D., Jin, H., Hu, N.-X., Deen, M.J.: Fully integrated, simple, and low-cost electrochemical sensor array for in situ water quality monitoring. ACS Sensors **5**, 412–422 (2020)
3. Duffy, P., Woods, G., Walsh, J., Kane, M.: Online real-time water quality monitoring and control system. Orlando, FL, ICCT (2010). http://arrow.dit.ie/engschmanconn
4. Organization, W.H.: Guidelines for Safe Recreational Water Environments: Coastal and fresh waters. World Health Organization (2003)

5. Senthilkumar, K., Zen, J.: Free chlorine detection based on EC mechanism at an electroactive polymelamine-modified electrode. Electrochem. Commun. **46**, 87–90 (2014)
6. https://iwaponline.com/jwh/article/17/2/227/65345/Variability-of-residual-chlorine-in-swimming-pool, Accessed 04 Sept 2021
7. Ford, R.L.: Certified pool-spa operator handbook. National Environmental Health Association (2005)
8. Donohue, J.M.: Water conditioning, industrial. In: Meyers, R.A. (ed.) Encyclopedia of Physical Science and Technology (Third Edition), pp. 671–697. Academic Press, New York (2003)
9. Morris, J.C.: The acid ionization constant of HOCl from 5 to 35. J. Phys. Chem. **70**, 3798–3805 (1966)
10. Qin, Y., Kwon, H.-J., Howlader, M.M.R., Deen, M.J.: Microfabricated electrochemical pH and free chlorine sensors for water quality monitoring: recent advances and research challenges. RSC Adv. **5**, 69086–69109 (2015)
11. Anantha Naik, G.D.D.G.V.: IoT based real-time water quality monitoring system using smart sensors. Int. Res. J. Eng. Technol. (IRJET) **7**(7) (2020)
12. Koertge, H.H.: The turbidity of public swimming pool waters. Am. J. Public Health Nations Health **60**, 138–150 (1970)
13. ISO (1999) Water quality—Determination of turbidity. Geneva, International Organization for Standardization (ISO 7027:1999) (1999)
14. Kamidi, P., Sabbi, V., Sanniti, R.: IoT based smart water quality monitoring and prediction system. Int. J. Eng. Adv. Technol. **8**, 484–489 (2019)
15. https://www.swimmingpool.com/maintenance/pool-care-basics/pool-water-level/, Accessed 08 July 2021
16. https://jeffellismanagement.com/services/pool-maintenance/maintain-pool-water-level, Accessed 12 July 2021
17. Bansal, N.: Designing Internet of Things Solutions with Microsoft Azure: A Survey of Secure and Smart Industrial Applications. Apress, New York (2020)
18. Glória, A., Cercas, F., Souto, N.: Design and implementation of an IoT gateway to create smart environments. Procedia Comput. Sci. **109**, 568–575 (2017)
19. Uckelmann, D., Harrison, M., Michahelles, F.: An architectural approach towards the future internet of things. In: Uckelmann, D., Harrison, M., Michahelles, F. (eds.) Architecting the Internet of Things, pp. 1–24. Springer, Heidelberg (2011)
20. Manimegalai, R.: An IoT based smart water quality monitoring system using cloud. In: 2020 International Conference on Emerging Trends in Information Technology and Engineering (ic-ETITE), pp. 1–7 (2020)
21. Chowdury, M., et al.: IoT based real-time river water quality monitoring system. Procedia Comput. Sci. **155**, 161–168 (2019)
22. Manrique, J.A., Rueda-Rueda, J.S., Portocarrero, J.M.T.: Contrasting internet of things and wireless sensor network from a conceptual overview. In: 2016 IEEE International Conference on Internet of Things (iThings) and IEEE Green Computing and Communications (Green-Com) and IEEE Cyber, Physical and Social Computing (CPSCom) and IEEE Smart Data (SmartData), pp. 252–257 (2016)
23. Vijayakumar, N., Ramya, R.: The real time monitoring of water quality in IoT environment. 2015 International Conference on Innovations in Information, Embedded and Communication Systems (ICIIECS), pp. 1–5 (2015)
24. Kalpana, M.B.: Online Monitoring Of Water Quality Using Raspberry Pi3 Model B (2016)
25. Simões, G., Dionísio, C., Glória, A., Sebastião, P., Souto, N.: Smart system for monitoring and control of swimming pools. In: 2019 IEEE 5th World Forum on Internet of Things (WF-IoT), pp. 829–832. IEEE (2019)

26. Rahman, B.C., Hossain, M., Hassan, Z., Hossain, G., Islam, M.: Internet of Things (IoT) based water quality monitoring system. Educ. Res. **2**, 168–180 (2020)
27. Salim, T.I., Haiyunnisa, T., Alam, H.S.: Design and implementation of water quality monitoring for eel fish aquaculture. In: 2016 International Symposium on Electronics and Smart Devices (ISESD), pp. 208–213. IEEE (2016)
28. Warungase, P., Worlikar, A., Mhatre, J., Saha, D., Salunkhe, G.: IOT Based Water Monitoring System (2017)
29. Marais, J.M., Bhatt, D.V., Hancke, G.P., Ramotsoela, T.D.: A web-based swimming pool information and management system. In: 2016 IEEE 14th International Conference on Industrial Informatics (INDIN), pp. 980–985 (2016)
30. Gouws, R., Nieuwoudt, A.: Design and cost analysis of an automation system for swimming pools in South Africa. In: 2012 Proceedings of the 20th Domestic Use of Energy Conference, pp. 9–15 (2012)
31. Hamid, S.A., Rahim, A.M.A., Fadhlullah, S.Y., Abdullah, S., Muhammad, Z., Leh, N.A.M.: IoT based water quality monitoring system and evaluation. In: 2020 10th IEEE International Conference on Control System, Computing and Engineering (ICCSCE), pp. 102–106 (2020)
32. Elmas, S., et al.: Photometric sensing of active chlorine, total chlorine, and ph on a microfluidic chip for online swimming pool monitoring. Sensors **20**, 3099 (2020)
33. Cloete, N.A., Malekian, R., Nair, L.: Design of smart sensors for real-time water quality monitoring. IEEE Access **4**, 3975–3990 (2016)

The Preliminary Study of Traffic Impact Analysis for Developing Countries in Southeast Asia

Anton Budi Dharma[1,2] and Rabiah Abdul Kadir[2(✉)]

[1] Dumai, Riau, Indonesia
p94464@siswa.ukm.edu.my
[2] Institute of IR4.0, Universiti Kebangsaan Malaysia, 43650 Bangi, Selangor, Malaysia
rabiahivi@ukm.edu.my

Abstract. Traffic Impact Analysis (TIAs) is an effective way to identify traffic generated by new developments in transportation systems so that it can reduce the impact of heavy traffic on the construction of new land. The traffic impact analysis model that has been developed in developed countries is very helpful in dealing with the problem of transportation disruption caused by development. Analysis of the impact of traffic in the development of new land uses is very influential in making a policy to overcome traffic congestion in developing countries such as Indonesia, Malaysia, The Philippines, and Thailand. There were two categories of nations with substantial differences in motorization rates: Sri Lanka, India, Nepal, Philippines, Pakistan, Indonesia, and Thailand have faster motorization rates than the rest of the world. The priority in analyzing the impact of traffic on the development of new land uses is used as a guide for the government in overcoming traffic congestion caused by development. The traffic impact analysis (TIAs) is designed to address traffic congestion and to improve the level of service (LOS) in new land-use developments. The problem faced by developing countries in overcoming traffic congestion at this time is that they do not have standard guidelines such as land-use models and planning implications in traffic impact analysis. Currently, a country like Indonesia does not have standard guidelines that can be applied in traffic impact analysis. So, it is necessary to provide a better traffic impact analysis that can be applied to reduce traffic congestion which is very bad for the surrounding network transportation, and to improve road services caused by the use of new land.

Keywords: Traffic impact analysis · Traffic congestion

1 Introduction

In Traffic Impact Analysis (TIAs) is critical to understanding how a proposed development will impact the surrounding transport network. TIA aims to assess the impact of new land-use developments on all aspects of the transport network. Therefore, by offering transport and land use planning, practitioners' knowledge of technological advances

© Springer Nature Switzerland AG 2021
H. Badioze Zaman et al. (Eds.): IVIC 2021, LNCS 13051, pp. 342–349, 2021.
https://doi.org/10.1007/978-3-030-90235-3_30

will make important development decisions that are more effective, low cost, and time-efficient. Transportation, social and environmental aspects will be considered during development planning.

The main factor which influences the traffic impact analysis is the development of new land which causes traffic congestion in every developing country. Therefore, it is necessary to develop standard guidelines in traffic impact analysis. There are some fundamentals differences in the countries' policymaking. The differences are presented in the policy-making of transportation conditions, land use, culture, and the surrounding environment. Standard guidelines have to be developed to determine the level of service (LOS) of new land development. To determine the level of service, supporting data is needed from traffic congestion, generation and attraction, traffic demand volume, traffic capacity, land, road length and width, and population density.

Traffic impact analysis (TIA) proposes a new method to enable regional accessibility of the proposed land use development project, this method is able to measure the impact of small-scale projects on the transportation system. In TIA development, special events would also be considered by the researchers. For example, The Federal Highway Administration (FHWA), proposes a special event TIA approach, and the approaches are designed similar to the TIA requirements for a planned development (Wang et al. 2019). Although there are many different TIA guidelines in most countries, the flexible limits for TIA transport impact analysis are not well reached through guidelines, or even in practice (Cooley et al. 2016).

In this case, the level of service (LOS) is one of the most frequently used congestion measurements, which is specifically intended to measure traffic congestion and assess the operational efficiency of the existing road network (Jolovic et al. 2021).

2 Related Work

The prerequisite to evaluate the TIA induced by traffic congestions is based on the evaluation indicators on two objects: land use and planning implication. Generally, the level of service (LOS) has been used to measure the operating conditions of transportation system elements for a long time and has been adopted by the Highway Capacity Manual. In line with the Highway Capacity Manual, the LOS ratings of transportation system elements range from A (best) to F (worst, or failure). Considering the data availability and comparability, we utilize the v/c ratio (v is hourly traffic demand volume and c is the capacity) to determine the LOS of roadway section and anticipating traffic congestions (Wang et al. 2019). Recent guides to TIA practice promote multimodal LOS analysis and the adjustment of trip generation rates based on local data. (Combs et al. 2020).

2.1 The Relationship Between Traffic Density and Congestion

There are three types of the density of traffic conditions: light, medium, and heavy which have a relationship with the level of perceived congestion density for the three traffic conditions showing the same tendency (Khoo and Asitha 2016). Figure 1 shows the relationship of the perceived traffic congestion level with density for three types of traffic conditions (i.e. light, medium, and heavy).

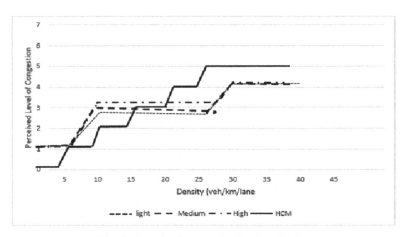

Fig. 1. Perceived congestion level vs density

In general, drivers feel a high level of congestion when travel speed is low, besides that drivers are more sensitive to travel speed during heavy traffic conditions (Senbil et al. 2007; Khoo and Asitha 2016). Figure 2 shows the relationship of perceived congestion level with speed.

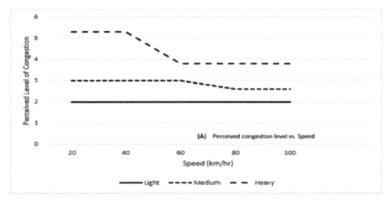

Fig. 2. Perceived congestion level vs speed

Drivers are more sensitive to changes in density compared to traffic flow and speed when evaluating traffic congestion levels. The reason is that when the density increases, the drivers' freedom to maneuver (e.g. change lanes) becomes limited and driving becomes less comfortable (Khoo and Asitha 2016). Figure 3 shows the relationship of perceived congestion level with traffic flow for three traffic conditions (i.e., light, medium, and heavy).

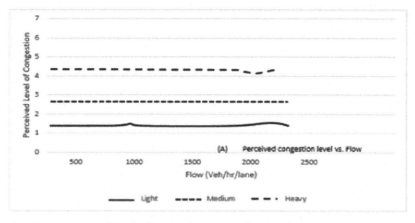

Fig. 3. Perceived congestion level vs flow

2.2   Guidance Framework for Traffic Impact Analysis (TIA)

Methodological frameworks and workflows in analyzing the impact of construction traffic during special events are designed according to traditional TIA but differ due to different goals and concerns. The analysis process must be closely combined with the data and the planned special event management (Wang et al. 2019). In general, data collection, traffic request requests, and evaluation are the main steps of TIA project construction during special events. However, the process does not last the same as a traditional TIA. The detailed steps are shown in Fig. 4.

3   Improper Traffic Impact Analysis

This is the initial stage where the overall research planning is carried out by identifying problems, determining research scope, conducting a literature review, and finding how to overcome traffic congestion using traffic impact analysis (TIA) development on new land and guidelines results. Theories and concepts in the research field will be explored and analysed. The analysis will be applied in developing countries in Southeast Asia.

This research collects and analyses the primary and secondary data. The source of primary data is speed data, traffic inventory data, estimated future traffic values, traffic forecasts, and respondent selection. Secondary data is used to be integrated into the analysis data process. Secondary data is the data that was obtained from the ministry of transportation officials, the ministry of public works office, and the central statistics agency.

Based on the framework of the analysis, the data process consists of various formats and types that will be carried out in the performance of evaluating the network of the road before or after construction. The results of the analysis can be used as guidelines for developing countries. This is used by the government as consideration for decision-making. Implementation of traffic impact analysis (TIA) is an analysis of road network performance in evaluating traffic congestion. Selecting the problems obtained from the evaluation includes recommendations and implementation that are the responsibility of

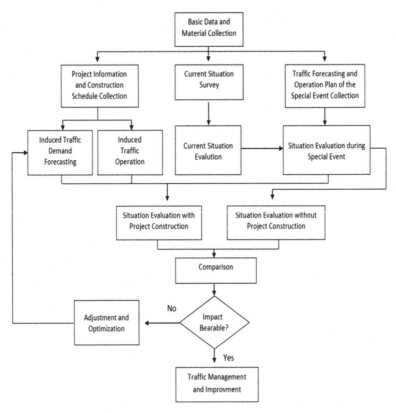

Fig. 4. Traffic impact analysis process of project construction during planned special events.

the government, monitoring, and evaluating plans to be implemented as well as providing appropriate guidelines in traffic impact analysis (TIA) in developing countries in overcoming congestion. Figure 5 shows the flow of traffic impact analysis (TIA) in studying the factors that caused of improper TIA in Southeast Asia developing countries.

3.1 Service Level Evaluation Criteria (LOS)

A prerequisite for evaluating the impact of extra traffic caused by project construction during a special event is the definition of evaluation indicators on two objects: road sections and intersections. As is known, the level of service (LOS) has long been used to measure the operating conditions of transportation system elements and has been adopted by the Highway Capacity Manual (Wang et al. 2019). We provide evaluation criteria for LOS of road sections and intersections for project construction caused by traffic impacts during special events in Table 1.

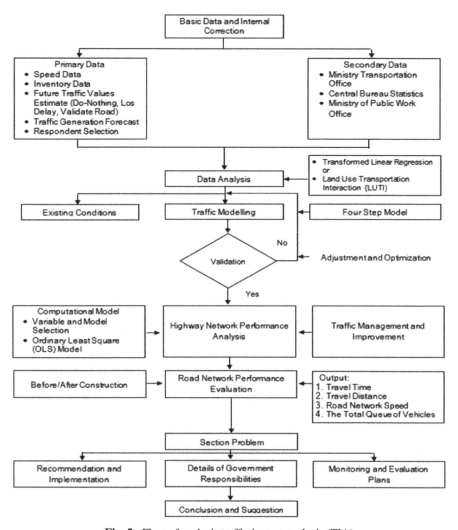

Fig. 5. Flow of analysis traffic impact analysis (TIA)

Evaluation criteria for construction project-induced traffic impacts during special events are suggested to determine impacts (see Table 2). The impact is significant if the LOS before (such as B) has an LOS after accounting for a construction project that is equal to or lower than the appropriate level (C or lower), and vice versa is not significant.

Table 1. Evaluation criterion for level of service.

Roadway section						
LOS	A	B	C	D	E	F
v/c ratio	v/c ≤ 0.27	0.27 < v/c ≤ 0.57	0.57 < v/c ≤ 0.70	0.70 < v/c ≤ 0.85	0.85 < v/c ≤ 1.00	v/c > 1.00
Intersection						
LOS	A	B	C	D	E	F
Average Vehicular delay (d, s)	d ≤ 10	10 < d ≤ 20	20 < d ≤ 35	35 < d ≤ 55	55 < d ≤ 80	d > 80

Note; LOS = level of service; v = hourly traffic demand volume; c = capacty

Table 2. Critical impact evaluation criteria for traffic due to project construction during special events.

LOS without project construction	A	B	C	D	E	F
LOS with project construction	B	C	D	E	F	F

Note; LOS = level of service

4 Discussion

This study is to provide accurate standard guidelines in the form of land use models and planning implications in traffic impact analysis (TIA). With the proposed guidelines in the form of existing models in the traffic impact analysis, it is hoped that they will be able to plan the transportation of a new city that can reduce traffic congestion. and predict future traffic both before and after development related to land use. The standard guidelines will be used as a determinant of government policy to make decisions in recommending development proposals on new land.

A traffic impact analysis (TIA) will have a good impact on areas that are still developing. It can also be used as a guide for developing countries in managing transportation to overcome traffic congestion. Traffic impact analysis is used as material for the government (policymakers) in making decisions on the development of new land that causes congestion.

The researchers further used traffic impact analysis in evaluating the development of land-use models and their implications for developing areas, and rearranging areas that previously had problems in traffic jams when development was carried out. The decrease in the level of road service (LOS) caused by the construction of new land causes traffic congestion. The standard guideline is expected to overcome and reduce traffic congestion.

5 Conclusion

Developed countries have well-managed transportation so that traffic congestion is not a major factor in development because those countries have already had a standard guideline for traffic impact analysis (TIA) which is used as a policy determination in making decisions for new areas. Standard guidelines for traffic impact analysis (TIA) in developed countries cannot be used and implemented in developing countries in general. This is due to differences in transportation, population, land area, high levels of traffic congestion, vehicle growth, and the surrounding environment.

This study aims to provide standard guidelines with a new model for optimizing traffic impact analysis (TIA) in the development of new land developments and assisting the government in making policies to address traffic congestion problems that arise as a result of development in developing countries.

Acknowledgement. The authors would like to express gratitude to the National University of Malaysia (UKM) for providing the opportunity and funding under the Student Research Project Code TAP-K020558.

References

Combs, T.S., McDonald, N.C., Leimenstoll, W.: Evolution in local traffic impact assessment practices (2020). SAGE Journals. Collection. https://doi.org/10.25384/SAGE.c.4880457.v1

Cooley, K., Gruyter, C.D., Delbosc, A.: A best practice evaluation of traffic impact assessment guidelines in Australia and New Zealand. Australasian Transport Research Forum 2016 (2019). 30 June 2019, https://www.atrf.info/papers/2016/files/ATRF2016_Full_papers_resubmission_155.pdf

Jolovic, B., Choi, K.A.: Land-use clustering approach to capturing the level-of-service of large urban corridors: a case study in downtown Los Angeles. Environ. Plan. B: Urban Anal. City Sci. **48**(7), 2093–2109 (2021)

Khoo, H.L., Asitha, K.S.: An impact analysis of traffic image information system on driver travel choice. Transp. Res. Part A: Policy Pract. **88**, 175–194 (2016)

Senbil, M., Zhang, J., Fujiwara, A.: Motorization in Asia: 14 countries and three Metropolitan areas. IATSS Res. **31**, 46–58 (2007)

Wang, Z., Bai, Y., Zhu, R., Wang, Y., Wu, B., Wang, Y.: Impact analysis of extra traffic induced by project construction during planned special events. Transp. Res. Rec. **2673**(7), 402–412 (2019)

Search Operators Based on TRIZ
for Optimising PCB Assembly Time

Jian Ching Lim[1], Kok Weng Ng[1], and Mei Choo Ang[2(✉)]

[1] Department of Mechanical, Materials and Manufacturing Engineering,
Faculty of Science and Engineering, University of Nottingham Malaysia, Sememyih, Malaysia
[2] Universiti Kebangsaan Malaysia, Institute of IR 4.0, Bangi, Malaysia
amc@ukm.edu.my

Abstract. PCBs are present in most modern electronics. Manufacturers have placed a heavy emphasis on optimising manufacturing to remain competitive, especially assembly time per board in order to reduce assembly cost. The target of this research is to evaluate and study the possibilities of applying a new search operator derived based on TRIZ principles into a meta-heuristic search algorithm, the Bees Algorithm, to solve the optimisation problem of PCB assembly using a Chip Shooter Machine. The TRIZ inventive principle selected for this research was "The Other Way Around" principle. This principle was applied into Bees Algorithm, alongside proven search operators of Segmentation, Local Quality and Dynamisation. The impact of the new operator was determined by average shortest assembly time and PCB travel distance. Introducing the new operator with older operators provided shorter average solution times in 10 runs experiments and resulted in faster convergence times with lower iterations.

Keywords: Bees algorithm · Printed circuit board assembly · Optimization · Algorithm operators · TRIZ

1 Introduction

Modern day electronics are heavily reliant on PCBs. Due to the type of electronics available, PCB sizes range from small to large along with the amount and types of components to be assembled on them. PCB manufacturers are keen in reducing costs for PCB assembly in order to remain competitive and a multitude of research work has been done in this field. Component assembly time is one of the key factors in PCB assembly performance and its cost. Any improvements to this factor will be able to increase productivity of assembly lines while reducing overhead costs of the factory by increasing hourly production [1, 2].

Since PCB component assembly involves assembling multiple components across asymmetrical positions, the total assembly time of a PCB board will be highly reliant on the component assembly sequence (PCB distance pathing) and the component feeder sequencing. Thus, due to the possible permutations possible with these 2 factors, researchers have used mathematical modelling to approach optimisation of PCB assembly [3].

© Springer Nature Switzerland AG 2021
H. Badioze Zaman et al. (Eds.): IVIC 2021, LNCS 13051, pp. 350–361, 2021.
https://doi.org/10.1007/978-3-030-90235-3_31

In this study, Bees Algorithm (BA) and its operators were selected to optimize the PCB assembly time problem set. It is a relatively new population search algorithm developed by Pham, et al. [4]. BA has shown to be able to solve complex combinatorial problems with high efficiency and strong fitness solutions. The goal of this study is to translate and implement a new operator from the 40 inventive principles of TRIZ into the BA. The performance and effectiveness of the new operator in BA were also benchmarked to prior works to evaluate the effectiveness of the new operator based on earlier works of Ang, Pham, Ng, etc. [5–7].

2 PCB Assembly Optimization

2.1 History of PCB Assembly Optimisation

This optimisation for PCB assembly problem is usually classified as a Non-Polynomial (NP)-complete or a NP-hard problem [1, 5]. Early development into this problem was initiated by Ball and Magazine [8]. They proposed a heuristic algorithm for component sequencing, Chan and Mercier then classified the PCB assembly problem as a Travelling Salesman Problem (TSP) [9]. The apparatus in use was the PnP machine (different from this study which uses a Chip Shooter machine), with their computational results reported a 35% decrease in travel distance.

2.2 Meta-heuristic Approach to Solving PCBA Optimisation Problem

Various algorithms have been used to solve optimization problems. A few algorithms that have been historically employed to solve optimisation problems are: Genetic Algorithm (GA) [10], Simulated Annealing (SA) [11], Particle Swarm Optimization [1], Bees Algorithm (BA) [3, 12–14]. These algorithms have been widely used and adopted for NP-complete and NP-hard problems. Bees algorithm, a relatively new optimisation algorithm developed by Pham and colleagues, operates based on the foraging behaviour of bees. It is based on a combination of neighbourhood search and random search, the algorithm will quickly focus on exploring the neighbourhood of high fitness solutions, which are assessed with a fitness function. An initial random global search is done to provide a sample solution, then the fitness of the sample solution is tested. The solutions with high fitness are then selected as the local search area or the "flower patch" and neighbouring solutions are then explored for other solutions. The fitness test is then applied again recursively to the solutions, resulting in recursive improvement and optimisation of the solution [4, 15].

The potential of BA and the trend of BA offered top solutions for the optimisation problem with the least number of iterations [5, 12, 13]. According to Pham and Castellani, improvements have been made to BA by introducing new functionalities to it, namely neighbourhood shrinking and site abandonment. Neighbourhood shrinking involves reducing neighbourhood search area when fitness levels of solutions found are stagnating while site abandonment is introduced when no significant improvements are made after neighbourhood shrinking and the potential of the search area is deemed saturated [12].

2.3 Operators and Their Functions in Optimisation Algorithms

In the case of Bees Algorithm, the leading published research work with the shortest assembly time of 23.46 s was achieved by Castellani and Pham [13]. The operators utilized by the algorithm were Block Insertion Operator, Single-Point Insertion Operator, 2-Opt Operator, Simple Swap Operator, and Neighbour Swap Operator. In essence, the insertion operators rearrange the solution set; the 2-Opt operator introduces rearrangement and inverse of sections of the solution, while the swap operators exchange elements in the solution set with its neighbouring elements [10]. The pseudo-randomness of the operators can result in improvement or regression in the solution, which will be filtered out by the fitness function.

2.4 Brief Introduction of TRIZ

TRIZ (/'triːz/; Russian: теория решения изобретательских задач, teoriya resheniya izobretatelskikh zadatch) is an engineering methodology developed by Altshuller. It is known as "the theory of inventive problem solving" [16, 17]. Ilevbare, Probert and Phaal described TRIZ as a systematic approach to finding solutions to technical problems and innovating technical systems [18]. The main focus of this case study is on TRIZ's 40 inventive principles (Table 1), although not all 40 inventive principles can be translated into operators.

TRIZ principles have been successfully applied to various design concepts and have met with varying degrees of success. Most of it in solving technical (engineering-related) problems. The most useful tools were found to be the 40 inventive principles based on a study on technology innovation done in 2013 [18]. The paper also found a small amount of business or management-related issues that researchers have applied TRIZ to, even if the field of study was different from intended use [18–20]. In this research work, certain principles such as No. 18 - Mechanical Vibration/Oscillations and No. 31- Use of Porous Materials cannot be translated into effective operators. As such, the interpretation of the 40 inventive principles is also very subjective as an individual might perceive a certain principle differently from others.

2.5 Prior Work on Search Operators Based on TRIZ

Ang, Ng, and Pham [6, 7] initiated application of TRIZ-inspired operators for BA optimization problems. Their work focused on 3 TRIZ-inspired operators which work in tandem, the three principles used are: Segmentation, Local Quality, and Dynamisation. The segmentation operator fragments the solution set into smaller groups and works with the local quality operator which compares inter- and intra- group fitness, while the dynamisation operator randomises the group size in the segmentation operator. The research work concluded that with the new operators, the assembly time found was better than BA with basic operators. The paper also concluded that the BA with TRIZ-inspired operators could perform well with or without seeding (initial solution generation with good fitness) [7].

This study is meant to be a continuation of Ang, et al.'s earlier work [7]. Since the effects and translation of the 3 said principles, Segmentation, Local Quality and Dynamisation have been developed, they were not evaluated again in this work.

Table 1. The 40 inventive principles of TRIZ [7]

1. Segmentation	2. Taking Out	3. Local Quality	4. Asymmetry	5. Merging
6. Universality	7. "Nested Doll"	8. Anti-Weight	9. Preliminary Anti-Action	10. Preliminiary Action
11. Beforehand Cushioning	12. Equipotentiality	13. "The Other Way Around"	14. Spheroidal	15. "Dynamisation"
16. Partial or Excessive Action	17. Another dimension	18. Mechanical vibration	19. Periodic Action	20. Continuity of Beneficial Action
21. Skipping	22. "Blessing in Disguise"	23. Feedback	24. Intermediate medium	25. Self-service
26. Copying	27. Cheap Short-lived Objects	28. Mechanics Substitution	29. Pneumatics/Hydraulics	30. Flexible and Thin Films
31. Porous Materials	32. Colour Changes	33. Homogeneity	34. Discarding and recovering	35. Parameter Changes
36. Phase Transitions	37. Thermal Expansion	38. Strong Oxidants	39. Inert Atmosphere	40. Composite Materials

3   Methodology

Ang, et al. [7] has provided the optimization problem breakdown for the Moving Board with Time Delay (MBTD) PCB assembly machine as shown in Fig. 1.

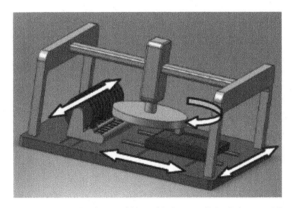

Fig. 1. MBTD PCB assembly machine with its possible degrees of freedom [7].

Similar mathematical models [6, 7, 10] were used in this work. By using Chebyshev metric, the time between component placement and feeder location can be found using Eq. (1).

$$t_1(c_i, c_j) = \max(\frac{|x_j - x_i|}{v_x}, \frac{|y_j - y_i|}{v_y}) \tag{1}$$

where x_i, y_i denotes component initial position and x_j, y_j denotes component final position. v_x, v_y is constant at 60 mm/s.

Feeder travel time, t_2 can be found with the Euclidean metric as shown in Eq. (2). For this case study, the feeder carrier was arranged in a straight line.

$$t_2\left(f_i, f_j\right) = \frac{\sqrt{\left|x_j^f - x_i^f\right|^2 + \left|y_j^f - y_i^f\right|^2}}{v_f} \tag{2}$$

where v_f is constant at 60 mm/s. Distance between feeder nodes were set at 15 mm in this study. A consistent indexing time was also needed by the machine to process movement commands and this was set at 0.25 s/index.

Component pathing sequence was denoted as:

$$C = \{c_1, c_2, c_3 \cdots c_{n-1}, c_n\}$$

For this research work, the number of components were set to 50. The feeder sequence was denoted as:

$$F = \{f_1, f_2, f_3 \cdots f_{m-1}, f_m\}$$

For this research work, ten types of components was used (Table 2).

Table 2. Summarised parameters for case study

Parameters	Values
No. of turret heads	2
Indexing time of turret	0.25 s/index
Average PCB mounting table speed	60 mm/s
Average feeder system speed	60 mm/s
Distance between feeder	15 mm
Total number of components, n	50
Total types of component, m	10

3.1 Optimisation Process Flow

The process flow for the proposed novel optimisation process is shown in Fig. 2. Multi-stage operators consisted of mentioned TRIZ inspired operators in prior works as well as the newly developed operator. In each iteration, this process flow was applied to the initial component pathing sequence to derive minimums for distance, which were followed by optimization of feeder sequence. The code was based on Ang, et al.'s prior work done in 2009 [7].

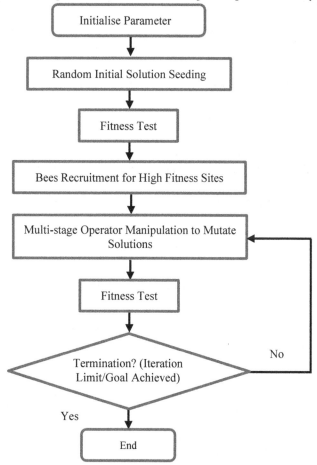

Fig. 2. The Bees Algorithm flow process with four TRIZ search operators.

Three of the 40 inventive principles have been developed by Ang, et al. [7] in prior works. In this research work, the 13th principle - "The Other Way Around" was developed to supplement these prior TRIZ-inspired operators. Operator 1 is the newly developed search operator based on TRIZ while Operators 2–5 were prior operators inspired by TRIZ.

Operator 1: "The Other Way Around" Operator. After the random segmentation process, the "The Other Way Around" operator would flip the entire segment as shown below:

Pre- "The Other Way Around":

| 1 | 2 | 3 | | 4 | 5 | 6 | | 7 | 8 | 9 |

Post "The Other Way Around":

1	2	3		6	5	4		7	8	9

The "The Other Way Around" command would flip the entire segment for segment sizes equal to or greater than 2, depending on the segmentation operator.

Operator 2: "Dynamisation" Operator. This operator randomly selected a group size in each iteration to undergo segmentation in "segmentation" operator.

Operator 3: "Segmentation" Operator. This operator randomly split the order into smaller groups. Group sizes could possibly be unequal [6, 7].

1	2	3	4	5	6	7	8	9	10	11

1	2	3		4	5	6	7	8		9	10	11

Operator 4: Local Quality Operator. After the segment swap operator was performed, a check for any improvements in fitness (PCB travel distance and time) Pre and post operator would be conducted. If there were no improvements in fitness relative to the original solution, then the original solution was retained. For example, the local quality operator would accept the segment fitness due to reduced travel distance, and post process segment 1 would be utilised. Local Quality operator would reject segment fitness due to the larger travel distance and post process segment 2 would not be utilised [5, 7].

Pre-process Segment

1	7	8	...	...	3	2	10

Travel distance of: 120 mm

Post Process Segment 1:

1	2	3	...	...	6	4	9

Travel distance of: 80 mm

Post Process Segment 2:

10	4	3	...	...	2	7	9

Travel distance of: 150 mm

Operator 5: "Point Insertion" Operator. This insertion operator caused a single point mutation, where it extracts and reinserts a random element from inside the segmented group:

Pre-Insertion:

1	2	3	4	5

Post Insertion:

1	2	5	3	4

Insertion can be at any location inside the segment with all possible permutations [16].

Operator 6: Segment Swap Operator. This segment swap operator resulted in a segment mutation where the segmented group elements were rearranged.

Pre-Segment Swap.

1	2	3	4	5	6	7	8

Post Segment Swap.

1	2	5	6	4	3	7	8

The segment swap would retain the order of some of the segment's units. The number of units swapped were also randomised but would not exceed half the size of the segment. This swap only occurred within the segment [21].

Since the "The Other Way Around" operator might perform similar operations to the segment swap operator in certain cases, three sets of experiment were conducted in this research as shown in Table 3. The new search operator, "The Other Way Around" Operator (Operator 1) was applied sequentially with operator 2, 3, 4, 5 and 6 and represented by NewOp. The Bees Algorithm with NewOp were tested and compared with NewOpNoSwap as well as the TRIZ-inspired search operators developed by Ang et al. [6, 7]. The NewOpNoSwap was a set of search operators consisted of operators 1, 2, 3, 4 and 5. Table 3 shows the experiment sets and all related operators applied in the experiments. Ten runs for each experiment set were conducted and each run stopped at 1000 iterations. The average best solution time was calculated and compared as shown in Table 4.

Table 3. Experiment sets and operators

Experiment Set name	Operators applied
Ang et al. [6, 7]	2,3,4,5,6
NewOpNoSwap	1,2,3,4,5
NewOp	1,2,3,4,5,6

4   Results

From the experiment results, it was found that the new "The Other Way Around" operator performance was affected by the removal of the old Swap operator as shown in the results using NewOpNoSwap (refer to Table 4). "The Other Way Around" operator performed better with existing operators in the NewOp as shown in Table 4. This can be seen in Fig. 3. The best solution time found in 1000 iterations was 24 s. The best component path from all data sets can be seen in Fig. 4. In Table 4, NewOp showed a 0.17% reduction in average solution time compared to Ang et al. [6, 7], while NewOpNoSwap showed an increase of 6.2%. However, this average solution was just from 10 runs experiments. The search operators by Ang et al. managed to obtain better average time, 24.290s, when 100 runs of experiments were conducted.

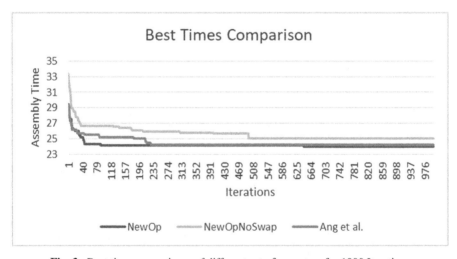

Fig. 3. Best time comparisons of different set of operators for 1000 Iterations

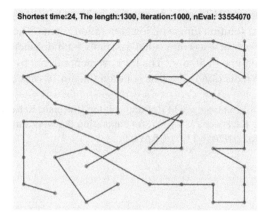

Fig. 4. Simulation of the optimum assembly path from NewOp

Table 4. Average solution time for 10 runs (each run contained 1000 iterations)

NewOp	NewOpNoSwap	Ang et al. [6, 7]
24.475s	26.033s	24.517s

5 Discussion

From Fig. 3, the Bees Algorithm with NewOp appeared to converge faster than the NewOpNoSwap and Ang et al. operators in ten runs experiment as shown in Fig. 3. The results from the NewOp operator converged to the best assembly time in 50 iterations. The solution time for the NewOpNoSwap appeared to converge slower and didn't achieve good assembly time when compared to the other set of operators. Therefore, the "The Other Way Around" operator should not be implemented as a core operator function due to this ineffectiveness, but instead should be utilized as a supporting operator. However, the performance of the NewOp were highly dependent on how the "the way around" inventive principle was interpreted.

The best time obtained by the Bees algorithm with NewOp represents the minimum time required to complete the assembly of the 50 component, which was only 24s. This best time was not as fast as the fastest time obtained by Ang et al [6, 7] and Castellani [13] and this fastest time was obtained within a limited number of runs. More runs are needed to verify whether this best time can be improved.

6 Conclusion

The newly developed "The Other Way Around" operator has shown improvements in the case study PCB assembly time. This criterion is only met when the "The Other Way Around" operator is partnered with the 3 operators developed earlier by Ang, et al. [6, 7]. The "The Other Way Around" operator cannot be used to substitute the previous segment swap operator. The four TRIZ inspired operators in NewOp of BA is shown to be able to converge to the best solution time with lower iteration counts. The best assembly path from this case study was at 1300 mm (total assembly path distance) with an assembly time of 24 s with a runtime of 50 min. The improvement offered by the new operator is found to be at 0.17% reduction in the best solution time in 10 runs experiments.

Acknowledgements. The authors would like to thank the Universiti Kebangsaan Malaysia and the Ministry of Higher Education, Malaysia, for supporting the work through research grants, GUP-2018–124 and FRGS/1/2018/TK03/UKM/02/6.

References

1. Hsu, H.: solving feeder assignment and component sequencing problems for printed circuit board assembly using particle swarm optimization. IEEE Trans. Autom. Sci. Eng. **14**, 881–893 (2017)
2. Ho, W., Ji, P.: Optimal Production Planning for PCB Assembly. Springer, London (2007)
3. Duman, E., Or, I.: The quadratic assignment problem in the context of the printed circuit board assembly process. Comput. Oper. Res. **34**, 163–179 (2007)
4. Pham, D.T., Ghanbarzadeh, A., Koç, E., Otri, S., Rahim, S., Zaidi, M.: The bees algorithm — a novel tool for complex optimisation problems. In: Pham, D.T., Eldukhri, E.E., Soroka, A.J. (eds.) Intelligent Production Machines and Systems, pp. 454–459. Elsevier Science Ltd., Oxford (2006)
5. Ang, M.C., Ng, K.W., Pham, D.T., Soroka, A.: Simulations of PCB assembly optimisation based on the bees algorithm with TRIZ-inspired operators. In: Zaman, H.B., Robinson, P., Olivier, P., Shih, T.K., Velastin, S. (eds.) IVIC 2013. LNCS, vol. 8237, pp. 335–346. Springer, Cham (2013). https://doi.org/10.1007/978-3-319-02958-0_31
6. Ang, M.C., Pham, D.T., Soroka, A.J., Ng, K.W.: PCB assembly optimisation using the Bees Algorithm enhanced with TRIZ operators. In: IECON 2010 - 36th Annual Conference on IEEE Industrial Electronics Society, pp. 2708–2713 (2010)
7. Ang, M.C., Pham, D.T., Ng, K.W.: Application of the bees algorithm with TRIZ-inspired operators for PCB assembly planning. . In: Soroka, A.J., Pham, D.T., Eldukhri, E.E. (eds.) Proceedings of 5th Virtual International Conference on Innovative Production Machines and Systems Virtual Conference (I*PROMS 2009), pp. 405–410. Whittles Publishing, Cardiff Unversity, Cardiff (2009)
8. Ball, M.O., Michael, J.M.: Sequencing of insertions in printed circuit board assembly. Oper. Res. **36**, 192–201 (1988)
9. Chan, D., Mercier, D.: IC insertion: an application of the travelling salesman problem. Int. J. Prod. Res. **27**, 1837–1841 (1989)
10. Leu, M.C., Wong, H., Ji, Z.: Planning of component placement/insertion sequence and feeder setup in PCB assembly using genetic algorithm. ASME J. Electron. Pack. **115**, 424–432 (1993)
11. Kirkpatrick, S., Gelatt, C., Vecchi, M.: Optimization by simulated annealing. Science **220**, 671–680 (1983)
12. Pham, D.T., Castellani, M.: The bees algorithm: Modelling foraging behaviour to solve continuous optimization problems. Proc. Inst. Mech. Eng. C J. Mech. Eng. Sci. **223**, 2919–2938 (2009)
13. Castellani, M., Otri, S., Pham, D.: Printed circuit board assembly time minimisation using a novel bees algorithm. Comput. Ind. Eng. **133**, 186–194 (2019)

14. Baronti, L., Castellani, M., Pham, D.: An analysis of the search mechanisms of the bees algorithm. Swarm Evol. Comput. **59**, 100746 (2020)
15. Ercin, O., Coban, R.: Comparison of the artificial bee colony and the bees algorithm for PID controller tuning. In: 2011 International Symposium on Innovations in Intelligent Systems and Applications, pp. 595–598 (2011)
16. Orloff, M.A.: Inventive thinking through TRIZ : a practical guide (2006)
17. Altshuller, G.S., Fedossev, U., Shulyak, L.: 40 principles, Triz keys to technical innovation. Technical Innovation Center, Worcester, Mass (2002)
18. Ilevbare, I.M., Probert, D., Phaal, R.: A review of TRIZ, and its benefits and challenges in practice. Technovation **33**, 30–37 (2013)
19. Ahmad, S.A., Ng, K.W., Airdzaman, S.H., Ang, M.C., Suliano, S.B.: Improving queuing system with limited resources using TRIZ and arena simulation. Int. J. Innov. Technol. Explor. Eng. (IJITEE) **9** (2020)
20. Ang, M.C., Ng, K.W., Ahmad, S.A., Wahab, A.N.A.: Using TRIZ to generate ideas to solve the problem of the shortage of ICT workers. Appl. Mech. Mater. **564**, 733–739 (2014)
21. Kahraman, C. (ed.): Computational Intelligence Systems in Industrial Engineering : With Recent Theory and Applications. Atlantis Press, Pari (2012)

A Model for Teaching and Learning Programming Subjects in Public Secondary Schools of Malaysia

Faridah Hani Mohamed Salleh[1]([✉]) [iD], Deshinta Arrova Dewi[2], Nurul Azlin Liyana[3], and Naziffa Raha Md Nasir[4]

[1] Department of Foundation and Diploma Studies, College of Computing & Informatics, Universiti Tenaga Nasional, Jalan IKRAM-UNITEN, Kajang, Selangor, Malaysia
faridahh@uniten.edu.my

[2] INTI International University, Persiaran Perdana BBN, Putra Nilai, 71800 Nilai, N. Sembilan, Malaysia
deshinta.ad@newinti.edu.my

[3] College of Graduate Studies, Universiti Tenaga Nasional, Jalan IKRAM-UNITEN, Kajang, Selangor, Malaysia

[4] Department of Computing, College of Computing and Informatics, Universiti Tenaga Nasional, Jalan IKRAM-UNITEN, Kajang, Selangor, Malaysia
naziffa@uniten.edu.my

Abstract. In recent years, more and more countries have included programming as one of the subjects in the national education curriculum. However, comparatively less attention has been paid to reviewing the methodologies and tools, according to our observations. This paper aims to review methods and tools that have been applied in higher education levels and identify the most effective one to be applied in teaching and learning programming in high schools. The possible methods to be applied in high schools are highly dependent on the education landscape of the country itself. Therefore, the methods proposed in this paper are identified by considering education issues in Malaysia such as language of communication, digital divide and schools' teaching and learning time. We conducted an interview with the teachers and students to identify the real problems of teaching and learning programming in Malaysia public secondary schools. From the interview and extensive review of literature, possible model elements have been identified. We found that teaching and learning programming at high school level should incorporate the following main features; incorporating computational thinking, IDE-centric learning, relation to life-example, reiterative method and spaced exercise, effective questioning, support multi-language and self-study. However, all of these recommendations should be studied for their effectiveness by conducting a detail testing. Thus, we conducted an expert evaluation by using a learning management system (LMS) that we created specifically to represent our suggested model components. The findings gathered from the expert evaluation confirms on the needs to give high priority to the following model components; reiterative and chunking, effective questioning, designing instructional materials, followed by adaptive learning, language and self-study. The components identified during the research process that are worthwhile to continue to prove their level of efficiency are AI, support think-pair, competition-based, gamification, mobile

© Springer Nature Switzerland AG 2021
H. Badioze Zaman et al. (Eds.): IVIC 2021, LNCS 13051, pp. 362–373, 2021.
https://doi.org/10.1007/978-3-030-90235-3_32

friendly and low usage of system resources (small memory footprint or RAM usage and low CPU usage). It is hoped that our model can be adopted by public secondary schools in Malaysia to produce the best tools or methods for teaching programming. Finally, we discuss the implications of our findings and suggest future research directions that could develop a more holistic understanding of this pedagogical technique.

Keywords: Programming · Secondary schools

1   Introduction

Programming has been introduced in Malaysia schools since 2016, starting with year six primary school. In a Malaysia public education system, year six of primary school is referred as a student aged 12 years old. A subject named Information and Communication Technology is taught as a subject for preparation for high school. In 2017, under the new curriculum for lower secondary students, the ministry introduced two subjects called Basic Computer Science for form 3 student who is a student aged 15 years old. The fourth-form and fifth-form students (age 16 and 17) can further study coding in a subject named Science Computer, which is an elective subject which is only be taken by the schools that are equipped with computer lab and have a teacher with a computer science qualification.

Our proposed model can be used by schools and Malaysia institute of teaching education to train teachers in programming languages. Our proposed model can also be used to train new graduates to reinforce basic knowledge before entering the industry. Apart from programming subjects, our model can be extended its usage to teach pure Science subjects that are technical in nature and require students to remember certain basic concepts. Several technology-based learning has been widely applied to the teaching of programming subjects [1, 2]. However, to the best of our knowledge, until today, there is no one dedicated tool or system has been built for schools in Malaysia. Our model can be developed to be a proprietary in-house solution. By having our own in-house design system, we can keep the assurance of customization and meet local needs. In terms of commercialization value, the output of this project can be offered to the other learning institutions of similar characteristics and challenges. With the uncertainty of the Covid-19 pandemic, our nation has embraced a new norm by adopting online technology, especially in the education industry. Thus, we strongly believe our proposed model will be able to produce the next generation of technology talents starting from secondary education level.

This paper presents results of interview conducted with the teachers and students in order to identify the existing problems of teaching and learning programming of the national secondary schools' students in Malaysia. Then, from the interview findings, we formulate a learning programming model by maintaining the existing national education setting. The feasibility of the proposed model components was simulated using a LMS that we crafted specifically for the testing purpose. An expert who is the teacher that teaches the subject was involved as the respondent. Our research contributes in such a way that a design of an in-house solution has been created to tailor to the specific needs of the national school students and teachers.

2 Students' Perception and Teachers' Experience in Teaching Programming Subjects

2.1 Interview and Field Study

The techniques of interview and field study were chosen to be conducted in this research because these techniques are best to be applied for our research that aims to identify the real problems of teachers and students in the field of programming. The participants of this study involve two teachers who taught Basics of Computer Science subject for form 3 students and two students that studied Basics of Computer Science. The participants were from one of the secondary schools located in Kelantan, Malaysia. As part of the procedure, we prepared a formal letter to the school principal prior to the to interview days. This procedure was very crucial as the country was still in the COVID-19 pandemic season, where the school restricts number of visitors going to the school. A list of questionnaires for teachers and students were prepared as a guide of the interview. Some short briefing was given via phone calls to explain to the school principal on the purpose of the research and the for the interview session to be recorded. The interview took place around the school, computer lab and teacher's office. The interviews were audio recorded based on the permissions given by the participants. All the recorded data obtained from the interviews were transcribed manually into text. In average, the interview was completed in 40 min for each of the teachers. The student's interview session was conducted after the school hours to avoid interruption to their learning session at school. The findings of our interview are divided into 5 sub-sections as shown in Sect. 3 of this paper.

3 Interview Findings

3.1 Language of Communication and Perception Towards Programming

Our study found that students and teachers were aware that there is a connection and interdependence between Basics of Computer Science subject (form 3) and Computer Science (form 4 & 5). However, since not all students master the Basics of Computer Science, this causes students not to be interested in taking Computer Science in form 4. Based on the interview conducted with the teachers, we found out that most of the form 3 students also did not want to continue taking Computer Science subject in their next year of study because they already knew that this subject was not easy to get a good grade based on their experience taking computer-science related subject before. The students we met also stated that they had a perception that computer-related subjects were difficult. Currently, most of the national schools use Bahasa Malaysia in school for teaching Computer Science subject. The students will start to show the signs of unexciting when they are required to search for additional information pertaining to programming by themselves. The difference between language used in schools and the language used later when to search for information has caused some problems because many of the external online resources are in English. Furthermore, programming has many special nouns such as arrays, pointers, passing values, which if you want to do an Internet search, these keywords need to be known. This issue becomes more prominent due to the gap in English proficiency between urban and rural students as been reported previously reported in [3].

Thus, our model suggests for using two languages with highlighted programming keywords for students to make additional searches. To change the perception of programming that is said to be difficult, our proposed model is built by selecting specific concepts to show the concept graphically.

One of the teachers agreed that Basics of Computer Science subject and Science Computer subject are interesting subjects that shall be learning by school students in Malaysia: *'The science computer-related subjects are very good to be introduced in school but students should be interested in the subject so that they do not get bored quickly.'* However, the teacher said that the syllabus used is a bit difficult for school students. The following quote summarized the information: *'The topic of form 3 is a little difficult. For example, in a topic of form 4 students, there are PHP questions almost on par with the university'*. Based on the interview conducted with the schools, we found out that the school selects students to take Basics of Computer Science subject based on the academic achievement of science and mathematics subjects. As for the teaching strategy, we found that the basics of computational thinking are taught at an early stage. Pseudocode and algorithm development are taught either in the lab or in the classroom. As for the teacher's training, the teacher said that even though there are courses provided for the teachers, the teachers learn programming by themselves. They also use the knowledge gained from university before.

3.2 Digital Divide and Computer Facilities

A research by [4] addresses there are certain places in Malaysia that have poor Internet service. As a developing region, in Southeast Asia, many students in Malaysia are from economically vulnerable families. Their access to computers is limited to school-provided computer labs, and many do not have access to unlimited Internet on their mobile devices.

Currently, Computer Science subjects are only offered by schools that have computer labs and teachers trained in IT. Or in other words, programming is just an optional skill or value-added for students rather than a compulsory subject. Our interview found that, despite having a computer lab, the number of computers was insufficient and students had to share computers. A teacher said that she normally encouraged the students to use their own laptop to complete the project: *'I encourage students to use their own laptops to make it easier for students to complete their projects because the school does not have enough computer equipment and time to teach programming is limited.'*

3.3 Quality Digital Content

In Malaysia, text books are used as the main teaching and learning resources. The contents of the textbooks produced by the ministry have undergone many evolutions. As been previously reported in [5], the content of the book is now very interesting. According to the teacher: *'For exercise, we use reference books. However, textbooks are mandatory because textbooks have followed the Co-Curriculum and Assessment Standard Document (DSKP) issued by the co-curriculum development center. The textbook syllabus is a guide for teachers to teach because we cannot teach students who are still new with a program with a syllabus with too high a level of difficulty.'*

In total, students learn 4 different programming languages (Python, XHTML, CSS, PHP) in different years. Through interviews with teachers, students were found not to be able to feel the excitement of a programming before switching to another programming language. The following quote summarized the information: *'Science Computer subject thought in form 4 and form 5 are different from Basics of Computer Science subject taught to form 3 students especially at programming part. Students of Basics of Computer Science learns Scratch, HTML and Python, whereas form 4 students learn JAVA. As for project of form 4 students, they are required to use PHP and CSS. When all these topics are mixed, it is a bit confusing to teach to students.'*

Students' interest in practical versus theory was obtained through the following quote: *'Students like to learn practical for programming as opposed to theoretical topics students quickly get bored. Nevertheless, theory needs to be taught before the practice of reason to explain the concept of programming. For example, problem analysis. I explained the theory first, even though it was boring to the students because they didn't see it. Students prefer the things they see. So, I would ask students to try programming on their own and learn from those errors.'*

Our study also found that students had difficulty completing projects that contributed a certain percentage to the overall score due to lack of practical skills. Despite of all these difficulties, teachers take the initiative to teach programming on Fridays or weekends to ensure no students are left behind. Based on the answers from the students, they said they rely a lot on friends to learn and like to use YouTube to learn on their own.

3.4 Teaching and Learning Time

Programming requires hands-on learning. Students are usually able to improve their skills as they are exposed to these new concepts progressively. However, since students need to study some other subjects, the time allotted for Computer Science subjects are very limited. Due to the time constraints, teachers have to work hard to finish the syllabus and students struggle to also focus on other subjects. Teacher said that they are interested to use a tool for teaching programming. However, they do not know what tools to use. As for experience teaching in computer lab, the teacher said: *'When students share a computer to do practical programming exercises, one student will do it, and another will just look without participate in the learning process. Software to control student activities in computer labs is no longer available. Before this there was NetSupport.'*

4 Identifying the Proposed Model Components

4.1 Methodology

Detail study on the syllabus of secondary schools Computer-Science related subjects were conducted by gathering the text books and reference books. More than 15 books had been studied. This study is important as the proposed model will be applied to school level programming later. An interview and field study were conducted with teachers and students to get an overview of teaching programming landscape in Malaysia and identifying the real problems facing by them. The model components were identified by performing an extensive literature review. The findings of interview and field study were taken into consideration. A prototype, which in this case is a LMS created using Moodle (with extra features) was developed to simulate the model design. Pilot test was conducted prior to the actual expert evaluation. The original plan was to include only model elements in LMS without any teaching materials. However, the pilot study disclosed the fact that respondent was unable to proceed with completing exercises without went through notes. Meaning that, they did not want to learn by studying text book and then shifted to LMS. After LMS was completed, an empirical study via an expert evaluation was conducted to quantify the efficiency level of the proposed model. The teacher is a respondent of an expert evaluation that aims to test the proposed model components that were embedded into the LMS before. Lastly, analysis and conclusion were made based on all the research activities conducted before (Fig. 1).

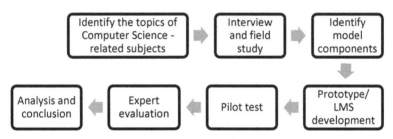

Fig. 1. Research methodology

5 Expert Evaluation

We conduct an additional experiment with the expert to support the findings of the interview conducted before. In this experiment, one teacher from one of the secondary schools in Kelantan has been chosen to be the respondent of our experiment. The respondent was given an access to our LMS, which is Moodle that has been specially created by incorporating all the possible components for our model. Our respondent took about 48 min to complete study and answering questions of two major topics in our LMS. Since our expert evaluation session occurred during pandemic season, respondent was unable to spend more time to avoid direct interactions occurring over a long period of time. The objectives of this expert evaluation session are (1) to identify the components required to formulate model for developing programming teaching tool for secondary school students in Malaysia, (2) to assess the feasibility of the proposed model components and (3) to involve experts that are working in the environment that the model will be applied in reality.

Moodle (with advanced features) has been chosen as a tool used for experiment because of its flexibility in creating an adaptive learning module, without restricting too much on the flow of learning and it is also a feature-rich software platform that runs on any computer server. The activities conducted using LMS was recorded and the video can be accessed from: https://tinyurl.com/programmingModelExperiment. Refer to https://tinyurl.com/appendixLMS for some screen captures of our LMS pages and the mapping between materials included in LMS and the proposed model components. The LMS was designed with an intention of testing the feasibility of model components without realizing by the respondent.

5.1 Responses from the Respondent

We required the respondent to navigate to all the pages in our LMS till complete. This is important as we want the respondent to experience the possible model components by themselves before answering more detail questions. The respondent answered quizzes that had been categorized and designed in such a way that the respondent would be excited to use IDE to identify the answer. We observed the actions performed by the respondent when navigating through the LMS. Table 1 shows the questions we asked after the session and responses given by our respondent. The questions marked with asterisks requires the respondent to rate the response in a scale of 5; 1- Do not agree, 2- Slightly agree, 3- Somehow agree, 4- Agree, 5- Very agree.

Table 1. Interview questions and the responses

Question	Responses
1. I realize that the questions are designed in such a way that the difficulty level increases as you progress forward?	Very agree **
2. At which part of Moodle make you realize that adaptive learning is being applied?	I do not realize that adaptive learning is being applied
3. How does the categorization help you to understand the lesson?	Aim high because I want to achieve highest level (difficult level)
4. Did you use the compiler when Moodle require you to do so? What is the reason of use?	Yes. Use compiler to try the given program example
5. After using Moodle, which language you preferred?	Dual language
6. The usage of compiler helps me to understand programming more	Very agree **
7. The usage of practical-type of questions helps me to understand programming more	Agree **
8. What do you think of asking questions with similar concepts repeatedly?	My understanding of the topics has been strengthened
9. What do you think of asking questions with similar concepts repeatedly?	My understanding of the topics has been strengthened

(*continued*)

Table 1. (*continued*)

Question	Responses
10. Did you realize that question with similar concepts were asked before?	Yes
11. How do you find the usage of English in certain keywords in Moodle?	It helps me to remember
12. Which video do you prefer?	Video uploaded by someone else
13. The usage of real-life examples helps me to remember the information	Agree **
14. The examples provided in the computational thinking lesson help me to link the examples with a program	Very agree **
15. Which part of the computational thinking lesson that you think help students to understand programming? (May choose maximum up to two answers)	The real life examples The presentation of the notes (colours, font, pictures)

5.2   Summary of the Findings from Experiment and Model Formulation

Firstly, we found that expert evaluation shall include real users from both categories; teacher and student. Testing with limited testers or respondents are insufficient to prove the effectiveness of the proposed methods. The current situation of the pandemic further limits the duration of sessions with respondents. Secondly, customized functions of LMS shall be developed instead of using a readily available one. Complex features such as adaptive learning requires custom-made system to avoid unnecessary complex system. Competition-based or goal-oriented concept shall be applied because we noticed that the respondent was looking for a reward or major goal but was unable to find one.

System to be developed later shall be user-friendly and has up-to-date design. When plain design was used, the respondent did not feel interested to further explore. Our respondent stated that she was interested in the design we used on the LMS. During a pilot test, we discovered that teaching contents shall be included because a self-study without teaching contents was inefficient. The tester got stuck even from beginning when there were no teaching notes provided. Dual language shall be applied for programming subject as majority of the online programming resources use English. Many argue that, having many components in the model to be implemented by the programming teaching system is good. However, we do not agree with that statement because having too many components will cause the system to be too heavy and require high -performance computers that may not be affordable by all, especially the low-income family. Referring to the Table 2 shown below, the statements with double asterisks were very much agreed by our respondent. The italicized statements were agreed by our respondent but the level of agreement was not as strong as the statements with double asterisks.

We conclude that these italicized components are required for the model but not at the highest level of priority. It is worth discussing these interesting facts revealed by the

Table 2. Summary of the model components and the research activities that discovered them.

Model Components	Literature	Interview	Experiment
A1 Reiterative and chunking Ask the same questions after some time, gradually and eventually form one big concept ** Questions increase of difficulty after mastering the earlier stage of learning **	•	•	•
A2 Adaptive learning Customized learning paths to engage each student	•	•	•
A3 Effective Questioning Categorize into different level of difficulties (easy, moderate, difficult) ** *The usage of practical-type of questions *	•	•	•
A4 Language Use Bahasa Melayu to sync with medium of learning (at school), text books and reference books *Selected keywords in English for easy searching of external resources*	•	•	•
A5 Self-study Learn through exercises only, study using conventional method	•	•	•
A6 Designing instructional materials Encourage the use of compiler to identify answer ** Relation to life-example, continuation between one slide to another ** Incorporating computational thinking **	•	•	•
New Model Components (** efficiency is yet to be tested)	Literature	Interview	Experiment
Artificial Technology in assessing students' performance and adaptive learning	•	•	•
Gamification	•	•	•
Support think-pair	•	•	•
Mobile-friendly	•	•	•
Competition-based	•	•	•
Low usage of system resources (small memory footprint or RAM usage and low CPU usage)	•	•	•

results of several components that we thought important but the experiment proves that these components were not so critical to the formulation of the model. For example, our respondent did not even realize an adaptive learning was applied in our LMS. Adaptive learning which allows the users to begin their lesson from the last point they stopped studying before seems not giving much excitement to the respondent.

However, it may be too early for us to make such conclusion as the respondent may not visibly show the excitement because she was concentrating on the other components of the LMS. In addition, from the recorded screen activities, we found that the respondent did not even have a chance to leave the LMS and came back to continue from the page she left due to time constraint. This could be one of the reasons why the respondent was not aware of the existence of adaptive learning in the LMS.

5.3   Limitations of the Study

The intention of this study is to assess the efficiency of the possible model components and to identify a new component, if any. The teaching approaches described by teachers in this study are not claimed to be representative of all teachers teaching Computer Science-related subjects in Malaysia. One limitation of our study is that the interview and survey were conducted to only one selected school. Interview and experts' evaluation shall be conducted at many more secondary schools from various locations in Malaysia. However, this plan will be able to be implemented if there is a direction from the Minister of Education as getting involvement of teachers and students in study is not easy in Malaysia, especially during movement control order that is imposed due to COVID-19. Thus, this study does not in any way attempt to claim that the findings of this research relate generally to all teachers of Computing. Another limitation in our works involves the issue of effective learning. Currently, we are not able to provide evidence suggested which particular model components are more effective in helping students to learn. Thus, another useful angle following on from this study would be to examine students' own perspectives on how programming is taught. As another area of further investigation, we suggest that more research is carried out on the implementation of these strategies for learning programming and the impact on students' learning. On top of that, there are several newer components that are yet to be tested because we discovered them while

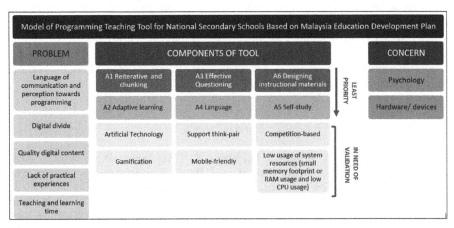

Fig. 2. Model of programming teaching tool for national secondary schools based on Malaysia education development plan.

conducting the current research. The newer possible components are support think-pair [6], mobile-friendly, competition-based, and low usage of system resources (small memory footprint or RAM usage and low CPU usage) (Fig. 2).

6 Conclusion

The formulation of model for learning programming, which later contributes to the development of a proper system or tool for programming subjects is in line with the policy stated in the Malaysia Education Blueprint (MEB) (2013–2025). In the MEB, it is the government's intention to provide students towards becoming a skilled workforce to meet the needs of Industrial Revolution 4.0 and beyond. The MEB has outlined a national long-term plan to introduce programming from year 6 to form 5 students. By having a proper system or tool for programming subjects, our country will be able to produce students with excellent logical thinking who will become skilled workers in high-tech field. Skilled works are experts in their field, and they will help to improve the country's businesses profitability and reputation. The skilled workforce reduces reliance on foreign skilled manpower. The uncertainty scenario caused by the COVID-19 pandemic forces the people to look for other alternatives to gain knowledge. A proper system or tool for programming subjects can prepare teachers and students in facing any future challenges. The interview conducted with the real potential users of this model reveals several important findings. Firstly, the students were unable to do self-study and had to rely completely on the limited teaching hours of Computer Science subject. Next is, digital divide. Not all families have computer at home. In addition, the number computers at schools are still insufficient. Secondly, current learning method is less focused on practical coding, which is the main attraction of Computer Science subjects. Thirdly, in term of language of communication and perception towards programming, where different language used in learning materials than global source of information. Lastly, we found that the teaching and learning time for Computer Science subjects is limited. While conducting the research, we identify several components to be tested in future, which are; support think-pair, mobile-friendly, competition-based, and low usage of system resources; small memory footprint or RAM usage and low CPU usage.

Acknowledgement. This work was carried out within the framework of BOLD2021 project and was sponsored by Universiti Tenaga Nasional.

References

1. Intisar, C.M., Watanobe, Y., Poudel, M., Bhalla, S.: Classification of programming problems based on topic modeling. In: Proceedings of the 2019 7th International Conference on Information and Education Technology, pp. 275–283 (2019)
2. Wang, X.-M., Hwang, G.-J.: A problem posing-based practicing strategy for facilitating students' computer programming skills in the team-based learning mode. Educ. Tech. Res. Dev. **65**(6), 1655–1671 (2017). https://doi.org/10.1007/s11423-017-9551-0
3. Gobel,P., Thang, S.M., Sidhu, G.K., Oon, S.I., Chan, F.Y.: Attributions to success and failure in english language learning: a comparative study of urban and rural undergraduates in Malaysia. Asian Soc. Sci. 9(2) (2013). https://doi.org/10.5539/ass.v9n2p53

4. A. Sharina, A. Latef, D. Frohlich, J. Calic, and N. H. Muhammad, "Teachers' Perceptions towards Implementing Mobile Learning in Rural Malaysia," 2018 http://www.blueoceanstrategy.com/, (2018).
5. Salleh, F.H.M., Dewi, D.A., Liyana, N.A.: Issues and challenges for teaching successful programming courses at national secondary schools of Malaysia. In: Alfred, R., Iida, H., Haviluddin, H., Anthony, P. (eds.) Computational Science and Technology. LNEE, vol. 724, pp. 501–513. Springer, Singapore (2021). https://doi.org/10.1007/978-981-33-4069-5_41
6. Luxton-Reilly, A., et al.: Introductory programming: A systematic literature review, no. December (2018)

GPU-Accelerated Enhanced Marching Cubes 33 for Fast 3D Reconstruction of Large Bone Defect CT Images

Daniel Jie Yuan Chin[1] , Ahmad Sufril Azlan Mohamed[1(✉)] ,
Khairul Anuar Shariff[2,3] , and Kunio Ishikawa[4]

[1] School of Computer Sciences, Universiti Sains Malaysia, 11800 Gelugor, Penang, Malaysia
sufril@usm.my
[2] School of Materials and Mineral Resources Engineering, Universiti Sains Malaysia,
14300 Nibong Tebal, Penang, Malaysia
biokhairul@usm.my
[3] Dental Materials Science and Technology Division, Faculty of Dental Medicine, Airlangga
University, JI. Prof. Dr. Moestopo No. 47, Surabaya 60132, East Java, Indonesia
[4] Department of Biomaterials, Faculty of Dental Science, Kyushu University, 3-1-1 Maidashi,
Higashi-ku, Fukuoka 812-8582, Japan
ishikawa@dent.kyushu-u.ac.jp

Abstract. With the advancement in three-dimensional technologies, three-dimensional reconstruction of medical images serves as reliable assistance for doctors and surgeons in evaluating and diagnosing bone defects. Amongst the existing reconstruction methods, the Marching Cubes algorithm is highly popular in the surface rendering research study. There are many improvements made over the Marching Cubes algorithm, but due to the relatively small image datasets used during evaluation, it is difficult to judge the effectiveness of the improvements on large image datasets and the reconstructed models may not be viewable in lower-end specs digital devices like tablets and smartphones. Thus, an enhancement over the extended Marching Cubes 33 with graphics processing unit acceleration to improve the reconstruction accuracy, execution time, and model portability for large image datasets is proposed in this study. The obtained results show that the proposed enhancement successfully increased the accuracy by 5.29%, decreased the execution time by 11.16%, and decreased the number of vertices and faces by 73.72%. This shows that it is possible to view bone defect models with a high similarity percentage on lower-end spec digital devices and print them out with a three-dimensional printer.

Keywords: Fast 3D reconstruction · Enhanced marching cubes 33 · Large CT images

1 Introduction

Three-dimensional (3D) reconstruction is the process of visualizing a set of two-dimensional (2D) images in its equivalent 3D form. The 3D profile is captured and

© Springer Nature Switzerland AG 2021
H. Badioze Zaman et al. (Eds.): IVIC 2021, LNCS 13051, pp. 374–384, 2021.
https://doi.org/10.1007/978-3-030-90235-3_33

visualized as a 3D model in a 3D space. 3D reconstruction plays an important role in visualizing bone defects in the medical field. It has been proven that 3D models can improve the visualization and diagnosis of bone defects [1]. In this specific study, 3D reconstruction methods are applied on a set of 2D micro-computed tomography (CT) bone defect image slices so that the 3D model of the bone defect can be visualized.

There are two main subdomains in 3D reconstruction, namely surface rendering and volume rendering. Surface rendering allows the 3D data to be visualized as a stack of isosurfaces formed through triangulation of vertices and faces whereas volume rendering allows the volume visualization of the 3D data. Between the two main subdomains, surface rendering is selected to visualize the bone defects. This is because by extracting and rendering the mesh from the volumetric data into a 3D solid object, which can be 3D printed, the structure and shape of the bone defects can be visualized and studied effectively.

There are many existing algorithms under the surface rendering technique, one of them is the Marching Cubes algorithm, which is a popular surface rendering technique in the 3D reconstruction domain due to its simplicity in implementation and fast computation with parallel processing. However, the ambiguity issue affects the reconstruction accuracy, which leads to the generation of redundant triangular faces, affecting the overall 3D model size and portability. Even though this issue is actively addressed like the Marching Cubes 33 [2] and the extended Marching Cubes 33 [3], the image datasets used are relatively smaller in size, which may question the effectiveness of the improvements. Also, the 3D model portability is rarely addressed. Hence, this paper aims to improve the reconstruction accuracy, execution time, and portability of the 3D models between higher-end spec digital devices and lower-end spec digital devices like tablets and smartphones for large image datasets.

The large image dataset used in this study is a rabbit femur defect micro-CT dataset collected from Dr Khairul Anuar Shariff, School of Materials and Mineral Resources Engineering, Universiti Sains Malaysia, using SkyScan 1076. A sample image is as illustrated in Fig. 1. The dataset consists of 952 images with every image slice having 1400 dots per inch (DPI) horizontal resolution and 1400 DPI vertical resolution. It is preprocessed through thresholding, the Canny edge detector, and area opening before the data is reconstructed into a 3D model using a laptop with 12 gigabytes (GB) random-access memory (RAM). The 3D models are then loaded to a smartphone with 4 GB RAM for visualization purposes using a 3D visualization application.

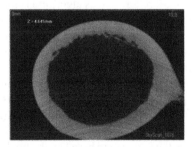

Fig. 1. Sample rabbit femur defect micro-CT image slice.

The rest of the paper is organized into several sections. In Sect. 2, the Marching Cubes, the Marching Cubes 33 and the extended Marching Cubes 33 are reviewed. In Sect. 3, the proposed enhancement over the extended Marching Cubes 33 (GPU-accelerated enhanced Marching Cubes 33) is elaborated. In Sect. 4, the obtained results on the reconstruction accuracy, execution time, and model portability are discussed. In Sect. 5, a conclusion is made about the work. This is followed by an acknowledgement and a list of references made in this paper.

2   Marching Cubes and Marching Cubes 33

The original Marching Cubes algorithm [4] first divides the input 3D volumetric data into n number of cubes with each cube representing a unit on isosurface. The defined n number of cubes are then placed between every two surfaces as elucidated in the 3D volumetric data.

When a cube is placed between two surfaces, the vertices of the cube are labelled as follows: a vertex is labelled as 1 when it falls within the boundary of the target object whereas the same vertex will be labelled as 0 when it is otherwise. Based on the labelling of all eight vertices, the index of the cube can be calculated and compared with the predefined lookup table consisting of various cube configurations. The index is then used to retrieve the configuration of the labelled cube.

In the original Marching Cubes algorithm, the cube configurations are categorized into 15 unique patterns identified by the authors [4]. The cube configuration consists of edges intersected by the vertices labelled as 1. In the triangulation step, the midpoint of the edges serves as vertices of the triangular faces. Finally, the algorithm marches on to the next cube in place.

The advantage of the Marching Cubes algorithm is the support for parallel processing. As each cube can be processed independently of one another, the overall reconstruction time can be reduced by processing the cubes in parallel. However, the number of triangular faces increases greatly when the size of the 3D volumetric data increases as well. This leads to bigger 3D models, affecting their portability between higher-end spec digital devices and lower-end spec digital devices. Also, ambiguity issue exists which leads to the formation of holes on the surfaces in certain cube configuration combinations. Despite that, the Marching Cubes algorithm is still a popular 3D reconstruction algorithm in recent years. For example, it is used in assisting the diagnosis of lumbar intervertebral disk herniation [5].

An improvement over the Marching Cubes algorithm is introduced by redefining all the 15 cube configurations into 33 cube configurations, which is named Marching Cubes 33 [2]. This improvement is introduced to cover the majority of the complex trilinear function of topology cases, effectively addressing the ambiguity issue on not just the surface but also within the cube itself [2]. The Marching Cubes 33 is further extended in a recent study by grouping all 33 cube configurations into 3 different categories during the triangulation step [3]. Through the three triangulation groupings, an extended Marching Cubes 33 triangulation is performed to support all complex cube topology cases in trilinear interpolation.

The groupings defined by the authors are based on the final shape of the isosurface in the cube after deformation. For deformed isosurface resembling a disc without requiring an additional point to support the representation, it is grouped into the simple leaves triangulation group [3]. For a deformed isosurface resembling a cylinder, it is grouped into the tunnel triangulation group [3]. For deformed isosurface resembling a disc requiring an additional vertex in the center of the cube to ensure its correct representation, it is grouped into the interior point leaves triangulation group [3]. After verifying all the connectivity between vertices and grouping all the cubes into any of the three categories, triangulation is performed following every category's triangulation rules and processes.

The advantage of the extended Marching Cubes 33 is the triangulation quality of the reconstructed 3D models are vastly improved due to the support for complex cube topology cases which solves the ambiguity issue [3]. However, it is noticed that the image dataset used in the study are relatively small, which questions the performance of the algorithm when large image datasets are used in testing. It is also noticed that there is no mention of whether the execution time is improved.

3 GPU-Accelerated Enhanced Marching Cubes 33

In this study, an enhancement over the extended Marching Cubes 33 is proposed to improve not just the reconstruction accuracy, but also the execution time and the portability of the reconstructed 3D models. The flowchart of the proposed enhancement is as illustrated in Fig. 2.

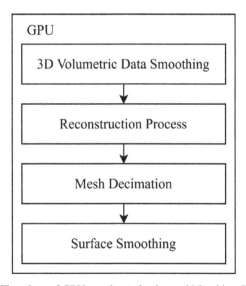

Fig. 2. Flowchart of GPU-accelerated enhanced Marching Cubes 33.

The proposed enhancement included three additional steps in addition to the extended Marching Cubes 33 algorithm. The first additional step is the smoothing of the 3D volumetric data before the reconstruction process. 3D data smoothing is a commonly applied technique in removing noises from the volumetric data itself. Noises, in this context, refer to the outliers in the 3D volumetric data which leads to wrong triangulation. Wrong triangulation often leads to surface mesh with redundant triangular faces and sharp edges, affecting the reconstruction accuracy. In this proposed enhancement, a 3-by-3-by-3 Gaussian filter is chosen as the smoothing method due to its simple implementation. Also, the result of the smoothing is independent of the starting point and the direction of the smoothing, which means better control over the smoothing result.

The reconstruction process is where the extended Marching Cubes 33 take place. The input is the smoothed 3D volumetric data from the 3D volumetric data smoothing step, and the output is a rendering of the reconstructed 3D model, a list of vertices and a list of faces. The rendering time is also recorded as part of the execution time evaluation. The list of vertices and faces are then used in the next step, which is the mesh decimation.

The second additional step is the mesh decimation, or in this case, faces and vertices decimation after the reconstruction step. Mesh decimation, or also known as mesh simplification, reduces the number of triangular patches, or in this case, the faces and vertices, resulting in a smaller 3D model size. This is achieved by manipulating the vertices' position which removes duplicated vertices. While mesh decimation is an effective step in improving the portability of the 3D models between higher-end spec digital devices and lower-end spec digital devices, it often leads to deformed surfaces, which affects the overall view of the 3D model when visualized. In this study, remeshing applied to the whole 3D model with a reduction factor specifying the percentage of the vertices and faces that should be maintained is implemented for the mesh decimation step. After computing the contraction cost between two vertices by combining the error matrices calculated for both vertices, the vertices are collapsed one by one, and vertices affected by this contraction will also be collapsed. The error metric is based on the quadric error metric [6]. This is repeated until the reduction factor is met. Two additional conditions are added to the remeshing rule, which preserves the mesh boundary and the vertex normal. This is to prevent extreme mesh deformation.

The third additional step is mesh smoothing after the mesh decimation step. Similar to 3D volumetric data smoothing, the purpose of mesh smoothing is to improve the visual representation of the surface meshes by manipulating the vertices' position. This results in reduced noises, or outliers in vertices, and smoother surface meshes. In this proposed enhancement, the Laplacian smoothing with preserved surface meshes is applied for the mesh smoothing step to prevent further deformation of the 3D model. The vertices are adjusted towards the average position of their neighboring vertices only if their new position still lies on the surface mesh. This is achieved by making sure that the displacement angle of the new position from its original position does not exceed a specified threshold. This is repeated for i number of iterations. It is recommended that the threshold is kept to a smaller degree. In this study, the threshold is kept at $0.5°$, which is half of the maximum recommended threshold.

Finally, the whole reconstruction method, which includes the three additional steps namely 3D volumetric data smoothing, mesh decimation, and surface smoothing is executed with a graphics processing unit (GPU) to speed up the execution and rendering time of the 3D model. The GPU used in this work is the NVIDIA Geforce RTX 2060, which uses the Turing microarchitecture, supports core speed of up to 1680 megahertz (MHz) when boosted and memory speed of up to 14 gigabits per second (Gbps), memory bandwidth of up to 336 GB per second, and memory type of Graphics Double Data Rate 6 (GDDR6).

4 Results and Discussion

The reconstruction accuracy is evaluated by calculating the similarity percentage between the reconstructed model and the original model. Due to hardware limitations, 2D black and white images are captured for the 3D models at the same orientation and compared with the original 2D images in the image dataset which serves as the ground truth. Root mean squared error (RMSE) and structural similarity index measure (SSIM) are used to evaluate the similarity between both images. RMSE is used instead of mean squared error (MSE) as MSE can be easily biased towards higher values. The execution time is evaluated by recording the time taken, in seconds, for the whole reconstruction and rendering process five times and the time taken is averaged out. The execution time does not include the time taken for loading the image stack, image preprocessing, and exporting the 3D models. The model portability is evaluated by calculating the percentage decrease in the number of vertices and faces, and the smoothness of the 3D model manipulation and visualization on a smartphone.

For the results in Table 1, the extended Marching Cubes 33 will be represented as MC33, the extended Marching Cubes 33 accelerated with GPU as MC33GPU, and the proposed enhanced Marching Cubes 33 as EMC33GPU with different parameter values combination, namely the reduction factor for the remeshing and the number of iterations for the Laplacian smoothing.

There are a few things to be noted on the obtained results tabulated in Table 1. Firstly, reduction factors of 0.0 and 0.1 are excluded in this study as the reconstructed model is unable to be opened and viewed. Secondly, reduction factors 0.8 and 0.9 are also excluded in this study as the reconstructed models have the same number of vertices and faces as the reconstructed models with a 0.7 reduction factor. Thirdly, reduction factor 1.0 is excluded in this study as there is no reduction in the number of vertices and faces. Any reduction factors that do not fall in the range of 0.0 and 1.0 are rejected as the values are out of the parameter's acceptable value range. Lastly, for the number of Laplacian smoothing iterations, 100 and any number higher than that are excluded in this study as the results similarity percentages showed no further increase and the increase in execution time is very huge. As the execution time is also evaluated in this study, it is determined that any parameter value combination that leads to an increase in execution time but zero increase in similarity percentages is ignored. Negative-numbered and 0 iterations are rejected as it is impossible to run Laplacian smoothing with zero and negative iteration.

Using the obtained results in Table 1, the best parameter value combination is selected by first computing the percentage of increase in similarity percentage for RMSE and SSIM, percentage decrease in execution time, and percentage decrease in vertices and faces. The calculated percentages are divided by 100 to obtain the percentages in decimal form. This is followed by multiplying the percentage of increase/decrease in decimal form with a weighted score. The weightage score is assigned based on the focus of the enhancement. In this case, the weightage score assigned to reconstruction accuracy is 0.6,

Table 1. Results for MC33, MC33GPU, and EMC33GPU.

Methods	Reduction factor	Iterations	RMSE (%)	SSIM (%)	Reconstruct (s)	Rendering (s)	Faces	Vertices
MC33	–	–	69.48	85.47	72.24	14.23	5837093	2798075
MC33GPU	–	–	69.48	85.47	66.97	14.64	5837093	2798075
EMC33GPU	0.2	1	74.09	88.84	72.14	0.36	1503286	750127
EMC33GPU	0.2	5	74.08	88.83	72.84	0.40	1503286	750127
EMC33GPU	0.2	10	74.08	88.83	73.33	0.39	1503286	750127
EMC33GPU	0.2	25	74.08	88.83	77.62	0.42	1503286	750127
EMC33GPU	0.2	50	74.08	88.83	85.69	0.40	1503286	750127
EMC33GPU	0.3	1	74.14	88.83	73.84	0.45	2254929	1125945
EMC33GPU	0.3	5	74.16	88.81	75.58	0.41	2254929	1125945
EMC33GPU	0.3	10	74.16	88.81	77.64	0.47	2254929	1125945
EMC33GPU	0.3	25	74.16	88.81	84.59	0.43	2254929	1125945
EMC33GPU	0.3	50	74.16	88.81	94.63	0.40	2254929	1125945
EMC33GPU	0.4	1	74.14	88.84	74.06	0.42	3006572	1501400
EMC33GPU	0.4	5	74.18	88.82	76.28	0.44	3006572	1501400
EMC33GPU	0.4	10	74.19	88.82	79.14	0.41	3006572	1501400
EMC33GPU	0.4	25	74.19	88.82	87.29	0.39	3006572	1501400
EMC33GPU	0.4	50	74.19	88.82	91.16	0.44	3006572	1501400
EMC33GPU	0.5	1	74.12	88.83	70.95	1.27	3758215	1876913
EMC33GPU	0.5	5	74.14	88.80	73.42	1.26	3758215	1876913
EMC33GPU	0.5	10	74.15	88.80	73.70	1.28	3758215	1876913
EMC33GPU	0.5	25	74.14	88.78	87.19	1.29	3758215	1876913
EMC33GPU	0.5	50	74.13	88.76	104.06	1.26	3758215	1876913
EMC33GPU	0.6	1	74.12	88.84	71.48	1.98	4509859	2252288
EMC33GPU	0.6	5	74.13	88.83	74.64	2.01	4509859	2252288
EMC33GPU	0.6	10	74.16	88.84	78.58	2.06	4509859	2252288
EMC33GPU	0.6	25	74.18	88.84	90.9	2.04	4509859	2252288
EMC33GPU	0.6	50	74.19	88.84	110.15	2.01	4509859	2252288
EMC33GPU	0.7	1	74.14	88.86	73.37	2.67	4863552	2427460
EMC33GPU	0.7	5	74.17	88.87	76.74	2.61	4863552	2427460
EMC33GPU	0.7	10	74.22	88.88	81.17	2.61	4863552	2427460
EMC33GPU	0.7	25	74.25	88.89	93.78	2.63	4863552	2427460
EMC33GPU	0.7	50	74.28	88.89	115.67	2.62	4863552	2427460

0.3 for the reduction in vertices and faces, and 0.1 for execution time, which totals to 1.0. Execution time is given the lowest weightage score as it is hardware dependent and the execution time obtained per run is not consistent. After multiplying every percentage of increase/decrease in decimal form by the weightage score, the total enhancement score is obtained by adding them up. Parameter value combination with the enhancement score closest to 1.0 is selected for comparison with the original algorithm. The values are tabulated in Table 2.

Table 2. Enhancement score for every parameter value combination.

Reduction factor	1 iteration	5 iterations	10 iterations	25 iterations	50 iterations
0.2	0.2641	0.2631	0.2625	0.2572	0.2473
0.3	0.2226	0.2205	0.2179	0.2094	0.1972
0.4	0.1829	0.1803	0.1769	0.1669	0.1621
0.5	0.1461	0.1431	0.1428	0.1261	0.1054
0.6	0.1052	0.1013	0.0966	0.0816	0.0096
0.7	0.0837	0.0798	0.0747	0.0594	0.0326

Based on the calculated enhancement scores in Table 2, it seems that GPU-accelerated enhanced Marching Cubes 33 with remeshing reduction factor of 0.2 and 1 iteration of Laplacian smoothing is the best parameter combination with the highest enhancement score of 0.2641. From Table 1, it is noticed that the increase in similarity percentages when the reduction factor is increased is only by a very small margin while the number of vertices and faces increased by a very huge margin and the execution time increased as well. Similarly, when the number of Laplacian smoothing iterations increased, the similarity percentages showed very small changes while the execution time greatly increased and the number of vertices and faces remained the same. This means that to achieve a good balance between the increase in reconstruction accuracy, the decrease in execution time and the number of vertices and faces, it is better to use a lower value for Laplacian smoothing iterations and remeshing reduction factor. The reason behind the same number of vertices and faces despite the increase in Laplacian smoothing iteration is because the mesh surface is preserved.

Comparing with original extended Marching Cubes 33 for reconstruction accuracy and reduction in vertices and faces, and with the GPU-accelerated extended Marching Cubes 33 for execution time to prove that the reduction in execution time is not solely due to GPU, the proposed enhancement increased in reconstruction accuracy by an average of 5.29%, reduced the execution time by 11.16%, and reduced the number of vertices and faces by an average of 73.72%. The average percentage increase in the reconstruction accuracy is obtained by averaging out the percentage increase in RMSE and SSIM. The percentage decrease in the execution time is obtained by calculating the percentage decrease in the total execution time, which is the reconstruction time added with the rendering time. The average percentage decrease in the number of vertices and faces is obtained by averaging out the percentage decrease in number of vertices and faces. It is also noted that comparing both models, the proposed enhancement's model can load and manipulate with no major delay, whereas the original algorithm's model loads slowly with delays in manipulation. Besides that, the proposed enhancement's model can be 3D printed at a shorter time than the original algorithm's model with Ultimaker Cura. Screenshots of the 3D models reconstructed using the extended Marching Cubes 33 and the proposed enhancement are elucidated in Fig. 3.

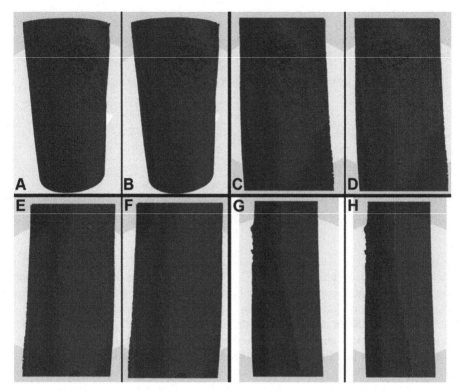

Fig. 3. Tilted view of MC33 3D model (A), tilted view of EMC33GPU 0.2 reduction factor 1 iteration 3D model (B), front view of MC33 3D model (C), front view of EMC33GPU 0.2 reduction factor 1 iteration 3D model (D), back view of MC33 3D model (E), back view of EMC33GPU 0.2 reduction factor 1 iteration 3D model (F), side view of MC33 3D model (G), side view of EMC33GPU 0.2 reduction factor 1 iteration 3D model (H).

The execution time for the extended Marching Cubes 33 and the proposed enhancement (with and without GPU) in GPU and central processing unit (CPU) environments is also tabulated in Table 3. This is to compare the performance of both methods in different environments using the same device.

Table 3. Execution time with GPU and CPU.

Reconstruction methods	Reconstruct (s)	Rendering (s)
Extended Marching Cubes 33 with CPU	72.24	14.23
Extended Marching Cubes 33 with GPU	66.97	14.64
Proposed enhancement with CPU	85.62	0.44
Proposed enhancement with GPU	72.14	0.36

Based on the obtained results, it is noted that the total execution time, which is the reconstruct time added with the rendering time, for the proposed enhancement and the original method ran in CPU environment is roughly the same, with the proposed enhancement only slightly faster than the original method by 0.41 s. This is because although additional processes are involved in the proposed enhancement, the increase in reconstruction time is offset by the decrease in the time needed to load the 3D model. When both methods are performed in a GPU environment, the difference in the total execution time increased to 9.11 s. The reason behind such drastic improvement in the execution time is because the 3D volumetric smoothing, mesh decimation, and surface smoothing steps are all boosted by GPU besides the reconstruction process. Assuming that the extended Marching Cubes 33 is considered as one process and the three additional steps in the proposed enhancement are considered as three processes, while the reconstruction time for the original method is decreased from boosting one process, the reconstruction time for the proposed enhancement is decreased from boosting four processes. While it is proven that the improvement in the execution time is not solely due to GPU, with the proposed enhancement running faster than the original method by 0.41 s in the CPU environment, it is also proven that GPU played a huge role in drastically improving the execution time.

It is also noted that the rendering time is roughly the same when running both methods in GPU and CPU environments. This is because the 3D models are rendered using the native renderer instead of loading the models with 3D rendering software. If the 3D models are rendered with a 3D rendering software and the software is also configured to run in GPU, the rendering time will be drastically improved as well.

5   Conclusion

In conclusion, the proposed enhancement (GPU-accelerated extended Marching Cubes 33 with Gaussian smoothing, remeshing reduction factor of 0.2 and Laplacian smoothing 1 iteration) has successfully increased in reconstruction accuracy by 5.29%, reduced the execution time by 11.16%, and reduced the vertices and faces number by 73.72%. This proved that the proposed enhancement generates 3D models with greater accuracy, at a faster rate, and better portability than the original method. An extension on the proposed enhancement is possible with more different parameters and values combinations and tested with more large image datasets.

Acknowledgement. The authors are grateful to Universiti Sains Malaysia and ASEAN University Network/Southeast Asia Engineering Education Development Network (AUN/SEED-Net) Japan International Cooperation Agency (JICA) project for supporting this documented work through Special Program for Research Against COVID-19 (SPRAC) grant [304/PBA-HAN/6050449/A119].

References

1. Alasal, S.A., Alsmirat, M., Al-Mnayyis, A., Baker, Q.B., Al-Ayyoub, M.: Improving radiologists' and orthopedists' QoE in diagnosing lumbar disk herniation using 3D modeling. Int. J. Electric. Comput. Eng. **11**(5), 4336–4344 (2021)

2. Chernyaev, E.V.: Marching cubes 33: construction of topologically correct isosurfaces. In: GRAPHICON'95, pp. 1–8. Technical Report CERN CN95-17, Saint-Petersburg, Russia (1995)
3. Custodio, L., Pesco, S., Silva, C.: An extended triangulation to the marching cubes 33 algorithm. J. Braz. Comput. Soc. **25**(6), 1–18 (2019)
4. Lorensen, W., Cline, H.: Marching cubes: a high resolution 3D surface construction algorithm. In: SIGGRAPH'87 Proceedings of the 14th Annual Conference on Computer Graphics and Interactive Techniques 1987, vol. 21, no. 4, pp. 163–169. ACM, NY (1987)
5. Al-Mnayyis, A., Alasal, S.A., Alsmirat, M., Baker, Q.B., Alzu'bi, S.: Lumbar disk 3D modeling from limited number of MRI axial slices. Int. J. Electric. Comput. Eng. **10**(4), 4101–4108 (2020)
6. Garland, M., Heckbert, P.S.: Surface simplification using quadric error metrics. In: SIGGRAPH'97 Proceedings of the 24th Annual Conference on Computer Graphics and Interactive Techniques 1997, pp. 209–216. ACM, NY (1997)

Cyber Security & Machine Learning and Digital Innovation

Malware Classification Based on System Call

Mohamad Redza Izudin Abu Zaharin[1] and Shafiza Mohd Shariff[2]([✉])

[1] East Coast Infosec Sdn. Bhd, Petaling Jaya, Selangor, Malaysia
admin@ecinfosecurity.com
[2] Universiti Kuala Lumpur (UniKL) Malaysian Institute of Information Technology,
Kuala Lumpur, Malaysia
shafiza@unikl.edu.my

Abstract. It has always been a never-ending battle between security analysts and malware developers due to the complexity of malware changing as quickly as innovation grows. Current research focuses on the application of machine learning techniques for malware detection due to its ability to combat the malware evolution. Furthermore, malware is hard to identify due to the enormous number of samples and its unknown activities. Therefore, a platform is needed to analyze the malware samples and identify their activities. A comparison between classification models via system calls made by the malware is implemented within the platform that capable of differentiating between a normal program and malware. The development incorporated DRAKVUF and Debian OS. The result is determined by the ability to log and identify the malware activities via system calls based on classification model in order to differentiate between malware and a normal program. In conclusion, the integration of malware analysis techniques and classification techniques will help provide more information to identify and distinguish malware from normal applications.

Keywords: Malware analysis · Malware behaviour classification

1 Introduction

Recent days, we are presented with a lot of advancement in technology. Following with this undeniable fact, the use of technology and people's intellectual properties are prone to attacks or unauthorized access by irresponsible parties. One of its ways includes malware attack. News have also reported that cyber-related events such as hacktivism, cyber warfare, cyber vandalism have deployed malware as one of the attack mechanisms.

The malware attack prevention is becoming popular as the consumers have started to aware on its effects on their computer system. According to Sanders [17], referring to the Verizon's 2018 Breach Investigations Report, it was found that 76% of attackers are driven by the monetary benefits. Behind this percentage, almost 2 billion records are being hacked and these immoral activities are

© Springer Nature Switzerland AG 2021
H. Badioze Zaman et al. (Eds.): IVIC 2021, LNCS 13051, pp. 387–398, 2021.
https://doi.org/10.1007/978-3-030-90235-3_34

affecting enormous number of victims. Following by the breaches, average cost for the data violation has reached 3.86 million, which is calculated as increasing by 6.4% in 2018. While the cost of data breach keeps increasing, the global cost for loss to malware attacks has grown to 2 trillion USD where this total number is estimated to be rising to 6 trillion by 2021.

Malware, or malicious software, is computer code designed to disrupt, disable or take control of a computer system. Extracted from "An Introduction of Malware" book, malware could be defined as all kinds of harmful software which its purpose is to violate one's computer system's while disregards the confidentiality, integrity or availability [21]. Considering that software is a wide dimension to be discussed, malware can also be classified according to its targets and its maliciousness. This kind of definition is also agreed by Milošević [11] in his journal, "History of Malware". He interpreted malware as a software that are invented by perpetrator to interrupt one's system operation in order to do harmful actions towards the system, be it collecting private information or to gain control over one's computer.

Malware comes in many forms, usually hidden or disguised as a benign application in another file. It operates by manipulating technological defects or bugs in hardware, software and operating systems. Malware is different from standard programs in such a way that most of them can spread themselves across the network, remain undetectable, cause changes or harm to the infected machine or network and persistence. Referring to Landage and Wankhade [8], malware can be classified into 7 categories, where these malwares are categorised according on how it attacks and its effects on the system. The categories are virus, worms, trojan horses, spyware, scareware, adware, and lastly botnet. Ozsoy et al. [15] stated that a system can entirely be compromised with only single vulnerability and this shows the importance to invest in finding a better and faster malware detection method so that the infections can be interrupted and contained before the damage becomes a high risk to the victim.

Most malware AV relies on the malware definition stored in the malware identification script, which is a part of the signature recognition technique for static analysis. This signature is the written fixed code inside the malware captured from the antivirus database being discovered and stored. The description file for malware contains the particular signature (a code snippet). When the antivirus program begins scanning, a particular signature is searched for in the files and applications. If no known signature is found in the file, it declares it secure. However, this method is not foolproof.

In regards to this issue, in this paper we make the following contributions:

– developing a sandbox in a virtual machine environment as a testing environment to test out malware for malware detector and gaining information on malware behaviour. This sandbox will help malware analysts to have a safe place to run malicious software without compromising the live environment or live host.

– with all the data gained from the sandbox, the system will be able to classifies and differentiate malware and normal application based on their behaviour via system call.

2   Related Work

Malwares use a similar technique to taint a personal computer (PC) which is dictated by its compose. For example, viruses, spyware or adware and Trojan horse can harm your PC when an individual operates or installed the afflicted program. As the tainted program provides malicious, this kind of contamination may show up through something downloaded from the web or stacked utilizing the PC from removable media. A few sorts of malware can harm a PC when the owner downloaded the malware through the web program by visiting a burdened site. Worms can be particularly tricky, in light of the fact that they can taint a PC without an individual doing anything. At the point when a programmer finds a weakness inside a working framework, they can program software that searches for PCs on the web with this powerlessness and taints them consequently. Frequently, the clearest outward indication of a malware diseases be that the PC ends up noticeably unusual. The PC may crash, reboot suddenly or decelerate with irrational clarification.

Malware detectors take the information from two sources. One info is its malicious behaviour learning. In the detection of anomalies, the opposite of this information comes from the learning stage. Moreover, hypothetically, identification based on anomaly knows what anomaly activity is based on their knowledge. Because anomaly activity subsumes malicious behaviour, anomaly-based detection catches some sense of malevolence. The other information source comes from the programme that is being examined. When the malware detector knows what is considered malicious activity and the software being evaluated, it will use its detection technique to determine whether the software is malicious or benign. Therefore, the malware detector is usually embedded as a part of a complete Intrusion Detection System (IDS).

The malware detector system based on the detection techniques of static analysis and dynamic analysis. Features are extracted from static data for the static analysis techniques whereas, the techniques for dynamic analysis is based on the features extracted from software implementation. Instead of traditional signature generation techniques, data mining and machine learning have been incorporated together with the byte code analysis focused static analysis techniques [6]. Since malware are packaged, encrypted, or embedded on other software, entropy-based byte code analysis techniques have also been proposed to detect such malware [20]. Imported libraries, file headers, external application programming interface (API) calls and string that are present in a static executable file are also other useful static features proposed by Ye et al. [24]. Another feature that uses the authoring dates of the program functions and the control flow information are also useful for malware detection. Using the control flow information, [3] proposed the use of formal semantic to describe common malicious behaviour of a malware.

However, semantically equivalent code detection techniques have been shown to be successful only against unique obfuscations [16]. Furthermore, static analysis techniques based on relatively high-level features such as control flow graphs are constrained by the difficulty of extracting the necessary information. The difficulty faced is due to the situation where malware is designed to complicate the process of deriving the codes due to them being encrypted, compressed or other complex design by the malware authors.

Researchers also studies dynamic analysis techniques to resolve the shortcomings of static analysis techniques. Taint analysis, one of the dynamic analysis, detects malicious activity by monitoring the flow of information [12]. The taint analysis is especially useful for the detection of malware infringement privacy. The technique will be able to identify potentially malicious use of sensitive data and monitor their access. However, taint analysis is high false-positive rate (FPR), have vulnerability to simple countermeasures, and is also having computational overhead, therefore limiting its practical applicability [18].

Hardware performance counters have been used by dynamic analysis techniques to provide information on processor use, such as cache failures [4]. CPU monitoring, memory, network, and application-specific resource use information are some of the useful software performance indicators features for malware detection [13]. Other techniques such as Java Virtual Machine-specific sensors have also been used to detect malicious Java application execution [9]. Mining audit data or monitor registry and file system operations is also another technique for malware infection indicators.

3   Classification of Malware Detection Techniques

3.1   Anomaly-Based Detection

Anomaly-based detection typically takes place in two stages, the field of training (learning) and the detection (monitoring) process. The detector attempts to learn normal behaviour during the training period. A significant benefit of anomaly-based detection is its ability to identify zero-day attacks. Weaver et al. [23] describe zero-day violations as threats that are already hidden by the malware detector. The two fundamental drawbacks of this approach are its high false alarm rate and the difficulty involved in deciding what features will be mastered in the training stage.

- Dynamic Anomaly-based Detection - Data obtained from the execution of the program is used in dynamic anomaly-based detection to detect malicious code. Throughout the detection phase, the system under review was monitored, and anomalies were matched with what was observed during the training phase.
- Static Anomaly-based Detection - A malware detection that uses the characteristics of the program's file structure. This detection technique could be used to recognize malware without allowing it to communicate program execution to the host system.

– Hybrid Anomaly-based Detection - A combination of both dynamic and static anomaly-based detection. This technique has been proposed by Wang et al. [22] to detect the type of malware the researchers depicted as "ghostware."

3.2 Specification-Based Detection

A specification-based detection is a form of anomaly-based detection. The detection method aims to resolve most anomaly-based detection techniques related high false alarm rate. The detection method can also be branched out for specification-based detection. A specification-based detection attempt is made to calculate the requirements for an application or framework, rather than trying to approximate the use of a framework. Identifying all the correct behaviour that any program may demonstrate for protected system or for the program under investigation (PUI) is part of the training for this specification-based detection.

– Dynamic Specification-based Detection - Approaches known as dynamic specification-based using actions found during run-time to assess the maliciousness of the executable.
– Static Specification-based Detection - The structural properties of the PUI is used by this method to assess the level of its maliciousness.
– Hybrid Specification-based Detection

3.3 Signature-Based Detection

Signature-based detection are based on the display of malicious malware behaviour. The pattern of malicious behaviour is often referred to as a signature. The detection system will detect any malware that displays the signature represented on the malware behaviour model. As any information that resides in large quantities requiring power, the signatures will be archived.

– Dynamic Signature-based Detection - The use of distinguishes dynamic signature-based detection only of data gathered during the execution of the PUI to select its maliciousness. The detection model will look for patterns of behaviour that would uncover the program 's real malicious intent.
– Static Signature-based Detection - Inspect the software under investigation for code arrangements that would reveal a malicious target. The goal is to obtain a code that reflects the program 's behaviour that will be known as the malware's signature. This technique provides an estimation of the run-time conduct of the executable under evaluation.

4   Detecting and Classifying Malwares Using Machine Learning

Schultz et al. [19] introduce the concept of data mining to detect malware by using various static malware classification tools. One of the methods, Portable

Executable (PE), uses the DLLs list of binary, function calls, and the number of specific systems calls used by each DLL are the features deployed in the model. The data collection used in this research consisted of 3265 malicious and 1001 benign programmes.

Another technique in machine learning proposed by Nataraj et al. [14] uses image processing methods. Visualising and classifying malwares are combined in the research. The visualisation technique is shown as grayscale images for malware binaries and for the malware classification, K-nearest neighbour with Euclidean distance strategy is used. The researchers compared binary texture analysis to complex investigation analysis that identifies a significant number of malwares in both packed and unpacked samples. However, the approach allows sophisticated attackers to bypass texture analysis by blurring the malicious code.

Kong et al. [7] proposed an automated malware classification system based on cultural malware data. The similarity is measured by applying differentiated distance metric analysis, which clusters malware samples belonging to the same family. All the while it will keep the various clusters slightly apart. The researchers then used a series of classifiers to identify malware in their respective families based on the distances.

5   System Call

System call is a way for programmes to connect to the operating system. A machine programme makes a system call as it asks the kernel of the operating system. System call is used for hardware facilities, to render or execute a value, and to communicate with kernel offers, along with an application and arranging procedures. System calls happen in several ways depending on computer used. The precise type and amount of information varies in line with the procedure system and call. For example, to get a type we have to specify the record of device to use as source and the address and amount of ram buffer into that your source should be read.

There are five (5) distinct kinds of framework calls: process control, file manipulation, device manipulation, information management, and communication. Process control is a working project that ought to be in a position to stop execution either typically or strangely. In the event that the execution is finished unusually, conventionally a dump of memory is considered and can be dissected with a debugger. File manipulation is a system calls such as erase, read and compose. Likewise, there's a need to search for the document highlights, for example, get and set record include. Device manipulation is a movement that a few assets required to perform where they will be conveyed to a client procedure when discovered.

Information management is a system call that exist only to move data between the client program and the working framework. A decent case of this is time, or specific date. The working framework likewise will keep data about every one of its strategies and gives framework call to report these points of interest. In communication, there are two sorts of interprocess correspondence, the message-passing model and the mutual memory. The mutual memory show which message-passing keeps running on the basic letter drop to cross message between techniques. All the while sharing memory to utilize certain framework calls to make and access locales of memory territory had by different process. The two capacities trade data by analysing and writing in the circulated information.

5.1   System Call Tracing

System call traces are a particularly way to obtain behavioural characteristics for malware detection. In-depth accounting of the system calls developed on the host are desirable for malware detection. The system call traces provide details about how precisely running software binds to the host operating system [5].

Two types of events log on system trace are system call inputs, and system call outputs. Information about the processor that comes from the system calls is what considered as the inputs, whereas the outputs are data returned by a system call. Speed of the processor, the nature and strength of computational load, and the number of processor cores are what makes the rate of device calls to the host. Therefore, having the system call tracks obtained on production hosts in real-time is what makes the use of system call monitoring an advantage for malware detection.

6   Methodology

In this study, we will be using classification models to identify malware based on their behaviour. The malware behaviour will be based on the infected host's system call. For this study, the host will do a web browser process trace starting with the development of a web browser tab. The systems calls for these processes ranged from hundreds to hundreds of thousands of systems calls per second. The system calls observed are based by the web browser's related system call input events. Only the first thirty machine trace calls are collected. The call traces from the host, programme, process, and thread levels are gathered. Since we are gathering malware's behaviour information, a sandbox is designed to ensure a safe environment to analyse the malware without harming the host's system.

The sandbox used in this study are designed by installing an operating system (Debian) on Xen Server. The Debian OS needs to build a logical volume for virtual machines (VM). In Windows 7 virtual machine, a logical volume for storage volume is required. After creating a volume, DRAKVUF is installed to successfully capture the device call log for this study. Figure 1 shows the system architecture for the malware analysis sandbox.

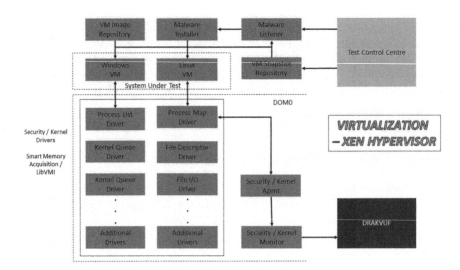

Fig. 1. Sandbox system architecture

DRAKVUF is a dynamic analysis tools that can monitor malware behaviour. Based on the works by Lengyel et al. [10], DRAKVUF is a virtualization-based agentless black-box binary evaluation system. The tool will enable in-depth execution tracing of arbitrary binaries (including operating system), all and never have to mount any special software within the virtual machine used for analysis.

This system use Xen Hypervisor to observe the execution of the samples in a sandbox while collecting its behavioral characteristic, mainly, the system call. It also collects artifacts such as PCAP, unpacked binaries, etc. So that analyst can quickly find the outliers. In the sandbox environment, no in-guest artifact to thwarts malware technique to avoid detection will occur. DRAKVUF's footprint is nearly undetectable from malware's perspective and therefore it serves as a good platform to analyse malware stealthily.

The sandbox system is then injected with the malware code. In this study, two hundred malware codes is used. The malware codes came from 'contagiodump.blogspot.com' site and virusshare.com site. Figure 2 shows the normal application that is free from malware flowchart and Fig. 3 shows the abnormal application flowchart in the system, applications that have been injected with malware code.

The system call log is captured by using DRAKVUF in both two hundred abnormal and one hundred ninety five normal application samplings. This log represents a big part in dataset generation. There are three types of data sets which are training, dev, and test that are used at various stages of development.

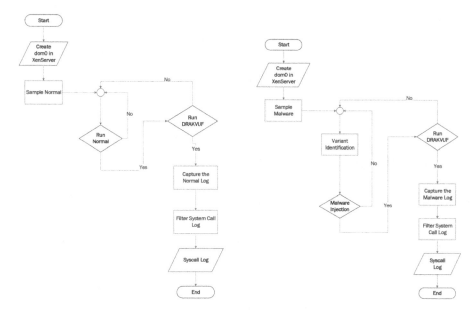

Fig. 2. Normal application flowchart   **Fig. 3.** Abnormal application flowchart

7   Findings

In this study, the malware dataset that has been collected from the Windows 7 sandbox environment is pre-processed. Using java code, the frequency of system calls is created and labeled with 0 for normal binaries and 1 for malware binaries in CSV format. The labeled dataset is then run through a series of classifier tools in WEKA. Three data mining classifiers, J48, Naive Bayes and Random Forest are applied to the extracted features. The three classifiers are chosen based on previous works.

The performance evaluation was considered using a set of classification metrics such as Precision, Recall, True Positive Rate (TPR), and False Positive Rate (FPR). Table 1 shows the classification accuracy results between the three classifier model.

Table 1. Comparison of classification model

Classification	True positive	False positive	Precision	Recall
J48	91.8%	7.6%	92.2%	91.8%
Random forest	93.7%	5.8%	94.0%	93.7%
Naïve Bayes	93.0%	6.3%	93.4%	93.0%

Based on Table 1, it states that the Random Forest classifier gives the highest precison in predicting malware based on system call with the accuracy of 94.0% compare to the other classifiers and the recall is also the highest with 93.7%. J48 has the lowest value of precision and recall with 92.2% and 91.8% respectively. While Random Forest and Naïve Bayes classification model is not that much of a difference, the false positive in Random Forest is the lowest compared to Naïve Bayes and thus it make the Random Forest the highest malware detection attack rate based on the malware's system call.

We then compared the results with the classification models for detecting malware based on the system call on android platform [1,2]. Both results show that Random Forest classification model works the best to classify malware attack using the system calls. The highest Random Forest model rate comes from [1] with a 95.85%, and [2] only shows a rate of 76.6%. This shows that our findings is at par with other malware detection classification model that uses system calls as a detection mechanism. It is assumed that the differences in the number of system call features and the volume of malware dataset used may have been affecting the result as [1] uses a 4949 samples, the highest between our work and [2].

As we have managed to developed the a good precision rating classification model, we also conducted a user acceptance test with a malware analyst to verify whether the features of this sandbox malware detection system via system call using classification model are working as intended. Conficker worm sample was used for the testing. The worm run inside sandbox of windows7, while using web application UI which result in system call log data of the worm samples.

The test case took part in two parts. The first part is the functional testing of the sandbox that are used for uploading malware and collecting behavioural data of the malware. The second part is to test the classifying algorithm. The results show that the malware was successfully uploaded on the web-based sandbox and the classification analysis report of the uploaded malware samples can be viewed by the user. The malware analyst also stated that the report of the comparison of classification models give extra information for them to analyse the malware's behaviour.

8   Conclusion

In this study, we have found that detecting worm need to use more than signature-based detection method because worm scatters or spread itself. In the wake of lessening the server's detection, the worm acted like a customer to another number of trusting devices, tainting more machines, utilising similar weakness. We also found that Random Forest classification model shows the best in detecting malware from normal application based on the collected log of both malware associated system call and normal application system call.

While this study only uses limited number of malware, future study can test on many more types of malware and compare different scenarios of infestation. Another possible future work is embedding more logs into DRAKVUF other than poolmon, syscall, and filetracer so that more features can be added to enhance the classification model based on the malware's bahaviour. Since currently our sandbox is a manual malware analysis, we recommend of making DRAKVUF into an automated malware behaviour analysis that can automatically generate the logs.

References

1. Ananya, A., Aswathy, A., Amal, T., Swathy, P., Vinod, P., Mohammad, S.: Sysdroid: a dynamic ml-based android malware analyzer using system call traces. Cluster Computing, pp. 1–20 (2020)
2. Anshori, M., Mar'i, F., Bachtiar, F.A.: Comparison of machine learning methods for android malicious software classification based on system call. In: 2019 International Conference on Sustainable Information Engineering and Technology (SIET), pp. 343–348. IEEE (2019)
3. Christodorescu, M., Jha, S., Seshia, S.A., Song, D., Bryant, R.E.: Semantics-aware malware detection. In: 2005 IEEE Symposium on Security and Privacy (S&P 2005), pp. 32–46. IEEE (2005)
4. Demme, J., et al.: On the feasibility of online malware detection with performance counters. ACM SIGARCH Comput. Architecture News $41(3)$, 559–570 (2013)
5. Forrest, S., Hofmeyr, S.A., Somayaji, A., Longstaff, T.A.: A sense of self for unix processes. In: Proceedings 1996 IEEE Symposium on Security and Privacy, pp. 120–128. IEEE (1996)
6. Kolter, J.Z., Maloof, M.A.: Learning to detect and classify malicious executables in the wild. J. Mach. Learn. Res. 7, 2721–2744 (2006)
7. Kong, D., Yan, G.: Discriminant malware distance learning on structural information for automated malware classification. In: Proceedings of the 19th ACM SIGKDD International Conference on Knowledge Discovery and Data Mining, pp. 1357–1365 (2013)
8. Landage, J., Wankhade, M.: Malware and malware detection techniques: a survey. Int. J. Eng. Res. Technol. (IJERT) $2(12)$, 2278–0181 (2013)
9. Lanzi, A., Balzarotti, D., Kruegel, C., Christodorescu, M., Kirda, E.: Accessminer: using system-centric models for malware protection. In: Proceedings of the 17th ACM Conference on Computer and Communications Security, pp. 399–412 (2010)
10. Lengyel, T.K., Maresca, S., Payne, B.D., Webster, G.D., Vogl, S., Kiayias, A.: Scalability, fidelity and stealth in the DRAKVUF dynamic malware analysis system. In: Proceedings of the 30th Annual Computer Security Applications Conference, pp. 386–395 (2014)
11. Milošević, N.: History of malware. arXiv preprint arXiv:1302.5392 (2013)
12. Moser, A., Kruegel, C., Kirda, E.: Exploring multiple execution paths for malware analysis. In: 2007 IEEE Symposium on Security and Privacy (SP 2007), pp. 231–245. IEEE (2007)
13. Moskovitch, R., Elovici, Y., Rokach, L.: Detection of unknown computer worms based on behavioral classification of the host. Comput. Stat. Data Anal. 52, 4544–4566 (2008)
14. Nataraj, L., Karthikeyan, S., Jacob, G., Manjunath, B.S.: Malware images: visualization and automatic classification. In: Proceedings of the 8th International Symposium on Visualization for Cyber Security, pp. 1–7 (2011)

15. Ozsoy, M., Donovick, C., Gorelik, I., Abu-Ghazaleh, N., Ponomarev, D.: Malware-aware processors: a framework for efficient online malware detection. In: 2015 IEEE 21st International Symposium on High Performance Computer Architecture (HPCA), pp. 651–661. IEEE (2015)
16. Preda, M.D., Christodorescu, M., Jha, S., Debray, S.: A semantics-based approach to malware detection. ACM Trans. Programm. Lang. Syst. (TOPLAS) **30**(5), 1–54 (2008)
17. Sanders, A.: 15 (CRAZY) Malware and Virus Statistics, Trends & Facts 2020. Technical report, January 2020. https://www.safetydetectives.com/blog/malware-statistics/
18. Sarwar, G., Mehani, O., Boreli, R., Kaafar, M.A.: On the effectiveness of dynamic taint analysis for protecting against private information leaks on android-based devices. In: SECRYPT, vol. 96435 (2013)
19. Schultz, M.G., Eskin, E., Zadok, F., Stolfo, S.J.: Data mining methods for detection of new malicious executables. In: Proceedings 2001 IEEE Symposium on Security and Privacy, S&P 2001, pp. 38–49. IEEE (2000)
20. Shafiq, M.Z., Khayam, S.A., Farooq, M.: Embedded malware detection using Markov n-Grams. In: Zamboni, D. (ed.) DIMVA 2008. LNCS, vol. 5137, pp. 88–107. Springer, Heidelberg (2008). https://doi.org/10.1007/978-3-540-70542-0_5
21. Sharp, R.: An Introduction to Malware (2017)
22. Wang, Y.M., Beck, D., Vo, B., Roussev, R., Verbowski, C.: Detecting stealth software with strider ghostbuster. In: 2005 International Conference on Dependable Systems and Networks (DSN 2005), pp. 368–377. IEEE (2005)
23. Weaver, N., Paxson, V., Staniford, S., Cunningham, R.: A taxonomy of computer worms. In: Proceedings of the 2003 ACM Workshop on Rapid Malcode, pp. 11–18 (2003)
24. Ye, Y., Li, T., Jiang, Q., Wang, Y.: CIMDS: adapting postprocessing techniques of associative classification for malware detection. IEEE Trans. Syst. Man Cybern. Part C (Applications and Reviews) **40**(3), 298–307 (2010)

A Conceptual Model: Securing Resources Through a Decentralized Access Control Using Blockchain Technology for Smart Farming

Noor Afiza Mat Razali[1][✉], Normaizeerah Mohd Noor[1], Nor Asiakin Hasbullah[1], Liew Ching Chen[1], Khairul Khalil Ishak[2], and Norlisa Francis Nordin[3]

[1] National Defence University of Malaysia, Kuala Lumpur, Malaysia
noorafiza@upnm.edu.my
[2] Management and Science University, Shah Alam, Malaysia
[3] OK Blockchain Center, Nusajaya, Malaysia

Abstract. Securing high number of IoT devices and sensors in smart farming ecosystem became a challenge especially when it comes to access control. Traditional approaches for access control mostly rely on a central authority which is a centralised server that is risky as it possesses a single point of failure and could be compromised with malicious attacks. Hence having a centralised model for access control does not seem to be an ideal solution. Meanwhile, blockchain technology, a decentralised Distributed Ledger Technology potentially can be applied to manage the access control. This study aims to propose a secure decentralised access control model using blockchain technology to secure the resources in smart farming ecosystem with a multi-tenant deployment model.

Keywords: Smart farming · Internet of things · IoT · Access control · Blockchain

1 Introduction

As technology is advancing day by day, people's lives are changing due to the advancement in technologies. Urban planning in developing country including farming is different from the last decade. Smart farming could be the future of urban development that aims to improve the quality of life and build a sustainable environment. Smart farming utilises smart technologies and the collected data to make themselves smart. Apart from there, a wide array of Internet of Things (IoT) based technology is widely implemented in smart farming to collect data (*sensors*) and perform actions (*actuators*). Hence, for a successful smart farming solution, it shall be implemented in a multi-tenant deployment model [1].

The heterogeneous IoT ecosystem in a smart farming consists of huge resources such as smart devices, sensors, and actuators. Unauthorised access to these resources could cause data leakage to malicious users and will cause catastrophic losses to the affected parties. Therefore, access control plays an important role in protecting these resources

© Springer Nature Switzerland AG 2021
H. Badioze Zaman et al. (Eds.): IVIC 2021, LNCS 13051, pp. 399–410, 2021.
https://doi.org/10.1007/978-3-030-90235-3_35

in the heterogeneous ecosystem. However, the traditional access control approach relies on a central authority which is a centralised server that possess a great threat as it is the single point of failure, especially when the server is compromised [2, 3]. Once the server is compromised, the malicious user may tamper with the access control policy of a system. Therefore, having a centralised server to manage the access control policies of a system opens a potential cybersecurity threat to the system. Other than that, depending on a centralised server to handle a large-scale system such as a smart farming in smart city may become a bottleneck as there are many resources need to be managed [4–6]. Blockchain, a technology that is decentralised by design and tamper-proof in nature, is a great solution to solve cybersecurity issue that relying on a central authority. It is not controlled by any central authority due to its decentralisation approach. Every node in the network has the ledger of the blockchain and once the data is chained, it will not be able to be tampered with any other data that is not in the blockchain network. Moreover, it allows data verification without depending on any third parties. Therefore, the access control for the resources in a smart farming can be secured and protected by utilising blockchain technology. Researchers have been proposing to build a robust access control model/framework based on blockchain technology in recent years. However, the study on effective and efficient access control on blockchain in a heterogenous IoT ecosystem has yet to be addressed [7, 8]. Hence, this research aims to propose a novel blockchain-based access control model for a heterogenous IoT ecosystem in smart farming. In this research, current access control models will be investigated, and a novel robust blockchain-based access control model is proposed with objectives to secure the resources such as smart device, sensors, and actuators in smart farming. Ultimately, the novel model shall strengthen the security via a decentralised network in a smart farming with a multi-tenant deployment model using blockchain technology.

2 Background Study

2.1 Smart Farming

A smart farming or smart agriculture that utilizes information and communication technologies (ICT) to achieve its ultimate goals such as to improve the efficiency of farming operations and to promote sustainable development farming systems. Smart farming equipped with smart devices, sensors and actuators in operation. These devices will help to collect data and provide intelligent services to the stakeholders and bring positive impacts by optimizing the public services and utilities. One of the key areas in smart farming is automation, by utilising intelligent monitor to collect a ground-based and aerial drones for crop health evaluation, fertilization, crop monitoring, soil and field analysis. This provides farmers with information into a whole plant health index, yield prediction and plant counting. This can be achieved by integrating the intelligent system with the smart devices in the farm. With the emerging technologies to support the establishment of IoT in smart systems, smart farming has endless possibilities to offer.

2.2 Cybersecurity

In today's world, with most of the objects are being digitalized, the objects to be secured no longer limited to a physical form and there are increasing efforts being invested into securing the resource such as our data in digital form on the internet. Cybersecurity is the practice of securing our data, software, network, and computing machines/devices etc. from malicious cyberattack. Cybersecurity plays an important role in protecting resources against cyberattacks that cause sensitive data leakage, system failure and loss of productivity. The impact of cyberattacks could potentially lead to catastrophic losses due to a cybersecurity breach. Thus, this research will focus on access control in cybersecurity. Access control is a method to perform authentication and authorization. Authentication will make sure that users are who they say they are. On the other hand, authorization is to allow access to a permitted resource only. In cybersecurity practice, access control policies help to ensure the resources and can only be accessed by authorized users and prevent malicious users from accessing restricted resources. However, traditional access control relies on a central authority which may lead to a severe security issue when the central authority is compromised. Hence, this research aims to propose a decentralized access control mechanism to overcome the security issues in traditional centralized access control.

2.3 Internet of Things

The Internet of Things (IoT) is a blanket term for all physical devices that are connected to the internet and used to collect data, share data and can be a part of any intelligent systems. It has become a buzzword in recent years due to the advancement in smart technologies integrated with IoT devices that can be as simple as a motion sensor to as powerful as an actuator to perform actions based on certain conditions. In smart farming, IoT plays an essential role in collecting data, monitoring and performing actions. The IoT applications are enabling smart farming to be smarter and more efficient with minimal human intervention. However, it also brings a huge challenge to cybersecurity as there are many resources to manage and secure.

2.4 Blockchain

Since the rising of cryptocurrency, blockchain technology has been gaining attention due to it characteristic that is secure by design. Blockchain is a Distributed Ledger Technology (DLT) that is based on peer-to-peer (P2P) topology. In blockchain technology, every data block in the chain is append-only and tamper-proof, every block will contain the cryptographic hash of the previous block except the genesis block (the first block in a chain). The node is the device in the blockchain P2P network, every node in the network will have a copy of the blockchain and the validation will be done by all the nodes in the network. The cryptographic hash will be utilised to check if there is an attempt to append a new block to the existing chain of block. This mechanism provides the strong security of blockchain technology. In recent years, there are attempts to solve the security concerns with having the decentralize authority for the access control policies by using blockchain technology. Blockchain is decentralized by nature and has a strong security feature to prevent malicious users from tampering with the data in the blockchain. Based on the background studies, in this research, a blockchain-based access control model is proposed as a solution to the centralized access control model.

3 Related Works

Blockchain technology started to gain a significant amount of attention when cryptocurrency started to become popular. Researchers are trying to solve the security issues of having access control relying on a third-party centralized authority with a decentralized model. Pinno et al. presented a blockchain-based architecture for IoT access authorization which based on the decentralized principle that aim to enable the scalable approach compare to the traditional access control methods like XACML, OAuth and User-Managed Access (UMA) [9]. However, in that architecture, the growth of blockchain has become an issue for devices with low stage space. On the other hand, Ouddah et al. proposed the design for a user-driven and fine-grained access control mechanism as a solution for the resources constrained environment [10]. Meanwhile, FairAccess has a disadvantage due to scalability limitation and the low speed in response due to utilization of the Proof of Work (POW) as the consensus algorithm. It results in low transaction throughput that is capped at 7 transactions per second and bloating block size problem. Thus, FairAccess being determined as not suitable for applications in a smart city that are hosting thousands of devices. Hence, it is an important factor to consider the limitation of resource constrained IoT devices when designing the decentralization solution for access control using blockchain technology. Zhang et al. proposed model that use private blockchain (Hyperledger Fabric), which is a permissioned model by implementing the Practical Byzantine Fault Tolerance (PBFT), a voting mechanism consensus algorithm instead of POW which is relatively computational expensive [11]. However, this model is difficult to scale well as PBFT will have high communication overhead when having a large number of nodes. Bezahaf et al. proposed that the network access control should be replaced with the blockchain and the central core network should be removed [12]. However, for edge nodes, the Proof-of-Work (PoW) may not be suitable as this is a computational power-based method of consensus voting. Xu et al. proposed a partially decentralized federated Capability-based Access Control framework that leverages smart contract and blockchain technology. The risk of performance bottleneck and single point of failure is mitigated by using the federated delegation mechanism and blockchain technology [13]. However, it is not suitable for resource-constrained IoT devices due to the increased overhead on the storage and computing resources when the blockchain grows larger. The proposed BlendCAC is susceptible to majority attack (51% attack) too. Le et al. proposed a blockchain-based access control framework that treats access right policies as types of assets that can be transferred between users via transactions, which are called capabilities. It allows users to share and delegate their access rights to other devices using capabilities. It implements the Proof of Work consensus method, generating a new block (which is also the access right, known as capability) that takes 3 min on average for the new block generation [14]. A less computationally expensive and lower latency consensus algorithm shall be implemented so that it is suitable for the IoT environment. Apart from that, Yu et al. proposed a Lightweight and Vote-based Blockchain (LVChain) that is a new decentralized and lightweight architecture that is scalable and fault-tolerant. A vote-based consensus algorithm is less dependent on computing and storage resources. It implements a vote-based consensus algorithm instead of proof-based, no mining is required and hence reduce the computational power needed. However, if more than half of the votes from the authorized users fail or act maliciously, it will fail [15]. Huang et al. proposed a Directed Acyclic Graph (DAG)-Structured Blockchain system with credit-based consensus algorithm mechanism for IoT. The proposed mechanism known as B-IOT is scalable and secure for IoT environments that utilise a moderate-cost credit-based PoW mechanism. It implements a self-adaptive PoW algorithm for power constrained IoT devices which will increase the difficulty of PoW for malicious nodes and decrease the difficulty of PoW for honest nodes. When it comes to a large scale system like a smart city, the storage limitation may be a challenge [16]. As PoW can be very computationally expensive for low power IoT devices, Xu et al. proposed to use a permissioned blockchain network that is implemented in microservice architecture to enable data sharing and access control mechanism using smart contract [17]. All entities in the permissioned blockchain network are implemented as containers. The containers perform their task autonomously. Although it is validated that this architecture could provide efficient and effective identity authentication and access control policy in a distributed IoT-based system, a lightweight consensus algorithm is much desired for the security solution in the IoT ecosystem. Bai et al. proposed a light-weighted Blockchain-based platform for Industrial IoT called BPIIoT, this platform is using an idea that is comprised of the on-chain network and the off-chain network. All the transactions on the platform such as digital signature based on admission control and programmable permissions are carried out on the on-chain network while the off-chain network deals with the storage, computational expensive processes and other problems that is not suitable to solve on blockchain [18]. In this way, the responsibilities can be split into different networks instead of doing everything in the blockchain network. Another interesting idea using DAG was proposed by Tekeoglu et al. using an experimental lightweight distributed ledger for IoT devices called TangoChain. It is utilizing the DAG as the underlying ledger data structure [19]. The key difference between TangoChain and traditional blockchain is the data structure, where there are no blocks in the chain, but it uses transaction instead. The key motivation for this design is to overcome the challenges in IoT devices such as low computational power, limited memory, restricted storage, and low networking bandwidth. The verification in a DAG blockchain is comparatively more lightweight compared to the algorithm like Proof of Work and no miners are required. A blockchain-based secure data sharing platform and fine-grained access control (BSDS-FA) combined with Attribute-Based Encryption (ABE) was proposed in [20]. Meanwhile, a smart contract of blockchain technology is being utilized in this platform to secure access control. There are 2 smart contracts namely the Validation Contract and Decryption Contract. The Validation Contract is responsible for detecting the validity of user access right. The author chose the Hyperledger Fabric, a permissioned blockchain which is a private blockchain that implements Raft ordering service instead of using a computational expensive consensus algorithm like PoW. Hence, it is more resource-friendly for resource constrained IoT devices. To overcome the challenges in supporting access control system in a large-scale IoT environment using traditional centralized access control methods due to the limited performance of IoT devices, Ding et al. proposed an access control system based on Hyperledger Fabric blockchain framework and attributed based access control (ABAC). The author also stated the reasons why a permissioned (private) blockchain is chosen over a permissionless(public) blockchain due to some disadvantages in public blockchain such as low transaction throughput, long transaction confirmation time, waste of resources, consistency issues and privacy issues. The author chose the Hyperledger Fabric, a permissioned blockchain which is a private blockchain that implements Raft ordering service instead of using a computational expensive consensus algorithm like PoW [21]. Hence, it is more resource-friendly for resource constrained IoT devices. Using a private blockchain is computationally efficient, Liu et al. proposed an access control system for IoT called fabric-iot that is based on a private blockchain, Hyperledger Fabric blockchain framework and ABAC. The author addressed that IoT devices have limited performance and traditional centralized access control methods may find it difficult to support the access control in a large-scale IoT environment. Experiments had been carried out in that research to compare the performance of the system and the result had shown that the fabric-IoT can maintain high throughput in a large-scale request environment and reach consensus efficiently in a distributed environment, with the use of private blockchain such as Hyperledger Fabric has high throughput and a low-cost time [22]. Nithin et al. proposed HyperIoT as a decentralized, distributed, private blockchain network that is based on Hyperledger Fabric framework on the current IoT architecture [23]. The HyperIoT aims to address the primary concern on security and privacy for IoT application and the challenge in the vulnerability to cyberattacks in IoT system due to the rapid growth of connected devices that has led to more access points in the network. However, there are many limitations such as coping with the computational and storage requirements when integrating blockchain technology into the traditional IoT architecture. A modern IoT architecture with decentralization by design shall be considered. Based on the reviewed research that utilised blockchain as the decentralized solution for access control in the IoT ecosystem, using a private blockchain could reduce the computational power required for processing and could achieve an efficient consensus algorithm as compared to pubic blockchain. Some researchers had tried various consensus algorithm in IoT ecosystem that uses blockchain technology, consensus algorithm like PoW is too computationally expensive. Hyperledger Fabric had been proven on its capability of maintaining high throughput with a high number of concurrent requests. Hence, applying private blockchain for access control shall be considered when designing a blockchain-based access control model to secure IoT resources in smart farming with a multi-tenant deployment model.

4   Conceptual Model: Securing Resources in Smart Farming Through a Decentralized Access Control Using Blockchain Technology

4.1   Secure Access Control Using Private Blockchain with On-Chain and Off-Chain Networks in Smart Farming

Based on the study on the related works, this research suggests a conceptual model with aims to secure resources in smart farming through a decentralized access control using blockchain technology with a multi-tenant deployment model. A private blockchain such as Hyperledger Fabric with on-chain and off-chain terminology proposed to be the combination that served as a foundation to design a secure decentralised access control model. Our proposed model that shows in Fig. 1 is a decentralized access control model that uses permissioned blockchain to manage access control in a multi-tenant deployment environment. We proposed the *Off-chain Hub*, a standalone server to handle tasks that require heavy processing power and storage such as metadata of the IoT systems and devices. Meanwhile, the *On-chain Hub* functioned as a permissioned blockchain using the Hyperledger Fabric that responsible to manage the access control policies of the resources. The proposed design parameters are storage constraint, consensus algorithm and security.

Storage Constraint. In a heterogenous IoT ecosystem, there are power/memory-constrained devices. The storage capacity issue could be mitigated by implementing Off-chain and On-chain networks. The off-chain network is responsible for storing the data that is not related to access control such as the metadata. On the other hand, the on-chain network is a blockchain network that is responsible for access control to secure the resources in smart farming. Hence, the block in the On-chain network will only contain the necessary data related to access control while reducing the size of the block in blockchain network to optimize usage on storage.

Consensus Algorithm. Computational expensive consensus algorithm such as PoW is not feasible in a heterogenous IoT ecosystem due to there are power constrained devices. These algorithms require heavy computational effort and usually have high time cost. In a private blockchain like Hyperledger Fabric, Raft ordering service is much more resource friendly as it is comparatively computational less expensive. Therefore, applying Hyperledger Ledger blockchain framework is resource efficient to large scale IoT system in smart farming.

Security. Traditional access control approaches normally rely on a centralized authority and is prone to single point of failure. The problem with single point of failure is mitigated via a decentralized model. The access control policies are being decentralized and tamper-proof by using blockchain technology.

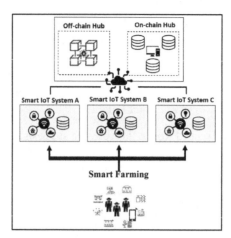

Fig. 1. Secure access control using private blockchain with on-chain and off-chain networks in a smart farming with multi-tenant deployment

4.2 Access Control via Permissioned Blockchain

To secure resources, we propose the implementation of the access control via a permissioned blockchain using Hyperledger Fabric as shows in Fig. 2. This research design allows secure resource protection and sharing in smart farming with multi-tenant model.

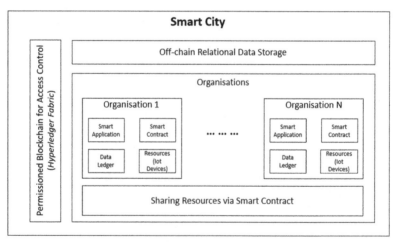

Fig. 2. Research design for securing resources by implementing the access control via a permissioned blockchain, Hyperledger Fabric

4.3 Multi-tenant Enabled

As today's technology is adapting collaboration over competition as what we can see in the cloud technology vendors. In a huge platform like a smart farming, it is nearly impossible to have smart systems that are only belong to a single organisation. Hence, enabling multi-tenant model is essential for a scalable platform. In our proposed conceptual model, different organisations will be registered under different *channels* in the Hyperledger Fabric. Each organisation could register its smart systems in the permissioned blockchain as nodes. Hence, it allows the smart farming platform to accommodate more than one organisation. The smart systems in each organisation are clearly segmented and easier to maintain too.

4.4 Decentralisation

Traditional server-client model is a centralised design that has single point of failure and scalability issue due to it is dependency on a single trusted third-party authority. When the centralised server goes down, the system will be not be able to work and could potentially cause catastrophic damage. On the other hand, this model is decentralised design. The smart systems of an organisation will be nodes of a channel in the permissioned blockchain. Every node will store the ledger of their access control policies to secure the resources of their smart systems such as IoT devices. The access control policies are distributed among nodes as every node will have a copy of the ledger.

4.5 Data Privacy

When there are multiple organisations on the same platform, the privacy of the data is a huge concern to the organisations, especially there could be competitors on the same platform. In the permissioned blockchain Hyperledger Fabric, each channel has a separate ledger. In this model, every organisation has their own separate channel and each organisation will have their ledger kept with themselves only. Each organisation will not be able to view other organisation's ledger unless intended. Moreover, the data can be stored in the off-chain storage. Consequently, the data privacy of each organisation is safely protected within themselves.

4.6 Secure Sharing Between Smart Farming Organisations

In this research, we propose secure sharing between organisation is possible via Smart Contracts which is known as *chaincode* in Hyperledger Fabric Framework. Although each organisation is treated as each channel in this famework and smart applications of each organisation are assigned to its respective channel, a smart application may connect to more than 1 channel.

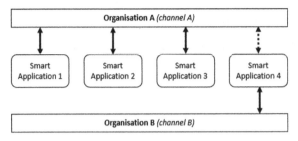

Fig. 3. Smart application design for resource sharing

In the Fig. 3 above, Smart Application 1, 2 and 3 belong to Organisation A, and Smart Application 4 belongs to Organisation B. However, there may be scenarios that two different organisations will have to collaborate and hence will need to share resources. Smart Application 4 could be connected to Organisation A and the resources being shared from Organisation A can be restricted by applying *chaincode* with well-defined conditions. Ultimately, secure sharing between organisations could be achieved in our proposed research design.

5   Discussion and Future Works

A secure, efficient and decentralised access control model is needed to protect the resources such as smart devices in smart farming due to the rapid growth in number of IoT devices in recent years. The proposed model aims to secure the resources in smart farming with a multi-tenant deployment model. This model is decentralised using blockchain technology and resilient to a single point of failure. The Hyperledger Fabric Framework is proposed in the model due to the proven track record to be very efficient for resource constrained IoT devices in term of processing power compared to public blockchain that uses PoW as a consensus algorithm. The access control policies are well protected as blockchain is tamper-proof by nature. This model implements the On-chain and Off-chain architecture to mitigate the performance bottleneck issue where the storage and computationally expensive tasks are handled by the Off-chain Hub and the access control related operations are handled by the On-chain Hub that contains private blockchain. This model is designed and proposed based on the theoretical findings, an empirical analysis will be carried out by prototyping and establishing the simulation of the proposed model in the testing environment. The validation will be done using virtual machines that will be simulating smart IoT systems in the smart farming and will be connected to the On-chain hub and Off-chain hub. The metrics for validation of the proposed model includes cybersecurity, computational effectiveness and storage efficiency. However, it could be challenging in a practical setting due to smart IoT systems may have different infrastructure and implementation standard. Future works to improve the proposed model include further research on solving semantic heterogeneity and adaptable to a heterogeneous IoT ecosystem.

Acknowledgement. This research is fully supported by the National Defence University of Malaysia (UPNM) under Short Grant UPNM/2020/GPJP/ICT/4. The authors fully acknowledged UPNM and Ministry of Higher Education Malaysia (MOHE) for the approved fund, which made this research viable and effective.

References

1. Esposito, C., Ficco, M., Gupta, B.B.: Blockchain-based authentication and authorization for smart city applications. Inf. Process. Manag. **58**(2), 102468 (2021). https://doi.org/10.1016/j.ipm.2020.102468

2. Shi, N., et al.: BacS: a blockchain-based access control scheme in distributed internet of things. Peer-to-Peer Netw. Appl. **14**(5), 2585–2599 (2020). https://doi.org/10.1007/s12083-020-00930-5

3. Gauhar, A., et al.: XDBAuth: blockchain based cross domain authentication and authorization framework for internet of things. IEEE Access **8**, 58800–58816 (2020). https://doi.org/10.1109/ACCESS.2020.2982542

4. Xu, J., et al.: Healthchain: a blockchain-based privacy preserving scheme for large-scale health data. IEEE Internet Things J. **6**(5), 8770–8781 (2019). https://doi.org/10.1109/JIOT.2019.2923525

5. Islam, M.A., Madria, S.: A permissioned blockchain based access control system for IOT. In: Proceedings - 2019 2nd IEEE International Conference Blockchain, Blockchain 2019, pp. 469–476 (2019). https://doi.org/10.1109/Blockchain.2019.00071

6. Urmila, M.S., Hariharan, B., Prabha, R.: A comparitive study of blockchain applications for enhancing internet of things security. In: 2019 10th Int. Conference Computer Communications Networking Technology, ICCCNT 2019 (2019). https://doi.org/10.1109/ICCCNT45670.2019.8944446

7. Muzammal,S.M., Murugesan, R.K.: A study on leveraging blockchain technology for IoT security enhancement. In: Proceedings - 2018 4th International Conference Advanced Computer Communications Automation ICACCA 2018 (2018). https://doi.org/10.1109/ICACCAF.2018.8776806

8. Riabi, I., Ben Ayed, H.K., Saidane, L.A.: A survey on blockchain based access control for internet of things. In: 2019 15th International Wireless Communication Mobile Computer Conference IWCMC 2019, pp. 502–507 (2019). https://doi.org/10.1109/IWCMC.2019.8766453

9. Pinno, O.J.A., Gregio, A.R.A., De Bona, L.C.E.: ControlChain: blockchain as a central enabler for access control authorizations in the IoT. In: 2017 IEEE Global Communication Conference GLOBECOM 2017 - Proceedings, vol. 2018-Janua, pp. 1–6 (2017). https://doi.org/10.1109/GLOCOM.2017.8254521

10. Ouaddah, A., Abou Elkalam, A., Ait Ouahman, A.: FairAccess: a new Blockchain-based access control framework for the Internet of Things. Secur. Commun. Networks **9**(18), 5943–5964 (2016). https://doi.org/10.1002/sec.1748

11. Zhang, Y., He, D., Choo, Kim-Kwang Raymond.: BaDS: Blockchain-based architecture for data sharing with ABS and CP-ABE in IoT. Wirel. Commun. Mob. Comput. **2018**, 1–9 (2018). https://doi.org/10.1155/2018/2783658

12. Bezahaf, M., Cathelain, G., Ducrocq, T.: BCWAN: a federated low-power WAN for the internet of things (industry track). In: Middleware Industry 2018 - Proceedings of the 2018 ACM/IFIP/USENIX Middleware Conference (Industrial Track), pp. 54–60 (2018). https://doi.org/10.1145/3284028.3284036

13. Xu, R., Chen, Y., Blasch, E., Chen, G.: BlendCAC: A smart contract enabled decentralized capability-based access control mechanism for the IoT. Computers **7**(3), 1–27 (2018). https://doi.org/10.3390/computers7030039

14. Le, T., Mutka, M.W.: Capchain: a privacy preserving access control framework based on blockchain for pervasive environments. In: Proceedings - 2018 IEEE Int. Conf. Smart Comput. SMARTCOMP 2018, pp. 57–64 (2018). https://doi.org/10.1109/SMARTCOMP.2018.00074

15. Yu, Y., Zhang, S., Chen, C., Zhong, X.: LVChain: a lightweight and vote-based blockchain for access control in the IoT. In: 2018 IEEE 4th International Conference Computer Communications ICCC 2018, pp. 870–874 (2018). https://doi.org/10.1109/CompComm.2018.8780687

16. Huang, J., Kong, L., Chen, G., Cheng, L., Wu, K., Liu, X.: B-IoT: blockchain driven internet of things with credit-based consensus mechanism. In: Proceedings - International Conference Distribution Computer System, vol. 2019-July, pp. 1348–1357 (2019). https://doi.org/10.1109/ICDCS.2019.00135

17. Xu, R., Nikouei, S.Y., Chen, Y., Blasch, E., Aved, A.: BlendMAS: a blockchain-enabled decentralized microservices architecture for smart public safety. In: Proceedings - 2019 2nd IEEE International Conference Blockchain, Blockchain 2019, pp. 564–571 (2019). https://doi.org/10.1109/Blockchain.2019.00082

18. Bai, L., Hu, M., Liu, M., Wang, J.: BPIIoT: a light-weighted blockchain-based platform for industrial IoT. IEEE Access **7**, 58381–58393 (2019). https://doi.org/10.1109/ACCESS.2019.2914223

19. Tekeoglu, A., Ahmed, N.: TangoChain: a lightweight distributed ledger for internet of things devices in smart cities. In: 5th IEEE International Smart Cities Conference ISC2 2019, pp. 18–21 (2019). https://doi.org/10.1109/ISC246665.2019.9071753

20. Xu, H., He, Q., Li, X., Jiang, B., Qin, K.: BDSS-FA: a blockchain-based data security sharing platform with fine-grained access control. IEEE Access **8**, 87552–87561 (2020). https://doi.org/10.1109/ACCESS.2020.2992649

21. Ding, Y., Sato, H.: Bloccess: towards fine-grained access control using blockchain in a distributed untrustworthy environment. In: Proceedings - 2020 8th IEEE International Conference Mobile Cloud Computing Service Engineering MobileCloud 2020, pp. 17–22 (2020). https://doi.org/10.1109/MobileCloud48802.2020.00011

22. Liu, H., Han, D., Li, D.: Fabric-IoT: a blockchain-based access control system in IoT. IEEE Access **8**, 18207–18218 (2020). https://doi.org/10.1109/ACCESS.2020.2968492

23. Nithin, M., Shraddha, S., Vaddem, N., Sarasvathi, V.: HyperIoT: securing transactions in IoT through private permissioned blockchain. In: Proceedings CONECCT 2020 - 6th IEEE International Conference Electronics Computer Communications Technology (2020). https://doi.org/10.1109/CONECCT50063.2020.9198474

Traffic Flow Prediction Using Long-Short Term Memory Technique for Connected Vehicles in Smart Cities

Nuraini Shamsaimon[1], Noor Afiza Mat Razali[1(✉)], Khairani Abd Majid[1],
Suzaimah Ramli[1], Mohd Fahmi Mohamad Amran[1], Khairul Khalil Ishak[2],
and Raslan Ahmad[3]

[1] National Defence University of Malaysia, Kuala Lumpur, Malaysia
noorafiza@upnm.edu.my
[2] Management and Science University, Shah Alam, Malaysia
[3] Malaysian Industry-Government Group for High Technology, Cyberjaya, Selangor, Malaysia

Abstract. An intelligent transportation system is an advanced application that aims to improve the efficiency and safety of various modes of transportation. It works by providing innovative services related to different modes of transportation and traffic management. Machine and deep learning have become an integral part of improving the efficiency of traffic flow prediction. In this study, we proposed a traffic flow prediction using Long-Short Term Memory (LSTM) technique to improve a traffic flow prediction. Our experimental design and algorithm to investigate the accuracy of traffic flow prediction are presented in this paper. For data simulation, the VISSIM simulator is utilised to generate data for classification training and testing. Validation will be done by applying other techniques discussed in the literature. This study will serve as a confirmatory study for traffic flow prediction using LSTM.

Keywords: Traffic flow · Congestion prediction · Machine learning · Deep learning · Long-short term memory

1 Introduction

Recently, developments emphasized making the planet a "smarter" place by implementing smart technologies such as smart cities, smart industry, smart transportation, and others with the rise of IoT technology. The Intelligent Transportation System (ITS) is a ground-breaking technology that is a component of intelligent transportation. ITS helps to lessen traffic issues especially, traffic congestion and, to improve traffic quality. The establishing transportation networks to facilitate the connectivity and mobility of travellers within a given location allows the most use of the networks. The establishment also offers an array of cost-effective, accessible travel alternatives, monitors collisions and congestions, and offering the highest quality of support to road users and travellers [1, 2]. Connected vehicles (CV) are part of ITS implementation which allows travellers

© Springer Nature Switzerland AG 2021
H. Badioze Zaman et al. (Eds.): IVIC 2021, LNCS 13051, pp. 411–422, 2021.
https://doi.org/10.1007/978-3-030-90235-3_36

to arrive at their destination safely, cost-efficient, and quickly [3]. Besides communicating with other cars, CV technology also enables connectivity with roadside facilities, providing critical warning and information.

One of the central concerns that researchers seek to address with the CV progress and growth is congestion [4]. The prediction of traffic flow and congestion has been the subject of several works and studies. Even though information sharing in congested areas is critical, the invention of the CV has made it much easier to disseminate the information. The use of Artificial Intelligence (AI) technologies, particularly Machine Learning (ML), to create and generate traffic flow predictions is innovative. It gives a more accurate technique of developing and generating traffic flow predictions [5]. DL is a subcategory of ML which are closely related to each other in AI methods. As a result, a comprehensive analysis of traffic flow prediction for connected vehicles using machine learning will be conducted in this study. The implementation of CV encouraged the use of ML methods to enhance the capability of the technology through the generation of vast amounts of data which demand a better and faster analysis of data that could not be performed well by traditional methods [6]. One of the main applications of ML in CV is for traffic flow prediction.

Several research questions have been raised and discussed to lead and inspire this study of Traffic Flow Prediction using LSTM Technique in Connected Vehicles. Several studies are currently underway examining the congestion prediction model in CV using the LSTM technique, with differing results and consequences. This study aims to review studies that implement the LSTM technique for traffic flow prediction and based on the review, to propose and come out with a conceptual model for traffic flow prediction using the LSTM technique.

2   Related Works

2.1   Smart City

The emergence of the Internet of Things (IoT) has led to developing Smart City. This concept is composed of various elements such as education, healthcare, transportation, and infrastructure. Sensors, cameras, mobile phones, high-speed wireless Internet, and emerging new technologies that are part of the Internet of Things are the leading technologies in Smart City. These devices create large amounts of data that can be used in Smart Cities for various purposes. Big data is defined as information that is large in volume, diversity, velocity, and validity [7]. As a part of smart cities development, the Intelligent Transportation System (ITS) advancements can change how people commute. Different types of transportation, advanced infrastructure, traffic and mobility management technologies are all available with ITS [2].

2.2   Machine Learning Techniques Approach in Traffic Flow Prediction

Most studies implement or integrate one machine learning approach with various methodologies and systems based on the literature reviewed. A model called SG-CNN is proposed by Tu et al. [8] in which a method of training data is enhanced through an algorithm where road segments are grouped up that make use of the CNN algorithm. A multi-task learning perspective for extracting both temporal and spatial data in numerous cities was demonstrated in [9]. In [10], the authors proposed a combination of distributed LSTM with normal distribution and time window formed on the MapReduce framework. Romo et al. [11] came out with a framework based on machine learning techniques through the conduct of a comparative study of three algorithms XGBoost, LSTM-NN and CNN. An efficient automated system for congestion classification is proposed in [12], which are formed on CNN and concise image representation. Abdelwahab et al. [13] present an LSTM model for IoT traffic forecast according to time series. Another LSTM based model called LSTM_SPLSTM is proposed by Lin et al. [14] to predict traffic flow. Shin et al. used the LSTM model for a prediction formed on absent spatial and temporal data [15]. Elleuch et al. [16], in their study, introduces a neural network model that uses floating car data (FCD) called Intelligent Traffic Congestion Prediction System. Another method called SSGRU is proposed by Sun et al. [17], where the focal point is on various road segments. Zafar and Haq [18] conducted a case study comparing different ML algorithms for the traffic congestion predicting based on the ETA congestion index. Yi and Bui [19] propose a deep neural network model using LSTM for data analysis derived from a Vehicle Detection System. Another study uses LSTM to develop a model called C-LSTM in an end-to-end neural network [20]. A CNN-based model called MF-CNN is introduced in [21] based on spatiotemporal features, capable of conducting a significant network scale prediction of traffic flow. In the study by C. Chen et al. [22], the authors develop a framework named MRes-RGNN, which are formed on various residual repetitive graph neural networks. A comparative analysis study is conducted in [23] to determine the performance of three ML techniques k-NN, ANN and SVR, in predicting traffic flow. Xu et al. [24] demonstrate the use of C4.5 and k-NN algorithms to predict the traffic flow by considering the network status like a video. Kong et al. [25] and Tian et al. [26] proposed a model that utilizes the LSTM technique for traffic flow recommendation.

Based on our observation through the reviews, most of the researchers commonly use CNN and LSTM models, which indicates the capability of the models to perform well to predict traffic congestion.

2.3 Hybrid Machine Learning Techniques for Traffic Flow Prediction

A few studies exhibit the usage of a combination of ML techniques by integrating ensemble and hybrid techniques. As an example, Ranjan et al. [27] introduces a hybrid neural network that involves CNN, Transpose CNN and LSTM, in which they also put forward a systematic strategy for data collection. Liu et al. [28] combine LSTM and GCN techniques in their model of traffic flow prediction. In [29], Chou et al. came up with a deep-stacked LSTM model called DE-LSTM to predict traffic flow during peak and non-peak hours. Study by J. Wang et al. [30] demonstrates the combination of LSTM and CNN that produces a traffic flow prediction for urban areas based on spatiotemporal aspects. Another author, W.Jin et al. [31], also combines LSTM and CNN algorithms that have STRNC, a model capable of capturing temporal dependency simultaneously throughout traffic flow prediction. Duan et al. [32] also utilize the combination of LSTM and CNN for spatiotemporal data extraction to produce a deep neural network model integrated with a greedy algorithm.

2.4 Parameters Involved

Since most studies are for traffic flow prediction, the traffic dataset differs due to the involvement of different countries and cities. Nevertheless, most of the dataset consists of standard variables and parameters used for the analysis of data, and the classification of traffic flow calculations. Based on our findings, the commonly used parameters are traffic speed, volume, density, time and traffic flow. Table 1 is the summary of the listed parameters and their description.

Table 1. List of parameters and description based on other studies.

Parameters	Description	Citations
Velocity (Traffic speed)	Speed of the vehicles	[8, 10–12, 15, 16, 19, 20, 22, 24, 26, 28, 32]
Time	Time of day, periods of time, passage of time, or duration of time	[9, 16, 18, 21, 26, 30, 31, 33, 34]
Traffic flow	The number of vehicles passing through a particular point	[9, 11, 12, 14, 25]
Traffic volume	The number of vehicles crossing a section of road per unit time	[8, 10, 17, 19, 23]

3 Research Design

In this research, we are proposing a research design as shown in Fig. 1. Future traffic conditions are predicted using real-time traffic data and the LSTM algorithm. LSTM is proposed to be used as algorithm to indicate the level of traffic congestion. Due to the nature of machine learning in data mining, it is vital that the data must be collected and analysed in a proper manner [24].

Figure 1 illustrates the research design for the conceptual model proposed for traffic flow prediction in this study. The method of this research consists of several phases to perform the traffic flow prediction.

Figure 2 represents the experimental design illustration, in which the figure graphically depicts the process using a variety of software, techniques, and procedures. The data used in this study are in the form of geographical data, collected from map applications and software such as OpenStreetMap, Google map and others. The location selected will be within urban Kuala Lumpur. The extracted map view will then be set up in VISSIM to run the simulation and collect parameters such as traffic speed, time, traffic density, traffic flow and traffic volume. The collected data then will be analysed using LSTM. A collection of training data is used to provide classification accuracy for future prediction. The result of the prediction will be compared with other ML techniques to determine the accuracy of the performance further.

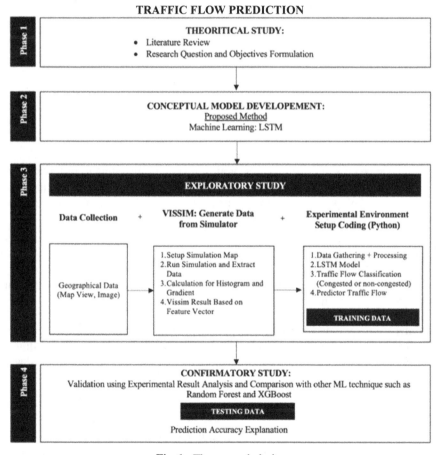

Fig. 1. The research design

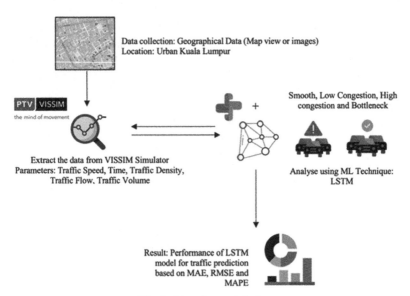

Fig. 2. Experimental design

3.1 Phase 1 – Theoretical Study

Phase 1 is the process of conducting theoretical reviews of literature to further explore the topic. Through these reviews, can produce the formulation of the research questions and objectives. The parameters used for traffic flow prediction are also studied. The outcome of this phase is explained in Sect. 2.

3.2 Phase 2 – Conceptual Model and Algorithm Development

Phase 2 is involving the process of developing a conceptual model, as well as an algorithm for the operation of traffic prediction using LSTM.

Standard Measurement for Congestion Status. To express the status level of traffic, speed performance index (*SPI*) is used, where SPI can evaluate urban traffic conditions [35]. *SPI* value ranges from 0 to 100, which is defined by the ratio of vehicle speed with the maximum speed limit as shown as below:

$$SPI = \left(v_{avg}/v_{max}\right) \times 100 \tag{1}$$

Where v avg is average vehicle speed, and v max is the maximum speed limit. SPI adopts three thresholds value consisting of 25,50 and 75 as the classification criteria for level of traffic congestion. The classification includes smooth, low congestion, high congestion and bottleneck. Table 2 below enlists the ranges of SPI, their levels of traffic congestion and description.

Table 2. Level of traffic congestion based on *SPI*

Traffic congestion level	SPI	Description
Bottleneck	0–25	If average speed is low = Road traffic state is poor
High congestion	25–50	If average speed is lower = Road traffic state is weak
Low congestion	50–75	If average speed is higher = Road traffic state is better
Smooth	75–100	If average speed is high = Road traffic state is good

LSTM Structure Model. In this research, the chosen deep learning technique for this study is Long short-term memory (LSTM). This technique is selected based on the literature review conducted and the performances in different studies, which will further explore in this study. LSTM is a variation that comes from RNN, where RNN solves the issue of other traditional neural networks in handling sequential data [13]. Traditional neural networks are only able to process current time-series information. they could not use its historical information to good use, in which RNN can retain information from the history and use it for the calculation of the current sequence. But RNN Could not effectively utilize the length of historical details [13, 25].

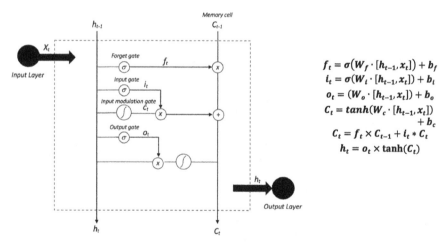

$$f_t = \sigma(W_f \cdot [h_{t-1}, x_t]) + b_f$$
$$i_t = \sigma(W_i \cdot [h_{t-1}, x_t]) + b_i$$
$$o_t = (W_o \cdot [h_{t-1}, x_t]) + b_o$$
$$C_t = tanh(W_c \cdot [h_{t-1}, x_t]) + b_c$$
$$C_t = f_t \times C_{t-1} + i_t * C_t$$
$$h_t = o_t \times tanh(C_t)$$

Fig. 3. LSTM structure and formula [13, 25].

LSTM is an extension of RNN, with the inclusion of a memory unit or cell which is used to hold historical information. The memory unit uses a "gate" to add or remove information to the cell state. There are three main gates in an LSTM Structure: input gate, output gate, and forget gate as illustrated in Fig. 3 and the calculation formula.

Where σ is the sigmoidal function, b_j is the bias, and W is the matrices weight. The main component of LSTM is the cell state, where C_{t-1} or memory from the preceding block runs to C_t, the memory from the actual block. x_t is the current input, and h_{t-1} is the former output. For a traffic flow prediction, the information to the LSTM structure includes traffic time, traffic speed, traffic density, traffic volume, and traffic flow. The outputs of the LSTM structure are the predicted state of current traffic flow, whether it is congested or non-congested.

LSTM Algorithm for Traffic Flow Prediction

Algorithm for Machine Learning Traffic Flow Prediction using LSTM
1. **Load Training set from VISSIM**   traffic_data ← load(data.csv)

2. **Input:**
    Training data X = {X, X, ...,Xᵢ)
    X ← traffic_data['Traffic Speed''Traffic Volume''Time''Density''Traffic Flow']

3. **Output:**
    MAE, MAPE and RMSE
    The Result of the Test Set {Congested or Non-Congested}

4. **Initialize:**   A pre-trained model

5. **Create Arrays of Training and Test Set:**
    80% training and 20% testing data
    X_train,X_test,

6. **Normalize the dataset (Xᵢ) into value from 0 to 1**
7. **Define:**   LSTM Structure Model
8. **For _n_ epoch and batch size to**   Train the LSTM model
9. **End for**
10. **Execute Prediction using LSTM()**
11. **Calculate using SPI to define smooth, low congestion, High congestion and bottleneck**
12. **Calculate the performance error using MAE, MAPE and RMSE**
13. **Predict the Result of the Test Set**   Prediction ← Predict(X-test)

Fig. 4. Algorithm for traffic flow prediction using LSTM

Figure 4 above is the algorithm for traffic flow prediction using LSTM, which will be used in this research. In this algorithm, first, a training data set is loaded and used as the input, which contains data such as Traffic Speed, Traffic Volume, Traffic Density, Traffic Flow and Time. The expected output from the LSTM model calculation is the value of Mean Absolute Error (MAE), Root Mean Square Error (RMSE) and Mean Absolute Percentage Error (MAPE) to determine the performance of the prediction classification, which will be calculated as below:

$$\mathbf{MAE} = \frac{1}{n}\sum_{i=1}^{n}|X_t - F_t| \quad \mathbf{MAPE} = \frac{\sum \frac{|X_t - F_t|}{X_t} \times 100}{n} \quad \mathbf{RMSE} = \left[\frac{1}{n}\sum_{i=1}^{n}(X_t - F_t)^2\right]^{\frac{1}{2}}$$

Then, a pre-trained model is initialized, and an array of training data and testing data is created, and data is split into 80% training data and 20% testing data. The series of size, train and test are determined. The dataset is then normalized into values between 0 and 1. The LSTM structure model is then defined and trained for _n_ epoch and batch size classification. After all, process is done, the prediction using LSTM model is run, and from the output, the performance is calculated through metrics MAE, RMSE, and MAPE.

3.3   Phase 3 – Exploratory Study

Phase 3 is the process of conducting the experiment, which starts with data collection, where geographical data such as the chosen area or location in urban Kuala Lumpur for the experiment will be taken from map view images generated from existing map providers such as OpenStreetMap and Google Maps. The data will then be used in traffic simulator applications such as VISSIM. The simulator will run a simulation and extract parameters such as traffic speed, traffic flow, traffic density, traffic volume and time. The data extracted from VISSIM will then be processed with the LSTM technique through Python and classified whether congested or non-congested. The result of this classification will act as training data.

3.4   Phase 4 – Confirmatory Study

The final phase of this research focuses on validating the outcome of the experiment through the analysis of experimental results and comparing the performance of the LSTM with other ML models and techniques, such as Random Forest and XGBoost. Testing data will be used to compare the results with the training data. Based on the outcome of the prediction, the accuracy will be further explained during this phase.

4   Conclusion and Future Work

Recent growth in the development of smart cities as a part of IoT technologies contributes to new innovative ideas and technologies, including the advanced development of ITS for smart transportation. Researchers and academicians have proposed various methodologies to enhance transportation experience and resolve traffic problems that contribute to a negative effect on the environment and community, such as safety and traffic congestion. Along with the introduction and growth of CV technology, various ideas have been thrown out and proposed to solve traffic problems, especially traffic congestion. In this study, a conceptual model is proposed for traffic flow prediction using a ML technique which is the LSTM. The model was developed based on the review of several related literatures which uses ML techniques for traffic flow prediction. Even when other reviewed literature shows that CNN is one of the most used techniques, in this study, we decide to exclude it due to the characteristic of CNN, which takes input from image data, where our analysis does not include. The chosen parameters, evaluation methods and evaluation metrics are also thoroughly discussed. The research design of the conceptual model with the experimental setup is illustrated and explained simply. In the future, the conceptual model will be implemented in an experiment to test the capability of finding the prediction accuracy performance of using ML techniques for traffic flow prediction.

Acknowledgements. This research is fully supported by the National Defence University of Malaysia (UPNM) under Short Grant UPNM/2020/GPJP/ICT/3. The authors fully acknowledged UPNM and Ministry of Higher Education Malaysia (MOHE) for the approved fund, which made this research viable and effective.

References

1. Hassn, H.A.H., Ismail, A., Borhan, M.N., Syamsunur, D.: The impact of intelligent transport system quality: drivers' acceptance perspective. Int. J. Technol. **7**(4), 553–561 (2016). https://doi.org/10.14716/ijtech.v7i4.2578
2. M. of works Malaysia, Malaysian Its Blueprint (2019–2023), vol. 53, no. 9 (2013)
3. "How Connected Vehicles Work | US Department of Transportation," U.S. Department of Transportation, (2020). https://www.transportation.gov/research-and-technology/how-con nected-vehicles-work, Accessed 12 May 2021
4. Miglani, A., Kumar, N.: Deep learning models for traffic flow prediction in autonomous vehicles: a review, solutions, and challenges. Veh. Commun. **20**, 100184 (2019). https://doi.org/10.1016/j.vehcom.2019.100184
5. Kamble, S.J., Kounte, M.R.: machine learning approach on traffic congestion monitoring system in internet of vehicles. Procedia Comput. Sci. **171**(2019), 2235–2241 (2020). https://doi.org/10.1016/j.procs.2020.04.241
6. Bhavsar, P., Safro, I., Bouaynaya, N., Polikar, R., Dera, D.: Machine learning in transportation data analytics. In: Data Analytics Intelligent for Transport System, no. December, pp. 283–307 (2017). https://doi.org/10.1016/B978-0-12-809715-1.00012-2
7. Ekler, P., Balogh, T., Ujj, T., Charaf, H., Lengyel, L.: Social driving in connected car environment. In: Proceedings of European Wireless 2015; 21th European Wireless Conference, pp. 1–6 (2015)
8. Tu, Y., Lin, S., Qiao, J., Liu, B.: Deep traffic congestion prediction model based on road segment grouping. Appl. Intell. **51**, 1–23 (2021). https://doi.org/10.1007/s10489-020-021 52-x
9. Zhang, Y., Yang, Y., Zhou, W., Wang, H., Ouyang, X.: Multi-city traffic flow forecasting via multi-task learning. Appl. Intell. **51**, 1–19 (2021). https://doi.org/10.1007/s10489-020-020 74-8
10. Xia, D., et al.: A distributed WND-LSTM model on MapReduce for short-term traffic flow prediction. Neural Comput. Appl. **33**(7), 2393–2410 (2020). https://doi.org/10.1007/s00521-020-05076-2
11. Romo, L., Zhang, J., Eastin, K., Xue, C.: Short-term traffic speed prediction via machine learning. In: Wang, J., Chen, L., Tang, L., Liang, Y. (eds.) GPC 2020. CCIS, vol. 1311, pp. 31–42. Springer, Singapore (2020). https://doi.org/10.1007/978-981-33-4532-4_3
12. Abdelwahab, M.A., Abdel-Nasser, M., Taniguchi, R.-I.: Efficient and fast traffic congestion classification based on video dynamics and deep residual network. In: Ohyama, W., Jung, S.K. (eds.) IW-FCV 2020. CCIS, vol. 1212, pp. 3–17. Springer, Singapore (2020). https://doi.org/10.1007/978-981-15-4818-5_1
13. Abdellah, A., Koucheryavy, A.: Deep learning with long short-term memory for iot traffic prediction. In: Galinina, O., Andreev, S., Balandin, S., Koucheryavy, Y. (eds.) Internet of Things, Smart Spaces, and Next Generation Networks and Systems: 20th International Conference, NEW2AN 2020, and 13th Conference, ruSMART 2020, St. Petersburg, Russia, August 26–28, 2020, Proceedings, Part I, pp. 267–280. Springer International Publishing, Cham (2020). https://doi.org/10.1007/978-3-030-65726-0_24

14. Lin, Y., Wang, R., Zhu, R., Li, T., Wang, Z., Chen, M.: The short-term exit traffic prediction of a toll station based on LSTM. In: Li, G., Shen, H.T., Yuan, Y., Wang, X., Liu, H., Zhao, X. (eds.) KSEM 2020. LNCS (LNAI), vol. 12275, pp. 462–471. Springer, Cham (2020). https://doi.org/10.1007/978-3-030-55393-7_41

15. Shin, D.H., Chung, K., Park, R.C.: Prediction of traffic congestion based on LSTM through correction of missing temporal and spatial data. IEEE Access **8**, 150784–150796 (2020). https://doi.org/10.1109/ACCESS.2020.3016469

16. Elleuch, W., Wali, A., Alimi, A.M.: Neural congestion prediction system for trip modelling in heterogeneous spatio-temporal patterns. Int. J. Syst. Sci. **51**(8), 1373–1391 (2020). https://doi.org/10.1080/00207721.2020.1760957

17. Sun, P., Boukerche, A., Tao, Y.: SSGRU: a novel hybrid stacked GRU-based traffic volume prediction approach in a road network. Comput. Commun. **160**(April), 502–511 (2020). https://doi.org/10.1016/j.comcom.2020.06.028

18. Zafar, N., Haq, I.U.: Traffic congestion prediction based on estimated time of arrival. PLoS One 15(12), 1–19 (2020). https://doi.org/10.1371/journal.pone.0238200

19. Yi, H., Bui, K.-H.: VDS data-based deep learning approach for traffic forecasting using LSTM network. In: Moura Oliveira, P., Novais, P., Reis, L.P. (eds.) EPIA 2019. LNCS (LNAI), vol. 11804, pp. 547–558. Springer, Cham (2019). https://doi.org/10.1007/978-3-030-30241-2_46

20. Gao, H., Wang, X., Yin, Y., Iqbal, M. (eds.): CollaborateCom 2018. LNICSSITE, vol. 268. Springer, Cham (2019). https://doi.org/10.1007/978-3-030-12981-1

21. Yang, D., Li, S., Peng, Z., Wang, P., Wang, J., Yang, H.: MF-CNN: traffic flow prediction using convolutional neural network and multi-features fusion. IEICE Trans. Inf. Syst. **E102D**(8), 1526–1536 (2019). https://doi.org/10.1587/transinf.2018EDP7330

22. Chen, C., et al.: Gated residual recurrent graph neural networks for traffic prediction. In: 33rd AAAI Conference Artificial Intelligence, AAAI 2019, 31st Innovation Application Artificial Intelligence Conference IAAI 2019 9th AAAI Symposium Education Advanced Artificial Intelligence EAAI 2019, pp. 485–492 (2019). https://doi.org/10.1609/aaai.v33i01.3301485

23. Bartlett, Z., Han, L., Nguyen, T.T., Johnson, P.: A machine learning based approach for the prediction of road traffic flow on urbanised arterial roads. In: Proceedings - 20th International Conference High Performance Computer Communications 16th International Conference Smart City 4th International Conference Data Science System, HPCC/SmartCity/DSS 2018, pp. 1285–1292 (2019). https://doi.org/10.1109/HPCC/SmartCity/DSS.2018.00215

24. Xu, W., Yang, G., Li, F., Yang, Y.: Traffic congestion level prediction based on video processing technology. In: Zeng, B., Huang, Q., El Saddik, A., Li, H., Jiang, S., Fan, X. (eds.) PCM 2017. LNCS, vol. 10736, pp. 970–980. Springer, Cham (2018). https://doi.org/10.1007/978-3-319-77383-4_95

25. Kong, F., Li, J., Lv, Z.: Construction of intelligent traffic information recommendation system based on long short-term memory. J. Comput. Sci. **26**, 78–86 (2018). https://doi.org/10.1016/j.jocs.2018.03.010

26. Tian, Y., Zhang, K., Li, J., Lin, X., Yang, B.: LSTM-based traffic flow prediction with missing data. Neurocomputing **318**, 297–305 (2018). https://doi.org/10.1016/j.neucom.2018.08.067

27. Ranjan, N., Bhandari, S., Zhao, H.P., Kim, H., Khan, P.: City-wide traffic congestion prediction based on CNN, LSTM and transpose CNN. IEEE Access **8**, 81606–81620 (2020). https://doi.org/10.1109/ACCESS.2020.2991462

28. Liu, D., Hui, S., Li, L., Liu, Z., Zhang, Z.: A method for short-term traffic flow forecasting based on GCN-LSTM. In: Proceedings - 2020 International Conference Computer Vision, Image Deep Learning CVIDL no. Cvidl, pp. 364–368 (2020). https://doi.org/10.1109/CVIDL51233.2020.00-70

29. Chou, C.-H., Huang, Y., Huang, C.-Y., Tseng, V.S.: Long-term traffic time prediction using deep learning with integration of weather effect. In: Yang, Q., Zhou, Z.-H., Gong, Z., Zhang, M.-L., Huang, S.-J. (eds.) PAKDD 2019. LNCS (LNAI), vol. 11440, pp. 123–135. Springer, Cham (2019). https://doi.org/10.1007/978-3-030-16145-3_10

30. Wang, J., Cao, Y., Du, Y., Li, L.: DST: a deep urban traffic flow prediction framework based on spatial-temporal features. In: Douligeris, C., Karagiannis, D., Apostolou, D. (eds.) KSEM 2019. LNCS (LNAI), vol. 11775, pp. 417–427. Springer, Cham (2019). https://doi.org/10.1007/978-3-030-29551-6_37

31. Jin, W., Lin, Y., Wu, Z., Wan, H.: Spatio-temporal recurrent convolutional networks for citywide short-term crowd flows prediction. In: ACM International Conference Proceeding Series, pp. 28–35 (2018). https://doi.org/10.1145/3193077.3193082

32. Duan, Z., Yang, Y., Zhang, K., Ni, Y., Bajgain, S.: Improved deep hybrid networks for urban traffic flow prediction using trajectory data. IEEE Access **6**, 31820–31827 (2018). https://doi.org/10.1109/ACCESS.2018.2845863

33. Sani, A.S., Yuan, D., Jin, J., Gao, L., Yu, S., Dong, Z.Y.: Cyber security framework for Internet of Things-based Energy Internet. Futur. Gener. Comput. Syst. **93**, 849–859 (2019). https://doi.org/10.1016/j.future.2018.01.029

34. Wang, S., Li, F., Stenneth, L., Yu, P.S.: Enhancing traffic congestion estimation with social media by coupled hidden Markov model. In: Frasconi, P., Landwehr, N., Manco, G., Vreeken, J. (eds.) ECML PKDD 2016. LNCS (LNAI), vol. 9852, pp. 247–264. Springer, Cham (2016). https://doi.org/10.1007/978-3-319-46227-1_16

35. Afrin, T., Yodo, N.: A survey of road traffic congestion measures towards a sustainable and resilient transportation system. Sustain **12**(11), 1–23 (2020). https://doi.org/10.3390/su12114660

A Machine Learning Classification Application to Identify Inefficient Novice Programmers

Ijaz Khan[1(✉)], Aysha Al-Mamari[1], Bashayer Al-Abdulsalam[1],
Fatma Al-Abdulsalam[1], Maryam Al-Khansuri[1], Sohail Iqbal Malik[1],
and Abdul Rahim Ahmad[2]

[1] Information Technology Department, Buraimi University College, Al-Buraimi, Oman
{ijaz,f201500665,f201500677,f201500674,f201500501,
sohail}@buc.edu.om
[2] College of Graduate Studies, Universiti Tenaga Nasional, Kajang, Malaysia
abdrahim@uniten.edu.my

Abstract. To preserve their reputation and prestige, the educational institutes are required to provide evidences of their students' academic performance to the governmental bureaus and accreditation agencies. As a consequence, the monitoring individual student academic performance is emerging as a vital task for the educational institutes. The indispensability of this prediction amplifies when it comes to programming language course; which emerges as backbone for Computer Science students. Machine Learning classifiers are considered as productive tools to develop models which can identify the students with inefficient academic performance. The early identification of inefficient students will provide an opportunity to instructor to take appropriate precautionary measures. This paper proposes a prediction model with an added application layer with graphical user interface. The experimental part of paper compares the performance of several machine learning algorithms and comes up with k-NN as appropriate classifier in the addressed context. Further, the application layer of the proposed architecture facilitates instructor with a Graphical User Interface to execute a wide range of operations.

Keywords: Educational data mining · Machine learning · K-Nearest neighbor · Supervised learning

1 Introduction

Introductory programming courses are considered as the basis for computer-related degree programs. These courses cover the basic concepts and structure of computer programming language [1]. However, due to the newness and complex constitution of these courses, these courses appear terrifying for the students. The student tends to face hardships which may result in failure to obtain satisfactory grades [2]. These courses have been classified amongst the seven major challenges in computing education [3]. These are obligatory courses for programming; therefore, the students have to perform convincingly.

© Springer Nature Switzerland AG 2021
H. Badioze Zaman et al. (Eds.): IVIC 2021, LNCS 13051, pp. 423–434, 2021.
https://doi.org/10.1007/978-3-030-90235-3_37

To increase the success rate, the institutions must adopt novel procedures in these courses. A number of researchers, for instance [4–6], highlights the behaviour of students towards programming courses, the error they make and their response to the errors. Similarly, several researchers, for example [7], make use of applications to assess the problem solving skills of the students. Additionally, the modern technological advancements have enabled the institutions to collect huge amount of data about the students.

Machine learning is a prolific to develop models having aptitude of forecasting the final outcome of the students [8]. Several models, for instance [9, 10], take training dataset, searches for the hidden patterns, and develop prediction models. A number of authors have developed machine learning prediction models. This provides an opportunity to instructor to identify the students with insufficient programming skills in a good time. The instructor can prepare appropriate supporting and preventive measures. Several authors [11–13] have prepared machine learning prediction models for predicting students in programming courses. For example, Quille et al. [14] developed a model to predict students' final grades at early stages of semester in an introductory programming course.

This paper proposes a prediction model to identify the inefficient novice programmer at an early stage of the semester. The prediction model is integrated into application software so as to provide a graphical user interface to the instructor. The underlying architecture of the application comprises of machine learning algorithms. Prior to the system design, several prediction models have been developed with distinct machine learning algorithms. The structure of the paper is: in next section, we provide an overview of Machine Learning and highlight the related work Sect. 3 provides the methodology and the experimental evaluation of the entire process. It also explains the structure of application software. Section 4 concludes the paper and provides future plans for extending our work.

2 Literature Review

Machine learning, an application of artificial intelligence, endow modern systems with the ability to learn from experience and perform accurate predictions without being explicitly programmed [15]. These models bestow computers the ability to learn automatically without human assistance [16]. Machine learning cclassification algorithms receive a dataset which consists of prearranged instances and the known outputs. Each instance consists of independent variables (prediction features) and a dependent variable (prediction class). The algorithms process the entire dataset and identify the patterns and rules hidden in the training data. A model, constructed on the basis of the identified rules, gets unseen instances and classifies them in appropriate classes.

Numerous prediction models have been developed aiming at forecasting the final academic outcome of the student. These models have a propensity to identify the students with unsatisfactory outcome. This provides opportunity to the instructor to pursue these students and bring them back to satisfactory pathway, thus, the students get a chance to transform their academic behavior. Ahadi et al. [12] utilized machine learning algorithms to classify the programming course students as "high performing" or "low performing" programmers at an university in Finland. This model helps to identify the students who need extra care and assistance. The authors evaluated several families of machine learning classifiers over a data of 86 instances. Random Forest appeared as the leading classifier. The significant attributes of the dataset were student's CGPA and the grades in different assessment tools.

Khan et al. [11] tracked student academic performance in the introductory programming courses. This study, carried out in University College in Oman, implemented several classifiers over a dataset of 50 students. Decision Tree and Neural network appeared with the highest prediction accuracy. Osmanbegovic et al. [17] compared several algorithms for the binary classification of student at at University of Tuzla. Naive Bayes prevails Decision tree and neural network algorithms. The dataset comprised of 257 instanced. Rawat et al. [18] developed a hybrid classification model based on machine learning classifiers to predict students' academic performance in an university in India. Costa et al. [19] evaluated the effectiveness of educational data mining techniques for early prediction of students' academic failure in introductory programming courses at an university in Brazil. The authors found Support Vector Machine as the leading algorithm in their context. Asif et al. [20] presents a case study to forecast the final outcome of student at an early stage of the study of a 4-years degree program in an University in Pakistan.

3   Methodology and Experiments

This architecture resembles the essential structure of machine learning model. Figure 1 shows the phases of the methodology. The Data Preparation phase is dedicated to the collection of data and executing various aspects to prepare the dataset. The dataset is transformed into a form readable by the machine learning algorithms. The next phase is devoted to the pre-processing of data, which refines the dataset to produce better results. Since, it is a binary classification model with High (majority class) and Low (minority class). Model selection phase compares several machine learning algorithms and then selects the one which appears most suitable in the addressed pedagogical context. The application phase involves the application software which provides graphical user interface to the instructors. Each of the phases has been further explained in the subsequent sections of this paper.

In this research, the data pre-processing and model selection is performed in Waikato Environment for Knowledge Analysis (WEKA). WEKA is free software which contains numerous machine learning algorithms for data mining researchers. In the model implementation phase, we used Python programming language. The analysis is carried out through Confusion Matrix [21].

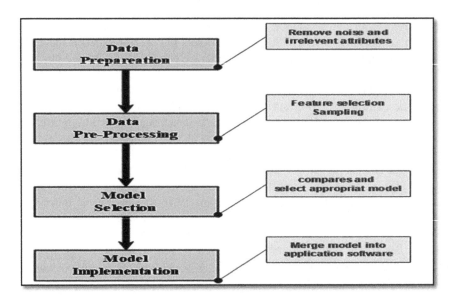

Fig. 1. An overview of the proposed model

3.1 Data Preparation

The dataset in this research consists of the student academic records for introductory programming course taught at all majors of Information Technology department et al.-Buraimi University College (BUC), Oman. The data spans over a time periods of 6 semesters. The data is collected from registration department of the college and all the ethical issues are followed carefully.

Prior to Machine learning classification, the dataset must transformed into a form acceptable by the classifiers. In order to do so, we initially eliminated the attributes which do not play any role in the prediction but to a certain extent they are associated with the student's privacy. These attributes include the student ID and name.

The classifier cannot understand and interpret the noisy data. This may include missing values where attributes in an instance may have irrelevant or missing value. The existence of such instance affects classification; therefore, we removed the noisy instances. In our case, the students who dropped the course at certain stage of the semester or those who did not attend the final exam are eliminated.

By the end of data preparation phase, there are total of 185 instances in the training dataset with 14 attributes and one prediction class. The prediction class categorizes students into 2 classes ("High" and "Low"). The "High" class includes the students having grades more than 65%.

Table 1. The list of attributes in the dataset

Attribute	Description	Values	Correlation
Previous Sem. GPA	GPA in previous semester	Continuous (0–4)	0.554075
Midterm Grade	Grades in Midterm Exam	Percentage	0.523422
CGPA	Cumulative Grade Points of student	Continuous (0–4)	0.389276
Hours Registered	Hours registered in current semester	Nominal	0.144507
Year	Year of study	Nominal	0.093237
Days of classes	The number of days classes are held in a week	Nominal	0.082673
Major	Major of the student	Nominal	0.082144
Section	Class section	Nominal	0.070136
Gender	Gender of the student	Nominal	0.052063
Sponsorship	Whether sponsored for study by government	Nominal	0.030429
Dorm	Whether resides in hostel	Nominal	0.015693
Nationality	Nationality	Nominal	0.006785
Program	Degree	Nominal	0.00358
Session	Study in morning or evening	Nominal	0.000694
Status	Class Variable	Nominal (Pass, Fail)	

3.2 Data Pre-processing

The data pre-processing prepares the data for the machine learning classification algorithms. This includes the steps which makes dataset easily interpretable by the machine learning algorithm. High Dimensionality (dataset having large number of attributes) and Imbalanced Data (dataset where the number of instances from one class is much larger than the number of instances from other class) are the two major problems likely to affect the performance of classification [22]. The high dimensionality is eliminated through the process of attribute selection which yields a set of most significant attributes for machine learning classification. Imbalanced data can be dealt by implementing sampling algorithms; which balances the instances in both classes.

Feature Selection. There are a number of algorithms meant for selecting the significant attributes from the dataset. We chose CorrelationAttributeEvaluator [23]. This technique evaluates the worth of an attribute by measuring the Pearson's correlation between it and the prediction class. Table 1 demonstrates, the features in the dataset, their description and the Pearson correlation with the prediction feature.

Sampling. Training with an imbalance dataset poses challenges for machine learning algorithms and it tends to predict the majority class more than the minority class. However, applying suitable techniques for class balancing can decrease the difference between the classes and can enhance the classifier's performance [24]. There are several class-balancing algorithms which either perform undersampling or oversampling. In order to minimize the class imbalance problem, we use SMOTE [25]. This algorithm makes use of oversampling technique to rebalance the original training dataset [26].

3.3 Model Selection

We implemented a set of state-of-the arts classifiers for classification purpose. The experiments aim to come up with the classification performance of machine learning algorithms in classifying students into binary classes. In order to partition the dataset, 10-fold cross validation is used. In order to measure the performance of classifiers, we use accuracy, Recall, Sensitivity, F-measure and Mathew Correlation Coefficient (MCC).

Accuracy. Classification accuracy assesses the overall performance of the prediction models. It shows how successful is the model in identifying the correct true classes.

F-Measure. Precision and recalls are amongst the supreme evaluation metrics for machine learning classifiers. Recall is the ratio of positive instances that are predicted correctly and the actual number of positive instances. Precision shows, out of all the positive instances that model predicted correctly, how many are actually positive. However, it is sometimes exigent to assess a model based on precision and recall values. F-Measure takes into consideration both precision and recall and calculates their harmonic average.

$$\text{Recall } = TP/(TP + FN) \tag{1}$$

$$\text{Precision} = TP/(TP + FP) \tag{2}$$

$$\text{F} - \text{Measure} = (2 * (\text{Precision} * \text{Recall }))/((\text{Precision } + \text{Recall})) \tag{3}$$

Matthews Correlation Coefficient (MCC). This metric demonstrates ranking capabilities of the classification model. It utilizes the entire confusion matrix information (TP, FN, FP, TN) and assess the performance of binary classification model proportionally both to the size of dataset [27].

$$\text{MCC } = ((TP.TN - FP.FN))/\sqrt{((TP + FP).(TP.FN).(TN.FP).(TN.FN))} \tag{4}$$

Figure 2 compares the accuracy of the classifiers. It illustrates k-NN achieving an accuracy of above 80% while the remaining classifiers stay slightly below. This demonstrates that all of the models are showing a good understanding of the training dataset. However, High accuracy, alone, does not guarantee the sophistication of prediction model. Therefore, we compare the F-Measure and MCC of the classifiers. Figure 3 illustrates F-measure and MCC of the classifiers. The chart demonstrates k-NN achieving the highest F-Measure followed by Support Vector Machine. k-NN produces the highest MCC as well, followed by decision tree and Support Vector Machine.

This evaluation concludes that Machine learning algorithms have the potential to appear handy in predicting student's academic performance. We observe that k-NN is more suitable for our educational context since it is providing higher accuracy, F-Measure and MCC. Therefore, we choose k-NN based prediction model for our education context and to convert it prediction model into application software.

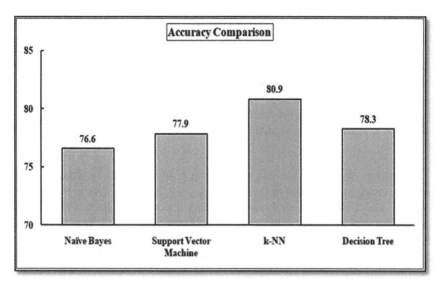

Fig. 2. The comparison of accuracy of classifiers

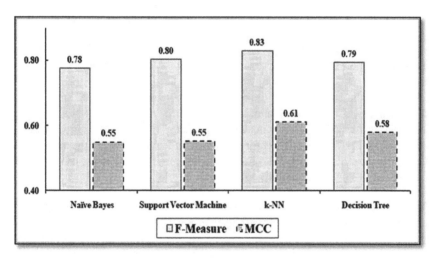

Fig. 3. Comparing the F-Measures of classifiers

3.4 Model Implementation

One of the core aims of this research is to transform the developed model into an easily explicable format so the instructors having minimum computer knowledge can execute it. In order to achieve this objective, we developed application software which provides a Graphical User Interface (GUI) to enable an instructor to take advantage of the prediction model without gaining in-depth knowledge of machine learning. Figure 4 demonstrates general architecture of the application. The whole training and prediction process is encompassed within 3 major tracks. The application has been developed in Python programming language.

Prediction Interface. The instructor runs the prediction model at the end of midterm exam. The model classifies the students as either "pass" or "fail". This provides an opportunity to the instructor to identify the struggling students in a good time and take necessary measures so they do not end up with unsatisfactory final results. The instructor has an option to either predict the final outcome of the whole class or for a single student individually.

The instructor compiles a file with CSV format in MS Excel. The architecture of the file must be exactly same as that of the training dataset. The student features, in training dataset, includes Midterm Grade, Hours_Resitered, Previous Semester GPA and CGPA (Table 1). The final column (prediction feature) "Status" must be filled with a question mark ("?"). This file is provided, as input, to the application. The application executes the prediction model and predicts the final outcome of each student. The "?" in the input file is filled with either "pass" or "fail".

The instructor fills the form (Fig. 5) in case the aim is to forecast the final outcome of a single student. The form in Fig. 5 includes the same 4 significant features as in the training dataset. Once the form is submitted, Python generates a CSV file with only single record in it with "?" in the last column. The prediction model executes for the single unseen instance and expected "pass" or "fail" is generated.

Settings Interface. The elementary principle of k-NN is that the instances having analogous properties exists in close immediacy [28]. The distance of unseen instance is calculated from the entire set of training instances. A voting procedure, among predefined k-neighbors, decides the label of unseen instance. Therefore, k-NN is considered an unstable classifier due to the fact that an alteration the value of k and distance function can change their performance. Therefore, an essential feature added in the application is to allow the instructor to modify the values of the essential parameters of k-NN. Figure 6 depicts the options available in this application.

The instructor can provide a positive integer value for k. The value of k is preferred to be an odd number to break the ties in case of an equal number of votes for both classes. The value of k must not be high to promote over-fitting. Most of the author prefers it to be the square root of the total instances in the training dataset. The application provides a set of distance function. The instructor can choose from Manhattan, Euclidean and Chebyshev function which are derived from Minkowski.

Evaluation Interface. The application provides an opportunity to look into the technical details of the prediction model. It provides the accuracy, precision, recall, specificity, and F-Measure of the model.

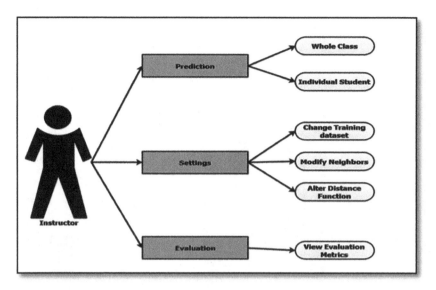

Fig. 4. General illustration of the application software

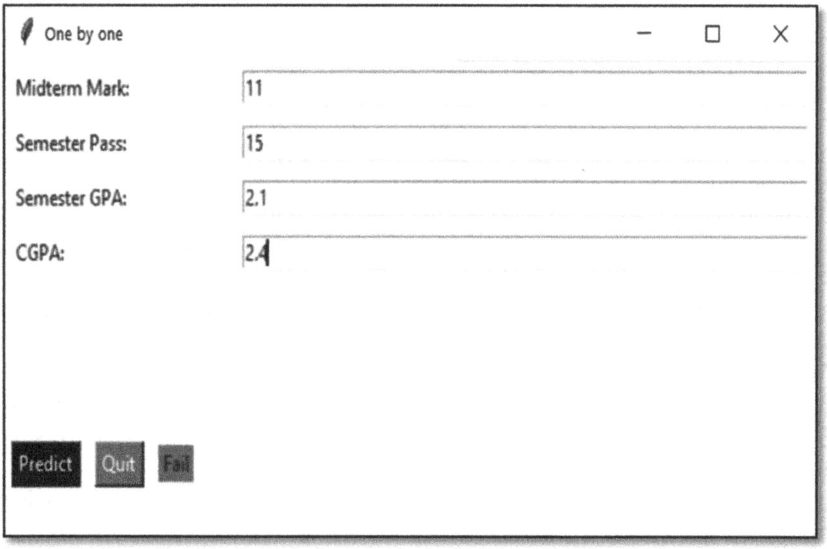

One by one	— □ ×
Midterm Mark:	11
Semester Pass:	15
Semester GPA:	2.1
CGPA:	2.4

Predict Quit Fail

Fig. 5. Predicting individual student's final outcome

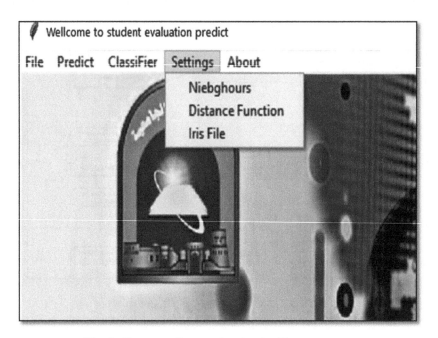

Fig. 6. The menu allows to alter the classifiers parameters

4 Conclusion

The literature highlights the effectiveness of machine learning in the student performance academic performance prediction model. In this research, we performed several experiments to come with a machine learning algorithm which appears appropriate for the addressed context. We implemented several state-of-the-art algorithms over a dataset of 185 instances with intention to identify the students who are performing inefficiently in the introductory programming course. The initial model selection phase concluded k-NN overcomes other algorithms.

We propose application software which provides a graphical user interface, so the instructor can perform prediction of the whole class or individual student. The interface executes k-NN algorithm and the instructor has an access to modify the essential parameters.

The proposed model is aimed for the prediction of students who perform inefficiently in programming courses. In future, we aim to include several other attributes which might be helpful in enhancing the prediction model. At application level, we aim to add an adaptive consultation module, where the application will have a command to send adaptive consolations to the students.

References

1. Malik, S.I., Coldwell-Neilson, J.: A model for teaching an introductory programming course using ADRI. Educ. Inf. Technol. **22**(3), 1089–1120 (2016). https://doi.org/10.1007/s10639-016-9474-0

2. Alturki, R.A.: Measuring and improving student performance in an introductory programming course. Inf. Educ. Int. J. **15**(2), 183–204 (2016)
3. Isa, N.A.M., Derus, S.: Students experience in learning fundamental programming: an analysis by gender perception. Adv. J. Tech. Vocat. Educ. **1**(1), 240–248 (2017)
4. Grover, S., Pea, R.: Computational thinking in K–12: a review of the state of the field. Educ. Res. **42**(1), 38–43 (2013)
5. White, G., Sivitanides, M.: An empirical investigation of the relationship between success in mathematics and visual programming courses. J. Inf. Syst. Educ. **14**(4), 409 (2003)
6. Watson, C., Li, F.W., Godwin, J.L.: No tests required: comparing traditional and dynamic predictors of programming success. In: Proceedings of the 45th ACM Technical Symposium on Computer Science Education (2014)
7. Malik, S., Mathew, R., Hammood, M.: PROBSOL: a web-based application to develop problem-solving skills in introductory programming. In: Al-Masri, Ahmed, Curran, Kevin (eds.) Smart Technologies and Innovation for a Sustainable Future. ASTI, pp. 295–302. Springer, Cham (2019). https://doi.org/10.1007/978-3-030-01659-3_34
8. Khan, I., et al.: A conceptual framework to aid attribute selection in machine learning student performance prediction models. Int. J. Interact. Mob. Technol. **15**(15), 4 (2021)
9. Asif, R., et al.: Analyzing undergraduate students' performance using educational data mining. Comput. Educ. **113**, 177–194 (2017)
10. Al-Sudani, S., Palaniappan, R.: Predicting students' final degree classification using an extended profile. Educ. Inf. Technol. **24**(4), 2357–2369 (2019). https://doi.org/10.1007/s10639-019-09873-8
11. Khan, I., et al.: Tracking student performance in introductory programming by means of machine learning. In: 2019 4th MEC International Conference on Big Data and Smart City (ICBDSC). IEEE (2019)
12. Ahadi, A., et al. Exploring machine learning methods to automatically identify students in need of assistance. In: Proceedings of the eleventh annual International Conference on International Computing Education Research. ACM (2015)
13. Liao, S.N., et al.: A robust machine learning technique to predict low-performing students. ACM Trans. Comput. Educ. (TOCE) **19**(3), 1–19 (2019)
14. Quille, K., Bergin, S.: CS1: how will they do? how can we help? a decade of research and practice. Comput. Sci. Educ. **29**(2–3), 254–282 (2019)
15. Mitchell, R., Michalski, J., Carbonell, T.: An artificial Intelligence Approach. Springer, Heidelberg (2013). https://doi.org/10.1007/978-3-662-12405-5
16. Giacoumidis, E., et al.: Harnessing machine learning for fiber-induced nonlinearity mitigation in long-haul coherent optical OFDM. Future Internet **11**(1), 2 (2019)
17. Osmanbegovic, E., Suljic, M.: Data mining approach for predicting student performance. Econ. Rev. J. Econ. Bus. **10**(1), 3–12 (2012)
18. Rawat, K., Malhan, I.V.: a hybrid classification method based on machine learning classifiers to predict performance in educational data mining. In: Rama Krishna, C., Dutta, M., Kumar, R. (eds.) Proceedings of 2nd International Conference on Communication, Computing and Networking. LNNS, vol. 46, pp. 677–684. Springer, Singapore (2019). https://doi.org/10.1007/978-981-13-1217-5_67
19. Costa, E.B., et al.: Evaluating the effectiveness of educational data mining techniques for early prediction of students' academic failure in introductory programming courses. Comput. Hum. Behav. **73**, 247–256 (2017)
20. Asif, R., Merceron, A., Pathan, M.K.: Predicting student academic performance at degree level: a case study. Int. J. Intell. Syst. Appl. **7**(1), 49 (2014)
21. Tharwat, A., Classification assessment methods. Applied Computing and Informatics (2018)

22. Márquez-Vera, C., Morales, C.R., Soto, S.V.: Predicting school failure and dropout by using data mining techniques. IEEE Revista Iberoamericana de Tecnologias del Aprendizaje **8**(1), 7–14 (2013)
23. Hall, M.A., Correlation-based feature selection for machine learning (1999)
24. Tan, P.-N.: Introduction to Data Mining. Pearson Education, Noida (2007)
25. Chawla, N.V., et al.: SMOTE: synthetic minority over-sampling technique. J. Artif. Intell. Res. **16**, 321–357 (2002)
26. Fernández, A., et al.: SMOTE for learning from imbalanced data: progress and challenges, marking the 15-year anniversary. J. Artif. Intell. Res. **61**, 863–905 (2018)
27. Chicco, D., Jurman, G.: The advantages of the Matthews correlation coefficient (MCC) over F1 score and accuracy in binary classification evaluation. BMC Genomics **21**(1), 6 (2020)
28. Kotsiantis, S., Pierrakeas, C., Pintelas, P.: Predicting students' performance in distance learning using machine learning techniques. Appl. Artif. Intell. **18**(5), 411–426 (2004)

Minimizing Classification Errors in Imbalanced Dataset Using Means of Sampling

Ijaz Khan[1,2]([✉]), Abdul Rahim Ahmad[3], Nafaa Jabeur[4],
and Mohammed Najah Mahdi[5]

[1] College of Graduate Studies, Universiti Tenaga Nasional, Kajang, Malaysia
[2] Information Technology Department, Buraimi University College, Al-Buraimi, Oman
ijaz@buc.edu.om
[3] College of Computing and Informatics, Universiti Tenaga Nasional, Kajang, Malaysia
Abdrahim@uniten.edu.my
[4] Computer Science Department, German University of Technology, Muscat, Oman
nafaa.jabeur@gutech.edu.om
[5] Institute of Informatics and Computing in Energy, Universiti Tenaga Nasional,
Kajang, Malaysia
najah.mahdi@uniten.edu.my

Abstract. Classification, a significant application of machine learning, labels each instance of the dataset into one of the predefined classes. Problems occur when the number of instances in the classes is not uniform. The exceptional lyuneven class distribution gives rise to class imbalancing issues which tend to demote the overall performance of the classifier. A set of data-level algorithms are available which are applied to adjust the class distribution. The class imbalancing emerges frequently in datasets from educational domains where the number of students with unsatisfactory performance general appears in low number comparing to the students with satisfactory outcomes. This paper applies a set of data-level sampling algorithms over a dataset taken from an educational domain. It underlines the consequences rising from classification with imbalanced dataset. This research confirms that a classification model achieving higher accuracy may not appear effective in correct identification of instances in minority class. Classification with an imbalance dataset may produce low recall, precision and F-Measure for classes with lower number of instances. The performance of classification model improves with application of data level algorithm. However, it highlights the supremacy of oversampling algorithm over undersampling algorithms.

Keywords: Machine learning · Oversampling · Undersampling · Spread subsampling · SMOTE · Class imbalance · Student performance prediction

1 Introduction

A dataset comprises of instances which are grouped in two (binary classification) or more than two categories (multiclass classification). For instance, a dataset may comprise of students academic results, in a course, where each student is labeled as 'pass' or 'fail'. The

© Springer Nature Switzerland AG 2021
H. Badioze Zaman et al. (Eds.): IVIC 2021, LNCS 13051, pp. 435–446, 2021.
https://doi.org/10.1007/978-3-030-90235-3_38

class having larger number of instances is referred as 'majority' while the less appearing class is called 'minority' class. The class imbalance issues emerge if the class distribution is not uniform [1]. This poses challenges for classification process. If a classifier is trained with an imbalance dataset then it possess a propensity for predicting majority class more than the minority class and thus influences the accuracy of the classifier [2]. Although the minority class makes up the least of the dataset but its identification gets the prime significance [3]. The standard classifiers are designed to lessen the classification error irrespective of the distribution of instances in the classes [4]. Generally, It is difficult for the classifiers to learn from the minority class [5].

Educational Data Mining (EDM) mines the data, collected from educational domain, to discover significant patterns in an attempt to optimize the learner and the learning environment [6]. Due to advancements in Information and Communication Technology, there has been a gigantic increase in the production of data. The educational institutes are desperate to scrutinize the available data and extract information useful in making productive decisions [7]. Several machine learning classifiers, primarily supervised, have emerged useful to develop student performance prediction models [8].

The imbalanced class distribution can adversely affect the performance of a model. However, authors usually give inadequate concentration to the class distribution. Several authors, for instance [9–13], developed models with imbalanced dataset. Due to high imbalance ratio in [10], the recall for several classes fall below 0.20. Similarly in [11], some classes achieves a recall of less than 0.10 comparing to other classes which attain 0.70. The model in [13] illustrates a higher difference in F-Measure of prediction classes. It accentuates towards the need of careful attention to the class distribution prior to applying machine learning classifiers.

The contribution of this research is to highlight the consequences of training classifiers with a dataset having uneven class distribution. This work confirms that the performance of classifiers can be enhanced if standard sampling algorithms are applied. The paper is organized as; the next section provides literature review of the sampling techniques. Section 3 provides the experimental setups and Sect. 4 provides details of experimental evaluation. Section 5 is dedicated to discussion and Sect. 6 concludes the paper.

2 Literature Review

A number of data level and algorithm level algorithm have been developed to handle the class imbalancing issues [14]. The data level algorithms include a variety of techniques for undersampling and oversampling. The algorithmic level comprises of techniques for instance, fine-tuning of the probabilistic estimation at the decision tree leaf, cost-sensitive learning, fine-tuning decision threshold, and recognition-based learning in binary classification [15]. Despite the fact that there is no incorporated rule for balancing the class distribution, still it can be inferred that applying sampling techniques over training dataset generate optimal results than proceeding without sampling [16].

Preferably, all the classes in the dataset must have equal number of instances [17]. The Imbalance Ratio (IR) measures imbalancing in a dataset, and is computed as the ratio of majority and the minority classes [18]. The dataset having an IR of 1 is absolutely balanced. Imbalancing rises with an increase in the IR. The aim of data balancing is to reduce the IR and bring it closer to 1. The literature demonstrates that minimizing IR can enhance classification performance.

2.1 Data Level Sampling

The data-level algorithms, oversampling and undersampling, apply algorithms to adjust the Imbalance Ratio. Oversampling algorithms add additional instances in the minority class. On the contrary, undersampling removes instances from the majority class [19]. Figure 1 portrays undersampling and oversampling techniques. The dataset in the middle is having additional apples. Undersampling (left-side) removes apples, while oversampling (right side) adds bananas to adjust the class distribution.

Undersampling removes instances from the majority class to reduce the difference between the classes. Spread Subsampling, an undersampling algorithm, adjusts the class distribution by randomly removing instances from the majority class [20]. This algorithm accepts a parameter (Spread-Distribution) which denotes the ratio between the classes.

Synthetic Minority Over-sampling Technique (SMOTE) [21] is the most prevailing data level algorithm [22]. It makes use of oversampling technique to balance the dataset [23]. SMOTE generates new instances for minority class by interpolating among several minority class instances that recline together [24]. It computes the k-nearest neighbors of minority class and subsequently selects several neighbors which take part in generating new synthetic instances. This algorithm does not change the instances in majority class. The (percentage) parameter denotes the increase in the minority class.

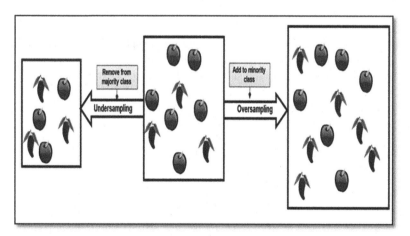

Fig. 1. Illustration of undersampling (left) and oversampling (right) over an imbalanced dataset (middle)

Asif et al. [10] performed a multiclass classification to forecast student academic performance. The dataset has highly uneven distribution of instances and at some point, for instance class A and C, the imbalance ratio is 1:46. Subsequently, some of the classes have as low as 0–20% of recall comparing to a higher recall for other classes.

Osmanbegovic et al. [9] classified students into binary classes with a dataset where the majority class has over three times more instances than the minority class. Consequently, all the applied classifiers generate a higher precision and recall for the majority class. In Kabakchieva [11], due to high imbalance ratio, decision tree (J48) achieved less than 0.10 recall for 'average' and 'excellent' classes as compare to other classes that achieve nearly or more than 0.70. Similarly Kaur et al. [13]and Ramesth [18] made use of imbalanced datasets and thus the classifiers bias specific classes. The literature emphasizes the need of sampling prior to applying machine learning classifiers.

3   Experimental Setups

We use Waikato Environment for Knowledge Analysis (WEKA) [25] for experiments. For classifiers' training we choose 10-fold cross validation [26]. We choose k-Nearest Neighbors (k-NN), Artificial Neural Networks (ANN), Support Vector Machine (SVM), Naive Bayes (NB), and Random Forest. We assess the performance of models using Confusion Matrix [27] (Table 1).

Table 1. Confusion matrix for binary classification model

	Majority	Minority
Majority	True Positive (TP)	False Negative (FN)
Minority	False Positive (FP)	True Negative (TN)

We use several evaluation metrics to evaluate and compare performance of the classifiers. Recall is a measure of all positive instances and the number of instances the model predicted correctly. Precision shows out of all the positive instances that model predicted correctly, how many are actually positive. F-Measure takes precision and recall in account and computes their weighted average. Accuracy is the ratio of the correctly classified and the total instances in the dataset.

$$\text{Recall} \ = \ \text{TP}/(\text{TP} + \text{FN}) \tag{1}$$

$$\text{Precision} \ = \ \text{TP}/(\text{TP} + \text{FP}) \tag{2}$$

$$\text{F} - \text{Measure} = 2 * ((\text{Precision} * \text{Recall})/(\text{Precision} + \text{Recall})) \tag{3}$$

$$\text{Accuracy} \ = \ (\text{TP} + \text{TN})/(\text{TP} + \text{FN} + \text{FP} + \text{TN}) \tag{4}$$

The dataset is taken from Al-Buraimi University College, Sultanate of Oman. It consists of the records of 151 students from a course. The instances are classified as "Low" and "High".

4 Experimental Evaluation and Results

The imbalanced dataset, in this research, is having an Imbalance Ratio of 1 to 3.19. Approximately 66% of the instances fall in majority class (High) class. There is low number of instances in minority (Low) class. We perform 3 sets of experiments a) with imbalanced dataset b) with undersampling and c) with oversampling. Figure 2 illustrates the class distribution in original/imbalanced dataset (centre), after undersampling (left) and oversampling (right).

4.1 Classification with Imbalanced Dataset

To begin with, we perform classification with an imbalance dataset (original dataset). The upper part of Table 2 illustrates the confusion matrixes from the models generated in this set of experiments.

Figure 3 compares the accuracy and F-Measure (in percent) for both minority and majority classes for the generated models. It illustrates that a higher accuracy (near to 80%) is achieved by most of the classifiers. Even though, the classifiers achieved higher accuracy and F-Measure for majority class, however, F-Measure for minority class is low. Support vector machine has achieves low F-Measure for minority (75.8%) class comparing to its accuracy (89.4%). Moreover, the difference between F-Measure of majority and minority class is high for all classifiers. It illustrates the biasness of classifiers towards majority class for an imbalanced dataset. Even though, the classifiers attain higher accuracy but are not able to accurately classify the instances from the minority class.

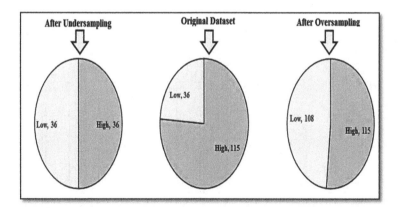

Fig. 2. Class distribution; original dataset, after undersampling (left) and oversampling (right).

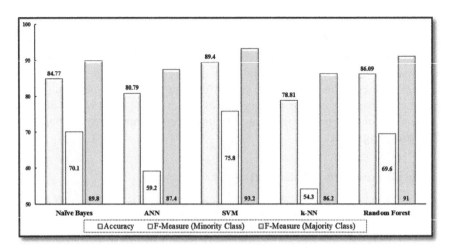

Fig. 3. A comparison of classifiers' accuracy, F-Measures (majority class), F-Measure (minority class) with imbalanced dataset

4.2 Classification with Undersampling Dataset

We apply undersampling algorithm (Spread Subsampling) to balance the dataset. The middle part of Table 2 illustrates the confusion matrixes of the models generated in this set of experiments. Figure 4 compares the accuracy of classifiers achieved with imbalanced datasets against the accuracy achieved subsequent to applying undersampling of dataset.

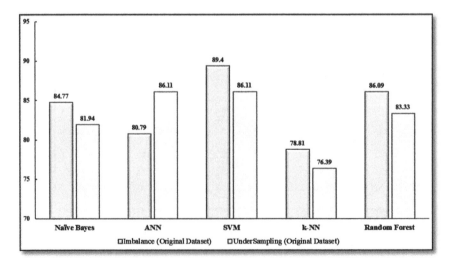

Fig. 4. Comparing the accuracy of classifiers before and after undersampling

Figure 4 also illustrates a decrease in accuracy of most of the classifiers after undersampling. This indicates an enhancement in the classifiers' performance when the dataset is subjected to undersampling. To further investigate, Fig. 5 compares the increase (in percent) in precision and recall for the minority class. It illuminates an increase in their precision and recall.

4.3 Classification with Oversampling

We make use of SMOTE, an oversampling algorithm with 200% as percentage value. SMOTE increases the minority class instances to 108 (Fig. 2). SMOTE creates new instances and appends them at the end of the dataset. In order to eliminate over-fitting, we randomize the instances to come up with a dataset having randomly scattered instances. The bottom part of Table-2 provides the confusion matrixes of the models generated in this set of experiments.

The chart in Fig. 6 compares classifiers' performance using average F-Measure, and the net increase in the precision of minority class with the dataset processed with oversampling algorithm (SMOTE). It demonstrates that the average F-Measure increases with oversampling. It also illustrates that oversampling has increased the precision of the minority class. The highest increase is achieved by Artificial Neural Networks and the lowest is achieved by Support Vector Machine. It shows an enhancement in the classifiers' performance with the dataset oversampled with SMOTE.

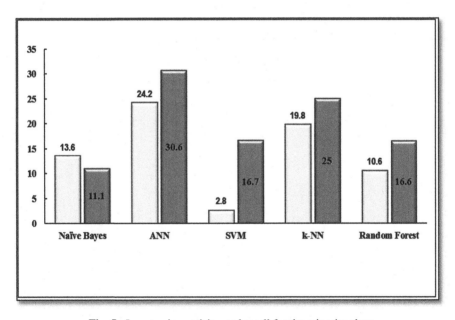

Fig. 5. Increase in precision and recall for the minority class

5 Discussion

This section compares the results obtained from all three sets of experiments. Figure 7 displays the variation in F-Measure and accuracy of classifiers. The charts show that the overall accuracy of classifiers fluctuates when we move from imbalanced dataset towards sampling. It shows a rise in the accuracy of most of the classifiers. In order to conclude the F-Measure, we produced the chart in Fig. 8 which shows the variation in F-Measure of the minority class.

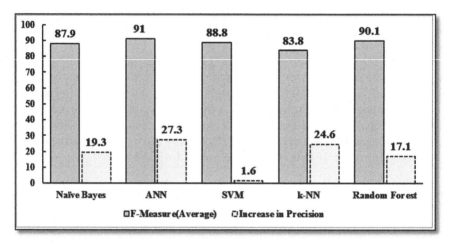

Fig. 6. Comparison average F-Measure and increase in precision

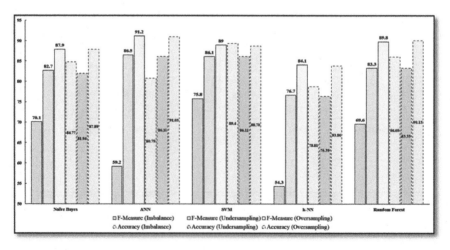

Fig. 7. Fluctuation in F-Measure and accuracy with imbalanced and sampled datasets

Table 2. Confusion matrixes of the classification with imbalance and sampled datasets

	Classifier	True Positive (TP)	False Negative (FN)	False Positive (FP)	True Negative (TN)
Imbalanced Dataset	Naïve Bayes	101	14	9	27
	Artificial neural network	101	14	15	21
	Support vector machine	110	5	11	25
	k-NN	100	15	17	19
	Random forest	106	9	12	24
Undersampling	Naïve Bayes	28	8	5	31
	Artificial neural network	30	6	4	32
	Support vector machine	31	5	5	31
	k-NN	27	9	8	28
	Random forest	30	6	6	30
Oversampling	Naïve Bayes	98	17	10	98
	Artificial neural network	100	15	5	103
	Support vector machine	97	18	7	101
	k-NN	92	23	13	95
	Random forest	104	11	11	97

The analysis in the chart in Fig. 7 also reveals a significant rise in the F-Measure of minority class after sampling. Further, it illustrates oversampling (SMOTE) prevailing undersampling in term of F-Measure of the minority class. In this aspect, SMOTE shows dominance over Spread Subsampling.

The classifiers having F-Measure close to 1 and with the minimum difference between F-Measure of both classes are considered the better choices. Figure 8 shows the difference between the F-Measure of both majority and minority classes. The difference decreases from imbalanced dataset to undersampling and then to oversampling.

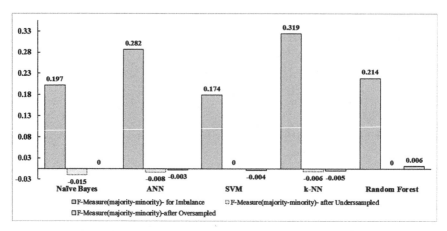

Fig. 8. Decrease in the difference between the F-Measure

Figure 8 shows that the difference between the F-Measure of majority and minority classes is higher for the imbalance dataset. However, the difference is negligible after balancing with undersampling and oversampling. It confirms that data level algorithms (undersampling and oversampling) appear effective in reducing the difference between the F-Measure. However, it also concludes the dominance of oversampled datasets.

This research verifies that the classifiers with an imbalanced dataset have the tendency to incorrectly classify instances as majority class. We observed that both undersampling and oversampling algorithms are effective in decreasing the difference between the F-Measures of majority and minority classes. In both sampling techniques, the classifiers achieve reasonable accuracy and F-Measure. However, it shows that oversampling (SMOTE) has performed better than Spread Subsampling. It also shows that solely accuracy does not confirm the supremacy of a classifier. Other evaluation metrics, for instance F-Measure, precision, and recall, should be taken into account while assessing a model's performance.

6   Conclusion

This research compares the performance of classifiers with imbalanced datasets, from an educational institute, to the dataset which is balanced with oversampling and undersampling algorithms. We conclude that classification with an imbalanced dataset tends to generate higher accuracy, but produce lower F-Measure for the minority class. This shows that the classifiers misclassify the minority class instances. We apply data level algorithms (Spread Subsampling and SMOTE). Spread subsampling and SMOTE increase F-Measure for the minority class. However, SMOTE performs better than Spread Subsampling in attaining higher F-Measure and accuracy.

References

1. Luque, A., et al.: The impact of class imbalance in classification performance metrics based on the binary confusion matrix. Pattern Recogn. **91**, 216–231 (2019)
2. Tyagi, S., Mittal, S.: Sampling approaches for imbalanced data classification problem in machine learning. In: Proceedings of ICRIC 2019, pp. 209–221. Springer (2020). https://doi.org/10.1007/978-3-030-29407-6_17
3. Leevy, J.L., Khoshgoftaar, T.M., Bauder, R.A., Seliya, N.: A survey on addressing high-class imbalance in big data. J. Big Data **5**(1), 1–30 (2018). https://doi.org/10.1186/s40537-018-0151-6
4. Elreedy, D., Atiya, A.F.: A comprehensive analysis of synthetic minority oversampling technique (SMOTE) for handling class imbalance. Inf. Sci. **505**, 32–64 (2019)
5. Raghuwanshi, B.S., Shukla, S.: SMOTE based class-specific extreme learning machine for imbalanced learning. Knowl.-Based Syst. **187**, 104814 (2019)
6. Romero, C., Ventura, S.: Educational data mining and learning analytics: an updated survey. Wiley Interdisc. Rev. Data Mining Knowl. Disc. **10**(3), e1355 (2020)
7. Leitner, P., Khalil, M., Ebner, M.: Learning analytics in higher education—a literature review. Learn. Anal. Fundaments Appl. Trends **94**, 1–23 (2017). https://doi.org/10.1007/978-3-319-52977-6_1
8. Khan, I., et al.: A conceptual framework to aid attribute selection in machine learning student performance prediction models. Int. J. Interactive Mob. Technol. **15**(15) (2021)
9. Osmanbegovic, E., Suljic, M.: Data mining approach for predicting student performance. Econ. Rev. J. Econ. Bus. **10**(1), 3–12 (2012)
10. Asif, R., Merceron, A., Pathan, M.K.: Predicting student academic performance at degree level: a case study. Int. J. Intell. Syst. Appl. **7**(1), 49 (2014)
11. Kabakchieva, D.: Predicting student performance by using data mining methods for classification. Cybern. Inf. Technol. **13**(1), 61–72 (2013)
12. Ramesh, V., Parkavi, P., Ramar, K.: Predicting student performance: a statistical and data mining approach. Int. J. Comput. Appl. **63**(8), 35–39 (2013)
13. Kaur, P., Singh, M., Josan, G.S.: Classification and prediction based data mining algorithms to predict slow learners in education sector. Procedia Comput. Sci. **57**, 500–508 (2015)
14. Ali, A., Shamsuddin, S.M., Ralescu, A.L.: Classification with class imbalance problem. Int. J. Advance Soft Compu. Appl. **5**(3) (2013)
15. Huang, Y.-M., Du, S.-X.: Weighted support vector machine for classification with uneven training class sizes. In: 2005 International Conference on Machine Learning and Cybernetics. IEEE (2005)
16. Khan, I., et al.: Tracking student performance in introductory programming by means of machine learning. In: 2019 4th MEC International Conference on Big Data and Smart City (ICBDSC). IEEE (2019)
17. Loyola-González, O., et al.: An empirical study of oversampling and undersampling methods for lcmine an emerging pattern based classifier. In: Mexican Conference on Pattern Recognition, Springer (2019). https://doi.org/10.1007/978-3-642-38989-4_27
18. Verbiest, N., et al.: Preprocessing noisy imbalanced datasets using SMOTE enhanced with fuzzy rough prototype selection. Appl. Soft Comput. **22**, 511–517 (2014)
19. Mohammed, R., Rawashdeh, J., Abdullah, M.: Machine learning with oversampling and undersampling techniques: overview study and experimental results. In: 2020 11th International Conference on Information and Communication Systems (ICICS). IEEE (2020)
20. Hernandez, J., Carrasco-Ochoa, J.A., Martínez-Trinidad, J.F.: An empirical study of oversampling and undersampling for instance selection methods on imbalance datasets. In: Iberoamerican Congress on Pattern Recognition. Springer (2013). https://doi.org/10.1007/978-3-642-41822-8_33

21. Chawla, N.V., et al.: SMOTE: synthetic minority over-sampling technique. J. Artif. Intell. Res. **16**, 321–357 (2002)
22. García, S., Luengo, J., Herrera, F.: Tutorial on practical tips of the most influential data preprocessing algorithms in data mining. Knowl.-Based Syst. **98**, 1–29 (2016)
23. Fernández, A., et al.: SMOTE for learning from imbalanced data: progress and challenges, marking the 15-year anniversary. J. Artif. Intell. Res. **61**, 863–905 (2018)
24. Elreedy, D., Atiya, A.F.: A novel distribution analysis for smote oversampling method in handling class imbalance. In: International Conference on Computational Science. Springer (2019). https://doi.org/10.1007/978-3-030-22744-9_18
25. Hall, M., et al.: The WEKA data mining software: an update. ACM SIGKDD Explor. Newsl. **11**(1), 10–18 (2009)
26. Franklin, J.: The elements of statistical learning: data mining, inference and prediction. Math. Intelligencer **27**(2), 83–85 (2005). https://doi.org/10.1007/BF02985802
27. Tharwat, A.: Classification assessment methods. Appl. Comput. Inf. (2018)

The Mediating Role of Cloud Computing and Moderating Influence of Digital Organizational Culture Towards Enhancing SMEs Performance

Muhammad Ramzul Abu Bakar[1,2], Noor Afiza Mat Razali[1(✉)], Muslihah Wook[1], Mohd Nazri Ismail[1], and Tengku Mohd Tengku Sembok[1]

[1] National Defence University of Malaysia, Kuala Lumpur, Malaysia
noorafiza@upnm.edu.my
[2] Malaysian Investment Development Authority, Kuala Lumpur, Malaysia

Abstract. Usage of Industry4.0 enablers such as cloud computing, IoT and data analytics is still not common among SMEs. Many SMEs had failed in adopting digital transformations due to the conflicting values of digitalization with the company's organizational culture. There is a gap in examining the moderating influence of digital organizational culture and its effect on cloud computing technology adoption within the organization. Thus, we aim to explore, develop, and propose the conceptual framework consisting of constructs from the technology-organization-environment (TOE) framework combined with cloud computing as a mediator and the effect of digital organizational culture as a moderator. The study outcomes should address the gap in the role of cloud computing and digital organizational culture to further enhance the SME's performance. The research is still ongoing work, with field data will be collected using the structured survey questionnaire with managers of SMEs, including owners, senior executives or supervisors as the target responders. Then an empirical study using Structural Equation Model (SEM) will be proposed to validate the hypotheses of the conceptual framework.

Keywords: Technology-Organization-Environment (TOE) Framework · Cloud computing · Digital organizational culture · Firm's performance

1 Introduction

The Industry4.0 revolution brought the speed and measure of the changes to the world and resulted in shifts of power, wealth, and knowledge. Traditional manufacturing companies are being transformed into Smart Factories due to recent technological advancements that integrate humans, goods, information, and technology-based machines into automated, digitalized, and context-aware manufacturing systems to optimize business model execution [1]. New equipment, knowledge, concepts, standards, interconnectivity, technical aid, information transparency, and decentralized decision-making within the organization are all part of the new revolutionary of Industry 4.0 [2, 3]. The main issues faced by

© Springer Nature Switzerland AG 2021
H. Badioze Zaman et al. (Eds.): IVIC 2021, LNCS 13051, pp. 447–458, 2021.
https://doi.org/10.1007/978-3-030-90235-3_39

companies were organizational flexibility and agility in response to fast-changing market trends and the critical need to react to technology advancements and increase technical efficiency [4]. Industry and academia build and redevelop self-assessment models that can evaluate the industry's performance [5]. However, for Small and Medium Enterprises (SMEs), there is still a long way to go due to the more challenging to adopt digital technologies [6].

Furthermore, the organization has been hampered by a lack of digitalization culture and knowledge of the benefits of utilizing Industry 4.0 tools at the organizational level [7, 8]. Another obstacle SMEs face is substantial financial investments and expenditures to computerize the process by installing new software, tools and equipment [7]. Additionally, companies must provide employees with adequate training to ensure that the tools are operated efficiently and that the equipment is used optimally in line with industry 4.0 standards [9].

The Malaysia Digital SME Study 2018 [10] highlighted significant gaps in using other ICT technologies beyond basic computing. The study shows that 71% of SMEs use social media for product communication and marketing, whereas just 44% used e-commerce. When looking at the utilization of business apps that influence business productivity (other than Finance and Accounting and Human Resource software), less than 20% of SMEs used administrative solutions that impact business operations. The use of digitalization enablers including cloud, IoT, and data analytics is also uncommon among SMEs. Cloud computing is used by 44% of SMEs, and the primary use is cloud storage usage such as Dropbox to store personal documents, photos, and videos. SMEs have not taken advantage of cloud software as a service to optimize software processes. A total of 35% of SMEs have implemented an IoT solution. Still, these are mostly isolated building security and surveillance and fleet tracking solutions, not solutions that might be provided to the market as a service. SMEs must break free from the computerization trap and transform their companies through digitization to achieve the next efficiency level and unleash business growth through new business models, products, and services [10].

SMEs are still hesitant to adopt cloud computing due to unclear guidelines and the absence of adequate standards [11, 13]. Furthermore, SMEs' lack of understanding has hampered their acceptance of the technology. As a result, SMEs are unable to reap the full advantages of cloud computing technology during its adoption [14]. SMEs that refuse to use cloud computing will lose out on the benefits and competitive advantages that the technology may provide. It may jeopardize their firms' long-term viability and economic impact [15, 16]. One of the barriers to SME cloud computing adoption is a lack of cloud computing understanding or knowledge. This barrier creates a gap between cloud computing's technological improvement and its adoption by SMEs, which fail to capitalize on new advances and hence miss out on opportunities [13, 17]. To address this gap, this research focuses on SMEs in Malaysia's manufacturing and services industries to understand how to improve their performance using cloud computing technologies. This study will be addressing three (3) research questions as follows:

1. What are the technological, organizational, and environmental factors influencing cloud computing adoption in SMEs in Malaysia?

2. Does cloud computing technology adoption mediate the effects between technological, organizational, and environmental factors and SMEs performance?
3. Does digital organizational culture moderate the effects of technological, organizational, and environmental factors and adoption of computing technology?

The rest of this paper is structured with Sect. 2 discusses relevant studies and literature reviews regarding Industrial 4.0, especially cloud computing technology as a mediator and digital organizational culture as a moderator. In Sect. 3, the development of the proposed theoretical model and the hypotheses is discussed, and finally, in Sect. 4, the data collection method, future work, and study conclusion are concluded.

2   Theoretical Background

2.1   Industry 4.0 and Cloud Computing

The fourth industrial revolution, also known as Industry4.0 is the current industrial revolution brought forth by the advancement of technology [18]. The term itself, introduced by German researchers, has attracted the attention of academicians and industries over the past decades. Industry4.0 is driven by intelligence and digitalization with 9 pillars, namely, Cybersecurity, Cloud Computing, the Internet of Things (IoT), Additive Manufacturing, Augmented Reality, Big Data Analytics, Autonomous Robots, Simulation and System Integration [19]. Implementing Industry4.0 in the SME will give a better competitive advantage and bring various opportunities to an organization [20]. According to the National Institute of Standards and Technology (NIST), cloud computing is a model for enabling convenient, on-demand network access to a shared pool of configurable computing resources such as networks, servers, storage, applications, and scalable computing services. Cloud computing can be rapidly provisioned and released with minimal management effort or service provider interaction [21]. The NIST defines cloud computing according to three popular service models which are Technology Software as a Service (SaaS), Platform as a Service (PaaS), and Infrastructure as a Service (IaaS) [21]. Interoperability between cloud computing systems and apps, however, can be difficult. Cloud computing can hold SMEs data while also lowering the cost of data analytics and making it more accessible.

2.2   SME in Malaysia and Firm Performance

SMEs have a critical role in ensuring the sustained growth and the success of country economies. SMEs play a key role in today's economy because they help large corporations and industries meet customer expectations and increase the profitability of their supply chain partners [22]. According to the SME Annual Report 2019/2020 [23], SMEs play a significant role in Malaysia's economic development and make up 98.5% of the total business establishment in Malaysia and contributed 38.9% of Gross Domestic Product (GDP) in 2019. SMEs also employed 48.4% of the country's workforce, with a total of 907,065 business establishments [23].

A manufacturing company is defined as an SME if the annual revenue is less than RM50 million or less than 200 people, full-time employees. On the other hand, companies in the services or other sectors with annual revenue not exceeding RM20 million or less than 75 full-time employees are defined as SMEs [23]. This study covers both SMEs in manufacturing and services and other sectors.

The effectiveness of implementing IT innovation to enhance performance has piqued the curiosity and interest of scholars. Scholars have studied IT investments' financial and non-financial returns at the firm level [24–26]. Various tools for defining SMEs' performance have been identified in the literature. The sustainability and competitiveness of SMEs and the degree of innovation in product, process, and management systems are considered significant indicators in the majority of research [27–29]. There are three main components in evaluating the SMEs' performance: (1) survival, growth, and profit, (2) philosophy and value, and (3) public image [30]. According to Beamon [31], however, many output performance measures are challenging to quantify, one of which is product quality.

2.3 Technology-Organization-Environment (TOE)

The technology-organization-environment (TOE) framework is frequently applied in technology innovation and technology adoption usage studies to investigate the variables that affect the adoption of technology by organizations. Tornatzky, Fleischer, Chakrabarti [32] has developed the TOE framework to explain how the technological, organisational, and environmental factors influence the decision to adopt technological innovations [33].

The technology dimension covers all the technologies accessible to an organization and how the attributes of those technologies affect the adoption process. The organization dimension includes elements such as globally present, adoption cost and size of the firm. The environment dimension covers how an organization operates, competitors, laws and regulations [32].

Although the original TOE was established in 1990, numerous researchers are still widely using TOE framework to model and measure the influence of technological-organisational-environment constructs when researching new emerging technologies and various applications such as technological factors in influencing cloud computing adoption [34–36], information system innovations [37] and TOE for SMEs [38]. As such, for this paper, the TOE framework offers an appropriate theoretical groundwork for analyzing the factors influencing cloud computing in SMEs, based on empirical evidence from previous studies and combined with relevant literature.

2.4 Digital Organizational Culture

Throughout the years, many researchers have proposed numerous definitions of organizational culture. Organizational culture is a reflection of an organization's members' collective values, beliefs, and ideals. Organizational culture is a set of shared mental assumptions that guide interpretation and action in the workplace by outlining appropriate behaviour for specific positions [39]. Suppose we adopt the term organizational culture to the digital domain. In that case, we may argue that an organization's culture must encompass its digital organizational culture [40].

In this regard, previous research has discovered a relationship between organizational culture and performance[41], innovation [42], leadership [43], knowledge management [44], and information technology [45]. Some companies that pursued digital revolutions with highly expected commercial advantages for their clients and the organization have failed due to cultural conflict [46]. Hence, digitalization transformation necessitates the adoption of digital organizational culture that supports the transition of digital revolutions. More research is needed to see how digital organizational culture may help firms with their digital transformation in this area. This study will explore digital organizational culture role as a moderator to increase the effect between TOE constructs and cloud computing use in SMEs.

3 Conceptual Framework and Hypotheses Development

3.1 Conceptual Framework

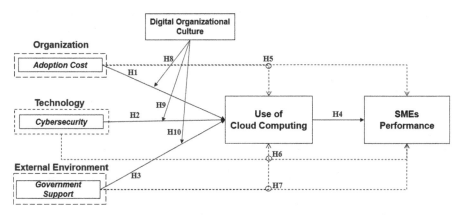

Fig. 1. Conceptual framework of the study

This research has selected several models based on the published articles and journals to establish the theoretical model. The models were then consulted and discussed with the panel of experts to get their views on the best conceptual framework and constructs for this study. Two (2) industry experts from SMEs and one (1) expert from the government agency in charge of industrial development in Malaysia were consulted for this research. The panel of experts suggested that this research focuses on the most critical constructs from each technological, organizational, and environmental dimension. Secondly, the panel of experts stated that previous researchers had made minimal effort to explore the relationship between TOE constructs and digital organizational culture in the organization. Often organizations forgot to include the digital culture as considerations in their adoption process of any new technologies. A conceptual framework for this study was then developed based on feedback and comments from the expert panel and presented in Fig. 1.

3.2 Hypotheses Development

Adoption Cost. The Malaysia Digital SME Study 2018 [10] shows that the highest factor that has hindered digitalisation among SMEs is adoption cost or financing. 49% of respondents report that this is due to SMEs' doubts about returns on their digitalisation investment. Furthermore, many SMEs believe that information and communication technology (ICT) is costly. For instance, 34% of SMEs believe cloud computing is extremely expensive. There is a need to educate and enlighten SMEs about the funding options available to help them accelerate their digital transformation and the fact that cloud computing has made business improvement software, data storage, and analytics more inexpensive [10]. The argument is that the lower the cost of technology implementation, the more likely it will be adopted [47]. Due to SMEs' limited resources, such as cash, labour, and materials, the relative cost of innovation is more critical for small businesses [48]. Due to this, transaction costs and company performance have a negative relationship [49]. Therefore, more information is needed at the firm level to explore the effect of adopting cloud computing technology and its utilization by SMEs. Various innovation costs have varying degrees of impact on a firm's performance [50]. Hence, the literature focusing on the indirect association between cloud computing adoption costs and firm performance is still in its early stages. To study this, we came up with the hypothesis that:

H1: Adoption cost has a significant effect on the use of cloud computing.
H5: The use of cloud computing mediates the relationship between adoption cost and firm performance.

Cybersecurity. Cloud computing systems, technologies, applications, and services have seen rapid and accelerating development in recent years. This is due to the numerous advantages that this technology provides for businesses. Furthermore, one of the most critical challenges and concerns for the widespread use of cloud computing in cybersecurity is data security, intrusion assaults, confidentiality, and data integrity [51]. Cybersecurity is also defined as a set of tools, policies, security concepts, security safeguards, guidelines, risk management approaches, procedures, training, best practices, assurance, and technologies that can be utilized to safeguard the cyber environment, company, and users' assets [52]. It also ensures the availability, integrity, authentication, confidentiality, and nonrepudiation of computers, electronic communications systems, electronic communications services, wire communication, and electronic communication, as well as the information contained therein, by preventing any damage, protecting, and restoring them [53]. Developing cybersecurity skills involves addressing digital threats using technology and complementary factors, including policy guidelines, organizational processes, and education and awareness strategies [54]. Furthermore, security has been as identified as one of the technological factors under the TOE framework by Aleem [55], Gupta [56] and Lian [57] that affecting the organization's decision to adopt cloud computing. Hence, it is hypothesized that:

H2: Cybersecurity has a significant effect on the use of cloud computing.

H6: The use of cloud computing mediates the relationship between cybersecurity and firm performance.

Government Support. Government support and a lack of implementation of innovation are the primary influencers on SMEs growth [58]. The government should undertake several initiatives to encourage SMEs to invest in technology improvements to improve their products and services. Previous research has revealed that government support is one of the most critical determinants for SMEs' success for innovation usage like e-marketing, e-government, e-banking, and e-learning [48, 59, 60]. In Malaysia, the National Technology and Innovation Sandbox (NTIS) is a crucial initiative announced to drive Malaysia's aspirations to be a high-income and high-tech nation through enhancing development and access to advanced technology. NTIS aims to create high-skilled jobs, boost growth in GDP and Gross National Product, social inclusion, and enhance investment and collaboration in research in the private sector. Participants in the NTIS programme will receive support in the form of capacity-building programmes, facilitation for market access and procurement, funding facilitation and facilitation for testbed and testing environment. The government also assists SMEs by offering grants and loans through the SME Digitalization Matching Grant, SME Technology Transformation Fund, and Smart Automation Grant programmes. These efforts encourage SMEs to digitize their operations and trading platforms and spur the digital economy from the recovery phase due to the Covid19 pandemic. Hence, it is hypothesized that:

H3: Government support has a significant effect on the use of cloud computing.
H7: The use of cloud computing mediates the relationship between government support and firm performance.

Role of Cloud Computing and SME Performance. A firm's competitiveness and long-term success in a worldwide market are heavily reliant on the efficiency and productivity of its operations [61, 62]. These are the factors that represent a company's long-term and sustainable profitability. According to theories, a technological upgrade in a firm leads to improvement in the firm's productivity. The innovation-based literature further cites the significance of energy efficiency technologies, e-commerce, information and communication technologies, and environmental management systems in business growth via productivity increases [63]. Therefore, this study will examine the mediator role of cloud computing technology in improving a firm's performance. The study proposes hypothesis as follows:

H4: The use of cloud computing has a significant effect on firm performance.

Role of Digital Organizational Culture. The history of technological advancement in business is filled with firms focusing on technologies without looking at organisational culture to ensure their overall impact. According to Hoffman and Klepper [64], managers have frequently overlooked or underestimated the impact of organizational culture when measuring the success or failure of new technology adoption. Prior work by Mohtaramzadeh [48] also suggests that companies with a "strong culture" have an easier time adopting new technologies than companies with a "poor culture." Hence, this paper will explore the critical moderating role of the digital organizational culture to strengthen the effect between TOE contracts and the use of cloud computing and formulates the following hypothesis:

H8: Digital organizational culture moderates the relationship between adoption cost and cloud computing adoption.
H9: Digital organizational culture moderates the relationship between cybersecurity and cloud computing adoption.
H10: Digital organizational culture moderates the relationship between government support cloud computing adoption.

4   Conclusion and Future Work

This study has explored the current challenges and problems that SMEs in Malaysia face in fully adopting cloud computing technology. This paper has also elaborated on the effect between the TOE framework, cloud computing as a mediator, and the gap often overlooks by the organization, which is digital organizational culture as a moderator to improve the firm's performance. Hence, a conceptual framework was developed to emphasise the details regarding these issues.

The study is still ongoing work. Future work will include data collection using the structured survey questionnaire adopted based on prior research and tailored to this study's requirements. A 7-point Likert scale will be used in the structured questionnaire to give more thorough response possibilities that reflect individual opinions. The survey will be subsequently distributed to the target population's respondents, such as managers of SMEs, including owners and senior executives and supervisors. Managers or supervisors were chosen as the most relevant respondents for this study because they were well-positioned within the company and were familiar with its IT resources and technological environment. Then, using a Structural Equation Model (SEM), an empirical study will be carried out to validate the conceptual framework's hypotheses.

The outcomes of the study are expected to contribute in two ways. The first contribution is that of a theoretical contribution. First and foremost, the study will examine the mediation effect of cloud computing and the moderator effect of digital organizational culture within the TOE framework. These integrations of a mediator, a moderator, and TOE constructs are expected to contribute theoretically to this study.

The second aspect of contribution is the practical contribution. This contribution will lead to a significant contribution to increase SME performance by adopting cloud computing technology among SMEs in Malaysia. The study has important practical implications, particularly for Malaysian SMEs, as it helps them determine which significant constructs should be used when deploying cloud computing technologies. Lastly, the findings will increase empirical evidence on constructs of the TOE framework, mediating the impact of cloud computing and moderating effects of digital organizational culture and how it can improve the firm's performance. Eventually, the empirical results will benefit other researchers theoretically and practically.

Acknowledgement. The authors would like to express their gratitude to the National Defence University of Malaysia for the financial support to conduct this research through Short Grants UPNM/2020/GPJP/ICT/4.

References

1. Chen, B., Wan, J., Shu, L., Li, P., Mukherjee, M., Yin, B.: Smart factory of industry 4.0: key technologies, application case, and challenges. IEEE Access **6**, 6505–6519 (2017). https://doi.org/10.1109/ACCESS.2017.2783682
2. Gerrikagoitia, J.K., Unamuno, G., Urkia, E., Serna, A.: Digital manufacturing platforms in the Industry 4.0 from private and public perspectives. Appl. Sci. **9**(14) (2019). https://doi.org/10.3390/app9142934
3. Castelo-Branco, I., Cruz-Jesus, F., Oliveira, T.: Assessing Industry 4.0 readiness in manufacturing: evidence for the European Union. Comput. Ind. **107**, 22–32 (2019). https://doi.org/10.1016/J.COMPIND.2019.01.007
4. Witkowski, K.: Internet of things, big data, industry 4.0 - innovative solutions in logistics and supply chains management. Procedia Eng. **182**, 763–769 (2017). https://doi.org/10.1016/j.proeng.2017.03.197
5. Hizam-Hanafiah, M., Soomro, M.A., Abdullah, N.L.: Industry 4.0 readiness models: a systematic literature review of model dimensions. Inf. **11**(7), 1–13 (2020). https://doi.org/10.3390/info11070364
6. Sommer, L.: Industrial revolution - Industry 4.0: are German manufacturing SMEs the first victims of this revolution? J. Ind. Eng. Manag. **8**(5), 1512–1532 (2015). https://doi.org/10.3926/jiem.1470
7. P. PwC: Industry 4.0: Building the digital enterprise. In: 2016 Global Industry 4.0 Survey London, Great Britain (2016)
8. Kellner, T., Necas, M., Kanak, M., Kyncl, M., Kyncl, J.: Assessment of readiness for Industry 4.0 implementation in ceramic industry. Manuf. Technol. **20**(6), 763–770 (2020). https://doi.org/10.21062/MFT.2020.110
9. Drath, R., Horch, A.: Industrie 4.0: hit or hype? [Industry Forum]. IEEE Ind. Electron. Mag. **8**(2), 56–58 (2014). https://doi.org/10.1109/MIE.2014.2312079
10. S. C. M. & Huawei: Accelerating Malaysian digital SMEs," SME Corp Malaysia, p. https://www.huawei.com/minisite/accelerating-malay (2018)
11. Oliveira, T., Thomas, M., Espadanal, M.: Assessing the determinants of cloud computing adoption: an analysis of the manufacturing and services sectors. Inf. Manag. **51**(5), 497–510 (2014). https://doi.org/10.1016/j.im.2014.03.006
12. Senyo, P.K., Addae, E., Boateng, R.: Cloud computing research: a review of research themes, frameworks, methods and future research directions. Int. J. Inf. Manage. **38**(1), 128–139 (2018). https://doi.org/10.1016/j.ijinfomgt.2017.07.007
13. Lee, Y.C.: Adoption intention of cloud computing at the firm level. J. Comput. Inf. Syst. **59**(1), 61–72 (2019). https://doi.org/10.1080/08874417.2017.1295792
14. Molinillo, S., Japutra, A.: Organizational adoption of digital information and technology: a theoretical review. Bottom Line **30**(1), 33–46 (2017). https://doi.org/10.1108/BL-01-2017-0002
15. Armbrust, M., et al.: A view of cloud computing. Commun. ACM **53**(4), 50–58 (2010). https://doi.org/10.1145/1721654.1721672
16. Marston, S., Li, Z., Bandyopadhyay, S., Zhang, J., Ghalsasi, A.: Cloud computing - the business perspective. Decis. Support Syst. **51**(1), 176–189 (2011). https://doi.org/10.1016/j.dss.2010.12.006

17. Seifu, S.D., Dahiru, A.A., Bass, J.M., Allison, I.K.: Cloud-computing: adoption issues for ethiopian public and private enterprises. Electron. J. Inf. Syst. Dev. Ctries. **78**(1), 1–14 (2017). https://doi.org/10.1002/j.1681-4835.2017.tb00575.x
18. Yin, Y., Stecke, K.E., Li, D.: The evolution of production systems from Industry 2.0 through Industry 4.0. Int. J. Prod. Res. **56**(1–2), 848–861 (2018)
19. Palka, D., Ciukaj, J.: Prospects for development movement in the industry concept 4.0. Multidiscip. Asp. Prod. Eng. **2**, 315–326 (2019)
20. Frank, A.G., Dalenogare, L.S., Ayala, N.F.: Industry 4.0 technologies: implementation patterns in manufacturing companies. Int. J. Prod. Econ. **210**, 15–26 (2019)
21. Mell, P., Grance, T.: The NIST-National Institute of Standars and Technology- definition of cloud computing. NIST Spec. Publ. **800–145**, 7 (2011)
22. Ward, M., Rhodes, C.: Small businesses and the UK economy, Stand. Note SN/EP/6078. Off. Natl. Stat. (2014)
23. SMECorporationMalaysia: PKS dalam Normal Baharu: Membangun Semula Eknonomi, p. 98 (2021)
24. Chan, Y.E.: IT Value: the great divide between qualitative and quantitative and individual and organizational measures. J. Manage. Inf. Syst. **16**(4), 225–261 (2000). https://doi.org/10.1080/07421222.2000.11518272
25. Gallivan, M.J.: Organizational adoption and assimilation of complex technological innovations: development and application of a new framework. Data Base Adv. Inf. Syst. **32**(3), 51–85 (2001). https://doi.org/10.1145/506724.506729
26. Iacovou, C.L., Benbasat, I., Dexter, A.S.: Organizations : and impact adoption of technology. MIS Q. **19**(4), 465–485 (1995)
27. Florido, J.S.V., Adame, M.G., Tagle, M.A.O.: Financial strategies, the professional development of employers and performance of sme's (AGUASCALIENTES Case). Procedia - Soc. Behav. Sci. **174**, 768–775 (2015). https://doi.org/10.1016/J.SBSPRO.2015.01.613
28. Singh, R.K., Garg, S.K., Deshmukh, S.G.: Strategy development by SMEs for competitiveness: a review. Benchmarking Int. J. **15**(5), 525–547 (2008). https://doi.org/10.1108/14635770810903132
29. Hogeforster, M.: Future challenges for innovations in SMEs in the Baltic sea region. Procedia - Soc. Behav. Sci. **110**, 241–250 (2014). https://doi.org/10.1016/j.sbspro.2013.12.867
30. Duygulu, E., Ozeren, E., Işildar, P., Appolloni, A.: The sustainable strategy for small and medium sized enterprises: the relationship between mission statements and performance. Sustain. **8**(7) (2016). https://doi.org/10.3390/su8070698
31. Beamon, B.M.: Measuring Supply Chain Performance, vol. 19, no. 3. (2007)
32. Tornatzky, L.G., Fleischer, M., Chakrabarti, A.K.: Processes of Technological Innovation. Lexington books, Lanham (1990)
33. Lin, H.F.: Understanding the determinants of electronic supply chain management system adoption: using the technology-organization-environment framework. Technol. Forecast. Soc. Change **86**, 80–92 (2014). https://doi.org/10.1016/j.techfore.2013.09.001
34. Okai, S., Uddin, M., Arshad, A., Alsaqour, R., Shah, A.: Cloud computing adoption model for universities to increase ICT proficiency. SAGE Open **4**(3), 1 (2014). https://doi.org/10.1177/2158244014546461
35. Ross, P., Blumenstein, M.: Cloud computing: the nexus of strategy and technology. J. Bus. Strategy **34**(4), 39–47 (2013). https://doi.org/10.1108/JBS-10-2012-0061
36. Willcocks, L.P., Venters, W., Whitley, E.A.: Cloud sourcing and innovation: slow train coming?: A composite research study. Strateg. Outsourcing Int. J. **6**(2), 184–202 (2013). https://doi.org/10.1108/SO-04-2013-0004
37. Kuan, K.K.Y., Chau, P.Y.K.: A perception-based model for EDI adoption in small businesses using a technology-organization-environment framework. Inf. Manag. **38**(8), 507–521 (2001). https://doi.org/10.1016/S0378-7206(01)00073-8

38. Ardito, L., Petruzzelli, A.M., Panniello, U., Garavelli, A.C.: Towards Industry 4.0: mapping digital technologies for supply chain management-marketing integration. Bus. Process Manage. J. **25**(2), 323–346 (2019). https://doi.org/10.1108/BPMJ-04-2017-0088

39. Ravasi, D., Schultz, M.: Responding to organizational identity threats: exploring the role of organizational culture. Acad. Manage. J. **49**(3), 433–458 (2006)

40. Duerr, S., Holotiuk, F., Wagner, H.-T., Beimborn, D., Weitzel, T.: What is digital organizational culture? Insights from exploratory case studies (2018)

41. O'Reilly, C.A., Caldwell, D.F., Chatman, J.A., Doerr, B.: The promise and problems of organizational culture: CEO personality, culture, and firm performance. Gr. Organ. Manage. **39**(6), 595–625 (2014). https://doi.org/10.1177/1059601114550713

42. Hogan, S.J., Coote, L.V.: Organizational culture, innovation, and performance: a test of Schein's model. J. Bus. Res. **67**(8), 1609–1621 (2014). https://doi.org/10.1016/j.jbusres.2013.09.007

43. Ke, W., Wei, K.K.: Organizational culture and leadership in ERP implementation. Decis. Support Syst. **45**(2), 208–218 (2008). https://doi.org/10.1016/j.dss.2007.02.002

44. Rai, R.K.: Knowledge management and organizational culture: a theoretical integrative framework. J. Knowl. Manag. **15**(5), 779–801 (2011). https://doi.org/10.1108/13673271111174320

45. Alavi, M., Kayworth, T.R., Leidner, D.E.: An empirical examination of the influence of organizational culture on knowledge management practices. J. Manage. Inf. Syst. **22**(3), 191–224 (2005). https://doi.org/10.2753/MIS0742-1222220307

46. Wokurka, G., Banschbach, Y., Houlder, D., Jolly, R.: Digital culture: Why strategy and culture should eat breakfast together. In: Shaping the digital enterprise, pp. 109–120. Springer (2017)

47. Premkumar, G., Roberts, M.: Adoption of new information technologies in rural small businesses. Omega **27**(4), 467–484 (1999). https://doi.org/10.1016/S0305-0483(98)00071-1

48. Mohtaramzadeh, M., Ramayah, T., Jun-Hwa, C.: B2B E-Commerce adoption in Iranian manufacturing companies: analyzing the moderating role of organizational culture. Int. J. Hum. Comput. Interact. **34**(7), 621–639 (2018). https://doi.org/10.1080/10447318.2017.1385212

49. Gunday, G., Ulusoy, G., Kilic, K., Alpkan, L.: Effects of innovation types on firm performance. Int. J. Prod. Econ. **133**(2), 662–676 (2011). https://doi.org/10.1016/j.ijpe.2011.05.014

50. Prajogo, D.I., Hong, S.W.: The effect of TQM on performance in R&D environments: a perspective from South Korean firms. Technovation **28**(12), 855–863 (2008). https://doi.org/10.1016/j.technovation.2008.06.001

51. Bennasar, H.: State-of-The-Art of Cloud Computing Cyber-Security (2015)

52. International Telecommunication Union: Overview Cybersecurity, ITU-T X.1205 Recomm., vol. 1205, no. Rec. ITU-T X.1205 (04/2008), pp. 2–3 (2008)

53. Committee on National Security Systems: CNSSI 4009 – Glossary, no. 4009 (2015)

54. Bada, M., Nurse, J.R.C.: Developing cybersecurity education and awareness programmes for small- and medium-sized enterprises (SMEs). Inf. Comput. Secur. **27**(3), 393–410 (2019). https://doi.org/10.1108/ICS-07-2018-0080

55. Aleem, A., Sprott, C.R.: Let me in the cloud: analysis of the benefit and risk assessment of cloud platform. J. Financ. Crime **20**(1), 6–24 (2012)

56. Gupta, P., Seetharaman, A., Raj, J.R.: The usage and adoption of cloud computing by small and medium businesses. Int. J. Inf. Manage. **33**(5), 861–874 (2013). https://doi.org/10.1016/j.ijinfomgt.2013.07.001

57. Lian, J.W.: Critical factors for cloud based e-invoice service adoption in Taiwan: an empirical study. Int. J. Inf. Manage. **35**(1), 98–109 (2015). https://doi.org/10.1016/j.ijinfomgt.2014.10.005

58. Humphreys, P., McAdam, R., Leckey, J.: Longitudinal evaluation of innovation implementation in SMEs. Eur. J. Innov. Manage. **8**(3), 283–304 (2005). https://doi.org/10.1108/14601060510610162

59. Sánchez-Torres, J.A., Canada, F.J.A., Sandoval, A.V., Alzate, J.A.S.: E-banking in Colombia: factors favouring its acceptance, online trust and government support. Int. J. Bank Mark. **36**(1), 170–183 (2018). https://doi.org/10.1108/IJBM-10-2016-0145

60. Kazungu, I., Panga, F.P., Mchopa, A.: Impediments to adoption of e-marketing by tanzanian small and medium sized enterprises: an explanatory model. Int. J. Econ. Commer. Manag. United Kingdom, vol. III(6), (2015)

61. Ahmedova, S.: Factors for increasing the competitiveness of small and medium- sized enterprises (SMEs) in Bulgaria. Procedia - Soc. Behav. Sci. **195**, 1104–1112 (2015). https://doi.org/10.1016/j.sbspro.2015.06.155

62. Nugroho, M.A., Susilo, A.Z., Fajar, M.A., Rahmawati, D.: Exploratory study of SMEs technology adoption readiness factors. Procedia Comput. Sci. **124**, 329–336 (2017). https://doi.org/10.1016/j.procs.2017.12.162

63. Meath, C., Linnenluecke, M., Griffiths, A.: Barriers and motivators to the adoption of energy savings measures for small- and medium-sized enterprises (SMEs): the case of the ClimateSmart Business cluster program. J. Clean. Prod. **112**, 3597–3604 (2016). https://doi.org/10.1016/j.jclepro.2015.08.085

64. Hoffman, N., Klepper, R.: Assimilating new technologies: the role of organizational culture. Inf. Syst. Manag. **17**(3), 36–42 (2000). https://doi.org/10.1201/1078/43192.17.3.20000601/31239.6

Arabic Speaker Identification System for Forensic Authentication Using K-NN Algorithm

Sarah Abdulwahid[1]([✉]), Moamin A. Mahmoud[2], and Nassren Abdulwahid[3]

[1] College of Graduate Studies, Universiti Tenaga Nasional, Kajang, Malaysia
[2] Institute of Informatics and Computing in Energy, Universiti Tenaga Nasional, Kajang, Malaysia
moamin@uniten.edu.my
[3] Department of Communication Engineering, University of Technology, Al-Sina'a Street, Baghdad, Iraq

Abstract. For many years, there was an increasing necessity for being capable of the identification of a person based on his/her voice. Judges, law enforcement agencies, detectives, and lawyers, wanted to be able to use the forensic authentication of voice for investigating a suspect or confirming a judgment of guilt or innocence. This study aims to design and build a comprehensive identification of the forensic speakers for the Arabic language. The suggested system has been utilized for the recognition of forensic speaker's isolated words for purposes of identification. It comprises two stages; the first stage is training the sentence of the forensic speaker in the case where it is not previously processed and stored; the second stage is testing; it is applied in the case where the sentence of the forensic speaker has been previously processed and stored. Every one of the phases involves utilizing audio features (standard division, mean, amplitude, and zero-crossing), pre-processing with the use of the MFCC, Hamming Window, vector quantization, and data mining classification approaches. The proposed system implementation provides removal of the noise in spoken sentences, processing speech sentences prior to the storing, and a correct classification with the use of a number of algorithms of data mining classification such as the Logistic Model Tree (LMT), and K-nearest neighbor (KNN) algorithms. KNN being given the highest accuracy of 91.53% and 94.56% respectively.

Keywords: Mel frequency cepstral coefficients (MFCC) · Speaker identification system · Logistic Model Tree (LMT) · K-nearest neighbor (KNN)

1 Introduction

Identical speakers present a difficult task to the technology biometrics that depends on measuring and distinguishing essential physical properties such as fingerprint, face, iris, voice, of individuals to conduct the process of human recognition. This issue served as an important stimulus for performing many multi-disciplinary research efforts, which

© Springer Nature Switzerland AG 2021
H. Badioze Zaman et al. (Eds.): IVIC 2021, LNCS 13051, pp. 459–468, 2021.
https://doi.org/10.1007/978-3-030-90235-3_40

concentrated considerably on the measurement of the similarity extent of biometric characteristics in speakers that are mentioned earlier [1].

Forensic Speaker Recognition (FSR) also referred to as Forensic Speaker Identification (FSI) aims to give a response to a common question in forensic casework: Could a person be identified by their voice beyond a reasonable doubt? i.e., could the recorded voice of a speaker who is not known be recognized by a known one? Typically, the questioned identity is that of an anonymous offender that has been recorded during a telephone or an environmental interception, whereas the known speaker is the one suspected to be the offender [2]. Generally, FSR is the term that is used for including all of the many various tasks of discriminating people according to the sound of their voices. Particularly, it is the procedure utilized to determine whether a certain person (suspected speaker) is the questioned voice recording source (i.e. trace). This procedure includes the comparison of recordings of an unknown voice (i.e. the questioned recording) to one or more recordings of a known voice (i.e. the suspected speaker's voice).

There are numerous FSR types. When the identification utilizes any trained skill or technologically-supported process, the term technical FSR is usually used. In contrast, the native FSR refers to the application of daily capabilities of individuals to identify known voices [3]. When we trying to build a technical FSR system, lots of problems will emerge, such as identifying a voice using forensic quality samples is, in general, a challenging process for automatic, semi-automatic, and human-based approaches. Additionally, the speech samples that are compared could be recorded in a variety of cases; for instance, a sample might be yelling over the phone, while another could be a whisper. Another problem is speech recognition based on pattern classification. This method of pattern classification must be capable of handling large speaker databases in a short time limit with accuracy. Also, the speech samples will possibly include noise, could be too short, and may not include a sufficient amount of relevant speech material for comparative reasons. The paper is organized as follows. Section 2 the related work. In Sect. 3, we describe the speaker identification system used throughout this work. In Sect. 4, we present an experimental result. Finally. Section 5 summarizes the main conclusions of this work.

2 Related Work

Several studies have explored the use of AI in the context of identification systems for forensic authentication. Noor A., Amar A., and Abbes A. [1] in 2014 this study, designed and implemented an innovative text-independent multi-modal SIS according to the wavelet analysis and NNs. The wavelet analysis includes the DWT, wavelet sub-band coding, wavelet packet transform, and Mel-frequency cepstral coefficients (MFCCs). The module of the learning comprises general regressive, radial basis function, and probabilistic NNs, which form the decisions via the majority voting method. This system has been discovered competitive and it has enhanced the rate of identification by 15% in comparison to the conventional MFCCs. Moreover, it decreases the time of the identification by 40% in comparison to back-propagation NN, principal component analysis (PCA), and Gaussian mixture model. The tests of performance which have been carried out with the use of GRID database corpora showed that this method consumed less time for identification and a higher level of precision in comparison to the conventional methods, and it can be applied to the real-time, text-independent SISs.

Noor K. [2] in 2016 this work is dedicated to present statistic method with dimensionality reduction for speaker identification. Where this research was performed by the following basic steps: 1. Pre-processing of the speech signal was performed on the input signal. 2. Feature extraction which was implemented using the LPC technique. 3. The process of the analysis and selection was performed using the PCA. 4. Distance method is used in the recognition phase. The experimental result revealed that the proposed work is achieved in better performance than without reduction.

Nagwa M. A., et al. [3] in 2016 this research improved the speed of the text-independent SIS, the suggested approach used the gender detection (PDA), MFCC, VQ for the training and the GMM for the testing. Results showed the fact that the proposed method has accomplished a high rate of recognition of up to 91% and the test time was 0.1051 s.

Zimeng H [4] in 2017 this research presents a real-time speaker gender identification system has been designed and it was capable of identifying the speaker gender via his/her voice automatically. This system utilized the mathematical calculations of voice frequency and voice fundamental frequency for features extracted. Machine learning classification technique (Naive Bayesian Classifier) is used for classification, this technique provides good performance about 92.75% for gender recognition.

Nassren N. Abd Alwahed et al. [5] in 2019. this research proposes a system that works on forensic speaker identification for the Arabic language. in this system, the VQ works to improve the MFCC technique. The extracted features which result from the mixing of uses the MFCC technique and (Mean, STD, Amp, and Zc) has given good results after being applied to a number of classification algorithms like; KNN, SMO, and NB with a better recognition rate; in male, 93.6%, 96.4%, and 100%, respectively, and in female, 98.1%, 98.1%, and 98.1%, respectively.

3   The Proposed Forensic Speaker System

The proposed forensic speaker recognition system consists of two phases applied to Arabic speech sentences, after applying the cross-validation to the dataset these two phases will be applied. As shown in Fig. 1.

3.1   Dataset/Speech Signal

The samples which were used in the search database is an Arabic-language isolated word are configured as private Arabic-language pronunciations (phonemes). These isolated words especially kidnappings and kidnappers are ten isolated words and pronounce this isolated word by 10 people, five men and five women of different ages and every one of those ten bands all isolated words, so a total of 220 samples and the samples were recorded on audio and wave extension form and address Several samples preprocessing, feature extraction, classification isolated words shown in Table 1.

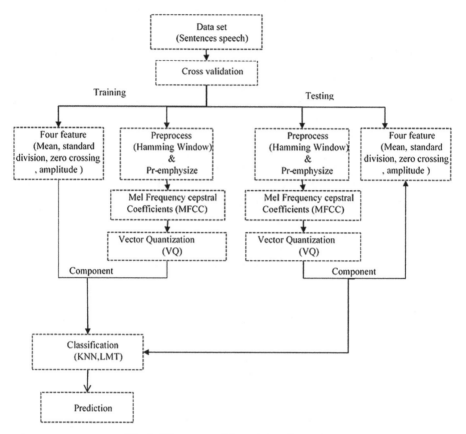

Fig. 1. The proposed forensic speaker system

Table 1. Dataset of isolated word

Isolated word	
يلقى	يكترث
يَنْظُرُ	يكافئ
يَنـامُ	نطق
مِنْ	الاثير
سَمِعَ	خَبَط
الشَّمس	أمسى
التَّوبة	فَرِحَ
اللَّيْلُ	طويلٌ
المَرْءُ	الصّدود
عـالِماً	كَتَبْتُ
تَـزالُ	يَتَكَلَّمُ

3.2 Preprocessing

Preprocessing stage has the main advantage which is organizing the data to simplify the recognition task. All operations that apply to audio is called preprocessing process.

K-fold Cross-Validation. Cross-validation extends the idea of holdout validation by repeating the splitting process several times and considers it as an alternative approach to a fixed partition. In cross-validation, multiple partitions are generated, potentially allowing for exploiting training and accuracy assessment samples multiple times for multiple purposes, with the overall aim of improving the statistical reliability of the results. Examples of cross-validation methods include k-fold [6].

The set DN is arbitrarily split to k mutually exclusive test partitions almost equally sized. The cases which aren't found in every test partition are exclusively utilized to select the hypothesis that is going to be tested on the partition itself. The mean value of the error over all the k partitions is the cross-validated error rate. Assume that k(i) is the part of DN that contains the ith sample. After that, the cross-validation estimate of the MISE prediction error will be calculated using the equation below,

$$\widehat{MISE_{cv}} = \frac{1}{N}\sum_{i=1}^{N}(y_i - \widehat{y}_i^{-k(i)})^2 = \frac{1}{N}\sum_{i=1}^{N}\left(y_i - \widehat{f}(x_i, \alpha^{-k(i)})\right)^2 \qquad (1)$$

Where $\widehat{y}_i^{-k(i)}$ represents the fitted value for the ith observation which is returned by the model that has been estimated with the k(i^{th}) part of the data eliminated [7].

The Training Phase. The first phase of the proposed system is the training of the dataset which will be produced from the cross-validation. In this phase the dataset will be processed using features extraction, preprocessing using hamming window and Re-emphasize, MFCC, VQ, and then the values of the processing will be mixed to prepare it for the classification using the algorithms (KNN, LMTs).

The Testing Phase. The second phase of the proposed system is the testing phase which will process the remained speech sentences dataset which results from the cross-validation processing. In this phase the dataset will be processed using features extraction, preprocessing using hamming window and Pr-emphasize, MFCC, VQ, and then the values of the processing will be mixed to prepare it for the classification using the algorithms (KNN, LMT).

3.3 Feature Extraction

Mel Frequency Cepstral Coefficients. The most predominant and prevalent approach which is utilized for the extraction of the spectral features is the calculation of the MFCC, which is a very common method of feature extraction which is utilized in the speech recognition based upon the domain of the frequency with the use of the Mel scale that has been based upon the ear scale of the humans. The MFCC is considered as features of the frequency domain which are considerably more precise compared to the features of the time domain [8].

The MFCCs represent the real cepstral of the windowed short-time signal which has been obtained from that signal's Fast Fourier Transformation (FFT). Its difference from real cepstral lies in the fact that it uses a non-linear scale of frequency, approximating the auditory system's behavior. In addition to that, those coefficients have robustness and reliability to the changes of the speakers and the conditions of the recording. MFCC is an audio feature method of extraction, it performs the extraction of the parameters from a speech like the parameters utilized by the humans to hear the speech, whereas simultaneously, deemphasizes every other type of information. Speech signals are initially fragmented to time frames which consist of a random number of the samples. In the majority of systems, frame overlapping is utilized for smoothing the transition from one frame to another. Every time frame is windowed by the Hamming window for the elimination of the discontinuities at edges [9]. The coefficients of the filter w (n) of the Hamming window which is n long will be computed based on the following equation:

$$w(n) = 0.54 - 0.46 \ cos\left(\frac{2\pi n}{N-1}\right), \quad 0 \le n \le N-1$$
$$= 0, \quad otherwise \tag{2}$$

N represents the entire number of the samples and n represents the current one. Following the process of windowing, FFT will be computed for every one of the frames for the extraction of the components of a signal's frequency in the time domain. The FFT has been utilized for speeding the process up. Logarithmic Mel-Scaled filter bank will be implemented on the frame that has been Fourier transformed. Such scale is almost linear up to 1 kHz, and it is logarithmic at higher values of the frequency [10]. The correlation between the speech frequency and the Mel scale may be represented in the following form:

$$Frequency(Mel \ Scaled) = [2595\log(1 + f(Hz)/700] \tag{3}$$

The MFCC uses the Mel-scale filter bank in which filters of the higher frequency are of a higher value of the bandwidth compared to filters of the lower frequency values, however, their temporal resolution values are identical.

Mean: The mean is referring to a central value, a discrete group of numbers particularly, the summation of the values that are divided by the number of values [11].

$$\bar{x} = \frac{x_1 + x_2 + x_3 + \ldots + x_n}{n} \ or \ \bar{x} = \frac{\sum_{i=1}^{n} x_i}{n} \tag{4}$$

Where Xi represents data values and n represent the number of data values.

Standard Deviation. A standard deviation is calculated by the summation of every value which is contained inside an informational index. This value is computed from the average. It indicates how to limit the characteristics in the information index are collected around the average. It is the most powerful and widely utilized scattering measure, unlike quadrature and scale; it takes every value in the dataset [11]. The value of the standard deviation is small when the dataset values are closely collected together, however, in the case where the values are separately scattered, the value of the standard deviation is rather large. Standard deviation is usually displayed together with the average, and it is calculated in similar units. For a certain group of numbers, the criterion perversion is obtained from the square root (Sqrt) of the average value of square deviations from their mean value [12].

$$S = \sqrt{\frac{\sum_{i=1}^{n}(x_i - \overline{x})^2}{n - 1}} \tag{5}$$

Where Xi represents data values, $\overline{x}$ represents the arithmetic Mean and n represents the number of data values.

Amplitude. The larger variations in the impressive pressure are allowed in height to low pressure, and this happens when the audio has a big value of capacitance. Capacity can be considered as a suitable measurement because at the lowest amplitude it ends with silence, almost air whit is in motion and at the highest end, the amount of compression and rarefaction although finite, is maximal. In electronic circuits, extended the alteration degree in varying electric current, could increase the amplitude. A woodwind player could increase their audio amplitude (i.e. blowing harder) via supporting the highest force in the column of air [13].

Zero Crossing. Zero-Crossings Rate In the concept of discrete-time signals, a zero-crossing happens in the case where consecutive samples have various algebraic signs, and the rate at which it happens is a simple measurement of a signal's frequency content. This rate measures the number of times in a specific interval of time which speech signals' amplitude passes through a value of 0, Fig. 2 the speech signals are broad-band signals and explanation of the mean rate of zero-crossing is thus considerably less accurate. Nonetheless, rough estimations of spectral characteristics may be obtained with the use of a representation according to the short-time average zero-crossing rate [14].

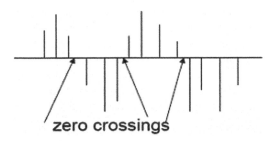

Fig. 2. Definition of zero crossing

3.4 Classification

Several classification algorithms were used as follows:

Logistic Model Tree (LMTs): The LMTs combine 2 complementary classifiers, tree induction, and linear logistic regression. LMTs' efficiency can be superior to a number of powerful classifiers like the boosted decision trees. Interpreting this tree is quite simple. The decision tree's structure includes the functions of the logistic regression at leaves. Based on the value of the threshold, the leaf node is divided into 2 child nodes in which the branch which is to the right contains the value of an attribute which is higher than the value of the threshold and the branch which is to left contains the attribute value which is smaller compared to the threshold[15]. It can be seen in Fig. 3.

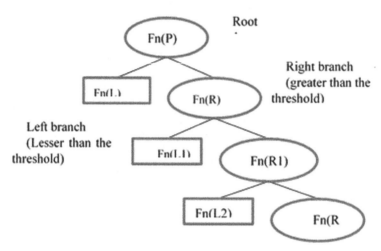

Fig. 3. Structure of logistic model tree.

K-Nearest Neighbor (K-NN). The K-NN algorithm computes the distance between the testing data and all available training data to obtain a list of nearest neighbors (with the total of k). Common distance metrics used in k-nearest neighbor (KNN) are such as Euclidean, Manhattan, or Murkowski. The choice of the number of neighbors (k) and the measure of distance depends on the data set to be classified. Idealistically, the choices should produce the highest accuracy for the given test data set. For a discrete-valued target function, the algorithm classified the test data to the majority class. For a real-value target function, the mean of the nearest neighbors will be computed as output. This approach is appropriate for the data sets with a large number of training data. Considered very fast because it merely stores the training data in memory without performing any further steps (hence the name lazy learner). Since all training will be used to be compared with the test data, there is also no loss of information [16].

4   Experiential Results

Tables 2 and 3 show the Average results for five speakers, of sex male, and female under two classification techniques KNN, LMT. These obtained results are based on the measurements of Mean, STD, Zc, and Amp. The performance of KNN with the default parameters was 94.2% and 96.7% for female that gave better result than LMT.

Table 2. Average results for five speakers, Sex: Male

Feature	Type algorithm	
	LMT	LMT
MFCC	75.1	80.3
MFCC-MEAN	55.1	61.4
MFCC-STD	69.1	78.4
MFCC-ZC	46.6	67.4
MFCC-Amp	70.8	76.1
MFCC-all	91.3	94.2

Table 3. Average results for five speakers, Sex: Female

Feature	Type algorithm	
	LMT	KNN
MFCC	81.8	88.2
MFCC-MEAN	84.5	86
MFCC-STD	91	94.1
MFCC-ZC	82.4	87.9
MFCC-Amp	93.3	92.7
MFCC-all	93.1	96.7

5 Conclusions

The proposed system work on forensic speaker identification for the Arabic language. In this system, the VQ works to improve the MFCC technique. The extracted features which result from the mixing of uses the MFCC technique and (Mean, STD, Amp, and Zc) has given good results after being applied to a number of classification algorithms like; KNN, LMT with a better recognition rate; in male, 94.2%, 91.3%, respectively, and in female, 96.1%, 93.1%. The processing time is reduced due to the use of cross-validation. For the future research, we shall examine the development of classification model that works on multi-languages recognition.

References

1. Zimeng, H.: Speaker gender recognition system. M.Sc. thesis, University of Oulu, Department of Communications Engineering (2017)
2. AboElenein, N.M., Amin, K.M.: Improved text-independent speaker identification system for real time applications. In: 4th International Japan-Egypt Conference on Electronics, Communications and Computers (JEC-ECC) (2016)

3. Shipra, G.: Application of MFCC in text independent speaker recognition. Int. J. Adv. Res. Comput. Sci. Softw. Eng. **6**(5) (2016). ISSN 2277 128X

4. Wahyuni, E.S.: Arabic speech recognition using MFCC feature extraction and ANN classification. In: 2nd International Conferences on Information Technology, Information Systems and Electrical Engineering (ICITISEE) (2017)

5. Abd Alwahed, N.N., et al.: A forensic speaker recognition system for the Arabic Language. J. Adv. Res. Dyn. Control Syst. **11**(04(Special Issue)), 1–7 (2019)

6. Tantithamthavorn, C., McIntosh, S., Hassan, A.E., Matsumoto, K.: An Empirical comparison of model validation techniques for defect prediction models. IEEE Trans. Softw. Eng. **43**(1), 1–18 (2019)

7. Jokinen, E., Saeidi, R., Tomi, K., Alku, P.: Vocal Effort Compensation for MFCC Feature Extraction in as Hooted Versus Normal Speaker Recognition Task. Elsevier (2019)

8. Abbas, M., Abdul Hassan, A.: Arabic handwritten words recognition using support vector machine and k-nearest neighbor. M.Sc. Thesis, Department of Computer Science of University of Technology (2017)

9. Shareef, S., Hashem, S.: Proposed hybrid classifier to enhance network intrusion detection system. M.Sc. Thesis, Department of Computer Science of University of Technology (2017)

10. Goeschel, K.: Reducing false positives in intrusion detection systems using data-mining techniques utilizing support vector machines, decision trees and naïve bayes for off-line analysis. In: IEEE International Conference on SoutheastCon 2016 (2016)

11. Shete, D.S., Prof, S.B., Patil, P., Patil, S.B.: Zero crossing rate and energy of the speech signal of devanagari script. IOSR J. VLSI Sig. Proces. **4**(1), 01–05 (2014). https://doi.org/10.9790/4200-04110105

12. Rajeswari, P., Juliet, K.: Text classification for student data set using naive Bayes classifier and KNN classifier. Int. J. Comput. Trends Technol. (IJCTT) **43**, 8–12 (2017)

13. Gill, M.K., Kaur, R., Kaur, J.: Vector quantization based speaker identification. Int. J. Comput. Appl. **4**(2), 1–4 (2010). ISSN 0975-8887

14. Bontempi, G., Ben Taieb, S., Le Borgne, Y.A.: Machine learning strategies for time series forecasting. In: Aufaure, M.A., Zimányi, E. (eds.) Business Intelligence. eBISS 2012. Lecture Notes in Business Information Processing, vol. 138. Springer, Heidelberg (2013). https://doi.org/10.1007/978-3-642-36318-4_3

15. Parlar, T., Özel, S.A., Song, F.: QER: a new feature selection method for sentiment analysis. HCIS **8**(1), 1–19 (2018)

16. Ramesh Nachiappan, M.: Performance of logistic model tree classifier using statistical features for fault diagnosis of single point cutting tool. Indian J. Sci. Technol. **9**(1), 1–8 (2016). https://doi.org/10.17485/ijst/2016/v9i47/107940

A Recent Research on Malware Detection Using Machine Learning Algorithm: Current Challenges and Future Works

Nor Zakiah Gorment[1,4], Ali Selamat[1,2,3,5(✉)] (iD), and Ondrej Krejcar[5] (iD)

[1] Malaysia-Japan International Institute of Technology, Universiti Teknologi Malaysia,
Jalan Sultan Yahya Petra, 54100 Kuala Lumpur, Malaysia
`aselamat@utm.my`

[2] Faculty of Engineering, School of Computing, Universiti Teknologi Malaysia,
81310 Johor Bahru, Johor, Malaysia

[3] MagicX (Media and Games Center of Excellence), Universiti Teknologi Malaysia,
81310 Johor Bahru, Johor, Malaysia

[4] College of Computing and Informatics, Universiti Tenaga Nasional, Jalan IKRAM-UNITEN,
43000 Kajang, Selangor, Malaysia

[5] Faculty of Informatics and Management, Universiti Hradec Kralove, Rokitanskeho 62, 50003
Hradec Kralove, Czech Republic
`ondrej.krejcar@uhk.cz`

Abstract. Each year, malware issues remain one of the cybersecurity concerns since malware's complexity is constantly changing as the innovation rapidly grows. As a result, malware attacks have affected everyday life from various mediums and ways. Therefore, a machine learning algorithm is one of the essential solutions in the security of computer systems to detect malware regarding the ability of machine learning algorithms to keep up with the evolution of malware. This paper is devoted to reviewing the most up-to-date research works from 2017 to 2021 on malware detection where machine learning algorithm including K-Means, Decision Tree, Meta-Heuristic, Naïve Bayes, Neuro-fuzzy, Bayesian, Gaussian, Support Vector Machine (SVM), K-Nearest Neighbour (KNN) and n-Grams was discovered using a systematic literature review. This paper aims at the following: (1) it describes each machine learning algorithm, (2) for each algorithm; it shows the performance of malware detection, and (3) we present the challenges and limitations of the algorithm during research processes.

Keywords: Malware detection · Machine learning algorithm · Systematic literature review · Comparative study

1 Introduction

Currently, the usage of the Internet and computer system are highly in demand. However, securing the data for personal or professional uses becomes a challenge because of malware attacks. As defined by Kaspersky Labs in 2017, malware is a computer program

© Springer Nature Switzerland AG 2021
H. Badioze Zaman et al. (Eds.): IVIC 2021, LNCS 13051, pp. 469–481, 2021.
https://doi.org/10.1007/978-3-030-90235-3_41

designed to disrupt a legal user's computer and wreak computer system harm in different ways. For example, it can access private computer systems without taking the systems owner's consent, gathering sensitive information, or disrupting computer operation. It can also disrupt the internet connection, the hosts' integrity, and the users' privacy.

Furthermore, malware threats keep growing by volumes, types, and functionality following the technological advances that provide various opportunities, including the Internet, social networks, smartphones, IoT devices, etc. This makes it possible to create intelligent and sophisticated malware. As such, malware is one of the significant digital dangers. For instance, in the third quarter of 2020, McAfee Labs [1] reported the volume of malware threats per minute is 588 threats averaged and increased to 648 threats averaged per minute in the fourth quarter of 2020. Meanwhile, AV-TEST institute [2] mentioned that over 450000 new malware and potentially unwanted applications were registered every day when this paper was written. Besides, the number of malware attacks was significantly increased for the last five years, from 2017 with 719.15 million attacks to 1256.73 million attacks in 2021.

Numerous surveys in malware detection explicitly using machine learning have been conducted. However, none of the work addresses the comparative study on the type of algorithms, including K-means, Meta-heuristic, Decision Tree (DT), Neuro-fuzzy, Bayesian, Naïve Bayes, Gaussian, Support Vector Machine (SVM), K-Nearest Neighbour (KNN) and N-grams for detecting malware. Thus, although malware detection techniques are increasingly studied, their performance (accuracy and detection rates), classification method, and analysis type are still not enough, limiting the utilization of malware detection in related research areas.

This paper aims to facilitate the research community with a comparative study using a systematic literature review (SLR) on machine learning algorithms chosen as their selection method in respective research activities. It presents an SLR to understand the machine-learning algorithms' processes in facilitating malware detection and identifying their performance. It also highlights the challenges and limitations of the chosen algorithms. The remaining sections of this paper, which are appropriately constructed, are: Sect. 2 presents malware's background and machine learning algorithm techniques used to detect malware. The selected methodology for this research study will be described in Sect. 3. Discussion of the results will be presented in Sect. 4. Finally, Sect. 5 reports the conclusion of this research study.

2 Background Study

The background of malware, related techniques, classification, and analysis type of malware detection will be presented in this section. Discussion on any similar systematic literature reviews that have been conducted during previous studies also will be discovered here.

2.1 Malware Types

Malware comes in a wide range of variations, including viruses, worms, trojans, spyware, botnets, ransomware, adware, rootkits, keylogger, and backdoor [3]. These variations of malware may simultaneously introduce the features of multiple variations because they are not mutually exclusive. Ilker kara [4] analyzes the ability of malware, a recovery plan for the potential damage, to identify the damage it can inflict on the targeted system, and if possible, discover specific information regarding the attacker. He proposed a method to analyze malware using digital material and an actual malware attack, including behavior analysis, memory analysis, and code analysis. It was found that malware can be traced using the server's Whois information to which the malware is connected, whereby research is conducted based on malware characteristic behavior. Furthermore, in this study, the author proposed the most current analysis programs and, at the same time, commonly used by the experts.

Meanwhile, the state-of-the-art for vulnerabilities and malware attacks for mobile were conducted [5]. A taxonomy that includes a vector of mobile malware attacks was highlighted to focus on loopholes and threat clusters where the impact of malicious widespread on communities was located. The study shows that malware tries to avoid the mechanism of detection by using techniques of evasion, including Obfuscation, a reflection of Java, encryption, repackaging, alteration of control flow, and Polymorphism in the mobile application domain. In this study, various techniques of evasion that are frequently applied by the malware were discovered as well.

Advanced Persistent Threats (APTs) [6] were discovered as an advanced type of malware that paves the way for most sabotages and Cyberespionage. APTs are target-specific, highly sophisticated, and work on a modern furtive mode. Based on continuous observation, APTs aim to exploit target-specific automated malware in a network or host to create attacks as on-demand. Besides, identifying APT is more challenging because of sophisticated attack techniques and encrypted covert communication used in APTs. On the other hand, common security systems, including anti-malware or anti-virus that rely on static analysis and signatures, failed to recognize APTs. Meanwhile, APTs use Advanced Evasive Techniques (AET), which can bypass the firewall's security in the computer system.

2.2 Taxonomy of Malware Detection

As a single malware attack can result in significant loss and damage, protecting the network and computer system from malware is highly required and crucial in cybersecurity tasks for a single user or the entire business. Thus, malware detection can be conducted in two phases: malware analysis and malware detection [7].

The malware analysis focuses on data collection of previously known malware whereby its features will be generated and extracted. The algorithm will then be developed based on those features. Furthermore, analysis of malware techniques can facilitate analysts to understand the intentions and risks which significant with a malicious code sample. The results gathered from the research can be applied to manage the new trends in the development of malware or as preventive measures to react with the threats coming in the future. Features obtained from the analysis of malware can be used to classify unknown malware and group them into their existing families.

The next phase, malware detection, will implement the algorithm developed on the new incoming malware to detect whether it is malware or benign. A different mechanism exists for malware detection, such as Data Mining, Deep Learning, Hypothesis

Exploration, etc. However, the Machine Learning algorithm is one of the most common techniques to detect malware. Two categories of malware detection are traditional signature-based approaches that detect the malware signature and modern behavior-based approaches that detect any possible attacks. Both categories can be classified as a hybrid, static, or dynamic [8]. Analysis of static is conducted by inspecting binary or the source code of applications and without executing the malware. Meanwhile, dynamic analysis traces the behavior or execution in a controlled environment such as virtual machine, emulator, sandbox, and simulator to monitors their behaviors. A hybrid study is a combination of the two types of analysis.

2.3   Machine Learning Algorithm

Malware detection was conducted by classifying using various machine learning algorithms [9], including Decision Tree, SVM, Naïve Bayes, K-nearest Neighbor (KNN), Random Forest, and Log Regression based on a system call on a computer system or Android. The study found that the highest accuracy rate at 76% is the Random Forest method. In comparison, False Positive Rate (FPR) is 13, 3% compared to other methods, and True Positive Rate (TPR) is 76%. In addition, these results show that the precision values are lower, but the accuracy and recall values are high. However, the lowest computation or fastest time is the KNN method followed by Random Forest and Naive Bayes. Besides, Log Regression is the highest computation time. Decision Tree and SVM came after that. These three methods used more parameters that reflect with high computation time.

Meanwhile, various machine learning algorithms [10], including Multilayer Perceptron Neural Network, Support Vector Machine, Decision Tree, Random Forest, Logistic Regression, Naïve Bayes, and KNN, were used to identify the application as malware or benign. Every algorithm was evaluated using several performance criteria to recognize which algorithm is more significant for malware detection. The random Forest method provides the best outcome, with a precision rate of 90.63%, and proves that the Random Forest method is still the most effective technique to detect malware. For other criteria, SVM is the second-best. The False Positive Rate of SVM is much better than Random Forest. Meanwhile, Naïve Bayes offers the lowest False Positive Rate, while in other criteria, the performance and True Positive Rate are pretty poor.

Furthermore, an empirical study and comparison performances [11] of six supervised algorithms of machine learning, including Random Forest, Logistic Regression, KNN, SVM, Naïve Bayes, and Decision Tree, for detecting zero-day and unknown Android malware apps were conducted to overcome the problems faced by conventional methods. The experiment results show that all machine learning algorithms have performed remarkably efficient detection on Android malware. The random forest method was obtained the best detection accuracy at 99%, while the lowest detection accuracy at 95.59% in the detection of Android malware is the Naïve Bayes.

2.4 Previous Preview

Several types of research work on systematic literature review have been conducted focusing on malware detection related issues, including the dataset used, the performance of method used, analysis type, and classification method.

According to [12], which conducted detection of malware for Android using a machine learning algorithm on hybrid analysis, the most common datasets are Android Malware Genome Project and Drebin. Most of the researchers use local app stores and Google Play Store to gather benign applications. Besides, VirusShare, VirusTotal, and ContagioDump, are also used for malware samples. Meanwhile, the authors found that the most commonly used machine learning algorithm is SVM in the current study. They were followed by Random Forest, Naive Bayes, and Logistic Regression. The Decision Tree is the least algorithm used in the study. Based on the analysis, the most frequent evaluation metrics are True Positive Rate (TPR), False Positive Rate (FPR), and accuracy.

Marvin [13] were employed several dynamic and static features in hybrid analysis, to detect malware on Android. Dynamic features such as Dynamically Loaded Code, Network Operations, Phone Events, and File Operations, while static features including Developers Certificate, Suspicious Files, API Calls, Permissions, and Intents were extracted. Linear Classifiers and SVM were adopted to build a model for detection where SVM is faster comparatively while Linear Classifiers' detection is more accurate. The accuracy is at 98.24% to detect malware with FPR is less than 0.04%. However, the accuracy is close to 90% for previous unseen malware. Although many features were considered, Marvin overlooked the system-level events which use System Calls as dynamic features.

The static features such as potentially dangerous functions, Receivers, Services, Intents, and Permissions, while dynamic features such as Network Traffic and investigated Native Code (Native API Calls) were used for Mobile-SandBox [14] to classify malware. However, the performance has lacked there are no solid performance metrics.

An on-device malware detection architecture [15] was proposed to reduce the memory overhead of local devices to ensure resource efficiency. A subset of Drebin's [16] with ten dynamic features predefined System Calls and features (6 out of 8) as static features was used. The accuracy rate is close to 98%, with 0.1% of FPR. However, since the old dataset was used and malware behavior frequently changes over time, the authors have failed to detect recent malware. They have also overlooked any additional dynamic features.

Furthermore, Kapratwar [17] were used System Calls and Permissions for analysis of hybrid. The result of the performance for static features is significantly better compared to dynamic features. However, the study has used an old dataset with a small size of samples (200 apps) and overlooked other dynamic and static features.

3 Methodology

The guidelines to conduct this SLR were proposed by Kitchenham [18]. Based on the guidelines, the creation of review questions will be the first process of SLR. The next process is developing a review protocol and validating each of it. They were followed by searching for and filtering the primary studies based on the criteria described in the review protocol. The process continues with reading the full text on selected studies and adopting any collaborative review methods to evaluate the quality of the studies. In the end, the gathered studies will be analyzed and synthesized. The result will then be extracted from the review. Details explanations for each process were presented in the following subsections.

3.1 Review Question

The malware detection process can be supported using various types of algorithms for machine learning. Thus, this paper aims to investigate and compare the relevant studies that are significant with the aims. In this SLR, the following review questions (RQ) have been identified to be addressed in this study:

- RQ1: What type of machine learning algorithm was used?
- RQ2: How does the machine learning algorithms work?
- RQ3: How does the performance of the algorithm used?
- RQ4: What is the classification method used?
- RQ5: What is the analysis type used?
- RQ6: What are the challenges and limitations found while implementing the algorithm?

3.2 Review Protocol

Based on the SLR guidelines adopted from Kitchenham [18], the following strategies, such as the strategy of search, exclusion and inclusion criteria, quality assessment, data extraction, and data synthesis, must be included for this protocol.

Strategy of Search. An automated search strategy was performed to address the review questions while different digital libraries' syntax and search algorithms were described database searching using the query string. The following are the scope of search and strings query:

- Query String - ("malware detection" OR "anti-malware" OR "malicious detection") AND ("machine learning algorithm" OR "machine learning approach") AND ("K-means" OR "Naïve Bayes" OR "Support Vector Machine" OR "Decision Tree" OR "Meta-heuristic" OR "Neuro-fuzzy" OR "Bayesian" OR "Gaussian" OR "K-Nearest Neighbour" OR "N-grams")
- Timespan is from 2017 to 2021, language is English, reference type including Book Chapter, Symposium, Conference, and Journal.

Digital libraries, including Mendeley (papers from Science Direct, Scopus, Web of Science, SpringerLink, and ACM Digital) and IEEE Explore, were used as a medium to facilitate the snowballing process of search to find related studies. All studies that fulfilled the exclusion and inclusion criteria were included for this SLR. The initial timespan of this SLR is from 2017 to 2021. The reasons are to get the most updated and relevant studies that considered the latest technology in managing the malware and to reflect the state-of-the-art machine learning algorithm for detecting malware and fit with the review questions.

Exclusion and Inclusion Criteria. In this study, the relevant papers were shortlisted using a set of exclusion and inclusion criteria described based on the review questions.

The following studies were included: if defined or applied a machine-learning algorithm to support malware detection processes, or if a review paper, the paper was separately treated, or if more than one paper was reported to the same study, the paper with the most updated version is selected. The following studies were excluded: if discussed machine learning algorithms but not related to malware detection, or if not written in English, or if identical to others. There were three phases in selecting the study. In the first phase, the author conducted the search and found all potential primary studies. Then, the author read the title and abstract of all possible studies obtained from the search results. After that, all the studies that fulfilled the exclusion and inclusion criteria were included. In the next phase, the author read the chosen papers in full for shortlisting the documents for final selection.

Assessment of Quality. The author evaluates the quality of the studies that fulfilled the exclusion and inclusion criteria to ensure the studies' relevancy, credibility, independence, and rigorousness according to the ten criteria. The full text was read for each paper, and the assessment criteria were applied to evaluate its quality. Table 1 shows the criteria set for questions of quality assessment and defined based on the checklists by [19]. Each question had four possible scores: not mentioned at all (score $= 0$), little mentioned (score $= 0.5$), discussed adequately (score $= 1$), and thoroughly addressed (score $= 1$). As such, based on their score, all primary studies were filtered.

Extraction of Data. All the required information to perform an in-depth analysis was collected to address all the review questions during this process.

Data Analysis. For each primary study, an in-depth data analysis was conducted to answer each review question. For RQ1, machine learning algorithms used were identified for each primary study. For RQ2, the algorithms used will then be analyzed to discover how it's work. Models or theories for each category also was discovered. For RQ3, the results from the algorithm implemented in terms of performance were analyzed. For RQ4, the classification methods and analysis type for RQ5 were identified. Lastly, for RQ6, any challenges and limitations found during the implementation of the algorithm are discovered.

4   Results Discussion

The summary of the results is presented in this section after all the methods that have been described in the previous section were implemented.

Table 1. Criteria of quality assessment

No.	Criteria
	Statement of problem
Q1	Is the aim of the study clearly described?
	Design of research
Q2	Is the performance of the algorithm for machine learning to support malware detection clearly explained?
Q3	Is the classification and analysis type of machine learning algorithms stated in the respective research paper?
	Collection of data
Q4	Are the measures and data collection sufficiently described?
Q5	Are the constructs and measures applied in the study are the most relevant to answer the review question?
	Analysis of data
Q6	Is the data analysis in the study sufficiently explained?
Q7a	Qualitative study: Is the explanation of proving clearly justified?
Q7b	Quantitative study: Is the significance of the data been evaluated?
Q8	Is it clear how machine learning algorithm works and has been applied?
	Conclusion
Q9	Are the findings of the study supported by the results and clearly presented?
Q10	Is the study address the validity or limitations?

4.1 Results of Primary Studies on Search and Selection

The process of searching and selecting the primary studies was conducted based on the search as mentioned earlier in Sect. 3. Figure 1 shows details of the process associated with establishing and identifying the significant studies. For the first process, by using the query strings defined in Sect. 3, the relevant studies were gathered from two electronic databases. From the automated searches, we found that 634 results were selected. Then, the selected studies were exported to Mendeley for reference management. The following process filters the studies based on the intended criteria, which identified only 74 studies are valid. Table 2 shows the 74 studies that were chosen after eliminating duplicate or irrelevant papers. The classification of studies based on the type of algorithm has been presented, indexed in IEEE Explore, Science Direct, Scopus, Web of Science, SpringerLink, and ACM Digital, as shown in Fig. 3.

Most of the studies are from research activities in 2018 which contribute 28%, followed by 2019 and 2020, which shared 23%. Meanwhile, research activities in 2017 are 20%, and only 6% contributed from 2021 since the studies were gathered from the first Quarter of 2021 only. Details of the contribution of the selected studies per year are shown in Fig. 2. Furthermore, the studies chosen per indexing type can be seen in Fig. 3, where IEEE Explore is a significant indexing database with 57% contribution, followed by Web of Science 11%. In comparison, Science Direct and Scopus shared 9% contribution, and the least 7% contribution shared by SpringerLink and ACM Digital. It shows that from 2017 to 2021, the related research works on malware detection using machine learning algorithms are continuously conducted and relevant for further direction.

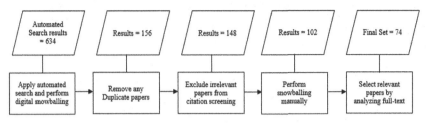

Fig. 1. Identification and selection of primary studies

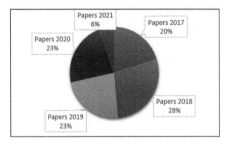

Fig. 2. Selected studies per year

Fig. 3. Selected studies per indexing type

Table 2. Search results

| No. | Approach | IEEE Explore | | Mendeley | | Total | Total |
		Returned Papers	Final Papers	Returned Papers	Final Papers	Returned Papers	Final Papers
1	K-Means	20	2	40	2	60	4
2	Naïve Bayes	42	7	27	2	69	9
3	Support Vector Machine (SVM)	156	12	33	6	189	18
4	Decision Tree	79	7	25	4	104	11
5	Meta-Heuristic	1	0	4	1	5	1
6	Neuro-fuzzy	1	1	4	3	5	4
7	Bayesian	11	3	14	3	25	6
8	Gaussian	10	2	10	2	20	4
9	K-Nearest Neighbour (KNN)	32	5	17	2	49	7
10	N-Grams	34	3	74	7	108	10
	Total	386	42	248	32	634	74

4.2   Quality Assessment and Performance Results

In this SLR, the final set of primary studies were identified, and predefined quality assessment criteria, as seen in Sect. 3, have been assessed to verify each selected study has fulfilled the required quality. Based on the score of quality assessment as shown in

Fig. 5, the overall score is above 7, which shows that all the studies fulfilled most of the criteria that have been set earlier. The highest score is 10 (20%, 15 studies), and the lowest score is 7.5 (7%, five studies). However, most of the studies achieved a score of 8 (34%, 25 studies). We can say that all ten criteria that were defined as a measurement can prove that our studies are relevant and have made a valuable contribution to the review. Based on the performance of machine learning algorithms, it shows that Support Vector Machine (SVM) [20], n-Grams [21], and Decision Tree [22] shows the highest performance at 100% detection accuracy rate, while the lowest performance is at 64.7% using Naïve Bayes [23]. However, the performance of Decision Tree and n-Grams on malware detection has been tested using a small dataset. Therefore, there is a possibility of biased analysis since not all the features may have been incorporated using the number of samples; as such, a larger scale of dataset needed to be used for future works as mentioned by authors.

Meanwhile, SVM is used to detect malware at the highest performance and is the most frequent algorithm researchers use due to its high detection accuracy rate. The average detection accuracy rate for each algorithm has been calculated as shown in Fig. 4, and the performance of SVM is still high, with 90.55%. The highest average detection accurate rate with 97.80% is n-Grams, followed by KNN 92.72%, Decision Tree 92.23%, K-Means 89%, Bayesian 89.08%, Gaussian 87.42%, Naïve Bayes 86.45%, Neuro-fuzzy 83.48%, and the lowest performance is Meta-Heuristic with 81.23%. On the other hand, Meta-Heuristic [24] is the least algorithm used by researchers.

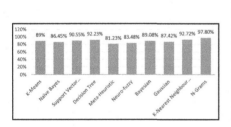

Fig. 4. Average of detection accuracy rate

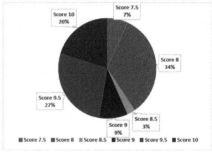

Fig. 5. Results assessment of quality

4.3 Challenges and Limitations

In the selected studies, we found that dataset is the most common issue faced by the authors. For instance, a small size of dataset [25], which then led to bias [22] results. Some authors have used outdated datasets [26], could not found suitable [21] datasets for their empirical study, has limited sources [28], and lack of standard benchmark datasets [26] that were led to the poor performance [29], in detection the malware. Other issues were high false positives rate [27], signature-based, and classification technique.

On the other hand, some authors also faced difficulties in handling the obfuscation technique [30]. Malware behavior cannot be performed in the Android application process [31], while security tools [24] and virtual environments were two mediums that the modern malware attacks can hide their behavior from being analyzed. During empirical studies, a longer time was needed to complete the detection process since two algorithm types were implemented together [32]. In contrast, the classification takes longer [38] time for better effectiveness.

Meanwhile, by using static analysis, updated attacks [33] cannot be detected. The existing approach used by authors [34] failed to detect some malware samples such as Pjapps and Geinimi since new malware samples constantly arise [35]. The difficulties occurred to detect new malware variants because some of them act differently in real environments [20]. Besides, the selected feature attributes need to be independent of each other or with a minor correlation coefficient [36]. The higher number of features might contribute to increasing the number of unrelated or redundant features, which might cause many problems such as confusing learning algorithms, reducing the classification accuracy, and over-fitting [37].

5 Conclusion

There were 74 studies that reflected this SLR study, which defined machine learning algorithms to keep up with malware detection. The results of this SLR will enable other researchers to understand the state-of-the-art in SLR to detect malware using machine learning algorithms. Gaps and future research directions also have been identified. The critical challenge in conducting SLR manually is time-consuming, prone to errors, and labor-intensive. Selecting and validating the available evidence gathered from different resources is also another challenge in performing SLR studies. Nevertheless, the findings facilitate the research community with a comparative research study on machine learning algorithms chosen as their selection method in respective research activities.

Acknowledgment. The authors sincerely thank Universiti Teknologi Malaysia (UTM) under Research University Grant Vot-20H04, Malaysia Research University Network (MRUN) Vot 4L876, for completing the research. This work was supported/funded by the Ministry of Higher Education under the Fundamental Research Grant Scheme (FRGS/1/2018/ICT04/UTM/01/1). The work is partially supported by the SPEV project (ID: 2102-2021), Faculty of Informatics and Management, University of Hradec Kralove. We are also grateful for the support of Ph.D. students Michal Dobrovolny and Sebastien Mambou in consultations regarding application aspects from Hradec Kralove University, Czech Republic.

References

1. McAfee Homepage (McAfee Labs Threats report April 2021). https://www.mcafee.com/ent erprise/en-us/lp/threats-reports/apr-2021.html. Accessed 18 Aug 2021
2. AV-TEST Institute Homepage (Statistic of malware). https://www.av-test.org/en/statistics/malware/. Accessed 18 Aug 2021
3. Qamar, A., Karim, A., Chang, V.: Mobile malware attacks: review, taxonomy & future directions. Fut. Gener. Comput. Syst. **97**, 887–909 (2019)
4. Kara, I.: A basic malware analysis method. Comput. Fraud Secur. **2019**(6), 11–19 (2019)

5. Yu, B., Fang, Y., Yang, Q., Tang, Y., Liu, L.: A survey of malware behavior description and analysis. Front. Inf. Technol. Electron. Eng. **19**(5), 583–603 (2018). https://doi.org/10.1631/FITEE.1601745

6. Chakkaravarthy, S.S., Sangeetha, D., Vaidehi, V.: A survey on malware analysis and mitigation techniques. Comput. Sci. Rev. **32**, 1–23 (2019)

7. Saeed, I.A., Selamat, A., Abuagoub, A.M.: A survey on malware and malware detection systems. Int. J. Comput. Appl. **67**(16), 25–31 (2013)

8. Shabtai, A., Moskovitch, R., Elovici, Y., Glezer, C.: Detection of malicious code by applying machine learning classifiers on static features: a state-of-the-art survey. Inf. Secur. Tech. Rep. **14**(1), 16–29 (2009)

9. Anshori, M., Mar'i, F., Bachtiar, F.A.: Comparison of machine learning methods for android malicious software classification based on system call. In: 2019 International Conference on Sustainable Information Engineering and Technology (SIET), pp. 343–348. IEEE (2019)

10. Al Ali, M., Svetinovic, D., Aung, Z., Lukman, S.: Malware detection in Android mobile platform using machine learning algorithms. In: 2017 International Conference on Infocom Technologies and Unmanned Systems (Trends and Future Directions) (ICTUS), pp. 763–768. IEEE (2017)

11. Abdullah, T.A., Ali, W., Abdulghafor, R.: Empirical study on intelligent Android malware detection based on supervised machine learning. Int. J. Adv. Comput. Sci. Appl. (IJACSA) **11**(4) (2020)

12. Galib, A.H., Hossain, B.M.: A systematic review on hybrid analysis using machine learning for Android malware detection. In: 2019 2nd International Conference on Innovation in Engineering and Technology (ICIET), pp. 1–6. IEEE (2019)

13. Lindorfer, M., Neugschwandtner, M., Platzer, C.: Marvin: efficient and comprehensive mobile app classification through static and dynamic analysis. In: 39th Annual Computer Software and Applications Conference, vol. 2, pp. 422–433. IEEE (2015)

14. Spreitzenbarth, M., Freiling, F., Echtler, F., Schreck, T., Hoffmann, J.: Mobile-sandbox: having a deeper look into android applications. In: Proceedings of the 28th Annual ACM Symposium on Applied Computing, pp. 1808–1815 (2013)

15. Arshad, S., Shah, M.A., Wahid, A., Mehmood, A., Song, H., Yu, H.: SAMADroid: a novel 3-level hybrid malware detection model for Android operating system. IEEE Access **6**, 4321–4339 (2018)

16. Arp, D., Spreitzenbarth, M., Hubner, M., Gascon, H., Rieck, K.: DREBIN: effective and explainable detection of android malware in your pocket. In: NDSS, vol. 14, pp. 23–26 (2014)

17. Kapratwar, A., Di Troia, F., Stamp, M.: Static and dynamic analysis of android malware. In: ICISSP, pp. 653–662 (2017)

18. Kitchenham, B.: Procedures for performing systematic reviews. Keele University and ESE, Nicta, UK, Australia, Technical report, TR/SE-0401, 0400011T.1 (2004)

19. Dybå, T., Dingsøyr, T.: Empirical studies of agile software development: a systematic review. Inf. Softw. Technol. **50**(9–10), 833–859 (2008)

20. Huda, S., et al.: Defending unknown attacks on cyber-physical systems by semi-supervised approach and available unlabeled data. Inf. Sci. **379**, 211–228 (2017)

21. Abiola, A.M., Marhusin, M.F.: Signature-based malware detection using sequences of N-grams. Int. J. Eng. Technol. **7**, 120–125 (2018)

22. Sethi, K., Chaudhary, S.K., Tripathy, B.K., Bera, P.: A novel malware analysis framework for malware detection and classification using machine learning approach. In: Proceedings of the 19th International Conference on Distributed Computing and Networking, pp. 1–4 (2018)

23. Irshad, A., Maurya, R., Dutta, M.K., Burget, R., Uher, V.: Feature optimization for run time analysis of malware in windows operating system using machine learning approach. In: 2019 42nd International Conference on Telecommunications and Signal Processing (TSP), pp. 255–260, IEEE (2019)

24. Mishra, P., et al.: VMShield: memory introspection-based malware detection to secure cloud-based services against stealthy attacks. IEEE Trans. Ind. Inf. **17**(10), 6754–6764 (2021). https://doi.org/10.1109/TII.2020.3048791

25. KP, A.M., Chandran, S., Gressel, G., Arjun, T.U., Pavithran, V.: Using dtrace for machine learning solutions in malware detection. In: 2020 11th International Conference on Computing, Communication and Networking Technologies (ICCCNT), pp. 1–7. IEEE (2020)

26. Cruz, S., Coleman, C., Rudd, E.M., Boult, T.E.: Open set intrusion recognition for fine-grained attack categorization. In: 2017 IEEE International Symposium on Technologies for Homeland Security (HST), pp. 1–6. IEEE (2017)

27. Lingam, G., Rout, R.R., Somayajulu, D.V.L.N.: Detection of social botnet using a trust model based on spam content in Twitter network. In: 2018 IEEE 13th International Conference on Industrial and Information Systems (ICIIS), pp. 280–285. IEEE (2018)

28. Rosli, N.A., Yassin, W., Faizal, M.A., Selamat, S.R.: Clustering analysis for malware behavior detection using registry data (IJACSA). Int. J. Adv. Comput. Sci. Appl. **10**, 12 (2019)

29. Al Zaabi, A., Mouheb, D.: Android malware detection using static features and machine learning. In: 2020 International Conference on Communications, Computing, Cybersecurity, and Informatics (CCCI), pp. 1–5. IEEE (2020)

30. Ibrahim, W.N.H., et al.: Multilayer framework for botnet detection using machine learning algorithms. IEEE Access **9**, 48753–48768 (2021)

31. Wei, L., Luo, W., Weng, J., Zhong, Y., Zhang, X., Yan, Z.: Machine learning-based malicious application detection of android. IEEE Access **5**, 25591–25601 (2017)

32. Qasim, O.M.: Detection system for detecting worms using hybrid algorithm of naïve Bayesian classifier and k-means. In: 2019 2nd International Conference on Engineering Technology and its Applications (IICETA), pp. 173–178. IEEE (2019)

33. Dhalaria, M., Gandotra, E.: A framework for detection of android malware using static features. In: 2020 IEEE 17th India Council International Conference (INDICON), pp. 1–7. IEEE (2020)

34. Khariwal, K., Singh, J., Arora, A.: IPDroid: Android malware detection using intents and permissions. In: 2020 4th World Conference on Smart Trends in Systems, Security and Sustainability (WorldS4), pp. 197–202. IEEE (2020)

35. Coban, O., Ozel, S.: Adapting text categorization for manifest based android malware detection. Comput. Sci. **20**(3), 383 (2019). https://doi.org/10.7494/csci.2019.20.3.3285

36. Wu, F., Xiao, L., Zhu, J.: Bayesian model updating method based android malware detection for IoT services. In: 2019 15th International Wireless Communications & Mobile Computing Conference (IWCMC), pp. 61–66. IEEE (2019)

37. Altaher, A.: An improved Android malware detection scheme based on an evolving hybrid neuro-fuzzy classifier (EHNFC) and permission-based features. Neural Comput. Appl. **28**(12), 4147–4157 (2016). https://doi.org/10.1007/s00521-016-2708-7

38. Cucchiarelli, A., Morbidoni, C., Spalazzi, L., Baldi, M.: Algorithmically generated malicious domain names detection based on n-grams features. Exp. Syst. Appl. **170**, 114551 (2021)

Symptoms-Based Network Intrusion Detection System

Qais Saif Qassim[1]([✉]), Norziana Jamil[2], and Mohammed Najah Mahdi[2]

[1] University of Technology and Applied Sciences – Ibri, Ibri, Sultanate of Oman
`qais.aljanabi@ibrict.edu.om`
[2] College of Computing and Informatics, Universiti Tenaga Nasional,
Kajang, Malaysia
`{norziana,najah.mahdi}@uniten.edu.my`

Abstract. Protecting the network perimeters from malicious activities is a necessity and essential defence mechanism against cyberattacks. Network Intrusion Detection system (NIDS) is commonly used as a defense mechanism. This paper presents the Symptoms-based NIDS, a new intrusion detection system approach that learns the normal network behaviours through monitoring a range of network data attributes at the network and the transport layers. The proposed IDS consists of distributed anomaly detection agents and a centralised anomaly classification engine. The detection agents are located at the end nodes of the protected network, detecting anomalies by analysing network traffic and identifying abnormal activities. These agents will capture and analyse the network and the transport headers of individual packets for malicious activities. The agents will communicate with the centralised anomaly classification engine upon detecting a suspicious activity for attack prioritisation and classification. The paper presented a list of network attributes to be considered as classification features to identify anomalies.

Keywords: Signature · Anomaly · False alarms · Classification · Features · Machine learning

1 Introduction

Protecting asset's information from inside and outside threats can be a very demanding task. The primary purpose of an Intrusion Detection System (IDS) is to identify attackers trying to expose vulnerable resources on information systems and network services. Practically most of the existing intrusion detection systems are signature-based [1]. The performance of these systems is limited by the signature database of previously seen instances or attacks [2]. Therefore, the inability of signature-based IDS to detect novel attacks whose nature is unknown has stimulated the need for intelligent and efficient intrusion detection methods. The anomaly-based intrusion detection system is designed to uncover

© Springer Nature Switzerland AG 2021
H. Badioze Zaman et al. (Eds.): IVIC 2021, LNCS 13051, pp. 482–494, 2021.
https://doi.org/10.1007/978-3-030-90235-3_42

abnormal behaviour patterns [3]. It establishes a baseline of normal usage patterns and flags anything that widely deviates from it as a possible intrusion. The major benefit of anomaly-based detection methods is that they can effectively detect previously unknown threats. However, they cannot provide utterly accurate detection and are prone to generate high false alarms [4]. This is a serious concern in information security because false alarms can severely impact the protected information systems, such as the disruption of information availability because of IDS blockage in suspecting an attack attempt is overburdened by false alarm.

Deploying an anomaly-based intrusion detection system is usually implemented in two stages [5]; during the first stage, the system learns the network's normal behaviours under the assumption of the absence of attacks and/or malicious activities. In the second stage, the system monitors network traffic and system activates and compares them to the learned normal behavioural patterns. If a mismatch occurs, a level of "suspicion" is raised, and when the suspicion, in turn, trespasses a given threshold, the system triggers an alarm.

Typical attack definition consists of a combination of attack symptoms that are abnormal values of the observed network variables. Context knowledge can significantly improve intrusion detection accuracy and minimise the rate of false alarms. This work presents a new two-tier intrusion detection system that learns the normal ranges of values for network data attribute at the network and the transport layers. The proposed IDS work within a distributed multi-agent Intrusion Detection System architecture; the algorithm uses attack symptoms vectors for attack prioritisation and classification.

The rest of the paper is structured as follows; in Sect. 2, we present a brief review of intrusion detection systems and highlight the primary goal of this work. In Sect. 3, we introduce our symptoms based intrusion detection system. Section 4 presents the system implementation and finally Sect. 5 describes the future research plan and concludes the paper.

2   Literature Review

It is well known that intrusion detection systems play a vital role as the second line of defence against network-based and host-based attacks behind the firewall [6]. The key usage of an intrusion detection system is to detect abnormal or suspicious activities and raise the alarm whenever such activities are detected. Therefore, intrusion detection systems are becoming a prominent tool for many organisations after deploying firewall technology at the network perimeter [7].

Typically, the IDS systems are classified based on the method used in detecting malicious activities into one of the two approaches [8]; anomaly detection and signature detection. An anomaly detection approach is used to detect deviations from a previously learned behaviour, whereas any activity that significantly deviates from the normal behaviour is considered as intrusive. On the other hand, the misuse detection approach detects intrusions in terms of the characteristics of known attacks or system vulnerabilities; any action that conforms to the pattern of a known attack or vulnerability is considered intrusive.

Due to the diversity of cyberattacks and zero-day attacks signature-based IDS will likely miss an increasingly large share of attack attempts. In spite of this, most intrusion detection systems in use today are signature-based; whilst few anomaly-based IDSs have been deployed to date [9]. The reason behind that is, a signature-based IDS is easier to implement and simpler to configure and maintain than the anomaly-based. On the other hand, the deployment of an anomaly-based IDS typically requires training time, crucial system's attributes to monitor, and expert personnel [10,11]. To configure the anomaly-based IDS, several parameters need to be set, such as the duration of the training phase and the similarity metric. In addition to that, different environments may require a different set of attributes to monitor and parameters to configure. Therefore, common detection guidelines for anomaly-based IDS are hard to dedicate. Each anomaly detection mechanism has its unique requirements such as training time, system parameters and dataset collection, while all signature-based IDSs perform similarly in various environments.

Anomaly-based IDSs are mainly criticised based on three aspects, each of which increases the security specialist effort needed to configure and run. Firstly, as discussed previously, anomaly-based IDS generally raise a high number of false alarms. Secondly, an anomaly-based IDS usually works as a black-box [12]. Lastly, an anomaly-based IDS raises alarms without a precise classification or context detection information clarifies the rationale of generating the alarm [13]. As a matter of fact, the classification of a certain instance for a signature-based IDS is predetermined. In contrast, the classification for an anomaly-based IDS depends on the training dataset. Thus, different anomaly-based model instances could classify the same instance differently [14].

False alarms are well-known problems of IDSs in general and anomaly-based IDSs in particular [15]. Security analysts have to verify each raised alarm; thus, systems prone to raise a high amount of false alarms will require many personnel and excessive time for alarm verification. Two distinct trends affect the rate of false alarms; primarily, most anomaly-based detection engines utilise statistical models, a distance function, and a threshold value to detect anomalies [13]. For that reason, there is an intrinsic tie between attacks detected and false alarms raised; when adjusting the threshold value to detect a larger number of attacks, the number of false alarms increases as well. Therefore, it is practically difficult to achieve ideal attack detection with no false alarms all at once [16,17].

Consequently, anomaly-based IDS have to be tuned by setting an appropriate threshold value. Secondly, since intrusions are rare events, and because detection engines cannot achieve both optimal detection rate and a negligible false alarm rate, a greater rate of false alarms will be generated than the desired and expected rate. This problem is commonly known as the base-rate fallacy, and it stems directly from Bayes' theorem [18].

Another limitation of an anomaly-based system is that it carries out the detection process as a black-box [19]. System administrators have little control over the process flow and its configuration; reasonably, they can merely configure the similarity metric used to discern legitimate traffic from malicious activities. Most anomaly-based IDSs employ complex mathematical models (such as neural networks, genetic algorithms and data mining algorithms) [20]. Therefore, system administrators can neither precisely understand how the IDS engine distinguishes normal instances nor refine the IDS model to avoid certain false alarms or improve attack detection.

Unlike signature-based IDS, the anomaly-based IDS lack attack classification. The main concept of an anomaly-based IDS is that it raises the alarm every time it detects an activity that deviates from the baseline model of the normal behaviour [19]. Therefore, the cause of the anomaly itself is unknown to the intrusion detection system. The generated alarm holds little information to determine the attack class. Network-based systems generally include the targeted IP address, network port used, and the IP source of the attack. This is because the detection engine's model is implemented based on learning the normal behaviours during a certain time. Therefore, it is difficult to develop an offline classifier suitable for any anomaly-based IDS instance.

An anomaly-based IDS is hypothetically supposed to detect unknown attacks or slight modifications of well-known attacks. Manual classification and the application of some heuristics-based approaches are possible options [19]. However, manual classification is not feasible due to a large number of false alarms generated, and the heuristics deliver results in a restricted context only because the "traits" of each attack must be known. In addition to that, because alarms are generated unclassified and hold little information to determine the attack class, no automatic countermeasure can be activated to react to a certain threat [6]. Because of all the limitations listed above for an anomaly-based IDS, the primary objectives of this work is to propose a method that can enhance and improve the usability of the anomaly-based intrusion detection system

3   Symptoms-Based Network Intrusion Detection System

The proposed IDS consists of two interacting components: the Anomaly Detection Agent (ADA) and the Attack Classification Engine (ACE). The ADA processes network traffic, analyse traffic statistics and extracts significant network traffic attributes. Once ADA has detected an abnormal activity, the collected information is passed to the ACE that automatically determines the attack class. This section presents the proposed system in detail.

3.1   An Overview

The proposed IDS is a completely network-based intrusion detection system that identifies intrusions by examining network traffic. As illustrated in Fig. 1, it consists of anomaly detection agents distributed in the networks' end nodes and a centralised correlation engine. The distributed agents are responsible for interpreting the data stream (network traffic) arriving at the particular node. The main function of these agents is to capture all network traffic generated by the specified host and analyse the content of individual packets for malicious activities. The ADA communicates with the anomaly classification engine upon detecting suspicious activities for attack prioritisation and classification.

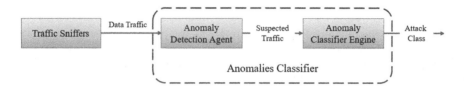

Fig. 1. conceptual framework of the proposed system

3.2   Attribute Vector

Before proceeding with system architecture any further, some concepts used in this paper should be explained in detail. The proposed IDS learns the normal behaviour of the network by monitoring and analysing several network data attributes at the network and the transport layers. The attributes have to be collected from the network protocol stack. The collected attributes will be used to produce a feature set containing statistical information that reflects the amount of change within each time interval. The monitored attributes can be arranged under two general categories: attributes extracted from the IP header and attributes extracted from the TCP header listed in Table 1.

As illustrated, twenty attributes to be monitored and analysed have been collected from the network protocol stack. The monitored attributes will be represented as a vector of 20 elements as shown in Eq. 1, where each element represents its designated value as described in Table 1.

$$f = [F_1, F_2, F_3, F_4, ...F_{20}] \tag{1}$$

For instance, F_1 represents the value of the IP header's Time To Live (TTL) field, an eight-bit field that holds a value specified in seconds and helps prevent datagrams from persisting on the Internet.

3.3   Anomaly Detection Agent (ADA)

Any network attack causes a certain abnormal behaviour, and it is imperative to be able to identify this abnormal behaviour accurately. To meet this challenge, the proposed IDS utilises decision correlation metrics to measure the attributes of the network that will most likely identify an attack in progress.

The proposed IDS works as follows; the distributed agents monitor the incoming traffic by analysing selected network data attributes at the network and the transport layers and estimate its deviation from the normal behaviours (baseline) learned during the training phase. The agents then generate symptoms vector based on the magnitude that the monitored network data attributes that deviate from the baseline, which represents the strength of the participation of each monitored attribute.

The central tendency rule backed by the arithmetic mean plays a vital role in the detection mechanism. They have been used to calculate the central value that the magnitude of deviations is trend to cluster around. In other words, if

Table 1. IP and TCP considered features

Attribute	Description
F1	The number of distinct values of the Time To Live field of the IP header
F2	The number of foreign IP addresses
F3	The number of inbound packets that were discarded due to errors in their IP headers
F4	The number of inbound packets for which this host was not their final IP destination
F5	The number of inbound packets received successfully but discarded because of an unknown or unsupported protocol
F6	The number of inbound packets which were discarded because of the IP checksum
F7	The average number of packets sent and received
F8	The ratio of packets sent and received to the number of foreign IP addresses
F9	Weigthed sum of TOS field
F10	The number of distinct values of the header checksum field of the IP header
F11	The number of TCP connections
F12	The number of half open connections
F13	The maximum value permitted by a TCP implementation for the retransmission timeout, measured in milliseconds
F14	The minimum value permitted by a TCP implementation for the retransmission timeout, measured in milliseconds
F15	The limit on the total number of TCP connections the host can support
F16	The number of times TCP connections have made a direct transition to the SYN SENT state from the CLOSED state during the observation period
F17	The number of times TCP connections have made a direct transition to the SYN RCVD state from the LISTEN state during the observation period
F18	The number of times TCP connections have made a direct transition to the CLOSED state from either the ESTABLISHED state or the CLOSE WAIT state during the observation period
F19	The total number of segments received, including those received in error
F20	The total number of segments sent

the central tendency of the generated symptoms vector is greater than zero (or a selected threshold value), it indicates the presents of an anomaly due to the deviation from the normal network behaviours. To reduce the rate of false alarms, a threshold value greater than zero to be considered based on the protection level required. Therefore, in this work, ranges of threshold values have been considered for comparison. Once the central tendency exceeds the defined threshold, an alarm will be generated indicating malicious activity. When a malicious activity has been indicated, the symptoms vector will be directed to the correlation module to identify the attack class.

3.4   Anomaly Classification Engine (ACE)

The anomaly classification engine is responsible for identifying the anomaly mechanism based on a predefined set of patterns of known attack mechanisms that are defined in the CAPEC and CVE databases. The ACE represents a modified signature-based intrusion detection system. However, it traces the symptoms vector to the most identical attack mechanism instead of detecting an attack. Identifying the attack mechanism (class) is an easy and effortless task comparing to detecting the attack itself. The attack class identified will help measure the risk exposed by the detected attack. The ACE is trained with several types of attack mechanisms to build a classification model. The attack mechanism information can be provided in several ways, either manually by an operator or automatically by extracting specific information from the known attack signatures.

3.5   The Proposed IDS Architecture

This section describes the main components and the working modes of the proposed IDS in detail. Figure 2 depicts system architecture and its principal sub-systems. As mentioned earlier, the proposed IDS consists of two interacting components: the ADA and the ACE. As described earlier, the anomaly detection agent processes network traffic, analyse traffic statistics and extracts significant information. Once ADA has detected an abnormal activity, the collected data is passed to the ACE, which automatically determines the attack class.

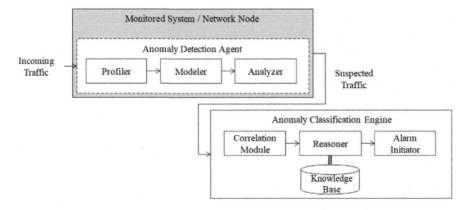

Fig. 2. System architecture.

The general modules of the system are described as follow; The Profiler sub-system is responsible for extracting the required information from the incoming traffic to generate an appropriate traffic representation (traffic vector); it is responsible for tracing the presence of every monitored network attribute in the IP and TCP header packets for a specified period of time. The Modeler sub-system is responsible for applying the specified conditional mapping criteria to transform the generated traffic vector, and as a result, it generates the symptoms vectors. At this stage, the analyser module estimates the weight of abnormalities by calculating the central tendency. The analyser then tests the result in opposition to the defined threshold value. Once the central tendency exceeds the defined threshold, an alarm will be generated indicating malicious activity. When a malicious activity has been indicated, the symptoms vector will be directed to the anomaly classification engine to identify the attack class.

The alarm correlation module sub-system plays an essential role in anomaly classification; it examinations the correlation strength of the detected anomaly against the defined pattern. This work uses matrices to describe the correlation strengths between the detected anomalies against the defined patterns; the strengths are calculated based on weighted absolute differences.

The alarm correlation module works in solidarity with the Reasoner. The reasoned or reasoning engine is in charge of inferring logical evaluation of correlation strength of the detected anomaly against the defined pattern. The reasoning engine will generate the attack probability score and direct the result to the Alarm Initiator. The Alarm Initiator generates an alarm with a standard data format using the Intrusion Detection Message Exchange Format (IDMEF).

3.6   System Implementation

The proposed detection system has been implemented in two stages; during the first stage, the system learns the network's normal behaviour (the normal range of values of the monitored network attributes) under the assumption of the absence of attacks and malicious activities. In the second stage, the system monitors network traffic activates and compares them to the learned normal behavioural patterns. If a mismatch occurs, a level of "suspicion" is raised, and when the suspicion, in turn, trespasses a given threshold, the system triggers an alarm. The alarm is not considered an incident yet and is not forwarded to the prevention system; instead, it will be forwarded to the correlation engine for further analysis. To better understand the mechanism of the proposed system, the operational phases of the system have been divided into two phases as follows;

Phase I: Learning the Normal Activities. During the learning phase, the agents learn the normal network behaviours by monitoring network data attributes at the network and the transport headers. The agents observe and record every network attribute in the IP and TCP header packets for a specified period of time. The proposed IDS uses the average rate of occurrence (arithmetic mean) and the variation from the average during the training phase to estimate an anomaly's chance while in the detection phase. If a network attribute is observed n times with m values for a defined period of time, then the mean M_{Fi} and the standard deviation σ_{Fi} for each attribute can be calculated as follow;

$$M_{Fi} = \frac{1}{n} \sum_{j=1}^{n} m_j \tag{2}$$

$$\sigma_{Fi} = \sqrt{\frac{1}{n} \sum_{j=1}^{n} (m_j - M_{Fi})^2} \tag{3}$$

The process flow of the learning phase is illustrated in Fig. 3. As shown, the proposed IDS starts extracting the required data from the IP and TCP header packets. A new vector should be created for every new connection.

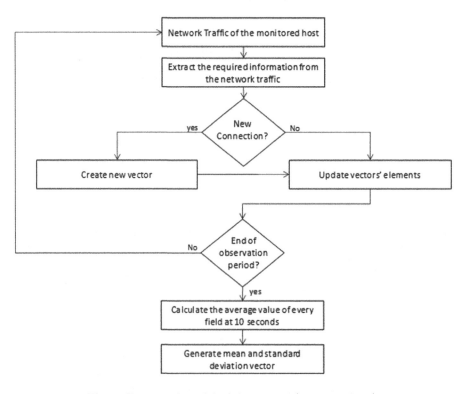

Fig. 3. Functional model of the system (training phase)

At the end of the observation period, the system starts to calculate the average value (M_{benign}) and the standard deviation (σ_{benign}) of every connection at t seconds window to generate the normal behaviour vectors. The calculated mean and standard deviation are represented as vectors, where each element represents its designated value as follows;

$$M_{benign} = [M_{F1}, M_{F2}, M_{F3}, M_{F4}, ...M_{F20}] \tag{4}$$

$$\sigma_{benign} = [\sigma_{F1}, \sigma_{F2}, \sigma_{F3}, \sigma_{F4}, ...\sigma_{F20}] \tag{5}$$

Phase II: Testing Phase/Detection Phase. In the detection phase, the agents observe and record (count the presence of) the 20 attributes from the network protocol stack for every t seconds. The process flow of this phase is illustrated in Fig. 4. The monitored attributes will be represented as a vector (traffic vector), as shown in Eq. 1, where each element represent its designated value. The agents then generate a symptoms vector based on the magnitude that the monitored network data attributes have deviated from the baseline (normal behaviour vector). The elements of the symptoms vector represent the strength of the participation of each monitored attribute. The estimated symptoms elements are represented as a vector (symptoms vector), as shown in Eq. 6.

$$F_{symptoms} = [S_1, S_2, S_3, S_4, ...S_{20}] \tag{6}$$

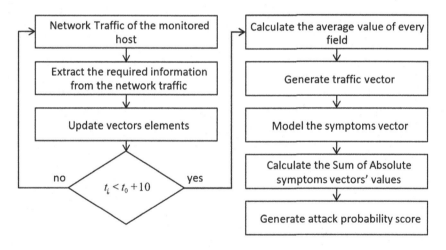

Fig. 4. Functional model of the system (detection phase)

The agents will use predefined conditional criteria to estimate the values of the symptoms vector. In this work, we have proposed five conditional rules defined as follow:

$$S_i = \begin{cases} 2, & \text{if } (M_{Fi} + 2 * \sigma_{Fi} \leq F_i) \\ 1, & \text{if } (M_{Fi} + 2 * \sigma_{Fi} < F_i < M_{F}i + \sigma_{Fi}) \\ 0, & \text{if } (M_{Fi} + \sigma_{Fi} \leq F_i \leq M_{F}i - \sigma_{Fi}) \\ -1, & \text{if } (M_{Fi} - \sigma_{Fi} < F_i < M_{F}i - 2 * \sigma_{Fi}) \\ -2, & \text{if } (F_i \leq M_{Fi} + 2 * \sigma_{Fi}) \end{cases}$$

For example, symptoms elements S_i can be represented by value 2, if the network attribute F_i is greater than or equal to its normal behaviours' mean value M_{Fi} plus twice its standard deviation σ_{Fi}. The sign of deviation (positive or negative) represents the direction of that difference (it is larger when the sign is positive and smaller if it is negative). The magnitude of the value indicates the size of the difference. The agents will be generating the new symptoms vector every t seconds. Then, the agents will calculate the weight of abnormalities by calculating the central tendency using the following formula:

$$M_{Fi} = \frac{1}{n} \sum_{j=0}^{n} m_j \tag{7}$$

If the central tendency T is greater than or equal to a defined threshold value, then an alarm will be generated indicating a malicious activity; otherwise, it is considered as benign activity. Once a malicious activity has been detected, the symptoms vector will be directed to the correlation module for identifying the attack class. Upon receiving the traffic vector, the central system will compare it with the knowledge base K of the attack pattern and generate an attack symptoms correlation matrix.

The symptoms correlation matrix will determine the possible attack class based on correlating the symptoms vector of the examined instance to the symptoms vector of the attack patterns stored in the knowledge base. The attack pattern that scores the highest value of will determine the class of the attack.

$$\mu = (1 - \sum_{i=1}^{n} |K_i - F_i|) * 100\% \tag{8}$$

4   Conclusion and Future Work

With the rapidly increasing rate of network attacks in recent years, network-based intrusion detection systems have become a critical network defence mechanism. However, these systems typically generate a vast amount of alarms that can be unmanageable and mixed with a large number of false alarms, especially in large-scale networks, which result in a huge challenge on the efficiency and accuracy of network attack detection. Recent research has shown that anomaly-based intrusion detection systems are more vulnerable to positive false alarms than signature-based detection systems. This is because of the detection nature of anomaly-based IDS. It raises the alarm every time it detects an activity that deviates from the baseline model of the normal behaviour. Therefore, the cause of the anomaly itself is unknown to the intrusion detection system.

The alarm classification approaches have become a popular solution in the alarm management process. It tends to enhance the quality of the generated alarms through filter-out the false alarms. Many researchers have considered classifying the generated alarms to reduce false alarms in intrusion detection systems. As a result, the amount of alarms presented to the security personnel is reduced, and the time required to validate and manage the IDS alarms is minimised. Therefore, this work considers the alarm classification approach to propose a new alarm classification method to enhance the quality of the generated alarms by filter-out false alarms. The main goal of this work is to present a new anomaly-detection system that embraces two stages for malicious activity detection and alarm classification. The first stage involves detecting unusual activities based on a previously learnt model. On the other hand, The alarm classification stage is intended to classify the detected activity based on known attack patterns. The alarms which are unable to be classified will be tagged as possible false alarms for further analysis. This work presents the concept of the proposed detection system, out future research will attempt to construct a testbed to generate the required dataset to evaluate the proposed architecture.

Acknowledgement. The research leading to these results has received funding from the Research Council (TRC) of the Sultanate of Oman under the Open Research Grant Program. TRC Grant Agreement No [BFP/RGP/ICT/20/377]

References

1. Khraisat, A., Gondal, I., Vamplew, P., Kamruzzaman, J.: Survey of intrusion detection systems: techniques, datasets and challenges. Cybersecurity **2**(1), 1–22 (2019). https://doi.org/10.1186/s42400-019-0038-7
2. Einy, S., Oz, C., Navaei, Y.D.: The anomaly- and signature-based IDS for network security using hybrid inference systems. Mathematical Problems in Engineering 2021 (2021)
3. Torabi, M., Udzir, N.I., Abdullah, M.T., Yaakob, R.: A review on feature selection and ensemble techniques for intrusion detection system. Int. J. Found. Comput. Sci. **12**, 1–13 (2021)
4. Singh, R.R., Gupta, N., Kumar, S.: To reduce the false alarm in intrusion detection systems using self-organizing. Int. J. Soft Comput. Eng. **1**(2), 27–32 (2011)
5. Chandola, V., Banerjee, A., Kumar, V.: Anomaly detection: a survey. ACM Comput. Surv. **41**(3), 1–58 (2009)
6. Rhee, M.Y.: Internet Firewalls for Trusted Security. Wiley (2013)
7. Sundaramurthy, S.C., Case, J., Truong, T., Zomlot, L., Hoffmann, M.: A tale of three security operation centers. In: Proceedings of the 2014 ACM Workshop on Security Information Workers - SIW 2014, pp. 43–50. ACM Press, New York (2014)
8. Ghorbani, A.A., Lu, W., Tavallaee, M.: Network Intrusion Detection and Prevention: Concepts and Techniques. Springer, Boston (2010)
9. Xue, Y., Wang, D., Zhang, L.: Traffic classification: issues and challenges. In: 2013 International Conference on Computing, Networking and Communications (ICNC), pp. 545–549. IEEE (2013)

10. Guimaraes, M., Murray, M.: Overview of intrusion detection and intrusion prevention. In: InfoSecCD '08: Proceedings of the 5th Annual Conference on Information Security Curriculum Development. Association for Computing Machinery. Kennesaw Georgia (2008)

11. Thottan, M., Liu, G., Ji, C.: Anomaly detection approaches for communication networks. In: Cormode, G., Thottan, M. (eds.) Algorithms for Next Generation Networks, pp. 239–261. Springer, London (2010)

12. Siraj, M., Hashim, M.: Zaiton: network intrusion alert correlation challenges and techniques. Jurnal Teknologi Maklumat. **20**, 12–36 (2008)

13. Om, H., Hazra, T.: Statistical techniques in anomaly intrusion detection system. Int. J. Adv. Eng. Technol. **5**, 387–398 (2012)

14. Bolzoni, D., Etalle, S., Hartel, P.H.: Panacea: automating attack classification for anomaly-based network intrusion detection systems. In: Kirda, E., Jha, S., Balzarotti, D. (eds.) RAID 2009. LNCS, vol. 5758, pp. 1–20. Springer, Heidelberg (2009). https://doi.org/10.1007/978-3-642-04342-0_1

15. Om, H., Kundu, A.: A hybrid system for reducing the false alarm rate of anomaly intrusion detection system. In: 2012 1st International Conference on Recent Advances in Information Technology (RAIT), pp. 131–136. IEEE (2012)

16. Spathoulas, G., Katsikas, S.: Methods for post-processing of alerts in intrusion detection. Int. J. Inf. Secur. Sci. **2**, 64–80 (2013)

17. Stiawan, D., Yaseen, A.L.A., Shakhatreh, I., Idris, M.Y., Bakar, K.A.B.U., Abdullah, A.H.: Intrusion prevention system: a survey. J. Theoretical Appl. Inf. Technol. (2011)

18. Karasek, D.Y., Kim, J., Kemmoe, V.Y., Bhuiyan, M.Z.A., Cho, S., Son, J.: SuperB: superior behavior-based anomaly detection defining authorized users' traffic patterns. In: International Conference on Computer Communications and Networks, ICCCN. Hawaii, USA (2020)

19. Bolzoni, D.: Revisiting anomaly-based network intrusion detection systems. University of Twente, Enschede (2009)

20. García-Teodoro, P., Díaz-Verdejo, J., Maciá-Fernández, G., Vázquez, E.: Anomaly-based network intrusion detection: techniques, systems and challenges. Comput. Secur. **28**, 18–28 (2009)

Impact Analysis and Correlation Study on the Spread of Fake News During Pandemic COVID-19 in Malaysia

Ahmad Qayyim Nordin[1], Norziana Jamil[1], Zuhaira Muhammad Zain[2], and Md Nabil Ahmad Zawawi[1(✉)]

[1] College of Computing and Informatics, Universiti Tenaga Nasional, 43000 Kajang, Selangor, Malaysia
ahmadqayyimm@gmail.com, {Norziana,MdNabil}@uniten.edu.my
[2] Department of Information Systems, College of Computer and Information Sciences, Princess Nourah Bint Abdulrahman University, Riyadh, Saudi Arabia
zmzain@pnu.edu.sa

Abstract. The issue of fake news spread on social media especially during the pandemic of COVID-19 has become a major threat to various sectors and agencies in Malaysia. It is observed that the new norm that requires Malaysian to work and stay at home during Movement Control Order (MCO) has contributed to the rapid spread of the fake news. In this research, we study the impact of the fake news during the COVID-19 pandemic in Malaysia and how the number of COVID-19 positive cases in the country would affect the number of fake news being spread locally. We also conducted a correlation analysis between the number of fake news and the number of COVID-19 cases. Result shows a significant strong positive correlation between the two studied variables. Besides, we built a fake news prediction model using linear regression algorithm to predict the number of fake news based the number of COVID-19 cases. However, the model did not show a good performance. This paper is targeted to assist the government, especially Majlis Keselamatan Negara, during the formulation of action plan and decision making in the effort to hinder the spread of fake news, by implying the constructed formula to predict the number of fake news in a day based on the number of COVID-19 positive cases.

Keywords: Fake news · COVID-19 · Correlation analysis · Impact analysis · Linear regression · Movement Control Order

1 Introduction

In this globalization era, news has been spread in second, reaching every people in the world. With the assist of highly advanced technology, people gained profits by providing data and information to their audience [13]. These people consist of [16] official reporters, newscasters, non-government bodies, academicians, influencers on social media, etc. They can earn real money through broadcasting information to the targeted patronage.

© Springer Nature Switzerland AG 2021
H. Badioze Zaman et al. (Eds.): IVIC 2021, LNCS 13051, pp. 495–507, 2021.
https://doi.org/10.1007/978-3-030-90235-3_43

This shows that people globally seek new information and are not restricted to a certain topic only. People look for something interesting or arguable, such as political issues, entertainment and celebrity, economic growth, healthcare, academic writing, sports update, and many more. With the advancement of information and communication technology (ICT), digital information spread faster than the non-digital information.

At the end of 2019, the world is shocked by a new pandemic that was perceived to be originated from Wuhan, China, known as COVID-19 [2]. The virus spread to the whole world rapidly as interstate travelling were allowed at that time. At the beginning of the outbreak, most of the countries were taking this newly born virus lightly, without taking any precautious measure to stop the spread of COVID-19. Malaysia is not excluded since we were still opening our airport for visitors from other countries, to enter our country.

While the world fights with COVID-19, people try their best not to get infected by the virus by staying at home. It was reported that were also people trying to prevent the infection by following some unofficial statements or steps to eliminate' the virus [4]. There were also videos and articles promoting unverified steps to kill the virus, which have attracted people to watch and some of them, to try the steps [8]. Some irresponsible people even spread false statistics, such as the number of positive cases in their state.

We represent the problem statement as research questions as follows:

1. What is the trend of fake news spread during COVID-19 pandemic?
2. What are the impacts of fake news to the country?
3. Is there any correlation between the number of COVID-19 cases and the number of fake news?
4. Can we predict the number of fake news based on the number of COVID-19 cases?

Hence, in this research, we aim at investigating further the impact of fake news during the COVID-19 pandemic specifically to our country. To do that, we gather the required data in our country, Malaysia and construct a new dataset that contains verified fake news and their enclosures.

This paper is organized as follows: Sect. 2 provides the literature review on fake news during the COVID-19 pandemic. Section 3 explains the materials and methodology involved in this study and how the impact analysis is conducted. Section 4 demonstrates how we can see the correlation between the number of COVID-19 cases and the number of fake news spread in a day. Section 5 accumulates the outcome of the findings from the research. Section 6 concludes everything throughout the research progress.

2   Literature Reviews

2.1   Fake News Related to COVID-19 in Malaysia

To fight COVID-19, our government has officially announced that Malaysia will be going through a new phase of lifestyle to help flatten the curve of COVID-19 cases in Malaysia; "Perintah Kawalan Pergerakan (PKP)" or Movement Control Order (MCO). It started on the 18th of March 2020 [6]. During this phase, people were told to stay at home, workers will be working from home, and students will be learning from home.

The number of fake news was risen rapidly during MCO, most probably because of people having plenty of leisure time staying at home. People are using their gadgets almost 24 h per day, scrolling through social media and messaging apps. These communication platforms have been a great contributor to the spread of fake news. Since they are using social media leisurely, some people might accidentally spread the news that is not from the official body.

During MCO, the government has released numerous announcements to keep the people update regarding the nation's latest decision on the COVID-19 cases in Malaysia. For every announcement, there must be at least one fake news being spread to the netizen. Some people really wanted to have that feeling to be the first person to know about everything and be the one to spread it, no matter what the status of that news, and even if our Prime Minister quoted that information. This kind of fake news was commonly spread on WhatsApp (messaging apps).

Each day, new fake news is being spread, to the extent that Pasukan Respon Pantas (PRP) under Kementerian Komunikasi dan Multimedia (KKMM) had to filter and do checking on every news being spread on social media, especially Facebook, Instagram, Twitter, and WhatsApp. PRP had to take a maximum of 3 h to ensure that certain news is fact or fake. The result is then written into an official statement named "PEMAKLUMAN BERITA PALSU" and released on Majlis Keselamatan Negara (MKN) Telegram channel for the public to notice. This statement is published almost every day during MCO, showing that people still lack the sense to filter every information they received [7].

Our government needs to filter and detect every fake news on social media because, according to Malaysia Digital Marketing Statistics 2020 [11], average Malaysians spend their time surfing through the internet for 8 h and 5 min a day. The popularity of social media among Malaysian is as followed (Fig. 1):

The data above might have slight changes during MCO, but that does not mean the percentage is dropped since everyone stays at home. The usage time of Malaysian on social media is a big factor for the spread of fake news. When almost everyone is online, any news being published will be spread immediately and even reached someone that is not initially active on social media.

2.2 Detected Fake News by PRP

It is a commendable action of our government to publish the "PEMAKLUMAN BERITA PALSU" statement that contains the list of fake news on social media. The statement will lower the rate of fake news and bring a sense for Malaysian to not take every news without investigating first. Below are some of the fake news detected by PRP.

1.	YouTube	93%	6.	WeChat	47%
2.	WhatsApp	91%	7.	Twitter	44%
3.	Facebook	91%	8.	LinkedIn	29%
4.	Instagram	70%	9.	Skype	26%
5.	FB Messenger	64%	10.	Pinterest	25%

Fig. 1. Top social media app among Malaysia (2020).

From 24th March 2020, PRP has released the statement regularly. There are at least 2 confirmed fake news for each statement, and for some days, PRP had to release 3 statements to clarify which news is genuine or fake. This shows that MCO is a critical period for spreading fake news related to COVID-19 in Malaysia. The statements were released on MKN Telegram Channel, making it easy for Malaysian people to keep up to date with the trending fake news as the channel has more than 1 million subscribers. However, after June's month, the statements have stopped being released since the government announced that MCO would be changed to Condition/Recovery Movement Order.

2.3   Fake News Related to COVID-19 Worldwide

The impact of the coronavirus pandemic is not limited to Malaysia but the whole world. Hence, the crime of spreading fake news is happening in almost every nation [15] even though government and authorities have warned the people by giving a severe penalty and arrested those who were caught spreading fake news about the virus.

In Indonesia, some people believed that plentiful sunshine would help them ward off the virus. This is due to multiple claims suggested that warm weather might slow down the spread of the COVID-19 virus. As usual, this kind of claim is spread on social media. Dr. Dirga Sakti Rambe at Jakarta's OMNI Pulomas Hospital said that exposing your skin to sunlight is good to obtain Vitamin D. Still, it is not helpful indirectly preventing the disease [9]. Up in South Korea, the River of Grace Community Church in Gyeonggi Province believed that saltwater could help prevent coronavirus spread. We can see their church official spraying saltwater inside the followers' mouth without disinfecting the nozzle during a prayer. This resulted in 46 infected people, including the pastor and his wife [3].

While in Africa, various conspiracies on COVID-19 were created by the media. Some said that this virus is a biological weapon from which to break China's economic power against other nations. There were also claims saying that using sodium chloride mixture with citric acid may cure the virus. However, The American Food and Drug Administration said that this solution might cause life-threatening low blood pressure, acute liver failure, and severe vomiting [1]. Over in Arizona, United States, a couple, was hospitalized for taking chloroquine phosphate, believing that chemical is a treatment for the virus. This, however, ended up in death for both [5]. There were also beliefs such as Harvard Professor Charles Lieber sold the coronavirus to China.

All these beliefs and claims lead to confusion over what information is genuine or fake. This confusion has affected the whole world since every nation has positive cases of COVID-19. If one misinformation is spread within the country today, it is not surprising that people live 10,000 km away to receive that information the next day. Even though the information might sound ridiculous such as eating sea lettuce will help prevents you from getting COVID-19, some people will believe in that.

3   Materials and Methods

3.1   Materials

There are numerous public datasets available on the internet—for example, LIAR, BuzzFeedNews, BS Detector, and CREDBANK [12]. However, for this research, a newly design dataset is needed as we are trying to study the fake news in Malaysia only.

To construct a dataset, numerous data are needed in a large amount. Hence, we collected the fake news statements from MKN Telegram Channel to see the trend of fake news spread in a certain period. Apart from that, we also gathered the statistic for COVID-19 cases in the same period as the fake news.

3.2   Methods

Figure 2 shows the overview of the research methodology used in this study. It consists of 4 main phases: data collection, impact analysis, correlation analysis, and fake news prediction. The detail of each phase was described in the next subsection.

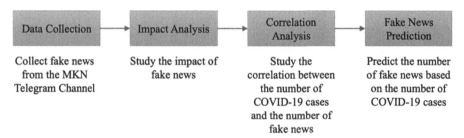

Fig. 2.   Research methodology.

3.3   Data Collection

A total of 293 confirmed fake news had been collected from Majlis Keselamatan Negara (MKN) Telegram channel. An analysis has been done from the collected fake news to see the trend of fake news being spread during MCO. The confirmed fake news has also been used to see the correlation between the number of COVID-19 cases with the number of fake news being spread.

Collected Fake News from MKN. One of the initiatives that our government took to stop the spread of fake news during MCO in Malaysia is by releasing a statement containing the confirmed fake news that has been spread on social media. This statement is published for public information to confirm what news is fact or fake. In March 2020, 22 statements were published in the telegram channel, with 64 news confirmed to be fake from 24th March. The number has been rapidly increased to 72 statements being announced in the following month, with a total of 159 confirmed fake news. Fortunately, in May, the number has decreased to 20 statements with 43 fake news. Lastly, in June, 17 announcements have been made containing 27 confirmed fake news.

In only 99 days during MCO, a total of 293 fake news has spread widely on social media. In Fig. 3, we can see the trend of fake news spread on social media is dropping slowly day by day. In Malaysia, MCO officially begins on 18th March, and everyone is ordered to stay at home. Since everyone has nothing important to do at home, they spent most of their time using a smartphone, navigating through social media.

Simultaneous people spending their time on social media during MCO is a big factor why fake news spread faster than before. The government had to release an official statement to inform the people which news is genuine and fake. The graph reached its highest point at the end of March, the beginning of the MCO. The graph slowly dwindles as people may already have the common sense not easily to spread any information on social media.

It is an applaudable act by our government during that time to verify which news and information is trustworthy and then publish it for public information. We can clearly see its effectiveness in Fig. 3.

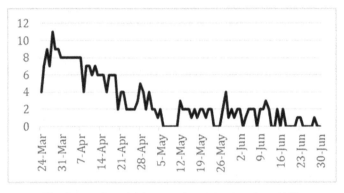

Fig. 3. Number of fake news from March to June 2020.

COVID-19 Cases in Malaysia. To investigate the correlation between fake news and COVID-19 cases using linear regression, we collected the daily data of COVID-19 cases in the same duration as the number of fake news.

For fake news, the duration is from 24th March until the end of June. Hence the same for the number of COVID-19 cases. In March, a total of 1248 cases have been reported. Followed by April, where the cases increased to 3236. In May, cases decreased to 1817 to 820 in June. Based on Figs. 3 and 4, we study its correlation and develop a fake news prediction model using RStudio.

3.4 Impact Analysis

An impact analysis was conducted to see which fake news' categories have the highest impact. First, the collected fake news from the MKN Telegram Channel was divided into several categories based on its purpose. Second, a bar graph (Fig. 4) was plotted to present the number of fake news based on the categories where each bar presents each category.

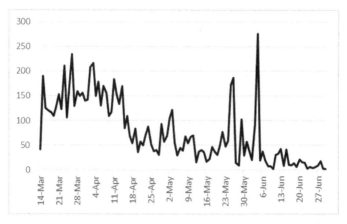

Fig. 4. Number of COVID-19 cases from March to June, 2020.

3.5   Correlation Analysis

In this phase, a correlation analysis was conducted using RStudio to investigate the association between the number of fake news and the number of COVID-19 cases. First, we plotted a scatter plot to see how the two variables correlate. The direction of the slope on the scatter plot represents the positivity or negativity of the relationship. An upward slope indicates positive relationships, while a downward slope shows negative relationships.

The correlation coefficient was then computed using the cor() function. The value of the correlation coefficient is always between −1 and +1. Table 1 shows how the correlation coefficient can be interpreted.

Table 1.   Interpretation of correlation coefficient values.

Correlation coefficient value	Interpretation
−1	A perfect negative linear relationship
−0.7	A strong negative linear relationship
−0.5	A moderate negative relationship
−0.3	A weak negative linear relationship
0	No linear relationship
0.3	A weak positive linear relationship
0.5	A moderate positive relationship
0.7	A strong positive linear relationship
1	A perfect positive linear relationship

3.6 Fake News Prediction

In this phase, we built a simple linear regression model using R to predict the number of fake news based on the number of COVID-19 cases. Simple linear regression is one of the simplest algorithms when it comes to machine learning. Linear regression is a statistical way of measuring the relationship between variables [10, 14]. For instance, as time increases, so does cost. To put it simply, people can predict the future using linear regression.

The math behind linear regression is quite simple; the formula is shown in Eq. 1:

$$y = mx + b \tag{1}$$

where 'y' is what we are trying to predict, 'm' is the slope, 'x' is the input, 'b' is the bias.

For this study, we attempt to predict the number of fake news being spread in a day based on the daily number of COVID-19 cases. Hence, 'y' is the number of fake news as the dependent variable and 'x' is the number of COVID-19 cases as the independent variable. The simple linear regression model was constructed by using lm() function. The summary() function was then run to view the detailed information on the coefficients and performance of the model. 'm' and 'b' values could be obtained from the coefficients part of the model output.

4 Findings

In this section, we present the results in 3 subsections based on research questions 2–4. In the first subsection, we present the result of the impact analysis to see which fake news' categories have the highest impact. In the second subsection, we present result of the correlation analysis. In the third subsection, we came up with a model for predicting the number of fake news spread in a day based on the number of COVID-19 cases reported daily.

4.1 Impact of Fake News

The collected fake news was categorized into 7 main categories based on its purposes:

(1) Politic: Fake news with the attention to grow hate or threat to our nation's political issue. It might be related to an individual in the parliament or any government organization.
(2) Economy: Fake news with the attention to affect our nation's economic growth. The news might intentionally spread to increase or decrease the stock market.
(3) Social: Fake news with the attention to cause panic or uncontrolled movement among citizens. It could be corresponding to an individual's benefit.
(4) Politic + Economy: Fake news with the attention to grow hate or threat to our nation's political issue, at the same time, will affect our economic growth.
(5) Economy + Social: Fake news with the attention to affect our nation's economic growth, at the same time, might cause panic among citizens.

(6) Politic + Social: Fake news with the attention to cause panic or uncontrolled movement among citizens, at the same time, to grow hate to the government.

(7) Politic + Economy + Social: Fake news with the attention to affect our national political issue, economic growth, and citizens' social life.

Figure 5 shows the number of fake news based on seven categories. We can conclude that fake news related to COVID-19 in Malaysia has the highest impact on the social category. As mentioned, this fake news' purpose is to cause panic or uncontrolled movement among the citizens.

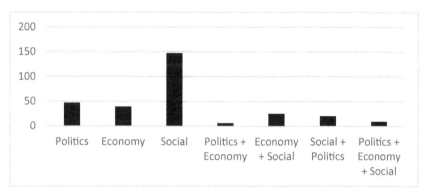

Fig. 5. Number of fake news based on categories.

4.2   Correlation Between COVID-19 Cases and Fake News

Using the fake news collected from MKN Telegram Channel and collected COVID-19 cases from March to June, the simple Linear Regression model was created using RStudio.

By importing the excel file consisting of several COVID-19 cases and the number of fake news spread in 99 days into RStudio, we plotted a scatter plot to visualize the correlation between the number of COVID-19 cases and the number of fake news.

From the upward slope on the scatter plot shown in Fig. 6, we can expect that there is a positive correlation between the number of COVID-19 cases with the number of fake news. To verify our expectation, we run 'cor' command to obtain the correlation value. The correlation value of 0.6636729 verifies that the number of COVID-19 cases has a strong positive linear relationship (correlation value close to 0.7) with the number of fake news. This indicates that the number of fake news will increase when the number of COVID-19 cases increase.

4.3   Fake News Prediction Based the Number of Covid-19 Cases

A linear regression model was built by using the 'lm' command to predict the number of fake news based on the number of COVID-19 cases. We run 'summary' command

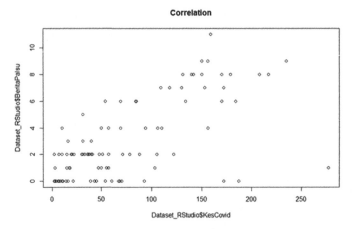

Fig. 6. Scatter plot of the number of fake news based on the number of COVID-19 cases.

to summarize the linear regression model (Fig. 7). The summary shows six important outputs for the built fake news prediction model: Call, Residuals, Coefficients, Residual Standard Error, Adjusted R-squared, and F-statistic.

The Call section shows the formula used by R script to fit the data. In the formula, the number of COVID-19 cases daily is set as the predictor and the number of fake news is set as the target.

The Residuals section shows the descriptive statistics about the residuals of the model. Residuals are the difference between the actual observed target values (the number of fake news) and the target values that the model predicted. The residuals must be in Gaussian distribution where the mean or median is approximately 0. In our case, the median = 0.0725 which is close to zero indicates that the distribution of the residuals is somewhat symmetrical.

The Coefficient section helps us in determining the value of m (slope) and b (intercept) from Eq. 1 to predict the number of fake news when the number of COVID-19 cases is given. The first row of the Coefficient-Estimate shows the intercept value, and the second row shows the slope value. The small p-values of the intercept (0.0221) and slope (7.08e-14) corroborate the correlation result we obtained in the correlation analysis that there is significantly strong positive relationship between the number of COVID-19 cases and the number of fake news. After substituting m = 0.030420 and b = 0.771475 in Eq. 1, we finally get the linear regression model for predicting the number of fake news being spread in a day based on the number of positive COVID-19 cases on a particular day as in Eq. 2.

$$y = 0.030420x + 0.771475 \tag{2}$$

If the number of COVID-19 cases in a day is 100, the predicted number of fake news being spread is 4.

The residual standard error is a measure used to assess how well a linear regression model fits the data. The residual standard error is the average amount that the real values of the number of fake news differ from the predictions provided by the regression line.

The residual standard error = 2.164 indicates that for 100 COVID-19 cases, the true number of fake news that can be predicted is between 2 – 6.

The R-squared is another measure to assess how well is the model fitting the data. The adjusted R-squared of 0.4347 shows that roughly 43% of the variance found in the number of fake news can be explained by the number of COVID-19 cases. Taking into consideration 0.5 as a threshold of a good model, we can conclude that our model still needs an improvement.

The F-statistic of 76.36 (>1) with p-value = 7.7077e−14 (<0.05) again validates the significant relationship between the number of COVID-19 cases and the number of fake news.

```
Call:
lm(formula = Dataset_RStudio$BeritaPalsu ~ Dataset_RStudio$KesCovid)

Residuals:
    Min      1Q  Median      3Q     Max
-8.1979 -1.1252  0.0725  1.1409  5.3917

Coefficients:
                          Estimate Std. Error t value Pr(>|t|)
(Intercept)               0.771475   0.331673   2.326   0.0221 *
Dataset_RStudio$KesCovid  0.030420   0.003481   8.738 7.08e-14 ***
---
Signif. codes:  0 '***' 0.001 '**' 0.01 '*' 0.05 '.' 0.1 ' ' 1

Residual standard error: 2.164 on 97 degrees of freedom
Multiple R-squared:  0.4405,     Adjusted R-squared:  0.4347
F-statistic: 76.36 on 1 and 97 DF,  p-value: 7.077e-14
```

Fig. 7. Summary of the linear model.

5   Discussion

To validate the built fake news prediction model, it was tested on COVID-19 cases reported daily in December 2020 using Eq. 2. Figure 8 shows the trend of the expected/predicted fake news based on the number of COVID-19 cases in December 2020. The expected values were compared with the actual values of fake news in December 2020 obtained from sebenarnya.my (Fig. 9).

The results shows that the difference/error between the expected and actual values is high. There are 2 possibilities why the built model is not giving us a good result, although there is a significant strong positive correlation between the number of fake news and the number of COVID-19 cases:

(1) Malaysian netizens have taken precaution measures before spreading fake news.
(2) Majlis Keselamatan Negara has given less priority to update the fake news on their platform (Telegram and sebenarnya.my)

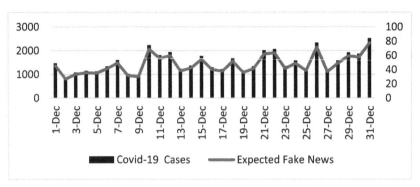

Fig. 8. Number of COVID-19 cases and expected fake news.

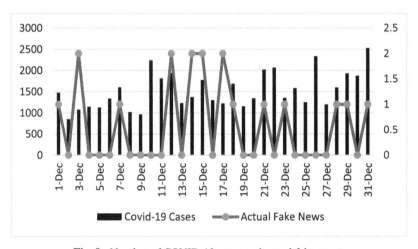

Fig. 9. Number of COVID-19 cases and actual fake news.

6 Conclusion

Most of the social media users in Malaysia tend to consume news from the internet without studying its status first. We must do our part in spreading awareness about the impact of fake news on our nation. This paper aims to study the impact of fake news during pandemic COVID-19 in Malaysia and to conduct a correlation study between the number of COVID-19 cases and the number of fake news spread in a day.

As mentioned, fake news can cause major problems to our community and environment, mainly in politics, economics, and society. The correlation study shows a significant strong positive relationship between the number of fake news and the number of COVID-19 cases. A fake news prediction model was built using a simple linear regression algorithm to predict the number of fake news based on the number of COVID-19 cases. However, because of our limitation in collecting more "Pemakluman Berita Palsu" from Majlis Keselamatan Negara after June 2020, it has caused our predicted fake news values to vary from the actual values.

For future works, we may have to do a correlation study using different variables by collecting the fake news from consistent sources such as sebenarnya.my only. The fake news prediction model can be optimized to increase its performance.

Acknowledgement. We would like to thank Yayasan Canselor Universiti Tenaga Nasional for funding our study under the YCU Grant number 202101017YCU. Also to our project member and research officers.

References

1. Bright, O., Ameyaw, E.K., Hagan, J.E., Seidu, A., Schack, T.. Rising Above Misinformation or Fake News in Africa: Another Strategy to Control COVID-19 Spread (2020). https://www.fro ntiersin.org/articles/. https://doi.org/10.3389/fcomm.2020.00045/full#B11. Accessed 1 Aug 2021
2. Bryner, J.: 1st known case of coronavirus traced back to November in China (2020). https:// www.livescience.com/first-case-coronavirus-found.html. Accessed 1 Aug 2021
3. Chan-kyong, P.: Coronavirus: saltwater spray infects 46 church-goers in South Korea (2020). https://www.scmp.com/week-asia/health-environment/article/3075421/coronavirus-salt-water-spray-infects-46-church-goers. Accessed 1 Aug 2021
4. Hauser, C., Diaz, J.: F.D.A. Warns 7 Companies to Stop Claiming Silver and Other Products Treat Coronavirus (2020). https://www.nytimes.com/2020/03/09/health/fda-letter-cor onavirus-cures.html. Accessed 1 Aug 2021
5. Hickok, K.: Husband and wife poison themselves trying to self-medicate with chloroquine (2020). https://www.livescience.com/coronavirus-chloroquine-self-medication-kills-man.html. Accessed 1 Aug 2021
6. Negara, M.K.: Kenyataan Media MKN: Perincian Perintah Kawalan Pergerakan (2020). https://www.pmo.gov.my/2020/03/kenyatan-media-mkn-18-mac-2020/. Accessed 1 Aug 2021
7. Negara, M.K.: Pemakluman Berita Palsu (2020). https://t.me/MKNRasmiK. Accessed 1 Oct 2020
8. Mark, M.: Missouri is suing a televangelist who falsely suggested on his show that colloidal silver could cure coronavirus patients (2020). https://www.insider.com/missouri-sues-televa ngelist-jim-bakker-false-coronavirus-cure-colloidal-silver-2020-3. Accessed 1 Aug 2021
9. The Asean Post Team. COVID-19: Facts And Fakes (2020). https://theaseanpost.com/article/ COVID-19-facts-and-fakes. Accessed 20 Mar 2020
10. The Concept Center, Linear Regression Explained Simply (2017). https://www.youtube.com/ watch?v=iIUq0SqBSH0. Accessed 11 Feb 2020
11. The Digital Influence Lab, Malaysia Digital Marketing Statistics (2020). https://digitalinflu encelab.com/malaysia-digital-marketing-stats/. Accessed 1 Aug 2021
12. The Elon University Poll, What is dataset? (2014). https://www.youtube.com/watch?v=eHo ZnQmSEzs. Accessed 1 Aug 2021
13. UiHua, What Does It Take To Be A "Macai" Online? An Ex-Cybertrooper Confesses (2016). https://cilisos.my/what-does-it-take-to-be-a-macai-online-an-ex-cybertrooper-confesses/. Accessed 10 Feb 2020
14. Uyanık, K., Neşe, G.: A study on multiple linear regression analysis. Procedia – Soc. Behav. Sci. **106**, 234–240 (2013). https://doi.org/10.1016/j.sbspro.2013.12.027. Accessed 1 Feb 2020
15. Wright, C.L.: COVID-19 Fake News and Its Impact on Consumers (2020). https://www.psy chologytoday.com/us/blog/everyday-media/202004/COVID-19-fake-news-and-its-impact-consumers. Accessed 1 Aug 2021
16. ZipRecruiter, Social Media Journalist Salary (2021). https://www.ziprecruiter.com/Salaries/ Social-Media-Journalist-Salary. Accessed 1 Feb 2020

Machine Learning Classification for Blood Glucose Performances Using Insulin Sensitivity and Respiratory Scores in Diabetic ICU Patients

Athirah Abdul Razak[1]([✉]), Radiyati Umi Partan[2], Normy Norfiza Razak[1]([✉]),
Asma Abu-Samah[3], Norliyana Nor Hisham Shah[1], and Mohd Shahnaz Hasan[4]

[1] Universiti Tenaga Nasional, Kajang 43000, Selangor, Malaysia
Normy@uniten.edu.my
[2] Universitas Sriwijaya, Palembang, Jakarta 30128, Indonesia
[3] Universiti Kebangsaan Malaysia, 43600 Bangi, Selangor, Malaysia
[4] University Malaya Medical Centre, Lembah Pantai, 59100 Kuala Lumpur, Malaysia

Abstract. Diabetes Mellitus (DM) patients with acute respiratory failure in the Intensive Care Unit (ICU) are susceptible to hyperglycaemia with adverse outcome of mortality. Clinically, Partial Pressure of Oxygen over a Fraction of Inspired Oxygen (P/F) scores is use as an indicator for acute respiratory failure and studies have shown that Insulin Sensitivity (S_I) can be used as the glycaemic control biomarker for DM patients. Since the elevation of blood glucose in ICU patients is linked to the progression of the acute respiratory system, this preliminary study initiates the combination of S_I, P/F, and DM status as the main predictors for machine learning classification. This assessment was done to identify which classification models and predictors between insulin sensitivity (S_I), (P/F) scores, and diabetic status will give higher accuracy on Blood Glucose (BG) performance with 7 types of classifier models. In total, 5684 total inputs from 3 predictors extracted from 76 ICU patients were split into 80:20 ratio for training and test sets with five-fold cross-validations. BG performances using three predictors from training vs. test data show that the k-Nearest Neighbor and Neural Network classifiers showed that the highest accuracies achieved were 54.1% and 54.5%, respectively. The sensitivity and specificity evaluated for both model's robustness demonstrated the possibility of using k-Nearest Neighbor and Neural Network for future BG performance prediction. Based on the model's robustness increment result, 8% vs. 12% and 10% vs. 4% shows a possibility that S_I, P/F scores, and DM can be utilized together as an input to classify glycemic level using both classifier models with a larger dataset from respiratory failures patients.

Keywords: Classification models · Machine learning · Diabetes mellitus · Insulin Sensitivity · Respiratory score · Blood glucose performance

1 Introduction

Critical care patients with or without history of diabetes are commonly linked to hyperglycemia (Blood Glucose (BG) > 11.1 mmol/L) [1, 2] during their stay at the Intensive

© Springer Nature Switzerland AG 2021
H. Badioze Zaman et al. (Eds.): IVIC 2021, LNCS 13051, pp. 508–517, 2021.
https://doi.org/10.1007/978-3-030-90235-3_44

Care Unit (ICU). This condition may occur when the cortisol and counterregulatory hormones increased with insulin resistance [3]. These patients, especially the diabetics, are additionally vulnerable to multiple organ failures, sepsis, or infection, and worst, a higher rate of mortality and morbidity [4]. The pandemic of Coronavirus Disease (COVID-19) cases raised concerns as 42.5% of critically ill patient's mortality had Diabetes Mellitus (DM) [5]. Lim et al. [5] showed that 9.8% of COVID-19 patients have a comorbidity of DM and from the study, 1.2% mortality rate was reported. To date, From The Desk of the Director General of Health Malaysia report as of 27 July 2021, 1,044,071 Malaysian have been detected positive with COVID-19 and the numbers of mortality are 8,201 (0.78%) in cumulative [6]. This report [7] illustrated that out of 125 mortality cases, 52% had DM. Moreover, COVID-19 also had similar symptoms as a Severe Acute Respiratory Syndrome (SARS) [8]. Additionally, according to the Malaysian Registry of Intensive Care quarterly report, 35.8% of the ICU admitted patients suffer from multiple organ failures in the first 24 h of admission. Respiratory failures represented one-third of the single organ failure by patient, with 21.9%. In the first 24 h of admissions, 15.7% patients were reported to have Acute Respiratory Distress Syndrome (ARDS) [9]. Few studies have also demonstrated that respiratory failures are relatively high in acute patients with diabetes [10–12]. From these studies, an interrelationship and correlation were observed between respiratory failure and diabetes. Logette et al., [13] showed evidence that linked elevated BG to COVID-19 patients. When the glycemic level of diabetic patients is uncontrolled, these patients are susceptible to various adverse outcomes such as multiple organ failures. Thus, if the early prediction of BG level in critically ill diabetic patients can be known using daily medical data available from the ICU charts to ease glycaemic control, the occurrence of respiratory failure might be improved in critically ill patients.

Respiratory failure can be assessed with P/F scores of oxygenation index based on the Partial Pressure of Oxygen (PaO$_2$) and Fraction of Inspired Oxygen (FiO$_2$) [14]. One of the standard procedures in diagnosing diabetes is to measure insulin resistance and through euglycaemic clamp [15], but this method can be time-consuming for ICU use [16]. Therefore, Insulin Sensitivity (S$_I$) estimation is used to replace insulin resistance for glycemic control as S$_I$ reflects the inversed parameter of insulin resistance. Moreover, S$_I$ has been suggested as biomarker in several various glycemic control studies [17–19]. In achieving the targeted BG performances, S$_I$ was used in stochastic targeted studies [20–23] for glycaemic control, predicting the BG within 5 to 95%. Since S$_I$ has been used for glycaemic control, we hypothesized that it can predict the BG performance by exploiting medical data available in the ICU charts. Additionally, P/F scores can give an early prediction for glycaemic control by stratifying the BG in time of the target bands using classification technique.

A study [24] has shown that there might be an association between insulin resistance and lung dysfunction. Therefore, there is a need to examine if respiratory P/F score and S$_I$ information can be used together as strong factors in predicting ICU glycemic control, especially for diabetic patients. Thus, this paper's objective is to assess classification of ICU patients' BG performance by classifying three different BG bands using P/F score, S$_I$, and diabetes mellitus (DM) status as predictors. In order to identify which model has the best performance accuracy, seven different classifiers are compared: Decision Tree, k-

Nearest Neighbor (kNN), Support Vector Machine (SVM), Naïve Bayes, Discriminant, Ensemble and Neural Network model. This preliminary study was done to identify which classifier models are more feasible towards glycaemic level prediction if P/F scores and DM status are included in model-based glycaemic control.

2 Materials and Method

2.1 Study Population

Retrospective patients' data for the case study in total were 76 (47 DM and 29 NDM) with 10704 h of length of stay and collected from University Malaya Medical Centre (UMMC) in 2018. These patients' dataset has examined the following factors: P/F score (in k/Pa), S_I (continuous in L/mU.min), diabetes mellitus (DM) status (binary, with 1 for DM and 0 for Non-DM), and the BG performance (three discrete classes). Instead of using a daily worst representative P/F score as usually done for Sequential Organ Failure Assessment (SOFA) score to decide on respiratory failure, P/F scores were extracted directly from the clinical chart whenever they were available. FiO_2 data were assumed similar to the previous value whenever the value of PO_2 and BG are available. On average, patients have three recorded P/F scores daily. Using BG measurements, provided nutrition and insulin, hourly S_I(L/mU.min) were fitted first with Intensive Care Insulin Nutrition Glucose (ICING) model [25] through integral fitting process method [26]. Instead of using a constant value to represent individual insulin resistance, S_I was estimated from the fitting process method to represent the patient's hourly varying metabolism.

Patients demographics are shown in Table 1. Patients' age and Acute Physiology and Chronic Health Evaluation (APACHE II) scores, S_I and P/F scores are presented in the average and standard deviation ($\pm$SD). Rank sum p-value test was used to determine the differences in age demographics (years old), the total of ICU stay (hours) distribution, S_I and P/F score. A P-value less than 0.05 is considered significantly different. The distribution of age and the total hours of ICU stay show no significant difference. Patients with diabetes status were presented by 11 and 7 female patients in the training and test datasets, respectively. In total, 1902 rows of input variables were divided randomly into training and testing data, with a ratio of 80:20. Three of the attribute variables, that is, S_I, DM, and P/F scores, were used as the predictors also known as features, and BG performance with three different classes was selected as the desired output to represent BG in time of the target bands. The data were divided into two partitions, where 4269 data points (1423 rows × 3 input variables) of the data were used for training and 1437 (479 rows × 3 input variables) for testing. Five-fold k cross-validation was used in training data to validate the accuracy of the model during the learning process.

2.2 Classification Learners

The seven classifiers model used in the study were supervised machine learning techniques [27]. The seven classifiers model used in training the dataset were Decision Tree (Model 1), Discriminant (Model 2), Naïve Bayes (Model 3), Support Vector Machine (Model 4), k-Nearest Neighbor (Model 5), Ensemble (Model 6) and lastly Neural Network (Model 7). Classification is often being used as the prediction for medical diagnosis

Table 1. Patients demographic for train and test data.

Demographics	Total	Train data	Test data	P-value
Number of patients (%)	76 (100%)	61 (80.2%)	15 (19.8%)	–
Total ICU stay (hours)	10704	8016	2688	Not significant
Mean (±SD) of age (years old)	59 (±14)	58 (±15)	61 (±9.7)	Not significant
Gender (%) • Male • Female	56 (73.7%) 20 (26.3%)	47 (77%) 14 (23%)	9 (60%) 6 (40%)	–
Ethnicity • Malay • Chinese • Indian • Foreigner	26 (34.2%) 30 (39.4%) 19 (25%) 1 (1.4%)	22 (35.4%) 24 (39.3%) 14 (22.9%) 1 (2.4%)	4 (26.7%) 6 (40%) 5 (33.3%) –	–
Diabetes status (%)	47 (61.8%)	38 (62.2%)	9 (40%)	–
Respiratory failures (%)	16 (21%)	15 (24.5%)	1 (6.6%)	–
Mean (±SD) of APACHE II Scores	18 (±7)	17 (±7)	20 (±7)	0.293
Mean (±SD) of PaO$_2$/FiO$_2$ Scores	299 (±130)	299 (±132)	300 (±132)	0.8879
Mean (±SD) of S$_I$	3.9e^{-4} (±5.7e^{-4})	3.6e^{-4} (±4.7e^{-4})	4.9e^{-4} (±8.4e^{-4})	0.8879
Number of data input (rows)	5684 (1902)	4247 (1423)	1437 (479)	–

[28], and showed efficiency in using small data for decision-making, [29]. Haque *et al.* showed an observation between 8 different machine learning algorithm performance for diabetes neuropathy diagnosis and Random Forest had outperformed among all those classifiers techniques [30]. Meanwhile, Singh *et al.* [28] showed that out of 8 classifiers used, the SVM classifier had the best accuracy to detect the relationship between diabetes and hypertension. From the previous studies, there are various types of classifiers that had classified patients with diabetes status. However, our focus of classification in this study is to observe BG performance with 7 types of classifiers using S$_I$, P/F, and DM as input predictors within diabetic ICU patients. P/F was included as one of the features to represent the respiratory score of the patients with 7 types of classifiers. BG performances as the desired output were classified into three BG level target ranges:

- Class 1: BG ≤ 7.7 mmol/L
- Class 2: BG = 7.8 to 11.1 mmol/L
- Class 3: BG ≥ 11.2 mmol/L

Figure 1 shows the framework for the usage of difference classifiers using MATLAB version 2021a.

Model accuracy results was demonstrated in Eq. 1. The confusion matrix represented will be used to illustrate the model with the highest performance. From the confusion matrix, the cohort train and test data results of True Positive (TP), True Negative (TN),

Fig. 1. Framework for classification learner

False Positive (FP), and False Negative (FN) were classified. To further test the classifier model robustness, sensitivity and specificity are calculated as represented in Eqs. 2 and 3, respectively. The nearer the value of sensitivity to 1, the more robust the classifier.

$$Accuracy = \frac{TP + TN}{TP + TN + FP + FN} \times 100\% \tag{1}$$

$$Sensitivity = \frac{TP}{TP + FN} \times 100\% \tag{2}$$

$$Specificity = \frac{TN}{TN + FP} \times 100\% \tag{3}$$

3   Results and Discussion

The accuracies of seven classifiers based on the 3 input predictors for train data are shown in Table 2. The test data accuracy was examined only with the three predictors as it is important to find out how all the three predictors especially P/F can influence the BG performance for critically ill DM patients. We hypothesized that P/F score, DM, and S_I could be used in classifying BG performances. When the three predictors of S_I-P/F-DM were used, the training Model 3, 4 and 7 showed the highest accuracy with results of 55.4%, 53.5% and 54.1% respectively. Meanwhile, when only two predictors of S_I-P/F were used, the training model results of 3 and 7 accuracies were observed and had decreased by 1.4%, and 0.6% respectively. The result for S_I-DM predictors shows that Models 5 and 7 had increased accuracy from 53.0% to 55% and 54.1% to 55.3% respectively.

At first, amongst all classifiers, the Kernel Naive Bayes (Model 3), Fine Gaussian SVM (Model 4), and Narrow Neural Network (Model 7) classifiers give the highest performances compared to other model functions during the training. However, after the trained classifiers were tested, the accuracy shows that Models 2, 5 and 7 had better results using three predictors with 53.2%, 54.1%, and 54.5%, respectively. Despite having low prediction performance result during training, using all the three predictors indicate that P/F is feasible to be included in giving early prediction BG performance for patients with DM.

Figure 2 shows the tabulation of sensitivity and specificity of BG performance results for both data in k-Nearest Neighbour (Model 5) and Neural Network (Model 7) classifiers to compare model robustness with three predictors. These two classifiers were presented and further tested for model robustness as the results were the top two highest. For both training and test data, Model 5 had sensitivity of 0.62 and 0.54, respectively. Meanwhile, specificity for Model 5 shows 0.66 and 0.76 based on the test set, respectively. Then,

Table 2. Models accuracies.

Model	Train (Accuracy %)				Test (Accuracy %)
	SI-P/F-DM	SI-P/F	SI-DM	P/F-DM	
Model 1	52.4	52.1	54.1	50.7	51.5
Model 2	52.8	51.5	51.6	51.2	53.2
Model 3	**55.4**	**54.0**	54.8	51.2	52.6
Model 4	53.5	53.5	54.8	50.5	49.6
Model 5	53.0	51.1	**55.0**	50.8	54.1
Model 6	52.9	53.0	54.6	**51.4**	52.8
Model 7	54.1	53.5	55.3	50.9	**54.5**
Mean (±SD)	53.4 (±0.9)	52.6 (±1.0)	54.3 (±1.1)	50.9 (±0.2)	52.6 (±1.5)

Model 7 shows the sensitivity of 0.65 and 0.53 for train and test data. The specificity for Model 7 of train and test data are 0.63 and 0.67, respectively. Model 5 has better ability to stratify BG performance while Model 7 is more sensitive and robust classifying the predictor.

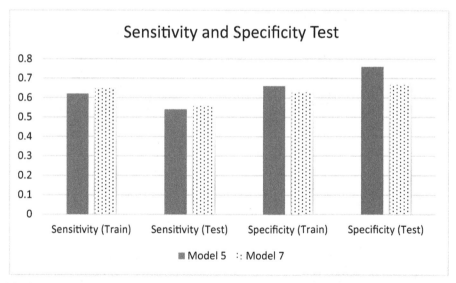

Fig. 2. Sensitivity and specificity for training and test data of k-Nearest Neighbour (Model 5) and Neural Network (Model 7).

Figure 3 shows that BG bands in Class 1,2 and 3 positively predicted in training data for Model 5 are 24, 680 and 50 respectively. Meanwhile, in test results for Model 5 are 33, 208 and 18. As for Model 7, 80, 582 and 108 of the predicted Class 1, 2 and 3 are true in train data. The test results that classified true for Class 1, 2 and 3 are 44, 192, and 25. Our findings show that k-Nearest Neighbor (k-NN) had better classification for larger data such as Class 2. In comparison to k-NN, Neural Network classifier had higher accuracy in classifying Class 1 and 3 meaning that Neural Network is more feasible for data with small volumes. From the specificity values, there are increment of 10% and 4% for Model 5 than Model 7.

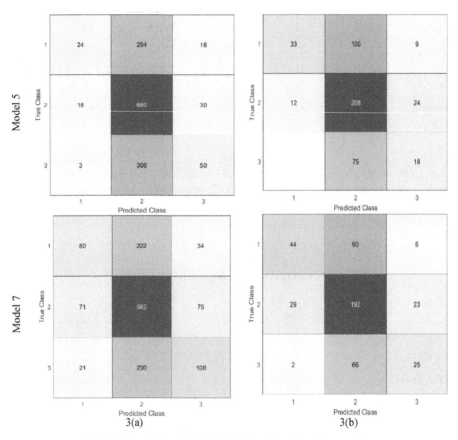

Fig. 3. Confusion matrix of the (a) training data (b) test data

Based on the classification results, TP predictions for both data partitions need to be calculated by two stages, one for model accuracy and followed by model sensitivity for robustness. This is because there are more than two classes to be classified. From the overall mean of classifier models, there is an increment of 4% from train to test data showing that the combination of S_I, P/F and DM status shows positive potential for classifying the BG within the time band. Moreover, sensitivity and specificity showed the highest test data accuracies for Model 5 and Model 7. This indicates an improvement in classifier robustness whereby the results are increased by 8% vs 12% and 10% vs 4% from train to test data. There are several possibilities that contribute to low prediction. First, a study by Razak et al. [31] suggested increasing the value of S_I to a physiologically relevant one that represented the human biomarker. Our study showed that the value of S_I used most of the time had 0 value which is not acceptable. Thus, improving S_I to a physiologically relevant value range of $1e^{-3}$ to $1e^{-5}$ may also help improve the classifiers features. Second, the PaO2 and FiO2 data collected from ICU charts whenever both data are available. Thus, in this study, we assumed the data of FiO_2 to complete the PO_2 data. However, since S_I represented the hourly varying parameter of ICING model, the data collected for P/F score can be interpolated to hourly as well for future study to complement all the features used.

In summary, this study was done to classify the BG performance bands using S_I, P/F, and DM. P/F scores can be used to predict the classes of BG, this input predictor can be used as a non-invasive and time-consuming method to predict glycemic levels. In the future, if these attributes were selected for further research, P/F predictors can be partitioned earlier based on the different ranges of SOFA score or partitioning the S_I based on days of stays. Additionally, data collected for this study was before the occurrence of the pandemic and only 16 out 76 patients had pneumonia cause respiratory failures. In the future, it is interesting to study on how P/F can influence sample size that involved COVID-19 patients as well, as COVID-19 are categorized in the severe acute respiratory system.

4   Conclusion

This preliminary work showed that k-Nearest Neighbor and Neural Network models are feasible to classify BG performance. Although the model's accuracy is only 54.1% and 54.5%, P/F scores can be used to make an early prediction of glycemic level through classification. Based on the test result using S_I-P/F-DM as predictors, the accuracy was increased for both models. Similarly, model robustness test using sensitivity, and specificity demonstrated a total increase of 20% and 14% for both models. This increment shows that there is a likely possible relationship between P/F scores and diabetes status and may influenced BG performances. In future, if we have data set from COVID-19 patients, we can make early prediction for BG performance with the train model for those two classifiers.

Acknowledgement. Thank you to Ministry of Education for funding our study via Fundamental Research Grant Scheme (FRGS) 2019 (Grant Code No: FRGS/1/2019/STG05/UNITEN/02/1), Universiti Tenaga Nasional, and Universitas Sriwijaya with UNSRI Grant (Grant Code: 2021005UNSRI). The data were collected under a collaborative study with Universiti Malaya Medical Centre under ethics number MECID No. 20171115754.

1. References

1. McCowen, K.C., Malhotra, A., Bistrian, B.R.: Stress-induced hyperglycemia. Crit. Care Clin. **17**, 107–124 (2001)
2. Dungan, K.M., Braithwaite, S.S., Preiser, J.C.: Stress hyperglycaemia (2009)
3. Preiser, J.-C. (ed.): The Stress Response of Critical Illness: Metabolic and Hormonal Aspects. Springer, Cham (2016). https://doi.org/10.1007/978-3-319-27687-8

4. Marik, P.E., Bellomo, R.: Stress hyperglycemia: an essential survival response! Crit Care **17**, 305 (2013)
5. Lim, B., et al.: Clinical characteristics and risk factors for severe COVID-19 infections in Malaysia: a nationwide observational study. Lancet Reg. Health - West. Pac. **4**, 100055 (2020)
6. D.G Of Health: From the Desk of the Director-General of Health Malaysia Kenyataan Akhbar KPK 31 Disember 2020 – Situasi Semasa Jangkitan Penyakit di Malaysia (2021). https://kpkesihatan.com/2020/03/11/kenyataan-akhbar-kpk-11-mac-2020-situasi-semasa-jangkitan-penyakit-coronavirus-2019-covid-19-di-malaysia/
7. D.G Of Health: From the Desk of the Director-General of Kenyataan Akhbar KPK 13 Julai 2021 – Situasi Semasa Jangkitan Penyakit Coronavirus (2021)
8. Zheng, X.y., Guan, W.j., Zhong, N.s.: Clinical characteristics of COVID-19 in developing countries of western pacific: low case-fatality rate unraveled. Lancet Reg. Health - West. Pac. **6**, 100073 (2021)
9. Ling, T.L., Har, L.C., Nor, M.R.M., Ismail, N.I., Ismail, W.N.W.: Malaysian Registry of Intensive Care Report (2016)
10. Edriss, H., Selvan, K., Sigler, M., Nugent, K.: Glucose levels in patients with acute respiratory failure requiring mechanical ventilation. J. Intensive Care Med. **32**, 578–584 (2017)
11. Ardigo, D., Valtuena, S., Zavaroni, I., Baroni, M.C., Delsignore, R.: Pulmonary complications in diabetes mellitus: the role of glycemic control. Curr. Drug Targets Inflamm. Allergy **3**, 455–458 (2004)
12. Abu-Samah, A., Razak, A.A., Razak, N.N., Suhaimi, F.M., Jamaludin, U.: The correlation of model-based insulin sensitivity and respiratory P/F score. In: Ibrahim, F., Usman, J., Ahmad, M.Y., Hamzah, N. (eds.) ICIBEL 2019. IP, vol. 81, pp. 54–62. Springer, Cham (2021). https://doi.org/10.1007/978-3-030-65092-6_6
13. Logette, E., et al.: A machine-generated view of the role of blood glucose levels in the severity of COVID-19. Front. Public Health **9**, 1–53 (2021). https://doi.org/10.3389/fpubh.2021.695139
14. Villar, J., et al.: Assessment of PaO2/FiO2 for stratification of patients with moderate and severe acute respiratory distress syndrome. BMJ Open **5**, e006812 (2015)
15. Holzinger, U., Kitzberger, R., Fuhrmann, V., Funk, G.C., Madl, C., Ratheiser, K.: Correlation of calculated indices of insulin resistance (QUICKI and HOMA) with the euglycaemic hyperinsulinaemic clamp technique for evaluating insulin resistance in critically ill patients. Eur. J. Anaesthesiol. **24**, 966–970 (2007)
16. Muniyappa, R., Madan, R.: Assessing insulin sensitivity and resistance in humans. In: Endotext, pp. 1–21 (2000)
17. Abu-Samah, A., et al.: Model-based glycemic control in a Malaysian intensive care unit: performance and safety study. Med. Devices Evid. Res. **12**, 215–226 (2019)
18. Chase, J.G., et al.: Insulin sensitivity, its variability and glycemic outcome: a model-based analysis of the difficulty in achieving tight glycemic control in critical care. In: IFAC (2011)
19. Blakemore, A., et al.: Model-based insulin sensitivity as a sepsis diagnostic in critical care. J. Diabetes Sci. Technol. **2**, 468–477 (2008)
20. Stewart, K.W., et al.: Safety, efficacy and clinical generalization of the STAR protocol: a retrospective analysis. Ann. Intensive Care **6**(1), 1 (2016). https://doi.org/10.1186/s13613-016-0125-9
21. Abu-Samah, A., et al.: Model-based insulin-nutrition administration for glycemic control in Malaysian critical care: first pilot trial. In: Ibrahim, F., Usman, J., Ahmad, M.Y., Hamzah, N., Teh, S.J. (eds.) ICIBEL 2017. IP, vol. 67, pp. 189–196. Springer, Singapore (2018). https://doi.org/10.1007/978-981-10-7554-4_33
22. Evans, A., et al.: Stochastic targeted (STAR) glycemic control: design, safety, and performance. J. Diabetes Sci. Technol. **6**, 102–115 (2012)

23. Fisk, L.M., Le Compte, A.J., Shaw, G.M., Penning, S., Desaive, T., Chase, J.G.: STAR development and protocol comparison. IEEE Trans. Biomed. Eng. **59**, 3357–3364 (2012)
24. Sagun, G., Gedik, C., Ekiz, E., Karagoz, E., Takir, M., Oguz, A.: The relation between insulin resistance and lung function: a cross sectional study. BMC Pulm. Med. **15**, 1–8 (2015)
25. Lin, J., et al.: A physiological intensive control insulin-nutrition-glucose (ICING) model validated in critically ill patients. Comput. Methods Programs Biomed. **102**, 192–205 (2011)
26. Hann, C.E., et al.: Integral-based parameter identification for long-term dynamic verification of a glucose-insulin system model. Comput. Methods Programs Biomed. **77**, 259–270 (2005)
27. Brink, H., Richards, J., Fetherolf, M.: Real-World Machine Learning. Manning Publications Co., Greenwich (2016)
28. Singh, N., Singh, P., Bhagat, D.: A rule extraction approach from support vector machines for diagnosing hypertension among diabetics. Expert Syst. Appl. **130**, 188–205 (2019)
29. Yahyaoui, A., Yumuşak, N.: Decision support system based on the support vector machines and the adaptive support. Biomed. Res. **29**, 1474–1480 (2018)
30. Haque, F., et al.: Performance analysis of conventional machine learning algorithms for diabetic sensorimotor polyneuropathy severity classification. Diagnostics **11**, 801 (2021)
31. Razak, A.A., Abu-Samah, A., Razak, N.N., Baharudin, S., Suhaimi, F.M., Jamaludin, U.: Endogenous glucose production variation assessment for Malaysian ICU patients based on diabetic status. In: Ibrahim, F., Usman, J., Ahmad, M.Y., Hamzah, N. (eds.) ICIBEL 2019. IP, vol. 81, pp. 129–136. Springer, Cham (2021). https://doi.org/10.1007/978-3-030-65092-6_15

Forecasting of Carbon Monoxide Concentration Based on Sequence-to-Sequence Deep Learning Approach

Nur'atiah Zaini[1]([✉]) [iD], Lee Woen Ean[1] [iD], and Ali Najah Ahmed[2] [iD]

[1] Institute of Sustainable Energy (ISE), Universiti Tenaga Nasional, Kajang, Selangor, Malaysia
{Nur_Atiah,LeeWoen}@uniten.edu.my
[2] Institute of Energy Infrastructure (IEI), Universiti Tenaga Nasional, Kajang, Selangor, Malaysia
Mahfoodh@uniten.edu.my

Abstract. Carbon monoxide (CO) is one of the dangerous air pollutants due to its negative impact on human health. Therefore, accurate forecasting of CO concentration is essential to control air pollution. This study aims to forecast the concentration of CO using sequences to sequence models namely convolutional neural network and long short-term memory (CNN-LSTM) and sequence to sequence LSTM (seq2seq LSTM). The proposed forecasting models are validated using hourly air quality datasets from six monitoring stations in Selangor to forecast CO concentration at 1 h to 6 h ahead of the time horizon. The performances of proposed models are evaluated in terms of statistical equations namely root mean square error (RMSE), mean square error (MAE) and mean percentage error (MAPE). CNN-LSTM and seq2seq LSTM model excellently forecast air pollutant concentration for 6 h ahead with RMSE of 0.2899 and 0.2215, respectively. Additionally, it is found that seq2seq LSTM has slightly improved CNN-LSTM indicates the effectiveness of the architecture in the forecasting. However, both proposed architectures illustrate promising results and are reliable in the forecasting of CO concentration.

Keywords: Air quality · Forecasting · Long short-term memory · Deep learning · Artificial intelligence

1 Introduction

In recent years, air pollution has become a vital issue in most developing countries and gained worldwide attention due to its negative effects on health, economic and environmental sustainability [1, 2]. Rapid development in industrialization, infrastructure, and urbanization has caused serious air quality deterioration, especially in urban areas [3]. One of the most dangerous air pollutants namely carbon monoxide (CO) can cause negative impacts on human health such as respiratory infections, lung cancer, and heart diseases that may lead to mortality [4]. CO is a colourless, tasteless and odourless gas that is commonly emitted from the combustion of fossil fuel and coal [5]. Concentration

© Springer Nature Switzerland AG 2021
H. Badioze Zaman et al. (Eds.): IVIC 2021, LNCS 13051, pp. 518–529, 2021.
https://doi.org/10.1007/978-3-030-90235-3_45

levels of CO are generally higher in urban areas as compared to the rural areas where the industrial, commercial and busy traffic particularly focus on the area [6]. Therefore, reliable forecasting of air pollutant concentration is essential and beneficial to provide accurate information on the air quality in the affected area and support environmental management [4].

Forecasting of time series air pollutants based on intelligent modelling strategies has been proven in illustrating higher accuracy as compared to statistical modelling such as Auto Regressive Integrated Moving Average (ARIMA) [7]. Deep learning is a subset of machine learning based on the neural network that also has been successfully implemented to solve problems in speech recognition and image classification [8]. On the other hand, deep learning strategies such as convolutional neural network (CNN) and recurrent neural network (RNN) has gained popularity in numerous studies of air quality forecasting due to their advantages over traditional machine learning models such as artificial neural network (ANN) and support vector machine (SVM) [3, 4, 9]. However, RNN is known to have a drawback during the learning process called the vanishing gradient problem [10]. Considering the limitation in RNN, an improved method namely long short-term memory (LSTM) that used memory block for recurrent learning process is introduced and have been widely applied in air quality forecasting [11, 12].

Besides that, hybrid architectures of multiple deep learning methods such as CNN-LSTM [13, 14] and sequence to sequence (seq2seq) model [15, 16] are able to improve the individual models in air quality forecasting. For instance, Wang et al. [17] developed a hybrid seq2seq model based on Bidirectional LSTM and gated recurrent unit (GRU) and Jia et al. [18] used stacked GRU layer to forecast hourly ozone concentration. Besides that, Sharma et al. [19] and Du et al. [20] developed hybrid CNN-LSTM in the forecasting of particulate matter. From the literature study, it is found that proposed hybrid architectures outperform individual deep learning models and yield the highest forecasting accuracy. However, the studies do not compare the forecasting performance between CNN-LSTM and seq2seq LSTM hybrid architectures. The comparison analysis between different hybrid models may provide new insight into the effectiveness and efficiency of hybrid architectures in air quality forecasting. Although sequence to sequence deep learning models have been previously developed for air quality forecasting, the model's evaluation in multistep forecasting of CO concentration is still limited.

The objective of this study is to establish two multistep hybrid deep learning models namely CNN-LSTM and seq2seq LSTM in hourly forecasting of CO concentration in Selangor, Malaysia. It involves hourly air quality datasets at six air quality monitoring stations for 1 to 6 h ahead forecasting of CO concentration, development and comparison of the proposed deep learning architectures. The comparison study was conducted in order to highlight the performances of different architectures and evaluate the impact of each architecture network on forecasting accuracy. The performances of the forecasting models were evaluated based on statistical evaluation such as root mean square error (RMSE), mean absolute percentage error (MAPE) and mean absolute error (MAE).

2 Data and Methods

2.1 Study Area and Data

Study Area and Data Collection. Hourly historical air quality data consist of six air pollutants namely $PM_{2.5}$, PM_{10}, SO_2, NO_2, O_3 and CO were obtained from the Department of Environment Malaysia from 1 January 2019 to 31 December 2019. The datasets were collected at six air quality monitoring stations in Selangor. Figure 1 shows the location of monitoring stations considered in this study. The hourly dataset contains 8760 records for each station. The mean hourly air pollutants concentration for the six monitoring stations are calculated and summarized in Table 1.

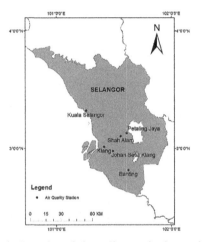

Fig. 1. Location of air quality monitoring stations

Table 1. Statistics of the parameters for Selangor

Variable	$PM_{2.5}$ ($\mu g/m^3$)	PM_{10} ($\mu g/m^3$)	SO_2 (ppm)	NO_2 (ppm)	O_3 (ppm)	CO (ppm)
Minimum	229.715	206.199	0.014	0.048	0.075	3.902
Maximum	7.533	3.792	0.000	0.002	0.000	0.282
Mean	41.170	31.489	0.001	0.017	0.016	0.983
Standard deviation	24.886	22.304	0.001	0.006	0.015	0.375
Total number	8760	8760	8760	8760	8760	8760

Data Preprocessing. The datasets collected contains missing values that may be due to instrumental error, invalid values and regular maintenance. In this study, mean value of the particular attribute is used to substitute the missing data. Then, mean hourly air pollutants of multiple monitoring stations were computed to represent the air quality for Selangor. The dataset was split into two sets namely training and testing. Training set is set for 80% of total records, while testing set was set to 20%. The dataset values were normalized in the range of [0, 1] to avoid the negative impacts on model's learning process due to nonuniform value ranges. The equation for data normalization is defined in Eq. 1.

$$z = \frac{x - \min(x)}{\max(x) - \min(x)} \tag{1}$$

where x is the actual value and z is the normalized value.

2.2 Long Short-Term Memory

LSTM is an updated version of RNN that is capable to learn long-term dependencies and solve vanishing gradient problems in RNN by performing self-loop memory blocks [4]. An LSTM unit consists of a memory block that includes three different gates namely forget gate, input gate and output gate as illustrated in Fig. 2. All three gates having functions of writing information from the input, forget the information, and determining the final outputs. The gate unit aims to control the information flow from one LSTM unit to another and allow the network to learn over many times steps [9].

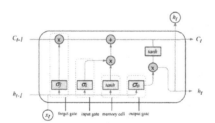

Fig. 2. LSTM unit architecture

LSTM takes current information x_t, previous output from hidden layer h_{t-1} and previous cell state, C_{t-1} as input. However, gate structures help LSTM to learn the long-term dependencies in sequential series and allow the information to pass through LSTM network. Therefore, LSTM is an effective model for learning sequential data. The forget gate, input gate, output gate and memory cell in the structure can be defined based on the following equations:

$$f_t = \sigma\left(W_f x_t + U_f h_{t-1} + b_f\right) \tag{2}$$

$$i_t = \sigma\left(W_i x_t + U_i h_{t-1} + b_i\right) \tag{3}$$

$$o_t = \sigma(W_o x_t + U_o h_{t-1} + b_o) \tag{4}$$

$$\tilde{C}_t = ReLU(W_C x_t + U_C h_{t-1} + b_C) \tag{5}$$

where U_f, U_i, U_o and U_C are the weight matrices connecting the preceding output to the gate units and memory cell. b_f, b_i, b_o and b_C are the bias vectors. W_f, W_i, W_o and W_C are the weight matrices mapping the hidden layer input to the gate units and a memory cell. σ denotes sigmoid function as defined in Eq. 6 and ReLU activation function is defined in Eq. 7. Then, the cell output and the layer output can be implemented using Eq. 8 and Eq. 9, respectively.

$$\sigma(x) = \frac{1}{1 + e^{-x}} \tag{6}$$

$$R(z) = \max(0, z) \tag{7}$$

$$C_t = f_t \circ C_{t-1} + i_t \circ ReLU(U_C h_{t-1} + W_C x_t + b_C) \tag{8}$$

$$h_t = o_t \circ ReLU(C_t) \tag{9}$$

2.3 Convolutional Neural Network

CNN is a biologically inspired network that has been successfully implemented in image recognition, object detection and text processing [21]. CNN is also able to work on multiple arrays of data where 1D is for signals and sequences data as well as text, 2D is for images and 3D is for images taken across time and videos [22]. General CNN network architecture consists of different layers namely convolutional, max pooling, dropout and fully connected layer as illustrated in Fig. 3. In CNN, a convolutional layer is important to extract the features of input variables using the convolutional kernel [8]. The pooling layer is introduced after the convolutional layer to speed up the filtering and reduce the number of operations. Pooling layers simplifies and downsamples the output received from convolutional layers to avoid overfitting [10]. After convolutional and pooling layers, the output was flattened into 1D array for successive forecasting.

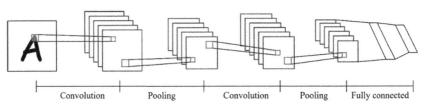

| Convolution | Pooling | Convolution | Pooling | Fully connected |

Fig. 3. CNN architecture

Considering the ability of 1D CNN in solving time series data, the application has gained worldwide attention in various fields. The equations for 1D CNN are as follows [20]:

$$c_j^l = \sum_i x_i^{l-1} * \omega_{ij}^l + b_j^l \tag{10}$$

$$x_j^l = ReLU\left(c_j^l\right) \tag{11}$$

$$x_j^l = Flatten\left(x_j^l\right) \tag{12}$$

$$x_k^{l+1} = FC(\omega_{kj}^{l+1} x_j^l + b_k^{l+1}) \tag{13}$$

The convolutional layer learning process is modelled based on Eq. 10 and Eq. 11, where $*$ denotes a convolution operator, ω_{ij}^l is filter, b_j^l is bias and l is the involved layer. ReLU activation function was used within the layer. x_i^{l-1} and c_j^l represent input and output vector to a convolution layer.

2.4 Experimental Design

This study aims to evaluate the performances of two hybrid LSTM based models for CO concentration forecasting at 1 to 6 h ahead of time horizon incorporating historical air quality datasets at six air quality monitoring stations. Besides that, a comparative analysis was conducted in order to highlight the effectiveness of different hybrid architectures in forecasting 1 to 6 h ahead of CO concentration in terms of error assessments.

Seq2Seq LSTM model consists of two LSTM layers with 128 units and 64 units, respectively for both encoder and decoder processing layers. A manual search is performed to find the optimum hyperparameters of the models. The activation function used in the network is rectified linear unit (ReLU) which has the advantage of reducing the vanishing gradient and has better convergence performance. Besides that, adaptive moment estimation (ADAM) is used as an optimizer within the network where the optimizer can successfully work in online and stationary settings. The exponential decay rate for first moment estimates and second-moment estimates are 0.9 and 0.999, respectively. The learning rate is set to 0.001. Then, the forecasting models are fitted with a batch size of 128 and mean square error (MSE) is used as the loss function. Early stopping criteria is implemented for learning epoch in the model. The description of hyperparameters used in this study is summarized in Table 2.

CNN-LSTM model consists of a 1D convolution layer with a filter number of 32 and kernel size of 3. The hyperparameters of LSTM in CNN-LSTM architecture is set equal to the seq2seq LSTM model. The architecture of seq2seq LSTM and CNN-LSTM model proposed in this study are illustrated in Fig. 4 and Fig. 5, respectively.

Table 2. Hyperparameters of proposed models

Model	Hyperparameters
Seq2seq LSTM	Encoder and decoder: LSTM layer = 2, num. of nodes = {128, 64}, activation function = ReLU, learning rate = 0.001, optimizer = Adam, dropout = 0.1, batch size = 32, epoch = early stopping
CNN-LSTM	CNN: 1D convolutional layer, kernel size = 3, num. of filter = 32, activation function = ReLU LSTM: num. of layer = 2, num. of nodes = {128,64}, dropout = 0.1 Optimizer = Adam, learning rate = 0.001, batch size = 32, epoch = early stopping

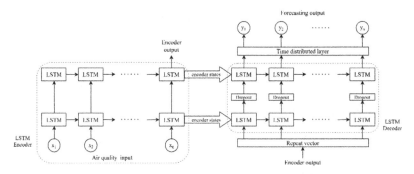

Fig. 4. Sequence to sequence LSTM architecture

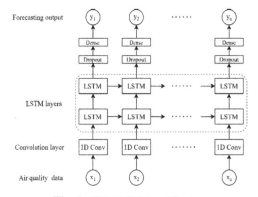

Fig. 5. CNN-LSTM architecture

2.5 Performance Evaluation

Proposed forecasting models were evaluated using statistical equations namely root mean square error (RMSE), mean absolute error (MAE) and mean absolute percentage error (MAPE). The RMSE represent the difference between the observed and forecasted value at a different time interval. The MAE shows the absolute difference between observed and forecasted values on overall data points. The MAPE presents the average absolute error of forecasts in terms of percentages that measure the model's forecasting accuracy. The smaller value of RMSE, MAE and MAPE indicate better forecasting performances.

The equations of performances criteria are defined as follows:

$$RMSE = \sqrt{\frac{1}{n} \sum\nolimits_{i=1}^{n} \left(y_i - \hat{y}_i \right)^2} \tag{14}$$

$$MAE = \frac{1}{n} \sum\nolimits_{i=1}^{n} \left| y_i - \hat{y}_i \right| \tag{15}$$

$$MAPE = \frac{1}{n} \sum\nolimits_{i=1}^{n} \left| \frac{y_i - \hat{y}_i}{y_i} \right| \times 100 \tag{16}$$

where n is the number of data points; y_i and $\hat{y}_i$ are the observed and forecasted values, respectively.

3 Results and Discussion

The performances of CNN-LSTM and seq2seq LSTM model in the forecasting CO concentration at 1 h to 6 h ahead in terms of RMSE, MAE and MAPE are demonstrated in Fig. 6, Fig. 7 and Fig. 8, respectively. From the graphs, the error values gradually increase as the forecasting time horizon increase. It can be perceived that both forecasting models show the same trend of evaluation scores which indicate forecasting accuracy is lower for a larger forecasting time horizon [3]. Therefore, it is important to decide on the high and low resolution for optimum forecasting accuracy and reduce bias in the dataset.

The forecasting performances of proposed architectures were compared to highlight their effectiveness and impact in air quality forecasting. Both forecasting models were developed to extract input data features using the first processing layer and forecast future CO concentration using the second processing layer. In this case, encoder-decoder frameworks were proposed with different architectural designs. Seq2seq LSTM architecture yields RMSE of 0.1623, 0.1823, 0.1980, 0.2082, 0.2153 and 0.2215 for 1 h to 6 h ahead forecasting, respectively which are lower as compared to CNN-LSTM model.

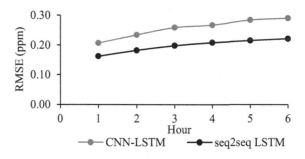

Fig. 6. RMSE of proposed models

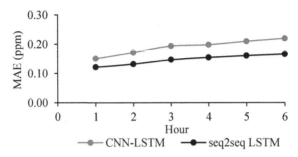

Fig. 7. MAE of proposed models

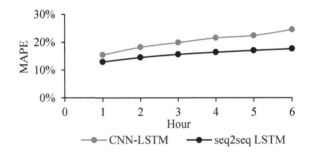

Fig. 8. MAPE of proposed models

Similar to MAE and MAPE, the error values of seg2seq LSTM are lower than CNN-LSTM. Therefore, seq2seq LSTM model outperforms CNN-LSTM in terms of RMSE, MAE and MAPE at multi-hour step ahead forecasting.

Seq2seq LSTM reduces the RMSE, MAE and MAPE of CNN-LSTM by 23.6%, 24.2% and 28.0%, respectively at 6 h ahead forecasting. Table 3 summarizes the error values of both proposed forecasting architectures. Higher performances of seq2seq LSTM indicates the architecture successfully extracted important features and captured temporal distribution in time series air quality dataset to successfully forecast multi-hour ahead of CO concentration [15]. Therefore, the architectural design of a forecasting model affects the performances in terms of the learning process and future forecasting. However, the architecture depicts slight improvements from CNN-LSTM illustrates that CNN-LSTM may still be consistent in multi-hour CO concentration forecasting.

Overall, both CNN-LSTM and seq2seq LSTM models yield promising forecasting performances where the models are able to forecast CO concentration near the observed values. It is indicated that proposed hybrid models have the ability to extract the important features in multiple input variables and successfully forecast future CO concentration. The comparison of observed and forecasted CO concentration at 6 h ahead forecasting is presented in Fig. 9. It can be concluded that both forecasting models are reliable to forecast multistep ahead of air pollutant concentration. Different designs of architectural networks and hyperparameter combinations can be further explored to enhance forecasting performances.

Table 3. RMSE, MAE and MAPE of proposed architectures at 6 h forecasting

Model	RMSE	MAE	MAPE
CNN-LSTM	0.2899	0.2195	24.51%
Seq2Seq LSTM	0.2215	0.1663	17.66%

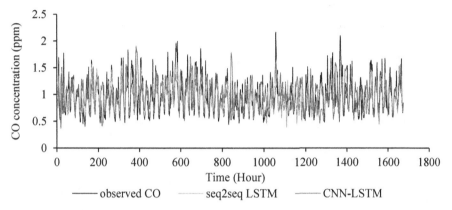

Fig. 9. Forecasted value and observed value of CO concentration

4 Conclusion

In this study, two hybrid architectures based on LSTM were proposed to forecast hourly CO concentration using air quality datasets from multiple monitoring stations in Selangor. CNN-LSTM consists of a 1D convolutional layer and two layers of LSTM. Meanwhile, seq2seq LSTM contains two LSTM layers in both decoder and decoder processing layers. Both models are designed to extract the features in multiple input variables using the first processing layer and forecast future CO concentration using the second processing layer. Seq2seq LSTM model illustrates slightly higher forecasting performances as compared to CNN-LSTM at 1 h to 6 h ahead of forecasting. However, both hybrid architectures depict superior forecasting performance and yield forecasted CO concentration near the observed values. Overall, the design of optimum hybrid architecture may depend on variational input parameters and forecasting requirements. There are many ways in which the study can be extended. First, considering other parameters such as weather and traffic data may enhance the forecasting performances which is exclusively considered in this study due to data source limitation. Second, the study can be extended by including spatiotemporal analysis among multiple air quality monitoring stations. Lastly, the hybrid architectures of deep learning approaches can be extended using more sophisticated methods such as bidirectional LSTM to handle larger datasets and optimization techniques to find optimum deep learning hyperparameters.

Acknowledgement. The authors would like to acknowledge Universiti Tenaga Nasional, Malaysia for financially support this research under BOLD RESEARCH GRANT 2021 (BOLD 2021): J510050002/2021089.

References

1. Ahani, K., Salari, M., Shadman, A.: An ensemble multi-step-ahead forecasting system for fine particulate matter in urban areas. J. Clean. Prod. **263**, 120983 (2020). https://doi.org/10.1016/j.jclepro.2020.120983
2. Pak, U., et al.: Deep learning-based PM2.5 prediction considering the spatiotemporal correlations: a case study of Beijing, China. Sci. Total Environ. **699**, 133561 (2020). https://doi.org/10.1016/j.scitotenv.2019.07.367
3. Chang, Y.S., Chiao, H.T., Abimannan, S., Huang, Y.P., Tsai, Y.T., Lin, K.M.: An LSTM-based aggregated model for air pollution forecasting. Atmos. Pollut. Res. **11**(8), 1451–1463 (2020). https://doi.org/10.1016/j.apr.2020.05.015
4. Zhang, B., Zhang, H., Zhao, G., Lian, J.: Constructing a PM 2.5 concentration prediction model by combining auto-encoder with Bi-LSTM neural networks. Environ. Model. Softw. **124** (2020). https://doi.org/10.1016/j.envsoft.2019.104600
5. Wong, P.-Y., et al.: Incorporating land-use regression into machine learning algorithms in estimating the spatial-temporal variation of carbon monoxide in Taiwan. Environ. Model. Softw. **139** (2021). https://doi.org/10.1016/j.envsoft.2021.104996
6. Breitner, S., et al.: Ambient carbon monoxide and daily mortality: a global time-series study in 337 cities. www.thelancet.com/. Accessed 10 May 2021
7. Liu, H., Yan, G., Duan, Z., Chen, C.: Intelligent modeling strategies for forecasting air quality time series: a review. Appl. Soft Comput. J. **102**, 106957 (2021). https://doi.org/10.1016/j.asoc.2020.106957
8. Neapolitan, R.E.: Neural Networks and Deep Learning. Springer, Heidelberg (2018). https://doi.org/10.1201/b22400-15
9. Navares, R., Aznarte, J.L.: Predicting air quality with deep learning LSTM: towards comprehensive models. Ecol. Inform. **55**, 101019 (2020). https://doi.org/10.1016/J.ECOINF.2019.101019
10. Mueller, J.P., Massaron, L.: Deep Learning for Dummies. Wiley, Hoboken (2019)
11. Yan, R., Liao, J., Yang, J., Sun, W., Nong, M., Li, F.: Multi-hour and multi-site air quality index forecasting in Beijing using CNN, LSTM, CNN-LSTM, and spatiotemporal clustering. Expert Syst. Appl. **169**, 114513 (2021). https://doi.org/10.1016/j.eswa.2020.114513
12. Rao, S., Lavanya Devi, G., Ramesh, N.: Air quality prediction in Visakhapatnam with LSTM based recurrent neural networks. Intell. Syst. Appl. **2**, 18–24 (2019). https://doi.org/10.5815/ijisa.2019.02.03
13. Li, S., Xie, G., Ren, J., Guo, L., Yang, Y., Xu, X.: Urban PM2.5 concentration prediction via attention-based CNN-LSTM. Appl. Sci. (Switzerland) (2020). https://doi.org/10.3390/app10061953
14. Huang, C.-J., Kuo, P.-H.: A deep CNN-LSTM model for particulate matter (PM2.5) forecasting in smart cities. Sensors (Switzerland) (2018). https://doi.org/10.3390/s18072220
15. Zhang, B., et al.: A novel encoder-decoder model based on read-first LSTM for air pollutant prediction. Sci. Total Environ. **765**, 144507 (2021). https://doi.org/10.1016/j.scitotenv.2020.144507
16. Du, S., Li, T., Yang, Y., Horng, S.-J.: Multivariate time series forecasting via attention-based encoder–decoder framework. Neurocomputing **388**, 269–279 (2020). https://doi.org/10.1016/j.neucom.2019.12.118,(2020)

17. Wang, H.-W., Li, X.-B., Wang, D., Zhao, J., He, H.-D., Peng, Z.-R.: Regional prediction of ground-level ozone using a hybrid sequence-to-sequence deep learning approach. J. Clean. Prod. **253**, 119841 (2020). https://doi.org/10.1016/j.jclepro.2019.119841(2020)
18. Jia, P., Cao, N., Yang, S.: Real-time hourly ozone prediction system for Yangtze River Delta area using attention based on a sequence-to-sequence model. Atmos. Environ. **244**, 117917 (2021). https://doi.org/10.1016/j.atmosenv.2020.117917
19. Sharma, E., Deo, R.C., Prasad, R., Parisi, A.V., Raj, N.: Deep air quality forecasts: suspended particulate matter modeling with convolutional neural and long short-term memory networks. IEEE Access **8**, 209503–209516 (2020). https://doi.org/10.1109/ACCESS.2020.3039002
20. Du, S., Li, T., Yang, Y., Horng, S.-J.: Deep Air quality forecasting using hybrid deep learning framework. IEEE Trans. Knowl. Data Eng. **33**(6), 2412–2424 (2021). https://doi.org/10.1109/TKDE.2019.2954510
21. Kranthi Kumar, K., Dileep Kumar, M., Samsonu, Ch., Vamshi Krishna, K.: Role of convolutional neural networks for any real time image classification, recognition and analysis. Materials Today: Proceedings (2021). https://doi.org/10.1016/j.matpr.2021.02.186
22. Lecun, Y., Bengio, Y., Hinton, G.: Deep learning. Nature **521**(7553), 436–444 (2015). https://doi.org/10.1038/nature14539

Infodemiology Framework for COVID-19 and Future Pandemics Using Artificial Intelligence to Address Misinformation and Disinformation

Mohamad Taha Ijab[1]([⊠]) (ID), Mohamad Syahmi Shahril[1] (ID), and Suraya Hamid[2] (ID)

[1] Institute of IR4.0, Universiti Kebangsaan Malaysia, 43600 UKM, Bangi, Selangor, Malaysia
{taha,syahmishahril}@ukm.edu.my
[2] Faculty of Computer Science and Information Technology, Universiti Malaya, 50603 Kuala Lumpur, Malaysia
suraya_hamid@um.edu.my

Abstract. The global fatality caused by the deadly COVID-19 already took 4.5 million lives and is still rapidly increasing. At the same time, Malaysian citizens have been inundated with the overabundance of news and information about COVID-19 since it hit the world in December 2019. Recent study by ISIS Malaysia discovered that WhatsApp and Facebook are the most used social media for misinformation at 39% and 34%, respectively. This phenomenon is termed as an infodemic which occurs when there is an excessive amount of information with undetermined level of accuracy. Hence, this situation makes it difficult for people to find reliable and truthful sources of information when they require it. Infodemiology is the scientific term used to describe the massive spread of information in a digital format particularly on the Internet which aims to guide the stakeholders such as the government on public health policy. Artificial Intelligence (AI) techniques hold potential solutions to address infodemic issue. This paper conceptualizes an Infodemiology Framework for COVID-19 and future pandemics towards addressing the proliferation of misinformation and disinformation on the Internet. Leveraging on AI techniques such as classification via clustering and decision tree algorithms, the research works will be conducted in five phases beginning with dataset collection phase, model building and algorithm selection phase, model refinement phase, model verification phase, and the model deployment phase. The proposed infodemiology framework has the potential to be integrated into the nation's healthcare data warehousing system, the Malaysian Health Data Warehouse (MyHDW).

Keywords: Infodemiology Framework · COVID-19 · Artificial Intelligence · Misinformation · Disinformation

1 Introduction

Everywhere in the world today, the populations are experiencing an overloaded stream of COVID-19 information [1–3]. With the rising number of infection and death cases,

© Springer Nature Switzerland AG 2021
H. Badioze Zaman et al. (Eds.): IVIC 2021, LNCS 13051, pp. 530–539, 2021.
https://doi.org/10.1007/978-3-030-90235-3_46

as well as loaded of new information, there are always the issue of misinformation and disinformation, either done intentionally or not-intentionally. Conceptually, [4] define misinformation as incorrect information based on experts' opinions at that particular time. Disinformation on the other hand is defined as the spread of falsified information with bad intention of causing discomfort, uneasiness or hate [5]. However, it is an accepted fact that it is difficult to understand the real motives of the individuals who create and spread the information, either intentionally or unintentionally [1].

In a recent study by [6] on the fact-checking portal of the Malaysian government, Sebenarnya.my have discovered that the most widely used application to spread fake news is WhatsApp (39%) and Facebook (34%). This is in line with [3] who claimed that social media channels were distinguished as the most prevalent information source (63.3%) and also as a medium to spread misinformation at 67.2%. Further to this, according to the ISIS Malaysia researchers, the way the fact-checking portal Sebenarnya.my is used to perform fact-checking process is generally poor. This is due to unavailability of a strong fact-checking mechanism since the current model is depended on either "truthful or fake" information statement made by the government agency in clarifying the status of unknown claims. This indicates that intricate information are basically hard to ascertain their truthfulness. Secondly, in some instances, the source of such information originated from official statements from the government agency leading to a high level of trust among the public, despite the fact that government information could also be not accurate at some point of time. ISIS Malaysia proposed for the enactment of a law to regulate COVID-19's misinformation and disinformation. Such law should incarcerate those who intentionally create and spread disinformation that causes harm while those who distributed the information without ill intention will not be severely punished.

Yet, beyond this recommendation from ISIS Malaysia on the enactment of a new law, no technological option was suggested by ISIS Malaysia or other parties. Hence, there is a need for a study to be conducted on addressing the propagation of misinformation and disinformation pertaining to COVID-19 and future pandemics via a new and novel Infodemiology Framework by leveraging on technologies such as AI and the machine learning (ML) techniques. Using such AI and ML solutions, the accuracy of information shared on the social platforms on the Internet can be enhanced through the fact-checking portal such as Sebenarnya.my. Thus, the overarching research question posed in this study is "How is the infodemiology framework can be formulated to address propagation of misinformation and disinformation using artificial intelligence technique?". This paper is divided into five sections. The following section provides background information related to infodemic, infodemiology, and the potential uses of AI for developing an infodemiology framework from detection of misinformation and disinformation in the context of COVID-19 and future pandemics. This is followed by the proposed research methodology and subsequently, a discussion on how the infodemiology framework can be developed for COVID-19 and other future pandemics. The last section concludes the paper by providing salient points and how this work would potentially address the nation's needs pertaining to dissemination of truthful and authentic information to the citizens during public health crisis.

2   Literature Review

A brief conceptual review on infodemic and infodemiology is offered in this section. The use of AI techniques for detecting misinformation and disinformation in the extant literature is then reviewed.

2.1   Infodemic and Infodemiology

The WHO deems infodemic on COVID-19 as a second "disease" which needs fighting, and they define infodemic is an excess of information with undetermined level of accuracy making it difficult for people to find reliable and truthful sources of information when they require it [7]. After nearing two decades "infodemiology" term being coined by [8], it is now acknowledged that infodemiology is an important academic field during the spread of COVID-19 today by public health organizations including the WHO [9]. Infodemiology is directly linked to online misinformation and disinformation. According to [10] and [5], misinformation and disinformation are critical social issues which leverage new media, messaging applications and news portal as the major vehicles to spread it. The implications of unmonitored spread of false news may cause disharmony, triggering violence, and diminishing citizens' trusts towards the government [10].

2.2   Uses of AI for Detecting Misinformation and Disinformation

AI can be used to understand the impact of "infodemic" and to solve the production and generation of more misinformation and disinformation [11, 12, 33]. Much of the initial research on COVID-19 using AI has concentrated on the kinds, sources, and virality of the virus [1] and the impacts of news which purported conspiracy theory on the purposeful released of the coronavirus. Those investigations were mostly conducted by the academics, industry, and media agencies [13, 14, 33–37].

In formulating the proposed Infodemiology Framework, datasets from public sources such as the Twitter and Facebook accounts, official government websites (such as The Ministry of Health Malaysia website), blogs, news portals, and messaging applications are available to supply the big data which usually appear in unstructured format. This is mainly due to the facts that social platforms of the government agencies have become the most used channels to disseminate information in a very fast manner for the public consumptions [11]. Managing vast information from such social platforms require deployment of efficient tools to detect misinformation and disinformation. Therefore, the use of AI and ML are advantageous. Unfortunately, not many studies have been conducted surrounding the social dynamics of the COVID-19 false news dissemination using AI and ML.

[16] argues that there is a gaining number of research works with the objectives of responding to misinformation and disinformation issues. The Duke Reporters' Lab claims the existence of close to three hundred projects on fact-checking works in more than eighty-four countries [17]. Until today, most of the fact-checking process have been performed manually by human checkers in verifying the authenticity of the information. This is also the case for this country's fact-checking website, Sebenarnya.my which is not an automated process. The fully robust fact-checking automation is still not a mature field

of research and most AI models are still largely unreliable towards recognizing either the content are fake or otherwise [16]. Further, such automated capabilities are questionable in terms of their accuracy in detecting subjective statements. As of now, social network platforms are dependent on AI for doing repetitive tasks, and the dependency on human reviewers are needed for detecting the more subtle statements [18]. According to [19], Facebook hired more than seven thousand moderators to review contents generated by its members. Thus, as disinformation is growing in volumes, the efficiency of human checking is being questioned.

While there are studies to produce full automation solutions to assist human checkers to identify, validate and rectify contents on social media, however, this is still not prevalent and such efforts are still on the way. AI via ML can employ huge datasets and specific algorithms to teach and instruct computer systems in identifying unique patterns previously unrecognized, and the capability of such automated systems to understand big data, and extract useful information. Thus, this paper proposes the use of AI via ML techniques such as classification via clustering and decision tree to automatically recognize questionable content and social media accounts, as well as to facilitate better judgment of human checkers.

3   Research Methodology

This study is proposed to be conducted over five phases namely dataset collection phase, model building and algorithm selection phase, model refinement phase, model verification phase, and the model deployment phase. The first four phases will be more technical in nature while the fifth phase is more strategic in nature as it involves potential strategic integration or deployment with the existing fact-checking portal, Sebenarnya.my and the bigger vision of integrating the Infodemiology Framework with the Malaysian Health Data Warehouse [20, 21].

3.1   Research Phases

In the first phase, the research starts with dataset collection. For this research, potential data will be crawled, scraped and collected from various infodemiology sources such as social media (Facebook; Twitter), blogs, news portals, messaging applications (such as WhatsApp), and other data corpus on COVID-19 pandemics. These datasets will be compared against the "gold standard" or "ground truth" sources of information, namely the official portal of MoH on COVID-19 (i.e., the Crisis Preparedness & Response Centre (CPRC) http://covid-19.moh.gov.my/); MoH social media accounts including MoH's Facebook and Twitter accounts, and the fact-checking portal, Sebenarnya.my. For example, the data types used for the stated infodemiology data source will include case counts (for CPRC data), articles (for news portal data), post/tweet on social media, sentiments such as like or share or retweet or forward (on Facebook, Twitter and WhatsApp), and will be calculated for the whole country (Malaysia) per week for the duration of the data collection phase. Data pre-processing will be performed to assess the data quality while some techniques will be adopted to find erroneous data and glaring outliers. For data preparation, the mining of textual data will consist of three steps: tokenization, removal of stop words, and stemming. Using feature extraction and selection, it will select the terms for stemming which are larger than the set threshold. Following this process, the collected datasets from the documents would be weighted and transformed into a term weights vector using Vector Space Model (VSM). Here, individual word will be given a value representation to indicate the word's weight within the document. The Term Frequency-Inverse Document Frequency (TF-IDF) will be developed in order to calculate the weights.

The second phase is the model building and algorithm selection phase. Diagnostics will be used to seek the relationships as well as the interactions among the dependent variables (i.e., accuracy of the information) and independent variables (such as information prevalence, information occurrence ratios, as well as search and navigation behaviour -- for detail please refer [8]. This will be helpful to discover dominant outliers and various collinearity of variables' source. Supervised learning of classification via clustering and decision tree will be performed. In this phase, the supervised AI algorithms will train the data which have been labelled and provide a return function to the data that has been supervised. The function's task is to appraise the output having the minimum error rate from the input. In the classification via clustering, clustering is the mechanism used to group similar samples. Clustering is a step during the pre-processing prior to data classification. The classification via clustering will use SVM as the chosen algorithm. Tree-based learning algorithm which is decision tree will also be used because they have a predefined target variable and said to have higher accuracy. The modelling using classification via clustering and decision tree will analyze and contrast the performances of the AI algorithms that have been supervised for misinformation and disinformation. A confusion matrix will be produced to evaluate the performance of misinformation and disinformation. From the matrix, misinformation/disinformation or correct information of samples are then classified. This is summarized as below:

- True Positive (TP): The prediction is labelled as TP if the prediction of misinformation/disinformation is indeed misinformation/disinformation.
- False Positive (FP): The prediction is labelled as FP if the misinformation/disinformation is indeed correct information.
- True Negative (TN): The prediction is labelled as TN if correct information is indeed correct information.
- False Negative (FN): The prediction is labelled as FN if the correction information is indeed misinformation/disinformation.

Based on the developed confusion matrix, Fig. 1 shows the performance evaluation criteria which will be used.

In the third phase, model refinement will be conducted in order to inspect the effects of the interaction more thoroughly. Complete assessment on accuracy, precision, recall and F-measure value will be conducted iteratively to obtain appropriate classification via clustering and decision tree models. Several iterations may be needed until reaching satisfactory performance.

In the fourth phase, after thorough checking, the models' validity will be conducted through the model verification phase. Accuracy is the most important measure in this

$$Accuracy \ = \ \frac{|TN| + |TP|}{|FN| + |FP| + |TN| + |TP|}$$

$$Precision \ = \ \frac{|TP|}{|FP| + |TP|}$$

$$Recall \ = \ \frac{|TP|}{|FN| + |TP|}$$

$$F\text{-}measure \ = \ 2 \ X \ \frac{Recall \ x \ Precision}{Recall + Precision}$$

Fig. 1. Performance evaluation criteria

research. Hence, this study will propose algorithms with higher accuracy. A graph representing the performance accuracy of the classification via clustering model will be shown using the ROC Curve and the decision tree model will be produced. Interpretation as well as the analysis of data will also be performed in this phase. It is proposed that the Waikato Environment for Knowledge Analysis or WEKA will be used to run all the AI algorithms and models in this research.

Finally, the fifth phase will take place when the ML models are integrated into the final Infodemiology Framework proposed in this research. Continuous monitoring of the models and its deployment into the Infodemiology Framework will be conducted. Conceptually and ideally, when the accuracy performance result from the models are 90% or above of accuracy level, then only those information can be published in timely basis on the Sebenarnya.my portal and other news portal that supply credible information for citizens' consumption. Strategically, stakeholders' engagement (i.e., with MoH and the Malaysia Communications and Multimedia Commission, MCMC) will be held in this phase where incorporation of infodemiology framework onto the fact-checking portal and mobile application Sebenarnya.my; as well as potential future integration into the Malaysian Health Data Warehouse [20].

4 Discussion

[3] have stated that algorithms harnessing on AI (43.8%) were recommended as solutions, however their research did not specify what are the AI algorithms that can be used for addressing the propagation of misinformation and disinformation. However, before models can be developed, [22] have separated fake news detection into three typologies: malicious fabrication, massive hoaxes, and irreverent false information. [1] identify six distinct typologies of misinformation on COVID-19: definitive agency, animosity, efficacy, enmity, prognostic, and sarcasm. In formulating the Infodemiology Framework using AI, it is proper to ratify the differing typologies of misinformation and disinformation, and to review some previous methods used detect fake news, which form part of misinformation and disinformation.

- The vector space model (VSM) is used to authenticate news as the originators attempt to distinguish misleading information in digital information sources [22].
- [23] attempted to group news into different grouping using TFIDF and SVM.
- For distinguishing false news and mere opinions, [24] have deployed ML classification techniques to public datasets.
- [25] has conducted numerical investigations on the false news, deceiving information and dubious arguments in social media.
- [26] have suggested a model which target the exchange of preceding fake information and the revised information to minimize the impact of misinformation/disinformation.
- [27] have used deep learning model based on geometry to identify false news using information from Twitter to evaluate their proposed model.

The above are not the exhausted list as there are more studies done by other researchers. However, according to [28], the algorithms that are providing higher accuracy level are classification and decision tree which use supervised learning approach. Hence, this research will experiment these two algorithms, namely classification via clustering, and decision tree. It is argued that classification is the most useful technique to predict a certain phenomenon [29, 30]. While clustering in generally an unsupervised technique used to group elements that are similar into clusters, classification can be performed based on clustering too [29, 31]. The algorithm that can be used for classification via clustering is support vector machine (SVM) algorithm.

One of the most employed supervised learning algorithm is decision tree-based learning which can produce high accuracy. Algorithms such as Decision Trees and Random Forests are widely used for data analytics. Structurally, these algorithms provide a top-down strategy. Using DT, dataset can be divided from huge number of records into clusters with smaller records by applying a certain decision rule [31].

The measures for the models will be their accuracy, recall, precision, and F-measure value. In this study, accuracy is the fraction of the total sum of predictions that are correct, precision is the fraction of cases that are positive and are identified correctly, and F-measure is the computation of average of the precisely retrieved information and recall metrics. The following Fig. 2 depicts the preliminary research framework proposed for this study.

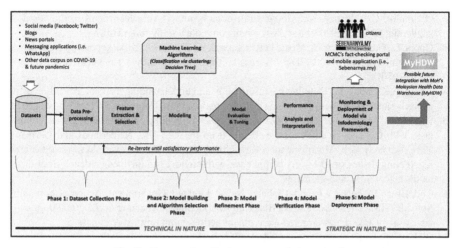

Fig. 2. Proposed preliminary research framework

5   Conclusion

Today, it is becoming harder for users to access information that are accurate and reliable due to the overwhelming amount of information available on the social news platforms and portals. This paper conceptualizes a model to detect misinformation and disinformation (i.e., fake news) in social media and other portals including messaging applications by integrating data mining techniques and certain supervised AI algorithms (i.e., classification via clustering and decision tree). The model will combine, test and train the real datasets and will evaluate it according to specific measurements of accuracy, recall function, precision, as well as F-measure value. Using AI models and algorithms to process accurate information from the ocean of data seems to hold promise in addressing the propagation of misinformation and disinformation. The dissemination of false news is precarious to individuals, society, businesses and also the government. The spread of misinformation and disinformation on the Internet pertaining to COVID-19 is disheartening. The Ministry of Health Malaysia (MoH) is struggling to cope with fake information being spread causing unnecessary panic or wrong information taken by the general public. While this research is still in the conceptualisation stage, the proposed Infodemiology Framework is expected to assist the respective stakeholders especially the MoH, the Ministry of Communications and Multimedia, as well as fact-checking website Sebenarnya.my to identify the sources of wrong or inaccurate information from being disseminated to the public.

Acknowledgements. The authors would like to thank Universiti Kebangsaan Malaysia under GP-2019-K021538 for sponsoring this publication.

References

1. Brennen, J.S., Simon, F.M., Nielsen, R.K.: Beyond (Mis)Representation: visuals in COVID-19 misinformation. Int. J. Press/Polit. **26**(1), 277–299 (2021)

2. O'Connor, C., Murphy, M.: Going viral: doctors must tackle fake news in the covid-19 pandemic. BMJ J. (2020). https://www.bmj.com/content/369/bmj.m1587

3. Gupta, L., Gasparyan, A.Y., Misra, D.P., Agarwal, V., Zimba, O., Yessirkepov, M.: Information and misinformation on COVID-19: a cross-sectional survey study. J. Korean Med. Sci. **35**(27), e256 (2020)

4. Vraga, E.K., Bode, L.: Defining misinformation and understanding its bounded nature: using expertise and evidence for describing misinformation. Polit. Commun. **37**(1), 136–144 (2020)

5. Hameleers, M., van der Meer, T.G.L.A., Brosius, A.: Feeling 'disinformed' lowers compliance with COVID-19 guidelines: evidence from the US, UK, Netherlands and Germany. Harv. Kennedy Sch. Misinformation Rev. (2020). https://misinforeview.hks.harvard.edu/art icle/feeling-disinformed-lowers-compliance-with-covid-19-guidelines-evidence-from-the-us-uk-netherlands-and-germany/

6. CodeBlue, Malaysia's Covid-19 Fake News Targeted Government Action, Community Spread: ISIS, Galen Centre, CodeBlue. https://codeblue.galencentre.org/2020/09/03/malays ias-covid-19-fake-news-targeted-government-action-community-spread-isis/

7. WHO: Infodemic management - Infodemiology. https://www.who.int/teams/riskcommunic ation/infodemic-management

8. Eysenbach, G.: Infodemiology: the epidemiology of (mis)information. Am. J. Med. **113**(9), 763–765 (2002)

9. Eysenbach, G.: How to fight an infodemic: the four pillars of infodemic management. J. Med. Internet Res. **22**(6), e21820 (2020)

10. Avram, M., Micallef, N., Patil, S., Menczer, F.: Exposure to social engagement metrics increases vulnerability to misinformation. Harv. Kennedy School (HKS) Misinformation Rev. **1**, 5 (2020)

11. Bullock, J., Luccioni, A., Pham, K.H., Lam, C.S.N., Luengo-Oroz, M.: Mapping the landscape of artificial intelligence applications against COVID-19. J. Artif. Intell. Res. **69**, 807–845 (2020)

12. Demartini, G., Stefano, M., Damiano, S.: Human-in-the-loop artificial intelligence for fighting online misinformation: challenges and opportunities. Bull. IEEE Comput. Soc. Tech. Committee Data Eng. **43**(3), 65–74 (2020)

13. Freeman, D., et al.: Coronavirus conspiracy beliefs, mistrust, and compliance with government guidelines in England. Psychol. Med. 1–13 (2020). https://www.cambridge.org/core/ journals/psychological-medicine/article/coronavirus-conspiracy-beliefsmistrust-and-compli ance-with-government-guidelines-inengland/9D6401B1E58F146C738971C197407461

14. Swan, B.W.: State Report: Russian, Chinese and Iranian Disinformation Narratives Echo One Another. POLITICO. https://www.politico.com/news/2020/04/21/russiachina-iran-disinform ation-coronavirus-state-department-193107

15. Hollowood, E., Mostrous, A.: Fake News in the Time of C-19. Tortoise, 23 March. https://mem bers.tortoisemedia.com/2020/03/23/the-infodemic-fake-news-coronavirus/content.html

16. Kertysova, K.: Artificial intelligence and disinformation. Secur. Hum. Rights **29**(1–4), 55–81 (2018)

17. Duke Reporters' Lab, Fact checking count tops 300 for the first time,

18. https://reporterslab.org/fact-checking-count-tops-300-for-the-first-time/

19. Zuckerberg, M.: A Blueprint for Content Governance and Enforcement. https://www.fac ebook.com/notes/mark-zuckerberg/a-blueprint-for-content-governance-and-enforcement/ 10156443129621634/

20. Lagorio-Chafkin, C.: Facebook's 7,500 Moderators Protect You from the Internet's Most Horrifying Content. But Who's Protecting Them? https://www.inc.com/christine-lagorio/fac ebook-content-moderator-lawsuit.html

21. Malaysian Health Data Warehouse. https://myhdw.moh.gov.my/public/home

22. Kelleher, J.: Malaysian Health Data Warehouse: Director General of Health cites as the Source of True Comprehensive Healthcare. https://opengovasia.com/malaysian-health-data-wareho use-director-general-of-health-cites-as-the-source-of-true-comprehensive-healthcare/

23. Rubin, V.L., Chen, Y., Conroy, N.J.: Deception detection for news: three types of fakes, In: Proceedings of the 78th ASIS&T Annual Meeting: Information Science with Impact: Research in and for the Community, Missouri (2015)

24. Dadgar, S.M.H., Araghi, M.S., Farahani, M.M.: A novel text mining approach based on TF-IDF and support vector machine for news classification. In: Proceedings of IEEE International Conference on Engineering and Technology (ICETECH), India, pp. 112–116 (2016)

25. Ahmed, H., Traore, I., Saad, S.: Detecting opinion spams and fake news using text classification. Secur. Priv. **1**(1), e9 (2017)

26. Bessi, A.: On the statistical properties of viral misinformation in online social media. Physica A Stat. Mech. Appl. **469**, 459–470 (2017)

27. Zhu, H., Wu, H., Cao, J., Fu, F., Li, H.: Information dissemination model for social media with constant updates. Physica A Stat. Mech. Appl. **502**, 469–482 (2018)

28. Monti, F., Frasca, F., Eynard, D., Mannion, D., Bronstein, M.M.: Fake news detection on social media using geometric deep learning. arXiv preprint arXiv:1902.06673 (2019)

29. Ozbay, F.A., Alatas, B.: Fake news detection within online social media using supervised artificial intelligence algorithms. Physica A Stat. Mech. Appl. **540**, 123174 (2019)

30. Lopez, M.I., Luna, J.M., Romero, C., Ventura, S.: Classification via clustering for predicting final marks based on student participation in forums. In: EDM, pp. 148–151 (2012)

31. Mandapati, S., Bhogapathi, R.B., Rao, S.: Classification via clustering for anonymzed data. I.J. Comput. Netw. Inf. Secur. **3**, 52–58 (2014)

32. Esmail, F.S., Senousy, B., Ragaie, M.: Predication model for leukemia diseases based on data mining classification algorithms with best accuracy. Int. J. Comput. Electr. Autom. Control Inf. Eng. **10**, 842–851 (2016)

33. Choudhary, A., Arora, A.: Linguistic feature based learning model for fake news detection and classification. Expert Syst. Appl. (2020). https://doi.org/10.1016/j.eswa.2020.114171

34. Alameri, S.A., Mohd, M.: Comparison of fake news detection using machine learning and deep learning techniques. In: Proceedings of the 3rd International Conference on Cyber Resilience, pp. 1–6 (2021)

35. Amin, Z., Mohamad Ali, N., Smeaton, A.F.: Attention-based design and selective exposure amid COVID-19 misinformation sharing. In: Kurosu, M. (ed.) HCII 2021. LNCS, vol. 12764, pp. 501–510. Springer, Cham (2021). https://doi.org/10.1007/978-3-030-78468-3_34

36. Azzwan, M.D., Mat Jusoh, N.: Spreading misinformation in social media: a case in a renowned public university. In: Malaysia Indonesia Conference on Economics, Management and Accounting, pp. 299–304 (2016)

37. Masngut, N., Mohamad, E.: Association between public opinion and Malaysian government communication strategies about the COVID-19 crisis: content analysis of image repair strategies in social media. J. Med. Internet **23**, e28074 (2021)

38. Nilashi, M., et al.: Recommendation agents and information sharing through social media for coronavirus outbreak. Telematics Inform. **61**, 101597 (2021)

39. Zainul, H., Said, F.: The COVID-19 Infodemic in Malaysia: Scale, scope and policy response, Institute of Strategic and International Studies Malaysia (ISIS Malaysia) (2020). https://www.isis.org.my/wp-content/uploads/2020/08/FAKE-NEWS_REV.pdf

Object Detection Model Training Framework for Very Small Datasets Applied to Outdoor Industrial Structures

M. Z. Baharuddin[1]([✉]) [iD], D. N. T. How[1] [iD], K. S. M. Sahari[1] [iD], A. Z. Abas[2], and M. K. Ramlee[2]

[1] Department of Electrical and Electronics Engineering, Universiti Tenaga Nasional, Kajang, Malaysia
{zafri,dickson,khairuls}@uniten.edu.my
[2] Tenaga Nasional Berhad, Kuala Lumpur, Malaysia

Abstract. Visual inspection of electrical utility assets is crucial in ensuring the continuous operation of a system or plant. With the advent of digital imagery using mobile devices, it has become easy to collect a vast amount of asset pictures from sites. To further enhance inspection efficiency, we propose RetinaNet, a deep learning-based object detection model that can be trained to automatically detect specific objects and features from images of outdoor industrial structures. The model is capable of detecting features such as intrusions, tree or bushes in the vicinity of the lattice towers. We also introduce a model training framework for use with very small datasets which consists of rigorous data augmentation, image pre-sizing, focal loss function, progressive resizing, learning rate finder, and the Ranger optimizer. Experiment results show that the proposed model used in conjunction with the aforementioned training framework results in the lowest validation loss and highest mean average precision of 31.36

Keywords: Object detection · Deep learning · Convolutional neural network · RetinaNet · Small dataset · Industrial inspection

1 Introduction

Monitoring the condition of electrical utility assets is essential for a stable electricity network. Mobile smart devices with built in cameras have enabled the collection of a vast amount of on-site asset imagery. It is desired to create a system that can extract meaningful information from these images to further enhance the inspection efficiency in terms of accuracy and speed.

Recent advances in the area of deep learning has allowed computers to match or even surpass the accuracy of human experts on visual inspection tasks [1,2]. Given the rapid development pace of deep learning, there are a plethora of deep

Supported by Uniten R&D Seed Grant U-TS-RD-19-31.

H. Badioze Zaman et al. (Eds.): IVIC 2021, LNCS 13051, pp. 540–551, 2021.
https://doi.org/10.1007/978-3-030-90235-3_47

learning-based object detector models that can be used depending on the nature of the task and data the availability of labeled dataset. In most modern deep learning object detectors, the models are usually composed of three components: backbone, neck and head. These three components are stacked atop one another to form the overall model. The backbone functions acts as a feature extractor, whereas the head is trained to predict the bounding boxes and object classes. Meanwhile the neck is an intermediate component that facilitates the head to better process the features extracted from the backbone [3]. Advances in deep learning object detectors are being made in all three components. To date, most prominent works on the backbone structure are residual networks (ResNet) [4], VGG16 [5], EfficientNet [6], SpineNet [7], CSPResNeXt50 and CSPDarknet53 [8]. Recent works on the neck includes feature pyramid network (FPN) [9], bidirectional feature pyramid network (BiFPN) [10] and path aggregation network (PAN) [11]. For the head, the two most common form is the one-stage and two-stage detection heads, each with its own pros and cons. In each form there are also anchor-based and anchor free approaches. One-stage detection heads are known to be faster and less accurate compared to its counterpart. Notable works include region proposal networks (RPN) [12], You Only Look Once (YOLO) [13], Single-shot multibox detector (SSD) [14] and RetinaNet [15]. Anchor free one-stage detectors include CornerNet CenterNet and Fully convolutional one-stage (FCOS) object detectors [16]. Two-stage detection heads are known to be more accurate at the expense of heavier computation. Anchor based versions include Faster Region Based Convolutional Neural Networks (Faster-RCNN) [17], Mask RCNN [18], and R-FCN [19]. An example anchor free version is Point Set Representation (RepPoint) [20]. Figure 1 succinctly illustrates the related works on components of a deep learning object detector.

In this study we propose a deep learning model training framework based on RetinaNet to assist in the detection of activities or features in outdoor industrial images. The main contributions of this paper are as follows:

i. We propose the RetinaNet model to detect specific activities or features in outdoor industrial images.
ii. We introduce a model training framework that enables the proposed model to be trained with a limited number of labeled images.
iii. We evaluate the performance of the proposed framework against several modern object detection models such as RetinaNet, Faster-RCNN and FCOS.

2   Proposed Framework

A new training framework is introduced to enable training of the RetinaNet model using a small dataset. The framework consists of augmentation and pre-sizing of the dataset images. The training optimization uses the focal loss function and progressive resizing. To select the learning rate, α hyperparameter, we used the learning rate finder and Ranger optimizer.

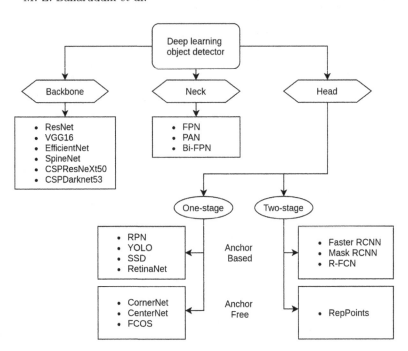

Fig. 1. Components of a modern deep learning object detectors and prominent architectures.

2.1   Dataset

In this work, we utilized proprietary images from the Malaysian national electricity utility. The images were sampled by employees as part of their routine to perform periodic inspections on transmission towers. The raw images are manually annotated and curated into three separate sets namely train, validation, and test dataset. The number of samples forming each dataset are 66, 31, and 15 images respectively. Images were resized to a 512×512 pixels image resolution. Figure 2 illustrates a few sample images from the train dataset. Due to the limited number of images, a data augmentation pipeline was used to artificially increase the number of samples for training. The images from the training dataset was subjected to the random combination of the following augmentation techniques:

i. Rotation - Image is subjected to a random rotation of 15° clockwise or counter-clockwise.
ii. Brightness - Image is subjected to a random change in brightness.
iii. Horizontal Flip - Image is subjected to a random chance of horizontal flip.
iv. Translation - Image is subjected to a random translation in the x and/or y-axis.

To boost the performance of the proposed model, a technique known as presizing was used in the augmentation pipeline. Pre-sizing is a technique used in [21] whereby images were resized to a larger size than the original image and augmented before feeding them into the model. This reduces the number of lossy operations and computations so that they can be more efficiently processed on the graphical processing unit (GPU). A more in-depth explanation on presizing is detailed in [22]. In this work, all images were presized to a resolution of 640×640 pixels.

Fig. 2. Sample images and ground truth bounding boxes from the training dataset, augmented with (a) horizontal flip, (b) brightness increase, (c) rotation with reduced brightness, (d) rotation, (e) translation, and (f) translation with brightness increase.

2.2 Model

The proposed model is the RetinaNet architecture, first introduced in [15] consisting of a backbone, neck and head as shown in Fig. 3. The backbone uses ResNet, an artificial neural network first introduced in [4] that has become a standard backbone for many object detection models.

The proposed model utilizes feature pyramids as the neck which allows the model to robustly detect objects at varying scales. The various types of feature pyramids is illustrated in Fig. 4. In Fig. 4(a) is a feature pyramid mostly used for hand-engineered features such as HOG and SIFT. Figure 4(b) is commonly found in one-stage detectors such as YOLO. Figure 4(c) is commonly used in one-stage detectors such as the SSD. Figure 4(d) was proposed by [15] to be used in RetinaNet and is also known as a feature pyramid network (FPN).

Additionally, the proposed model also includes the use of a specific loss function known as the Focal Loss (FL) instead of the conventionally used Cross-Entropy (CE) loss. The FL is designed to alleviate the class imbalance problem for one-stage object detectors and has shown to improve the effectiveness of the model. FL and CE loss is given in Eqs. 1 and 2.

$$CE(p,y) = -\log(p_t) \tag{1}$$

$$FL = -\alpha_t(1 - p_t)^\gamma \log(p_t) \tag{2}$$

The term $(1 - p_t)^\gamma$ in known as the modulating factor and is a key addition to the original CE loss that improved the performance of RetinaNet over other one-stage object detectors. α_t is the weighting factor. The notation p_t is defined as

$$p_t = \begin{cases} p & \text{if } y = 1 \\ 1 - p & \text{otherwise} \end{cases} \tag{3}$$

where $y \in \{\pm 1\}$ is the ground truth class, and $p \in [0,1]$ is the model's estimated probability of the class.

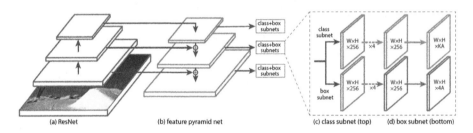

(a) ResNet   (b) feature pyramid net   (c) class subnet (top)   (d) box subnet (bottom)

Fig. 3. Illustration of the model architecture [15]. (a) Backbone of the model, (b) Neck of the model, (c) and (d) Head of the model.

2.3   Training

To train the proposed model, we utilized a technique known as progressive resizing, introduced in [21]. In this technique, an initial model was trained using a small image size of 64×64 pixels as input. Next we used the trained weights as a starting point and re-train the model again with a larger image resolution of 128×128 pixels. With each successive training the input resolution of the images were increased until the desired resolution (512×512 pixels). In this study the image resolution was increased in the order: $64 \times 64 > 128 \times 128 > 256 \times 256 > 384 \times 384 > 512 \times 512$ pixels. The benefit of progressive resizing is that it allows the model to be trained quickly, and also generalizes better by mitigating the

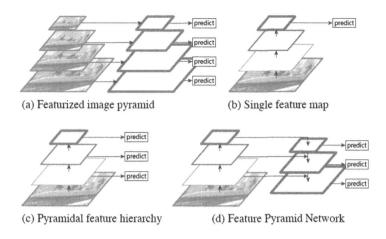

(a) Featurized image pyramid   (b) Single feature map

(c) Pyramidal feature hierarchy   (d) Feature Pyramid Network

Fig. 4. Different feature pyramid architectures [9].

overfitting tendency due to data scarcity [23]. For consistency, all models used in this study utilized backbones pretrained on the ImageNet dataset.

Learning rate, is arguably one of the most important hyperparameter that significantly influences model performance [24]. Instead of empirically choosing the learning rate, the proposed model was trained using a learning rate finder as a guide. The learning rate finder was first introduced in [25]. In combination with the Ranger optimizer [26], this allowed the proposed model to be trained quickly with less overfit on the training dataset. Figure 5 illustrates the learning rate finder plot showing the optimal learning rate range of values. According to [25] optimal learning rate values lie within the minimum and valley point in the plot where the loss descents most rapidly. The proposed model was trained on a learning rate, $\alpha = 2e - 4$.

All models in this study were trained of a Ubuntu 20.04 LTS with Intel core Intel Core i7-4790K CPU at 4.00GHz, 32GB RAM and a single Nvidia RTX3090 GPU. We utilized the open source PyTorch 1.8.0 [27], IceVision 0.8.0 [28] and Fastai 2.4.1 [21].

3   Results and Discussions

3.1   Performance Metrics

In this section we present the performance of the proposed model against other models (RetinaNet and Faster-RCNN) with different pretrained ResNet backbones. The RetinaNet and Faster-RCNN model is based on the implementation from [15] and [17] respectively. The ResNet architecture is based on the implementation from [4]. The numbers following the model name indicate the number of layers in the ResNet model and the length of pretrained epoch on the ImageNet dataset. For example, ResNet50_2x indicates a 50-layer deep residual

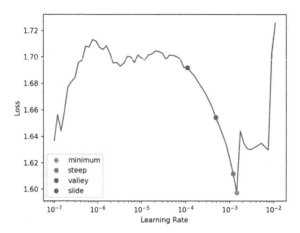

Fig. 5. Learning rate finder algorithm estimates the optimal range of values that results in the rapid decrease in loss function. Show in this figures are four suggested learning rate values: minimum, steep, valley and slide.eps

network trained for 24 epochs (twice the normal training epoch of 12) on the ImageNet dataset.

Table 1 shows cross-model comparison on mAP metric performance on the train, validation and test dataset. We observe that for all models, the mAP on the training dataset surpasses the mAP for the validation and test dataset significantly. The difference in performance could indicate overfitting on the training dataset which is expected given the small amount of available training images. The performance of all models on the validation dataset is close to the test dataset indicating the validation data is representative of the test dataset. The proposed model achieves a mAP of 31.36% on the test dataset, outperforming others.

We observe that ResNet101 backbones tend to perform poorer than ResNet50 backbones. This is also consistent with a plausible overfitting of the training data since ResNet101 twice the number of layers compared to ResNet50 and hence contains significantly more parameters. As for the ResNet pretraining duration, we observe no significant trend in performance on the test dataset. The proposed model outperformed all other models in the mAP metric for the test dataset. Despite similar model architecture, the performance of the proposed model is slightly better compared to RetinaNet-ResNet50_2x on the test dataset. We attribute the performance increase to the training method of the proposed model.

The proposed model was trained with a more recent Ranger optimizer in combination with pre-sizing and progressive resizing while all other models were trained on the Adam optimizer with no pre-sizing and progressive resizing. The combination of Ranger optimizer, pre-sizing and progressive resizing seems to slightly mitigate the overfitting issue encountered across all models. This can also be observed in the validation loss graph of the proposed model as show in

Fig. 6(a). Compared to all other models, the validation loss of the proposed model dived below all the others approximately halfway through training. Note also that the validation loss of all models tend to increase with prolonged duration of training. This shows that increasing training duration contributes to more overfitting. However, the validation loss curve of the proposed model is not only lower than the others, but it does not progress in an upward trend resulting in better performance as shown in Fig. 6(b). For all other models, the validation mAP generally stops improving about halfway through training. However, for the proposed model the validation mAP continue to increase until the end of the training.

Table 1. Mean average precision performance metric on the train, validation and test dataset across all models and backbones.

Model Type	Backbone	mAP (%)		
		Train	Valid.	Test
RetinaNet(Proposed)	ResNet50_2x	52.75	30.01	31.36
RetinaNet	ResNet50_1x	49.63	31.01	29.82
RetinaNet	ResNet50_2x	56.30	29.10	30.27
RetinaNet	ResNet101_1x	53.12	31.24	27.39
RetinaNet	ResNet101_2x	54.27	27.80	28.11
Faster RCNN	ResNet50_1x	48.35	27.42	30.74
Faster RCNN	ResNet50_2x	48.71	27.45	30.37
Faster RCNN	ResNet101_1x	44.82	24.10	24.81
Faster RCNN	ResNet101_2x	47.56	24.85	27.11
FCOS	ResNet50_1x	47.22	22.82	23.16
FCOS	ResNet101_1x	54.65	24.55	24.08

3.2 Inference

We ran the images from the test dataset to visualize the inference bounding boxes in comparison to the ground truth boxes. In Fig. 8, the inference output on a portion of the test dataset images. The top row shows the ground truth images and bounding boxes, while the bottom row shows the inference output from the proposed model. Observe that in Fig. 8(a) and (d) interestingly, the model was able to correctly detect objects that were not labeled in the ground truth image. For example, Fig. 8(d), the model detects "tree" and "intrusion" near the bottom left corner which were absent in the ground truth image. Comparing Fig. 8(b) and (e), the ground truth image was incompletely labeled where the labels for tree and tower were mistakenly left out. However, the bounding boxes on the output image clearly shows that the model was able to detect objects that were not labeled as ground truth. This shows that the model has sufficiently learned good representations of the objects from the training dataset. Comparing to Fig. 8(c)

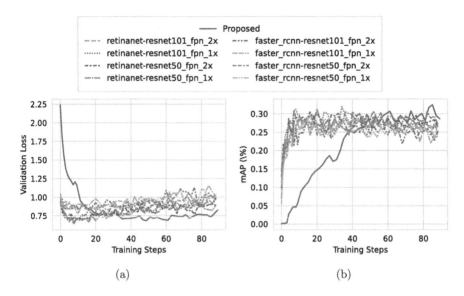

Fig. 6. Validation loss and mean average precision of all models on the validation set during training.

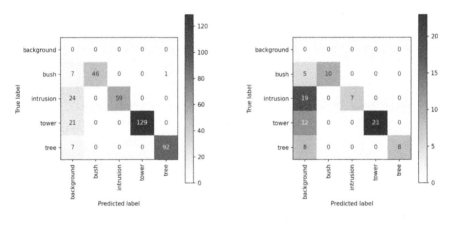

(a) Evaluation on the training dataset.   (b) Evaluation on the test dataset.

Fig. 7. Confusion matrix plot of the proposed model on the train and test dataset.

and (f), the model mistakenly detected the fencing around the transmission tower as an intrusion with low confidence level but correctly identified a patch of bushes not labeled in the ground truth. Figure 7 shows the confusion matrix on the training and test dataset. In both datasets "intrusion" and "tower" were the most frequently mis-detected classes.

Fig. 8. Ground truth with manual annotations (top row) and automatic inference bounding boxes performed by the proposed model (bottom row).

4   Conclusion

In this study we proposed the use of a RetinaNet deep learning-based object detection model for automatic detection of activities and features in outdoor industrial images. We also introduced a model training framework for use with very small datasets. This new model training framework was benchmarked with various deep learning based object detectors using the available dataset. The comparison showed that the introduced training framework resulted in a lower validation loss and a higher mAP metric, even with scarce data availability. Our model achieves the highest mAP of 31.36% on the test dataset, outperforming others.

References

1. Zhou, W., Yang, Y., Yu, C., Liu, J., Duan, X., Weng, Z., Chen, D., Liang, Q., Fang, Q., Zhou, J., et al.: Ensembled deep learning model outperforms human experts in diagnosing biliary atresia from sonographic gallbladder images. Nature Commun. **12**(1), 1–14 (2021)
2. Zhao, Z.-Q., Zheng, P., Xu, S.-T., Wu, X.: Object detection with deep learning: a review. IEEE Trans. Neural Networks Learn. Syst. **30**(11), 3212–3232 (2019)

3. Bochkovskiy, A., Wang, C.-Y., Liao, H.-Y.M.: Yolov4: optimal speed and accuracy of object detection. arXiv preprint arXiv:2004.10934, 2020

4. He, K., Zhang, X., Ren, S., Sun, J.: Deep residual learning for image recognition. In: Proceedings of the IEEE Conference on Computer Vision and Pattern Recognition, pp. 770–778 (2016)

5. Simonyan, K., Zisserman, A.: Very deep convolutional networks for large-scale image recognition. arXiv preprint arXiv:1409.1556 (2014)

6. Tan, M., Le, Q.: Efficientnet: rethinking model scaling for convolutional neural networks. In: International Conference on Machine Learning. PMLR, pp. 6105–6114 (2019)

7. Du, X., et al.: Spinenet: learning scale-permuted backbone for recognition and localization. In: Proceedings of the IEEE/CVF Conference on Computer Vision and Pattern Recognition, pp. 11 592–11 601 (2020)

8. Wang, C.-Y., Liao, H.-Y.M., Wu, Y.-H., Chen, P.-Y., Hsieh, J.-W., Yeh, I.-H.: Cspnet: a new backbone that can enhance learning capability of cnn. In: Proceedings of the IEEE/CVF Conference on Computer Vision and Pattern Recognition Workshops, pp. 390–391 (2020)

9. Lin, T.-Y., Dollár, P., Girshick, R., He, K., Hariharan, B., Belongie, S.: Feature pyramid networks for object detection. In: Proceedings of the IEEE Conference on Computer Vision and Pattern Recognition, pp. 2117–2125 (2017)

10. Tan, M., Pang, R., Le, Q.V.: Efficientdet: scalable and efficient object detection. In: Proceedings of the IEEE/CVF Conference on Computer Vision and Pattern Recognition, pp. 10 781–10 790 (2020)

11. Liu, S., Qi, L., Qin, H., Shi, J., Jia, J.: Path aggregation network for instance segmentation. In: Proceedings of the IEEE Conference on Computer Vision and Pattern Recognition, pp. 8759–8768 (2018)

12. Faster, R.: Towards real-time object detection with region proposal networks. In: Advances in Neural Information Processing Systems, vol. 9199 (2015)

13. Redmon, J., Divvala, S., Girshick, R., Farhadi, A.: You only look once: unified, real-time object detection. In: Proceedings of the IEEE Conference on Computer Vision and Pattern Recognition, pp. 779–788 (2016)

14. Liu, W., Anguelov, D., Erhan, D., Szegedy, C., Reed, S., Fu, C.-Y., Berg, A.C.: SSD: single shot MultiBox detector. In: Leibe, B., Matas, J., Sebe, N., Welling, M. (eds.) ECCV 2016. LNCS, vol. 9905, pp. 21–37. Springer, Cham (2016). https://doi.org/10.1007/978-3-319-46448-0_2

15. T.-Y. Lin, P. Goyal, R. Girshick, K. He, and P. Dollár, "Focal loss for dense object detection. In: Proceedings of the IEEE International Conference on Computer Vision, pp. 2980–2988 (2017)

16. Tian, Z., Shen, C., Chen, H., He, T.: Fcos: fully convolutional one-stage object detection. In: Proceedings of the IEEE/CVF International Conference on Computer Vision, pp. 9627–9636 (2019)

17. Ren, S., He, K., Girshick, R., Sun, J.: Faster r-cnn: Towards real-time object detection with region proposal networks. In: Advances in Neural Information Processing Systems 28, pp. 91–99 (2015)

18. He, K., Gkioxari, G., Dollár, P., Girshick, R.: Mask r-cnn. In: Proceedings of the IEEE International Conference on Computer Vision, pp. 2961–2969 (2017)

19. Dai, J., Li, Y., He, K., Sun, J.: R-fcn: object detection via region-based fully convolutional networks. In: Advances in Neural Information Processing Systems, pp. 379–387 (2016)

20. Yang, Z., Liu, S., Hu, H., Wang, L., Lin, S.: Reppoints: point set representation for object detection. In: Proceedings of the IEEE/CVF International Conference on Computer Vision, pp. 9657–9666 (2019)
21. Howard, J., Gugger, S.: Fastai: a layered api for deep learning. Information **11**(2), 108 (2020)
22. Howard, J.: Deep Learning for Coders with fastai and PyTorch. O'Reilly Media (2020)
23. Bhatt, A., Ganatra, A., Kotecha, K.: Covid-19 pulmonary consolidations detection in chest x-ray using progressive resizing and transfer learning techniques. Heliyon, p. e07211 (2021)
24. Van Rijn, J.N., Hutter, F.: Hyperparameter importance across datasets. In: Proceedings of the 24th ACM SIGKDD International Conference on Knowledge Discovery & Data Mining, pp. 2367–2376 (2018)
25. Smith, L.N.: A disciplined approach to neural network hyper-parameters: Part 1-learning rate, batch size, momentum, and weight decay. arXiv preprint arXiv:1803.09820 (2018)
26. Wright, L., Demeure, N.: Ranger21: a synergistic deep learning optimizer. arXiv preprint arXiv:2106.13731 (2021)
27. Paszke, A., et al.: Pytorch: an imperative style, high-performance deep learning library. Advances in neural information processing systems **32**, 8026–8037 (2019)
28. Vazquez, L., Hassainia, F.: Icevision: an agnostic computer vision framework (2020)

A Comparison of ML and DL Approaches for Crowd Analysis on the Hajj Pilgrimage

Muhammad Nur Hakim Bin Zamri[1] (ID), Junaidi Abdullah[1] (ID), Roman Bhuiyan[1(✉)] (ID),
Noramiza Hashim[1] (ID), Fahmid Al Farid[1] (ID), Jia Uddin[2] (ID), Mohd Nizam Husen[3] (ID),
and Norra Abdullah[4]

[1] Faculty of Computing and Informatics, Multimedia University, Cyberjaya, Persiaran
Multimedia, 63100 Cyberjaya, Malaysia
[2] Technology Studies Department, Endicott College, Woosong University,
Daejeon, South Korea
[3] Malaysian Institute of Information Technology Universiti
Kuala Lumpur, Kuala Lumpur, Malaysia
[4] WSA Venture Australia (M) Sdn Bhd, Rawang, Malaysia

Abstract. In proportion to the growth in human population, there has been a substantial rise in the number of crowds in public places. The more crowded a place, the more risk of stampedes. Therefore, crowd management is very critical to ensure the safety of the crowds. Crowd monitoring is an effective approach to monitor, control and understand the behavior of the density of the crowd. One of the efficient automated video monitoring techniques to ensure public safety is crowd density estimation. Crowd density analysis is used primarily in public areas that are usually crowded with people such as stadiums, parks, shopping malls and railway stations. In this research, crowd density analysis by machine learning is presented. The main purpose of this model is to determine the best machine learning algorithm with the highest performance for crowd density classification. This model is focusing on machine learning algorithms such as traditional machine learning algorithms and deep learning algorithms. For traditional machine learning algorithms, Histogram Oriented Gradients (HOG) and Local Binary Pattern (LBP) have been used to extract important features from the input crowd images before being fed into Support Vector Machine (SVM) for classification. For deep learning algorithms, custom Convolutional Neural Network (CNN) together with two famous CNN architectures named Residual Network (ResNet) and Visual Geometry Group Network (VGGNet) were implemented as other methods in this paper for comparison. Other than that, the performance evaluation of the algorithm was measured based on the accuracy of the models. The performance of all different models was recorded and compared.

Keywords: Crowd analysis · CNN · SVM · ResNet · HOG · VGGNet

1 Introduction

According to sociology, crowds can be defined as a disorganized human grouping formed during a certain period of time. Crowd density refers to the number of objects within a

© Springer Nature Switzerland AG 2021
H. Badioze Zaman et al. (Eds.): IVIC 2021, LNCS 13051, pp. 552–561, 2021.
https://doi.org/10.1007/978-3-030-90235-3_48

unit area, such as number of pedestrians per square meter [1]. As crowd density increases, the degree of mental stress and discomfort also increases. This affects the crowd behavior in which they become more chaotic and difficult to control [2]. In order to resolve safety issues, density is very critical to determine the optimum occupancy of a space, room or building. The analysis of crowd density is essential for security monitoring. The focus area includes public crowded areas such as shopping malls, rail stations and also religious or sports events, where the community is normally packed. Crowd density analysis may be used to help predict suspicious activities and irregular incidents at an early level, study of pedestrian traffic and advice on the construction of public spaces. However, over the past few years, there are many drawbacks faced throughout the studies in this area. Accordingly, crowd density can be quantified into 3 basic classes, which are low, medium and high or 5 classes called very low, low, medium, high, and very high. The qualitative knowledge is useful and various levels of monitoring sensitivity should be paid to crowds of different densities.

There are many crowd tragedies that have happened around the world. Some of the tragedies are 1426 pilgrims (mostly Malaysian and Indonesian) die in a stampede incident inside Al-Ma'aisim tunnel leading to Mecca in July 1990, at least 1000 Shia pilgrims (mostly woman and children) drown in the Tigris River because of panic about suicide bombing rumors in August 2005, up to 375 people die in a crush on a bridge on the Tonle Sap river in November 2010, at least 700 pilgrims die and 450 injured in a stampede near Mecca in September 2015 and many more. This model is a research-based paper on analysis of crowd density images. The paper will be focusing on crowd density classification by using machine learning. The main purpose of this model is to determine the best machine learning algorithm with the highest accuracy. Machine learning techniques that are implemented in this research are traditional machine learning algorithms, SVM and deep learning algorithms, CNN.

In the following order, the paper is presented. Section 2 in the related work; the proposed system is described in depth in Sect. 3. Section 4 you will find result discussion and comparison. Lastly, Sect. 5 the paper conclusion.

2   Related Work

There are various techniques proposed to analysis crowd density such as image processing, machine learning, deep learning and smartphone-based approach [3]. In order to analysis crowd density, the first step is to capture important features from the resources followed by classifying the feature results based on the density levels: very low, low, medium, high and very high [4].

2.1 Image Processing Approach

According to [5] there are two categories of image processing approach to estimate crowd density namely as direct (detection-based) approach and indirect (feature-based) approach. In direct approach, segmentation and classification algorithm is used to identify target objects while in indirect approach, the crowd density is estimated by the combination of feature extractor and machine learning algorithm [6].

For low occlusion situations, direct approach can be applied because it segments each individual from the scene to predict the number of people [3]. However, this approach is not applicable for high crowd situations. Therefore, the improved version of direct approach is implemented by using part-based detection such as head and shoulder detection [3].

Feature-based has become a famous field of study, especially in computer vision [7]. The objective of indirect (feature-based) approach is to extract global and local features from images. There are two methods in indirect approach: Pixel Based Method and Texture based method [3]. Pixel based methods aim to estimate the crowd by extracting very local features from a scene.

In[8] have proposed a method that uses Gaussian Background Modelling and binary image to predict crowd density. Gaussian Background Modelling is able to capture the target recognition, which is the foreground and the fixed background.

Besides that [9] used a CRF model to capture the foreground from the fixed background and get the binary image. The resulting binary image indicates that the white area as foreground and black area as fixed background.

In summary, the pixel-based method is applicable for very low and low crowd scenes with 100% accuracy [3]. However, it is not suitable for high crowd scenarios because it could extract false information.

Texture based method is more robust and accurate than pixel-based method because it captures detailed information from crowd image. Gabor Features, Local Binary Pattern (LBP) and Gray Level Co-occurrence Matrix are some of the methods used in texture feature extraction [3]. Other textures feature based approach is by combining two texture features namely Local Binary Pattern (LBP) and Gabor Filter [7].

2.2 Smartphone-Based Approach

In a smartphone-based approach, a sensing method is proposed where each individual location will be shared through their smartphone. In this case, the exact location of individuals in a crowd is very critical. The main techniques usually used to obtain the location of people are in-phone localization and in-network localization [3].

In[10] proposed a method to estimate crowd density based on the Received Signal Strength Indicator (RSSI) measurements and classify using K-Nearest Neighbors (KNN) classifiers.

2.3 Traditional Machine Learning Approach

Machine Learning is one of the recent techniques used in crowd density analysis [3]. Traditional machine learning is energy and time consuming and also less efficient [2]. There are a few steps involved to estimate crowd density using Machine Learning. Firstly, feature extraction algorithms are used to extract features for different density classes of images. In [10] proposed a method to estimate crowd density by combining RSSI and KNN. The RSSI works as a feature extractor on the input image dataset while KNN acts as a classifier. The result indicates good accuracy performance even though at the minimum cost.

Besides that, [7] proposed a method that used multi-class Support Vector Machine SVM to classify the vector feature result of the combination of LBP and Gabor Filter according to four levels of densities: Free, Restricted, Dense and Very Dense.

2.4 Deep Learning Approach

Deep learning has better robustness and adaptability in crowd density estimation compared to traditional methods [2]. The most famous deep learning algorithm for image classification is CNN. There are 3 main layers in CNN: input layer, hidden layer and output layer [3]. The input image is pushed into the input layer, then provided to a hidden layer that consists of Convolution Layer and Pooling layer for feature extraction [2, 3]. The last layer is an output layer that is also known as a fully-connected layer which performs classification. Pu et al. [4] have proposed two classic CNN, namely as Googlenet and VGGnet to estimate crowd density in surveillance scene.

In addition, [2] have proposed one of the structures in CNN based method which is GoogleNet to estimate crowd density in real-time. The model has been trained to classify crowd images according to 5 levels of density: Very Low, Low, Medium, High and Very High.

Besides that, in [6] the authors have proposed two neural network frameworks, CNN and Long Short-Term Memory (LSTM) to estimate crowd density from the crowd video. The first person that proposed this method is Hochreiter [11] to prevent the limitation in vanishing gradient.

2.5 Density Based Method

Detection and tracking are critical for crowd dynamics modeling because they provide the position and velocity characteristics of pedestrian dynamics. Counting camera systems [12], tablet sensors [13], and Wi-Fi sensors are examples of automated sensor technologies used in crowd dynamics. However, trained detectors are prone to failing in congested or dense groups. Counting by regression, as opposed to counting by detection, is based on hand-crafted features such as SIFT [14], HOG [15], and VLAD [16].

3   Proposed Research Method

Figure 1 indicates the general structure of this crowd density analysis research. Firstly, data collection is performed to gather related and useful datasets for the crowd density analysis. The dataset that is required for this project is a set of crowd images according to very low, low, medium, high and very high density. Secondly, these datasets has performed data cleaning process before it can be used for the next process. Thirdly, the preprocessed data undergo a feature extraction process to select and extract important and valuable features for the further analysis. Fourthly the feature extraction is fed into the classifier to get the output class. The output of the classification will be the density classes: very low, low, medium, high and very high.

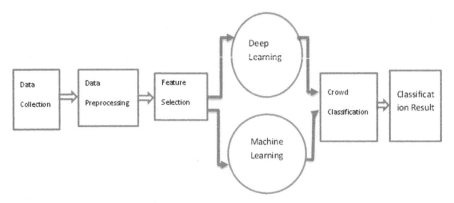

Fig. 1. Proposed crowd density analysis model

3.1 Data Collection

There are two image datasets that have been used in this project: Masjidil Haram dataset and Sai dataset. Both of the datasets are collected from the youtube live broadcast and captured by using video recording software such as Bandicam.

Masjidil Haram dataset. The dataset was collected from camera footage and live broadcast of annual hajj pilgrimage performed by Muslims to the Kaaba in Mecca. All of the images showed the view of pilgrims performing tawaf around the beautiful Kaaba. The frames of the video have been extracted and saved into jpg file format for further analysis. The dataset contains a total of 1250 crowd images with 250 very high density images, 250 high density images, 250 medium density images, 250 low density images and 250 very low density images.

Sai Dataset. Sai dataset is CCTV footage of muslims pilgrimage walk and run seven times between Mount Safa and Mount Marwah. The frames of the video have been extracted and saved into jpg file format for further analysis. The dataset contains a total of 2598 crowd images with 534 very high density images, 548 high density images, 512 medium density images, 504 low density images and 500 very low density images. Figure 2 example of the dataset as below:

3.2 Pre-processing

Pre-processing in this project can be defined as the transformations on the original crowd image dataset before it is fed into the machine learning or deep learning algorithm. Below are the pre-processes that will be done:

- **Data Partition** – In this project, the image datasets were partitioned into 80% for train and 20% for test
- **Image scaling** - In this project, the width and height of the crowd images will be resized to 224 × 224 pixels.
- **Image normalization** - The image pixel values are normalized (divide by 255) to get the values within the range 1 and 0.

Fig. 2. Proposed dataset

3.3 Feature Selection

The feature extraction model for traditional machine learning approaches is the LBP algorithm. The computation of LBP is by comparing the center pixel of an input image with the 8-neighborhood pixel (sometimes N- neighborhood). If the neighborhood pixel is bigger than the center, then the LBP for this location will be '1', otherwise '0'. Then, binary value is converted into decimal value. After extracting the important features from the input image, the final process will be the classification of features according to its density: very low, low, medium, high and very high density. For traditional machine learning, the machine learning model that is implemented to train the features is SVM.

4 Result Discussion and Comparisons

4.1 LBP with SVM

Table 1 and Table 2 show the accuracy results of LBP with SVM model using Sai and Masjidil Haram dataset respectively. For the Sai dataset, the overall accuracy that can be achieved by LBP with the SVM model is 86.6%. It also has high accuracy in predicting the class density for very low, medium and high with 93.75%, 92.5% and 90% respectively. Besides that, the overall accuracy of LBP with SVM using the Sai Masjidil Haram dataset is 78.81%.

Table 1. Accuracy results of LPB with SVM using Sai dataset

Model	Very low	Low	Medium	High	Very high	Overall
LBP with SVM	93.75	68.75	92.5	90.5	87.5	86.6

4.2 CNN

Table 3 and Table 4 shows the accuracy results of CNN model using Sai and Masjidil Haram dataset respectively. For the Sai dataset, the overall accuracy that can be achieved

Table 2. Accuracy results of LPB with SVM using Masjidil Haram dataset

Model	Very low	Low	Medium	High	Very high	Overall
LBP with SVM	83.75	82.3	72.5	75	80.5	78.81

is 88.25%. It also has high accuracy in predicting the class density for very low, low and high with 91.25%, 96.25% and 98.75% respectively. However, the accuracy to predict medium density class is quite low with only 67.5%. Besides that, the overall accuracy of CNN using the Masjidil Haram dataset is 85.6%. It also has high accuracy in predicting the very low class density with 90% accuracy.

Table 3. Accuracy results of CNN using Sai dataset

Model	Very low	Low	Medium	High	Very high	Overall
CNN	91.25	96.25	67.5	98.75	90.0	87.5

Table 4. Accuracy results of CNN using Masjidil Haram dataset

Model	Very low	Low	Medium	High	Very high	Overall
CNN	90	87	80	83	89.0	88

4.3 ResNet

Table 5 and Table 6 show the accuracy results of the ResNet model using Sai and Masjidil Haram dataset respectively. For the Sai dataset, the overall accuracy that can be achieved is 84.75%. It also has high accuracy in predicting the class density for very high with 93.75% accuracy and high with 98.75% accuracy. By using Masjidil Haram dataset, ResNet is able to achieve up to 88% overall accuracy. It also has high accuracy in predicting the very high and very low density category with 92% and 91.25% respectively.

Table 5. Accuracy results of ResNet using Sai dataset

Model	Very low	Low	Medium	High	Very high	Overall
ResNet	56.25	83.75	91.25	98.75	93.75	84.75

4.4 VGGNet

Table 7 and Table 8 show the accuracy results of the VGGNet model using Sai and Masjidil Haram dataset respectively. For the Sai dataset, the overall accuracy that can be

Table 6. Accuracy results of ResNet using Masjidil Haram dataset

Model	Very low	Low	Medium	High	Very high	Overall
ResNet	91.25	90	89	84	92	89.25

achieved is up to 90%. It also has high accuracy in predicting the class density for very low with 92.5%, high with 91.25% and very high with 95.5% accuracy. In addition, the overall accuracy of VGGNet using Masjidil Haram dataset is 89.35%. It also has high accuracy in predicting the class density for very low density and very high density with 92.5% and 91% respectively.

Table 7. Accuracy results of VGGNet using Sai dataset

Model	Very low	Low	Medium	High	Very high	Overall
VGGNet	92.5	83.75	82.50	91.25	95.5	90

Table 8. Accuracy results of VGGNet using Masjidil Haram dataset

Model	Very low	Low	Medium	High	Very high	Overall
VGGNet	92.5	86	89	88.25	91	89.35

4.5 Comparison

Figure 3(a) shows the accuracy for every model by each density class named as very low, low, medium, high and very high by training and testing on Sai dataset. The bar graph includes the accuracy of traditional machine learning algorithms that have been experimented in this project such as SVM, and LBP with SVM also deep learning approaches such as custom CNN, VGGNet and ResNet. From the graph, we can make a comparison and determine the best machine learning algorithm for a specific density class. For very low density class, LBP with SVM has the best performance with 93.75% accuracy. For low density class, CNN has the highest accuracy with 96.25% accuracy. For medium class density, SVM has the highest test accuracy with 98.75% accuracy. For high class density, both CNN and ResNet from deep learning approach have the highest performance with 98.75% accuracy. Lastly, VGGNet has the highest accuracy for very high density with 95.5% accuracy. Figure 3(b). Indicates the accuracy for every model CNN, ResNet and VGGNet have the best performance in which all three models are able to achieve more than 90% accuracy. For low density class, ResNet has the highest accuracy with 90% accuracy. For medium class density, both VGGNet and ResNet from deep learning approach have the highest performance with 89% accuracy. For high class density, VGGNet has the highest test accuracy with 88.25% accuracy. Lastly, ResNet,

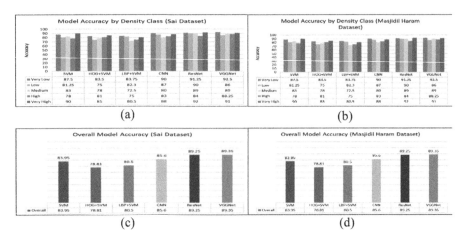

Fig. 3. 3(a) Model accuracy by density class using Sai dataset, 3(b) Model accuracy by density class using Masjidil Haram dataset, 3(c) Overall model accuracy using Sai dataset, 3(d) Overall model accuracy using Masjidil Haram dataset.

VGGNet and SVM are the top 3 highest accuracy for very high density with 92%, 91% and 90% respectively. Figure 3(c). Indicates the overall test accuracy for each of the models proposed HOG with SVM and VGGNet is among the top models with the highest overall performance as both models are able to achieve 90.5% and 90% accuracy respectively. Other than that, CNN is at the third place with 88.25% accuracy, followed by SVM, LBP with SVM and ResNet with 87.75%, 86.6% and 84.75% respectively. Figure 3(d). Shows the accuracy of the ResNet and VGGNet are among the top models with the highest overall performance as both models are able to achieve 89.25% and 89.35% accuracy respectively. Other than that, CNN is at the third place with 85.6% accuracy, followed by SVM, LBP with SVM and HOG with SVM with 83.95%, 80.5% and 78.81% respectively.

5   Conclusion

In summary, for this project, we address a problem to implement machine learning and computer vision algorithms to predict density class based on input of crowd images. We have proposed two algorithms, traditional machine learning algorithms and deep learning algorithms. We try to justify and determine the best model to predict crowd density with the highest performance. From all of the experiments that have been done, both traditional machine learning algorithms and deep learning algorithms that we have proposed are able to perform well in estimating the density of crowd images especially when we trained using Sai dataset. From the outcome of this project, some future work that can be done is to add people counting estimation functions in order to improve the performance of the model as our project only focuses on the estimation of density based on the features generated from the input of crowd images. Besides that, this project is only focusing on training the machine learning models by using crowd image datasets.

Acknowledgements. Multimedia University, Cyberjaya, Malaysia fully supported this research and this research also supported from the FRDGS Grant from the Multimedia University, Cyberjaya, Malaysia.

References

1. Ma, W., Huang, L., Liu, C.: Crowd density analysis using co- occurrence texture features. In: Proceeding - 5th International Conference Computer Science Convergance Informayion Technology, ICCIT 2010, pp. 170–175 (2010). https://doi.org/10.1109/ICCIT.2010.5711051.
2. Li, B., Han, X., Wu, D.: Real-time crowd density estimation based on convolutional neural networks. In: Proceedings - 3rd International Conference Intelligent Transport Big Data Smart City, ICITBS 2018, vol. 2018-Janua, pp. 690–694 (2018). https://doi.org/10.1109/ICITBS.2018.00179
3. Ahuja, K.R., Charniya, N.N.: A survey of recent advances in crowd density estimation using image processing. In: Proceedings 4th International Conference Communications Electronic System, ICCES 2019, no. Icces, pp. 1207–1213 (2019). https://doi.org/10.1109/ICCES45898.2019.9002291
4. Pu, S., Song, T., Zhang, Y., Xie, D.: Estimation of crowd density in surveillance scenes based on deep convolutional neural network. Procedia Comput. Sci. **111**, 154–159 (2017). https://doi.org/10.1016/j.procs.2017.06.022
5. Saleh, S.A.M., Suandi, S.A., Ibrahim, H.: Recent survey on crowd density estimation and counting for visual surveillance. Eng. Appl. Artif. Intell. **41**, 103–114 (2015). https://doi.org/10.1016/j.engappai.2015.01.007
6. Anees, M.V., Kumar, S.G.: Deep learning framework for density estimation of crowd videos. In: Proceedings 2018 8th International Symposium Embedded Computer System Design ISED 2018, pp. 16–20 (2018). https://doi.org/10.1109/ISED.2018.8704051
7. Pai, A.K., Karunakar, A.K., Raghavendra, U.: A novel crowd density estimation technique using local binary pattern and Gabor features. In: 2017 14th IEEE International Conference Advanced Video Signal Based Surveillance, AVSS 2017, no. January 2018, (2017). https://doi.org/10.1109/AVSS.2017.8078556
8. Liu, S., Xie, K., Zhu, Z., Ma, D.: Research on the estimation of crowd density based on video image processing. In: Proceedings - 2016 International Conference Industrial Informatics - Computer Technology, Intelligent Technology, Industries Information Integration, ICIICII 2016, pp. 10–13 (2017). https://doi.org/10.1109/ICIICII.2016.0014
9. Yanqin, W., Zujun, Y., Yao, W., Xingxin, L.: Crowd density estimation based on conditional random field and convolutional neural networks. In: 2019 14th IEEE International Conference Electronics Measurement Instruments, ICEMI 2019, pp. 1814–1819 (2019). https://doi.org/10.1109/ICEMI46757.2019.9101551
10. Taha, M., Atallah, R., Dwiek, O., Bata, F.: Crowd estimation based on RSSI measurements using kNN classification. In: 2020 3rd International Conference Intelligent Autonomous System, ICoIAS 2020, pp. 67–70 (2020). https://doi.org/10.1109/ICoIAS49312.2020.9081850
11. Hochreiter, S., Schmidhuber, J.: Long short-term memory. Neural Comput. **9**(8), 1735–1780 (1997). https://doi.org/10.1162/neco.1997.9.8.1735
12. Duives, D., Daamen, W., Hoogendoorn, S.: Monitoring the number of pedestrians in an area: the applicability of counting systems for density state estimation. J. Adv. Transp. (2018)
13. Nagao, K., Yanagisawa, D., Nishinari, K.: Estimation of crowd density ap- plying wavelet transform and machine learning. Physica A **510**, 145–163 (2018)
14. Lowe, D.G.: Distinctive image features from scale-invariant keypoints. Int. J. Comput. Vision **60**, 91–110 (2004)
15. Dalal, N., Triggs, B.: Histograms of oriented gradients for human detection. In: Proceedings of the IEEE Conference on Computer Vision and Pattern Recognition, pp. 886–893 (2005)
16. Jegou, H., Perronnin, F., Douze, M., Sánchez, J., Perez, P., Schmid, C.: Aggregating local image descriptors into compact codes. IEEE Trans. Pattern Anal. Mach. Intell. **34**, 1704–1716 (2012)

Movement Estimation Using Mediapipe BlazePose

Ainun Syarafana Binti Pauzi, Firdaus Bin Mohd Nazri, Salisu Sani,
Ahmad Mwfaq Bataineh, Muhamad Nurul Hisyam, Mohd Hafiidz Jaafar(iD),
Mohd Nadhir Ab Wahab(iD), and Ahmad Sufril Azlan Mohamed(✉)(iD)

School of Computer Sciences, Universiti Sains Malaysia, Minden, 11800 Penang, Malaysia
sufril@usm.my

Abstract. The paper describes a system to track the body movement of a person
from a video source while augmenting the labelled skeleton joints onto the body
of the person. This work has endless applications in the real world especially in
the physical-demanding working environment as well as in the sports industry by
implementing deep learning, the techniques can recognize the joints on a person's
body. An algorithm namely Mediapipe Blazepose has been applied using PoseNet
dataset to detect and estimate curated movements specifically designed for body
injury during heavy workload. The propose method has been compared to IMU
based motion capture and the difference accuracy is within 10% since IMU capture
real data of the sensors while the deep learning method using 2D image analysis.
The expected outcome from this project is a working system that is able to correctly
identify and label the skeleton joints on a person's body as well as perform various
calculation such as movement velocity and the angle of joints which could be
crucial for determining whether certain body movements could result in injuries
either in the short- or long-term period.

Keywords: Marker-less · Motion capture · Deep learning · Marker-based

1 Introduction

In the current augmented reality field, there exists numerous marker-based motion captured software which uses markers which are attached to a suit that has to be worn by
the subject. These markers act as sensors which will give input to the motion capture
software which will then calculate the subject's location and thus displaying the subject
to the display screen [1]. This model of motion capture is costly as it requires designated
tools such as the markers as well as specialized camera. Although the marker-based
system cost is high, the accuracy is very satisfactory [2, 3].

There are many applications such as Microsoft Kinect which uses Time-of-Flight
(ToF) and other sensors which uses Dynamic Time Warp (DTW) that measures the
distance of IR sensors and the time it takes to return to the sensor due to its reflections
[4, 5]. However, the data captured consists of heavy noise as the data captured everything
seen from the IR sensor and camera [6]. Other technology such as Inertia Measuring Unit

© Springer Nature Switzerland AG 2021
H. Badioze Zaman et al. (Eds.): IVIC 2021, LNCS 13051, pp. 562–571, 2021.
https://doi.org/10.1007/978-3-030-90235-3_49

(IMU) has the advantageous of capturing only the needed movements of the sensors; gyroscopes and accelerometer, in real time however, due to its hardware dependent system, a dedicated connection is needed, and sensors can be influenced by wireless reception and earth gravity giving some noise or error in detection. IMU is very useful as the system not required visual field to tracking a motion [7] (see Table 1).

Table 1. Comparisons of marker-less motion capture.

Software	Strength	Weakness
Microsoft Kinect [15]	Users are more free to explore the functionalities and can create their own variation of product	No support from Microsoft. User needs to tweak software on their own
Kinetisense [16]	The screen can be customized from a wide selection of 75 assessment which could prove beneficial for a more comprehensive workflow	Offers assessment for performance and sport but nothing beyond it. The focus of the application is just the analysis of motion
Human trak [17]	Real-time display of important data overlayed on the user. Among the data that could be displayed are the joint range of motion and balance metrics	For the top-tier hardware and performance, users are looking at an expensive yearly subscription when compared with other options in the market
Inertia measuring unit [7]	Uses real-time sensors capturing from gyroscope and accelerometer	Need dedicated network connection and prone to earth gravity noise

Therefore, the aim of this work is to explore a marker less motion capture method that is able to perform skeleton joint detection using 2D images that are more accessible to the general public. This would reduce the cost of motion capture as tools that are readily available [8].

2 Related Works

The existing system in the market also has a hard time detecting limbs that are performing fast paced movement or even subjects that are equipped with loose clothing. Furthermore, if the subject is placed far away from the camera, this will also result in poor tracking of their joints [9]. Another problem that existing systems have is detecting torso bending which is due to the systems unable to perform depth estimation correctly from the images obtained from the front part of the body and the inability to sense the back part of the body [10, 14].

Apart from that, the current existing system in the market does not provide an indication when a risk-prone injury movement is being performed by a subject. The risk-prone movement needs to be identified by the user of the system by further analysis using the data obtained from the system. The use of deep learning able to eliminate the complication of the hardware and by using the 2D digital image, features can be extracted and accurately in recognizing the human structure while using a suitable human pose dataset [11, 12]. The sparse Inertial Measurement Unit will paired with the Deep Learning model earlier gives a better estimation for the system for a more accurate detection of the joints. However, IMU [13] sensors need to be placed on subjects' body which irritates the process and constant recalibration needed due to its prone to magnetic interference.

The aim of the study is to propose a method that leads to marker-less motion capture with deep learning implementation to correctly recognized human body pose and movements. The threefold objectives that leads to the aim of the study are mainly focusing on integrating deep learning model for correctly estimating the movement of the body joints, to measure the distance between one joint to another creating the skeleton frames with each joint record individual velocity and angle at every successive frames, and to compare the accuracy between the proposed marker-less method and the marker-based motion capture.

3 Methodology

This proposed method aims to automatically give an indication during a risk-prone movement is being perform by a subject. Apart from that, existing motion capture that is in the market has a hard time capturing the motion of limbs accurately especially when subject is equipped with loose clothing or during subject performing motions that are fast paced. Furthermore, if the subject is placed far away from the camera, this will also result in poor tracking of their joints. In addition, movement such as torso bending makes the existing system of motion capture have a hard time detecting these movements accurately.

3.1 Application Architecture

The architecture of the proposed method is shown in Fig. 1 below, where the system is divided into 2 major subsections which are the front-end and the back-end. The front-end of the system involves in getting user input as well as displaying the necessary information to the user. The back-end of the system is responsible in processing the input provided by the user to produce an understandable output to be used by the user for further analysis. The underlying modules contained within the application architecture will be explained in the same order from the user of the system launches the program until the user exits the program.

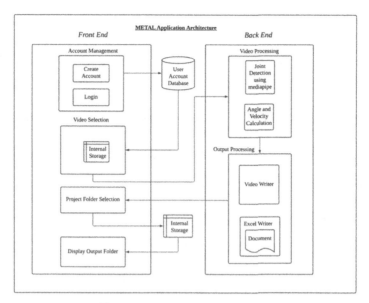

Fig. 1. System architecture diagram

3.2 Video Processing

The main focus of the method is the Video Processing module. The input video will be processed frame-by-frame, meaning that each frame of image of the video will be processed independently. The system will first take the first frame of the video and employs the holistic functionality of Mediapipe BlazePose. This package is a pretrained model package which was developed by Google. The difference between this model as compared to other models in the market is that mediapipe is able to accurately track human body pose almost in real-time. Mediapipe also offers more key points (33 key points) as compared to other body pose detection model which generally are built based on Common Objects in Context (COCO) topology (17 key points). Figure 2 below illustrates the pose detected by BlazePose model. The COCO topology is colored in green whereas the blue key points are the included key points offered by BlazePose model [12].

The difference in the number of key points is among the factors that allows Mediapipe to process the image input almost in real-time. For the sake of our system, we will only display 12 different key points which have been determined to be the most vital key points for analysis of body angle. Body parts such as feet, hand and face which are also detected by Mediapipe BlazePose are ignored by the calculation modules since they are not related to angle calculation.

Mediapipe's BlazePose algorithm works by utilizing two-step-detector-tracker Machine Learning pipeline. The pipeline will first locate the person's region-of-interest (ROI) within the frame. Once the ROI is determined, the tracker will predict the pose landmarks within the ROI. In the system's case, the detector will be invoked only in the first frame. For subsequent frames, the pipeline will derive the ROI of the new frame

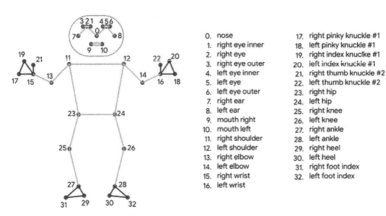

Fig. 2. COCO model in green, BlazePose model is inclusion of blue key points (Color figure online)

from the previous frame's pose landmarks. This is also one of many reasons that allows Mediapipe BlazePose to compute the landmark poses in almost real-time. The Pose Detection model of Mediapipe BlazePose is trained from an image dataset containing around 85,000 images including 30,000 of the images obtained from consented images of people using a mobile AR application captured with smartphone cameras in various "in-the-wild" conditions.

The model is used for predicting the human body center (middle of hip). Once the body center is determined, Mediapipe will use the body center to determine the pose landmarks located within the radius from the body center. Once the pose landmarks have successfully detected by Mediapipe BlazePose, the results will be stored in variables to denote the x and y coordinates of the respective pose landmark. Each pose landmark of a body part will be stored in different variable which will be used later for angle and velocity calculation.

Once the x and y coordinates have been obtained from the joint detection module, the values of the x and y coordinates will be passed to the angle and velocity calculation module. This module will perform mathematical computation based on the coordinates of the joint-of-interest and its 2 respective adjacent body parts connected to the joint-of-interest. This calculation is performed based on the mathematical principle called "The Law of Cosines" as shown in Eq. (1).

$$a^2 = b^2 + c^2 - 2bc \cos A \tag{1}$$

We can see that the formula (1) is used to calculate the length of side a given that the information of side b and c as well as angle A is known. For the case of our system, we need to rearrange the equation to a different form since we are interested in finding the angle A given that we have the values for side a, b and c. Rearranging the equation above for our system's will yield us the equation below in Eqs. (2–4).

$$2bc \cos A = b^2 + c^2 - a^2 \tag{2}$$

$$\cos A = \frac{b^2 + c^2 - a^2}{2bc} \tag{3}$$

$$A = cos^{-1}\left(\frac{b^2 + c^2 - a^2}{2bc}\right) \tag{4}$$

Now that the equation to compute the angle has been determined, we just have to pass the necessary arguments to the calculation module function.

To understand the approached used in the module, we will assume that we are interested in the angle of the right elbow labelled "13" in Fig. 2. The adjacent connected body parts of the right elbow are the right wrist labelled "15" and the right shoulder labelled "11". We can see visually that these 3 points make up a triangle which is why this particular principle can be used to calculate the angle of joint-of-interest. Since the joint-of-interest is the right elbow, we would need to find the distance between point "15" of the right wrist and point "11" of the right shoulder and denote it as a for the rearranged equation from The Law of Cosines.

The variable **b** of the equation will be taken from the distance between point "11" of the right shoulder and point "13" of the right elbow. Consequently, the c of the equation will be taken from the distance between point "13" of the right elbow and point "15" of the right wrist. The value of b and c can be interchanged since it does not affect the value of the angle. However, the value of a in the equation needs to be the value of the distance between the two adjacent connected body parts since it is the joint-of-interest. The distance between the two points can be calculated using the mathematical concept of the Distance Formula as shown in Eq. 5.

$$d = \sqrt{(x_2 - x_1)^2 + (y_2 - y_1)^2} \tag{5}$$

Since we had acquired the x and y coordinates of each joint from the joint detection module above, we can use these values to compute the distance between them. The distance value computed will be stored in a separate variable to be used by the angle calculation module above. For instance, we would need to pass the x and y coordinates of point "11" of the right shoulder and point "15" of the right wrist to the distance formula to get the distance between them. Once all the necessary distance variables have been calculated, we then pass the values to compute the angle of the joint-of-interest. For the velocity calculation, we employ the formula as Eq. 6.

$$v = \frac{d}{t} \tag{6}$$

where, v = speed, d = distance travelled and t is time taken.

From the equation above, we can see that in order to determine the velocity of a joint, we would need to determine the distance travelled in a given second. To do this, we can apply the same equation for distance above. For instance, if we were to compute the velocity of the right wrist labelled number "15" in a particular second, we would need to know the distance that the joint has travelled in a second. Since we already know the location of the particular joint in *0th* second and 1st second, we can use the distance formula to calculate the distance travelled by that particular joint in one second. However, the distance computed is the distance in terms of pixel. Thus, we need a reference of an object that we know the real-life length. The purpose of the real-life reference is for us to obtain a ratio between the pixel distance to the real-life distance. This is done by measuring beforehand the real-life distance between the right shoulder and the right hip of a participant. Once this length has been determined, we can set a variable of this constant. The next step is to measure the pixel distance between the right shoulder and the right hip of the participant which could be done by finding the distance between these two points that we have obtained in the joint detection module earlier. These two points will then be divided to obtain a ratio which will be used to multiply with the pixel distance travelled by a joint to obtain the real-life distance value travelled by that particular joint. This process is done on 4 different joints which are the left wrist, right wrist, left ankle and the right ankle. These 4 joints are chosen for the velocity calculation due to the nature that these joints are the joints identified to move at a higher speed and are more prone to injury due to speed.

3.3 Output Processing

After the angles and velocities of the joints has been calculated, these values will then be displayed on the respective image that was processed. Simultaneously, while the system is processing the frames in a video until it reaches the end, the calculated angles and velocities will be stored in an array. Once the frame processed reaches the end, this array will then be stored using 2 arrays, the angles array and the velocity array as input.

Since the reliability of the method will be based on the "gold standard" of the Inertial Measuring Unit (IMU), the calibration of the sensors are calibrated for offsets, scale factors and alignment errors in x,y and z-axes which can be formalized as:

$$w' = C_w S_w w' + b_w \tag{7}$$

$$a' = C_a S_a a' + b_a \tag{8}$$

where, w', a' are the true angular velocity and acceleration, b_w, b_c are the biases, C_w, C_a are the rotation matrices representing the misalignment between the actual and nominal sensitivity axes of the sensors, and S_w, S_a are the diagonal matrices containing the scale factors of the three axes of each sensor [18]. The calibration needs manual adjustment until the IMU sensors are aligned to the markers preset by the system. A controlled movements are needed so offsets measurement can be done by aligning the 2D plots of the proposed method with the 3D plots of the IMU (without the Z-axis).

4 Results

Comparisons were made between the proposed method and Rokoko Smartsuit (using IMU). Since Rokoko Smartsuit comes with real-time sensor reading of gyroscope and accelerometer which is the basis of IMU components, the data generated by the Rokoko smartsuit is used as the gold standard (Fig. 3).

The capture data are then compared frame-by-frame and evaluated based on its velocity, angles and x-y coordinates. The data that will be used for comparison is determined to be compared by each second. This means that for each second that passes by from

(a)   (b)

Fig. 3. The figure shows the comparisons between the proposed method and IMU where (a) is the initial pose with both hands raised up. The lower left is showing the IMU representation. (b) is the squatting position with both hands raised straight towards the camera. The camera is capturing simultaneously with IMU to get accurate readings.

the input video, an average value of a particular joint will be computed in order to be compared from the two sets of data. This is done because the output data that Rokoko provides comes at 100 frames per second whereas our system takes the video recording from a camera that is able to record only at 60 frames per second. To get an accurate representation for the comparison, an average value within one second will be taken. Table 2 shows the mean difference (%) between the data generated from the proposed method.

Table 2. Mean differences (%) between the proposed method and IMU.

Joint	Mean difference (%)
Right elbow	8.06
Left elbow	7.72
Right knee	10.99
Left knee	6.30
Right hip	0.19
Left hip	0.52
Right shoulder	23.67
Left shoulder	24.57

The table shown above exhibits the mean difference of approximately mean difference of 10% overall with the shoulder having the worst mean differences (Right: 23.67% and Left: 24.57%). The differences at the shoulders exist when each shoulder and arm are at the same angle which confuses the algorithm to estimate the joints' location.

5   Conclusion and Future Work

Based on the findings and interpretation of the results from the analysis performed on the developed system, it is apparent that proposed method has meet the functional and non-functional requirement that has been determined beforehand. The algorithms and implementation used has been selected properly and accurately for marker-less motion capture analysis.

In the future, improvements could be made to measure at two different perspectives and videos to be processed simultaneously and could provide a better output data for a more accurate representation for the angles and velocity calculations. Another improvement that could be adopted is to auto clean wrong joint detection made due to noise of the image or occlusion of one arm to the other side.

Acknowledgement. The authors are grateful to the Ministry of Higher Education Malaysia for Fundamental Research Grant Scheme with Project Code: FRGS/1/2020/STG07/USM/02/12 for supporting this documented work.

Conflicts of Interest. The authors declare that they have no conflicts of interest to report regarding the present study.

References

1. Eldar, R., Fisher-Gewirtzman, D.: Ergonomic design visualization mapping- developing an assistive model for design activities. Int. J. Ind. Ergon. **74**, 102859 (2019)
2. Maurice, P., et al.: Human movement and ergonomics: an industry-oriented dataset for collaborative robotics. Int. J. Robot. Res. **38**(14), 1529–1537 (2019)
3. Yunus, M.N.H., Jaafar, M.H., Mohamed, A.S.A., Azraai, N.Z., Hossain, M.: Implementation of kinetic and kinematic variables in ergonomic risk assessment using motion capture simulation: a review. Int. J. Environ. Res. Public Health**18**, 8342 (2021)
4. Bortolini, M., Gamberi, M., Pilati, F., Regattieri, A.: Automatic assessment of the ergonomic risk for manual manufacturing and assembly activities through optical motion capture technology. Procedia CIRP **72**, 81–86 (2018)
5. Zhang, Z., Fang, Q., Gu, X.: Objective assessment of upper-limb mobility for poststroke rehabilitation. IEEE Trans. Biomed. Eng. **63**, 859–868 (2016)
6. Ong, Z.C., Seet, Y.C., Khoo, S.Y., Noroozi, S.: Development of an economic wireless human motion analysis device for quantitative assessment of human body joint. Measurement **115**, 306–15 (2018)
7. Fletcher, S.R., Johnson, T.L., Thrower, J.: A study to trial the use of inertial non-optical motion capture for ergonomic analysis of manufacturing work. Proc. Inst. Mech. Eng. Part B: J. Eng. Manuf. **232**(1), 90–98 (2018)
8. Brownlee, J., What is Deep Learning? Accessed 25 Oct 2020. https://machinelearningmastery.com/what-is-deep-learning/ (2020)
9. Plantard, P., Auvinet, E., Le Pierres, A.S., Multon, F.: Pose estimation with a kinect for ergonomic studies: evaluation of the accuracy using a virtual mannequin. Sensors (Switzerland) **15**(1), 1785–1803 (2015)

10. Wang, X., Hu, Y.H., Lu, M.L., Radwin, R.G.: The accuracy of a 2D video-based lifting monitor. Ergonomics **62**(8), 1043–1054 (2019)
11. Schechter, S.: What is markerless Augmented Reality? Retrieved October 26, 2020. https://www.marxentlabs.com/what-is-markerless-augmented-reality-dead-reckoning/. Accessed 20 Oct 2020
12. Bazarevsky, V.: BlazePose: On-device Real-time Body Pose tracking. Accessed 18 Jun 2021. https://arxiv.org/abs/2006.10204 (2021)
13. Alessandro, F., Norbert, S, Markus, M., Gabriele, B., Emanuele R., Didier S.: Survey of motion tracking methods based on inertial sensors: a focus on upper limb human motion. Sensors **17**, 1257 (2017)
14. Mohamed, A.S.A., Chingeng, P.S., Mat Isa, N.A., Surip, S.S.: Body matching algorithm using normalize dynamic time warping (NDTW) skeleton tracking for traditional dance movement. In: Badioze Zaman, H. et al. (eds.) Advances in Visual Informatics. IVIC 2017. Lecture Notes in Computer Science, vol. 10645, pp. 669-680 Springer, Cham (2017). https://doi.org/10.1007/978-3-319-70010-6_62
15. Warren, T.: A closer look at Microsoft's new Kinect sensor. https://www.theverge.com/2019/2/25/18239860/microsoft-kinect-azure-dk-hands-on-mwc-2019. Accessed 28 Nov 2020
16. Kinetisense. What Is a Functional Movement Screening? (2020). https://www.kinetisense.com/a-functional-movement-screen/. Accessed 28 Nov 2020
17. VALD Performance (n.d.). News and Research. https://valdperformance.com/blog/. Accessed 28 Nov 2020
18. Mourkani, S.S.: IMU-based Suit for Strength Exercises: Design, Calibration and Track (Phd Thesis), Technische Universitat Kaiserslautern, Germany (2021)

Energy Informatics and Digital Innovation

Awareness on Energy Efficient Products as Prediction on Intention to Subscribe to and Purchase Energy Efficient Services and Products

Husni Mohd Radzi[(✉)], Farhaniza Ghazali, Nurshuhaida Mohd Shokri, and Hazleen Aris

Universiti Tenaga Nasional, Jalan IKRAM-UNITEN, 43000 Kajang, Malaysia
{Husni,farhaniza,nurshuhaida,hazleen}@uniten.edu.my

Abstract. Issues related to high energy consumption is contemporary and concerning socio-politic situation in this country. Thus, the study aims at gauging public awareness on energy efficient products that have been in the market and how this awareness may indicate the future intentions of consumers in subscribing to and purchasing energy efficient services and products. The data were gathered from an online survey that had been distributed using common social media, which received 548 responses from all over Malaysia. A questionnaire was developed in three sections that focus on demography information, energy efficient products (EEP) and energy awareness. Smart PLS Version 3.0 was used to determine the influence of the different constructs on sample's attitude and intentions to purchase energy efficient products. The final analysis indicates that there is awareness on EEP label and other energy efficient products, environmental concern and perceived benefits and prices of the energy efficient product that have moderate correlation by R^2 0.692. Consumers attitude also has a moderate correlation of 64% in prediction intention to purchase of the consumer by R^2 0.644. Thus, the study shows that public already have good awareness on the energy efficient product and has started to purchase EEP. The study predict that consumer will purchase more energy efficient services and products in future.

Keywords: EE product · Environmental concern · Consumer attitude

1 Introduction

Malaysia is moving towards sustainable energy development to reduce the use of conventional energy that produces CO2 emission. Tenaga Nasional Berhad (TNB) has pledged to support sustainability pathway with an aspiration to achieve net zero emissions by 2050, as a bold move towards decarbonisation and Renewable Energy (RE) [1]. In 2017, Malaysia's residential sector has been recorded to emit 2,347,538 tonnes of CO_2 and is expected to increase to 11,689,308 tonnes in few years [2, 3]. Households' energy efficiency behaviour is directly related to the monthly cost of energy which mean they have more direct control over energy consumption and the potential for savings through

© Springer Nature Switzerland AG 2021
H. Badioze Zaman et al. (Eds.): IVIC 2021, LNCS 13051, pp. 575–586, 2021.
https://doi.org/10.1007/978-3-030-90235-3_50

behaviour change [4, 5]. On January 1, 2014, residential customers have seen an increase in electricity consumption of 10.6% on average which also showed the increase of tariff in the last decade [5, 6]. Hence, renewable energy resources have emerged as a viable option for achieving Malaysia's long-term energy development [6, 7]. Thus, it is important to take a step forward in educating the public regarding their energy consumption habits and cultivating a strategic mind set to conserve for sustainable living in the future [8, 9]. This is definitely a responsibility for all individuals in our society to be energy literate and wise consumers [10]. In line with Malaysia aspiration of revolutionizing the energy sectors in the aspect of smart grid, renewable energy and liberalization, it is important to make sure that the public is made aware and ready to move towards the direction that government is preparing. Since domestic consumer is the third biggest user of energy business, understanding the attitude and behavior pattern of the consumer is very important [2, 11, 12]. Thus, the study has two objectives that are i) to create public awareness on energy efficient products in the market and ii) to measure consumers' intention to purchase the energy efficient products in the future.

2 Energy Efficiency, Energy Efficiency Product and Consumer Behavior

The terms energy conservation, energy efficiency and renewable energy (RE) are often interchangeable as to lessen demand for energy and to safeguard the fast-depleting natural fossil fuel resources and to preserve the environment from harmful carbon emission [13]. Energy efficiency (EE) is recognized worldwide as the most powerful and cost-effective strategy for achieving goals of sustainable development [12]. Function of EE label is to promote consumers to buy energy efficient product and to encourage manufacturers to produce more EE appliances. In Malaysia 5 domestic appliances are issued with EE Star rating label Certification of Approval (COA) which are domestic fans, domestic lights, air conditioning units, refrigerator and TV. Performance Standards, Minimum Energy Performance Standards (MEPS), are types of energy measurements and class-average for energy efficient product manufactured [5]. Rating starts with 2 Star (minimum level of EE) and the highest is 5 Star (highest level of EE) [10]. Energy labels are informative labels to describe the manufactured product's energy performance in the form of energy use, efficiency, or energy cost [5]. The EE label is issued by the Energy Commission to manufacturers of electrical appliances who comply with the standards and requirements of the energy performance test for a star [14].

Households' electricity consumption varies more directly with household composition and social standing, and thus may be more responsive to behaviour change programs [15]. Kollmuss and Agyeman [16] conclude that behavior is the result of a complex interplay of demographic factors, external factors (including institutional, economic, and social and cultural factors), and internal factors (including motivation, environmental knowledge, values, attitudes, environmental awareness, environmental involvement, locus of control, and others). Psychological ownership and behavioral models are necessary to understand what consumers do, and why they do so [17–19]. It is predicted that social and emotional influences, issues of learning and awareness, and access to technologies will all play a role in formulating effective behavioral change among Malaysia's domestic consumer [20]. Thus, by identifying the factors that influence consumers' attitude, may influence their intention in purchasing energy efficient product.

3 Study Design and Methodology

This study frames its conceptual framework from the theory of planned behavior (TPB) and electricity saving intention (ESI) concept developed in [22]. Based on the theory and concept, a questionnaire was designed and distributed.

3.1 Theory of Planned Behavior (TPB) and Electricity Saving Intention (ESI)

TPB is the theory that most typically used to anticipate pro-environment behavior [21, 22]. Ajzen [23] who championed the TPB theory explained that intention can predict actual behavior. Intention in turn is motivated by attitude, subjective norms, and perceived behavior control. TPB allows other variables to be added to the frame-work as long as they explain a wide range of behavior [24–26]. ESI can be explained as individual commitment to perform certain behavior that facilitates electricity saving. Many studies on attitude on electricity saving intention found that a positive attitude towards a certain behavior resulted in a stronger intention to perform the behavior [27], such as attitude toward green product [25, 26]. In our study there is a total seven variables that is grouped under the ESI attitude (eg. energy efficient product, consumer attitude), subjective norm (eg. environment awareness, environment concern) and perceived behavior control (eg. perceived benefits, perceived price, purchase intention). Figure 1 shows how the current study used several foundations of this theory to develop the conceptual framework. The environmental awareness (EA), environmental concern (EC), energy efficient product (EEP), perceived benefits (PB) and perceived price (PP) are the independent variables that make the consumer attitude (CA), which will influence the dependent variable of purchase intention of energy efficient product (PIEP).

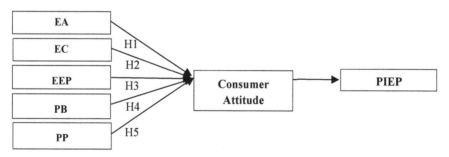

Fig. 1. Study framework and hypothesis

Attitude is a determinant as a product of psychological evaluation on the electric saving behavior that could lead to purchase intention of energy efficient product [16], subjective norm is how much consumers perceived that they are being pressured to conform to certain social expectation [23, 28]. Consumers are more likely to perform or refrain from performing specific behaviors based on whether or not the behavior meets social expectations [26, 29]. Perceived behavior control (PBC) is described as perceived difficulty or ease of conducting a behavior [30]. Several studies have found a positive causal relationship between PBC and purchase intention in a variety of contexts, including green products [24], energy-saving intention [17] and environmentally conscious consumption behavior [23, 31]. The paragraphs below describe the variables involved in the conceptual framework.

Energy Awareness (EA). High level of awareness about energy challenges can predict consumer orientation toward energy conservation behaviour [32] this may lead to consumers' positive attitudes toward changing their behaviour in response to energy challenges [26].

Environmental Concern (EC). Environmental concern is described as the extent to which people are aware of environmental issues and want to help solve or contribute to environmental on a personal level [33]. [34, 35] found that consumers' intentions to purchase energy efficient products are significantly influenced by EC.

Energy Efficient Product (EEP). People had higher chances of performing positive behavior towards environmental when they actually believed that they could do something about the matters through their action at personal level [26] such as purchasing EEP may indicate this environmentally responsible behavior.

Perceived Benefits (PB). [24, 27, 36] emphasized that people's willingness to buy environmentally friendly products can be influenced by perceived benefits. Consumers are more likely to buy a product if they believe there will be advantages to doing so. Akroush, et al. [36] discovered that perceived benefits influence EA consumers' purchasing intentions.

Perceived Price (PP). Perceived price is attitudinal influence that an energy efficient product has upon consumer purchasing EEP [36]. Previous study indicated that the price of EEP could outperform the perceived quality of the EEP. Consumers typically will evaluate the cost and benefits subjectively prior to purchase.

Consumer Attitude (CA). Consumer attitude is defined as the degree to which a person has a favourable or unfavourable evaluation or approval of a specific behavior [23]. Many studies have found that consumer purchase intentions for EEP are heavily influenced by their attitude toward such products in terms of energy awareness, perceived benefits, and perceived price [36].

Purchase Intention (PI). The degree to which consumers believe they will purchase such products is referred to as purchase intention [32]. Consumers who have a strong desire to buy are more likely to engage in purchasing behaviour than those who have no desire to buy [25]. A strong desire to purchase and use a green product can lead to actual purchase and use [25, 37].

Based on the TPB theory and ESI concept, the study aligns EA, EC, EEP, PB and PP to form consumer attitude variable towards ESI and this will predict positive PBC in the form of intention to purchase. To measure the relationship between each variable, the study will look at these hypotheses.

1. H1: Energy awareness have positive relationship with consumer attitude
2. H2. Environmental concern has positive relationship with consumer attitude
3. H3: Energy efficient product has positive relationship with consumer attitude
4. H4: Perceived benefits have positive relationship with consumer attitude
5. H5: Perceived price have positive relationship with consumer attitude
6. H6: Consumer attitude (EA, EC, EEP, PB, PP) has positive relationship with purchase intention

3.2 Questionnaire Design

Based on the above theory, a questionnaire was designed. The questionnaire was adopted from [21] and [36]. They were adjusted according to local need and the objectives of the study. The questionnaire is divided into three sections. Section A intended to collect the demographic information of the respondents. Section B, was arranged to gauge the awareness of EEP available in the market and C assessed the seven variables such as energy efficient product awareness, environmental concern, perceived prices of energy efficient product, perceived benefits of energy efficient product, and intention to purchase energy efficient product in the future as shown in Table 1.

Table 1. Questionnaire design.

Section	Description	Measurement
Section A	Demographics information	Descriptive
Section B	Energy efficient product in market	Descriptive
Section C	Energy efficient product awareness Energy awareness Environmental concern Perceived benefits Perceived price	Likert interval scale

3.3 Questionnaire Distribution

This quantitative study involved a set of self-administered questionnaires that are issued through online and social media channels; WhatsApp, Telegram, Facebook, Emails, Tweeter and Instagram. The survey questionnaire in Google Form was distributed around six weeks with every participant received Touch and Go e-voucher worth RM10 upon completion of the survey. The study uses simple random sampling methods targeting all population aged 18 and above.

4 Result and Analysis

A total of 553 responses received from which only 548 were usable responses received and analyzed. All statistical data were analyzed by using Smart PLS version 3.0 for correlational and regression. The data was analyzed to examine the study objectives which focus on:

1. public awareness on energy efficient products in the market and;
2. intention to purchase the energy efficient products in future.

Smart PLS Version 3.0 was used to conduct the inferential statistical analysis that determined the awareness of energy label, perceived benefits, energy awareness, environmental concern and perceived price influence, consumer attitude, and impact on purchase intention of energy products. The study used two phases of analysis. The first analysis is the descriptive analysis where it highlights the statistics and percentages of some of the variables. The second phase is the correlation and regression analyses that measure the possible and existing relationships between variables.

4.1 Validity and Reliability of the Study

Internal reliability and convergent validity tests were performed to validate the model. Internal reliability was evaluated using Cronbach's alpha and composite reliability tests. The results showed that the constructs' Cronbach's alpha coefficients had a large vertical extent to predict. Table 2 showed that the values of all constructs were between 0.746 and 0.917. It was established that all the constructs achieved values higher than 70% for composite reliability, thus meeting the standard level of reliability. Composite reliability values were identified as it was appropriate for both to be considered and disclosed based on composite reliability table below.

Table 2. Composite reliability table

Construct	Items	Outer loading	Cronbach's alpha	Composite reliability	Average variance extracted (AVE)
Energy efficient product	EEP1	0.827	0.777	0.857	0.601
	EEP2	0.833			
	EEP3	0.721			
	EEP4	0.713			
Perceived benefits	BEF1	0.828	0.909	0.929	0.687
	BEF2	0.848			

(continued)

Table 2. (*continued*)

Construct	Items	Outer loading	Cronbach's alpha	Composite reliability	Average variance extracted (AVE)
	BEF3	0.843			
	BEF4	0.790			
	BEF5	0.822			
	BEF6	0.841			
Consumer attitude	CA1	0.795	0.902	0.919	0.535
	CA10	0.670			
	CA2	0.760			
	CA3	0.820			
	CA4	0.812			
	CA5	0.728			
	CA6	0.673			
	CA7	0.737			
	CA8	0.719			
	CA9	0.568			
Energy awareness	EGAW1	0.670	0.749	0.833	0.502
	EGAW2	0.790			
	EGAW3	0.728			
	EGAW4	0.746			
	EGAW5	0.592			
Environmental concern	ENV1	0.840	0.845	0.897	0.685
	ENV2	0.871			
	ENV3	0.739			
	ENV4	0.856			
Purchase intention energy products	PI1	0.846	0.87	0.911	0.720
	PI2	0.800			
	PI3	0.903			
	PI4	0.841			
Perceived price	PRI1	0.939	0.917	0.947	0.857
	PRI2	0.911			
	PRI3	0.927			

4.2 Descriptive Analysis

The 548 valid returned responses consisted of almost equal gender distribution with 272 (49.6%) male and 276 (50.4%) female participants [30, 36]. Middle age adult of 29 to 38 years old group has been the main population of the study sample with 184 participants (33.6%). The majority of respondents have at least a bachelor's degree (284/51.8%) and also work in the private sectors (277/50.5%). The overall incomes of the majority of the respondents are in the range of between RM4000 to RM4850, which are in the B40 group living in a 3-bedroom double storey houses, with a minimum of 9 900 sq. ft. to 1200 sq. ft. The normal electricity bills that they have paid monthly are between RM51 and RM100. The gathered data also indicate that the study population is made up of educated people who are currently establishing their life in terms of work and financial status. They are also still having young children living together in the same residents.

It is worth to be noted that 153 respondents are satisfied with the Smart Meter that they have installed (27.9%). Another important input is that 40 respondents (7.3%) are satisfied with their solar panel system. Although majority is categorized in B40 groups, but the awareness regarding energy efficient product is high and this can be seen by their responses of product such as air conditioned, TV and refrigerator that they have already owned. Thus, it showed that the many respondents have certain level of awareness regarding energy efficiency as promoted by government. They are also keeping themselves updated with the sustainable technology like solar panel system and smart meter [3, 9, 11, 12].

4.3 Correlation and Regression

As described earlier, this study postulated six research hypotheses based on the developed conceptual research framework. The structural findings indicate that all of the hypotheses (H1-H6) are supported as shown in Table 3. For H2, the values of β-coefficient (0.388) and t (9.753) indicate the Environmental Concern (EC) as the primary determinant of Consumer Attitude (CA). Positive and significant relationships are also found between Energy Awareness (EA) and CA ($\beta = 0.093$, t $= 5.089$), Awareness on Energy Label (EA) and CA ($\beta = 0.187$, t $= 5.089$), Perceived Benefits (PB) and CA ($\beta = 0.158$, t $= 3.047$) and Perceived Price (PP) and CA ($\beta = 0.223$, t $= 7.656$), providing support for hypotheses H1, H3, H4 and H5. There is no negative relationship between the variables. For H6, it is supported by the strong relationship between CA and Purchase Intention of Energy Efficient Products (PIEP) ($\beta = 0.803$, t $= 52.588$). The correlation (R2) result for CA is 0.692, which is considered moderate as it indicates that 69.2% of the variance in consumer attitude could be justified by energy awareness, environmental concern, awareness on energy label, perceived benefits and perceived price. Meanwhile, R2 result for PIEP is 0.644, which is considered moderate as it indicates that 64.4% of the variance in purchase intention energy product could be justified by consumer attitude. This indicates that consumer attitude construct has a moderate connection with purchase intentions construct with R2 for both construct values above 0.6.

Table 3. Hypotheses testing results

	Path	*Beta, β	Standard deviation	T statistics	**P- values	Result
H1	Energy efficient product → Consumer attitude	0.187	0.037	5.098	0.00	Supported
H2	Perceived benefits → Consumer attitude	0.158	0.052	3.047	0.00	Supported
H3	Energy awareness → Consumer attitude	0.093	0.039	2.36	0.00	Supported
H4	Environmental concern → Consumer attitude	0.388	0.04	9.753	0.00	Supported
H5	Perceived price → Consumer attitude	0.223	0.029	7.656	0.00	Supported
H6	Consumer attitude → Purchase intention energy products	0.803	0.015	52.588	0.00	Supported

* Standardised Beta Coefficients. ** Significant at $P < 0.05$

5 Conclusion

The purpose of this study is to examine the factors influencing consumers' attitudes toward energy efficient products. The impact of consumer attitudes on purchasing intentions for energy-efficient products was also investigated. A conceptual framework was developed based on the TPB theory and ESI concept by including the vital constructs. Findings of this study show that the attitude is a predictor for consumers' intention to purchase energy efficient products. The attitude variable is influenced by several independent variables such as the energy awareness, environmental concern, awareness on energy label, perceived benefits and perceived price and consumer attitude. From this study, we understand that the consumers' attitude has been notable in predicting the purchasing intention towards EEP. The results also show us that the consumers also take into consideration the price, energy label, benefits and energy consumption when deciding to purchase the green products. The five factors studied also have significant influence on the consumer attitude that leads to the intention to purchase the EEP in future. These factors can aid as the elements to be considered in promoting the use of energy efficient products and appliances more actively from the household perspective.

The percentage of those who are considering to adopt smart meters and solar panels are also impressive. Financial and environmental advantages of energy efficient products should be emphasized to consumers more directly in comparison with non-energy efficient appliances. These factors should be the highlights of EEP promotional and marketing strategies to win public trust and confidence in using EEP. It is worth to note few limitations in this study. The research is formed on a survey of Malaysian residents that was conducted online in a short period of time. Apart from that, the demographic factors such the classification of the area, i.e. urban and rural, is unknown. The limitations may influence the economic activities, level of awareness, belief and wider access to EEP.

Acknowledgement. This project is funded by BOLD Grant number RJO 10517844/004, Universiti Tenaga Nasional, Malaysia.

References

1. Tenaga Nasional Berhad, TNB Sets Net Zero Emissions Aspiration by 2050 (2021)
2. Mohamad, H.F., Amran, S.N.M.E.: Electricity industry to undergo transformation with MESI 2.0, New Straits Times, p. 1, (2018)
3. Azlina, A.A., Kamaludin, M., Abdullah, E.S.Z.E., Radam, A.: Factors influencing household end-use electricity demand in Malaysia. Adv. Sci. Lett. **22**(12), 4120–4123 (2016). https://doi.org/10.1166/asl.2016.8189
4. Ahmed, M.S., Mohamed, A., Homod, R.Z., Shareef, H., Khalid, K.: Awareness on energy management in residential buildings: a case study in Kajang and Putrajaya, J. Eng. Sci. Technol. **12**(5), 1280–1294 (2017)
5. Majid, N.H.A., Salehudin, M.S., Rahim, Z.A., Othman, R.: Indoor Environmental Regulation hrough preference and behaviour of inhabitants in houses. Procedia Soc. Behav. Sci. **170**, 527–536 (2015). https://doi.org/10.1016/j.sbspro.2015.01.054
6. Energy Commision, National Energy Balance (2017)
7. Mahapatra, K., et al.: A behavioral change-based approach to energy efficiency in a manufacturing plant. Energ. Effi. **11**(5), 1103–1116 (2017). https://doi.org/10.1007/s12053-017-9581-9
8. TNB, Electricity Tariff Schedule, no. January. pp. 1–5, (2014)
9. Bakhtyar, B., Zaharim, A., Asim, N., Sopian, K., Lim, C. H.: Renewable energy in Malaysia : review on energy policies and economic growth. Recent Adv. Energy. Environ. Econ. Dev. 146–153 (2005)
10. Ting, L.S., Mohammed, A.H.B., Wai, C.W.: Promoting energy conservation behaviour : a plausible solution to energy sustainability threats. In: 2011 In International Conference on Social Science and Humanity, IPEDR, vol. 5, no. 1, pp. 372–376 (2011)
11. Rahman, K.A., Leman, A.M., Mubin, M.F., Yusof, M.Z.M., Hariri, A., Salleh, M.N.M.: Energy consumption analysis based on energy efficiency approach. In: Faculty of Mechanical and Manufacturing Engineering at the Universiti Tun Hussein Onn Malaysia, vol. 02003 (2017)
12. Mat, M., Harun, R.: Residential consumers behaviour towards efficient energy utilisations in Kajang Selangor. **1359**, 28–33 (2018)
13. Azizi, Z.M., Azizi, N.S.M., Abidin, N.Z., Mannakkara, S.: Making sense of energy-saving behaviour: a theoretical framework on strategies for behaviour change intervention. Procedia Comput. Sci. **158**, 725–734 (2019). https://doi.org/10.1016/j.procs.2019.09.108
14. Rahman, N.A.A., Kamaruzzaman, S.N., Akashah, F.W.: Scenario and strategy towards energy efficiency in malaysia: a review. MATEC Web Conf. **266**, 02012 (2019). https://doi.org/10.1051/matecconf/201926602012
15. Wiel, S., McMahon, J.E.: Governments should implement energy-efficiency standards and labels—cautiously. Energy Policy **31**(13), 1403–1415 (2003). https://doi.org/10.1016/S0301-4215(02)00199-4
16. Chik, N.A., Rahim, K.A., Radam, A., Shamsudin, M. N.: CO2 emissions induced by households lifestyle in Malaysia. Int. J. Bus. Soc. **14**(3), 344–357 (2013)
17. Kollmuss, A., Agyeman, J.: Mind the gap: why do people act environmentally and what are the barriers to pro-environmental behavior? Environ. Educ. Res. **8**(3), 239–260 (2002). https://doi.org/10.1080/13504620220145401

18. Brick, C., Lewis, G.J.: Unearthing the "Green" personality: core traits predict environmentally friendly behavior. Environ. Behav. **48**(5), 635–658 (2016). https://doi.org/10.1177/001391651 4554695

19. Koroleva, K., Melenhorst, M., Novak, J., Herrera Gonzalez, S.L., Fraternali, P., Rizzoli, A.E.: Designing an integrated socio-technical behaviour change system for energy saving. Energy Inf. **2**(1), 1–20 (2019). https://doi.org/10.1186/s42162-019-0088-9

20. European Environment Agency, Achieving energy efficiency through behaviour change: what does it take? (2013)

21. Ishak, M.H., Ahmad, M.F., Satar, M.A.A., Ting, K.L.: Energy saving patterns of personnel behaviour in Malaysian office. Int. Energy J. **18**(4), 353–364 (2018)

22. Fatoki, O.: Determinants of hotel employees' electricity saving intention: extending the theory of planned behavior. Entrepreneurship Sustain. Issues **8**(2), 86–97 (2020)

23. Xingjun, R., Wang, S., Yan, S.: Exploring the effects of normative factors and perceived behavioral control on individual's energy-saving intention: an empirical study in eastern China. Resour. Conserv. Recycl. **134**, 91–99 (2018). https://doi.org/10.1016/j.resconrec.2018. 03.001

24. Ajzen, I.: The theory of planned behavior. Organ. Behav. Hum. Decis. Process. **50**(2), 179–211 (1991). https://doi.org/10.1016/0749-5978(91)90020-T

25. Tommasetti, A., Singer, P., Troisi, O., Maione, G.: Extended theory of planned behavior (ETPB): investigating customers' perception of restaurants' sustainability by testing a structural equation model. Sustain. **10**(7), 1–21 (2018). https://doi.org/10.3390/su10072580

26. Yadav, R., Pathak, G.S.: Determinants of consumers' green purchase behavior in a developing nation: applying and extending the theory of planned behavior. Ecol. Econ. **134**, 114–122 (2017). https://doi.org/10.1016/j.ecolecon.2016.12.019

27. Ha, H.-Y., Janda, S.: Predicting consumer intentions to purchase energy-efficient products. In: Campbell, C.L. (ed.) The Customer is NOT Always Right? Marketing Orientations in a Dynamic Business World. DMSPAMS, pp. 897–897. Springer, Cham (2017). https://doi.org/ 10.1007/978-3-319-50008-9_249

28. Lin, S.-P.: Raising public awareness: The role of the household sector in mitigating climate change. Int. J. Environ. Res. Public Health **12**(10), 13162–13178 (2015). https://doi.org/10. 3390/ijerph121013162

29. Collins, S.E., Carey, K.B.: The theory of planned behavior as a model of heavy episodic drinking among college students. Psychol. Addict. Behav.s **21**(4), 498–507 (2007). https:// doi.org/10.1037/0893-164X.21.4.498

30. Apipuchayakul, N., Vassanadumrongdee, S.: Factors affecting the consumption of energy-efficient lighting products: exploring purchase behaviors of Thai consumers. Sustainability **12**(12), 4887 (2020). https://doi.org/10.3390/su12124887

31. Ajzen, I.: Consumer Attitudes and Behavior. In: Handbook of Consumer Psychol. Routledge, Milton Park (2015). https://doi.org/10.4324/9780203809570.ch20

32. Varman, M., Masjuki, H.H., Mahlia, T.M.I.: Electricity savings from implementation of minimum energy efficiency standard for TVs in Malaysia. Energy Buildings **37**(6), 685–689 (2005). https://doi.org/10.1016/j.enbuild.2004.10.001

33. Ali, S., Ullah, H., Akbar, M., Akhtar, W., Zahid, H.: Determinants of consumer intentions to purchase energy-saving household products in Pakistan. Sustainability **11**(5), 1462 (2019). https://doi.org/10.3390/su11051462

34. Li, G., Li, W., Jin, Z., Wang, Z.: Influence of environmental concern and knowledge on households' willingness to purchase energy-efficient appliances: a case study in Shanxi. China Sustain. **11**(4), 1–18 (2019). https://doi.org/10.3390/su11041073

35. T. A. N. C. Seang.: A Moral Extension of the Theory of Planned Behavior To, (2014).

36. Irfan, M., Zhao, Z.-Y., Li, H., Rehman, A.: The influence of consumers' intention factors on willingness to pay for renewable energy: a structural equation modeling approach. Environ. Sci. Pollut. Res. **27**(17), 21747–21761 (2020). https://doi.org/10.1007/s11356-020-08592-9

37. Akroush, M.N., Zuriekat, M.I., Al Jabali, H.I., Asfour, N.A.: Determinants of purchasing intentions of energy-efficient products: the roles of energy awareness and perceived benefits. Int. J. Energy Sect. Manage. **13**(1), 128–148 (2019). https://doi.org/10.1108/IJESM-05-2018-0009

Algebraic Operations-Based Secret-Key Design for Encryption Algorithm (ASKEA) for Energy Informatics and Smart Internet of Things (IoT) Applications

Abbas M. Al-Ghaili[1,2]([⊠]) [iD], Hairoladenan Kasim[2], Ridha Omar[2],
Zainuddin Hassan[2], Naif M. Al-Hada[3]([⊠]) [iD], and Jihua Wang[3]

[1] Institute of Informatics and Computing in Energy (IICE), Universiti Tenaga Nasional
(UNITEN), 43000 Kajang, Selangor, Malaysia
[2] College of Computing and Informatics (CCI), UNITEN, 43000 Kajang, Selangor, Malaysia
abbas@uniten.edu.my
[3] Shandong Key Laboratory of Biophysics, Institute of Biophysics,
Dezhou University, Dezhou 253023, China
alhada@dzu.edu.cn

Abstract. This paper designs a secret key that has the ability to behave in a different way based on plaintext input. This paper proposes two schemes of secret key length which are: 2^i and $2^i + 2^{i-1}$. The aim is to increase unpredictability and privacy of plaintext. A series of algebraic operations has been used to create a specific coefficient by which the relation between plaintext size and key length is adjustable. This design of secret key increases privacy of sensitive data used with energy informatics and smart Energy Internet-of-Things (EIoT) applications. The proposed design has been evaluated in terms of time complexity computation time to generate one secret key and encrypt plaintext. Additionally, results show that the proposed Algebraic Operations-based Secret-Key Design for Encryption Algorithm (ASKEA) has less computation time and complexity than other competitive research works. Privacy and unpredictability of plaintext and secret key could be preserved and achieved.

Keywords: Security scheme · Secret key · QR-code · Energy informatics ·
Energy Internet-of-Things

1 Introduction

Many Internet-of-Things (IoT) applications have lately been using the technique of Quick Response Code (QR-Code) to allow many smart services and tasks be done in a very short period of time [1–3]. The number of researches [4–8] focusing on the use of QR-Code is gradually increasing [9, 10]. Such researches produce smart services to the user whereas private data are used. Thus, there is a continuous need to protect data from being used by an unauthorized party.

Usually, Many IoT-based applications have become widely used to do many smart services and tasks which require a sufficient and precise process in a short period of time.

H. Badioze Zaman et al. (Eds.): IVIC 2021, LNCS 13051, pp. 587–599, 2021.
https://doi.org/10.1007/978-3-030-90235-3_51

Thus, a lot of information, caused by the huge portion of data being stored, requires fast processing.

The QR-Code is a very effective tool and has been used by many applications to with different purposes. Usually, QR tags store data in an encrypted form where scanners are used to extract data. Then, depending on the system or application the QR-Code is used for, a verification procedure follows the extraction step to make sure those extracted values are identical to original values before being encrypted [11].

Hence, various factors are taken into account when such a smart application is designed e.g., privacy, authentication, availability, data integrity, data recovery, responsiveness, reliability ... etc. Depending on the kind of the smart application being used for, certain security factors rise up to make that application as perfect as possible, more than other factors do. Smart home applications, for example, require privacy, safety, and responsiveness ...etc. Embedded systems such as health systems require more responsiveness and reliability. Sensor based collection systems reliability and maintainability. Hence, there is a need to consider all above mentioned security factors using a strong encryption scheme to include as many factors as it could.

Proposed works in [12, 13] have designed two different methods to generate a QR-Code. In [12], a graphical design has been used to make sure that documents being verified are secure whereas the document authentication factor has been considered. The design in [13] has considered both privacy and usability factors by using array of patterns that includes no much details. Similarly, another proposed QR-Code design [14] to protect private data, a print-and-scan (P&S) operation has been addressed whereas the data privacy factor has been investigated. Additionally, QR-Code designs have been used with root applications. In order to measure distances accurately and reliably, landmark images and image recognition processes have been used to head the robot to estimate the accurate location detection [15].

On the other hand, smart and IoT applications have numerous uses reviewed in literature. Some researches, for example, have proposed a security purposed method for smart home [16], monitoring purposed application [17], biometrics-based home access system [18], embedded physical evaluation method [19] ... etc. These IoT applications require, for example, reliable responsiveness, security, and authentication. IoT technology relies on some other essential tools to successfully and accurately build such a system. One of these tools is the encryption scheme by which the smart system is robust. The verification procedure is however another important tool for a robust smart application. Usually, the encryption scheme needs to be followed by a strong verification procedure. Therefore, any the encryption scheme is so essential for smart and IoT applications because it affects the whole smart system including the verification procedure as well.

In general, proposed methods have utilized the security and privacy of contents however the computation time and code complexity are still of importance to be considered by many IoT applications.

This paper focuses on designing a different way of encryption for both plaintext and secret key. It proposes an Algebraic Operations-based Secret Key Design for Encryption Algorithm (ASKEA) focuses on the authentication and integrity. ASKEA is used to increase privacy of several information-centric applications such as energy informatics, IoT, and smart home applications. In this work, QR-Code has been acted as a landmark image to ease the recognition process considering both reliability and responsiveness factors to attain integrity and availability. To protect data stored in a QR-Code which is used with IoT based smart applications, this paper proposes an unpredictable secret key design by which the QR-Code tag is encrypted.

ASKEA has used a strong encryption procedure in order to increase the time needed to decrypt the QR-Code information in case the secret key has been deduced. ASKEA however has focused to use a 1-session secret key policy with the most of encryption steps so that encrypted data will not be decrypted; this is to increase the privacy and secrecy of the user's information. In order to attain the availability, the encryption policy generates a random unpredictable key. Furthermore, the proposed design has considered a very long encryption key to reduce the vulnerability of being deduced; it takes very long time to attack and crack the key. So that data integrity could be achieved.

This paper is organized as follows: Sect. 2 is dedicated to explain the schematic representation for ASKEA. Section 3 is dedicated for Results and Discussion. Conclusion has been drawn in Sect. 4.

2 The Proposed ASKEA Schematic Representation

The proposed ASKEA is relevant to user information encryption. Its encryption scheme deals with the way the collected information is being protected. ASKEA is proposed to protect information from being modified in an unauthorized manner. This paper aims to design the secret key based on the ASKEA plaintext. A generalized schematic representation is shown in Fig. 1 to show ASKEA main steps and its relationship with such a verification tool.

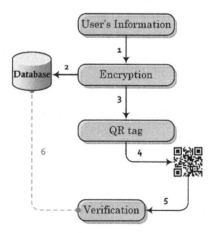

Fig. 1. A generalized ASKEA schematic representation

In Fig. 1, information will be encrypted and stored. Then, the QR-Code is generated based on the encrypted values. Then, the user interface starts. Once, an access is needed by the user, the ASKEA immediately is called to enable the verification. However, the encryption process is called two times; the first one, when it is used to encrypt original information collected from the user at the first time. Another call happens when there is a need to update the database with new values, such as SQ values, new hash values ...etc. One of the main uses for ASKEA, as marked in Fig. 1 with numerical labels: 5 and 6, is to be used as a verification tool for a number of IoT applications using QR-Code.

2.1 The Proposed ASKEA Design

This section is dedicated to explain the ASKEA basic design and how this proposed design could be used with a verification tool for energy informatics related applications.

2.2 Proposed ASKEA Inputs' Design

Initially, ASKEA encrypts whole information collected from the user. Information includes certain values that consist of pure characters, numbers, and a mixture of characters and numbers as described in Fig. 2.

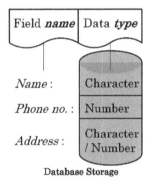

Fig. 2. User's information category

In Fig. 2, data types of 'character', 'number', and 'character/ number' are assigned to be stored in the 'name', 'phone no., fax ...etc.', 'address, website, email ...etc.' fields, respectively.

To increase the security of encryption scheme, further matter has been considered that is a variable with a property that is capable to frequently change its value and data type. Usually, the user has different activities. Thus, the user could be asked to answer a security question. This feature is so useful to create different answers with different values producing amounts by which the field can be increased or decreased in case the answer is a number. As expected, in case the SQ answer alters, for example, from text to number, its data type will be changing accordingly. This proposed scheme is illustrated in Fig. 3.

Unlike values of fields, shown in Fig. 2, are constants and related data types are fixed; the field in Fig. 3 is dynamically and periodically changing in value and data type. This has added a feature that is, the value is difficult to be predicted when a threat is trying to access or modify data contents.

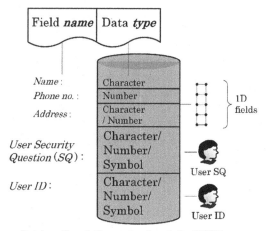

Database Description used as Inputs for ASKEA

Fig. 3. Proposed user's information category for ASKEA

As can be seen in Fig. 3, there will be two attributes considered as inputs for ASKEA which are: User SQ (USQ), and User ID (UID). Description of fields of which ASKEA inputs consist is provided in Table 1.

Table 1. Description of input items of ASKEA

		Data descriptor			
		Data type	Array size	Status	
				Data type	Field value
ASKEA Input Attribute/Field	User SQ (USQ)	num/char/ symbol	1	alt	var
	User ID (UID)	num/char	1	fix	const

As can be seen in this table, the field of '*User SQ (USQ)*' has the following data description: a *Data_Type* = 'number, character or symbol', *Array_Size* = '1D', *Status_of_Data_Type* can *alter* between 'numbers', 'characters', and 'symbols', and *Field_Value* = 'variable'.

2.3 Proposed ASKEA Secret-Key Length Design

In order to implement the ASKEA, a series of cascade encryption processes are applied on fields related values. The output of ASKEA is the QR-Code for User ID, User SQ. The technical procedures will be discussed in this section.

ASKEA has adopted to use two schemes for key length, which are 2^i and $2^i + 2^{i-1}$. However, the value of i is designed to be adjustable between key length and encrypted data size. The increment denoted by 2^{i-1} for the second key length is to take into account any increment caused by a potential change inside the 'field value' or 'data type'. Referring to Table 1, for example, the SQ increment could probably happen when it is increased or altered between numbers and characters. However, this design includes a limitation relates to the maximum length of the secret key by the value $2^i + 2^{i-1}$. Thus, the key length must be greater than or equal to the data size.

Therefore, the following two formulas are considered for the secret key length, shown in Eq. (1) and Eq. (2):

$$2^i \leq key_1 \ length \tag{1}$$

$$key_2 \ length \geq 2^i + 2^{i-1} \tag{2}$$

2.4 Mathematical Design of ASKEA Input (Plaintext)

The key length has a directly proportional relationship with user information being encrypted. That is, and from this information, the encryption scheme is going to extract a certain amount of data (i.e., plaintext) to be encrypted; and not whole user's information. This amount of data (plaintext) being encrypted is, as mentioned before, mutable due to it depends on alteration of data type(s). As a result, this amount of data is considered as an ASKEA plaintext input whereas it has a variable length producing two different sizes in bits/ Bytes. The design of key length has considered both minimum and maximum sizes of the plaintext input. This criterion is a must and is expressed in inequalities (1) and (2):

$$u_{data_{min}} < 2^i \tag{3}$$

$$u_{data_{max}} < 2^i + 2^{i-1} \tag{4}$$

whereas $u_{data_{min}}$ and $u_{data_{max}}$ minimum and maximum size(s) of data entered by the user, respectively.

Thus, in order to derive the relationship between the key length and data size with consideration of the adjustable variable (i): firstly, inequalities (2) and (4) are used to produce inequality (6); secondly, inequalities (3) and (5) are used to produce inequality (7), as follows:

$$u_{data_{min}} < 2^i \leq key_1 \ length \tag{5}$$

$$u_{data_{max}} < 2^i + 2^{i-1} \leq key_2 \ length \tag{6}$$

Thus, inequalities (6) and (7) could produce the following expression:

$$size \ of \ data < adjustable \ variable \leq key \ length \tag{7}$$

2.5   Proposed Mathematical Operations Based ASKEA Design

As discussed, there is a proportional relationship between the secret key size and data size with consideration of adjustable variable, therefore these two mathematical formulas are true:

$$f(key) \propto f(data) \tag{8}$$

$$f(key) = f(data) + c_{HEA} \tag{9}$$

where,

- $f(data)$ is an independent function to which user's information is assigned
- $f(key)$ is a dependent function and varies based on $f(data)$
- c_{HEA} is an ASKEA constant designed exclusively to normalize the size of $f(data)$ to a fixed size that is proportional to the length of $f(key)$

This equation relates mainly to the length of secret key and size of data being encrypted. Meaning, Eq. (9) is mathematically represented as in Eq. (10):

$$size_{f(key)} = size_{f(data)} + size_{c_{HEA}} \tag{10}$$

where,

- $size_{f(key)}$ is the function by which the key size is calculated
- $size_{f(data)}$ is the function used to store a piece of data extracted from user's information; data to be sent to ASKEA for encryption purpose
- $size_{c_{HEA}}$ calculates the size of c_{HEA} by which the plaintext size is normalized to the key length

Equation (10) could be mathematically re-formulated as:

$$k_{size} = P_{text_{size}} + c_{HEA_{size}} \tag{11}$$

where,

- k_{size} has two secret key sizes which are represented in Eq. (12):

$$k_{size} = \begin{cases} 2^i & f(data) = minimum\ size\ of\ data \\ 2^i + 2^{i-1} & f(data) = maximum\ size\ of\ data \end{cases} \tag{12}$$

- $P_{text_{size}}$ is an aggregation function relates to data entered by user, refer to Table 1, as mathematically represented in Eq. (13):

$$P_{text_{size}} = f(input_{user}) \tag{13}$$

- $c_{HEA_{size}}$ is an ASKEA constant and can be calculated using Eq. (14) producing two different values based on minimum and maximum size of data entered by the user:

$$c_{HEA_{size}} = \begin{cases} 2^i - P_{text_{size}} & 2^i \geq u\_data_{min} \\ 2^i + 2^{i-1} - P_{text_{size}} & 2^i < u\_data_{max} \end{cases} \tag{14}$$

2.6 $P_{textsize}$ Design

In this subsection, ASKEA inputs are in detail discussed. That aims to explain how to obtain appropriate values for length and sizes of ASKEA inputs. Following considerations are in detail discussed:

As for data entered by user, it is a function in which whole entered information is aggregated, see Eq. (13). Once the user has entered and filled up required fields, a series of algebraic operations extracts a piece of data from user's information in accordance with 'ASKEA Input Field' mentioned in Table 1. It is an aggregation function of several user inputs whereas it is simply formulated in (15):

$$f(P_{text}) = f(USQ, UID) \tag{15}$$

where,

- $f(P_{text})$ represents assigned data to ASKEA as a plaintext
- $f(USQ, UID)$ represents data-required input-fields (DRIFs).

In order to determine the size specified for each function, a size-purposed algebraic function has been proposed to obtain the bits-length needed (BLN) for each DRIF. To calculate BLN for each DRIF, a certain piece-of-data (PoD) is extracted from the related DRIF based on algebraic operations and then PoD's size is passed to the BLN.

Thus, to ease the procedure mentioned in Eq. (15), each BLN could be calculated for every DRIF using the following mathematical formulas shown in Eq. (16) and Eq. (17):

$$f(USQ) = inp(u_{SQ}) \tag{16}$$

$$f(UID) = inp(u_{ID}) \tag{17}$$

where,

- $f(USQ)$, and $f(UID)$ are DRIFs for user SQ and user ID, respectively
- $inp(u_{SQ})$ and $inp(u_{ID})$ are alphanumeric values of PoD for USQ and UID RFIDs, respectively.

Once $inp(u_{SQ})$ and $inp(u_{ID})$ have been calculated, the P_{text} is ready to feed the ASKEA, using Eq. (18). In order to find the appropriate ASKEA secret key size, BLNs need to be firstly calculated for each DRIF by using Eqs. (19) - (20):

$$f(P_{text}) = inp(u_{SQ}) + inp(u_{ID}) \tag{18}$$

$$BLN_{USQ} = size_{bits}\{inp(u_{SQ})\} \tag{19}$$

$$BLN_{UID} = size_{bits}\{inp(u_{ID})\} \tag{20}$$

By obtaining values of BLNs in Eqs. (19) - (20), Eq. (13) is re-formulated as in Eq. (21):

$$P_{textsize} = BLN_{USQ} + BLN_{UID} \tag{21}$$

Usually, a PoD for each DRIF consists of a number of alphanumeric/ numeric values. Thus, each PoD has a 'value' and 'data type'. The relation between PoD and DRIF items is provided in Table 2.

Table 2. DRIF and PoD

DRIF	PoD	
	Value	Data type
User SQ	Variable	alphanumeric
User ID	Constant	alphanumeric

As mentioned before in Table 1, fields requiring data entries whether by automatically or manually ways are supersets of ASKEA inputs. Thus, a series of mathematical subsets which can be derived from Table 2 are mathematically represented, as follows: $\{DRIFs\} \subset \{HEA\ Input\ Attributes\}$, the set DRIF is represented by Eq. (22):

$$\{DRIF\} = \{\{USQ\}, \{UID\}\} \tag{22}$$

Each subset is defined using the following algebraic description:

$$\{USQ\} = \{inp_{SQ} : \forall inp \in\ user\ inputs\ for\ SQ\}$$

$$\{UID\} = \{inp_{ID} : \forall inp \in\ user\ inputs\ for\ ID\}$$

Each PoD is a subset of its related DRIF's superset, which is mathematically represented as follows: $\{PoDs\} \subset \{DRIFs\}$.

As a result, further defined descriptions could be derived, as follows:

$$\{PoD_{USQ}\} \subset \{USQ\};\ \Leftrightarrow \{PoD_{USQ}\} \cap \{USQ\} = \{PoD_{USQ}\}$$

$$\{PoD_{UID}\} \subset \{UID\};\ \Leftrightarrow \{PoD_{UID}\} \cap \{UID\} = \{PoD_{UID}\}$$

Each of abovementioned algebraic definitions is true with every condition accompanied.

As per the design limitation, the user is allowed to enter an answer for the SQ with a length up to 8 Bytes.

In this design, the minimum size of an answer the user can type is '1' alphanumeric e.g., '1', '#', 'a', or 'z'. Thus, '1' alphanumeric can be written as: 2^b; whereas $b = 3$.

Therefore, 1 Byte is a minimum length of the SQ answer. As a result, the proposed algorithm has adopted that 1 character of 8-bits length is assigned to 'i'. That is represented in by Eq. (23):

$$i = 2^b \tag{23}$$

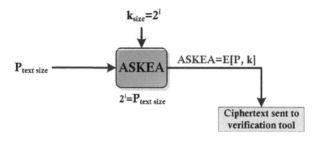

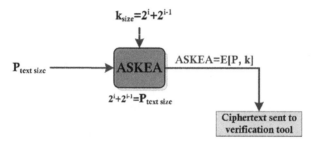

Fig. 4. ASKEA block-diagram – security scheme design

2.7 Proposed ASKEA Block-Diagram Design

A simple model of ASKEA ingredients for two schemes of plaintext size(s), which are $P_{text_{size}} < 2^i$ and $P_{text_{size}} < 2^i + 2^{i-1}$, is illustrated in Fig. 4.

3 Results and Discussion

This part presents results in terms of plaintext time complexity, computation time, security factors. Then, it evaluates the proposed design performance based on abovementioned obtained results.

3.1 Time Complexity

Big-O-Notation will be used for a further evaluation and comparative analysis. The running time for the proposed secret key design will be described. Two main procedures will be evaluated which are plaintext entries values and secret key variables. Usually, O(n) with the proposed design depends on user entries and values being extracted.

As for USQ and UID, O(n) depends on values being generated from equations. An array $A_{USQ}[k1]$ and $A_{UID}[k2]$ is dedicated to store k elements. Therefore: O(n) for this case is defined as in Eqs. (24) and (25):

$$O(n)_{A_{USQ}[k1]} = O(k1) \tag{24}$$

$$O(n)_{A_{UID}[k2]} = O(k2) \tag{25}$$

Totally, $O(n)$ for ASKEA is a summation formula of Eqs. (24) and (25). Since $k1$ and $k2$ are constants, therefore Eq. (26) is used to obtain value of $O(n)_{ASKEA}$:

$$O(n)_{ASKEA} = O(k) \tag{26}$$

A time complexity value equals to $O(k)$ looks reasonable when compared to other time complexity schemes.

3.2 Time Based Efficiency

The proposed design scheme of secret key design in term of computation time needed to generate one secret key. The proposed ASKEA in term of secret key and plaintext processing computation times has been compared to other methods which are Password and Certificate techniques. The obtained result is given in Fig. 5.

In this comparison, the procedure of how samples are taken is explained as follows: many tests using different samples of entries have been considered. There have been seven tests at which different number of samples is considered. In regard to the proposed design, the user entries of plaintext have been fed to the ASKEA inputs which are $P_{text_{size}}$ and k_{size}. For the first implemented test, 7 samples are considered to produce 7 secret keys accordingly. The computation time for each sample is recorded; whereas the computation time mentioned in Fig. 5 is the average computation time for whole samples of the related test. Similarly, this is repeated for the rest of tests with different number of samples. As for Password and Certificate techniques, both are used to create the same number of words.

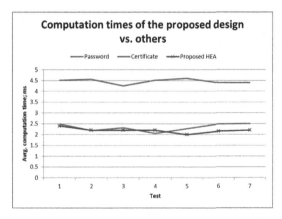

Fig. 5. Average computation times of the proposed secret key design vs. others

There are seven tests in which 10, 20, 50, 75, 100, 200, and 500 samples have been considered. Thus, the computation time for each sample is calculated and then the average computation time is obtained for whole samples for every test. The related result is provided as mentioned in Fig. 5.

As noticeable, the proposed design has less time than Certificate and Password techniques unless two tests in case of Password. The reason is that the length of secret key is the maximum length which is considered acceptable when comparing to the Certificate technique.

3.3 Security Factors Analysis - Confidentiality and Privacy vs. Unpredictability

The aim of choosing 2 schemes of key length is to increase the privacy of encryption algorithm by building an unpredictable behavior of key. Thus, the way the secret key changes help increase the confidentiality of plaintext being encrypted.

4 Conclusion

This paper has proposed a dynamical design for a secret key based on user plaintexts. Original inputs are encoded. To perform such a design, a number of algebraic operations have been derived and proposed. The essential part in designing such a secret key is to keep an unpredictable behavior of ASKEA in terms of key length and the way the values are generated. This design could be followed by a verification tool in which a QR-Code is used to achieve a high level of security and privacy to such energy informatics, smart home, and EIoT applications.

Acknowledgement. This research work is funded by Universiti Tenaga Nasional (UNITEN) with Grant Code: (J510050002/2021048).

References

1. Liu, L., Wang, Q., Wu, Y.: QR code positioning algorithm. In: The 2nd International Conference on Computing and Data Science, Stanford, CA, USA (2021)
2. Al-Ghaili, A.M., Kasim, H., Othman, M., Hassan, Z.: A New Encryption Scheme Method (ESM) using capsulated-layers conception for verified QR-Tag for IoT-based smart access systems. In: Balas, V.E., Solanki, V.K., Kumar, R., Khari, M. (Eds.) Internet of Things and Big Data Analytics for Smart Generation, Cham, Springer International Publishing, pp. 77–103 (2019)
3. Ramalho, J.F.C.B. et al.: Super modules-based active QR codes for smart trackability and IoT: a responsive-banknotes case study. npj Flexible Electron. **4**, (1), 11 (2020)
4. Liu, Z., Choo, K.K.R., Grossschadl, J.: Securing edge devices in the post-quantum internet of things using lattice-based cryptography. IEEE Commun. Mag. **56**(2), 158–162 (2018)
5. Neisse, R., Baldini, G., Steri, G., Ahmad, A., Fourneret, E., Legeard, B.: Improving Internet of Things device certification with policy-based management, In: 2017 Global Internet of Things Summit (GIoTS). Vol. 6–9, pp. 1–6 (2017)
6. Rane, S., Dubey, A., Parida, T.: Design of IoT based intelligent parking system using image processing algorithms. In: 2017 International Conference on Computing Methodologies and Communication (ICCMC), pp. 1049–1053 (2017)
7. Xiao-Long, W., Chun-Fu, W., Guo-Dong, L., Qing-Xie, C.: A robot navigation method based on RFID and QR code in the warehouse. In: 2017 Chinese Automation Congress (CAC), vol. 20–22, pp. 7837–7840 (2017)
8. Ghaffari, M., Ghadiri, N., Manshaei, M.H., Lahijani, M.S.: P4QS: a peer-to-peer privacy preserving query service for location-based mobile applications. IEEE Trans. Veh. Technol. **66**(10), 9458–9469 (2017)

9. Sha, K., Yang, T.A., Wei, W., Davari, S.: A survey of edge computing-based designs for IoT security. Digit. Commun. Netw. **6**(2), 195–202 (2020)
10. Parikh, S., Dave, D., Patel, R., Doshi, N.: Security and privacy issues in cloud, fog and edge computing. Procedia Comput. Sci. **160**, 734–739 (2019)
11. Al-Ghaili, A.M., Kasim, H., Othman, M., Hassan, Z.: Security factors based evaluation of verification algorithm for an IoT access system. In: Saeed, F., Gazem, N., Mohammed, F., Busalim, A. (eds.) Recent Trends in Data Science and Soft Computing, Cham, Springer International Publishing, pp. 384–395, (2019)
12. Tkachenko, I., Puech, W., Destruel, C., Strauss, O., Gaudin, J.M., Guichard, C.: Two-Level QR code for private message sharing and document authentication. IEEE Trans. Inf. Forensics Secur. **11**(3), 571–583 (2016)
13. Lin, S.S., Hu, M.C., Lee, C.H., Lee, T.Y.: Efficient QR code beautification with high quality visual content. IEEE Trans. Multimedia **17**(9), 1515–1524 (2015)
14. Lin, P.Y.: Distributed secret sharing approach with cheater prevention based on QR code. IEEE Trans. Industr. Inf. **12**(1), 384–392 (2016)
15. Nazemzadeh, P., Fontanelli, D., Macii, D., Palopoli, L.: Indoor localization of mobile robots through QR code detection and dead reckoning data fusion. IEEE/ASME Trans. Mechatron. **22**(6), 2588–2599 (2017)
16. Kirkham, T., Armstrong, D., Djemame, K., Jiang, M.: Risk driven Smart Home resource management using cloud services. Futur. Gener. Comput. Syst. **38**, 13–22 (2014)
17. Chen, Y.H., Tsai, M.J., Fu, L.C., Chen, C.H., Wu, C.L., Zeng, Y.C.: Monitoring elder's living activity using ambient and body sensor network in smart home. In: 2015 IEEE International Conference on Systems, Man, and Cybernetics, pp. 2962–2967 (2015)
18. Kanaris, L., Kokkinis, A., Fortino, G., Liotta, A., Stavrou, S.: Sample size determination algorithm for fingerprint-based indoor localization systems. Comput. Netw. **101**, 169–177 (2016)
19. Gentili, M., Sannino, R., Petracca, M.: BlueVoice: voice communications over Bluetooth Low Energy in the Internet of Things scenario. Comput. Commun. **89–90**, 51–59 (2016)

Comparison of Electricity Load Prediction Errors Between Long Short-Term Memory Architecture and Artificial Neural Network on Smart Meter Consumer

Nur Shakirah Md Salleh[1]($^{\boxtimes}$), Azizah Suliman[1], and Bo Nørregaard Jørgensen[2]

[1] Universiti Tenaga Nasional, 43000 Kajang, Selangor, Malaysia
{shakirah,azizah}@uniten.edu.my
[2] Mærsk Mc-Kinney Møller Institutte, 5230 Odense, Denmark
bnj@mmmi.sdu.dk

Abstract. Machine learning can perform electricity load prediction on the demand side. This paper compared the electricity prediction errors between two machine learning algorithms: Artificial Neural Network (ANN) and Long Short-Term Memory (LSTM) architecture. LSTM can solve the regression problem in time-series. Due to that, this paper applied LSTM. The traditional machine learning approach, ANN, was used to compare the effectiveness of LSTM in performing the time-series prediction. A dataset that consisted of historical electricity consumption data with independent variables was used in this study. The mean squared error (MSE) and mean absolute error (MAE) evaluation metrics were used to evaluate the models. The model generated using LSTM showed the lowest error with MSE value of 0.1238 and MAE value of 0.0388. These results indicated that choosing a suitable machine learning algorithm for the time-series problem could improve the model generated from the training session.

Keywords: Electricity load · Regression · LSTM · ANN · Time-series

1 Introduction

Electricity is a form of energy that being used widely [1]. Coal, solar, and wind energy are the examples of primary sources of energy. These primary energy sources were used in electricity generation. There are two types of primary energy sources: renewable and non-renewable. The conventional way of generating electricity was from non-renewable sources. This method affects the environment in negative way by releasing carbon emission. The drawback of using non-renewable sources is overcome by the implementation of renewable energy. However, the integration of renewable energy is challenging to ensure the supply meets the demand. Electricity power generator companies can use electricity load prediction based on the consumers' electricity usage pattern to estimate the power generation. The electricity forecasting able to predict for short-, medium, and long-term [2]. Short-term forecasting is suitable to predict the demand for less than a

© Springer Nature Switzerland AG 2021
H. Badioze Zaman et al. (Eds.): IVIC 2021, LNCS 13051, pp. 600–609, 2021.
https://doi.org/10.1007/978-3-030-90235-3_52

month [3]. As the prediction for a longer period such as monthly until decades, medium-, and long-term are more suitable. This study applied two machine learning algorithms in forecasting the electricity consumption pattern.

The research of machine learning in electricity area has been increased in recent years [4]. Supervised learning allows the machine to learn from historical electricity load data. In supervised learning, the training process learns based on the sample dataset. The training process produces a model, while the testing process evaluates the model quality using evaluation metric. The testing process uses a set of unknown data that only consists of features.

Regression is a machine learning algorithm used to predict in time-series [5]. There are many computational algorithms to solve regression problems such as Artificial Neural Network (ANN), Support Vector Machine (SVR) [3], and Regression Neural Network (RNN). These algorithms were revised into extended versions that include Deep ANN, Sequential Minimal Optimization (SMO) [6], Support Vector Regression (SVR) [7, 8], and Long Short-Term Memory (LSTM). RNN handles the sequential data and memorise previous inputs that are stored in the internal memory [7, 9]. The drawback of RNN is vanishing gradients caused by too small parameter updates. Gradients is important because it contain information used in RNN iteration. However, LSTM overcome this issue.

LSTM can memorise information for extended period because it has its own cell [10, 11]. LSTM works by repeating modules of a Neural Network (NN) with a few layers that communicate with each other [9].

The data input for machine learning represents by features and label. However, the data input for RNN and LSTM requires data transformation into features, time step, and label. The time step benefits LSTM in terms of prediction based on a specific period of time, whereby it is applied in time-series forecasting in predicting the future value derived from historical data patterns [12]. These algorithms apply in training phase to produce a model. The model is assessed using evaluation metric.

In RNN, the common evaluation metrics applied are mean absolute error (MAE), root mean square error (RMSE), and mean square error (MSE) [13, 14]. A lower evaluation metric value represents a better model [13–15].

The remainder of this paper is organised as follows: Sect. 2 provides a review of existing published works related to electricity load forecasting. Section 3 describes the case study applied to this paper. Section 4 describes the methodology employed in the chosen machine learning algorithm. Section 5 describes the experiment results that include the model quality and prediction values. Finally, Sect. 6 concludes the findings.

2 Review of Related Works

Liu et al. [16] applied historical electricity dataset on LSTM. The article generated two models from two machine learning algorithms, Elman Neural Network and LSTM. The article compared the prediction results made by these models for normal and special days. This article used mean absolute percentage error (MAPE) to evaluate the model. As the results, MAPE value for LSTM model is 2.13%, and Elman Neural Network is 5.19%. The model generated using LSTM achieved high precision compared to Elman Neural Network.

Hossen et al. [17] used the historical electricity load dataset with independent variables. Hossen et al. [17] used the two-year duration dataset, Almanac of Minutely Power Dataset (AMPDs) dataset. The data collected based on one-minute interval. The dataset consists of independent variables from the utility meters: power and water, and weather data. The article compared the execution between Deep Neural Network (DNN) using LSTM with Gated Recurrent Unit (GRU) and simple RNN. The result proven the lowest MAPE error rate, 24% is by the model generated from DNN using LSTM. The error rate of the model generated from GRU and simple RNN are 24.7% and 37.7% respectively.

Zheng et al. [2] used another set of independent variables in the dataset of study. Initially, the authors proposed to include independent variables such as temperature, humidity, rainfall, and wind speed. These independent variables went through the selection operator (Lasso) to identify which independent variables affect the electricity load. As the results, only average temperature added to the historical electricity load dataset. The dataset duration used was one year and 11 months. This research study applied Adaptive Moment Estimation (ADAM) optimiser in the execution. The study conducted in three categories: load dataset, load and temperature dataset, and load, time, and temperature dataset. The researcher used MAPE to evaluate the model. The best model was generated from the experiment that used the load, time, and temperature dataset with MAPE value of 6.00%. The MAPE result for the experiment that used only load feature is 8.52%. The model was used to predict electricity load in summer, autumn, winter, and spring seasons. Memarzadeh and Keynia [11] also compare the model performance on each season.

Wang et al. [18] compared the prediction performance among various traditional forecasting methods, such as Autoregressive Moving Average model (ARMA), Autoregressive Fractionally Integrated Moving Average model (ARFIMA), and Backpropagation Neural Network (BPNN) with LSTM. The RMSE result for LSTM showed the lowest error among other traditional methods.

Karunathilake and Nagahamulla [19] studied the implementation of ANN in electricity load prediction. The researcher used RMSE, MAE, and R-squared (R^2) to evaluate the model. The result of MAE value was 0.0211, RMSE value was 0.6328, and R^2 value was 0.7385.

Table 1 summarises the machine learning algorithm applied, and the evaluation metrics used in the reviewed research articles.

Table 1. Summary of machine learning algorithms and evaluation metrics used in the reviewed articles.

Reference	Machine learning algorithm	Evaluation metrics
Zheng et al. [2]	LSTM with ADAM optimiser	MAPE
Xuan et al. [9]	Chaos-SVR, Wavelet Decomposition-SVR, SVR, Back propagation	Error percentage, mean bias error, R^2
Salam and El Hibaoui [10]	Random forest, Linear regression, Decision tree, SVM, ANN	RMSE, MAE
Memarzadeh and Keynia [11]	LSTM	MAPE
Singla et al. [12]	ANN	MAPE, RMSE
Shabbir et al. [15]	Linear regression, Tree-based regression, SVM	RMSE
Liu et al. [16]	Elman, LSTM	MAPE
Wang et al. [18]	ARMA, ARFIMA, BPNN, LSTM	RMSE
Karunathilake and Nagahamulla [19]	ANN	MAE, RMSE, R^2

3   Case Study: Danish Electricity Usage Dataset

Denmark is one of the developed countries that leads the implementation of renewable energy. This article intends to assist in predicting residential consumers' electricity demand in Denmark. This study used the unpublished Danish electric power consumption dataset. The dataset was retrieved from a smart meter data of one household unit in Denmark with an hourly sampling rate throughout four years duration, between the year 2015 and year 2018. The dataset used consists of historical electricity load, year, month, day, hour, minute, weekend, holiday type, seasons, and day length columns.

The dataset is divided into the training, testing, and prediction dataset as shown in Table 2.

Table 2 summarises the total rows for each dataset. The training dataset consisted of 26,304 rows and ten columns. The target of the training data was the electricity load column. Other columns were used as features. The testing dataset had 8,760 rows that

Table 2. Summary of training, testing, and validation datasets.

Dataset	Duration	Total rows
Training	January 2015 – December 2017	26,304
Testing	January – December 2018	8,760
Prediction	Any day in between January – December 2018	24

contained one-year of data. The prediction set had 24 rows that represented 24 h in a day. The prediction dataset is the subset of testing dataset.

4   Modelling Using LSTM and ANN

The prediction was performed based on a periodic of time. The data input used in ANN were samples and features. In LSTM, the data input consisted of samples, time steps, and features. The optimizer used is ADAM optimizer [20]. The programme flow is illustrated in Fig. 1.

The difference between LSTM and ANN is in the input layer process. LSTM ap-plied the LSTM method with input_shape parameter values set to time steps value, 24, and number of features. The execution for ANN applied the Dense method with input_shape parameter value set based on the number of features. The ANN and LSTM algorithms applied consist of one input layer, one hidden layer, and one output layer.

The programme produced two models, one model produced by ANN algorithm, and the other model produced by LSTM algorithm. These models were used in the testing phase to evaluate the model quality based on the evaluation metrics, namely MSE and MAE. The model was used in prediction phase to predict the electricity load of a certain duration. The actual values were compared with the actual value. The results' pattern and difference were observed.

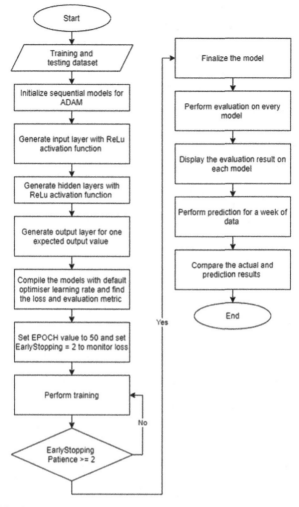

Fig. 1. Experiment methodology applicable for LSTM and ANN.

5   Experimental Results and Discussions

This section shows the results of the implementation of the proposed methodology. The models were trained, tested, and predicted on Intel® Core™ i7-3930K CPU with 6 cores and maximum clock frequency of 3.2 MHz. The software used was Jupyter Notebook on Anaconda Navigator. The TensorFlow Keras library was applied in the execution.

5.1   Training and Testing Datasets

The dataset used was a single household unit electricity load dataset comprising 35,064 rows of samples with nine columns representing features. The initial training data shape was 26,304 rows with nine columns, while the testing dataset shape was 8,760 rows and nine columns. This two-dimensional (2D) array data was applied with ANN algorithm.

For the implementation using LSTM, the time steps applied in this experiment were 24, which represented 24 h per day. The shapes were reshaped into three-dimensional (3D) array with 24 time steps. The new 3D training dataset shape was 1,096 samples, 24 time steps, and nine columns, while the testing set reshape value had 365 samples, 24 time steps, and nine columns.

5.2 Training and Testing Activities

The input for training activity was the training dataset. The output of the training activity was a model. The model generated was tested with the testing dataset. The result of testing activity was evaluated using evaluation metrics, MSE and MAE. Then, the prediction was made on the prediction set, represented for any of the day in 2018. The default epoch value was set to 50.

Table 3 summarises the result of testing process and the epoch required to complete the training on both datasets with ANN and LSTM.

Table 3. Training and testing activities results.

Model name	Machine learning algorithm	MSE	MAE	Epoch
modelLSTM	LSTM	0.1238	0.0388	26
modelANN	ANN	0.1479	0.0480	12

There were two models generated, modelLSTM and modelANN. The lowest error rate produced by modelLSTM with MSE values of 0.1238, and MAE values of 0.0388. The total epoch used in LSTM was 26, while the ANN algorithm completed its training phase with 12 epochs.

5.3 Prediction Activity

The prediction was made for 24-h duration on 2nd April 2018. It was on Monday, in the spring season, in the beginning of the week, and no special occasion on this day in Denmark. The prediction was in hourly, started on 0000 h and ended on 2300 h. Table 4 shows the execution result for actual and prediction values of electricity load derived from the modelANN and modelLSTM.

Table 4. Actual and prediction values generated by modelANN and modelLSTM for one day.

Datetime	Actual	modelANN	modelLSTM
2/4/2018 0:00	0.04	0.09	0.07
2/4/2018 1:00	0.11	0.07	0.07
2/4/2018 2:00	0.07	0.05	0.07
2/4/2018 3:00	0.03	0.06	0.07
2/4/2018 4:00	0.07	0.08	0.07
2/4/2018 5:00	0.15	0.13	0.07
2/4/2018 6:00	0.36	0.25	0.30
2/4/2018 7:00	0.71	0.48	0.54
2/4/2018 8:00	0.32	0.61	0.33
2/4/2018 9:00	1.12	0.33	0.27
2/4/2018 10:00	0.15	0.14	0.18
2/4/2018 11:00	0.34	0.07	0.13
2/4/2018 12:00	0.17	0.08	0.12
2/4/2018 13:00	0.05	0.16	0.12
2/4/2018 14:00	0.18	0.24	0.14
2/4/2018 15:00	0.11	0.29	0.19
2/4/2018 16:00	0.05	0.29	0.19
2/4/2018 17:00	0.15	0.26	0.20
2/4/2018 18:00	0.39	0.20	0.19
2/4/2018 19:00	0.21	0.13	0.16
2/4/2018 20:00	0.2	0.08	0.14
2/4/2018 21:00	0.23	0.05	0.13
2/4/2018 22:00	0.13	0.04	0.13
2/4/2018 23:00	0.05	0.04	0.16

Figure 2 illustrates the results of actual and predicted values by the ANN and LSTM models in Table 4.

Figure 2 shows the actual and prediction results by the modelANN and modelLSTM. The sample of one-day hourly electricity load was on 2nd April 2018. It falls in the spring season. The peak electricity load was identified in between 0600 h and 0900 h, and 1300 h and 1900 h. The electricity load decreased from 0000 h until 0600 h, followed by 1000 h until 1300 h.

The results by the LSTM algorithm was also proven to be better than the model generated by the ANN algorithm as stated in Table 3. This was obtained due to the ability of the LSTM algorithm in memorising the time-series input during the training session.

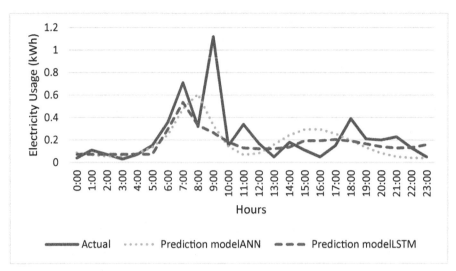

Fig. 2. Comparison between actual electricity load and prediction values from ANN and LSTM models.

6 Conclusion

Electricity power generator companies can use electricity load prediction based on the consumers' electricity usage pattern to estimate the power generation. This paper proposed the implementation of LSTM algorithm to predict electricity demand in time series. Experiments on the traditional machine learning algorithm, ANN, was executed to verify the performance of LSTM. The contribution of this paper is in the implementation with time-series prediction. The model generated using LSTM was proven to produce a lower error rate than the traditional algorithm, ANN, although independent variables were added into the input variables.

This experiment was conducted based on the historical electricity load data with independent variables of a single household unit. Future experiment should consider the implementation on Deep Learning algorithm.

Acknowledgement. The publication of this paper was funded by URND TNB Seeding Fund: U-TE-RD-20–08. The authors would like to thank the Institute of Informatics and Computing in Energy (IICE), Universiti Tenaga Nasional (UNITEN) for providing a platform to collaborate with the Center for Energy Informatics, Southern Denmark University (SDU).

References

1. Electricity explained - U.S. Energy Information Administration (EIA). https://www.eia.gov/energyexplained/electricity, Accessed 12 Dec 2020
2. Zheng, J., Chen, X., Yu, K., Gan, L., Wang, Y., Wang, K.: Short-term Power Load Forecasting of Residential Community Based on GRU Neural Network. 2018 International Conference on Power System Technology (POWERCON). (2018).

3. Md Salleh, N., Suliman, A., Jorgensen, B.: A systematic literature review of machine learning methods for short-term electricity forecasting. In: 2020 8th International Conference on Information Technology and Multimedia (ICIMU) (2020)

4. Zamee, M., Won, D.: Novel mode adaptive artificial neural network for dynamic learning: application in renewable energy sources power generation prediction. Energies **13**, 6405 (2020)

5. Dave, A.: Regression in Machine Learning - Data Driven Investor – Medium. https://medium.com/datadriveninvestor/regression-in-machine-learning-296caae933ec, Accessed 25 June 2019

6. Bai, D., Lee, J., Kim, S., Kang, I.: Near ML modulation classification. In: IEEE Conference on Vehicular Technology (VTC). IEEE (2019)

7. Sikiric, G., Avdakovic, S., Subasi, A.: Comparison of machine learning methods for electricity demand forecasting in bosnia and herzegovina. Southeast Europe J. Soft Comput. **2**, 12–14 (2013)

8. Basile, A., Napporn, T.: Current Trends and FUTURE Developments on (Bio-) Membranes. Elsevier, San Diego (2020)

9. Xuan, Z., Zhubing, F., Liequan, L., Junwei, Y., Dongmei, P.: Comparison of four algorithms based on machine learning for cooling load forecasting of large-scale shopping mall. Energy Procedia **142**, 1799–1804 (2017)

10. Salam, A., El Hibaoui, A.: Comparison of machine learning algorithms for the power consumption prediction : - case study of Tetouan city. In: 2018 6th International Renewable and Sustainable Energy Conference (IRSEC). IEEE (2019)

11. Memarzadeh, G., Keynia, F.: Short-term electricity load and price forecasting by a new optimal LSTM-NN based prediction algorithm. Electric Power Syst. Res. **192**, 106995 (2021)

12. Singla, M., Gupta, J., Nijhawan, P., Oberoi, A.: Electrical load forecasting using machine learning. Int. J. Adv. Trends Comput. Sci. Eng. **8**, 615–619 (2019)

13. Maklin, C.: R Squared Interpretation I R Squared Linear Regression. https://towardsdatascience.com/statistics-for-machine-learning-r-squared-explained-425ddfebf667, Accessed 02 Mar 2020

14. Kassambara, A.: Machine Learning Essentials: Practical Guide in R. CreateSpace Independent Publishing Platform (2018)

15. Shabbir, N., Ahmadiahangar, R., Kutt, L., Rosin, A.: Comparison of machine learning based methods for residential load forecasting. In: 2019 Electric Power Quality and Supply Reliability Conference (PQ) & 2019 Symposium on Electrical Engineering and Mechatronics (SEEM) (2019)

16. Liu, C., Jin, Z., Gu, J., Qiu, C.: Short-term load forecasting using a long short-term memory network. In: 2017 IEEE PES Innovative Smart Grid Technologies Conference Europe (ISGT-Europe) (2017)

17. Hossen, T., Nair, A., Chinnathambi, R., Ranganathan, P.: Residential Load Forecasting Using Deep Neural Networks (DNN). In: 2018 North American Power Symposium (NAPS) (2018)

18. Wang, H., Li, G., Wang, G., Peng, J., Jiang, H., Liu, Y.: Deep learning based ensemble approach for probabilistic wind power forecasting. Appl. Energy **188**, 56–70 (2017)

19. Karunathilake, S.L., Nagahamulla, R.K.H.: Artificial neural networks for daily electricity demand prediction of Sri Lanka. IN: 2017 Seventeenth International Conference on Advances in ICT for Emerging Regions (ICTer). p. 128–133. IEEE, Colombo (2017)

20. Md Salleh, N., Suliman, A., Jørgensen, B.: Experiment on electricity consumption prediction using long short-term memory architecture on residential electrical consumer. In: The International Congress of Advanced Technology and Engineering (ICOTEN 2021) (2021)

Study on the Contributing Factors in e-hailing Waste Management Systems for Mobile Application Adoption and Usage

Ozioma Alex Nwaogwugwu[1]([✉]) and Nazrita Ibrahim[2] [ID]

[1] College of Graduate Studies, Universiti Tenaga Nasional, Kajang, Malaysia
[2] Institute of Informatics and Computing in Energy, Universiti Tenaga Nasional, Kajang, Malaysia

Abstract. Efforts to curb household waste in Malaysia have been unsatisfactory despite numerous policies and regulations. With technological advancements, participation rates can be increased in communities if utilized. This study looks at the current e-hailing waste management technology being used in Malaysian's solid waste management, especially mobile applications usage. Additionally, the study investigates factors that can influence Malaysians to adopt and use e-hailing waste management technology in order to increase recycling participation rates in communities. A survey was carried out with recycling practitioners in Kuala Lumpur to identify their recycling interests, challenges faced while recycling and opinion on e-hailing waste management service. The data was analyzed using a descriptive statistical and thematic analysis methodology and findings from the study showed that the respondents were keen on reducing waste in communities. Based on findings, a design framework was established to boost participation rates and improve awareness in Malaysian communities. Therefore, in order to reduce household waste, it is advised that technologies such as e-hailing waste management be used to channel recyclable household waste to proper destination and cut off landfill dumping.

Keywords: e-hailing · Mobile application · Waste management · Recycling · Solid waste

1 Introduction

Waste generation in Malaysia is increasing as the country's population, both rural and urban, grows. The current municipal waste management system in Malaysia has created inconveniences and a difficult situation, particularly for households that want to recycle. Malaysia current waste separation is divided into four categories: food waste, recyclable waste, scheduled waste, and other waste. These four types of waste can be collected in various ways, including communal containers where collector workers are expected to pick up, house-to-house scheduled collection, and fixed time fixed location.

For effective waste management system, several studies [1–3] have suggested that recycling is the best strategy to minimize waste because of the economic, environmental, and social benefits it provides to a country. The cost of recycling must be low, and

© Springer Nature Switzerland AG 2021
H. Badioze Zaman et al. (Eds.): IVIC 2021, LNCS 13051, pp. 610–622, 2021.
https://doi.org/10.1007/978-3-030-90235-3_53

there must be an easy way to collect recyclables. People must also know how to recycle and be motivated to recycle in order for recycling to be successful. Ineffective dissemination of recycling information on what, where and how to recycle is lacking despite the government putting efforts in policies to drive waste minimization. Additionally, [4] also provided strategies and clear direction to spearhead the initiative to manage waste holistically in Malaysia.

Since E-hailing system is popular amongst Malaysian, implementing a similar system for waste management will not be strange to residents. The adoption of e-hailing amongst Malaysian would be a stimulant to adoption of sustainability lifestyle in Malaysia. Although a few applications bearing this concept had been introduced, not many studies have been carried out to understand what are the elements required in the application that can promote usage adoption among users.

Therefore, given the issues above, this study will review the current e-hailing waste mobile application and identify the factors that can encourage adoption of e-hailing waste management for application adoption and usage for promoting recycling in communities.

2   Literature Review

2.1   Situational Analysis of Municipal Solid Waste in Malaysia

Solid waste management is Malaysia's most pressing environmental concern, with landfilling serving as the primary disposal mechanism for the country's annual rise in solid waste generation. Malaysia depends on landfilling as a waste disposal method. Municipal Solid Waste (MSW) disposal via landfilling is becoming increasingly difficult as new landfill sites fill up. More specifically, constructing a new location would be difficult due to a lack of available land, an increase in land prices, and high demand, particularly in urban areas due to population growth [5]. Waste generated increased in 2018 from 30,987 tonnes to 31,089 in 2019 based on [6]. The reported increase in waste is a clear indication that waste generation will continue to rise by the year and the storage or disposal mechanism may be overloaded; hence, environmental hazard could happen.

In managing the household waste problem, several studies supported recycling as a practice. To reduce waste generation, [7] believe that it is critical to raise public awareness for behavioral change, recycling facilities and collection systems, according to [8], could be made more convenient and easily accessible which was supported by [9]. Besides that [10] identified that some households do not have adequate storage bins. Furthermore, there are no recycling bins for households to separate different types of waste. Residents needed to have a proper storage facilities to avoid waste being dumped besides the collection point or bin. Collections are done either by fixed time fixed location or communal bin being placed a centralized location or house-to-house collection across Malaysia [10, 11]. Hence, to improve the collection rate, proper container has to be assigned which will increase the participation and recycling rates in Malaysian communities. Another good strategy to increase participation in recycling is by the reward system. According to [12], rewards could be either monetary incentives received from recycling or a virtual reward system implemented to drive participation.

Since the technology era and use the use of mobile application has become the norm of the day, an application that would encourage and motivate the complete implementation of reduce, reuse and recycle (3R) would be needed to encourage residents to embrace sustainability lifestyle. E-hailing systems are widely used in Malaysia for ride –sharing or online food delivery. However, the same concept can be implemented in waste management application, as demonstrated by [12] who develop an application that uses e-hailing concept to monitor the level of waste in rivers and surrounding areas. Based on this recent development, driving recycling through e-hailing system could be an alternative solution to help improve the recycling lifestyle of Malaysians.

Table 1 shows the summary of four existing e-waste applications and feature supported by them. The four applications are RIIICYCLE, RECIRCLE, Gargeon and Internet Waste of Things (iOWT). The applications were selected based on the following selection criteria: Locally available in Malaysia, Used for waste collection and Mobile application.

Table 1. Review of existing e-waste application features.

	Reward / Incentives	Location Map	Redemption	Recycling Data Report	Educational Campaign	Request Pickup	Charges	Availability
RIIICYCLE	√	√	√	X	√	X	X	√
RECIRCLE	√	√	√	√	√	√	X	√
Gargeon	X	√	X	√	X	√	√	√
iOWT	√	√	√	√	√	X	X	√

Legend: X - Not available, √ - Available

Based on the review, it can be observed that there are eight (8) common features/functions provided by these apps.

Rewards/Incentives. It is believed that daily reward programs encourage the involvement of residents in waste recycling. According to various studies on human motivating factors to participate in waste management, reward is a motivating factor [13, 14].

Location Map. Solid waste management involves multiple steps, starting from the stage in which the waste is created before it reaches its final destination or at a stage in which the environment is no longer threatened. Therefore, it is important to implement a location map that makes it easier for its users to quickly and conveniently drop waste.

Redemption. Redemption refers to features, which allow users to Redeem reward points into vouchers, send cash to their bank account, or donate cash to the charity home [15]. There are several ways in which reward points can be turned. This is will also motivate users to recycle more and redeem their choice redemption.

Recycling Data Report. Tracking performance behavior is one type of motivation that can encourage individuals to continue participating in the waste reduction exercise, thereby increasing the rate of community participation. Tracking progress increases emotional and cognitive sense of actions [16].

Educational Campaign. With the era of mobile technology advancement, the awareness of residents should be easy and the way waste is handled should be improved. Recently, some campaigns are now using mobile apps as a way to engage users in improving waste recycling [17].

Request Pick Up. Humans always want a convenient way to do things. Convenience is a key factor in encouraging residents to participate in recycling activities [18]. If users are able to request the collection of waste at their convenience, there will be encouragement in the communities, and therefore a reduction in waste and increased participation rate.

Charges. The flat-rate charging model does not encourage households to reduce the amount of waste [19]. Although some users may be willing to pay for good quality of service. With 'Pay as you throw policy,' educating consumers on how to reduce waste is important from the point of view of municipalities, because they pay for landfills and waste disposal services. A minimal charge would encourage users to pay and recycle which could be regained by earning rewards and convert back into monetary value.

Availability. Service readiness and availability also encourages users. All the mobile applications reviewed above are available for use in Malaysia but may need to expand and engage more with the local councils for more awareness.

Efforts have been made in Malaysia to reduce waste, but many people are unaware of how waste management can be accomplished. Among the issues identified are a lack of storage facilities, a lack of awareness, insufficient collection, and environmentally unfriendly disposal methods. Implementing e-hailing system to boost the waste management in Malaysia could be the next smart move towards encouraging recycling among the residence. However, although the current features of the current system have been reviewed, it is unclear which factors are required to promote usage and adoption of the e-hailing waste application. The goal of this study is to identify the factors that encourage residents to use and adopt an e-hailing waste application, which would increase community recycling participation rates.

3   Methodology

The methods used in this research were Primary Data Collection through survey and Secondary Data Collection through literature review. In the secondary data collection, official papers, posts, newspapers, legal records, published and unpublished literature, and case studies are all included in desk studies. Four different e-hailing waste mobile applications were reviewed.

The Primary Data Collection was based on a survey of some households in the Klang Valley geographic area who were given online questionnaires. The study's target audiences are waste management/recycling practitioners of various genders, age group, working schedule, and housing property type from urban and rural settings. The target audience was selected due to their understanding of waste management. The questionnaire link was sent via instant message groups of focused group, face to face was avoided due to covid-19 situation. The survey was conducted between 1st June–30th June 2020.

Total of 61 respondents responded to the survey. The survey had five sections which include both the open-ended and closed-ended questions: Sect. 1 (Demography), Sect. 2 (To understand what motivates individuals to participate in waste management.), Sect. 3 (To understand what hinders individuals to participate in waste management), Sect. 4 (To identify issues with existing e-hailing services) and Sect. 5 (To gather views on the introduction of e-hailing waste management systems to participants). The closed ended was analyzed using descriptive analysis while open ended questions were analyzed using thematic analysis.

A design framework will be constructed based on the analyzed results and the framework will be discussed.

4   Data Analysis and Results

4.1   Demography

The number of female respondents is higher than male with 32 participants (52%) are female, and 29 participants (48%) are male. The majority of participants are between 41 and 50 years of age, with 24 participants (39%) in the group. There are 21 participants (34%) aged between 51 and above, 8 participants (13%) aged between 31 and 40 years, 6 participants (10%) aged between 25 and 30 years. Finally, 2 participants (3%) aged between 17 and 24 years participated in this study. Working schedule were considered in order to understand what a flexi working hour and a fixed time working hour residents may prefer. The participants with a flexible working hour will be able to make collection requests anytime at their convenience while those with the fixed working schedule time participants would only be able to request collection at a specific time due to their work schedule. Thirty-three participants (54%) have a flexible working schedule while twenty-eight participants (46%) have a fixed working schedule. Thirty-nine participants (64%) reside in a landed property kind of housing and twenty-two participants (36%) reside in condo/high rise apartments.

4.2   To Understand What Motivates Individuals to Participate in Waste Management

Based on the Pareto chart in Fig. 1 and 2, with 80/20 rule, 80% of those who recycle do so because they care about the environment, decreasing waste impact on the environment and reducing landfill waste. While 80% of those who do not recycle say they are unable to do so due to the dispiriting and inconvenient nature of the process, incapacity to recycle, and the unfriendliness of the overall process. 80% of residents would be motivated if rewards and elements that can instill environmental consciousness are provided in Fig. 3. Two important findings that can be used as a basis for the proposed e-hailing waste management design are: reward recognition system that would motivate those who recycle to continue recycling and quick tips that can assist those who find it difficult to recycle, to learn the easy way to recycle.

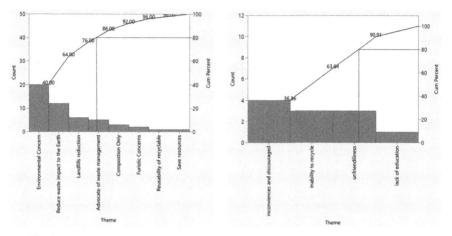

Fig. 1. Reason why people recycle   **Fig. 2.** Reason why people do not recycle

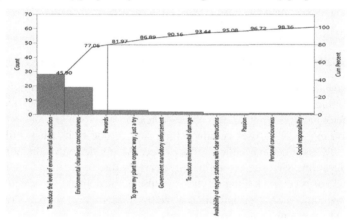

Fig. 3. Motivation to do recycling

4.3 To Understand What Hinders Individuals to Participate in Waste Management

Based on the Pareto chart in Fig. 4, with 80/20 rule, 80% of the participants face barriers of inadequate bins, poor educational awareness and poor collection timing, which hinders their involvement in participating in waste management. There is a significant hindrance within the 20% which does not know the waste final destination as it would motivate more participation. Several important findings that can be used as a basis for the proposed e-hailing waste management design are: Easy geotag location access to collection points/bins or pick up locations, waste end-of-life destinations data and educational awareness program.

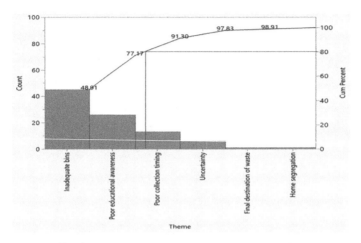

Fig. 4. What hinder participant from doing recycling

4.4 To Identify Issues with Existing e-hailing Services in Malaysia

Based on the Pareto chart in Fig. 5, with 80/20 rule, 80% of the participants believes the current e-hailing services in Malaysia is high cost, driver late arrival time, rider location inconsistencies and unfriendly user mobile application.

Based on Fig. 6, 39% uses certain hailing service due to its trustworthiness and reliability, 20% uses certain hailing services because it's the only common available hailing application, 8% uses certain hailing services due to its user friendliness and simplicity, 7% uses certain hailing services because of the delivery service functionality and 2% participants uses the application because of the regular coupon shared on the hailing service platform.

Therefore, three key findings that can be used as the basis for the proposed e-hailing waste management design are as follows: Collector punctuality, Easy to use application and Moderate cost.

4.5 To Gather Views on the Introduction of e-hailing Waste Management Systems to Participants.

Based on the pie chart in Fig. 7, 31% of participants would like to have user friendly application, 30% would like to have good collection service, 11% would like to have traceable waste data, 3% wants to see news feed on the application, 2% recommends a reduced fee and 23% are undecided about what should be in the application.

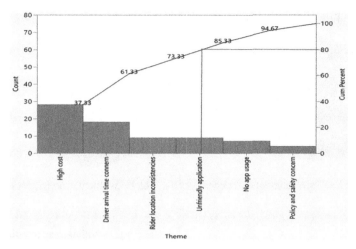

Fig. 5. Issues with current e-hailing service

Reason to use ehailing

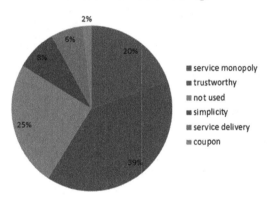

Fig. 6. Why use hailing application

Based on the pie chart in Fig. 8, 51% of participants are willing to pay for such service if implemented, 34% are unwilling while 13% are still undecided and 2% would still prefer self-service.

Based on the Pareto chart in Fig. 9, with 80/20 rule, 80% of the participants high-lighted potential issue that may be lacking or should be included such as professionalism of personnel, awareness program, user centric application and unwillingness to pay.

Based on the pie chart in Fig. 10, 69% of participants are willing to adopt the new e-hailing waste mobile application while 31% do not see the need for a mobile application.

Based on the results and observations in this section, five key findings that can be used as the basis for the proposed e-hailing waste management design are as follows:

Features needed

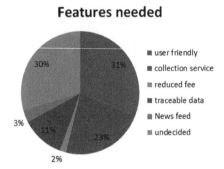

Willingness to pay

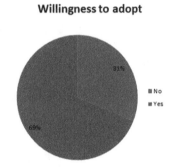

Fig. 7. What feature(s) are needed   **Fig. 8.** Willingness to pay for the service

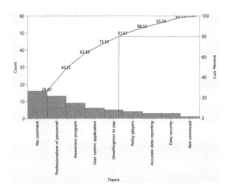

Willingness to adopt

Fig. 9. Concerns or suggestions of proposed system   **Fig. 10.** Willingness to adopt

Friendly User Interface, Collection service, Reduced charged fee, Traceable data and News Feed.

Therefore, based on results in this study, participants would like to see proper educational awareness provided to households through campaign programs, monetary incentives should be considered, collection system that would ease collection from source to storages, viewing collected waste data is also important to participants for psychological effect, convenient scheduling and reduced charges. As a result, a convenient and simple-to-use e-haling waste mobile application would encourage residents of various working classes and ages to participate in waste management at their convenience.

5   Discussion

This section is derived from data analysis. The responses of participants were collected and analyzed, yielding the following design framework shown in Table 2 to encourage adoption and usage of e-hailing waste management participation.

Based on this observation, six factors were proposed as framework for designing an e-hailing waste management for application adoption and usage in communities: Rewards, Friendly User Interface, Waste Analytics, News Feed, Convenient Scheduling and Convenient Payment as shown in Fig. 11.

Table 2. Design element for adoption and usage of e-hailing waste application in Malaysia

Factors	Design element
Rewards	a) Points b) Badges c) Merchant (allows rewards to be redeemed to products, monetary or donations) d) Leaderboard e) Levels
Friendly user interface	a) Input Controls (allow users to input information into the system) b) Navigation Components (help users move around the application) c) Informational Components (Share information with users.) d) Containers (hold related content together) e) Incorporate Clear Micro-Copy (small snippets of text that provide instructions to your audience.)
Waste analytics	a) Performance charts in graphical representations b) Waste destination tracking system via tabular representation
Campaign	Feed • Educational • Events • Announcement • Scoreboard ranking
Convenient scheduling	a) Schedule pick up b) Select vehicle size c) Calendar d) Upload photo
Convenient payment	Pay Now • Points • Bank transfer • Credit Card

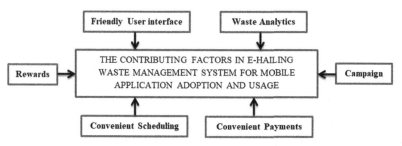

Fig. 11. Proposed design framework for e-hailing waste management system for mobile application adoption and usage.

Rewards: Anything given in appreciation for service, effort, or achievement is referred to as a reward. Reward encompasses any type of incentive provided by the government or competent authorities for recycling (separating recyclable materials from waste at home). Element such as Monetary incentives is a direct rewards to user while badges, merchants, a scoreboard, or levels, to encourage users to progress, complete actions and compare their results with other users that engage in waste management.

Friendly User Interface: A simple to use mobile application, according to several participants in this report, would allow more users to use it. Participants must have a positive user experience in order to remain engaged and involved in the application. A clear User Interface (UI) provides users with discoverability and comprehension. The first experience of a product or service has a significant influence on the user's attitude and relationship with the product.

Waste Analytics: Analytic waste representation that will allow users to see the progress made on waste management in their communities. Performance charts like waste trends, waste recycled, and carbon dioxide savings are needed to track individual progress and the emotional attachments that come with helping to reduce waste sent to landfills. It is also crucial to have the waste final destination traceability (from household to final destination).

Campaign. Raising public awareness about waste prevention is a critical first step in encouraging behavioural change. Awareness campaigns that are well-designed and well-executed will help to address the two major obstacles to recycling: a lack of knowledge about proper waste segregation and shifting attitudes and expectations, as well as keeping people motivated to avoid and sort waste. Therefore, the campaign should be aimed at creating relevant awareness programmed to communities.

Convenient Scheduling. The ability to schedule hailing on a mobile device would promote community engagement. To achieve an economically and environmentally sustainable practice, providing a convenient hailing scheduling is the best way to enable users to engage in waste management.

Convenient Payment. A reduced service charge and easy payment method would encourage residents to be interested in using the mobile application. Therefore it is very important to create a convenient experience.

6   Conclusion

Recycling is a campaign that aims to reduce waste in Malaysia's communities, but residents are hesitant to engage for a variety of reasons, including lack of educational knowledge, collection facilities, motivation, storage facilities, and, more broadly, a lack of interest.

The current waste mobile applications have not answered those concerns comprehensively. A design framework was design in this study to address the issues why residents do not participate in recycling. Incentives, points, badges, scoreboards, merchandize, and levels were recognized as reward element that can inspire a user to recycle more. A user interface that is easy to use for people of all ages. Waste analytics that can indicate a user's waste performance and trace waste dropped until it reaches its final destination have been shown to have a psychological impact to users. A public awareness program that disseminates information about waste management, recycling related events, public announcements to communities, and community rankings should be provided. Flexible scheduling is imminent to make recycling simple, as well as a simple payment option for costs incurred.

According to the study, a convenient waste management system, such as an e-hailing waste management system with mobile application adoption, would improve community participation in recycling exercises. Thus, this helps to reduce waste sent to landfills, promote a sustainable lifestyle, increase the amount of recyclable material recycled through proper channels and promote circular economy.

References

1. Chen, H.L., Nath, T.K., Chong, S., Foo, V., Gibbins, C., Lechner, A.M.: The plastic waste problem in Malaysia: management, recycling and disposal of local and global plastic waste. SN Appl. Sci. 3(4), 1–15 (2021). https://doi.org/10.1007/s42452-021-04234-y
2. Mentek, M.: Solid waste management in Malaysia: towards a holistic approach. In: International Solid Waste Association (ISWA) World Congress. Ministry of Urban Wellbeing (2017). Housing and Local Government. http://www.swcorp.gov.my/docfile/kertas-taklimat/TowardsaHolisticApproach.pdf
3. Jereme, I.A., Alam, M.M., Siwar, C.: Waste recycling in Malaysia: transition from developing to developed country. Indian J. Educ. Inf. Manage. 4, 1–14 (2015)
4. Solid Waste Management Lab (2015). https://jpspn.kpkt.gov.my/resources/index/user_1/fileupload/slaid_dapatan_makmal.pdf. Accessed 23 May 2021
5. Yatim, S.R.M., et al.: Study on waste generation and composition in rapid residential development of sub urban area in Kuala Selangor District, Selangor. J. Wastes Biomass Manage. (JWBM) 1(1), 1–5 (2019)
6. Compendium of Environment Statistics, Malaysia (2020). https://www.dosm.gov.my/v1/index.php?r=column/pdfPrev&id=TjM1ZlFxb3VOakdmMnozVms5dUlKZz09. Accessed 23 May 2021
7. Taušová, M., et al.: Analysis of municipal waste development and management in self-governing regions of Slovakia. Sustainability 12(14), 5818 (2020)
8. Geiger, J.L., Steg, L., van der Werff, E., Ünal, A.B.: A meta-analysis of factors related to recycling. J. Environ. Psychol. 64, 78–97 (2019)
9. Starr, J., Nicolson, C.: Patterns in trash: Factors driving municipal recycling in Massachusetts. Resour. Conserv. Recycl. 99, 7–18 (2015)
10. Ali, N.E., Siong, H.C., Mokhtar, K., Talmizi, N.M., Saleh, A.A.: Solid waste management in Shah Alam city residential area. J. Sustain. Sci. Manage. 13(1), 211–227 (2018)
11. Saipul, N.I.L., et al.: Parties and their roles in solid waste separation at the source: an example from Malaysia's award-winning residential area. J. Tourism 2(6), 10–21 (2017)
12. Rohana, S., Abdamia, N., Mohd, M.: Developing a pollution free environment framework through technology integration (e-hailing app). Environ. Behav. Proc. J. 4(10), 161–167 (2019)

13. Mahpour, A., Mortaheb, M.M.: Financial-based incentive plan to reduce construction waste. J. Constr. Eng. Manag. **144**(5), 04018029 (2018)

14. Amini, F., Ahmada, J., Ambalia, A.R.: The Influence of reward and penalty on households' recycling intention. APCBEE Proc. **10**, 187–192 (2014)

15. Abd Wahab, M.H., Abdul Kadir, A., Md Tomari, M.R., Jabbar, M.H.: Web-based reward and redemption system for smart recycle system (2015)

16. Goh, D.H.L., Pe-Than, E.P.P., Lee, C.S.: Perceptions of virtual reward systems in crowd-sourcing games. Comput. Hum. Behav. **70**, 365–374 (2017)

17. Bonino, D., Alizo, M.T.D., Pastrone, C., Spirito, M.: WasteApp: smarter waste recycling for smart citizens. In: International Multidisciplinary Conference on Computer and Energy Science 2016 (2016)

18. Mutang, J.A., et al.: Recycling motivations and barriers in Kota Kinabalu, Malaysia. Int. J. Psychol. Behav. Sci. **9**(8), 2911–2915 (2015)

19. Salminen, S.: Value of Waste Flow Monitoring Service for House Managers in Municipal Solid Waste (MSW) Management (2016)

Establishing Valid and Reliable Measures for Residential Consumer Behaviour Towards New Technology Electricity Appliances: An Exploratory Factor Analysis

Nor Salwati Othman[1]([✉]) [iD], Nor Hamisham Harun[1] [iD], Izzaamirah Ishak[2] [iD],
and Nurul Hezlin Mohamed Hariri[3]

[1] College of Business Management and Accounting, Universiti Tenaga Nasional, Kajang,
Malaysia
norsalwati@uniten.edu.my
[2] College of Energy Economics and Social Sciences, Universiti Tenaga Nasional,
Kajang, Malaysia
[3] Tenaga Nasional Berhad (TNB), Kuala Lumpur, Malaysia

Abstract. The government policies and initiatives to guarantee sustainable energy and clean environmental conditions contributed to the introduction of new technology electricity appliances in the market. This research intends to develop a valid and reliable survey instrument to measure consumer behaviour towards new technology electricity appliances. For that purpose, the pilot study randomly sampled 104 residential electricity consumers using an online survey with an interval scale between 1 and 10 is applied. Then, the Exploratory Factor Analysis (EFA) procedure on construct elements with the extraction method of Principal Component with Varimax Rotation is used to determine the adequacy of construct elements. The results of EFA indicate one of the elements of government policy needs to be dropped because it shows the lowest total variance explained and factor loading. Cronbach's Alpha was applied to test the reliability of the retained items. All eleven constructs have Cronbach's alpha values that exceed the threshold value of 0.7, which indicates high reliability. The development scale and validation confirmed that the instrument is consistent and stable across samples. As an implication, the field study can be conducted with the remaining and valid constructs and items.

Keywords: New technology electricity appliances (NTEA) · Consumer behaviour · Exploratory factor analysis · Residential sector

1 Introduction

Electricity has been one of the world's most important resources for human and economic activity in recent years. Its function becomes rigorous, along with economic development and modernisation [1]. Realising the importance of electricity to maintain the quality of life, the government needs to ensure an adequate supply of electricity to the Malaysian community by discovering alternative energy and increasing energy

© Springer Nature Switzerland AG 2021
H. Badioze Zaman et al. (Eds.): IVIC 2021, LNCS 13051, pp. 623–641, 2021.
https://doi.org/10.1007/978-3-030-90235-3_54

efficiency. Accordingly, several policies and initiatives have been implemented, starting with the National Energy Policy in 1979 [2]. The government introduced the Five-Fuel Diversification Policy in 2001 and Renewable Energy Act in 2011 to encourage the use of renewables in electricity production [3]. Other government initiatives such as Feed-in-Tariff (FiT) (2011), Net Energy Metering 1.0 (NEM 1.0) (2016), NEM 2.0 (2019), and the latest one, NEM 3.0 (2021) schemes had created awareness on solar energy and increased the new technology electricity appliances (NTEA) in Malaysia. These initiatives are quite challenging initially because Malaysians are unfamiliar with the aforementioned scheme [3, 4]. Then, with the information spreading, many Malaysians realised the benefit from FiT and NEM 1.0 and 2.0. In 2021 the government had introduced the NEM 3.0 due to overwhelming response from the PV industry and to boost the usage of Solar energy [5]. Moreover, through National Green Technology Policy in 2009 and National Energy Efficiency Action Plan (NEEAP) 2016–2025, the government had promoted energy efficiency to safeguard the productive use of energy and minimise waste from energy consumption through energy efficiency appliances. However, the Malaysia Energy Information Hub (MEIH) data show the electricity consumed by Malaysians and the electricity intensity[1] still rising in the same direction (Fig. 1). The electricity consumption and electricity intensity grew by 5.5% and 1.9%, respectively, for the 1980–2020 periods. This indicates the possibility of achieving energy saving from energy efficiency (EE) by 8% in 2025 could be impossible.

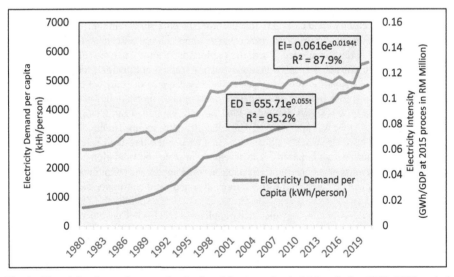

Fig. 1. Electricity demand per capita & electricity intensity in Malaysia for 1980–2020 period [6].

The adoption and success of that particular technology are beyond government control. The government and the producer (of that particular technology) need to understand

---

[1] Electricity intensity is the amount of electricity consumed divided with GDP. The higher the electricity intensity, the lower the level of efficiency.

the consumer behaviour intention, which also represents the gap of this research. Through it, the producer can predict market demand, the consumer willingness to pay, and benefit from the information to increase the sales of its products and gain the expected profit since it is the ultimate goal of their operation. Furthermore, household appliances have become the primary source of household energy consumption. Cultivating consumer purchasing intentions towards new electricity appliances (NTEA) and promoting energy-efficient (EE) appliances is crucial for Malaysia to achieve its sustainable development goals. Even though many empirical studies have been undertaken on behaviour intention, the past researcher focuses less on consumer behaviour intention on NTEA and therefore is relatively scant [7–11].

This research intends to develop a reliable instrument to measure consumer intention behaviour towards new technology electricity consumption. Through it, the researcher can proceed with a field study on assessing the status of Malaysian consumer behaviour intention on the aforesaid product. Instead of being beneficial to NTEA's producer, this information is also beneficial to electricity providers that enable them to plan the supply for electricity and cater to the demand of electricity mainly from the residential consumer.

The remainder of this paper is structured as follows. Section 2 is an overview of Malaysia's electricity consumption and policies. Section 3 and 4 present the literature on behaviour intention and research framework, respectively. Section 5 presents the methodology steps, and Sect. 6 presents the empirical results. Lastly, Sect. 7 concludes the findings.

2 Overview of Electricity Consumption in Malaysia

Electricity consumption in Malaysia has risen with increasing economic development. It can be shown that the annual growth rate for total Malaysian electricity consumption is 6.4% (Fig. 2). However, electricity demand in Peninsular Malaysia is likely to fall into the negative zone in 2020 due to the Movement Control Order (MCO). The anticipated sharp decline in electricity consumption is not entirely surprising, considering close to 80% of Tenaga Nasional Bhd's (TNB) sales in Peninsular Malaysia come from industrial and commercial customers [12]. The most notable decline was in the commercial sector, such as business complexes, shopping malls, and hotels, which decreased between 31 to 47% in electricity consumption [13]. Nevertheless, according to Datuk Shamsul Anuar Nasarah (Minister of Energy and Natural Resources), electricity consumption by residential users in Peninsular Malaysia soared by 23% during the MCO period compared to a decrease of 33% in the overall electricity consumption. Accordingly, the residential sector has the highest growth rate (6.9%) compared to commercial (6.7%) and industrial (5.9%) sectors (Fig. 2).

The consistent increase of electricity demand particularly comes from the residential sector, giving a negative signal to our environment with detrimental impacts on future generations. An important component of securing a sustainable future is to reduce the consumption of electricity while promoting an environmentally friendly culture.

The Malaysian government has launched the National Energy Efficiency Action Plan (NEEAP) for a ten-year implementation period from 2016 to 2025 after considering the socio-culture, policy, financial, and administration barriers. The NEEAP

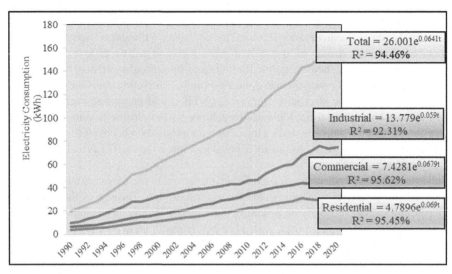

Fig. 2. Final electricity consumption in Malaysia for 1990–2020 period [6].

presents a strategy for a well-coordinated and cost-effective implementation of energy efficiency measures in the industrial, commercial and residential sectors, which will lead to reduced energy consumption and economic savings for the consumers and the nation. The plan aims to promote energy efficiency to meet the following policy direction: Promote energy efficiency to ensure productive use of energy and minimise waste to contribute to sustainable development and increased welfare and competitiveness. Accordingly, the government has initiated various initiatives for energy efficiency, especially for residential sectors, such as phasing out incandescent light bulbs, increasing energy performance labelling, and introducing Minimum Energy Performance Standards (MEPS) for selected household electric appliances. Given that, they give retailers incentives on sales of small capacity appliances and promotion of electrical appliances with Minimum Energy Performance Standards (MEPS) under the SAVE Rebate Programme. Currently, MEPS has introduced five electricity appliances: refrigerators, air-conditioners, televisions, fans, and lighting. By purchasing these appliances, the consumers will get a rebate of RM100–RM200 under the SAVE programme [14].

Furthermore, the Malaysian Electricity Supply Industry 2.0 (MESI 2.0) was reformed to liberalise the generation to distribute components of the power industry in Peninsular Malaysia and promote green energy in Malaysia. This was by establishing a hybrid generation market (honouring current Power Purchase Agreement—PPA and opening up for capacity and energy market); sourcing of own fuel (coal and gas); enabling Third Party Access (TPA) for transmission and distribution (T&D), and facilitating green energy producers and consumers. The establishment of MESI 2.0 is due to three emerging technologies disrupting the industry of electrification, digitalisation, and decentralisation. By reforming MESI 2.0, the potential outcome will be highlighted for better consumer experience, reasonable electricity supply, and generate additional economic activities [15].

In addition, having been dependent mainly on oil and gas generated power plants for half a century, Malaysia had realised the importance of adopting renewable energy as an alternative to conventional non-renewable energy resources and continuously reviewed its energy policy to ensure sustainable energy supply and security [16]. As a result, Malaysia could be self-sufficient ultimately with self-produced energy. The total production of all-electric energy-producing facilities is 148 billion kWh, which is 108% of the country's usage. Despite this, Malaysia is trading energy with foreign countries. Besides pure consumption, imports and exports play an important role [17].

3   Literature Review

Many past studies discussed household intention and behaviour with a variety of perspectives. A review of the literature found some of the previous scholarly work on behavioural intention on energy efficient (EE) usage [18], energy-saving behaviour [19], purchasing electric vehicle behaviour [20] and public intention to use solar energy [21]. Accordingly, numerous researchers applied the Theory of Planned Behaviour (TPB), Theory of Reasoned Action (TRA), and Technology Acceptance Model (TAM) as a theoretical basis for their study. However, several studies attempted to improve the explanatory power of TPB, despite the general usefulness of the theory in predicting behavioural intention, by adding additional constructs within the TPB model [22]. For example, [22] extended the TPB research by adding the items in the survey that consist of moral norms, environmental concern, and environmental knowledge to understand consumer's intention toward purchasing energy-efficient household appliances. Furthermore, the items or variables that were highlighted in their study are not much different from one study to another study, such as attitude, subjective norms, perceived behavioural control, environmental knowledge, and the intention to use renewable energy (Table 1). Thus, Table 1 shows the items/variables used in different countries, years, and contexts of the study.

This current study focuses on exploring the items towards new technology electricity appliances, namely smart meter, electricity vehicle, battery storage, solar PV, and energy efficiency appliances. Therefore, this study explores relevant items and develops an instrument for measuring residential consumer attitudes towards NTEA in Peninsular Malaysia.

Table 1. Past Studies on items/variables used

Author	Context	Country	Items/variables	Theory
Apipuchayakul & Vassanadumrongdee (2020) [18]	Household energy efficient	Thailand	Attitude, subjective norms, perceived behavioural control, intention, behavioural	Theory of Planned Behavior (TPB)

(*continued*)

Table 1. (*continued*)

Author	Context	Country	Items/variables	Theory
Akroush et al. (2019) [19]	Household energy saving	Amman, Jordan	Energy Awareness, perceived benefits, perceived price, consumers' attitudes, purchasing intention	Theory of Planned Behavior (TPB), Theory Reasoned Action (TRA), Technology Acceptance Model (TAM)
Tu & Yang (2019) [20]	Purchasing electric vehicle	China	Perceived usefulness, perceived ease of use, compatibility, personal innovativeness, interpersonal influences, external influences, self-efficacy, facilitating conditions, perceived behavioural control	Theory of Planned Behaviour (TPB), Technology Acceptance Model (TAM), Innovation Diffusion Theory (IDT)
Ali et al. (2019) [23]	Household energy efficient	Pakistan	Optimism, innovativeness, insecurity, discomfort, attitude, subjective norms, perceived behavioural control, intention to buy	Theory of Planned Behavior (TPB), Technology Readiness Index (TRI)
Alam et al. (2019) [24]	Household energy efficient	Malaysia	Purchasing intention of energy-efficient product, attitude, subjective norm, perceived control, knowledge, price	Extended Theory of Planned Behavior (TPB)
Kardooni et al. (2018) [25, 26]	Renewable energy usage	Peninsular Malaysia	Intention to use of renewable energy, knowledge, trust, cost	Conceptual Framework

(*continued*)

Table 1. (*continued*)

Author	Context	Country	Items/variables	Theory
Wang, Wang & Guo (2017) [27]	Household energy saving	China	Attitude, subjective norm, perceived behavioural control, residual effect	Theory of Planned Behavior (TPB)
Tan et al. (2017) [22]	Household energy saving	Malaysia	Attitude, subjective norm, perceived behavioural control, moral norms, environmental concern, environmental knowledge	Theory of Planned Behavior (TPB)
Park & Kwon (2017) [28]	Household energy saving	South Korea	Intention to use, perceived benefits, perceived trust, satisfaction, system quality, perceived cost, attitude	Theory of Planned Behavior (TPB)
Wallis et al. (2016) [29]	Electricity consumption in households	German	Electricity consumption, socio-demographic, economic factors, purchasing and use behaviours	–
Kim et al. (2014) [21]	Public intention to use solar energy	South Korea	Intention to use, perceived benefits, perceived trust, satisfaction, system quality, perceived cost, attitude	Theory of Reasoned Action (TRA), Technology Acceptance Model (TAM)
Wang et al. (2014) [30]	Household energy saving behavior	Beijing	Attitude, subjective norm, perceived behavioural control, information publicity, living habits, energy knowledge, demographic variable	Theory of Planned Behavior (TPB)

(*continued*)

Table 1. (*continued*)

Author	Context	Country	Items/variables	Theory
Ha & Janda (2012) [31]	Household energy saving	South Korea	Attitude, subjective norm, belief about energy efficient product, knowledge about energy efficient product, environmental awareness, confidence of consequence, eagerness of environmental engagement	Theory of Reasoned Action (TRA),

4   Consumer Behavior Framework on Residential Consumer Behavior Towards New Technology Electricity Appliances

The previous literature (Table 1) has demonstrated the majority of the studies measuring consumer behaviour are employing the theory of TPB, TRA, and TAM. Figure 3 shows the proposed research framework based on the finding in Sect. 3.

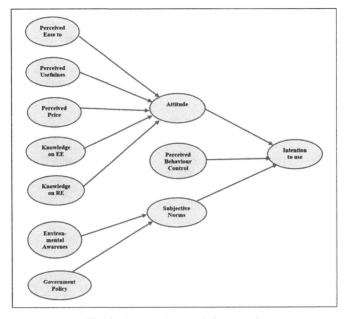

Fig. 3. Proposed research framework

The constructs employed in this study and its definition:

- Intention to use (ITU):

    The intention to use (ITU) refers to the extent to which consumers think they are willing to purchase or use such products. The TPB proposed by Ajzen stated that the behaviour of individuals is determined by their 'behavioural intention'. Therefore this study utilised TPB to determine residential consumer behaviour toward NTEA.
- Attitude (A):

    Attitude refers to consumer psychological evaluation of a certain product. According to [18], attitude is a determinant of purchase intention. The consumer with positive attitudes towards NTEA tends to have an intention to purchase the NTEA.
- Perceived behaviour control (PBC):

    According to [23] and [20] the perceived behaviour control (PBC) is an individuals' degree of control over the execution of certain behaviour. [22] defined the PBC as an individual's perceived ease or difficulty performing a specific behaviour. This study concluded the PBC as a consumer's confidence to perform a given behaviour with available resources (i.e., time, money, support, etc.) in hand.
- Subjective Norms (SN):

    The Subjective norms (SN) refer to consumers' perceived peer pressure, which dictates that they behave in a certain way to meet social expectations [18]. [23] state the SN as the influential degree of peers' opinion and perceptions while performing a specific behaviour. Based on previous literature, this study defines the SN as a consumer performance as a result of peers' opinions (friends, family, mass media, and internet information) about NTEA.
- Government policy (GP):

    The government policy (GP), in this case, refers to any related energy and environmental policies that are used to sway purchase, retail stocking, and production decisions towards NTEA. The study by [27], had classified government policy as one of the subjective norm's indicators. In the current paper, the GP purposely measures the influence of government policies and initiatives towards SN and consumer behaviour.
- Perceived ease to use (PEU):

    The perceived ease to use (PEU) refers to consumers' ability to learn the operation of NTEA and use the NTEA without much effort.
- Perceived usefulness (PU):

    The perceived usefulness (PU) is referring to consumers' perception of the efficiency of NTEA functions.
- Perceived price (PP):

    Many researchers have examined the effect of the perceived price (PP) on consumer attitude and intention to buy, and the results were found to contradict one another. The PP, in this case, is referring to consumers' perception of the price of NTEA, either affordable or unaffordable.
- Knowledge on EE (KEE) & Knowledge on RE (KRE):

    The knowledge is used to understand its influence on ITU and explain the gap between the consumers' attitudes and orientation towards energy conservation and their actual behaviour [19]. This study anticipates the better the knowledge on EE and RE, the higher ITU on NTEA.

- Environmental awareness (EA):

    Similar to KEE and KRE, environmental awareness (EA) is used to understand its influence on behavioural variables and explain the gap between the consumers' attitudes and orientation towards energy conservation and their actual behaviour [19, 32]. This study anticipates that the higher the degree of consciousness on environmental issues, the higher the ITU on NTEA.

5   The Methodology Steps

Choosing the correct methodology step is crucial in achieving the aim of any study, mainly from a psychological aspect. This is because the psychological aspect is not directly measured. It requires a few constructs to represent the indicator under investigation. Due to that, a detailed literature review was carried out to identify items measuring the consumer intention to use the NTEA construct. This study revealed the TPB and TAM as the best theory to be applied and suited to measure residential consumer behaviour towards NTEA and electricity consumption.

Next, the questionnaire with 11 constructs was measured using a 10-point interval Likert scale. As explained by [33] and [34], the 10-point interval scale presents the respondents with more response options that correspond with their specific judgment of a question. A score of 1 denotes 'strongly disagree', whereas a score of 10 denotes 'strongly agree'. The items in the instrument were adapted from past studies [3, 18, 24, 27, 32]. Accordingly, the questionnaire was structured as follows: Section A: To assess the socio-demographic aspects and the electricity consumption. Section B: To measure consumer actual electricity usage behaviour. Section C: To measure consumer attitude/behavioural intention to use the NTEA (such as solar, smart meter, battery storage, electric vehicles). And section D: To assess consumer comments and suggestions related to electricity consumption.

To ensure the quality, reliability, and validity are met, the questionnaire was reviewed and examined by an expert in the energy field and an expert in methodology (mainly the art of developing the questionnaire). Later the pilot test was conducted on 104 residential consumers in Peninsular Malaysia, covering consumers in the East Coast, Southern Region, Northern Region, and Central Region. Due to the Covid-19 pandemic, this questionnaire is distributed online via a Google Form mechanism, and convenient sampling is employed.

The Exploratory Factor Analysis (EFA) is employed to explore and assess the usefulness of items measuring the construct. In this case, the construct is used rather than variable because the construct cannot be measured directly. It requires several items/indicators to indicate or explain certain constructs (For example, attitude, perceived usefulness, and environmental awareness). The questions (items or survey instruments) are considered useful if they meet the validity and reliability criteria. Preceding EFA, the sample adequacy has to be measured, and this can be assessed by utilising Kaiser-Meyer-Olkin (KMO) and Bartlett's test of Sphericity with the following conditions. First, the value of the Kaiser-Meyer-Olkin (KMO) Measure of Sampling Adequacy (MSA) should be greater than 0.50. Secondly, Bartlett's test of Sphericity results should be significant at $p < 0.001$ as recommended by [35].

In EFA, the principal component analysis (PCA) was employed to determine the number of factors to be retained and dropped. In this case, the function of Varimax rotation was applied as it was the most widely used orthogonal factor rotation method as it can clarify the analysis of factors [35]. Items that attained factor loadings with an absolute value below ±0.5 were discarded, while items with factor loading values of more than ±0.55 were retained [35]. The higher factor loading indicates a higher interconnection/correlation between one item to another in that particular construct. Data analysis was performed using IBM SPSS Statistics. Once all the above criteria are met, this study can proceed with the field study and answer the objectives of the study highlighted in the earlier section. The abovementioned steps were summarised in Fig. 4.

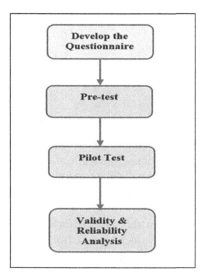

Fig. 4. Methodology steps

6 Research Finding

6.1 Exploratory Factor Analysis (EFA)

The data from the pilot study were concluded as suitable/adequate for EFA as the results from two tests which are Kaiser-Meyer-Olkin (KMO) and Bartlett's test of sphericity. These tests established that all constructs to measure attitude/behaviour and intention to use NTEA were significant. The values of KMO for all constructs exceeded 0.5, while Bartlett's test of sphericity for all constructs was significant ($p < 0.001$). Table 2 presents the results of KMO and Bartlett's test of sphericity for attitude/behaviour and intention to use technology.

Table 2. KMO and Bartlett's test of sphericity

Construct	No. of items in the construct	KMO	Bartlett's test of sphericity (<0.001)
Attitude/behaviour	7	0.917	0.000
Perceived usefulness	6	0.884	0.000
Perceived ease of use	6	0.915	0.000
Government policy	5	0.740	0.000
Intention to use	12	0.852	0.000
Perceived price	4	0.782	0.000
Environmental awareness	8	0.866	0.000
Knowledge of EE	6	0.772	0.000
Knowledge of RE	6	0.878	0.000
Perceived behaviour control	10	0.905	0.000
Subjective norms	6	0.769	0.000

Table 3 presents the retained items of the eleven constructs, namely, attitude, perceived usefulness, perceived ease of use, government policy, intention to use, perceived price, environmental awareness, knowledge of energy efficiency and renewable energy, perceived behaviour control, and subjective norms after exploratory factor analysis was conducted.

All the items in the eleventh construct obtained factor loading values of more than 0.5. The eigenvalue for the eleventh construct surpassed the recommended value 1 and above, as shown in Table 3. Instead, all the items explained at least 60% of the total variance,

Table 3. Exploratory factor analysis results

No.	Items	Factor loading	Eigenvalue	Total variance explains (%)
1	*Attitude/behaviour*			
	AT1	0.821	5.263	75.185
	AT2	0.910		
	AT3	0.928		
	AT4	0.912		
	AT5	0.682		
	AT6	0.902		
	AT7	0.890		
2	*Perceived usefulness*			
	PU1	0.894	4.840	73.397

(continued)

Table 3. (*continued*)

No.	Items	Factor loading	Eigenvalue	Total variance explains (%)
	PU2	0.469		
	PU3	0.933		
	PU4	0.920		
	PU5	0.948		
	PU6	0.877		
3	*Perceived ease of use*			
	PEU1	0.886	4.840	80.663
	PEU2	0.861		
	PEU3	0.903		
	PEU4	0.932		
	PEU5	0.889		
	PEU6	0.916		
4	*Government policy*			
	GP1	0.677 [0.626]	2.872 [2.565]	57.438 [64.115]
	GP2	0.640 [Dropped]		
	GP3	0.854 [0.882]		
	GP4	0.868 [0.894]		
	GP5	0.722 [0.772]		
5	*Intention to use*			
	ITU1	0.695	7.236	60.300
	ITU2	0.731		
	ITU3	0.687		
	ITU4	0.806		
	ITU5	0.849		
	ITU6	0.753		
	ITU7	0.717		
	ITU8	0.746		
	ITU9	0.826		
	ITU10	0.779		
	ITU11	0.826		
	ITU12	0.876		

(*continued*)

Table 3. (*continued*)

No.	Items	Factor loading	Eigenvalue	Total variance explains (%)
6	*Perceived price*			
	PP1	0.841	3.013	75.315
	PP2	0.824		
	PP3	0.875		
	PP4	0.928		
7	*Environmental awareness*			
	EA1	0.851	4.810	60.131
	EA2	0.880		
	EA3	0.688		
	EA4	0.203		
	EA5	0.831		
	EA6	0.836		
	EA7	0.855		
	EA8	0.823		
8	*Knowledge of EE*			
	KEE1	0.813	3.948	65.801
	KEE2	0.873		
	KEE3	0.783		
	KEE4	0.865		
	KEE5	0.829		
	KEE6	0.690		
9	*Knowledge of RE*			
	KRE1	0.845	4.698	78.300
	KRE2	0.901		
	KRE3	0.832		
	KRE4	0.951		
	KRE5	0.944		
	KRE6	0.827		
10	*Perceived behaviour control*			
	PBC1	0.716	6.593	65.929
	PBC2	0.680		
	PBC3	0.759		
	PBC4	0.825		
	PBC5	0.881		
	PBC6	0.818		

(*continued*)

Table 3. (*continued*)

No.	Items	Factor loading	Eigenvalue	Total variance explains (%)
	PBC7	0.858		
	PBC8	0.765		
	PBC9	0.879		
	PBC10	0.906		
11	*Subjective norms*			
	SN1	0.767	3.742	62.361
	SN2	0.835		
	SN3	0.747		
	SN4	0.743		
	SN5	0.786		
	SN6	0.853		

*Notes: The figure in the bracket is the new factor loading, eigenvalues, and total variance explained after taking out the GP2.

which also surpassed the recommended point as suggested by Hair et al. (2014), except for government policy with a total variance of 57.44%. Due to that, the GP2 is dropped because it has the lowest factor loading. As a result, GP1, GP3, GP4, and GP5 remained as the items to measure the government policy (Table 3).

6.2 Reliability

Next, the internal reliability of an instrument was measured to ensure that the instrument is free from random error and does not contain bias [36], Cronbach's alpha was utilised to examine the perceived usefulness, perceived ease of use, attitude, government policy, intention to use, perceived price, environmental awareness, knowledge of energy efficiency and renewable energy, perceived behaviour control, and subjective norms. This method was utilised as it is one of the most widely used methods to evaluate reliability where the value of 0.6 and above indicates acceptable internal consistency reliability [35].

Table 4 reported that all eleven constructs of perceived usefulness, perceived ease of use, attitude, government policy, intention to use, perceived price, environmental awareness, knowledge of energy efficiency and renewable energy, perceived behaviour control, and subjective norms were reliable as they surpassed the minimum reliability value of 0.6 [37]. Perceived ease of use achieved the highest reliability of 0.951, while the lowest reliability value was government policy at 0.788. Attitude/Behaviour came in second with 0.938. Table 4 also illustrates that no items were deleted among these eleven constructs as the factor loading for all items in every construct was satisfactory, as reported in Table 3. Thus, the construct reliability of these eleven constructs was established.

Table 4. Reliability results

Construct	No. of items after item deletion	Cronbach's Alpha
Attitude/behaviour	7	0.938
Perceived usefulness	6	0.894
Perceived ease of use	6	0.951
Government policy	4	0.796
Intention to use	12	0.937
Perceived price	4	0.887
Environmental awareness	8	0.854
Knowledge of EE	6	0.894
Knowledge of RE	6	0.944
Perceived behaviour control	10	0.935
Subjective norms	6	0.877

7 Conclusion

This research aims to develop a valid and reliable survey instrument to measure consumer behaviour towards new technology electricity appliances. For that particular purpose, the Exploratory Factor Analysis (EFA) was applied. Since the psychological aspect, in this case, is behaviour is not directly measured, a detailed literature review was carried out to identify items measuring the consumer intention to use the NTEA construct. This study revealed the TPB and TAM is the best theory to be applied and suited to measure residential consumer behaviour towards NTEA and electricity consumption. A set of questionnaires was developed, and it contains 11 constructs with a total of 72 items to be measured. The pilot study randomly sampled 104 residential electricity consumers using an online survey with an interval scale between 1 and 10. The EFA procedure on construct elements using IBM SPSS Statistics was performed. The Bartletts' Test of Sphericity and KMO test confirmed the adequacy of the sample size to assess a valid and reliable survey instrument to measure consumer behaviour towards NTEA. The result of EFA shows all the suggested items to measure attitude, perceived usefulness, perceived ease to use, intention to use, perceived price, environmental awareness, knowledge on EE and RE, perceived behaviour control, and subjective norms explained 60% and more of its variance changes. However, the suggested items to measure government policy explained less than 60%. One of the items (GP2) with the lowest factor loading is dropped from the construct to encounter the problem. The Cronbach Alpha indicates the constructs (with remaining items) are pretty reliable. The development scale and validation confirmed that the instrument is consistent and stable across samples. Based on the research findings, the field study can be conducted with valid constructs and items.

Acknowledgments. Information presented in this paper forms part of the research work granted by UNITEN R&D under TNB Seed Fund 2020; entitled Domestic Electricity Demand Model for TNB Regulation Strategy (U-TR-RD-20-01).

References

1. Othman, N.S., Hariri, N.H.M., Hanafi, W.N.D., Harun, N.H., Saad, N.M., Toolib, S.N.H.: Examining the Malaysian consumer attitude and expectation towards consumption of electricity - phase. Glob. Bus. Manag. Res. **12**(4), 431–441 (2020)
2. Bekhet, H.A., Othman, N.S.: Enlightening Malaysia's energy policies and strategies for modernization and sustainable development. world academy of science, engineering and technology. Int. J. Soc. Behav. Educ. Econ. Bus. Ind. Eng. **10**(9), 2747–2759 (2016). https://doi.org/10.5281/zenodo.1126269
3. Lau, L.S., et al.: Investigating nonuser's behavioural intention towards solar photovoltaic technology in Malaysia: the role of knowledge transmission and price value. Energy Policy **144**, 111651 (2020). https://doi.org/10.1016/j.enpol.2020.111651
4. Muhammad-Sukki, F., et al.: solar photovoltaic in Malaysia: the way forward. Renew. Sustain. Energy Rev. **16**(7), 5232–5244 (2012). https://doi.org/10.1016/j.rser.2012.05.002
5. Sustainable Development Authority (SEDA): Net Energy Metering (NEM) 3.0 (2021). http://www.seda.gov.my/reportal/nem/. Accessed 1 Jul 2021
6. Energy Commission. Malaysia Energy Information Hub (MEIH). https://www.st.gov.my/. Accessed 2 May 2021
7. Ozaki, R.: Adopting sustainable innovation: what makes consumers sign up to green electricity? Bus. Strateg. Environ. **20**(1), 1–17 (2011). https://doi.org/10.1002/bse.650
8. Gyamfi, S., Krumdieck, S., Urmee, T.: Residential peak electricity demand response—highlights of some behavioural issues. Renew. Sustain. Energy Rev. **25**, 71–77 (2013). https://doi.org/10.1016/j.rser.2013.04.006
9. Manjunath, M., Singh, P., Mandal, A., Parihar, G.S.: Consumer behaviour towards electricity-a field study. Energy Procedia **54**(1), 541–548 (2014). https://doi.org/10.1016/j.egypro.2014.07.295
10. Neaimeh, M., et al.: A probabilistic approach to combining smart meter and electric vehicle charging data to investigate distribution network impacts. Appl. Energy **157**, 688–698 (2015). https://doi.org/10.1016/j.apenergy.2015.01.144
11. De Dominicis, S., Sokoloski, R., Jaeger, C.M., Schultz, P.W.: Making the smart meter social promotes long-term energy conservation. Palgrave Commun. **5**(1), 1–8 (2019). https://doi.org/10.1057/s41599-019-0254-5
12. The Star. Electricity Demand to Shrink in 2020. https://www.thestar.com.my/business/business-news/2020/04/22/electricity-demand-set-to-shrink-in-2020, last accessed 2021/05/02.
13. Malay Mail. Residential Electricity Usage Soar 23pc During MCO, Says Energy Ministry. https://www.malaymail.com/news/malaysia/2020/05/30/residential-electricity-usage-soar-23pc-during-mco-says-energy-ministry/1870790. Accessed 02 May 2020
14. My Government. National Energy Efficiency Action Plan (NEEAP) (2021). https://www.malaysia.gov.my/portal/content/30919. Accessed 2 May 2021
15. Ministry of Science, Technology and Innovation, MOSTI. Malaysian Electricity Supply Industry 2.0 (MESI 2.0) (2021). https://www.mosti.gov.my/web/en/. Accessed 02 May 2021
16. Rahman, N.A.A., Kamaruzzaman, S.N., Akashah, F.W.: Scenario and strategy towards energy efficiency in Malaysia: a review. MATEC Web Conf. **266**, 02012 (2019). https://doi.org/10.1051/matecconf/201926602012

17. World Data Info. Energy Consumption in Malaysia (2021). https://www.worlddata.info/asia/malaysia/energy-consumption.php#google_vignette. Accessed 02 May 2021
18. Apipuchayakul, N., Vassanadumrongdee, S.: Factors affecting the consumption of energy-efficient lighting products: exploring purchase behaviors of Thai consumers. Sustainability 12(12), 4887 (2020). https://doi.org/10.3390/su12124887
19. Akroush, M.N., Zuriekat, M.I., Al Jabali, H.I., Asfour, N.A.: Determinants of purchasing intentions of energy-efficient products. Int. J. Energy Sect. Manage. 13(1), 128–148 (2019). https://doi.org/10.1108/IJESM-05-2018-0009
20. Tu, J.C., Yang, C.: Key factors influencing consumers' purchase of electric vehicles. Sustainability 11(14), 3863 (2019). https://doi.org/10.3390/su11143863
21. Kim, H., Park, E., Kwon, S.J., Ohm, J.Y., Chang, H.J.: An Integrated adoption model of solar energy technologies in South Korea. Renew. Energy 66, 523–531 (2014). https://doi.org/10.1016/j.renene.2013.12.022
22. Tan, C.S., Ooi, H.Y., Goh, Y.N.: A moral extension of the theory of planned behavior to predict consumers' purchase intention for energy-efficient household appliances in Malaysia. Energy Policy 107, 459–471 (2017). https://doi.org/10.1016/j.enpol.2017.05.027
23. Ali, S., Ullah, H., Akbar, M., Akhtar, W., Zahid, H.: Determinants of consumer intentions to purchase energy-saving household products in Pakistan. Sustainability 11(5), 1462 (2019). https://doi.org/10.3390/su11051462
24. Alam, S.S., Lin, C.-Y., Ahmad, M., Omar, N.A., Ali, M.H.: Factors affecting energy-efficient household products buying intention: empirical study. Environ. Clim. Technol. 23(1), 84–97 (2019). https://doi.org/10.2478/rtuect-2019-0006
25. Kardooni, R., Yusoff, S.B., Kari, F.B., Moeenizadeh, L.: Public opinion on renewable energy technologies and climate change in Peninsular Malaysia. Renew. Energy 116, 659–668 (2018). https://doi.org/10.1016/j.renene.2017.09.073
26. Koohang, A., Paliszkiewicz, J.: E-learning courseware usability: building a theoretical model. J. Comput. Inf. Syst. 56(1), 55–61 (2016). https://doi.org/10.1016/j.renene.2017.09.073
27. Wang, Z., Wang, X., Guo, D.: Policy implications of the purchasing intentions towards energy-efficient appliances among China's urban residents: do subsidies work? Energy Policy 102, 430–439 (2017). https://doi.org/10.1016/j.enpol.2016.12.049
28. Park, E., Kwon, S.J.: What motivations drive sustainable energy-saving behavior?: an examination in South Korea. Renew. Sustain. Energy Rev. 79, 494–502 (2017). https://doi.org/10.1016/j.rser.2017.05.150
29. Wallis, H., Nachreiner, M., Matthies, E.: Adolescents and electricity consumption; investigating sociodemographic, economic, and behavioural influences on electricity consumption in households. Energy Policy 94, 224–234 (2016). https://doi.org/10.1016/j.enpol.2016.03.046
30. Wang, Z., Zhang, B., Li, G.: Determinants of energy-saving behavioral intention among residents in Beijing: extending the theory of planned behavior. J. Renew. Sustain. Energy 6(5), 053127 (2014). https://doi.org/10.1063/1.4898363
31. Ha, H.Y., Janda, S.: Predicting consumer intentions to purchase energy-efficient products. J. Consum. Mark. 29(7), 461–469 (2012). https://doi.org/10.1108/07363761211274974
32. Kaffashi, S., Shamsudin, M.N.: Transforming to a low carbon society: an extended theory of planned behaviour of Malaysian citizens. J. Clean. Prod. 235, 1255–1264 (2019). https://doi.org/10.1016/j.jclepro.2019.07.047
33. Hoque, A., Awang, Z., Jusoff, K., Salleh, F., Muda, H.: Social business efficiency: instrument development and validation procedure using structural equation modeling. Int. Bus. Manage. 11(1), 222–231 (2017). https://doi.org/10.36478/ibm.2017.222.231
34. Hoque, A.S.M.M., Awang, Z.: The sway of entrepreneurial marketing on firm performance: case of small and medium enterprises (SMEs) in Bangladesh. In: Terengganu International Business and Economics Conference (TiBEC-V), Terengganu, Universiti Teknologi Mara (UiTM), pp. 174–194 (2016)

35. Hair, J.F., Gabriel, M., Patel, V.: AMOS covariance-based structural equation modeling (CB-SEM): guidelines on its application as a marketing research tool. Braz. J. Mark. **13**(2), 43–53 (2014)
36. Sekaran, U., Bougie, R. Research Methods for Business: A Skill Building Approach. Wiley (2010)
37. Ehido, A., Awang, Z., Halim, B.A., Ibeabuchi, C.: Developing items for measuring quality of worklife among Malaysian academics: an exploratory factor analysis procedure. Humanit. Soc. Sci. Rev. **8**(3), 1295–1309 (2020). https://doi.org/10.18510/hssr.2020.83132

Energy Efficiency Through a Wearable Device for the Elderly Based on the Integrated Smart Neighbourhood Framework of Malaysia 5.0 Model

Halimah Badioze Zaman[1(✉)], Azlina Ahmad[2], and Kien Sin Aw[3]

[1] Institute of Informatics and Computing in Energy, Universiti Tenaga Nasional (UNITEN), Jalan IKRAM-UNITEN, 43000 Kajang, Selangor, Malaysia
[2] Malaysian Information Technology Society (MITS), Bangi, Selangor, Malaysia
[3] Tunku Abdul Rahman (TAR) University College, Kuala Lumpur, Malaysia

Abstract. In reinventing a nation, Malaysia is moving from a social paradigm shift of an Agricultural-Industrial to a Digital one, moving towards the development of Malaysia 5.0. This human-centric concept portrays the citizens to be smart in using the right technology to help them conduct their daily activities. A Study conducted on dimensions of the concept of Malaysia 5.0 which is used in the design of the Integrated Smart Neighbourhood Framework (ISNF) of the Malaysia 5.0 model, comprised twelve dimensions: smart mobility/transportation, smart finance, smart economy, smart education, smart social & health, smart environment, smart governance, smart industry integration, culture, human capital, Information and Communications Technology (ICT) and spirituality. This paper highlights the integration between the smart social & health with the smart finance dimensions, through the use of a wearable device designed for the elderly for social and health, as well as financial purposes through energy efficiency. Based on an ambient interface, the tangible user interface (TUI), used in the design of the wearable device allows the elderly to control electrical and electronic appliances such as air conditioning, lights, lamp, fans, computer, as well their telephones for social and emergency calls, through the control system built in their homes. The wearable device was validated and its results have been published previously in another publication and will not be discussed in this paper. The energy efficiency which will be reported in this paper was measured based on the financial savings made for a span of three months when the experiments were conducted. Based on the study the findings showed that using the wearable device to control the use of electrical appliances in their homes, the elderly made financial savings of between 20%–25% of their normal electricity bill compared with the previous three months when they were not using the wearable device to control the electricity appliances in their homes. Thus, the efficient use of electricity or 'energy efficiency' function of the wearable device had resulted in financial savings for the elderly.

Keywords: Malaysia 5.0 · Smart neighbourhood framework · Wearable device · Control system · Energy efficiency · Energy savings

© Springer Nature Switzerland AG 2021
H. Badioze Zaman et al. (Eds.): IVIC 2021, LNCS 13051, pp. 642–654, 2021.
https://doi.org/10.1007/978-3-030-90235-3_55

1   Introduction

In reinventing a nation, Malaysia is transforming from a paradigm shift of agro-industrial to a digital innovative one. The term Digital Innovation emerged in the previous decade, by Nicholas Nigroponte [1], who had used an interesting metaphor about the changes that took place from atomic processing to bit processing. He discusses the advantages of atomic processing (e.g., Mass, material, transport) as well as the advantages of bit processing (e.g., weightlessness, virtual, real global movement). Thus, the digital innovative economy at that time was described as something based on electronic materials and services produced by an electronic business and traded through e-commerce using the internet, cloud, Internet of Things (IoTs) and web technology. To ensure that most Malaysians can benefit from this digital innovation economy, the elderly of the country that represents 9.9% of the 32 million of population are not left behind.

The convergence of knowledge, intelligent manufacturing (AI) technology and autonomous technology, industry, as well as markets of the "Cyber-Physical-Biological" Industry Revolution 4.0 (IR4.0) and the forthcoming "neuro-quantified" Industry Revolution 5.0 (IR5.0) [2], is transforming the process and meaning of innovation. The transfer of innovative knowledge for the purpose of social and economic development (with high income earnings), is showing signs that there are no significant differences between producers, innovators/inventors, and consumers. Today, the digital innovative economy, still has similar but much broader recognition. We see various types of economies have existed because of it such as Gig economy and Sharing economy. Anyone can market their innovations through digital infrastructure that has become so sophisticated and widespread, that they are called prosumers. What is important for Malaysia is to create a future generation with high scientific knowledge, and also strong digital skills based on fusion technologies. The economic era of digital innovation equipped with scientific knowledge and digital skills, at the same time envisions the development of a society that can build the nation and the well-being of society more effectively and efficiently, called a smart society or society 5.0 (Malaysia 5.0).

This smart society such as Malaysia 5.0, is a human-centric society equipped with digital fusion technologies that can help them in all their daily work and leisure time effectively. Smart society (Malaysia 5.0) can be defined as: *"A human-centric society that is moving progressively towards a socio-technical ecosystem, where the physical and virtual dimensions of life are integrated with humans and machines harmoniously. The society uses machines more than ever, to communicate for educational, social, political, administrative, governance, economic and business."* [3, 4]. The Smart Society concept model (Malaysia 5.0) can have multiple dimensions.

2   Dimensions of the Malaysia 5.0 Model

There are twelve (12) dimensions involved in the Malaysia 5.0 model as can be observed in Fig. 1 [4]. The dimensions include: Smart mobility/transportation, smart finance, smart economy, culture, smart education, human capital, ICT (Fusion technologies), smart industry integration, smart social and health, smart environment, smart governance and spirituality.

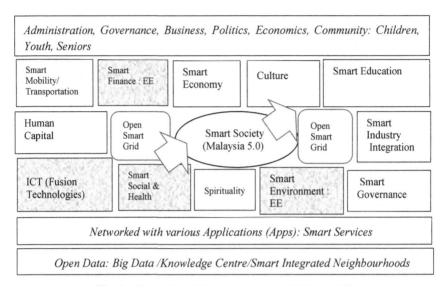

Fig. 1. Dimensions of the smart society (Malaysia 5.0)

Brief descriptions of the dimensions are as follows:

Smart Mobility/Transportation Dimension. The smart mobility or transportation dimension not only allows society to save energy but can also help to attain clean air environment. For example, the use of batteries from their electric cars be storage for other uses on applications at home. This dimension also deals with traffic congestion in a smart city and uses various mobility data to help drivers avoid traffic congestion and other road related matters.

Smart Finance. The smart financial dimension are widespread in mobilising financial institutions to build various platforms and ecosystems to enable the creation of new business models and services. Artificial intelligence (AI) technology and data are the two main drivers that drive financial business innovation. Smart financial and banking systems has changed people's lives by integrating new digital resources into every network and life scenario of financial services value chain not only to multinational institutions but also to rural and remote communities, medium and small institutions as well. We have also seen the emergence of FinTech which have further helped also individuals at the 'last mile'.

Smart Economy. The smart economy dimension involves the inclusive development of a country, including equitable distribution of all economic development facilities, and social spending across different income groups and low-income earners [5]. It is an economic-based activity using technology, and can measure its societal success in the economy such as income, poverty, economic stability, and equal participation in the workforce, which enables smart planning, such as a flexible way of working (especially during this unprecedented COVID19 pandemic (either from home or smart work centres). This can not only help in lessening the spread of the disease but also alleviate traffic jams on the roads, save time and increase work productivity.

Culture Dimension. The cultural dimension is important not only because society 5.0 is driven by technology and human beings, but it should also be driven by the process of innovative culture [6, 7], have proposed a cultural framework that contains a society that shares a set of values that motivates society with knowledge and technology that needs to be expressed through innovation and used as new business designs, new business products and new business competitions.

Smart Education Dimension. The smart education dimension means that digital technologies, especially fusion technologies should be used to provide attractive and effective smart learning environments (SLEs) [8–10]. Smart communities can learn anywhere and from anywhere, without enrolling in a physical learning institution. They can learn through flexible e-learning, engaging, adaptive, and personalised systems. In addition, the smart education system is effective and efficient, where students at all levels benefit from the smart education through SLEs such as science and technology parks and various smart learning systems, to enhance skills and competencies in order generate innovation.

Human Capital Dimension. Human capital dimension plays an important role in the development of reinventing the Nation State. Any development whether technological, economic or digital, will not benefit, unless it is related to human beings or society [11–13]. The smart society, not only needs technology to drive it, but it also needs value-based human capital to ensure it succeeds effectively. Human capital is recognised as an engine of economic development of a nation.

Information & Communications Technology (Fusion Technologies) Dimension. In a smart society such as Malaysia 5.0. Information and communication technology (ICT), especially fusion technologies play a significant role in a nation that is undergoing transformation into a human-centric technology savvy society. Fusion technologies that integrates motion and vision technologies will become more important, and this means that ICT has also moved rapidly away from the simple electronic networks but one that includes complex hardware and software, interconnected with various technical protocols; with fusion technologies that can capture, store, process, display, protect and manage information and data to more [14]; complex supercomputers that integrate AI, machine learning in physical, cyber & biological systems as well neuro-quantified systems of the future.

Smart Social and Health Dimension. This dimension is central in all areas of human life. Social aspects include among others, unity, cohesiveness and equality that need to be addressed in this dimension. The social aspect, too, is sometimes defined as social capital. Social capital is defined as social networks, groups, values as well as norms and behaviours commonly shared with a community [15]. A community is likely to benefit from better health care services when the social and health aspects are considered together.

Spirituality Dimension. This dimension is very important for Malaysia because "Belief in God" is one of the principles of "Rukun Negara", the fourth challenge in vision 2020 which emphasizes "*the challenge of establishing a fully moral and ethical society, whose* *citizens are strong in religious and spiritual values and imbued with the highest of ethical standards"* [16], and continued in the Vision of Inclusive Prosperity 2030. It is important to draw the attention of the Malaysia 5.0 in Malaysia, where the citizens are not only smart in terms of digital knowledge and skills, but has a high moral values and integrity. Actually, spirituality is different but almost the same as religion [17].

Smart Governance Dimension. The smart governance dimension involves various aspects such as the efficiency of a government, political stability, control of corruption, freedom of speech and freedom of information, and digital government [18]. Define governance as, *"the traditions and institutions by which authority in the country is exercised."* This involves a government's processes such as selecting, monitoring, and replacing its ministers, resources, and finance; the government's ability to formulate and implement policies; the government's ability to collect and maintain and share data for the purpose of national development and sovereignty; and earn the respect of the people for the state institutions involved in the administration and management of the economy and social interaction.

Smart Environment Dimension. The smart environment dimension is important as environmental degradation is an ongoing global challenge. Increasing population pressures, increasing consumption patterns, and rapid industrial development are major contributors to environmental degradation. Thus, the smart environment dimension is important to ensure that all data is shared and decisions made for the needs of the country are implemented without compromising the national environment. Environment also refers to environmental situations due to climate change that affect public health. Because environmental dimensions also need to take into account aspects of hygiene, waste management, climate change, global warming and pollution, a smart society model needs to integrate these dimensions with appropriate public policies for the well-being of smart societies.

Smart Industry Integration. As in Japan [19], where this dimension is considered paramount for its country' society 5.0 so will it be for Malaysia 5.0. Through this dimension, three important 'industrial' entities namely, government, academia and industry ingest the quality data they collect and store respectively, and share it together for the purpose of business decision making and national development. The data obtained and shared were analyzed using AI, ML, IoT, robotics and big data technologies. Based on this dimension as well, communities alongside the aforementioned industry entities, as well as systems are all integrated in cyberspace and large amounts of information obtained from sensors in physical space are shared and analysed using AI. The results will be used by the society 5.0 to balance the situation to solve the problems related to economic development, environmental conservation as well as social issues.

All these dimensions are sustained based on the *Administration, Governance, Business, Politics, Economics & Community* entity as well the *Networked with various Applications (Apps): Smart Services* entity and *Open data/Big data Knowledge Centre* Entity. The three entities ensure that all the dimensions are conducted effectively and efficiently. Within the Malaysia 5.0 model, there can be many specific developments like the smart cities and smart neighbourhoods. This paper highlights the integrated smart neighbourhood of the elderly.

3   Malaysia 5.0: Integrated Smart Neighbourhood Framework

The integrated Smart Neighbourhood framework can be observed in Fig. 2. As can be observed from the framework, the underpinning theories involved are the human-centric cognitive computing and the human behaviour and detection analysis theories. These theories take into consideration the ICT dimension, and social and health dimensions, Finance: Energy Efficiency dimension and Environment: Energy Efficiency dimension of the Integrated Smart Neighbourhood framework embedded in the Malaysia 5.0 model sharing the same dimensions in principle (as indicated in shaded boxes representing the dimensions in the model). Although the Integrated Smart Neighbourhood Framework (ISNF) identified three entities as crucial for an elderly neighbourhood: waste management system (to ensure clean environment), security (video surveillance security system) and Energy Efficiency/ Social & Health system (for electricity savings and emergency calls for health purpose). This paper highlights the latter.

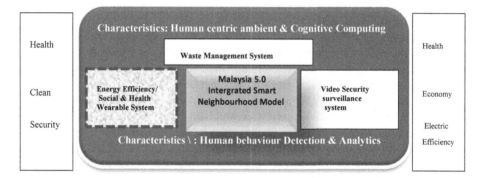

Fig. 2. Integrated Smart Neighbourhood (ISN) framework

4   Energy Efficiency Wearable Device/System for the Elderly (W-Emas)

W-Emas was developed for the elderly who are either living in the conventional neighbourhood or in an 'Integrated Smart Neighbourhoods' (presumably in the smart cities of the Malaysia 5.0 model). The wearable device was designed based on the Energy Efficiency: Social and Health: Wearable Systems dimension, of the ISN framework (shaded box), derived from the Malaysia 5.0 model (shaded boxes). The elderly involved in the research did not include those that were patients of Parkinson's disease or Dementia; as well as illiterates. Although the wearable device was created with specific attributes such as: to be 'easy to use' (for both literate and illiterate users); should apply the Tangible User Interface (TUI), instead of the Graphical User Interface (GUI) to ease understanding and use. Moreover, TUI is more natural, thus familiar to the natural behaviour of some of the elderly; the device must be designed in a non-digital form to avoid anxiety amongst some of the elderly when handling a digital device; the device must be easy to wear and detachable so that they can easily be taken off without the help of others. Lastly, the device must be able to transfer data to the control system that would eventually be detected at the 'Integrated Smart Neighbourhood' (ISN) dashboard if deemed necessary. Thus, this wearable device can be used by all elderly (literate or illiterate, any level of education, any location where they live (except for the last attribute-must be in an integrated neighbourhood).

4.1 Design of Wearable Device/System (W-Emas) for the Elderly

The wearable device or system was designed in the form of an Analog watch, that is easily put on and detachable, suitable for the elderly to use without much help (especially those whose physical functions are slow due to ageing). The wearable device or system was originally designed with three (3) basic functions and improved with one (1) optional administrative function (should the user wants to share information/data with the neighbourhood), that would then be sent to the dashboard of the ISN. The former, include functions: to control light/lamp brightness, control fan and air conditions and vice versa just by pressing the 'watch' button.

As mentioned earlier, the wearable device or system was designed in the form of an Analog watch, that is easily put on and detachable, suitable for the elderly to use. The wearable device or system was originally designed with three (3) basic functions and improved with one (1) optional administrative function (should the user wants to share information/data with the neighbourhood), that would then be sent to the dashboard of the ISN. The former, include functions: to control light/lamp brightness, control fan and air conditions and vice versa just by pressing the 'watch' button. The device can also assist the elderly in making emergency calls to a doctor or next of kin for social/health purposes. This emergency information will be linked automatically to the ISN dashboard in a case where the trigger was made by the elderly but did not receive response. This latter function, allows someone at the ISN control room can then attend to the emergency to help the elderly. Figure 3 shows the wearable watch (W-Emas) for the elderly for use in the ISN/smart home and emergency response.

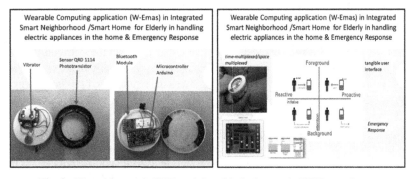

Fig. 3. Wearable watch (W-Emas) for elderly for use in ISN/smart home

4.2   Use of the Wearable Device/System (W-Emas) for the Elderly

The elderly can use the wearable device to change the control mode of the electrical appliances. They can change the mode control of the lights/lamps to fans/air conditioners and vice versa by pressing the watch button. An electronic vibrator is embedded in the watch to tell the elderly user, which control mode has been activated. When the watch vibrates once, the lamp/light mode is activated and when the watch vibrates twice, the fan/air condition mode is activated. However, the watch will vibrate for a longer time (2.5 s, stop 1 s and vibrate for another 2.5 s) for an emergency call mode.

Figure 4 shows the watch with its natural interaction interface (NII) using the TUI approach (natural pressing and rotation actions that is required to do by the elderly user).

Figure 4 shows the watch with its natural user interaction (NUI) using the TUI approach (natural pressing and rotation actions that is required to do by the elderly user). The elderly user needs to rotate the shaded triangle to associate it with the actions required to control the appropriate electrical appliances.

 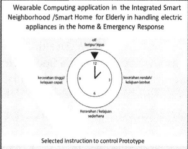

Fig. 4. W-Emas embedding natural user interaction using TUI

The selection made by the elderly user would be sent to control unit in the home via the blue tooth. Any selection made by the elderly user will be executed in the control unit and the data that wants to be shared will be Sent to the 'control room' of the Integrated Smart Neighbourhood System (ISNS). Figure 5 shows the design of the Control Unit linked to the Control Room of the Integrated neighbourhood System.

When the elderly user presses the watch three (3) times continuously, it will trigger the emergency call/response and the smartphone will automatically call the pre-set number. If the number does not answer, it will automatically be directed to the phone at the control room of the ISNS for emergency response. Figure 5 shows the ISNS architecture.

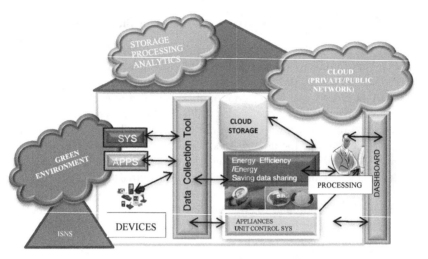

Fig. 5. Conceptual architecture integrated smart neighbourhood system

There were many aspects such as Cleanliness, Security and Energy Efficiency/Energy Savings as well as Social & Health that were monitored and managed for the elderly in a smart integrated neighbourhood. However, this paper only highlights the Energy Efficiency/Energy Savings: Social and Health: Wearable Systems Dimension/Element in Integrated Smart Neighbourhood (ISN) Framework of the Malaysia 5.0 model for the elderly.

5 Energy Efficiency/Energy Savings Experiments (W-Emas)

Experiments were conducted to study specifically on W-Emas, the wearable device/system designed for the elderly living in an integrated smart neighbourhood that could/exists in a smart society like Malaysia 5.0. Electrical Energy Efficiency is defined in this study as the reduction in power and energy demands or use without affecting the normal activities conducted in the house by the elderly. In short this study on energy savings and efficiency due to the use of the wearable device (W-Emas) designed for the elderly will involve three (3) basic assumptions:

i.   Use of the device will mean that less electricity consumption that will reduce economical cost of energy
ii. Efficient use of electricity, because energy consumption is efficiently use (elderly will switch on lights only in rooms where they are going in through their 'wearable watch' instead of having the light on all the time)
iii. Support the sustainability of the system and environment by reducing greenhouse emissions as a result of reducing energy use/demand.

In this study, the demographic profile of the samples were basically as follows: ten (10) elderly individuals between the age of 65–70 years old; Six (6) are males, four (4) females; education they possessed: four (4) had high school (Form 5) certificate: three (3) male, one (1) female, four (4) had diploma certificate: two (2) male and two (2) females and two (2) were degree holders: one (1) male, one (1) female; Five (50%) of them were still working: four (4) males and one (1) female and all were literate; and majority (7) have a spouse; whilst three (3) are living alone; and they all live in one of the 'smart city' in Selangor. The electrical energy efficiency and savings of the elderly involved in the study were based on a quasi-experiment conducted for a duration of six (6) months: for the first three months (months 1,2 & 3) experiments were conducted, the samples were required to either indicate in a notebook given to them-with the appliances and time indicated: 'morning, afternoon, evening and night' already prepared for them or any other methods that they were at ease. They only needed to tick in the appropriate columns in the note book provided. Two (2) of the elderly actually kept the notes in their hand phones. Since they were all literate, they did not find this task difficult to do at all. In fact, they were excited and want to see how much savings they can make from their electricity bills) on the efficiency use of the electrical appliances and electricity generally in their homes. For each of these three months the total electricity bills and the amount stated were also noted. The next three (3) months (months 4, 5 & 6), experiments were conducted on the use of the appliances based on the type of appliances and time use of the electricity generally, this time with the help of the wearable device (watch). The findings of the study can be observed in Table 1 and 2.

Table 1. Experiment I conventional approach

No	Elderly	Bill (Month 1)	Bill (Month 2)	Bill (Month 3)
1	EISN 1	400 kWh @0.516 = RM206.00	400 kWh @0.546 = RM218.40	400 kWh @0.571 = RM228.40
2	EISN 2	300 kWh @0.516 = RM154.80	300 kWh @0.546 = 163.80	300 kWh @0.571 = 171.30
3	EISN 3	400 kWh @0.516 = RM206.00	400 kWh @0.516 = RM206.00	400 kWh @0.546 = RM218.40
4	EISN 4	450 kWh @0.516 = RM232.20	450 kWh @0.516 = RM232.20	450 kWh @0.571 = RM256.95
5	EISN 5	200 kWh @0.334 = RM 66.80	250 kWh @0.516 = RM129.00	250 kWh @0.516 = RM129.00
6	EISN 6	370 kWh @0516 = RM190.992	400 kWh @0.516 = RM206.40	370 kWh @0516 = RM190.992

(continued)

Table 1. (*continued*)

No	Elderly	Bill (Month 1)	Bill (Month 2)	Bill (Month 3)
7	EISN 7	270 kWh @0.334 = RM90.18	300 kWh @0.516 = RM154.80	300 kWh @0.516 = RM154.80
8	EISN 8	350 kWh @0.516 = RM180.60	370 kWh @0.516 = RM190.92	400 kWh @0.516 = RM206.40
9	EISN 9	400 kWh @0.516 = RM206.00	420 kWh @0.516 = RM216.72	420 kWh @0.516 = RM216.72
10	EISN 10	350 kWh @0.516 = RM180.60	370 kWh @0.516 = RM190.92	400 kWh @0.516 = RM206.40

[*]Experiment: months 1, 2 & 3; *Exchange rate is US1\$ = RM4.16

Based on the above Table, it can be observed that ten (10) samples of elderly who were either living alone or with their spouse were involved in the study. They were told to use the appliances and electricity as usual taking care that the appliances were those that were really necessary to use. This also applies to the spaces in the house: the living room, the bedroom, kitchen, bathroom and study room (for some who were enjoying writing or collating photos in albums). The bills of the elderly generally ranged from 200 kWh (RM66.80), indicated as lowest amongst them to 450 kWh (RM256.95) indicated as highest amongst them. The highest bill was due to the fact that the elderly was using air condition for four (4) hours daily during the day.

Table 2. Experiment II W-Emas approach

No	Elderly	Bill (Month 1)	Bill (Month 2)	Bill (Month 3)
1	EISN 1	300 kWh @0.516 = RM154.80	300 kWh @0.516 = RM154.80	350 kWh @0.516 = RM180.60
2	EISN 2	200 kWh @0.516 = RM103.20	200 kWh @0.516 = 103.20	250 kWh @0.516 = 129.00
3	EISN 3	300 kWh @0.516 = RM154.80	350 kWh @0.516 = RM180.60	370 kWh @0.516 = RM190.92
4	EISN 4	390 kWh @0.516 = RM201.24	400 kWh @0.516 = RM 206.40	400 kWh @0.516 = RM206.40

(*continued*)

Table 2. (*continued*)

No	Elderly	Bill (Month 1)	Bill (Month 2)	Bill (Month 3)
5	EISN 5	150 kWh @0.334 = RM50.10	190 kWh @0.334 = RM63.46	200 kWh @0.516 = RM103.20
6	EISN 6	320 kWh @0516 = RM165.12	350 kWh @0.516 = RM180.60	350 kWh @0516 = RM180.60
7	EISN 7	190 kWh @0.334 = RM63.46	200 kWh @0.516 = RM103.20	200 kWh @0.516 = RM103.20
8	EISN 8	270kWh @0.516 = RM139.32	270kWh @0.516 = RM139.32	300kWh @0.516 = RM154.80
9	EISN 9	350kWh @0.516 = RM180.60	370kWh @0.516 = RM192.92	370 kWh @0.516 = RM192.92
10	EISN 10	270 kWh @0.516 = RM139.32	270 kWh @0.516 = RM139.32	300 kWh @0.516 = RM154.80

*Experiment: months 4, 5 & 6 *Exchange rate is US1$ = RM4.16

Based on Table 2, it can be observed that with the use of the wearable device (W-Emas) designed for the elderly, there are obvious savings on energy made to their homes. The bills for months 4, 5 and 6 showed a much lower amount compared to the months 1, 2 and 3. The bills on the months 4, 5 and 6 ranged from RM50.10, indicated as the lowest amount to RM206.40 indicated as the highest amount paid by the elderly. Thus, it can be observed that for majority of the elderly, they were saving between 20%–25%. They managed to make the savings due to the fact that they only switched on the light and other appliances using their wearable watch device when they entered the specific spaces. This meant that they were using less electricity and these savings have helped them not only financially, but has helped them to create a greener environment in the neighbourhood.

6 Conclusion

Although this is still at its preliminary stage, early findings show some very positive results. It can be observed that W-Emas is very useful for the elderly in many ways. This is because it can make them more independent and confident going around their homes, as they can switch on the lights whenever they enter the appropriate spaces/rooms. In the long run, the system which is integrated with the ISNS would not only help the elderly to feel more secure and independent in their homes and in the neighbourhood, but also will help them in terms of energy efficiency and energy savings and eventually contribute to more clean/green environment in the neighbourhood.

References

1. Nigroponte, N.: Being Digital. Knopf Doubleday Publishing Group, New York (1995)
2. Hussin, R., Peredaryenko, M.: Orwellian vs Humane 5IR? The Choice is Ours. Malay Mail. Telegram Channel. Monday, 22 March 2021
3. Badioze Zaman, H.: Membangun Masyarakat Pintar. Majlis Profesor Negara (2015)
4. Badioze Zaman, H., Ahmad, A.: Teknologi Fusion dan Pemikiran Komputational bagi Kesediaan Data Terbuka. Universiti Kebangsaan Malaysia, Bangi (2020)
5. UNDP: Malaysia human development report 2013: redesigning an inclusive future. United Nations Development Programme (UNDP), Washington (2013)
6. Tiffin, S., Jimenez, G.: Design and test of an index to measure the capabilities of cities in Latin America to create knowledge-based enterprises. J. Technol. Transf. 31(1), 61–76 (2006)
7. Levin, I., Mamlok, D.: Culture and society in the digital age. Information 12(68), 2–13 (2021)
8. Uzkov, V.L., Bakken, J.P., Pandey, A., Singh, U., Yalamanchili, M., Penumatsa, A.: Smart University Taxonomy: features, components, systems. In: Uzkov, V.L., Howlett, R.J., Jain, L.C. (eds.) Smart Education and e-Learning. Springer, Cham (2017). https://doi.org/10.1007/978-3-319-39690-3_1
9. Roumen, E.S., & Kovatcheva, N. E.: Conceptualising of Smart Education (2017). https://www.researchgate.net/publications/320623528_Conceptualiiing%20of%20Smart_Education
10. Uzkov, V.I., Howlett, R.J., Jain, L.C. (eds.): Smart Education and E-Learning. Springer, Singapore (2021). https://doi.org/10.1007/978-981-15-5584-8
11. Nasbitt, J.: Megatrends 2000: Ten New Directions for the 1990s. William and Morrow Company Inc., New York (1990)
12. Nasbitt, J., Nasbitt, N., Philips, D.: High Tech High Touch: Technology and Our Search for Meaning. Nicholas Brealy Publishing, London (1999)
13. Deloitte: Global Human Capital Trends: Special Report. Deloitte, New York (2021)
14. Pathan, S.: Development of Smart Fusion Technology Based on System for Light Intensity Management for Polyhouse. Researchgate (2021)
15. UNCTAD: Technology and Innovation Report. UNCTAD, New York (2021)
16. Mohamad, M.: Malaysia: The way forward. Centre for Economic Research and Services, Malaysian Business Council, Kuala Lumpur (1991)
17. Badioze Zaman, H., Ahmad, A.: Sustainable Smart Technologies in Visual Informatics in the Fourth Industrial Revolution for Societal Well-being. Penerbit Universiti Kebangsaan Malaysia, Bangi (2019)
18. Kaufmann, D., Kraay, A., Mastruzzi, M.: Governance matters VIII: Aggregate and individual governance indicators 1996–2008. World Bank Policy Research Paper No. 4978. World Bank, New York (2009)
19. Japanese Embassy. Discussion with Economic Attache, Japan, January 2020

Investigating the Contributing Factors of Continuance Use of Smart Meter in Melaka

Azlina Abdullah[1,2]([⊠]), Nor Shafiqah Yusoff[1], Nurul Wahilah Abdul Latif[3],
Abdul Rahman Zahari[4], Zeittey Karmilla Kaman[2], Zurina Ismail[4],
and Wan Hafiizhah Wan Mohamad Norafi[1]

[1] College of Graduate Studies, National Energy University, Selangor, Malaysia
azlina@uniten.edu.my
[2] Institute of Energy Policy and Research, National Energy University, Selangor, Malaysia
[3] College of Energy Economics and Social Sciences, National Energy University,
Selangor, Malaysia
[4] College of Business Management and Accounting, National Energy University,
Pahang, Malaysia

Abstract. The Malaysian government is currently implementing an initiative to install smart meter (SM) in all Malaysian homes. Hence, this study analyses the contributing factors that influence the continuance use of SM among SM users in Melaka. This study found that the existing SM users in Melaka were slightly willing to continue using SM. Among the contributing factors to the continuance use of SM are attitude toward SM, perceived ease of use, perceived usefulness, internal perceived locus of causality and external perceived locus of causality. Moreover, the findings have been used to develop an index called Continuance Use of Smart Meter Index (CUSMI).

Keywords: Smart meter · Continuance use · Acceptance

1 Introduction

Smart meter (SM) technology application and acceptance have been widely debated among researchers, local communities, industrial sector and decision makers [1, 2]. There are developed countries that have been equipped with SMs. For instance, the US have installed 4.69 million, Japan decided to replace 7.5 million SMs by the end of 2020, France 1.5 million, UK planned 2.975 million, the Netherlands 7 million, Spain 3.5 million, Australia 2.6 million, and New Zealand 1.12 million SMs respectively [3]. A smart or advanced meter is an electronic appliance capable of recording precise electricity consumption over time intervals of one hour or less, and of sending the data back to the utility provider through a two-way communication feature, enabling providers to respond to the data [4]. Hence the installation of SM has been endorsed by the Malaysian government and is currently being rolled out by the electricity provider, Tenaga Nasional Berhad (TNB). The first two states to have SM are Melaka and Putrajaya, where the pilot project was carried out before. Melaka has been selected since this state has adopted the

© Springer Nature Switzerland AG 2021
H. Badioze Zaman et al. (Eds.): IVIC 2021, LNCS 13051, pp. 655–664, 2021.
https://doi.org/10.1007/978-3-030-90235-3_56

Green City Action Plan. This initiative is a cooperation between the state government with The Asian Development Bank (ADB). TNB has started installing SM in Melaka since 2018. As of June 2020, a total of 287,078 (82.6%) TNB customers out of 347,585 target users have been provided with SMs [5].

Even though SM is a good technology and device, it also has many weaknesses. A few cases of inaccurate readings have been reported in Sweden. Electricity consumers have been billed twice as high as those issued before meter change [6]. A survey conducted by the Netherlands homeowners' association found that a group of consumers did not receive their monthly billing summaries at all and that many summaries received did not comply with applicable laws and were misleading [4]. Customers also believed that detailed information about household behaviours were not securely protected and led to privacy risks in using SM. Malaysia also witnessed the same scenarios: after the implementation of the SM initiative in Melaka, there have been some issues reported by users. According to Malek, for the month of May 2019, more than 300 complaints were lodged with the Energy Commission, which was 10 times more than the same month the previous year [7]. Most of the cases involved were the tremendous spike in electricity bills. Customers received high bills after changing to the SM and questioned the benefits of SMs to their lifestyles [8]. Users did not expect to be burdened with high bills with the change from conventional meters to the new SMs.

These arising issues show that users in Melaka are expecting more positive outcomes from SM installation. Due to this aspiration, the key factors to ensure the continuance use of the SM must be identified. Despite the negative feedbacks, there have been positive reactions from the users after SM installations. SM enables homeowners to view and track their daily electricity consumption levels via the provided application which is myTNB App or myTNB Portal. SMs are certainly among the important steps towards a smarter, sustainable, and greener future of our country. This is one of the benefits of SM to the environment where less paper is used to print the bill in line with Melaka's goal towards becoming a green city.

Nevertheless, considering the fact that some researchers have analysed potential users' pre-adoption behaviour of SMs, there is still a lack of studies on continuance use. Therefore, the current study proposed to determine the contributing factors that influence SM users' decision to continue using SM and to develop an index as a measurement of the continuance use of SM. This index known as Continuance Use of Smart Meter Index (CUSMI). This index is important to know the satisfaction and perception on SM adoption by customers. The value of indices generated through CUSMI will help the electricity provider to further improve the services rendered to customers related to SM. The proposed indices can be used as important benchmark of SM adoption in Malaysia. It can also be recognized as a useful tool to evaluate marketing strategies performance overtime. The listed factors are attitude towards SM, perceived benefit on environment, perceived privacy risk, perceived behaviour control, perceived ease of used, perceived usefulness, internal perceived locus of causality and external perceived locus of causality.

In the next section, this paper reviews related literature followed by the data and research methodology. The results and analysis of the findings is discussed before the conclusion of the study.

2   Literature Review

SMs are significant devices of next-generation smart grids because they allow remote metering of electricity consumption and deliver more data than conventional meters [9]. Users and electricity provider companies can experience the valuable features of SMs. One of the benefits is real-time dynamic tariffs and pricing. Customers who have SMs in their homes can also benefit from feedback information. Wood and Newborough found that display systems of electricity information can affect consumer consumption behaviour [10]. SMs features can detect unfamiliar electricity usage patterns based on past meter readings since this new device is equipped with difference detection tools, and can identify faulty meters or consumer theft [1]. However, for these benefits to be realised, it is vital to secure consumer acceptance of SMs and the connected features that come with SMs.

Earlier studies have highlighted that user acceptance and confidence are critical for further development of any new technology. Besides, acceptance has been observed as a function of user contribution in systems development. The factors that influence users' decisions to use a specific system need to be identified so that policy makers would be able to take them into account during the development stage [11]. One of the most common research models is technology acceptance model (TAM). This model was designed by Davis and also used to predict the adoption of technology and information systems by specific customers [12]. TAM has been widely tested and presented by different research that investigate individual's acceptance behaviour in different information technology constructs. There are two variables involved in this model: perceived usefulness and perceived ease of use [13]. According to TAM, perceived ease of use and perceived usefulness are the most significant factors of actual system use. Although initially TAM was used to emphasise the acceptance of new technology, scholars have proven that TAM is also suitable to examine continuance and post-adoption behavioural intention [12, 14]. TAM, with its emphasis on initial adoption of an information system, theorises that the use of the system is primarily influenced by behavioural intent to use, and in effect driven by the attitude of the consumer towards system use. In recent years, the expectation confirmation model (ECM) has been proposed to describe consumer behaviour in an information system. Attitude toward SM is a variable in this model. In addition, Wunderlich also added perceived privacy risk to this model [15]. Figure 1 below shows the conceptual model that has been developed for this study.

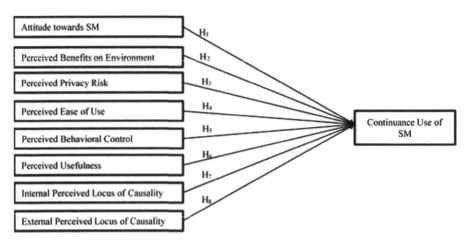

Fig. 1. Conceptual model

Based on the models discussed earlier, the review of literatures provided below defines the eight factors that influence continuance use of SM by users in Melaka. The hypothesis for each factor is also developed.

Attitude Towards SM. Wunderlich reported that attitude reflects the consumer's evaluative judgment about using the technology as either being harmful or beneficial [15]. Users' attitudes can be used to determine their behaviour towards SM use as proven in the TAM model. The literature suggests that the attitude has a significant impact on the information technology use and acceptance [14, 16, 17]. Based on the above statements, the proposed hypothesis is as follows:

H_1: Attitude towards SM has a significant influence on continuance use of SM.

Perceived Benefit on Environment. While never directly tested against SMs, environmental concern has been shown to influence attitudes toward home energy saving measures in alternative contexts. Bugden and Stedman (2019) demonstrated that environmental concern is one of the strongest indicators of willingness to accept home and transport energy saving measures [3]. Findings from Nanggong and Rahmatia highlighted that perceived benefit on environment has significant influence on technology adoption [18]. Numerous studies also demonstrated that environmental concerns play a key role in determining the continuance use of new technology [19]. Based on the above statements, the proposed hypothesis is as follows:

H_2: Perceived benefit on environment has a significant influence on continuance use of SM.

Perceived Privacy Risk. Perceived privacy risk describes the potential loss of control over personal information [15]. Evidence found that privacy issues will play a significant role in understanding why people are adopting (or not adopting) new technologies [20]. Studies have looked at the effect of privacy issues and a person's willingness to adopt SM technology. Few parts of the population claimed that after corporations have collected personal information via SMs, this information may be hacked or leaked to other entities [21]. Most recently, Chen and his colleagues discovered that privacy issues were negatively correlated to people's support for and plan to implement SMs [1]. Based on the above statements, the proposed hypothesis is as follows:

H_3: Perceived privacy risk has a significant influence on continuance use of SM.

Perceived Ease of Use. Perceived ease of use is the degree to which a person believes that using a particular system would be free from effort. If the technology is easy to use, then there will be zero barriers between the users and the technology in question. Davis pointed out that a user accepts effortless use of a technology [12]. Previous studies have exposed solid experimental support for a significant relationship between perceived ease of use and continuance used of SM [22]. Based on the above statements, the proposed hypothesis is as follows:

H_4: Perceived ease of use has a significant influence on continuance use of SM.

Perceived Behavioural Control. Perceived behavioural control reflects the "people's perceptions of ease or difficulty in performing the behaviour of interest". It is related with theories about the existence of control factors that could facilitate or delay the behaviour performance in question [23, 24]. Based on the above statements, the proposed hypothesis is as follows:

H_5: Perceived behavioural control has a significant influence on continuance use of SM.

Perceived Usefulness. Perceived usefulness refers to the degree to which the individual believes that using SM is enhancing his or her energy efficiency [12]. The literature shows that perceived usefulness can be a fundamental factor of the user's intention in using a new product [25] and findings from Chen stressed that perceived usefulness is positively related to continuance use of SM [1]. Based on the above statements, the proposed hypothesis is as follows:

H_6: Perceived usefulness has a significant influence on continuance use of SM.

Internal Perceived Locus of Causality. Internal perceived locus of causality refers to the extent to which individuals perceive their own actions as a result of internal reasons. Because it is involuntary, i.e. it is not determined by different incentives or other people's recommendations, but rather on laws, values, and results, helps explain why some social ideals and standards are accepted by individuals while others are not [26]. Previous studies showed that internal perceived locus of causality supports the relationship with the continuance use of SM [15]. Based on the above statements, the proposed hypothesis is as follows:

H_7: Internal perceived locus of causality has a significant influence on continuance use of SM.

External Perceived Locus of Causality. External perceived locus of causality refers to the extent to which individuals perceive their own actions as a result of external reasons. External PLOC is associated with perceived reasons for one's behaviour that is attributed to external authority or compliance [15]. Based on the above statements, the proposed hypothesis is as follows:

H_8: External perceived locus of causality has a significant influence on continuance use of SM.

3 Data and Research Methodology

Online surveys and face-to-face surveys were conducted from February 2020 to April 2020. Data were collected from 510 SM users within three districts in Melaka which were Melaka Tengah, Jasin and Alor Gajah. The questionnaire was divided into two sections: the users' willingness to continue using SMs and demographic profile. The questionnaire contained 22 items; variable attitude towards SM, perceived privacy risk, perceived ease of use, perceived behavioural control, perceived usefulness, internal and external perceived locus of causality using the instrument from [15] while the perceived benefits on environment variable was adopted from [3]. Some items needed to be reworded and rephrased. A 6-point Likert-scale was used in these questionnaires to best describe their views towards each statement that reflected the variables influencing users toward the continuance use of SM. The scale ranges from strongly disagree to strongly agree (1 = strongly disagree, 2 = disagree, 3 = slightly disagree, 4 = slightly agree, 5 = agree and 6 = strongly agree). In information system research, particularly in new technology adoption and acceptance, a similar scale had been used. Data were analysed using multiple regression analysis to test the relationship between variables of the developed model. Instrument reliability evaluation using Cronbach alpha with cut-off value of 0.6 was used to evaluate instrument reliability [27].

4 Results and Analysis

Results from the demographic profile is shown in Table 1 below. Fifty seven percent of the respondents were male as compared to female. Most respondents (32.9%) were in the 21–30 age groups and 92.0% were of Malay ethnicity. The majority of the respondents

Table 1. Respondents' profile

Profile	Category	Percentage (%)	Frequency
Gender	Male	57.0	291
	Female	43.0	219
Age	20 years old and below	1.6	8
	21–30 years old	32.9	168
	31–40 years old	28.6	146
	41–50 years old	22.2	113

(*continued*)

Table 1. (*continued*)

Profile	Category	Percentage (%)	Frequency
	51–60 years old	11.6	59
	More than 61 years old	3.1	16
Race	Malay	92.0	470
	Chinese	4.0	20
	Indian	3.0	16
	Others	1.0	4
Education	SPM and below	31.0	160
	Diploma	28.0	144
	Bachelor's degree	29.0	149
	Master/PhD degree	10.0	50
	Others	2.0	7
Job	Professional	19.4	99
	Top management	3.9	20
	Middle management	15.1	77
	Supervisory	4.3	22
	Administrative/Clerk	12.2	62
	Technical	11.6	59
	Housewife	6.1	31
	Retiree	5.7	29
	Others	21.8	111
Income	RM 3,000 and less	57.0	290
	RM 3,001–RM 6,000	28.0	141
	RM 6,001–RM 9,000	10.0	52
	RM 9,001–RM 12,000	3.0	18
	RM 12,001–RM 15,000	1.0	3
	RM 15, 001–RM 18, 000	0.0	2
	More than RM 18,001	1.0	4
Marital status	Married	64.0	325
	Single	33.0	167
	Divorced	2.0	12
	Widowed	1.0	6

(31.0%) only held Malaysian Certificate of Education (i.e., SPM) or below. A total of 21.8% responded "others" for their occupations and people in the monthly income group of RM 3,000 and less made up the highest percentage in this study. Lastly, 64.0% respondents were married.

Descriptive data showed responses from respondents on the variables. The mean response value of the all the variables are at a value above 4 as shown in Table 2.

For the hypothesis testing, attitude towards SM has a positive and significant influence on continuance use of SM ($\beta = 0.28$; t = 7.89; p < 0.01). These results indicate that the users' attitudes towards SM led to the continuance use of SM. Therefore, this finding supports hypothesis 1. Next supported hypothesis is H_4 where perceived ease of use showed a significant influence on continuance use of SM ($\beta = 0.16$; t = 4.13; p < 0.01). The test results for Hypothesis 6 confirmed the positive significance of perceived usefulness on continuance use of SM. The variables of internal and external perceived locus of causality ($\beta = 0.26, 0.32$; t = 6.60, 8.82; p < 0.01) also revealed the positive and significant factor in influencing users to continue the usage of SM.

These findings show that attitude toward SM, perceived ease of use, perceived usefulness, internal perceived locus of causality and external perceived locus of causality are significant factors that influence users in Melaka to continuously use the SMs.

Table 2. Analysis

Model	B	Mean	Beta	t-stats	Sig.	Index
(Constant)	−0.246			−2.391	0.017	
Attitude towards SM	0.280	4.469	0.284	7.892	0.000	1.142*
Perceived benefits on environment	0.013	4.321	0.014	0.414	0.679	
Perceived privacy risk	−0.059	4.559	−0.049	−1.862	0.063	
Perceived ease of use	0.155	4.175	0.141	4.134	0.000	0.591
Perceived behavioural control	0.000	4.123	0.000	0.005	0.996	
Perceived usefulness	0.091	4.436	0.088	2.367	0.018	0.368
Internal perceived locus of causality	0.256	4.231	0.259	6.596	0.000	0.987
External perceived locus of causality	0.315	4.321	0.275	8.817	0.000	1.240
Total B	1.098					4.327
						72.114**

*Note: * Construct B/Total B (significant construct only) x Mean; ** Total Index/6 X 100*

The steps involved to develop CUSMI are in line with industry requirement. The steps are as follows: checking the face validity (questionnaire), then testing on convergent and discriminant validity (unidimensional/multidimensionality), checking the balance number of item and testing the correlation between the dependent and independent variables before undergoing the multiple regression analysis.

To develop the model, some analyses had been carried out. The total sum of the attitude toward SM, perceived benefits on environment, perceived privacy risk, perceived ease of use, perceived behavioural control, perceived usefulness, internal perceived locus of causality and external perceived locus of causality equalled to the continuing use of the SMs. After running the multiple regression analysis, the significant factor that contributed to the continuance use of SM were attitude toward SM, perceived ease of use, perceived usefulness, internal perceived locus of causality and external perceived locus of causality. For the state of Melaka, the CUSMI is 4.327 or 72.11%. The percentage can be generalized as SMs users in Melaka were slightly willing to continue use the SM.

5   Conclusion

From the CUSMI value, this research found that in general, the SM users in Melaka were slightly willing to continue the usage of SMs in their houses. This project's findings could give new insights to the electricity provider to craft a better planning for SM installation. Since this study was limited to SM users in Melaka, the future research can be further expanded in other areas in Malaysia and identify other related factors to motivate the SM continuance use. This is important to ensure that the government initiative could be successfully implemented.

Acknowledgement. This research work was funded by TNB through TNB Seeding Fund (U-TD-RD-19–12).

References

1. Chen, C.F., Xu, X., Arpan, L.: Between the technology acceptance model and sustainable energy technology acceptance model: investigating smart meter acceptance in the United States. Energy Res. Soc. Sci. **25**, 93–104 (2017). https://doi.org/10.1016/j.erss.2016.12.011
2. Kaufmann, S., Künzel, K., Loock, M.: Customer value of smart metering: explorative evidence from a choice-based conjoint study in Switzerland. Energy Policy **53**, 229–239 (2013). https://doi.org/10.1016/j.enpol.2012.10.072
3. Bugden, D., Stedman, R.: A synthetic view of acceptance and engagement with smart meters in the United States. Energy Res. Soc. Sci. **47**(January 2018), 137–145 (2019). https://doi.org/10.1016/j.erss.2018.08.025
4. van Gerwen, R., Koenis, F., Schrijner, M., Widdershoven, G.: Intelligente meters in Nederland Herziene financiële analyse en adviezen voor beleid, pp. 1–4 (2010)
5. Harian, S.: Pemasangan meter pintar beri banyak manfaat (2019)
6. Livgard, E.F.: Electricity customers' attitudes to smart metering. Experiences from the Norwegian market. In: SPEEDAM 2012 - 21st International Symposium on Power Electronics, Electrical Drives, Automation and Motion, pp. 690–694 (2012). https://doi.org/10.1109/SPEEDAM.2012.6264476
7. Malek, N.H.A.: Smart meter implementation in Klang Valley by 2023. The Malaysian Reserve (2019)
8. TNB, R.D.: Smart Meter Related Issues and Challenges in Melaka (2019)
9. Qiu, Z., Deconinck, G.: Smart Meter's Feedback and the Potential for Energy Savings in Household Sector: A Survey (2011). https://doi.org/10.1109/ICNSC.2011.5874882
10. Wood, G., Newborough, M.: Dynamic energy-consumption indicators for domestic appliances: environment, behaviour and design. Energy Build. **35**(8), 821–841 (2003). https://doi.org/10.1016/S0378-7788(02)00241-4

11. Taherdoost, H.: A review of technology acceptance and adoption models and theories. Procedia Manuf. **22**, 960–967 (2018). https://doi.org/10.1016/j.promfg.2018.03.137

12. Davis, F.D.: Perceived usefulness, perceived ease of use, and user acceptance of information technology. MIS Q. Manag. Inf. Syst. **13**(3), 319–339 (1989). https://doi.org/10.2307/249008

13. Surendran, P.: Technology acceptance model: a survey of literature. Int. J. Bus. Soc. Res. **2**(4), 175–178 (2012). https://doi.org/10.1016/j.biortech.2015.06.132

14. Liao, C., Palvia, P., Chen, J.L.: Information technology adoption behavior life cycle: toward a technology continuance theory (TCT). Int. J. Inf. Manage. **29**(4), 309–320 (2009). https://doi.org/10.1016/j.ijinfomgt.2009.03.004

15. Wunderlich, P., Veit, D., Sarker, S.: Examination of the Determinants of Smart Meter Adoption : An User Perspective, no. December 2012 (2014)

16. Lee, M.: Computers and education explaining and predicting users' continuance intention toward e-learning : an extension of the expectation – confirmation model. Comput. Educ. **54**(2), 506–516 (2010). https://doi.org/10.1016/j.compedu.2009.09.002

17. Weng, G.S., Zailani, S., Iranmanesh, M., Hyun, S.S.: Mobile taxi booking application service's continuance usage intention by users. Transp. Res. Part D Transp. Environ. **57**(October), 207–216 (2017). https://doi.org/10.1016/j.trd.2017.07.023

18. Nanggong, A., Rahmatia: Perceived benefit, environmental concern and sustainable customer behavior on technology adoption. Asian J. Technol. Manag. **12**(1), 31–47 (2019). https://doi.org/10.12695/ajtm.2019.12.1.3

19. Joshi, Y., Rahman, Z.: Investigating the determinants of consumers' sustainable purchase behaviour. Sustain. Prod. Consum. **10**, 110–120 (2017). https://doi.org/10.1016/j.spc.2017.02.002

20. Xu, H., Gupta, S.: The effects of privacy concerns and personal innovativeness on potential and experienced customers' adoption of location-based services. Electron. Mark. **19**(2), 137–149 (2009). https://doi.org/10.1007/s12525-009-0012-4

21. Hmielowski, J.D., Boyd, A.D., Harvey, G., Joo, J.: The social dimensions of smart meters in the United States: demographics, privacy, and technology readiness. Energy Res. Soc. Sci. **55**(May), 189–197 (2019). https://doi.org/10.1016/j.erss.2019.05.003

22. Hamid, A.A., Razak, F.Z.A., Bakar, A.A., Abdullah, W.S.W.: The effects of perceived usefulness and perceived ease of use on continuance intention to use e-government. Procedia Econ. Finan. **35**(October), 644–649 (2016). https://doi.org/10.1016/s2212-5671(16)00079-4

23. Chen, C.C., Hsiao, K.L., Li, W.C.: Exploring the determinants of usage continuance willingness for location-based apps: a case study of bicycle-based exercise apps. J. Retail. Consum. Serv. **55**(129), 102097 (2020). https://doi.org/10.1016/j.jretconser.2020.102097

24. Liao, C., Chen, J.L., Yen, D.C.: Theory of planning behavior (TPB) and customer satisfaction in the continued use of e-service: an integrated model. Comput. Human Behav. **23**(6), 2804–2822 (2007). https://doi.org/10.1016/j.chb.2006.05.006

25. Karahanna, G., Straub, D.: Inexperience and experience with online stores: the importance of TAM and trust. IEEE Trans. Eng. Manag. **50**(3), 307–321 (2003)

26. Vansteenkiste, M., Simons, J., Lens, W., Sheldon, K.M., Deci, E.L.: Motivating learning, performance, and persistence: the synergistic effects of intrinsic goal contents and autonomy-supportive contexts. J. Pers. Soc. Psychol. **87**(2), 246–260 (2004). https://doi.org/10.1037/0022-3514.87.2.246

27. Hair Jr., J.F., Black, W.C., Babin, B.J., Anderson, R.E.: Multivariate Data Analysis (MVDA) (2010)

Highlighting the Contributing Factors of Smart Meter Adoption in Klang Valley

Azlina Abdullah[1,2(✉)], Wan Hafiizhah Wan Mohamad Norafi[1],
Nurul Wahilah Abdul Latif[3], Abdul Rahman Zahari[4], Zeittey Karmilla Kaman[2],
Zurina Ismail[4], and Nor Shafiqah Yusoff[1]

[1] College of Graduate Studies, National Energy University, Selangor, Malaysia
azlina@uniten.edu.my
[2] Institute of Energy Policy and Research, National Energy University, Selangor, Malaysia
[3] College of Energy Economics and Social Sciences, National Energy University,
Selangor, Malaysia
[4] College of Business Management and Accounting, National Energy University,
Shah Alam, Malaysia

Abstract. This study aimed to examine the contributing factors of smart meter adoption amongst household. A survey was conducted amongst 529 potential smart meter users in Klang Valley. The results indicated that the factors that contributed significantly to the willingness to adopt smart meter amongst potential users were smart meter awareness, social influence, perceived usefulness, user expected satisfaction and trust in utility company. The findings will assist the utility company in identifying the contributing factors to smart meter adoption and craft the right strategy to ensure that the installation of smart meter amongst all residentials can be successful. The findings were also used to develop an index called smart meter Adoption Index (SMAI).

Keywords: Smart meter · Adoption · Technology acceptance model

1 Introduction

Smart meter is a device to help households and businesses track their energy consumption. Smart meter rollout has various reasons in different countries. For instance, the rollout in Italy was due to reducing energy theft, while in Ireland, it was due to achieving accurate billing and demand management [1]. Smart meter is being studied and installed in many developed and some developing countries due to their expected benefits. Several countries in Europe, such as Italy and Sweden have already installed the smart meter system [2, 3]. In other countries, such as the USA, smart meter deployment is underway [4]. Meanwhile, in some developed countries or regions such as Korea and Taiwan, smart meter installation is still on going. Citizens of Korea prefer the adoption of smart meter because they expect positive implication such as instant saving [5]. By 2019, one million customers in Indonesia were expected to have access to smart meter

© Springer Nature Switzerland AG 2021
H. Badioze Zaman et al. (Eds.): IVIC 2021, LNCS 13051, pp. 665–675, 2021.
https://doi.org/10.1007/978-3-030-90235-3_57

too. Smart meter was initially installed in major cities and tourist destinations of the country [6].

Now, Malaysia is taking a step further with the smart meter. This is a government nationwide initiative and Tenaga Nasional Berhad (TNB)[1] was given responsibility by the Energy Commission[2] to install smart meter in all Malaysian homes. Smart meter operates similarly with traditional meters, except that the smart meter allows households to monitor and track their daily energy usage via the myTNB application or myTNB portal. Smart meters are certainly the first step towards a smarter, sustainable, and greener future of the country. TNB aims to install smart meter to most Malaysian households by 2022. To date, close to 340,000 smart meters were installed in Melaka from 2016 to 2018 and TNB has targeted to install the smart meter for 1.2 million consumers around Klang Valley from 2018–2021 as a start [7].

Since the installation of smart meter is considered new in Malaysian market, it is important to conduct a study to assess the factors that contribute to potential users' willingness to adopt smart meter in their houses and to propose SMAI as a measurement of willingness to adopt smart meter. This index could be used in the future to know the smart meter adoption willingness amongst potential users in any areas prior to smart meter installation. The paper is organised as follows; literature review is explained in the next section, followed by the research method. In the subsequent section, results and analysis are discussed and lastly the conclusion and recommendations of the study are presented.

2 Literature Review

This section presents some past studies regarding smart meter acceptance by using various theories, such as Theory of Perceived Behaviour (TPB), Unified Theory of Acceptance and Use of Technology (UTAUT) and Technology Acceptance Model (TAM).

With regard to adoption behaviour related to the new technology, TPB [8], UTAUT [9] and TAM [10] were the most fundamental and influential theories discussed by researchers. These model studied the attitude towards behaviour, subjective norm, perceived behaviour control, perceived ease of use, perceived usefulness, facilitating conditions, performance expectancy, effort expectancy and social influence [9, 10]. Therefore, to discuss the household adoption of smart meter, it is important to identify the factors that influence the willingness of potential users to adopt smart meter. Several studies have investigated respondents' intention to adopt a number of technologies, such as smartphone [11], smart watch [12] and smart grid [13] by using TRA, TPB, UTAUT or TAM. The positive belief towards a new technology will propel respondents to have the intention to adopt the new technology. In most cases, when the respondents perceived the usefulness of a technology, they will have the intention to adopt the new technology.

---

[1] Tenaga Nasional Berhad (TNB) is the largest electricity utility in Malaysia.

[2] Energy Commission is a statutory body established under the Energy Commission Act 2001, Suruhanjaya Tenaga (ST) or the Energy Commission is responsible for regulating the energy sector, specifically the electricity and piped gas supply industries, in Peninsular Malaysia and Sabah.

The construct of adoption intention refers to a person's subjective likelihood of engaging in a particular action [14].

Based on the theories discussed above, the review of literatures provided below defines the eight factors that influence potential users' willingness to adopt smart meter in their houses. The hypothesis for each factor is also developed.

2.1 Smart Meter Awareness

According to Alabdulkarim et al., smart meter awareness is defined as the extent to which users and target audience are familiar with the qualities or image of smart meter. They also stated that smart meter awareness have shown significant influence on the intention to adopt smart meter [15]. Chawla and Kowalska-Pyzalska also discussed that users who are aware with the function of smart meter will adopt it [16]. Therefore, a hypothesis was proposed as such:

H_1: Smart meter awareness has a significant influence on household intention to adopt smart meter.

2.2 Benefits on the Environment

According to Liobikienė and Poškus benefits on the environment are defined as beliefs about the positive environmental outcomes associated with behaviour in response to a real or perceived threat [17]. Kranz & Picot stated that benefit on environment influence positively on the intention to adopt smart meter [18]. Alkawsi and Baashar in their study confirmed that amongst the factors that influence utility users to adopt smart meter are associated with benefit to the environment [19]. Therefore, a hypothesis proposed as such:

H2: Benefits on the environment has a significant influence on household intention to adopt smart meter.

2.3 Energy Tariff or Cost

Energy tariff refers to the energy consumption price. Past study by Chou et al. Proved that this factor had a positive influence on smart meter adoption [20]. Previous study by Mah et al., mentioned that the energy users who were sensitive to tariff had increased because of the smart meter implementation and will affect users to adopt it [21]. Chawla et al., highlighted that one of the issues expressed by the studied participants was the extra burden caused by energy-rate fluctuations [6]. However, their study found that the energy tariff had a positive link with smart meter adoption. Conversely, Chou and Yutami demonstrated that the energy tariffs had a negative effect on smart meter adoption [20]. Therefore, such hypothesis is proposed:

H_3: Energy tariff/cost has a significant influence on household intention to adopt smart meter.

2.4 Privacy or Safety Concerns

Privacy or safety concern can be defined as beliefs regarding the processes, activities, systems, or tasks that protect the confidentiality, integrity, and accessibility of information or objects [22]. Many past studies found the negative influence of privacy or safety concerns with smart meter adoption. For instance, Chou and Yutami highlighted that privacy and security concerns negatively influence smart meter adoption amongst utility users in Indonesia [20]. Another study from Chawla et al., studied on the privacy and security concern in Indonesia. In their work, Chawla et al., found that privacy and security concern had a positive impact on smart meter adoption. The Chou and Yutami study was conducted amongst the general population, whereas the study by Chawla et al., was conducted amongst social media users. Regular users of social media were considered to be early adopters of new technology [6]. In most cases, the privacy concerns could be important when considering support for new technologies [23]. Therefore, a hypothesis is proposed as such:

H_4: Privacy or safety concerns has a significant influence on household intention to adopt smart meter.

2.5 Social Influence

According to Ahn et al., social influence is defined as the degree to which an individual perceives that it is important for others to believe that he should use the new system [24]. A few recent studies proved that social influence was identified as a critical element in increasing smart meter acceptance [16, 25].In addition, Kranz and Picot stated in their study that social influence also positively impacted the intention to adopt smart meter [18]. Koo et al., also found that social influence had a positive impact on smart meter adoption [26].Therefore, a hypothesis is proposed as such:

H_5: Social influence has a significant influence on household intention to adopt smart meter.

2.6 Perceived Usefulness

Perceived usefulness refers to the degree to which an individual believes that using smart meter will improve energy efficiency [27]. In addition, Chou et al., defined that perceived expected usefulness is the degree to which a person expects that using a particular technology will improve his performance [22]. A study by Kranz and Picot confirmed that smart meter adoption was significantly influenced by perceived usefulness [18]. Koo et al., found that perceived usefulness had a positive impact on smart meter adoption [26]. Therefore, a hypothesis is proposed as such:

H_6: Perceived usefulness has a significant influence on household intention to adopt smart meter.

2.7   User Expected Satisfaction

Another contributing factor that is used in this study is user expected satisfaction. User expected satisfaction refers to a person's belief that smart meter meets their needs or desires [28]. They added that the user expected satisfaction was never directly tested against smart meters. However, it was found that user expected satisfaction significantly affects behavioural intention to use, which was an important indicator of successful acceptance of new technology [28]. Chou and Yutami found that user expected satisfaction had a positive impact on smart meter adoption [20]. Therefore, a hypothesis is proposed as such:

H_7: User expected satisfaction has a significant influence on household intention to adopt smart meter.

2.8   Trust in Utility Company

Trust in the utilities that install, manage the smart meter, and handle the collected data is also important and has a positive influence on the smart meter adoption amongst residential users [29]. Huang & Palvia, stated that if a user had a high level of trust in the utility provider, he would not be so concerned that the provider would violate his obligations, and defined trusting beliefs as the degree to which consumers believe that utility providers are reliable in protecting their personal data [30]. Trust in the utility companies is crucial because it will impact people's positive opinion towards smart meter [4]. Therefore, a hypothesis is proposed as such:

H_8: Trust in utility company has a significant influence on household intention to adopt smart meter.

3   Data and Methodology

Figure 1 shows the research framework used in the current study. In this framework, smart meter awareness, benefits on the environment, energy tariff or cost, privacy or safety concerns, social influence, perceived usefulness, user expected satisfaction, and trust in utility company are considered as the independent variables, whereas the smart meter adoption willingness is a dependent variable. Data collected through a survey were analysed by using descriptive analysis, reliability, and multiple regression. All data were analysed by using IBM SPSS Statistics for Windows Version 24. Descriptive analysis simplifies the presentation of quantitative data [31]. This analysis enables researchers to rationalise a large amount of data. Reliability refers to the degree to which Likert scale questions can produce consistent results over time [32]. Reliability analysis measures scale reliability and provides information about the relation between individual items in the scale. Multiple regression analyses the relation between a single dependent variable and a collection of independent variables or predictors [32]. In the present study we will test the relation between smart meter awareness, benefits on the environment, energy tariff or cost, privacy or safety concerns, social influence, perceived usefulness, user expected satisfaction, trust in utility company and smart meter adoption willingness.

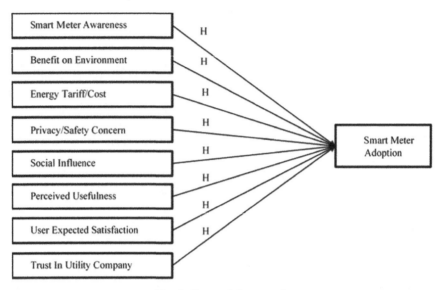

Fig. 1. Research framework

This study obtained 529 smart meter potential users amongst the residents living in Klang Valley as respondents. Klang Valley is the largest urban area in Malaysia and the main economic centre of the country with a population of 6.37 million in 2017 [33]. Data were collected through online survey by using a convenience sampling technique through Google form, which was distributed through social media platforms, such as Facebook, WhatsApp, Twitter, Telegram, and Instagram. The data collection period was executed from February to April 2020. The survey questionnaire used in this study consisted of two parts. The first part indicated the contributing factors that influence the potential users' willingness to adopt smart meter. A total of 22 questions were used in Part 1. The items were adapted/adopted from [4, 20, 34]. All items in Part 1 were measured by using a six-point Likert type scale, ranging from "strongly disagree (1) to strongly agree (6)". In addition, Part Two was designed to capture respondent demographic information. A total of 14 questions were asked in this section.

4   Results and Analysis

The sample demographic profiles are represented in Table 1. Based on descriptive analysis, 59% of respondents were females and 41% were males, with 33.6% of respondents being aged between 21 and 30 years old. The Malays made up 95% of the respondents. 50% of respondents had a bachelor's degree, and 44% had a monthly income of RM3,000 or less. Furthermore, 43.5% of respondents were homeowners.

In this study, Cronbach's alpha was used to identify the internal consistency of each item in an instrument. Coefficient Cronbach's alpha value must reach 0.7 and above to make the internal consistency of the survey acceptable, good and excellent [35]. The reliability test was conducted for the questionnaire, whereby the overall results indicated that the instrument was reliable.

Table 1. Demographic profiles (n = 529)

Profile	Percentage (%)	Numbers
Gender		
Male	41.0	217
Female	59.0	312
Age		
20 and below	2.5	13
21 – 30	33.6	178
31 – 40	30.2	160
41 – 50	20.6	109
51 – 60	10.2	54
61 and above	2.8	15
Race		
Malay	95.0	502
Chinese	2.0	11
Indian	2.0	9
Others	1.0	7
Education		
SPM and below	13.0	66
Diploma	18.0	97
Bachelor's degree	50.0	266
Master/PhD Degree	19.0	99
Others	0.0	1
Job		
Top Management	6.4	34
Middle Management	18.7	99
Supervisory	3.8	20
Administrative/Clerk	13.2	70
Technical	8.9	47
Housewife	6.4	34
Retiree	3.0	16
Others	13.4	71
Monthly Income		
RM3,000 and less	44.0	233

(continued)

Table 1. (*continued*)

Profile	Percentage (%)	Numbers
RM3,001 – RM6,000	32.3	171
RM6,001 – RM9,000	12.7	67
RM9,001 – RM12,000	4.9	26
RM12,001 – RM15,000	2.8	15
RM15,001 – RM18,000	1.3	7
RM18,001 and more	1.9	10
Marital Status		
Married	64.1	339
Single	33.5	177
Divorced	1.9	10
Widowed	0.6	3
House Ownership		
Owner	43.5	230
Family Member	19.8	105
Tenant	36.7	194

Multiple regression analysis was used to determine the relation between smart meter awareness, benefits on the environment, energy tariff or cost, privacy or safety concerns, social influence, perceived usefulness, user expected satisfaction, trust in utility company and smart meter adoption intention. For the hypothesis testing, smart meter awareness had a positive significant influence on household intention to adopt smart meter ($\beta = 0.73$; $t = 3.30$; $p < 0.01$). Next, social influence also had a positive significant influence on household willingness to adopt smart meter ($\beta = 0.13$; $t = 4.72$; $p < 0.01$). Hypothesis 6, perceived usefulness had a positive significant influence on household willingness to adopt smart meter ($\beta = 0.32$; $t = 7.19$; $p < 0.01$). User expected satisfaction had a positive significant influence on household willingness to adopt smart meter ($\beta = 0.24$; $t = 5.81$; $p < 0.01$). Lastly, trust in utility company also had a positive significant influence on household willingness to adopt smart meter ($\beta = 0.27$; $t = 9.32$; $p < 0.01$).

The steps taken to develop SMAI are in accordance with the industrial standards. The procedure is as follows: face validity is checked (questionnaire), followed by convergent and discriminant validity tests (unidimensional/multidimensionality). Prior to performing the multiple regression analysis, it is necessary to verify the item balance and determine the correlation between the dependent and independent variables.

Based on Table 2, factors that contributed significantly to potential users to adopt smart meter at Klang Valley were smart meter awareness, social influence, perceived usefulness, user expected satisfaction and trust in utility company. Therefore, the step to calculate SMAI is by calculating index (2). Second, total up the index by referring (1).

Table 2. Regression analysis

Model	B	Mean	Beta	t-stats	Sig	Index
(Constant)	−0.291			−2.519	0.012	
Smart meter awareness	0.073	4.22	0.084	3.299	0.001	0.301
Benefit on environment	0.015	4.57	0.015	0.492	0.623	
Energy tariff/cost	0.045	4.62	0.049	1.452	0.147	
Privacy/safety concerns	−0.019	4.56	−0.019	−0.636	0.525	
Social influence	0.124	4.51	0.131	4.716	0.000	0.546
Perceived usefulness	0.319	4.88	0.299	7.192	0.000	1.519
User expected satisfaction	0.236	4.68	0.231	5.807	0.000	1.078
Trust in utility company	0.273	4.82	0.262	9.316	0.000	1.284
Total B	1.025					4.726
						78.77

Lastly, use (3) to calculate the SMAI.

$$\text{Smart Meter Adoption} = \text{Awareness} + \text{Social} + \text{Usefulness} + \text{Satisfaction} + \text{Trust} \tag{1}$$

$$\frac{\text{Construct B}}{\text{Total B}} \times \text{Mean} = \text{Index} \tag{2}$$

$$\frac{\text{Total Index}}{6} \times 100 = \text{SMAI} \tag{3}$$

The SMAI for the respondents of this research was 4.726% or 78.77%. Therefore, it can be generalised that all smart meter potential users in the Klang Valley were willing to adopt smart meter in their house.

5   Conclusion

The research in Klang Valley investigated the contributing factors that influenced the adoption of smart meter by potential smart meter users. Based on the SMAI value, it was found that in general, potential smart meter users in the Klang Valley were willing to adopt smart meter usage in their houses. From all the eight factors analysed in the research model, five factors were found to significantly influence respondents' willingness to adopt smart meter, namely smart meter awareness, social influence, perceived usefulness, expected satisfaction, and trust in utility company. By knowing these factors, it will be easier to find ways to increase the willingness of public to adopt smart meter in other areas prior to smart meter installation.

Since this study was limited to potential users in Klang Valley, the future, research can be further expanded in other areas in Malaysia and identify other related factors to motivate the smart meter adoption.

Acknowledgement. This research work was funded by TNB through TNB Seeding Fund (U-TD-RD-19–12).

References

1. Darby, S.: Smart metering: what potential for householder engagement? Building Res. Inf. **38**(5), 442–457 (2010)
2. Ntouros, V., et al.: Smart Meter Awareness in Italy, Ancona, Smart and Sustainable Planning for Cities and Regions, p. 47 (2021)
3. Leysen, R.: An analysis of smart meter deployment in Sweden with applicability to the case of India. In: Book an Analysis of Smart Meter Deployment in Sweden With Applicability to the Case of India (2018)
4. Chen, C.-F., Xu, X., Arpan, L.: Between the technology acceptance model and sustainable energy technology acceptance model: investigating smart meter acceptance in the United States. Energy Res. Soc. Sci. **25**, 93–104 (2017)
5. Alkawsi, G., Ali, N.a., Baashar, Y.: The moderating role of personal innovativeness and users experience in accepting the smart meter technology. Appl. Sci. **11**(8), p. 3297 (2021)
6. Chawla, Y., Kowalska-Pyzalska, A., Widayat, W.: Consumer willingness and acceptance of smart meters in Indonesia. Resources **8**(4), 1–23 (2019)
7. Subhi, M.H.F.M.: Communication technology options for better customer experience–the case of advanced metering infrastructure (AMI) at TNB, iLEARNed **1**(1), 16–24 (2020)
8. Ajzen, I.: The theory of planned behavior. Organ. Behav. Hum. Decis. Process. **50**(2), 179–211 (1991)
9. Venkatesh, V., Morris, M.G., Davis, G.B., Davis, F.D.: User acceptance of information technology: toward a unified view. MIS quarterly, 425–478 (2003)
10. Davis, F.D.: Perceived usefulness, perceived ease of use, and user acceptance of information technology. MIS quarterly, 319–340 (1989)
11. Pan, D., Chen, N., Rau, P.-L.P.: The acceptance and adoption of smartphone use among Chinese college students. In: Book The acceptance and Adoption of Smartphone Use Among Chinese College Students, Springer, edn., pp. 450–458 (2013)
12. Dutot, V., Bhatiasevi, V., Bellallahom, N.: Applying the technology acceptance model in a three-countries study of smartwatch adoption. J. High Technol. Managem. Res. **30**(1), 1–14 (2019)
13. Abu, F., et al.: Technology Acceptance Model (TAM): empowering smart customer to participate in electricity supply system. J. Technol. Manage. Technopreneurship (JTMT) **2**(1) (2014)
14. Huang, Z., Palvia, P.: Consumers' privacy concerns about smart meters. In: AMCIS 2016: Surfing the IT Innovation Wave - 22nd Americas Conference on Information Systems, pp. 1–10 (2016)
15. AlAbdulkarim, L., Molin, E., Lukszo, Z., Fens, T.: Acceptance of ict-intensive socio-technical infrastructure systems: Smart metering case in the Netherlands. In: Book Acceptance of Ict-Intensive Socio-Technical Infrastructure Systems: Smart Metering Case in the Netherlands, IEEE, edn., pp. 399–404 (2014)
16. Chawla, Y., Kowalska-Pyzalska, A.: Public awareness and consumer acceptance of smart meters among Polish social media users. Energies **12**(14), 2759 (2019)
17. Liobikienė, G., Poškus, M.S.: The importance of environmental knowledge for private and public sphere pro-environmental behavior: modifying the value-belief-norm theory. Sustainability **11**(12), 3324 (2019)

18. Kranz, J., Picot, A.: Is it money or the environment? An empirical analysis of factors influencing consumers' intention to adopt the smart metering technology (2012)

19. Alkawsi, G.A., Baashar, Y.: An empirical study of the acceptance of IoT-based smart meter in Malaysia: the effect of electricity-saving knowledge and environmental awareness. IEEE Access **8**, 42794–42804 (2020)

20. Chou, J.-S., Yutami, I.G.A.N.: Smart meter adoption and deployment strategy for residential buildings in Indonesia. Appl. Energy **128**, 336–349 (2014)

21. Mah, D.N.-y., van der Vleuten, J.M., Hills, P., Tao, J.: Consumer perceptions of smart grid development: results of a Hong Kong survey and policy implications. Energy Policy **49**, 204-216 (2012)

22. Chou, J.-S., et al.: Cross-country review of smart grid adoption in residential buildings. Renew. Sustain. Energy Rev. **48**, 192–213 (2015)

23. Hmielowski, J.D., Boyd, A.D., Harvey, G., Joo, J.: The social dimensions of smart meters in the United States: demographics, privacy, and technology readiness. Energy Res. Soc. Sci. **55**(June), 189–197 (2019)

24. Ahn, M., Kang, J., Hustvedt, G.: A model of sustainable household technology acceptance. Int. J. Consum. Stud. **40**(1), 83–91 (2016)

25. Chawla, Y., Kowalska-Pyzalska, A., Oralhan, B.: Attitudes and Opinions of Social Media Users Towards Smart Meters Rollout in Turkey'. pp. 1–27 (2020)

26. Koo, C., Chung, N., Lee, Y.-C.: The Influential Motivations of Green IT Device Use and the Role of Reference Group Perspective. In: Book The Influential Motivations of Green IT Device Use and the Role of Reference Group Perspective, Citeseer, edn., p. 90 (2013)

27. Davis, F.D.: A technology acceptance model for empirically testing new end-user information systems: Theory and results. Science (1985)

28. Chin, J., Lin, S.-C.: A behavioral model of managerial perspectives regarding technology acceptance in building energy management systems, Sustainability. **8**(7), 641 (2016)

29. Nachreiner, M., Mack, B., Matthies, E., Tampe-Mai, K.: An analysis of smart metering information systems: a psychological model of self-regulated behavioural change. Energy Res. Soc. Sci. **9**, 85–97 (2015)

30. Huang, Z., Palvia, P.: Invasion of privacy by smart meters: an analysis of consumer concerns. J. Inf. Priv. Secur. **13**(3), 120–136 (2017)

31. Fisher, M.J., Marshall, A.P.: Understanding descriptive statistics. Aust. Crit. Care **22**(2), 93–97 (2009)

32. Hair, J., Black, W.C., Babin, B., Anderson, R., and Tatham, R.: Pearson new international edition, Multivariate data analysis, Seventh Edition. Pearson Education Limited Harlow, Essex (2014)

33. Cai, Y., Abdullah Yusof, S., Mohd Amin, R., Mohd, M.N.: The association between household debt and marriage satisfaction in the context of urban household in Klang Valley, Malaysia. J. Emerg. Econ. Islamic Res. **8**(1), 1–11 (2020)

34. Bugden, D., Stedman, R.: A synthetic view of acceptance and engagement with smart meters in the United States. Energy Res. Soc. Sci. **47**, 137–145 (2019)

35. Habidin, N.F., Zubir, A.F.M., Fuzi, N.M., Latip, N.A.M., Azman, M.N.A.: Sustainable performance measures for Malaysian automotive industry. World Appl. Sci. J. **33**(6), 1017–1024 (2015)

Virtualization Technology to Support Green Computing Among IT Personnel in the Public Sector

Mohd Yusri Jusoh$^{(\boxtimes)}$ ⓘ, Haryani Haron ⓘ, and Jasber Kaur ⓘ

Faculty of Computer and Mathematical Sciences, Universiti Teknologi MARA, Shah Alam, Selangor, Malaysia

Abstract. This paper presents virtualization technology that supports green computing among IT personnel in the public sector. The selection of effective technology in virtualization is crucial to reduce the negative impact of IT usage in the public sector by leveraging resources and maximizing the use of IT devices. Virtualization can provide important processes related to green computing implementation in the organization. However, the organization still faces problems in identifying suitable technology used by IT personnel in the organization. Thus, there is a need to understand the process to select the suitable technology based on the role of people, process, technology, and IT organization structure. The methodology comprises that the work process exploration, end-user segmentation, and technology evaluation process, which is validated by interviewing targeting IT personnel in government-based institutions in Malaysia that have in-house green data centers. The qualitative approach was adopted to understand the work activities of IT personnel and IT devices used to perform the task. A case study approach was used where the data was collected from open-ended interviews, observation, and report documents. The data was analyzed using a thematic analysis approach. Then, technology evaluation was conducted to select appropriate virtualization technologies to be used to support green computing in the IT work process by integrating four dimensions that consist of the people, process, technology, and IT organization structure. The results show a list of virtualization technology to support green computing based on the technology evaluation process.

Keywords: Technology evaluation · Virtualization · Green computing · It Personnel · Work process

1 Introduction

The term "green" has become widely used in recent years, referring to a perspective on the environmental impact of a product or service's development and production, as well as its use and disposal. Green refers to environmental improvement through the application of various green approaches in various sectors to reduce environmental impacts. For an organization to manage its IT devices while remaining environmentally friendly, it must consider ways to ensure that the type of end-user who brings IT devices is appropriate

H. Badioze Zaman et al. (Eds.): IVIC 2021, LNCS 13051, pp. 676–688, 2021.
https://doi.org/10.1007/978-3-030-90235-3_58

for the work task performed by an employee. As a result, the requirement for bringing IT devices and device selection to support green computing in the organization is critical.

Implementing green IT in organizations involves several different practices. They include the green data center approach, software, and deployment optimization, power management, and materials recycling, all of which have the potential to provide benefits to the organization in the form of energy savings, pollution reduction, improved performance, increased productivity, and cost reduction. Studies on green computing focused on practical emphasis on life cycle strategies such as Green design, Green production, Green procurement, Green operation, and Green disposal [1]. Green computing is becoming more popular in businesses as a way to reduce carbon emissions, energy consumption [2], the total cost of ownership [3], and e-waste [4, 5]. Existing green environmental practices emphasize the reduction of environmental impact through the use of green data centers, green IT equipment, power management, and product recycling, among other methods. Using these approaches, employees in IT industries can use information technology devices in the most environmentally friendly way. It is extremely beneficial to the organization in the form of electricity savings, pollution reduction, improved performance, increased productivity, and money savings on new hardware purchases. To ensure that the environmental impact of information technology is minimized, these advantages are critical in measuring green IT. Many key elements of green computing approaches are found in telecommuting, voice over internet protocol (VoIP), power management, algorithmic efficiency, virtualization, material recycling, and procurement [6] that show the benefit of green computing.

To improve business performance, virtualization technology has been identified as a significant strategy in many organizations [7]. In cloud computing, virtualization will be widely used as new technology. Virtualization also ensures high availability for operation and application areas while also making application deployment and migration easier [8]. Bring your own device (BYOD) encourages end-users to use IT devices to access virtualization technology [9]. In the organization, the high number of IT devices used by end-users in the data center will result in an increase in energy consumption and carbon emissions in the data center. Virtualization is an incredible strategy for reducing the environmental impact of data centers, particularly in terms of energy efficiency and the reduction of an organization's CO2 footprint. It also helps to increase flexibility while also lowering maintenance costs. However, the IT personnel spends a lot of money every year because the IT department fails to manage virtualization technology in the data center and integrate the work process based on the IT nature of work [14, 15]. It is even more concerning for IT organizations because they rely on the data center as their primary source of IT services to run their business. The business must therefore ensure that virtualization technology is implemented by IT workers (end-users) can reduce energy and carbon emissions within the data center.

2   Research Method

The study included observation and interviews to gather input from the organization's IT personnel. Observation between IT personnel and current work processes that are related to the IT were recorded to collect information relevant to green computing concerning the environment such as energy consumption, electricity consumption, CO_2 emission, paper-reduction, and e-waste. The personnel interviewed were IT personnel that perform work tasks or manage the IT work process. A qualitative approach is useful for our study because it allowed us to get more information faster and ask follow-up questions. This type can improve the interviewee's communication skills and focusing on subject knowledge. The organization targeted in the study presented in this paper is Ministry of Entrepreneur Development and Cooperatives (MEDAC) and Malaysian Administrative Modernisation and Management Planning Unit (MAMPU). It is a public sector organization in Putrajaya, Malaysia, which was chosen because it is an organization that has in-house green data centers wholly managed by the IT department. It undertakes all processes of the data center and provided IT services in organization; including planning, implementation, servicing, and IT supporting. The observation and interview were conducted with the IT personnel and the IT expert on August, the 30th, 2018, and finished in December 2018 (16 months). With 16 valid samples, content analysis using a thematic analysis approach was mapped to determine the suitable technology of virtualization based on the technology evaluation process.

The method proposed by references [12] was adapted so that the technology evaluation process can be carried out. This method also uses by [13] to introduce a new selection of technology using the technology evaluation process. Technology evaluation has provided a variety of functional criteria since starting of the process, including identify technological trends and current practices, assessing the effects of new technology, and propose an effective tool to a particular end-user.

This study uses this process to identify virtualization technology using by end-user to support green computing in the public sector. Based on this study, technology evaluation helps the researcher in exploring existing market technologies and determining their suitability for supporting ICT work processes and green computing in the IT department. The process was necessary to integrate four dimensions that consist of the people (end-user component), process (IT work activities), technology (virtualization), and IT organization structure (nature of work). The process used in this study is depicted in Table 1.

Table 1. Technology evaluation processes adapted from [12]

Steps	Detailed activities
Step 1	Define functional criteria
Step 2	Identify candidate technology based on the functional criteria
Step 3	Assessment of possible conflicts
Step 4	Selection or rejection of the proposed technology
Step 5	Evaluation results

3   Evaluation Process

This section explains how to evaluate technology using technology evaluation. Technology evaluation was helped to determine which virtualization technology is suitable to support end-user work activities and thus contributes to the green computing benefit. Technology evaluation assists the researcher in finding existing and new technologies on the market and determining their suitability for supporting the IT work process and issues discovered in the IT department as the functional criteria to be supported identified earlier in this study. Work activities at all levels of service, such as the type of work task, work sensitivity, and organization, must be managed by IT personnel in IT services.

3.1   Define Functional Criteria

First, to ensure that the process continues, the functional criteria provided by the technology should be defined. The functional criteria were based on the IT work process discovered in the ICT business in the IT department. Since the processes discovered in the ICT business work process use multiple IT devices to access organization resources, this research believes that when the technology can support end-user to perform work tasks, subsequently it will be able to resolve the work process issues. The functional criteria based on the issues are as Table 2 below:

Table 2. Functional criteria based on work process related to the issues

No.	Functional criteria (Work process)	Issues
1	Procurement	• Work process change with new technology • Different skill worker • Work task based on mobility
2	Booking	• Work process change with new technology • Work task based on mobility
3	Asset distribution	• Work process change with new technology • Work task based on mobility
4	Administrative support services	• Work process change with new technology
5	Data processing	• Difficult to handle data
6	System development	• Not standardize • Different skill worker
7	Onsite monitoring	• Work process change with new technology
8	Preventive maintenance	• Different skill worker
9	Corrective maintenance	• Different skill worker • Not standardize • Work task based on mobility
10	Disaster recovery	• Difficult to handle data • Work process change with new technology

3.2 Identify Candidate Technology Based on the Functional Criteria

Based on the functional criteria defined in Sect. 3.1 above, the study examined several virtualization technologies currently on the market and recognized the candidate technology that can support the functional criteria.

Application streaming is a type of virtual appliance (VA), in which applications are run directly from a virtual machine (VM) on a centralized server that is completely separate from the local computer. VA is a concept that entails creating and delivering a pre-configured package containing an application and operating system for easy installation and operation on incompatible devices [2]. Prefetching virtual packs on-demand significantly decreases the network's transmission time and bandwidth usage. The load on internal nodes' processing power also decreases as data size decreases. It will reduce CO_2 emission and energy consumption during the use of streaming applications. Virtualization-based sandboxes take advantage of virtualization technology to provide a virtual environment for unknown resources, ensuring that its parsing does not affect the host [14]. Sandboxing is a software management technique that isolates applications from important system resources and other processes. Sandboxing uses virtual servers to test software in a controlled environment. Because the testing environment is isolated from the actual production environment, it can be used to test software modifications before they are launched. It can save cost to buy, maintain, and managing physical server to test the application [3].

Data virtualization is virtual real-time data access from multiple heterogeneous systems on-premise and in the cloud. It can be used by a different approach such as data federation, metadata management, or data cloud. A virtual database (VDB) allows data to be retrieved and virtually integrated in real-time from several sources without copying or relocating data [15]. It is important for virtualization to support data management. Thus, the database management system can connect to other databases to store metadata. Virtualization improves speed deployment, maintenance, and encapsulation for a computing system by using an algorithm to route data to the data center [16].

The primary goal of the VM is to reduce the number of physical machines or hosts in centralized servers in the data center that can decrease the resource consumption rate, energy consumption, and carbon emission rate [17, 18]. Virtualization-based server consolidation improves system administration, lowers power and infrastructure costs, and enhances resources [19]. High availability (HA) ensures service continuity despite host, VM, or application failures. Failover is a backup operational method to support hardware and system failure, In a virtualized system, failover is achieved by creating an active VM and a standby VM [20]. By using HA, organizations can optimize data centers which can reduce CO_2 emissions and energy consumption.

Fault tolerance refers to a system's ability to continue performing tasks while experiencing a fault by using the self-healing method [21]. The term "live migration" refers to the process of moving a virtual machine from one host server or storage location to another in the following circumstances: preventive failure, fault tolerance, energy management, server maintenance, load balancing, resource scheduling, or server stabilization and high availability that which allows the virtual machine to restart automatically in the event of a hardware failure or failure [22]. Table 3 below lists the candidate technology to support functional criteria.

Table 3. Candidate technology to support functional criteria

No.	Functional criteria	Functional criteria details	Candidate technology
1	To support procurement work process	• To support procurement process used in purchasing ICT hardware or system • To promote mobility and multiple users so that the procurement process can be carried out at any time and in any location; • To support the existing government system by utilizing the system	• Application streaming • Sandbox Application
2	To support the booking work process	• To support booking system • To access booking system on various devices, for example, a laptop, iPad, smartphone • To promote mobility so that the process can be carried out at any time and in any location;	• Application streaming • Sandbox Application
3	To support asset distribution work process	• To support asset system • To access booking system on various devices, for example, a laptop, iPad, smartphone • To promote mobility so that the process can be carried out at any time and in any location;	• Application streaming • Sandbox Application
4	To support administrative support services work process	• To support admin support services system • To access system in various devices, for example, a laptop, iPad, smartphone	• Application streaming • Sandbox Application • Thin Client
5	To support data processing work process	• To support data management • To use an algorithm to route data to the data center	• Data virtualization using Data federation • Data virtualization using metadata management • Data virtualization using Data Cloud

(continued)

Table 3. (*continued*)

No.	Functional criteria	Functional criteria details	Candidate technology
6	To support system development work process	• To support the system development process	• Server consolidation • Online system
7	To support onsite monitoring work process	• To support hardware and system failure	• High Availability • Thin Client
8	To support preventive maintenance work process	• To prevent data loss	• Fault Tolerance Distributed power management
9	To support corrective maintenance work process	• To reduce boot time installation • To support multi-site telework • To support mobility	• Virtual Desktop Infrastructure (VDI)
10	To support the disaster recovery work process	• To support system real-time • To manage workload	• Live migration

3.3 Assessment of Possible Conflicts

In Sect. 3.2, the researcher has identified all of the candidate technologies that are already available in the market and that, in function, are capable of supporting the functional criteria stated in Sect. 3.1. There are multiple candidate technologies listed for certain functional criteria, which may result in some conflicts. When assessing potential conflicts, two or more candidate technologies are compared to see if they complement or contrast one another. This study sought expertise from two IT consultants from MAMPU to assist the researcher in resolving the potential conflict. The experts were selected based on their experience and knowledge in their respective fields. The experts helped the researcher to determine whether the candidate technologies proposed are suitable in supporting the functional criteria defined earlier and they do not conflict with each other.

3.4 Selection or Rejection of the Proposed Technology

After assessing the potential for conflict among the candidate technologies, the researcher selected the following technologies to support the work process, as recommended by experts. The evaluation result displays a list of technologies that were selected. Finally, the results of the technology evaluation were listed and presented in Table 4 below in Sect. 4.

4   Results and Discussion

This study develops end-user computing to support green computing using virtualization technology by integrating all of the components identified in the work processes with

Table 4. List of virtualization technology

IT work process	Virtualization technology	Justification	Green benefit
Procurement, ICT Booking, Asset distribution, Administrative support services	• Application streaming	Help IT workers to divide the system module into multiple packages that allow the module streamed toward the user location. It will help to develop environmental friendly software	• Reduce CO_2 emission and waste • Reducing travel requirements
	• Sandbox Application	IT workers use sandbox applications to executable procurement applications that can be distributed independently	• Reduce CO_2 emission and energy consumption
Data processing	• Data virtualization using metadata management	The use of metadata management could help IT workers, to retrieve and manipulate data from one or more data sources without requiring technical details about the data, such as how it is formatted or where it is physically located	• Reduce CO_2 emission and energy consumption • Reducing travel requirements
System development	• Server consolidation	The use of server consolidation could help IT workers to create a single-purpose server that running a single application per server using virtual machines on one physical server	• Reduce CO_2 emission and energy consumption • Optimization of data center

(*continued*)

Table 4. (*continued*)

IT work process	Virtualization technology	Justification	Green benefit
Onsite monitoring	• High Availability	Technology that continuously monitors all virtual machines running in virtual resources that looking for a hardware failure	• Reduce CO2 emission and energy consumption
Preventive maintenance	• Fault Tolerance	When the maintenance started, the IT worker can run an identical copy of the virtual machine on another server to prevent data loss	• Reduce CO2 emission and energy consumption and waste
Corrective maintenance	• Virtual Desktop Infrastructure (VDI)	The use of VDI could help the hosts (IT workers) of desktop environments to do the maintenance on a centralized server and deploys them to end clients on request	• Reduce CO2 emission and energy consumption • Reducing travel requirements
Disaster recovery	• Live migration	The use of live migration could help IT workers to move virtual machines across a different host of physical servers without any downtime	• Reduce CO2 emission and waste

the virtualization technologies that we're able to support green computing. Based on Sect. 3.1, ten work process in IT department was found and has been named procurement, ICT booking, asset distribution, administrative support services, data processing, system development, onsite monitoring, preventive maintenance, corrective maintenance, and disaster recovery. The researchers then find appropriate virtualization technology to support green computing within IT personnel in the public sector.

The qualitative analysis from the interviews with IT personnel at their workspace has been analyzed through thematic analysis in three themes. There are namely work process, virtualization, and green benefit. The main objective of this process is to find appropriate virtualization for end-users in the public sector who use IT devices. Before deciding on virtualization, an organization must determine the types of IT work processes that will be performed in the workplace, as well as the resources that employees will have access to. Thus, this study looks at how IT personnel perform work tasks using IT devices, and what services they provide to their users daily in the organization's premises.

The end-user is the most important dimension to consider when observing the IT work process, particularly when it comes to the use of IT devices by end-users. End-users may be required to use a variety of IT devices to complete a task depending on the work activity they are performing. IT devices play an important role in work activities to perform work tasks in the organization [23]. For IT devices can help to reduce and optimize the use of IT devices in work activities, job role-play is an important criterion in a work activity to improve productivity.

The virtualization technologies chosen are critical because they show how important the relationship between the IT work process and the end-user component is for green computing. It also determines whether the work process is green or not. In the public sector, the type of work process and IT device used is unique in that it is determined by the IT personnel and user involved. Once the work process is completed, the IT personnel selects the type of IT device he wants to use to perform the work task. In some cases, a combination of two or more virtualization technologies can be used to support green computing by ensuring an efficient work process.

The end-user usage pattern influenced the IT work process because of the use of virtualization technology. The process becomes greener when end-users access the system using an IT device to perform work tasks. The IT usage in the end-user component varies depending on the IT personnel who are using the IT device to perform a work task. End-users who have more roles in their tasks typically have more access to the IT department's system or application. As a result, IT personnel who performs the work task using virtualization determines the success of the IT work process to support green computing. It also depends on what type of IT work processes the end-user uses. As a result, the end-user plays a critical role in making the IT work process greener by implementing virtualization to complete a task.

This study found that a sandbox application and application streaming was used to access the system or application to perform work tasks. Both technologies could make it easier for IT personnel to access the system from different types of devices, including laptops, iPads, and smartphones. It also supports mobility, allowing IT work to be done from any location and at any time. As a result, this study focus on the work process pattern, this includes the IT personnel's job role to support green computing by substitute laptop for greener computers. IT functional support was created to aid the IT work process with users who require access to the IT department's IT system's functions. Sandbox applications and application streaming are suitable to support various types of systems that allow end-users to perform work tasks regardless of where and when they work. Both of this technology can reduce CO_2 emission and waste by the development of environmentally friendly software. The strategy also highlights the access system to support the ICT work process to perform work tasks through the use of virtualization technology as the main process in using own IT device. The access system is essential in the IT work process as the authoritative process must be done before the system could be accessed.

Data is stored in the data storage after it is ready. Data stored could be managed in a more structured manner using data virtualization technology. This is necessary to ensure that the user can retrieve the data later. The managing of data in the data center can help the server to optimize the existing resources that can reduce CO_2 emission and energy consumption.

The whole IT work process is also supported by virtual desktop infrastructure (VDI) [24]. VDI allows the ICT support process especially corrective maintenance to be carried out at any place and any time. This is a crucial task in the ICT business as the ICT department plays a role as a supporter to make sure the system and ICT process. VDI can provide easy maintenance, upgrade and the extension of the life cycle of hardware without problems. It also can minimize equipment disposal by using flexible technology and services for long-term use. Server consolidation could help with system development by converting a physical server into a virtual server that IT personnel can manage and enabling the virtual server using a hypervisor known as a virtual machine monitor (VMM). Virtualization by IT personnel refers to the creation of multiple isolated instances known as virtual machines, each with its operating system and application. Server consolidation can help to reduce hardware costs. It is also can minimize equipment disposal requirements (e-Waste) [19].

To support the onsite monitoring process, high availability (HA) technology can be used to monitor all virtual machines running on the physical server in real-time. It's critical to keep track of any hardware or physical server failures by restarting the VM on a different server. IT personnel can use video conferencing and telecommuting to communicate with other employees that can reduce travel requirements and costs. Table 4 shows the Virtualization technology matrix for green computing in public sector, highlighting how these organizations can minimize the negative impacts of IT work processes on the environment and maximizing energy efficiency during the IT work process of the IT department. Likewise, the organization can promote the optimization and reused existing IT hardware by concurrently implementing the green computing and virtualization technology strategies presented in Table 4. The development of this model will aid the ICT sector in better managing their work processes, ensuring the long-term viability and competitiveness of green ICT businesses.

5 Conclusion

This study focused on the technology evaluation process to evaluate and select the suitable technologies of virtualization in the public sector to support green computing. This study contributes towards a new process in the area of IT in providing the role of virtualization to support green computing and is significant in supporting the government's initiatives to enhance the performance of public servants from the Malaysian public sector. Technology evaluation can assist in determining the best virtualization approach to use in the public sector using IT devices that support green computing. The evaluation process began with the definition of functional criteria, which were derived from the current issues. The functional criteria that were mapped with appropriate technologies that can support green benefit are then assessed and verified by experts. This process resulted in a list of virtualization technologies that could be used to support the IT work process. The results can be valuable for practitioners and decision-makers in the green computing context as the results will help them to implement virtualization technologies effectively in the public sector based on end-user perspectives. Moreover, this is one of the first studies to explore end-user strategies for Green IT practices using virtualization technologies in government-based institutions.

However, this study only collected data from 16 IT practitioners in government-based institutions in Malaysia that have in-house green data centers; as such results from this research cannot be generalized to other organizations that owned their own data centers. Moreover, the developed virtualization technology for green IT practice in the public sector can only be fully deployed after the IT department has added green computing practice during IT work processes. More experimental work is needed on how to calculate and identify the green impact and outcomes of virtualization technology involvement in the study, including further green IT analysis and exploration of green impact when IT devices are using to perform a work task. It would also be helpful to measure energy consumption, electricity consumption, and CO_2 emission that have a negative impact on the environment.

Acknowledgment. This work is supported by the Faculty of Computer and Mathematical Sciences, UiTM Shah Alam, Selangor, Malaysia.

References

1. Anthony, B., Abdul Majid, M. Romli, A.A.: Descriptive study towards green computing practice application for data centers in IT based industries. MATEC Web Conf. **150**, 1–8 (2018). https://doi.org/10.1051/matecconf/201815005048
2. Malik, A.W., Rasool, R.ur., Anwar, Z., Nawaz, S.: A generic framework for application streaming service. Comput. Electr. Eng. **66**, 149–161 (2018). https://doi.org/10.1016/j.com peleceng.2017.09.029
3. Swamy, V.F., Sandbox, S.: A secured testing framework for applications. J. Technol. Eng. Sci.**4**, 1–8 (2020)
4. Kiruthiga, P., Vinoth Kumar, T.: Green computing – an ecofriendly approach for energy efficiency and minimizing E-Waste. Int. J. Adv. Res. Comput. Commun. Eng.**3**, 6318–6321 (2014)
5. Franklin, O.U. Zainul Abeeden, M.I.: The impact of green computing in higher institutions. Int. J. Inf. Syst. Eng.**2**, 199–210 (2014)
6. Haron, H., Ibraheem, Y.Y.A., Aljunid, S.A., Bakri, M.: Software reusability in green computing. Adv. Sci. Lett. **21**, 3283–3287 (2015). https://doi.org/10.1166/asl.2015.6454
7. Lambropoulos, G., Mitropoulos, S., Douligeris, C.: Improving business performance by employing virtualization technology: a case study in the financial sector. Computers **10**, 52 (2021). https://doi.org/10.3390/computers10040052
8. Sawant, A.G., Rasal, P.R.: Research on the virtualization technology in cloud computing environment. J. Emerg. Technol. Innov. Res. **8**, 237–242 (2021)
9. Jusoh, M.Y., Haron, H., Kaur, J.: The transformation of byod practices to support green computing in Malaysia public sector. Int. J. Eng. Technol. **7**, 361–365 (2018). https://doi.org/10.14419/ijet.v7i3.20.19273
10. Cloud Security Alliance. Best Practices for Mitigating Risks in Virtualized Environments (2015)
11. Kaviani, P.: Virtualization with data center. Int. J. Adv. Eng. Res. Dev. **4**, 682–685 (2017)

12. Md Sabri, S., Haron, H., Jamil, N.: Technology evaluation to support knowledge recall and transfer. in ICIET 2018. In: Proceedings of the 6th International Conference on Information and Education Technology, pp. 258–262 (2018). https://doi.org/10.1145/3178158.3178191

13. Aziz, N.H.N., Haron, H., Harun, A.F.: ICT-supported for participatory engagement within E-learning community. Indones. J. Electr. Eng. Comput. Sci. **20**, 492–499 (2020). https://doi.org/10.11591/ijeecs.v20.i1.pp492-499

14. Liang, Z., Zhang, X., Jiang, D., Shen, W., Li, H.: Simulation of operating system and hardware stripping based on sandbox technology. In: Abawajy, J.H., Choo, K.-K., Xu, Z., Atiquzzaman, M. (eds.) ATCI 2020. AISC, vol. 1244, pp. 633–638. Springer, Cham (2021). https://doi.org/10.1007/978-3-030-53980-1_93

15. Vu, X.S., Elmroth, E., Ait-Mlouk, A., Jiang, L.: Graph-based interactive data federation system for heterogeneous data retrieval and analytics. In: The Web Conference 2019 - Proceedings of the World Wide Web Conference, WWW 2019, vol. 2, pp. 3595–3599 (2019). https://doi.org/10.1145/3308558.3314138

16. Polkowski, Z., Mishra, S.K.: Concept of virtualization linked to energy storage and green computing: a case study. In: Mahapatra, S., Shahbaz, M., Vaccaro, A., Emilia Balas, V. (eds.) Advances in Energy Technology. ASST, pp. 57–65. Springer, Singapore (2021). https://doi.org/10.1007/978-981-15-8700-9_6

17. Zhuang, H., Esmaeilpour Ghouchani, B.: Virtual machine placement mechanisms in the cloud environments: a systematic review. Kybernetes **50**, 333–368 (2021)

18. Kaaouache, M.A., Bouamama, S.: An energy-efficient VM placement method for cloud data centers using a hybrid genetic algorithm. J. Syst. Inf. Technol. **20**, 430–445 (2018). https://doi.org/10.1108/JSIT-10-2017-0089

19. Wang, B., Song, Y., Sun, Y., Liu, J.: Analysis model for server consolidation of virtualized heterogeneous data centers providing internet services. Clust. Comput. **22**(3), 911–928 (2018). https://doi.org/10.1007/s10586-018-2880-x

20. Chang, X., Wang, T., Rodríguez, R.J., Zhang, Z.: Modeling and analysis of high availability techniques in a virtualized system. Comput. J. **61**, 180–198 (2018). https://doi.org/10.1093/comjnl/bxx049

21. Chen, C.C., Wang, J.H., Wang, H.W., Zhang, J.: Fault-tolerant content list management for media servers in the smart robot domain. Libr. Hi Tech (2021). https://doi.org/10.1108/LHT-07-2020-0179

22. Bahrami, M., Farahbakhsh, M., Haghighat, A.T., Gholipour, M.: Virtualization and live migration : issues and solutions. J. Comput. Based Parallel Program **6**, 10–15 (2021)

23. Modlo, Y.O., et al.: The use of mobile Internet devices in the formation of ICT component of bachelors in electromechanics competency in modeling of technical objects. CEUR Workshop Proc. **2433**, 413–428 (2019)

24. Awang, A., Jusoh, M.Y.: Implementation of BYOD and virtualized desktop in organization. J. Electr. Power Electron. Syst. **1**, 1–4 (2019)

Willingness of Electricity Consumer in Malaysia to Share Electric Energy Consumption Data

Salman Yussof[1]([⊠]) [iD], Nurul Nazeera Mohd Zulkefle[2], Yunus Yusoff[3] [iD], and Asmidar Abu Bakar[3] [iD]

[1] Institute of Informatics and Computing in Energy, Universiti Tenaga Nasional, Kajang, Malaysia
salman@uniten.edu.my
[2] Tenaga Nasional Berhad, Kuala Lumpur, Malaysia
nazeera.zulkefle@tnb.com.my
[3] College of Computing and Informatics, Universiti Tenaga Nasional, Kajang, Malaysia

Abstract. Data sharing is a process of interchanging data among multiple data sources in a controllable access manner. Successful data sharing of information belong to public depends on public support. Analyzing household electric consumption data and user behaviour profile based on household electricity demand are also vital to enhance energy efficiency in Malaysia. This research used quantitative methodology via survey method. A set of questionnaires was developed to identify the willingness of electricity consumer in Malaysia on sharing their electric energy consumption data and types of incentives preferred. A total of 424 responses were successfully gathered and was analyzed using SPSS software. This survey proves that electricity consumer in Malaysia are willing to share their energy consumption data regardless of demographic profiles, with or without awareness of PDPA and technology that may capture their data. These findings indicate that data sharing related to energy consumption can potentially be successful since statistic shows that the public are willing to share their energy consumption data. The result of this study may help researcher who are planning to develop data sharing platform to increase public willingness to share their energy data. The availability of data sharing platform can assist research community during data gathering process which later can be analyzed to identify areas of improvement to be undertaken by the industry.

Keywords: Data sharing · Energy consumption · Energy efficiency

1 Introduction

Driven by mutual benefits, there are demands for sharing transactional data among organizations or parties for research or business analysis purposes [1]. Transactional data has immense social value and is economical for revealing relationships, dependencies and performing predictions of outcomes and behaviors [2]. Information sharing in a community becomes more accessible with technology and technology such as cloud computing offers a collaborative platform for massive data sharing.

© Springer Nature Switzerland AG 2021
H. Badioze Zaman et al. (Eds.): IVIC 2021, LNCS 13051, pp. 689–700, 2021.
https://doi.org/10.1007/978-3-030-90235-3_59

In the energy industry, large amount of energy production and consumption data are generated and digitized by continuous application of sensors, network communication, wireless transmission, and internet of things. The huge volume of data produced may be shared among government agencies and various energy companies for efficient energy management. In United Kingdom, 84% of energy companies already explored opportunities to utilize data, potentially selling customers' personal data as new revenue stream [3]. 52% of the companies plan to use data to expand their current value chain, collaborating with firms in adjacent markets and transforming their business models. The process of collecting and sharing customers data is done with their customers' consent.

Data sharing between respective agencies are needed to allow the data management to run smoothly. Energy data sharing may involve personal data as well as consumption data. Sharing of personal data must be in line with the Malaysian Personal Data Protection Act 2010 (PDPA). This means, customers must give their consent prior to their data being shared. Report in [4] indicates that customers are willing to share their energy consumption data, hence it indicates that the energy data is less sensitive as compared to other personal data. Furthermore, the report also indicates that half of the consumers are willing to share their energy data if it is linked to benefits such as financial saving and improved energy efficiency.

This paper focused on the willingness of electricity consumer in Malaysia regarding data sharing. It is essential to measure the willingness of electricity consumer in Malaysia on data sharing before electricity company decided to embark on data sharing among organizations or parties for the purpose of research or business analysis. It has also been identified that offering incentives can also increase customers' willingness to share their data [5]. Thus, it is crucial to investigate what type of encouragement should be offered to the electricity consumer in order to increase the willingness level to share their data.

In this study, a survey on domestic consumers is carried out by considering four objectives. The first objective is to identify the target group willingness to share electricity consumption data. The second objective is to identify the willingness of electricity consumer in Malaysia to share the electricity consumption data. The third objective is to identify parties that electricity consumers are willing to share their data with. The final objective is to identify types of incentives that electricity consumers expect in return for sharing their data.

Section 2 of the paper highlights the research hypothesis, while Sect. 3 summarized the method used to collect the data. The survey results are analyzed and presented in Sect. 4 and the last section concludes the paper.

2   Related Work and Hypothesis Development

Hypothetico-deductive method requires hypotheses to be falsifiable [6]. Thus, null hypothesis (H_0) is developed to be rejected in order to support alternate hypothesis (H_a). Null hypothesis is presumed true until statistical evidence in the for-hypothesis test, indicate otherwise.

There are three dimensions of digital literacy in privacy related online behaviour, which are familiarity with technical aspects of the internet, awareness of common institutional practice and understanding of current privacy policy [7].

H_0 1:   There is no significant difference between PDPA Awareness (with / without) and willingness to share residency background detail

H_0 2:   There is no significant difference between PDPA Awareness (with / without)
and willingness to share electrical appliance energy consumption data

H_0 3:   There is no significant difference between Awareness on data capturing technology (with / without) and willingness to share residency background detail

H_0 4:   There is no significant difference between Awareness on data capturing technology (with/without) on willingness to share electrical appliance energy consumption data.

Usage of digital services and social network sites is also considered as gender sensitive. The same applies to privacy concern when using digital services which are more pronounced in women. In line with this, women report higher privacy concerns and fears of being the victims of cybercrime [7].

H_0 5:   There is no significant difference between Genders (Male & Female) and willingness to share residency background detail

H_0 6:   There is no significant difference between Genders (Male & Female) and willingness to share electrical appliance energy consumption data

Younger generations are more concerned with the accessibility of data access and are more interested to use datasets of others if the data can be accessed easily. In fact, data-sharing behavior increases significantly with each older age group [9].

H_0 7:   There is no significant difference between Age group and willingness to share residency background detail

H_0 8:   There is no significant difference between Age group and willingness to share electrical appliance energy consumption data

H_0 9:   There is no significant difference between education level and willingness to   share residency background detail

H_0 10:   There is no significant difference between education level and willingness to   share electrical appliance energy consumption data

Electrical energy consumption has direct relationship with the standard of living. Household with higher income will consume more electrical energy than lower income household [8]. Thus, this hypothesis will test the willingness of this high usage consumer to share their electric consumption data.

H_0 11:   There is no significant difference between income range and willingness to share residency background detail

H_0 12:   There is no significant difference between income range and willingness to share electrical appliance energy consumption data

3   Methodology

The questionnaires used as the survey instrument consisted of 24 questions grouped into 5 different sections, i.e., demographic, data sharing concern on residency household background, data sharing concern on electrical appliance detail, parties to receive data and data sharing reward. The participants considered in the study were customers of the largest electricity provider in Malaysia, Tenaga Nasional Berhad (TNB) with age of more than 18 years old. Prior to conducting the actual survey, the pilot survey was performed and a total of 30 responses were gathered to measure the reliability of the questionnaire. Measurement items of constructs were self-developed based on previous energy consumption research. The wordings were revised to fit the context of this research. Likert scale was used for most of the survey questions, where 1 represents "Strongly not willing" and 5 represents "Strongly willing".

The survey was conducted online using Google platform facility. The link to the online questionnaire was distributed via popular social media platforms in Malaysia such as WhatsApp, Facebook, Twitter and Telegram. By using Krejcie and Morgan's sample size table and stratified random sampling method [9], it has been identified that 384 respondents are required to represent a population size of 8.2 Million, which is a rough estimate of the total number of TNB customer under residential type.

4   Result and Analysis

In this research, the survey responses collected was 451. Out of 451 responses, 27 were rejected due to email duplication. Therefore, only 424 responses were processed, and the reliability result was examined. The data obtained from the respondent was analyzed using Statistical Package for Social Science (SPSS).

The result of Cronbach's alpha is 0.813 as shown in Table 1, which exceeds the recommended lowest threshold of 0.7. The composite reliability shows good reliability because all the values are above the 0.7 thresholds.

Table 1. Reliability measurement analysis

Construct	Cronbach's alpha
Residency detail	0.882
Appliance detail	0.938
Parties to share	0.813

4.1 Demographic Analysis

The gender of respondents participating in this survey is equally distributed. 208 (49.1%) were males, and 216 (50.9%) were females. A sizeable number of respondents, 48.6% (206) indicate that the most significant number of participants is within the age range between 18 to 29 years old. They are followed by 30 to 43 years age group, which consists of 27.4% (116) of total respondents. The balance 24.1% of the respondents is 44 years old and above.

The majority of the respondents, which is 79.5% (337), have a bachelor's degree or equivalent. The secondary school level is 12% (51) and 8.5% have master's degree and above.

A sizeable number of respondents, which is 43.2% (183), are earning income between RM 3001 and RM 6000 per month. This is followed by 34% (144) of respondents who earn income below RM 3000 and 19.6% (83) of respondents have earn income between RM 6001 and RM 10000. The balance, which is 3.3% (14) of respondents are earning more than RM 10,000. Most of the respondents are aware of PDPA (91.7%), and most of them are aware that the current technology is capturing their data with or without their permission (93.6%). Demographic information on the respondents is presented in Table 2.

Table 2. Demographic analysis

	Variable	Frequency	Percentage
Gender	Male	208	49.1
	Female	216	50.9
Age	18 years to 29 years	206	48.6
	30 years to 43 years	116	27.4
	44 years and above	102	24.1
Education level	High School	51	12.0
	Bachelors degree or equivalent	337	79.5
	Masters degree and above	36	8.5
Income	Below RM 3000	144	34.0
	RM 3001 - RM 6000	183	43.2
	RM 6001- RM 10,000	83	19.6
	Above RM 10,000	14	3.3
Aware on PDPA	Yes	389	91.7
	No	35	8.3
Aware on data capturing technology	Yes	397	93.6
	No	27	6.4

4.2 Descriptive Analysis

Table 4, Table 5, and Table 6 summarized the descriptive analysis of the perceived values that were tabulated in mean, median and standard deviation. Since the data is normally distributed (skewness value between −1 and 1), the mean is the most suitable to present this data. However, to avoid the matter of judicious use as to how well the mean represents the willingness of respondents to share the data, the 5 scales will be converted into 3 parts where 0 to 1.67 is considered as unwillingness to share data, 1.68 to 3.33 is considered neutral and 3.34 to 5 is considered as willingness to share data (refer to Fig. 1).

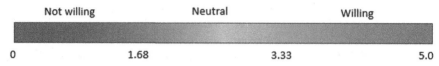

Fig. 1. Willingness scale

Residential Detail. In this study, there are six types of residential data identified as factors that may influence households' energy consumption. The most important one is the residential electricity bill (ResBill). Electricity bill will be the indicator of household's energy consumption. This data will determine the willingness of TNB customers to share their residential detail data. Next is the residential size (ResSize). This data is also essential to know how large the respondent's house or residential is, for example, 600 sqft, 1000 sqft or 1200 sqft. Information on residence type (ResType) is also required in most energy consumption studies. There are several types of residential in Malaysia, such as Semi-D, apartments, condominiums, and bungalows. Besides that, we also ask the respondents about their willingness to share their house location (ResLoc). Next is the residence occupant number (ResOccNum), which determines the number of electricity consumers in the house. Last but not least, respondents were asked about their willingness to share the age of occupants in the house (ResOccAge) so that we can identify how many high-energy consumers are in the house.

The results that appear in Table 3 indicate that most of the items had mean ratings that far exceeded the theoretical mean of 3.33, which means respondents are willing to share residential data. The residential electricity bill has the highest mean rating of 3.85 (SD = 0.83), indicating the respondents are willing to share the residential electricity bill. The reported high willingness to share residential electricity bills could be because the data itself is already available in TNB record. The least mean rating of 3.33 (SD = 1.12), which is the borderline between neutral and willingness to share, is the residential location. The low value may depend on how detail or accuracy the residential location is required to be shared.

Energy Appliance Data. For appliance data, there are six item codes identified to measure the willingness of respondents to share their electrical appliance detail such as type of electrical appliance (AppType) such as fan, refrigerator, washing machine, and air conditional. Next, most studies require respondents to share their number of electrical devices (AppNum) since it will affect the electricity consumption. A respondent may need to declare how many fans, air conditioning units, and other electrical appliances are available in the house.

Next is the model of electrical appliance used in the house. This data is required to understand customer product preferences. Examples of electrical appliance models

Table 3. Statistics for perceived willingness to share residential detail

Construct	Item code	Mean	Mode	Standard deviation
Residency detail	ResBill	3.85	4.00	0.83
	ResSize	3.70	4.00	0.86
	ResType	3.84	4.00	0.79
	ResLoc	3.33	4.00	1.12
	ResOccNum	3.57	4.00	0.99
	ResOccAge	3.50	4.00	1.03
Total		3.63	4.00	0.75

are Sharp, LG and Samsung. The most crucial data is energy efficiency appliance data (AppEE). From this data, researchers can determine the significant relationship between usage of energy efficiency appliance data and energy consumption. Besides that, respondents were asked for their willingness to share the number of years the appliance has been used (AppAge) since some study mention that old device may have decreased energy efficiency. Last but not least is the appliance usage frequency (AppFreq) which is to determine how many hours the appliance is used per day or week.

The results in Table 4 indicate that all the items had mean ratings that far exceeded the willing mean score of 3.33. Sharing on appliance age has the lowest mean rating of 3.90 (SD = 0.73). Although it has the least mean rating, the value of 3.90 substantially exceeds the theoretical mean of 3.33, indicating the willingness to share.

Table 4. Statistics for perceived willingness to share appliance detail

Construct	Item code	Mean	Mode	Standard deviation
Appliance detail	AppType	3.96	4.00	0.73
	AppNum	3.93	4.00	0.73
	AppModl	3.93	4.00	0.71
	AppEE	3.96	4.00	0.71
	AppAge	3.90	4.00	0.73
	AppFreq	3.93	4.00	0.74
Total		3.93	4.00	0.63

Sharing Parties. Data in Table 5 shows that respondents are more willing to share their data with TNB (4.03) compared to government (3.67), research center (3.61), and university (3.53). However, respondents are neutral (2.87) about sharing their residential detail and electricity consumption data with private companies. With this finding, we conclude that TNB is the best party to gather data for consumer energy consumption data in Malaysia.

Table 5. Statistics for perceived willingness to share data with sharing parties

Construct	Item code	Mean	Mode	Standard deviation
Parties to share	sTNB	4.03	4.00	0.70
	sGov	3.67	4.00	0.90
	sPrivate	2.87	3.00	1.01
	sUni	3.53	4.00	0.88
	sResearch	3.61	4.00	0.86
Total		3.54	3.80	0.66

Reward Preference. The pie chart in Fig. 2 shows the customers' reward preference as an incentive to their willingness to share their energy consumption data. Most of the respondents are interested in only two of the choices in the survey. Based on the result, most respondents are either interested in having a discount on their electricity bill or converting their points to e-wallet credits as their rewards.

More than 50% of respondents prefer a discount on electricity. The justification for this behavior is that the electricity bill is considered one of the monthly financial commitments. Thus, discount on electricity bills would help to reduce their monthly commitment. Next, respondents prefer to convert the reward points to their e-wallet credits, most likely due to the increasing use of e-wallets lately.

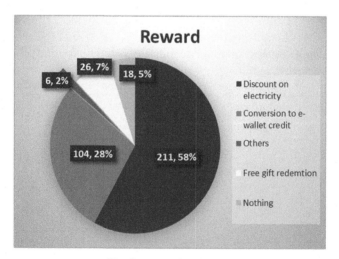

Fig. 2. Reward preference

4.3 Inferential Analysis

Six of the hypotheses will use the independent sample t-test method to evaluate the relationship between gender, awareness of PDPA, and awareness on data capturing technology towards the willingness to share data on residential and electric appliance. When the Sig-T (P) is less than the critical value ($\alpha = 0.05$), H_o is accepted [6], which means there is no significant relationship between the test variable and the tested groups. Based on the result in Table 6, all H_o is accepted.

Table 6. Summary of t-Test result

Hypothesis	Test variable	Groups	Sig-T (p)	Conclusion
H_{o1}	Residency background detail	With/without PDPA awareness	0.12	No significant effect
H_{o2}	Energy appliance detail	With/without PDPA awareness	0.22	No significant effect
H_{o3}	Residency background detail	With/without awareness on data capturing technology	1.00	No Significant effect
H_{o4}	Energy appliance detail	With/without awareness on data capturing technology	0.45	No significant effect
H_{o5}	Residency background detail	Male	0.91	No significant effect
		Female		
H_{o6}	Energy appliance detail	Male	0.78	No significant effect
		Female		

When the Sig-F is less than the critical value ($\alpha = 0.05$), H_o tested with ANOVA is accepted [6], which means that there is no significant relationship between the test variable and the tested groups. Based on the result in Table 7, for H7 there was statistically significant difference between groups (age group) as determined by one-way ANOVA ($F(2,421) = 3.88$, $p = 0.21$) at 0.05 level of significant. A Tukey post hoc test reveal that statistically significant difference in willingness of sharing residency background detail between age group 18 years and 29 years and 43 years and above ($p = 0.03$). However, there is no difference between age group 18 years to 29 years and 43 years and above ($p = 0.12$), as well as between age group 30 years to 43 years and 43 years and above ($p = 0.83$). The remaining hypothesis are as summarized in Table 8, where there is no significant difference between all test variables and test groups.

Based on the result from inferential analysis, all respondents exhibited about the same level of agreement concerning the willingness to share the residential data and electrical appliance detail for energy consumption study regardless of gender or awareness on PDPA or awareness of data capturing technology or level of education or level of income. From the respondents' ratings regarding the 11 types of data (5 for residential data and

Table 7. ANOVA result on Hypothesis 7

Test variable	Groups	n	Mean	SD	F	p
Residency background detail	18 years to 29 years	206	3.52	0.79	3.88	0.21
	30 years to 43 years	102	3.76	0.77		
	43 years and above	116	3.70	0.62		

Table 8. Summary of ANOVA result

Hypothesis	Test variable	Groups	Sig-F	Conclusion
H_o7	Residency background detail	18 years to 29 years	0.02	Significant difference
		30 years to 43 years		
		43 years and above		
H_o8	Energy appliance detail	18 years to 29 years	0.31	No significant difference
		30 years to 43 years		
		43 years and above		
H_o9	Residency background detail	High School	0.68	No significant difference
		Bachelors degree		
		Masters degree and above		
H_o10	Energy appliance detail	High School	0.41	No significant difference
		Bachelors degree		
		Masters degree and above		
H_o11	Residency background detail	Below RM 3000	0.63	No significant difference
		RM 3001 - RM 6000		
		RM 6001- RM 10,000		
H_o12	Energy appliance detail	Above RM 10,000	0.42	No significant difference
		Below RM 3000		
		RM 3001 - RM 6000		

6 for electrical appliance data), there was a high degree of uniformity in the level of willingness to share their energy consumption data.

5 Conclusion

In general, this survey was done to determine the willingness of electricity customers in Malaysia towards data sharing on energy consumption data. Quantitative research method was used via the use of online survey and distributed to TNB customers, where 424 valid responses were gathered and analyzed using the SPSS tool.

Statistical analysis showed that electricity consumer in Malaysia are willing to share their energy consumption data (residential detail and appliance detail). Besides that, inferential analysis using t-test and ANOVA showed electricity consumer in Malaysia regardless of gender, awareness on PDPA and awareness on capturing data technology, age groups, level of education, and level of income, shows high degree of uniformity with respect to the willingness to share their energy consumption data. This is a good indication for a successful data sharing platform deployment for residential energy sector since consumers are willing to share their energy data. Besides that, this information is also useful to researchers to properly target their potential respondents during their data gathering process.

Next, electricity consumer in Malaysia are willing to share their energy consumption data with TNB, Government, Research Centre and universities. However, respondents are taking a natural stance with regards to sharing their data with a private company. It may be due to their not fully trusting those private organizations who are handling their data. This means that during data gathering using data sharing platform, it is good if researcher can clearly specify that the data is gathered for which party or organization so that researcher may gain respondents' trust and increase the willingness of public to share their energy data. Last but not least, more than 50% respondents prefer to convert points gained from sharing their energy data to get discount on electricity bills which can reduce their monthly financial commitment. The second popular option is to convert the points gained to e-wallet credits since e-wallet are gaining popularities nowadays.

The research provides an important insight for researcher who are planning to deploy data sharing platform related to energy consumption usage. There are certain limitations to this study, however. First and foremost, the data used to measure the willingness of the study is only limited to the data used in previous energy consumption research. However, governments, private companies or university may require other types of data to meet their research objectives. Thus, for future study, the survey can be expanded to include additional types of data that the data users are interested in.

Acknowledgement. This work is funded by Tenaga Nasional Berhad (TNB) Seed Fund (Project No.: UTD-RD-19-24) in collaboration with TNB Distribution Network. We would like to thank UNITEN R&D Sdn. Bhd. for their role in fund management.

References

1. Wang, L.E., Li, X.: A clustering-based bipartite graph privacy-preserving approach for sharing high-dimensional data. Int. J. Softw. Eng. Knowl. Eng. **24**(7), 1091–1111 (2014). https://doi.org/10.1142/S0218194014500363
2. Zhang, D.: Granularities and inconsistencies in big data analysis. Int. J. Softw. Eng. Knowl. Eng. **23**(6), (2013). https://doi.org/10.1142/S0218194013500241
3. Husseini, T.: As energy companies race to cash in on data, should we be worried. https://www.power-technology.com/features/energy-companies-sharing-data/ (2019)
4. Ofgem.: Consumer views on sharing half-hourly settlement data, pp. 1–13 (2018). https://www.ofgem.gov.uk/publications-and-updates/consumer-research-datasets

5. Richter, H., Slowinski, P.R.: The data sharing economy: on the emergence of new intermediaries. IIC Int. Rev. Intellect. Prop. Compet. Law **50**(1), 4–29 (2018). https://doi.org/10.1007/s40319-018-00777-7
6. Space, W.L.: An easy way to help students learn, collaborate, and grow. www.wileypluslearningspace.com
7. Halder, D., Jaishankar, K.: Cyber gender harassment and secondary victimization: a comparative analysis of the United States, the UK, and India. Vict. Offenders **6**(4) (2011). https://doi.org/10.1080/15564886.2011.607402
8. Tuck, N.W.: A study on the electrical energy consumption characteristic of urban household in Klang valley, Malaysia. A dissertation submitted in fulfilment of the requirement for the degree of Master of Science in Building Services Engineering. Kul (2012)
9. Krejcie, R.V. Morgan, D.W.: Determining sample size for research activities. Educ. Psychol. Meas. **30**(3), (1970). https://doi.org/10.1177/001316447003000308

Challenges and Recommendations on the Development of Distributed Energy Resources (DERs) Datahub for Improved DERs Data Management in Malaysia

Ammuthavali Ramasamy[1(✉)], Hazleen Aris[2(✉)], Aliza Abdul Latif[1(✉)],
S. Nur Hidayah Malek[2(✉)], Syakir Abdul Latif[2(✉)], and Komal Deep Kaur[3(✉)]

[1] College of Computing and Informatics, Universiti Tenaga Nasional, Kajang, Malaysia
{ammutha,aliza}@uniten.edu.my
[2] Institute of Informatics and Computing in Energy, Universiti Tenaga Nasional,
Jalan IKRAM-UNITEN, 43000 Kajang, Selangor, Malaysia
{hazleen,hidayah.malek}@uniten.edu.my
[3] Distribution Network Division, Tenaga Nasional Berhad, Kuala Lumpur, Malaysia
komaldeepkuar@tnb.com.my

Abstract. The increase in Malaysia's energy demand has resulted in the rise of electricity generation. Specific policies and measures are therefore put in place to reduce the dependence on fossil fuels. The reduction is possible with the widespread adoption of distributed energy resources (DERs) technologies that produce electricity from renewable energy sources. With the increase of DERs and advanced metering infrastructure (AMI), more data need to be managed. DERs data come from various sources in different formats, making data management process more complex. The technical challenges faced by the utility companies are in terms of data integration, data interoperability and data model. The non-technical challenges include business model, access right and boundary, and data security and privacy. The aim of this research is therefore to find a wholesome solution to these challenges. To do that, DERs data management from six countries have been analyzed and compared. Taking the cue from the successful endeavors of the selected countries, this paper proposes the development of an energy datahub to address the challenges and provides recommendations in moving forward. A datahub is a central repository, which allows all DERs data to be stored, structured and shared with other systems. Datahub can be utilized to coordinate and manage the processes between complex data transactions, electricity suppliers and grid companies. Good data management can be ensured in datahub by implementing good data governance.

Keywords: Energy informatics · Renewable energy · Distribution grid · Smart meter · Advanced metering infrastructure · Energy efficiency

1 Introduction

The rising concerns over climate change and the mounting hype about achieving net zero carbon emissions by 2050 have intensified the efforts towards increasing the share

© Springer Nature Switzerland AG 2021
H. Badioze Zaman et al. (Eds.): IVIC 2021, LNCS 13051, pp. 701–714, 2021.
https://doi.org/10.1007/978-3-030-90235-3_60

of renewable energy to achieve the target. For Malaysia, the target set by the government is 31% of renewable energy share by 2025 and 40% by 2030 [1]. To meet the target, various schemes have been introduced to increase the share of renewable energy. At the moment, three schemes are available in Malaysia for the consumers (prosumers) to choose from at the distribution level. These are self-consumption (SELCO), feed-in tariff (FIT) and net energy metering (NEM). SELCO is a scheme where electricity generated by the consumers from renewable sources is for personal use and any excess is not transferred to the grid. FIT requires the utility company to purchase electricity produced from renewable resources by the feed-in approval holders at certain rate. For NEM, the electricity generated by the consumers will be consumed first, and any excess will be exported to the grid at the current displaced cost. While SELCO only involves behind-the-meter installation meant for personal consumption, FIT and NEM are connected to the distribution grid via smart meters that allow for bidirectional flow of electricity and provide opportunities of feeding back to the grid when there is excess of generated energy. In terms of the types of renewable energy generated, SELCO and NEM are only meant for solar while FIT can include other types such as biomass and biogas [2].

It was observed that the amount of renewable energy being fed back into the distribution grid has escalated. In 2019, an increase of 51.27% in rooftop solar installation was recorded [3]. Consequently, the energy infrastructure at the distribution level has to be upgraded to accommodate the surge of renewable energy penetration from these DERs into the distribution grid. One of the main challenges with respect to the increased penetration of renewable energy from DERs at the distribution level in Malaysia is the management of the DERs data. At present, there is a number of issues and challenges that are faced by the utility companies with respect to the gathering of the DERs data. Utility companies utilize many applications to support their business processes with respect to DERs. These applications provide various types of data. Data that come from different sources with different formats and types complicate the data management process in terms of consistency, redundancy and lack of interoperability [4]. Unstandardized data make it difficult to timely analyze and making sense of the data. As the data continue to grow with more and more DERs being commissioned and hence more and more data are being generated by the DER platforms, management of the data becomes even more critical [5]. If this matter is not addressed, data interoperability and transfer within and between the systems will become infeasible, which will lead to inefficiency in the distribution operation and planning.

In this paper, the problem with the management of DERs data is analyzed based on the information obtained from a study done by a utility company in Malaysia to assess the current state of the data quality. From the analysis, six challenges were identified, which were classified into technical and non-technical. By referring to the solutions adopted by countries, which have been successful in managing their DERs data, recommendations to address the challenges by means of the development of an energy datahub are proposed and discussed. Section 2 of this paper provides introduction to DER and its current state in Malaysia. Section 3 explains the data management challenges faced and Sect. 4 looks at the solutions of other countries. Recommendations are given in Sect. 5 and finally, Sect. 6 concludes the paper and presents future work.

2 Distributed Energy Resources (DERs) in Malaysia

DER is a new identity in energy landscape that has been introduced because of new technologies. A DER is a small-scale unit of power generation, often from renewable, that operates locally and is connected to a larger power grid at the distribution level, rather than to the bulk power transmission systems [6]. DERs are modular, small systems that can be combined with management and storage energy systems to improve the operation of the distribution system. From an environmental point of view, DER is considered clean, reliable and secure. DER will change the way electric power systems operate along with its types and operating technologies [6]. Figure 1 shows the setup of DERs which is directly connected to the distribution network [7].

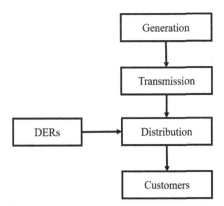

Fig. 1. Setup of DERs in the electricity value chain [7].

In Malaysia, there has been a substantial increase in the integration of DERs, mostly from solar photovoltaics (PVs), into electric power distribution systems over the last several years. Malaysia's solar energy capacity was roughly 1,493 megawatts in 2019, an increase from one megawatt in 2010 [8]. Multiple schemes have been introduced by the government in order to promote DERS. Most popular schemes are FIT and NEM as mentioned earlier. Customers who commit to installing solar PV panels are immediately enrolled in the Malaysian government's revamped NEM 2.0 scheme for 2019. The idea behind NEM is that the energy generated by the installed solar PV system would be utilized first, and any excess will be exported to the grid on a 'one-on-one' offset basis. If the buying rate (the rate that the customers buy from the utility company) is higher than the selling rate, it will be less attractive to the customer to inject power into the grid.

Figure 2 shows a DER that is connected to the grid at the distribution level. This includes many types of resources and technologies, which are located in front of or behind the meter. The real-time or near real-time monitoring capability of these information and communication technology (ICT) devices provides information on system operations, patterns of energy consumption application and load current monitoring, which are necessary for design, planning and operation of LV distribution grids.

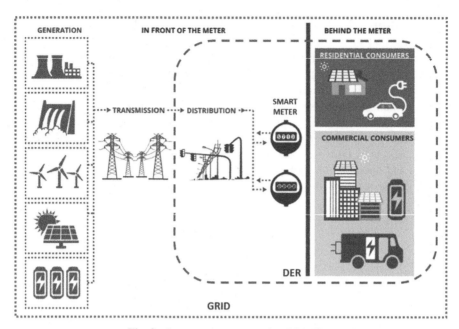

Fig. 2. Smart meter connected to DER [9].

When there is a large number of DERs in distribution systems, real-time monitoring and control in the grids will result in large amount of data to be managed, which give rise to data management challenges. Utilities need information such as generated capacity from DERs, their locations and their energy consumption. The data collected from DERs are one of the many sources of information in the distribution grid, which are expected to be used in combination with other sources of information collected from the actors that constitute the grid, including system operators, transmission system operator, regulators and electricity retailers. The collected DERs data are expected to be used for three kinds of purpose; billing, operations and value-added services. To achieve high interoperability and avoid collaboration difficulties resulting from multiple sources of data being exchanged across boundaries, a deeper understanding of data management issues related to DERs is thus required.

3   Potential Challenges in Managing DERs Data

This section focuses on the selected challenges that are encountered in managing energy data. A study conducted by a utility company in Malaysia had identified challenges to the management of energy data that can be broadly divided into technical and non-technical challenges as follows.

3.1   Technical Challenge

Data quality is defined and measured to the degree to which the data conform to their specified syntax and to the degree to which the data are appropriate and useful for a particular purpose. Data being used in the company undergo data quality monitoring and reporting, which are performed systematically in several data areas. However, opportunities for improvement are seen in several other data areas. More systematic approach in mitigating the data quality issues observed, such as dealing with root causes and promoting continuous improvements can be made. Quality of the data is also checked to the degree to which data correspond to that which they represent, i.e., when smart meters measure that 10 kW is being transmitted, the actual load should also be 10 kW at the point of measurement [10]. Therefore, from the data quality perspective, the technical challenges include data integration, data interoperability and data modelling.

Data Integration. Data integration concerns with the ability to combine data, possibly heterogeneous, residing in different sources and providing the end users with a unified and meaningful view of them. In this regard, one of the common challenges within utilities is when a number of systems and resources used in managing the energy resources are isolated and not connected with other systems. These may include the data storage, like the data lake, enterprise resource management systems, customer management systems and mobile applications that are used between customers and utility providers. Due to the disconnection, changes to some of the systems used may have to go through change request processes involving the vendors. Additionally, if other systems need data from any of the systems, some sort of arrangements that may incur payment, have to be made. Due to these, users needing any data from these systems need to get them manually, which is time consuming. Data involved therefore may not be easily extracted from and transferred to other systems due to the integration issues that prevent users from getting the unified and meaningful view of the data.

Data Interoperability. Data integration enables data in diverse formats and from different locations to be unified and used together. Data interoperability goes one step further to ensure data that cross the system or organizational boundaries (on their way to integration) are correctly interpreted. This means that one system (and its users) can understand and interpret the data that comes from another system (and its users). Data interoperability can become an issue in data integration, especially when we are talking about integrating existing systems that are already in use. The various systems are most likely developed by different vendors, and built with point-to-point proprietary interfaces. Maintaining point-to-point interfaces is costly and difficult under this circumstance as most of the systems may rely on specific vendors and platforms [10]. This can be worsened if multiple systems and disconnected data sources are used. Data from certain systems could not be correctly understood by other systems, or may even be misunderstood. For a system to be able to interpret the imported data correctly, the data have to be manually mapped to ensure interoperability and this has to be done for each system. Proper compatibility checking then needs to be performed to ensure that the data can be correctly used by the other system.

Data Modelling. Data model is an abstract model that organizes elements of data and standardizes how they relate to one another and to the properties of real-world entities. For instance, a data model may specify that the data element representing a car be composed of several other elements which, in turn, represent the color and size of the car and define its owner. Data modelling is the process of creating the data model by applying certain formal techniques, which can be iterative. Figure 3 depicts an example of a data model that represents the metering structure. In the model, it can be seen that for a meter, there should be at least two data elements required, which are supplier and meter reading, where the meter reading will be used for two purposes, monitoring and billing. One of the consequences of systems that are being developed by multiple vendors as described above is that data models being used in the systems are most likely proprietary, i.e., each system may have different data model. As a result, although certain data carry the same meaning or purpose in the context of the energy domain, each system would have its own naming convention and structure for the same data. Therefore, some details or elements of the data may be missing/incomplete when entered using different systems (due to the different data models referred to by the systems). As such, there is need to establish a well-defined and standardized data model across the systems to ensure completeness and consistency of the data entered. A well-defined and standardized data model can also help addressing the issues of integration and interoperability. Likewise, lack of common data model will increase risk of data integrity issues and duplication.

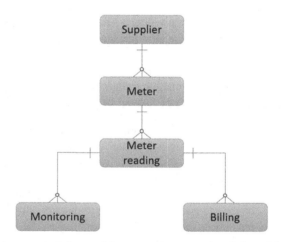

Fig. 3. A conceptual data model representing meter data (adapted from [11])

3.2 On-Technical Challenge

This section describes the non-technical challenges identified from the study. Three challenges are identified, namely business model, access right and boundary, and data privacy and protection.

Business Model. The energy industry is seeing more new business models being developed to create more values to the people. In Malaysia, innovative business models are emerging with the deployment of DERs that enable renewable energy to be supplied from the solar panels installed in houses. With the current promotion, it is expected that more consumers will install the panels resulting in more energy coming from DERs. However, the direction on how this information is used in operation and planning is currently not available. With several options of business model available, the utility companies need to identify the most suitable business models by studying the local market requirements and constraints.

Access Right and Boundary. The use of smart meters in datahub implementation resulting in more digital electricity data being produced and shared in multiple systems. The digital data has greater frequency and volume, and it also characterized by the granularity of collecting the data. Data being collected and stored for datahub include consumers' details and electricity consumption data, which are collected from different systems that are integrated. When large amount of data is being managed with a datahub, there are issues of who owns the data and have the authorization to access the data. This prompts the need to have a clearly defined access rights and boundaries of the collected data. Data that being put into datahub must be planned and identified to suit the aim of the datahub implementation. When companies do not set limits of data being managed by datahub, and the parameter of the data to be collected, it may turn the data lake in the datahub into a data swamp, flooded with information that is not needed by the company.

Data Privacy and Protection. The other non-technical issue with regards to the energy data management is concerning the privacy and protection of the data, especially those containing consumers' personal information. Some countries that use continuous wireless transmission in exchanging the data may transmit personally identifiable information (PII) which may lead to privacy breaches due to security vulnerabilities. By including smart meters and AMI in the datahub implementation, this has increased the concerns of customers relating to their safety and privacy of their personal data. Security models and access rules need to be designed properly with clear and strategic manner to protect the customers. Datahub implementor should design proper controls and put in place to prevent third parties from accessing and distributing the information for commercial gain [12].

4   DERs Data Management in Other Countries

DERs phenomena might be new in Malaysia. However, this is not the case for some other countries. Several countries have long started their energy generation by using solar PV panels. In these countries, DERs operating at the distribution network level are a big part of decentralized energy management systems.

In Germany where the smart grid technology has been implemented, German AMI technology is used to acquire the meter data. It has a specific feature that is referred as smart meter gateway (SMGW), which is a secure communication device installed at the customer's location. SMGW collects data from one or more connected smart meters, stores them, and even applies tariff rules to them before communicating the results to authorized external entities (AEE). Energy suppliers are part of AEEs who communicate with customers on metering data for billing purposes, efficiency consulting projects or controllable local system (CLS) aggregator severs. The metering data are collected for the grid operator to estimate power usage. The energy suppliers use meter data for energy consumption data, billing data and other customers data such as invoice verification, tariff updating, energy usage visualization as well as feed-in management [13].

Implementation and deployment of the national smart metering system project called FAHAM in Iran began in 2009. In FAHAM's ICT architecture, all data from smart meters and concentrators are stored in meter data management (MDM) centers via general packet radio service (GPRS) links. Data can be provided at the customer level and for other enterprise-level systems either on regular basis or on demand. Depending on the requirements of application systems, data collected from the smart meters are extracted from corresponding MDM centers by adding web service call mechanisms. FAHAM will communicate this data to a central location, sorting and analyzing it for a variety of purposes on profile data such as customer billing, outage response, system loading conditions and demand-side management. FAHAM as a two-way communication network will send this information to other systems, customers and third parties as well as send the information back through the network and meters to capture additional data, control equipment and update the configuration and software of equipment [14].

Canada introduced AMI technology as foundation of smart grid. The data storage is used to collect the data from group of meters in local data concentrators, and then transmits the data using a backhaul channel to central command where the servers, data storing and processing facilities as well as management and billing applications reside. The types of data are energy consumption data that are stored in MDM centers to be analyzed to provide information in a useful form to the utility service provider through backhaul data link. The data are from smart meters and contain customer's name and address information, which are stored for billing and in utility networks with four levels that are core back-bone, backhaul distribution, access point and home area networks with customer as an actor [15].

The United States had a program under the Smart Grid Investment Grant (SGIG) projects that implement AMI and customer system technology known as SGIG AMI projects. The communications network consists of MDM centers to store and process the interval load data from smart meters. These centers collect the customers data and billing data at high-speed using fiber optic with power-line communications (PLC), microwave, and RF-cellular systems for backhauling large volumes. The data usage is for control systems, including head-end systems, billing systems, customer information systems (CIS), geographic information systems (GIS) and outage management system (OMS) with customers and grid operators as actors [16].

Back to the Europe, Sweden used AMI for data sources from smart meters and the data storage via meter data center (MDC) system that gathers consumption data to a unique database. The communication is bidirectional from 3G wireless communication channels to broadband PLC, optical fiber, wireless radio et cetera. The data usage is for utility system, billing system, customer information system, distribution management system (DMS), IT system and tariff information. The distribution network

Table 1. Summary of DERs data management in Germany, Iran, Canada, US, Sweden and Denmark.

Countries	Germany [13]	Iran [14]	Canada [15]	U.S. [16]	Sweden [17]	Denmark [18]
Data sources	German Advanced Metering Infrastructure (AMI)	Advanced Metering Infrastructure (AMI)	Advanced Metering Infrastructure (AMI)	Smart Grid Investment Grant (SGIG) Advanced Metering Infrastructure (AMI)	Advanced Metering Infrastructure (AMI)	The Danish Distribution System Operators (DSOs) business models
Data storage	Servers at Authorized External Entities such as Supplier-metering data server and Aggregator Controllable Local System (CLS) communication server	Meter Data Management (MDMs) centers	Collect data in local data concentrators and transmit the data using a backhaul channel to central command. The server for data storage is Meter Data Management Systems (MDMS)	The AMI communications network consists a MDMS to store and process the interval load data	Meter data center (MDC) system is software tools and utilities required to gather data to a unique database	Distribution and Transmission network, The medium and long-range backbone network infrastructure, Value network
Types of data	Customer Data, Billing Data and Consumption Data	Profile Data	Energy Consumption Data	Customer Data and Billing Data	Consumption Data	Customer Data and Billing Data
Data collection	Smart Meter Gateway (SMGW)	General Packet Radio Service, GPRS links	Backhaul data link	Use high-speed, fiber optic, power-line communications (PLC), microwave, and RF-cellular systems for backhauling large volumes of data	Bidirectional communication, from 3G wireless communication channels to broadband PLC, optical fiber, wireless radio, etc	Bidirectional energy flow and Distributed Energy Resources (DERs)
Data usage	Estimating Power Usage Energy usage Bill Invoicing, Invoice verification Tariff Updating Energy usage visualization Feed-in management	Customer billing, outage response, system loading conditions, and demand-side management	Customer's name, address information, stored for billing and in utility	Control systems, including head-end systems, billing systems, customer information systems (CIS), geographic information systems (GIS), outage management systems (OMS), and distribution management systems (DMS)	Utilities system, billing system, customer information systems (CIS), distribution management systems (DMS), IT system, Tariff information	Billing and customer data management, real-time algorithms, online optimization solutions and forecasting systems

(*continued*)

Table 1. (*continued*)

Countries	Germany [13]	Iran [14]	Canada [15]	U.S. [16]	Sweden [17]	Denmark [18]
Actors	Customers, TSOs, DSOs	Customers, DSOs	Customers	Customers, Grid Operators,	Distribution network operator (DNO), DMS operators	Customers, DSOs

operator (DNO) and DMS operators are the actors in this system [17]. Denmark can be considered the most advanced amongst the other Nordic countries with regards to DERs data management. The Danish distribution system operators (DSOs) business model is the sink for smart meter data. The data streams are transferred over the backbone network infrastructure and value network are supposed to deliver the value proposition. The DERs data usage is in billing data and customer data management with real-time algorithms, online optimization solutions and also a forecasting system [18].

Table 1 presents a comparison of several technologies described above that can serve data management in terms of data sources, data storage, types of data, data collection, data usage and the actors involved. As can be seen, all the countries listed in Table 1 are collecting data related to DERs from AMI. This is because DERs are connected to the grid through the smart meters. The collected data are then sent through a gateway or communication link such as GPRS or high-speed fiber optic to a server that gathers the meter data. The collected data are used mainly for billing and energy efficiency management. Based on the comparison, AMI, data storage and capable communication channels are important elements in managing DERs data.

5   Discussion and Recommendations

Suitable recommendations are provided to act as potential solutions to the identified challenges presented above. Based on the DERs data management from other countries analyzed in Sect. 4, a centralized data storage, i.e. *datahub*, is crucial. The countries investigated in this study are using MDM centers to store the DERs data collected. Thus, datahub can be used as the centralized data storage. It is developed to allow all data to be stored, separated and sent to other systems. In fact, datahub is more than just data storage as it also has governance, security, indexing and transactional integrity [19].

With the creation of the datahub, there will be a single point of contact or single source of truth, which is from the centralized datahub. This can help to address the data integration challenge resulting from the conventional method of point-to-point connections [20]. A potential solution for the DERs data integration or energy data integration in general is the creation of an appropriate data integration architecture by implementing a communication system called enterprise service bus (ESB) or service-oriented architecture (SOA) for energy systems and applications. Through the implementation of ESB/SOA, data integration catalogue can be created in an easy way and less expensive, which improves the efficiency of data sharing between applications [10].

To enable interoperability, data have to be compatible. The use of a common data model can help to achieve this compatibility resulting in data that can interoperate, although they come from different systems. One of the steps in implementing a datahub is the creation of data model [19]. For this reason, a common information model (CIM) can be established to represent the data coming from the various actively used applications associated with the energy industry and the relation between them [21]. Having a common data model therefore overcomes the problems associated with proprietary data model that hinders data exchanges and interoperability. CIM also defines the general interfaces and communications, allowing applications and systems to communicate. The combination of CIM with ESB/SOA will together provide the solution to the data integration and interoperability issues [10]. This subsequently enables information sharing between applications in the power system [22].

Defining business models (or business objectives) is important to ensure clear direction on how the collected DERs data are going to be used to achieve objectives such as energy efficiency and efficient energy data management. If the business models are not defined properly, data cannot be used to its full potential. From the analysis, it can be understood that data from the smart meters are used for billing, energy consumption analysis and energy efficiency management such as demand response management. As explained above, the development of the datahub will entail the development of the data model for the datahub for interoperability. Through the data model, visibility of the data in the datahub is improved and this will facilitate the development of the business models when the types of data are known. Additionally, the business models developed can help increase the transparency and efficiency of the energy industry where access to the vast amount of valuable energy data can be given with clear reasons resulting from clear business models. For example, several business models for datahub implementation that have been proposed in the Nordic countries include aggregators, P2P trading, energy-as-a-service, community ownership model and pay-as-you-go model [23].

Concerning the issue of access right and boundary, it is important to identify the actors and their corresponding access rights especially when all data are pooled at one place, and these must be defined hand-in-hand with the development of the business models. Figure 2 illustrates that the actors for the datahub can be from generation, transmission and distribution. In the context of the DERs data in Malaysia, potential actors include the electricity providers' generation, transmission, distribution and retail, Energy Commission, Sustainable Energy Development Authority (SEDA) and Malaysian Green Technology Corporation (MGTC). The grid division of the main electricity provider company can potentially be the owner of the datahub, who needs to work with all the actors involved in defining their roles as well as their access rights to the data. This is the practice in the Nordic countries where the transmission system operator is made the owner of the datahub. However, it is worth to note that this is partly due to the unbundling structure of their electricity supply industries, which is not the case for Malaysia. With clearly defined actors and access rights, datahub can connect the energy industry players/actors, allowing them to benefit from advantages such as improved data interchange complexity and lower operational costs [12]. For example, datahub enables a systematic process for registration and use of energy data, ultimately allowing businesses, suppliers and consumers access to the required data at the same time.

Finally, DERs data collected from the AMI may include customers' private data, and there must be a means protect this information and its owner. Once the customer data are released to a third party, they are no longer under the control of the organizations collecting them, and the data owners are not able to control the way the data are used. Most customers are concerned with the security access and access privilege to their data stored in the datahub. Therefore, the datahub implementation must assure them on their security and privacy. This can be achieved as most datahub implementation also comply with some sort of data protection acts and/or regulations. For example, the implementation of datahub in Turkey is being supported by data privacy regulations that serve as a tool to protect the customers' data collected. As a result, any key activities related to the datahub must comply with the General Data Protection Regulation (GDPR) [12]. The same policy can be used in DERs datahub implementation in Malaysia where Personal Data Protection Act 2010 can be used as a compliance tool for the data shared by the customers.

In summary, the presence of a centralized repository or datahub can help to address the challenges identified in managing energy data as discussed above. It can also serve as a crucial component and information source, by having a means in ensuring a standardized processes in managing DERs data. The datahub will become the main support for greater integration, analysis and usage of data between internal and external of utility companies. It will also enable effective product and service development. Experience from the selected countries presented in this paper showed that the presence of a data storage has significantly improved the efficiency of the electricity industry. The datahub as the data storage is expected to improve interoperability, accountability, integrity and transparency in utilities' DERs data management [24]. More standardized and harmonized information sharing amongst the stakeholders also results in improved relationships [25]. Residential customers, prosumers that subscribe to NEM and bulk purchasers will have better engagement by having a datahub that helps the electricity company to achieve optimum demand response.

6 Conclusion and Future Work

This research seeks to contribute to a deeper understanding of the issues related to DERs data management in Malaysia specifically and energy data management in general. From the study done by a utility company in Malaysia, issues concerning the management of energy data are identified, which are categorized into technical and non-technical issues. These are data integration, data interoperability, data model, business model, access right and boundary, and data privacy and protection. Our findings show that these issues can be addressed with the implementation of datahub, a practice that has been implemented in several countries and has proven successful. The technologies, e.g. DERs and ICT related are important to support the establishment of the datahub. Although datahub rollout has not started in Malaysia yet, there is a strong demand for the datahub development to realize a smart energy system taking advantage of all energy resources. It is believed that datahub will be a natural product of the energy ecosystem as examples can be seen from the selected countries in this paper. With the need positioned, future work in this area includes conducting a series of engagements with the energy stakeholders as the first step to design and develop the energy datahub.

Acknowledgement. Project Design and Development of Distribution Network Datahub for a Future Proof Energy Efficient Utility (U-TD-RD-20-11) is funded by TNB Seed Fund. Special thanks to Tenaga Nasional Berhad for the funding opportunity and UNITEN R&D Sdn Bhd for assistance in fund management.

References

1. Malaysian Investment Development Authority, MIDA. https://www.mida.gov.my/mida-news/malaysia-aims-31-re-capacity-by-2025/. Accessed 13 Sept 2021
2. Sustainable energy Development Authority, SEDA. http://www.seda.gov.my/. Accessed 9 June 2021
3. Chenm W.N.: Invest in the Sun: What COVID 19 has taught us – Webinar. YouTube, 29 April 2020. https://www.youtube.com/watch?v=ZgBjLxzM0RY&t=2266s. Accessed 25 June 2021
4. Kristensen, S.D.: Transforming the Danish retail market. https://www.slideshare.net/Fingrid/transforming-the-danish-retail-market. Accessed 8 June 2020
5. Burger, S.P., Luke, M.: Business models for distributed energy resources: a review and empirical analysis. Energy Policy **109**, 230–248 (2017)
6. Akorede, M.F., Hizam, H., Pouresmaeil, E.: Distributed energy resources and benefits to the environment. Renew. Sustain. Energy Rev. **14**(2), 724–734 (2010)
7. Bayod-Rújula, A.A.: Future development of the electricity systems with distributed generation. Energy **34**(3), 377–383 (2009)
8. Vaka, M., Walvekar, R., Rasheed, A.K., Khalid, M.: A review on Malaysia's solar energy pathway towards carbon-neutral Malaysia beyond Covid'19 pandemic. J. Cleaner Prod. **273**, 1–16 (2020)
9. Johnson, R.C., Mayfield, M.: The economic and environmental implications of post feed-in tariff pv on constrained low voltage networks, Appl. Energy **279**, 1–15 (2020)
10. Wah, L.P., Kreuknie, G., Basrihuddin, H., Zur, S., Kaur, K.D.: Blueprint and Roadmap Report. (PowerPoint slides). Accessed 20 June 2021
11. Data Models for Smart Meters. http://www.databaseanswers.org/data_mod-els/smart_meters/index.htm. Accessed 13 Sept 2021
12. Kemal, M., Sanchez, R., Olsen, R., Iov, F., Schwefel, H.-P.: On the trade-off between timeliness and accuracy for low voltage distribution system grid monitoring utilizing smart meter data. Int. J. Electr. Power Energy Syst. **121**, 1–9 (2020)
13. Küfeoğlu, S., Üçler, Ş: Designing the business model of an energy datahub. Electr. J. **34**(2), 1–9 (2021)
14. Meister, J., Ihle, N., Lehnhoff, S., Uslar, M.: Smart grid digitalization in Germany by standardized advanced metering infrastructure and green button. Appl. Smart Grid Technol. pp. 347–371 (2018)
15. Gharehpetian, G.B., Salay Naderi, M., Modaghegh, H., Zakariazadeh, A.: Iranian smart grid: road map and metering program. Appl. Smart Grid Technol. 13–60 (2018)
16. Mohassel, R.R., Fung, A.S., Mohammadi, F., Raahemifar, K.: A survey on advanced metering infrastructure and its application in smart grids. In: 2014 IEEE 27th Canadian Conference on Electrical and Computer Engineering (CCECE), pp. 1–12 (2014)
17. Smartgrid.gov: Advanced Metering Infrastructure and Customer Systems – Results for the Smart Grid Investment Grant Program, U.S Department of Energy (2016)
18. Bago, R., Campos, M.: Smart meters for improved energy demand management. In: Eco-Friendly Innovation in Electricity Transmission and Distribution Networks, pp. 339–361 (2015)

19. Ma, Z., Sommer, S., Jorgensen, B.N.: The smart GRID impact on the Danish DSOS' business model. In: 2016 IEEE Electrical Power and Energy Conference (EPEC), pp. 1–5 (2016)
20. What is a data hub: concepts and guidelines. https://www.data4v.com/-what-is-a-data-hub-concepts-and-guidelines/. Accessed 5 Aug 2021
21. What is a data hub and why should you care?. https://www.actian.com/company/blog/what-is-a-data-hub-and-why-should-you-care/. Accessed 5 Aug 2021
22. Kim, H.J., et al.: A comprehensive review of practical issues for interoperability using the common information model in smart grids. Energies **13**(6), 1435 (2020)
23. Khisro, J.: Understanding the relation between interoperability and data quality: a study of data hub development in Swedish electricity market. Int. J. Public Inf. Syst. **14**(1), 1–21 (2020)
24. IRENA, Innovation landscape for a renewable-powered future: solutions to integrate variable renewables. Preview for policy makers. International Renewable Energy Agency, Abu Dhabi (2019)
25. Agarwal, U., Jain. N.: Distributed energy resources and supportive methodologies for their optimal planning under modern distribution network: a review. Technol. Econ. Smart Grids Sustain. Energy **4**(1), 1–21 (2019)

Author Index

Printed in the United States
by Baker & Taylor Publisher Services